Bouncing-Bomb Man

THE SCIENCE OF SIR BARNES WALLIS

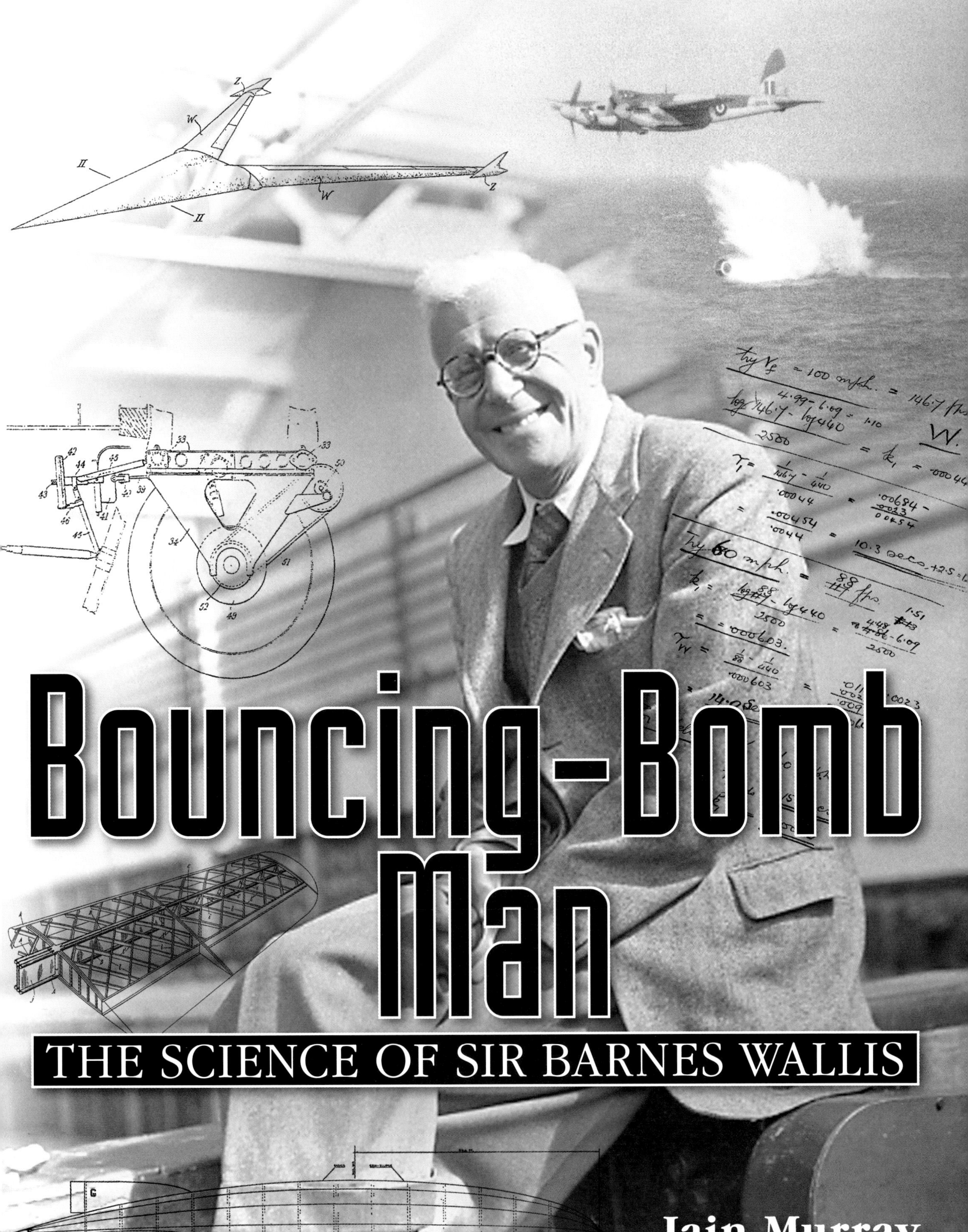

Bouncing-Bomb Man

THE SCIENCE OF SIR BARNES WALLIS

Iain Murray

This book is dedicated to those who lost their lives flying, dropping or testing the various inventions of Sir Barnes Wallis, and to those who lived on to tell of his genius.

First published in October 2009

A catalogue record for this book is available from the British Library

ISBN 978 1 84425 588 7

Library of Congress catalog card no 2009923645

Published by Haynes Publishing,
Sparkford, Yeovil, Somerset BA22 7JJ, UK
Tel: 01963 442030 Fax: 01963 440001
Int.tel: +44 1963 442030 Int.fax: +44 1963 440001
E-mail: sales@haynes.co.uk
Website: www.haynes.co.uk

Haynes North America Inc.,
861 Lawrence Drive, Newbury Park, California 91320, USA

Designed and typeset by Dominic Stickland
Printed and bound in the UK

Contents

Foreword

Iain Murray's book, *Bouncing-Bomb Man: The Science of Sir Barnes Wallis* is, for me, a fascinating and revelatory study of the complex and almost superhuman range of a brilliant but very practical mind.

I was very fortunate to have spent a variety of moments in his company, particularly during the period that we were preparing and later working on production details for the film *The Dam Busters*. It was probably his contribution to the effective bombing of the German dams in 1943 that brought to the public attention the brilliance and scientific achievements of this otherwise modest and unpretentious man.

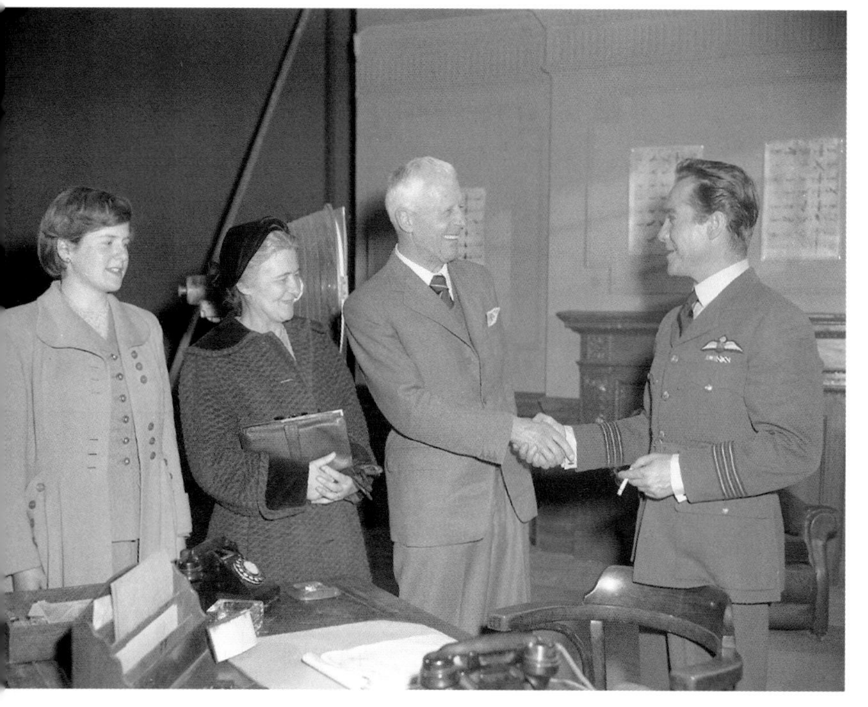

Richard Todd (as Wg Cdr Guy Gibson) on the set of *The Dam Busters* with (the real) Wallis, his wife Molly and daughter Elisabeth – watch out for Elisabeth's brief appearance in the film. *(Canal+Image UK Ltd)*

From what I knew of him, I gained the impression that, even in advanced old age, his brain was crammed with ideas and plans. Once when I asked him when he expected to retire he replied, with an enigmatic smile, that he had a lot of ideas which he hoped to bring to fruition long before he might cease to be active in the scientific and aeronautical world.

Among the future subjects to which he intended to apply his mind were the design and propulsion of a submarine that would travel faster for longer periods and at greater depths than any known craft; and a means of air travel that would 'make a modern jet airliner look like a Hansom Cab', by dint of its ability to reach the stratosphere by vertical take-off and then use the Earth's rotation to descend in Sydney, Australia, in about five hours.

Dr Murray's book makes compulsive reading, not only for the widely known achievements of Barnes Wallis, which included everything from the design of the *R.100* airship to the enormous success of the Wellington bomber.

A little secret which I have held for some years, and which has been unknown even to Dr Murray, was that Barnes had calculated the exact year of his own demise, which he had worked out using a series of factors using his parents' lifespans, his own health prospects and his personal expectations.

And he was right!

Richard Todd, OBE

Preface

What one fool can do, another can.

(Ancient Simian proverb, reprinted on the flyleaf of a calculus text book used by Wallis, and one of his favourite quotes)

I first encountered the name of Barnes Wallis as a boy, watching the film *The Dam Busters* on TV, where he appears rather as an absent-minded professor guiding his seemingly absurd 'bouncing bomb' through to triumph over technical and political adversity. During one of its frequent repeats, I was probably inspired to read Paul Brickhill's book, upon which the film was mostly based, and read more of the exploits of 617 Squadron and Wallis's later 'earthquake bombs'.

Perhaps most people know the name of Wallis through a similar route, or know that he was the designer of the Wellington bomber, whose rather strange structure made it better than its contemporaries. Such a series of important contributions to Britain's war effort, and the legendary status of the Dams Raid, would easily offer Wallis a place at the top table in any aviation hall of fame, but paradoxically his contributions to the aircraft industry are far wider in range than even his fame suggests. His working career began less than a year after the first powered flight by the Wright Brothers, and when Concorde first flew, he was still in paid employment in the industry, and continued to work enthusiastically on his ideas even after his considerably belated (and forced!) retirement. He can directly lay claim to groundbreaking ideas in airship design, aircraft structures, aerodynamics and weaponry, as well as making significant contributions to many related areas (and some unrelated).

In the 2002 BBC *Great Britons* poll, Wallis came a modest 95th, the lowest-placed of three 20th-century engineers. However, while the significance of Frank Whittle's jet engine and John Logie Baird's television is unquestionably great, both must be considered 'one hit wonders' of engineering, an epithet that can certainly not be attached to Barnes Wallis.

The Wallis researcher is blessed in that the importance of his work was recognised during his lifetime, and consequently much material has survived in numerous archives; however, the distribution between the various archives sometimes appears arbitrary with different parts of the same story having to be gathered together from many sources, and in some cases parts of the story are missing. A flood at Weybridge in the autumn of 1968 caused the loss of 'most of his records for the past 33 years',[1] which no doubt accounts for some of the holes in the story (many of the surviving archive papers also show signs of water damage), and George Edwards is reported to have allowed 'scrapping of heaps of stuff from the Brooklands clubhouse'[2] when Wallis retired, although some of the papers from there (including many personal documents) did go to the RAF Museum. It was suggested to me that 'the trail may have become so overgrown that it will be impossible to follow'[3] and while this has been true in parts (for example, many of the remaining plans of Swallow variants are undated, so it is difficult even to sequence them), the challenge of hacking at the undergrowth has been an immensely enjoyable and rewarding one.

There have been many books covering many of Wallis's inventions, the historical significance of their use, and the lives that were changed as a result. However, none have attempted to look in detail at the remarkable science and engineering skills that lay behind the inventions, and make these accessible to a general audience to reveal the true genius of Wallis. It is the thesis of this book to attempt to rectify this, and demonstrate that Wallis should be remembered not only for his eclectic inventions, but as one of Britain's greatest scientists and engineers.

Two aspects which I particularly wanted to bring out in this book have both come to nothing, for different pragmatic reasons. One was an intention to describe the ideas behind Wallis's inventions and discuss how each of them worked *in isolation* – however, I quickly realised that it was both desirable and necessary to contrast his ideas with contemporary alternatives in order to show how his solution was better (if it was), and also to set the ideas within the wider technical and political landscape of the time. Wallis was always part of a (sometimes quite large) team, and the second aspect that I wished to illuminate was which elements of the work were done by Wallis himself, and which by others on his staff (or elsewhere). In practice, it has proven difficult to trace the origins of many ideas as the majority of documents (other than those in Wallis's own hand) do not identify an author, and some of the more formal reports which bear Wallis's name may have been written collaboratively. Where specific ideas and inventions can definitely be (or not be) credited to Wallis, this is mentioned in the text. The nature of the material from Wallis's own files indicates that, even when he was not working on these projects directly, he was keeping in touch with those who were and offering guidance (and criticism).

Regarding the title of this book, Wallis would have considered his work to be engineering rather than science, but I use the term 'science' in its common contemporary context as a coverall word encompassing engineering, mathematics and technology as well as science itself. His son Barnes W. Wallis defined science as 'done by someone who requires absolute certainty from his work, time being immaterial' while engineering is 'done with externally selected and specific objectives, to which are attached times and . . . prices, with penalties for slippage in either'.[4] As such, Wallis was firmly in the engineering camp, but he clearly recognised the value of knowing the underlying science in order to help the engineering along the right path.

I have researched all of the principal archives with Wallis material, and have targeted all of the main files, but I cannot claim to have covered everything – over 250 files at The National Archives alone are potentially related to the Wallis story. As such, I am unable to state definitely that certain documents do not still exist, so within the text, I have used the shorthand 'it seems' or 'it appears' to indicate that I have been unable to find materials relating to the point in question, despite looking specifically for such material. Care has been taken when referencing documents which refer to forthcoming trials and developments, as these may have actually taken place in a modified form, or not at all. Note also that justification given for certain ideas may no longer be valid, resting as it does on theories and a state of knowledge quoted from archive materials 40 or more years old.

As will be seen, Wallis's expertise covered a wide range of domains, and where I myself have had no knowledge in a particular area, I have attempted to gain a sufficient understanding of the concepts in order to explain them as clearly as possible to a general audience, so I have not assumed any specialist knowledge, trying instead to define any new terminology as I go along. Under similar circumstances (selling the theories supporting his 10-ton bomb idea to an ambivalent military),[5] Wallis wrote:

> *This brief conspectus of an immense subject must inevitably exhibit the defects inherent in the work of a jack-of-all-trades.*

For such defects here, the responsibility is my own.

Iain Murray, 2009

Note: Generally, units have been left as they appear in the original; a conversion table can be found in the Glossary, together with a list of common terms and acronyms with definitions. Detailed notes on the text, including references, are included in Notes and Sources. Recommended publications appear in Further Reading.

Acknowledgements

I extend my grateful thanks to my wife Karen for proofreading the whole text, and for listening to all of my discursive ramblings about Wallis. I also thank Duncan McAra, my literary agent, and Jonathan Falconer, Senior Commissioning Editor at Haynes Publishing, for seeing the potential in this subject, and for giving their support to this, my first book. My thanks also go to Jane Hutchings, my editor, for many well-spotted observations.

In addition to those interviewed, the author is indebted to the many correspondents who have contacted him or replied to his enquiries (by telephone, letter or e-mail) over many years of researching into Wallis's work, or otherwise assisted in the preparation of this book, especially:

For comments on Wallis's later aircraft designs and assistance in obtaining comments: John Barnes, Bob Fairclough, John Farley, John Flower, Ollie Heath, Ralph Hooper, Peter Liddell, Phillip Ransom, Constantinos Soutis, Heinz Vogel, Tony Wilson.

For comments on Wallis's submarine designs: Jason Dobb and other staff of BAE SYSTEMS Submarine Solutions.

For their hospitality when visiting 617 Squadron at RAF Lossiemouth: Wg Cdr Dave Cooper, Flt Lt Cox, Flt Lt Jackson, Sqn Ldr Kent, Sqn Ldr Lawrence, Flt Lt Tait.

For their hospitality when visiting Brooklands Museum: Albert Kitchenside, Julian Temple (also Steve Adey and John Pulford).

For their hospitality when visiting the Science Museum library: Katy Allen, Allison Pollard, Mandy Taylor, John Underwood (also David Exton, Deborah Jones and others).

For his hospitality when visiting the RAF Museum: Ian Thirsk (also Ewan Cameron, Peter Elliott, Andrew Renwick and others).

Many others, including: Neil A. Armstrong, Professor John L. Arnott (University of Dundee), the late Henry Black, Patrick Bourdin (University of Bristol), Don Bradford (Vickers R&D), Jim Brookbank (9 Squadron), Eric Brown RN, Kevin Brown (Geodetic Preservation Society), Dan Burchmore (Airship Heritage Trust), ACM Sir Brian Burnett, Tom Buttery (Boom Defence Department, Greenock), Tony Buttler, Niamh Conlon (Fife Council), Alan Cooper, Jim Croll (Centre for Materials Research, UCL), Ted Crosbie (PDS Diving), Michael Dahlem, Veronica Davies (Shell UK), Kathleen Dickson (British Film Institute), Professor Dame Ann Dowling (University of Cambridge), Helmuth Euler,

John Evans, Mike Fielding (BAE SYSTEMS), Bill Finlay (The Flambards Experience), Martyn Ford-Jones (15 Squadron official historian), Holger Forstemann, Philip French (Brenzett Aeronautical Museum), Simon Fryer, Robert Gardner, Chris Gibson, John Godwin, Barry Guess (BAE SYSTEMS), Tony Hadland and other family of Herbert Jeffree, Andrew Hemsley, Caroline Herbert (Churchill Archives Centre), Megan Humphries (University of Bristol), Dicky James (9 Squadron), Angela Jeffreys, Alan Jones, Arthur Kearse (QinetiQ), Eric Knight (618 Squadron), Tony Knight, Bob Liebeck (Boeing), John Lorimer RN, Don MacIntosh (9 Squadron), Ben and Jean Mackay (Skitten Farm), the late John Marks, John Moffat RNVR, Richard Morris, the late Jean Mortimer and other family of Joseph 'Mutt' Summers, Stuart Moy (School of Civil Engineering, University of Southampton), Michael Nelmes (Narromine Aviation Museum), Michael Ogilvie (Museum of Islay Life), Robert Owen (617 Squadron official historian), Peter Pritchard (PDS Diving), Peter Rix (Barnes Wallis Memorial Trust), Tim Robinson, Tony Salter-Ellis (BAE SYSTEMS), 'Sandy' Sanderson (Explosive Ordnance Disposal), Jim Shortland (617 Squadron unofficial historian), Brian Spear, Brett Stolle (USAF Museum), Gay F. Sturt (Dragon School), John Sweetman, Ken Swift (University of Hull), Richard Thorp, Richard Todd, Reginald Turnill, Dave Wheeler (Abbotsbury Swannery), David Williams, John Woodcock (Ringwood Town & Country Experience), David Worrow.

Microsoft Flight Simulator screen shots are reprinted with permission from Microsoft Corporation.

The author would also like to thank the many anonymous contributors to the Internet, without which the wide-ranging research undertaken for this book would have been more difficult by several orders of magnitude. Although Internet-only resources have been cited in just a few cases, the web has been enormously helpful in chasing down new avenues of exploration, quickly revealing those that are blind alleys and those which, after exploring a little way, open out into whole new vistas of research. The Internet has also been invaluable in connecting to new sources of information, both written and human. How much more Wallis might have accomplished if he had access to the same facility can only be guessed at.

Chapter 1

Wallis, the Man

He who walks where others have trod leaves no footprints.
(Anonymous)

Wallis's early life

When Charles Wallis, recently qualified in classics from Oxford and medicine from Guy's Hospital, and his new wife Edith moved with their baby son John to Ripley, Derbyshire, in the summer of 1886, it was with great hopes for the future of the family. Their fortune continued with the birth of a second son, Barnes Neville Wallis on 26 September 1887. However, the appointment in Ripley had been the only one available at the time, and the people of Ripley did not warm to their new GP, nor the Wallises to them, so in 1891, the family moved to New Cross in London. Two years later, as the cries of his baby sister Annie echoed through 241 New Cross Road, Barnes's father was struck down by polio, and the clank of his leg callipers would reverberate in Barnes's mind down the years.[1]

Barnes and his siblings were taught to read by their mother, and he could read fluently and recite his tables by the time he was 5. He attended the kindergarten at the girls' school of Haberdashers' Aske's Hatcham College, just across the road from the family home, two years later moving to the boys' school further up the hill.

Both his parents aspired to a public school education for their children, but with the medical practice struggling due to Charles's illness, the family was never well off, and this was beyond their means. Consequently, in 1900 Barnes was fortunate to follow his older brother John to Christ's Hospital at Newgate Street in the shadow of St Paul's Cathedral; this was a long-established public school[2] which offered a number of scholarships to deserving cases who had secured appropriate nomination and, despite a poor performance in Latin, Barnes secured one of ten places competed for by over 100 applicants.

From unremarkable beginnings at the school (he was bottom of his form in his first term), his performance improved, invariably coming first in his form in mathematics, and close to top in other subjects too (the problematic Latin having been dropped). Key among the lessons were the science classes taught by Professor Henry Armstrong and his protégé Chas. E. Browne, and they fanned his emerging interest in science into a blue flame. They were pioneers of the use of heuristics (the use of reasoning and prior experience) in science teaching, encouraging their pupils to augment the rote learning of facts and method with practical experimentation, lessons which would inform Wallis's approach throughout his life, and others' too – five of Browne's pupils would become Fellows of the Royal Society.

School rules meant that scholars not taking classics and not proceeding to university had to leave at the end of the term prior to their 17th birthday. His father lobbied the school to let him stay on to take the Matriculation exam for the University of London, but they refused, though he did sit it – and fail it – two months after he left. However, Wallis was already set on a career in engineering, and wanted to 'get his hands dirty' in a real job, and to contribute financially to his family, rather than burden them with the costs of going to university.[3] Wallis thus left school with, by the standards of the day, an excellent education, and also a modern one – his science education was the best available anywhere at the time. The school itself had been undergoing modernisation at the same time, moving from central London to a new purpose-built complex at Horsham in West Sussex, much to the delight of Wallis and his compatriots. In a final flourish, he picked up not only the newly instigated Willcox Prize for Science (for which he had always been a contender, and with which he bought himself a lathe), but also the school's Rokeby French Prize.

His four years at the school were hard work, but he undoubtedly made the most of his time, forging, as did many Old Blues, a lifelong allegiance and obligation to the school, and an appreciation of the value of education in general. Later in life, Wallis would serve as Christ's Hospital Treasurer and Chairman of Almoners for over 12 years, allowing him to gratefully give something back to a school he felt had given him a great deal.

Working life

Out of school and unable to enter university, Wallis began an indentured apprenticeship with the Thames Engineering Works in Blackheath, working on marine engines. Shipbuilding on the Thames was already in decline and diversification was in the air, so Wallis found himself working on the first English racing car and the prototype London taxi.[4] He did not find this very satisfying, so in 1908 he got his indentures transferred to John Samuel White's shipyard at Cowes on the Isle of Wight, the company specialising in naval destroyers. Here he developed a lifelong love of ships, though it was a passion often swamped by his work on aircraft. White's gave earnest support to its young apprentices, and Wallis was promoted to the drawing office. The accompanying pay rise removed his financial dependence on his family in London and gave him a bit of free money to take up some sports. Following some evening classes, he also re-sat the Matriculation exam, and this time passed, though he seems to have shown no inclination to become a student at this time, taking up a full-time post with the company when his apprenticeship ended.

This was also a time of personal sadness – overtaken by gradually worsening asthma, his mother died in August 1911. Barnes had always been very close to her, and some people suggest that this removal of a personal burden was the touchpaper that ignited his career:

> *Extend the graph of professional progress in the direction that is indicated when Wallis was twenty-four years old and one places him ten years later as a senior in the drawing-office and twenty years later as a manager. At fifty or thereabouts, he joins the board of a middle-sized engineering firm and at sixty-five he retires with a decent pension, a large bungalow, and a small sailing-boat. For such men there are no biographies.*[5]

The reconstruction of Wallis's office at the Royal Air Force Museum, Hendon, features original artefacts from all stages of his career. *(Author)*

More likely, the true spark came the following year when Hartley Blyth Pratt joined White's drawing office after departing under a cloud from the great Vickers armaments company at Barrow-in-Furness. The two men quickly became friends, sharing a mutual love of running and sailing in Wallis's recently acquired dinghy. A change in the fortunes of airship construction meant that Pratt was recalled to Vickers in the spring of 1913, working in London premises rented for secrecy in the name of 'Mr Mountain'. After a few months, he called for Wallis to join him as his Chief Assistant, their friendship winning him around over worries about the company and his total lack of experience with airships. As their designs progressed, they moved up to Barrow where the airships would be built. By such chance began Wallis's association with Vickers, an association that would endure, through several changes of company name, to his retirement and beyond.

The start was rocky, with government vacillation on airship policy culminating in the cessation of all work on them in 1921. Wallis (with a £250 annual retainer from Vickers, later withdrawn) took the opportunity to obtain his BSc in Engineering from the University of London – in less than six months – and in 1922 found a post as a maths teacher at Chillon College near Lausanne in Switzerland.

Returning to England in 1923 when airships were again in the ascendancy, he married Molly Frances Bloxam on

St George's Day in 1925, in the church on the street where she lived in Hampstead, London, following a courtship conducted largely by mail beneath the veneer of a correspondence course in mathematics.[6] Molly was 17 years his junior and daughter of Wallis's patent agent Arthur Bloxam, whose sister had become Wallis's stepmother in 1916. Barnes and Molly had four children (Barnes 1924–2008, Mary b. 1927, Elisabeth b. 1933, and Christopher 1935–2006) and also brought up Molly's niece and nephew after their parents were killed in an air raid on London. After Wallis's move to Weybridge in 1930, they bought a newly-built house in Effingham, Surrey, overlooking the golf course, and remained there until frailty forced a move to a smaller house nearer the centre of the village in the spring of 1979,[7] just a few months before his death.

Wallis suffered from occasional migraine headaches, which affected him from his time at Christ's Hospital and were often so severe as to be virtually crippling. During a brief spell in hospital in 1962 he extrapolated from the ages at death of his ancestors to calculate his own death at the age of 90 – though in the event he underestimated by two years. He died at Leatherhead Hospital in October 1979 after a short illness, and is buried in Effingham. A memorial service was held for him in St Paul's Cathedral in February 1980, attended by the Prince of Wales, with the address given by his biographer and fellow Old Blue, Jack Morpurgo. Molly died in 1986.

Wallis's values

From his family Wallis had inherited a Victorian attitude to family life, and a fierce loyalty to those he depended on and who depended on him. He was a devout Christian and a habitual attender at church, other than during the war years when he sought to serve his God in other ways. He was also a faithful believer in England[8] as the geographical, but also intellectual, centre of the world, and a theme of bonding the British Empire for practical and patriotic purposes runs throughout his work, as does one of helping his fellow man as much as possible.

His work was characterised throughout by 'breadth of vision, definition of purpose and pursuit of elegant solutions' as well as his 'ability to understand those fundamental principles supporting a particular work and to isolate its potential holding problems'.[9] He was a workaholic, often working 12-hour days, sometimes even more – partly as his philosophy of leading from the front meant that he wanted to be available at all times, which in turn inspired great loyalty and affection from his workers. At many points in his career, most notably during the Second World War, he was also engaged on a large number of different projects at the same time, and was masterfully able to juggle the requirements and deadlines of all.

Something of a perfectionist, he did not want to give his customer a product that just met their specification – the simplest and cheapest option. He wanted to give his customer 'quality at almost any cost',[10] offering a specification over and above that which was called for, but with these extras being such that any additional costs were met by an even greater increase in value. Despite having a drawing office staff of up to 50, he did a lot of drawings himself – he had a drawing board in his office, and was a good draughtsman – and also had an excellent ability to interpret a set of drawings into three dimensions.

While other engineers progressed their art by tweaking at the edges of existing designs to squeeze out an extra few percent, Wallis's work is characterised by quantum leaps in new directions, his thinking 'out of the box' offering more than simply marginal improvements in performance. This originality is also a defining feature of his genius, inventing a number of concepts that no-one else would have thought of.

Probably the reason for his success in such a broad range of areas was that he was well read in many fields and so could make useful connections between disciplines (including the arts) which others had not seen. It is notable that his third fellowship, that of the Royal Aeronautical Society (1938), was preceded by fellowships of both the Institute of Civil Engineers (1929) and the Royal Society of Arts (1937). This wide knowledge base helped to nurture a number of his projects – and where he felt he did not know enough about a particular area, he would readily undertake further reading or consultation with his wide range of acquaintances in order to strengthen his knowledge of the science underlying the idea. He would often not show his hand on an idea until he was sure that he had covered all the bases in his research, so that a reader could not easily knock down or refute his proposals, which were often presented in tightly written and well-argued reports (see Appendix 2). His search for an elegant solution in the aesthetics, mechanics and production values is seen throughout his designs.

As an inventive genius, he was often put in the position of a salesman trying to sell a wholly new concept to a reluctant customer who needs prompt and satisfactory results. In this role he excelled, being able to construct a carefully reasoned argument for his ideas, while foreseeing and explaining away the most likely objections. Reading some of the 'sales pitches' in some of his reports, it is difficult not to be completely carried along by his train of thought, but this was the seed of conflict. He researched the background and theory to his ideas very thoroughly, and his confident explanation of them could be mistaken for arrogance. Further, those who could not or did not agree with his arguments he thought to be foolish or too timid to try something new, despite the obvious potential benefits of the scheme, and his undisguised disdain could lead to animosity from those to whom he was trying to sell his ideas and to frustration on the part of Wallis. He also brimmed over with so many ideas and possible applications, that he was often seen as unfocused. These combined to form a widely held opinion that he was a difficult person to work with, and consequently led to the establishment (and individuals within it) often being less co-operative than they might have been. Sir Edward Bullard at Cambridge wrote 'he is a very old friend and a splendid engineer and I have the greatest admiration for him but I would not work with him for all the tea in China'.[11]

He 'did not suffer fools gladly'[12] and was renowned for occasional use of a fiery temper (even being rebuked by his mother for it), perhaps putting down some member of the press who had asked a particularly inane question, but sometimes also on his own staff; on occasion he would rip an unsatisfactory drawing from the board of an apprentice and tear it up.

Wallis, however, was unrepentant in light of any criticism of him or his ideas:

> *I have found that the more opposition and the more criticism one gets, the more one has to perfect one's ideas in putting it forward. Half the joy consists of the fight and not the subsequent success. I think you've got to be tough, I think you have to express your own opinions definitely and firmly, but I don't say that it follows that you're always right.*[13]

Retiral

Wallis retired from BAC in 1971, which he did with considerable reluctance, despite his 83 years. Budgets were being slashed (partly due to government funding cut-backs following the bail-out at Rolls-Royce) and men much younger were retiring, but it was recognised that Wallis would take careful handling. The task fell to Sir Geoffrey Tuttle, an ex-Air Marshal who had joined BAC in 1960 and been General Manager at Weybridge for a time. He was a friend of Wallis's so he was able to state the case politely but firmly. 'Wallis then accused the company of throwing him out when all of his ideas were just coming to fruition at the height of his career'[14] and although the media made much of this, he eventually relented. To be fair, the company remained faithful to him in his retirement, allowing him to take home everything from his office (including his fine draughting machine and even the carpet) and if he needed slides made for a talk, or a car, then they continued to oblige. It is notable that the date of his retiral is not marked in his 1971 diaries, nor does the pattern of diary entries change after this date; his retiral was, however, marked by the BBC, who showed *The Dam Busters* on television for the first time that weekend.

Recognition and celebrity

Although his name was known to the public from the time of his work on *R.100* and the Wellington, Wallis's fame achieved epic proportions after the release of *The Dam Busters* book in 1951[15] and even more so after it was made into a film, released in May 1955. Wallis was also often in the press during the 1960s, commenting (usually negatively) on Britain's prevailing aircraft and airport policies. Despite foreseeing impending large increases in passenger air traffic, he opposed airport expansions for the pragmatic reason that he believed the country should be using larger numbers of smaller aircraft, and that consequently runways should be getting shorter (not longer) and more numerous. He was also often asked to comment on other aspects of science and education policy, and a recent appraisal of Wallis says that 'in interesting and important ways, however, Wallis stood for engineers as a whole and their power and influence, or lack of it, for many decades'.[16] He recognised that the United States posed the greatest threat to Britain's commercial aircraft industry by producing inferior aircraft at lower cost, and that Britain would be doubly affected if it bought these aircraft rather than developing her own. One can only imagine the thoughts in his head on the day in 1967 that Britain ordered the American F-111, which not only filled the gap left by BAC's cancelled TSR.2, but also incorporated some of his key variable-geometry concepts.

He was often called upon to give lectures, both to expert and general audiences, and undertook many to both; most notable were his Christmas lecture to the Institution of Civil Engineers in 1959, when he described details of Swallow publicly for the first time,[17] and a series of lectures entitled *The Strength of England* throughout the 1960s[18] (he also wrote a substantial article for *The Times* under this title in 1963, but BAC management told him that some of the material was confidential and was not to be published).[19] His later lecture engagements were increasingly disrupted by ill-health.[20] Jack Morpurgo, a fellow Old Blue of Christ's Hospital and Professor of American Studies at Leeds University, began a biography of Wallis in 1968; although Wallis gave the author his full support, he was keen that it should only be published after his death, but

Barnes Wallis and Michael Redgrave pose together on the set of *The Dam Busters* (1955). *(Canal+Image UK Ltd)*

friends and colleagues persuaded him to the contrary, and it was published in 1972.[21]

His numerous awards (see Appendix 3) included a CBE in 1943,[22] Fellowship of the Royal Society in 1945 (which he prized above all others) and many honorary degrees. After the Dams Raid, 'Bomber' Harris had promised his support for a knighthood but was unable to deliver against the opposition of others, even including that of Sir Charles Craven, Chairman of Vickers-Armstrongs.[23] Wallis did eventually receive a knighthood in 1968[24] – Harris (who referred to Wallis as the RAF's 'number one wizard') sent him a telegram of congratulation saying simply 'My Dear Sir'. For his wartime work, he was awarded £10,000 from the Royal Commission for Awards to Inventors,[25] and he donated this to Christ's Hospital to enable it to set up the RAF Foundationers' Trust, which continues to offer scholarships to enable the children of RAF personnel killed or injured in action to attend the school.[26]

Summary – Wallis, the man

Wallis was a man of paradoxes: a pacifist who spent much of his life working on more efficient weapons; a mathematical engineer who was equally comfortable in the role of design engineer and production engineer; a scientist with the eye of an artist; a man of deep faith who was happy to produce experimental proof for unbelievers; a futurist with a deep knowledge of history; a man born before powered flight who worked on hypersonic aircraft in his retirement; a man who relied on the establishment to support his work yet was unashamed to criticise that establishment for any shortcomings he perceived in it. In summary, he was a man with Victorian values but with ideas years ahead of his time.

'His prodigious energy, his brisk intellect, and his dancing imagination'[27] were a combination that has ensured that his genius will be long remembered.

Chapter 2

Airships

Discovery consists of seeing what everybody has seen and thinking what nobody has thought.
(Albert von Szent-Gyorgy)

A brief history of airships

The story of airships is a complex one, with liberal helpings of drama, farce, excitement and tragedy. Spurred on by a series of spectacular German successes in the first decade of the 20th century, the story in the UK was one of lukewarm political support leading to fitful progress and some measure of technical triumph, before disaster saw an end to UK development in advance of the worldwide abandonment of airships following the *Hindenburg* disaster in 1938. Rebirths of the airship phoenix continued post-war, and airships feature at both ends of Barnes Wallis's career.

Before the First World War, attempts to produce airships had generally been small efforts, the most significant being the German Zeppelin programme, which had produced 25 airships of various types by the turn of the century. Between 1909 and 1914, four passenger airships of up to 636,500cu ft capacity were built, and these had flown over 100,000 miles (with no fatal accidents) by the outbreak of war. In Britain, it was realised that the aerial scouting capability of the Zeppelins could give the German navy a serious advantage (the airship's potential as a bomb carrier was also of interest), and the Imperial Committee decided that the Royal Navy should commence a rigid airship programme. In 1909 the huge armaments firm Vickers was awarded the contract for the first ship, which was designed by it in conjunction with some naval officers, though much based on what could be gleaned about the best Zeppelin practice. As a Navy vessel, His Majesty's Airship *No.1* was built in (or rather, in the shed above) the Cavendish Dock at the Barrow shipyard of Vickers. Beset by design and weight problems, she was successfully 'launched' from her shed in May 1911, her long gestation and date of 'birth' earning her the unofficial and rather cynical name *Mayfly*. Following some tests, she was put back into the shed for modifications, and while being taken out again in September, a gust of wind caused her to break her back – she was not repaired.

In February 1912, the Naval Airship section was disbanded, but with storm clouds gathering over the continent, it was re-formed in September and began to build or procure a variety of airships. The Army had also been experimenting with airships as battlefield scouts, but on 1 January 1914 it disbanded its airship programme, and its four remaining airships (and some officers and men) were transferred to the Naval Air Service.

In this rather ad hoc manner a total of 22 rigid airships had been planned, built or acquired by the Royal Navy by early 1915. They were each allocated a serial number, even if the airship was not commonly known by this number. With the German submarine campaign getting under way, the British authorities realised that the airship offered the best way available of countering the threat. For expediency and speed of construction, small short-range non-rigid designs were also built in large numbers, and these were designated 'submarine scouts' or SS airships. They were very successful, 150 of various classes up to 360,000cu ft capacity having been built by the end of the war – making up the bulk of the 90,000 flying hours and 2 million miles covered by British airships during the war.

The SS size was about the largest possible for a non-rigid, due to limitations on the

BACKGROUND

AIRSHIPS

Airships are classed as either non-rigid (the single gas envelope maintaining its shape by internal pressure alone, with engines and payload suspended from the envelope by netting and wires), or rigid (a rigid framework of aerodynamic shape containing multiple gasbags, with engines and payload attached to the framework either internally or externally). Non-rigids are restricted in size by the strength of the gas envelope material, rigid airships being scalable to almost any size and hence able to lift more weight (cargo, engines and fuel), thus offering greater range and payload capacity. Hot air balloons are not usually formally classed as airships.

The main framework of rigid airships consisted of a series of parallel polygonal hoop girders (normally with a dozen or more sides, thus appearing roughly circular), with the same number of longitudinal girders holding the hoops together to form the overall shape of the airship. The framework was thus divided into a series of sections or 'bays', with (usually) one gasbag within each bay. The hoop girders were kept in shape by a series of radial cables, and the longitudinals were strengthened by cables or girders usually running diagonally across each quadrilateral of the outer surface. In early airships, the central bays of the envelope were mainly parallel-sided of the same diameter (for ease of fabrication), but this gave way to more aerodynamic shapes later. Early ships also often had a stronger 'keel' structure protruding along the bottom of the frame which supported the cars, engines and tanks for fuel and water ballast; in later ships, this became internal to the envelope, and later still was dispensed with entirely.

Airships were usually built within large sheds. The framework was built hanging from the roof,[i] and when the airship was inflated and thus bearing its own weight, it could be detached and floated out of the shed, a process as a rule requiring the services of hundreds of handlers on ropes.

A detailed contemporary guide to some of the particulars of rigid airship construction is given by Cole[ii] and a guide to the early evolution of the rigid airship by Pritchard.[iii]

[i] Although the airship frame was hung from the roof of the building, the latter was always referred to as a 'shed', never a 'hangar'.
[ii] Cole, A.P., 'The Principles of Rigid Airship Construction', *Flight* (1920), 132–3, 159, 183–6, 205–9.
[iii] Pritchard, J.E.M., 'Rigid Airships and their Development', *Flight* (1920), 525–8, 554–7, 578–81, 597–600.

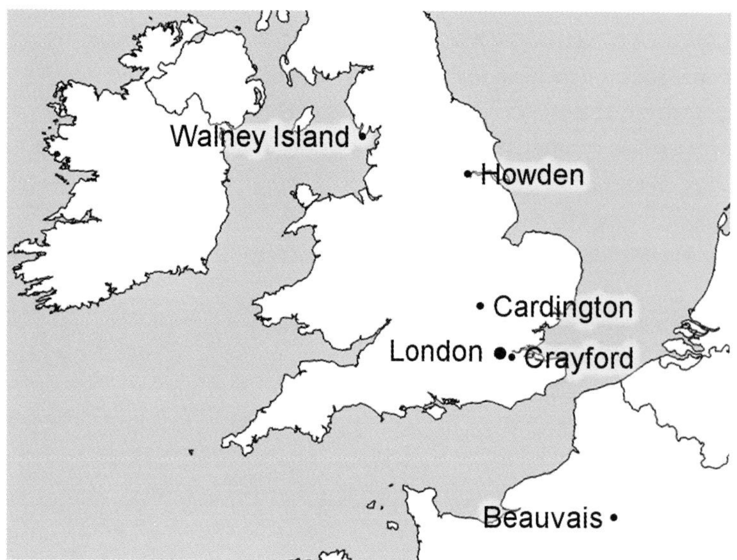

Locations associated with Wallis's work on airships. *(Author)*

envelope strength imposed by the available materials. The need to carry substantial loads, to travel faster (and thus carry more powerful engines) and travel further (and thus carry more fuel), all pointed towards rigid airships, as these allowed multiple gasbags to be used, making larger sizes more feasible.

Budget constraints and frequent suspensions or cancellations were a problem for the airship men during the war years, as many officials did not see the value in airship development, and the diet of limited funding and cancelled projects was to continue after the war. In both politics and technology, the Germans were far ahead (they relied entirely on rigid airships) and with the concept well proven before the war, there was no political wrangling about the efficacy of an airship programme; during the early war years, the Germans were launching a new rigid every ten weeks or so (the Americans lagged further behind the British).[1]

Wallis joins the Airship Programme

Although rather unremarkable in design, as it largely followed the known Zeppelin practices, HMA *No.1* was significant in being the first use of the new light alloy duralumin[2] (the German airships used either wooden or aluminium frames, not beginning to use duralumin until shortly before the war), the Admiralty insisting on duralumin over the protests of Vickers which wanted to use wood (as it was familiar with this material and working with duralumin produced some teething problems initially, even in making simple angle or channel components).[3] One critic of HMA *No.1*'s design at the Vickers works at Barrow was a young draughtsman named Hartley Blyth Pratt. Though not a member of the airship team, he independently did his own calculations on *No.1*'s structure, and predicted that she would break in two. Although he was proven right by events, this did little to endear him to his colleagues, and he chose to make a discreet exit from Vickers in 1912, joining the drawing office at White's Shipyard at Cowes where he found himself on the drawing board next to Wallis, recently having completed his apprenticeship as a shipbuilder. The two quickly became close friends, sharing a love of sailing and cross-country running.

Fresh orders for Zeppelins in Germany prompted the British government to commission the building of HMA *No.9*, and Vickers' Managing Director Sir Trevor Dawson realised that the intuitive skill shown by Pratt would be of use, and so sought him out and offered him the position of Chief Draughtsman: Airships. He was persuaded to return to Barrow, although soon did some persuasion of his own and got Wallis to come along with him as his Chief Assistant. By this turn of events, Wallis found himself with a senior post within the design team for the latest rigid airship, where he quickly proved to himself and his employers that he possessed the skills required for the job.

No.9 was to be a 846,000cu ft airship, again to be based closely on the standard Zeppelin layout – a straight-sided envelope with an external keel (the keel projected below the main gas envelope and was the primary structural element, additionally carrying concentrated loads such as ballast and fuel tanks) – though a number of innovations were included, such as swivelling propellers for improved handling at take-off and landing. She was to be strongly built, to withstand rough handling by unskilled crews on the ground and in the air. Design started in spring of 1913, in rented premises near Vickers House in central London (though the actual contract with Vickers was not signed until March 1914), and a new shed on Walney Island, near Barrow, was built for her, allowing erection to begin in August 1914.

During the spring of 1915, as *No.9* lay partly complete, work on her was stopped altogether as Churchill (then First Lord of the Admiralty) thought the war would be over before *No.9* would fly; Pratt and Wallis joined the Artists Rifles during the hiatus. As it became apparent that the war was not nearly won, work on *No.9* restarted in July. Pratt and Wallis were transferred to the RNVR and seconded to the Royal Naval Air Service to resume their design duties, Wallis at Barrow and Pratt at the RNAS Headquarters at Kingsnorth in Kent. Political and military machinations ground on between the Admiralty and Vickers, meaning that little practical work was done on the airship. The vagaries of the political process and time lost made a lasting impression on Wallis, especially as it was during wartime. He learned 'contempt for . . . the Establishment, suspicion of those who had influence without the professional knowledge to use it sensibly, and lack of patience for those who put position before creation'.[4] This would remain the backdrop to Wallis's work for the rest of his life – relishing the creation but having to battle with higher powers to get it adopted.

Ultimately, Wallis resigned his commission in November 1915, and the ship was finally completed in the autumn of 1916. However, she was found to be overweight, so Wallis put modifications in hand. These included the removal of the propeller swivelling gear and auxiliary control surfaces (her elevators were originally in triplicate), fitting of lighter gasbags, and replacement of two rear engines with a single lighter engine (which had been salvaged from the German Zeppelin *L.33* which had been brought down over Essex in September). These changes gave her a satisfactory lift, and HMA *No. 9* duly became the first British rigid to fly, in November 1916. She was formally accepted by the Admiralty in March 1917 and used mostly (as intended) for experimentation and crew training. In June 1918, after nearly 200 hours of flying, during which valuable experience in all aspects of airship building and handling had been gained, she was dismantled at Pulham, to give her shed space over to newer ships.

The resurgence of the fortunes of airships in the summer of 1915 also saw four new rigid airships being ordered – these would become known as the *R.23* class. The design was again by Pratt and Wallis, being similar to *No.9* but slightly larger (942,000cu ft capacity, with the addition of an extra bay in the envelope) and with additional armament, though the ships themselves were to be built by three different builders (two were built by Vickers) to the same initial specification. Construction of these airships proceeded faster than on *No.9*, and the first three (built by Vickers, Armstrong-Whitworth and Beardmore's) were completed by the end of 1917; work on *R.26* was started when *No.23* vacated the shed.[5]

The *R.80*

In 1917 Vickers was awarded the contract for *R.37*. This ship would be too large to be built in the Barrow shed, so Vickers planned to build a larger shed at Flookburgh in Lancashire; ultimately, the required steel could not be spared from the war effort (the Flookburgh works was never completed, and the *R.37* order was transferred to Shorts at Cardington). A design was thus required which could be built within the confines of the existing Barrow shed (about 530ft long and 70ft diameter) – the first completely original

British rigid design, being assigned the out-of-sequence serial number *R.80*.

Wallis set about designing a ship (Pratt was now mostly away from Barrow) and prepared a detailed specification within two months; this was submitted to the Admiralty in November 1917[6], and was accepted inside a week. *R.80* was to have a range of 6,400 miles at 50mph, a top speed of 65mph, and carry eight 230lb bombs, a two-pounder gun and Lewis guns (for self-defence) in patented mountings.

Now competent in all of the practicalities of airship design and construction, Wallis was able to add both aesthetic appeal and aerodynamic and structural innovation to the design. *R.80's* main visible innovation was her streamlined shape – unconvinced that the parallel-sided Zahm shape[7] was the most aerodynamic, Wallis abandoned it and by reducing the fineness ratio (i.e. making her comparatively fat for her length), he was able to create an airship of 1,200,000 cu ft with almost three times the disposable lift of *No.23*, despite being the same length (535ft). With his envelope shape offering only 3 per cent of the air resistance of a flat disc (compared to around 15 per cent for *No.23*) and the streamlining also carrying over into the design of the gondolas (which offered less than 40 per cent of the head resistance of the cars on *R.33*), the ship had a top speed of 60mph – 15 per cent faster than *No.23* despite having less powerful engines, and her manoeuvrability 'showed marked superiority over previous designs'. Further, she had a gross lift two tons above the specification – a major feat of design and construction compared to earlier ships.[8] Internally, Wallis attempted to standardise as many parts of

R.80 leaving Barrow on her maiden flight. *(© The Dock Museum (Air1_09))*

the structure as possible, to allow benefits of mass production.[9] She was equipped for mooring at a mast, but inflatable bags on her cars also meant that she could alight directly on the ground (or water) if required.[10] With the general slowdown in work following the Armistice, *R.80* would not make her maiden flight until 19 July 1920. There were a number of minor teething troubles,[11] but in her performance, *R.80* was unquestionably the finest British airship, and was in many ways equal to the contemporary Zeppelins.

Vickers attempted to promote all of its airships for civil applications, an article by the Managing Director[12] laying out the thesis, and a brochure[13] proposing designs for two 'Passenger and Mail Carrying Ships'. One was essentially *R.80* with the armament replaced by an extra car underneath for 50 passengers, the other a 3,500,000cu ft ship with six power cars and passenger accommodation for 100 along the top of the 800ft-long envelope, and a range of 4,000 miles. However, the government was unimpressed, the airship programme being wound down apart from some interest from the US Navy in *R.38*. *R.80* made a few training flights in connection with the sale in the spring of 1921,[14] and made her final flight in September 1921 to Pulham, where she was tested 'scientifically to destruction' in 1923 before her remains were finally dismantled in 1925. Britain's finest airship had flown for less than 75 hours.[15]

Of masts and men

Despite the superior German airship technology before and during the war, they had made little progress in ground handling, airships being brought down to land on the ground where a large team of men would tend to them like bees to their queen. In 1916 Cdr Masterman at the Admiralty conceived the idea of the mooring mast to simplify matters and to prevent the frequent accidents which occurred during ground handling. The concept was for the airship to fly up to the mast, where its nose would be captured by the tower (leaving the ship free to pivot in the wind), then fly off again directly. In addition to its anchoring function, an essential feature of the mast was an ability to pass supplies to the airship – hydrogen (to top up the gasbags) and water (to top up the ballast tanks) – as well as cargo and passengers, so some ingenuity was required. Masterman sketched out the requirements and Wallis performed the calculations to make them work.

This period also saw Wallis begin to apply for patents for his inventions (Vickers was keen to protect any developments by its staff). By the start of 1920 he had been awarded the first four of over 200 patents that he would ultimately be granted[16]. It is noteworthy that his first two patents[17] did not relate to airship technology directly, but to production engineering technology – for making holes and riveting.[18]

In 1918 two patent applications relating to mooring masts were submitted, one in Wallis's name mainly associated with rigid moorings and one in Masterman's relating to non-rigid moorings, though it seems likely that both men collaborated on both patents.[19] In the years that followed, Masterman attempted to give to Wallis some of the royalties earned from his patent (from at least one mast built in the USA and two in Japan),[20] but Wallis refused; Masterman instead bought him a grandmother clock from Harrods, and this remains a prized possession of the Wallis family.

Airships *vs* aeroplanes

While in the early years of the 20th century the airship's fortunes were in the ascendancy more than those of the aeroplane, by the end of the First World War the aeroplane was becoming dominant especially for military uses due to the combat vulnerability demonstrated by the airship – particularly after the invention of incendiary bullets. As the military had initially been the driving force behind airship development, there was thus a loss of impetus when the conflict ended (even in Britain, which was now the world leader in airship design; the German programme was largely dormant following the Armistice, her airships sold off as war reparations, and although the American navy continued to show some interest in airships, it would make slow progress). Despite the increasing speeds achieved by heavier-than-air machines, aircraft still had insufficient range for many commercial services, especially for the lucrative transatlantic route and other services to outposts of the empire, and were more

BACKGROUND

PATENTS

A patent is a means by which an inventor can protect the technical aspects of intellectual property rights (IPR) embodied in an invention (including copyright, trademarks and designs). A patent specification makes full public disclosure of the detail of the invention, and the inventor is then granted a monopoly right to the invention for a period, typically 20 years if renewal fees are paid. Anyone making use of the invention must license its use (usually with payment of a fee), otherwise the patentee can sue them for infringing their monopoly. A draft patent document is published around 18 months after filing, and in its final form around the time the patent is granted.

Each country has its own patent system, although there are many similarities. The legal requirements for a patent to be granted require the invention to undergo a technical search, from which three main conditions need to be met:

1. The invention described must be an original idea; stated formally, there is no 'prior art' of the same invention.

2. The invention should contain a leap of genius – something which another person well versed in the field concerned would not have thought of (in fact, many patents represent only a logical incremental improvement from what has gone before).

3. The invention must be able to be built (theoretical inventions cannot be patented, and the situation with mathematical methods and computer software is complicated).

When a patent is applied for (usually via a Chartered Patent Agent/Attorney), the Patent Office examines the patent, searching for prior art, practicality and inventiveness, and if satisfied, the patent is awarded. It should be noted that the patentee is permitted to make minor additions and alterations to the patent within the 12-month period following application and prior to the formal date of examination of the patent. Importantly, this means that the detailed content of the patent cannot be dated to the date of application (unless the original application is available), only to the date of the completed specification being submitted.

Typically, Wallis's patents were awarded between two and four years after initial application, although due to the secret nature of some, these only became public much later – for example two of the 'bouncing bomb' patents were applied for in 1942, but not published until 1963. Wallis was a voracious patenter of his inventions, being granted 140 UK patents (plus 42 in the USA and more than 60 in other countries) over the period between 1918 and 1969, either in his own name or that of his employer (most of his airship patents are in the name of the Airship Guarantee Company).

His stream of published patents stops abruptly in 1959, a further dozen applications submitted up to 1965 all being abandoned before publication for various reasons.[i] Consequently his later inventions (such as the cascade and vulture-wing aircraft, and the high-pressure submarine) were never covered by patents. A summary of the Wallis patents is given in a recent paper.[ii]

[i] SM Arch BNW EC7/2.

[ii] Spear, Brian, 'Sir Barnes Wallis, a radical engineer and his patents', *World Patent Information* (28, 2006), 20-33.

dependent on good weather for navigation. Further, the low reliability of piston engines was a serious problem for aeroplanes – an engine failure would normally lead to an aircraft being brought down, but as an airship did not rely on its engines for lift, a failure would merely result in it arriving late at its destination. Even by the end of the 1920s, practical short-haul airliners had a range limit of 500 miles or so. Crucially, this was not far enough to reach Gibraltar (1,000 miles from the UK and the closest British colony) which meant that an 'all red' route – across the empire using only British-controlled territories (coloured red on contemporary maps) was not possible using an aircraft.[21]

Governments and manufacturers were thus engaged in long debates about whether it was better to invest development effort into airships or aeroplanes, the initial rounds of this debate going to the aeroplane lobby.

In late 1919, with the war over and *R.80* nearing completion, Vickers produced a paper arguing the profound benefits of airships for commercial aviation, with full details and costings of a proposed passenger and mail service to Rome via Paris. Plans and models of a commercial transatlantic service were also prepared, but the ideas were largely rejected by the Air Ministry, and the Vickers Airship Department was closed down. Wallis still held out hope for the future of airships and, while initially kept on an annual retainer of £250 by Vickers, made the most of his career hiatus by entering the University of London where he gained a BSc in Engineering in the spring of 1923 after only six months' work. His practical experience meant that he hardly needed the qualification, but the respectability that it offered was something he had coveted in his graduate peers.

He then accepted a position as mathematics master at Chillon College, a private school near Lausanne in Switzerland. He enjoyed both his new job, where he relished the opportunity to impart to others the skills that he had learned from Armstrong and Browne, and the college, with the opportunity to improve his hesitant German, though he found himself yearning for home due to a blossoming personal relationship with the niece of his father's second wife, Molly Bloxam. She was 17 years his junior and then just 18 years old. Not experienced in matters of the heart, despite his age, Wallis fostered the blossoming friendship via a correspondence course with Molly in mathematics[22] and Cupid was to further assist Wallis with yet another revival of the rigid airship programme.

The Imperial Airship Scheme

During 1922 and 1923 Cdr C. Dennistoun Burney (see biography in Appendix 1), with Vickers' support, lobbied strongly for a new commercial airship programme for passenger services to India and Australia. Burney had invented the minesweeping paravane during the First World War (earning him considerable royalties) and was the Conservative MP for Uxbridge. In 1924, the new Labour government set up a Cabinet committee to consider the matter, under the new Air Minister, Lord Thomson of Cardington, who was a keen supporter of air travel. The committee resolved that the government should undertake an experimental airship development programme for services to Canada and India (initially with Australia, New Zealand, Kenya and other destinations to follow). Its initial budget was £1,350,000 over three years, but both proved to be very optimistic. The programme was to investigate the feasibility of using airships for long-distance travel, by building two airships and conducting a test programme to demonstrate the efficacy of the airships for this purpose. A memorandum prepared by the Air Minister outlined the building of the two ships, one funded and controlled directly by the Air Ministry, and the other as a commercial enterprise funded via a fixed-price contract. This scheme was seen as 'politically correct' while also ensuring the best design through scientific competition, and also preventing failure of the programme should an 'accidental failure' befall one ship (although the latter words were to prove hollow). It was expected that the best design features of both prototypes would be incorporated into the next generation of airships.

To support the programme, the National Physical Laboratory (NPL) carried out a series of wind tunnel tests to derive the most aerodynamic shape for the ships (which offered less than 2 per cent of the resistance of a circular plate of the same diameter as the hull), and *R.33* was reconditioned to carry out a series of experimental flight tests in support of the programme.[23] Sites were also sought for termini, with masts being constructed at St Hubert near Montreal in Canada, Ismailia in Egypt (as an intermediate stop) and Karachi in India (now in Pakistan)[24] – the latter also had a shed built to house *R.101*, and there were plans for a shed at Montreal too. Meteorological investigations of the proposed route to India were also undertaken to support the programme.

The broad specification of the ships was as follows:

1. To be built within the 1924 guidelines.[25]
2. To be of 5,000,000cu ft capacity, giving a gross lift of 150 tons and a disposable lift of 60 tons (40 per cent of gross lift).[26]
3. To be capable of 70mph with a cruising speed of 63mph (monetary penalties would be imposed if the design speeds were not met – £1,000 for each mph below specification).
4. Accommodation (for 100 passengers and mail) to be within the envelope (i.e. not in external cars) to reduce drag.
5. To be operated on fuel that could be safely used in tropical climates; this in effect meant that diesel engines were to be used (as petrol and its electric ignition system was considered too volatile for use in the tropics).

The new scheme had prompted Vickers to form the Airship Guarantee Company specifically to undertake the commercial airship contract (awarded 22 October 1924 at a fixed price of £350,000),[27] with Burney as Managing Director. He hoped to employ Wallis as Secretary to the Design Committee, comprising Maj George Scott and Wg Cdr Reginald Colmore (both experienced airship men, though as crew rather than designers) and two airship engineers, Lt Col Vincent Richmond (originally a chemist) and W. Nixon (originally a stockbroker). Wallis would have nothing to do with design-by-committee, and wanted sole charge of design (Pratt was initially involved too, but subsequently refused to work with Burney). Burney conceded when Wallis produced a draft design for the whole airship, and he was appointed Chief Designer in May 1923; the four others did not join the company, but went over to the rival design team, Scott leading and Richmond doing the main design work with Sqn Ldr Frederick Rope as his assistant. Looking back, Wallis said:

> *The ensuing seven years were years of great anxiety and responsibility and fertility on my part, for on the engineering side I was practically single handed. Fortunately, I was joined by Major P.L. Teed, barrister, chemist and metallurgist, who inflated all my ships during the war, and by J.E. Temple, an able but erratic mathematician who had been with me at Barrow and had specialised in the stress analysis of rigid airship hulls.*[28]

Temple left early on in the work to be replaced by Nevile Shute Norway – later to gain fame as novelist Nevile Shute (see biography in Appendix 1). The Airship Guarantee Company acquired the former RNAS station at Howden in Yorkshire, together with its shed, for construction of the new ship (design was begun at Vickers House in 1924, then continued at the Vickers works at Crayford in Kent, before transferring to Howden); the government ship was to be built at the Royal Airship Works at Cardington in Bedfordshire. Both sheds were double units, with the airship built in one and the other used for fabrication and laying out of materials.[29]

The commercial ship was allocated the serial *R.100*, and the government ship *R.101* – there have been various explanations put forward for the selection of these numbers, including a rather derogatory version told to Wallis by Scott that the *R.100* was the last of the old style of ships, and *R.101* the first of a new style, but the true source of the ships' numbering seems to be unrecorded. Newspapers of the time suggested many romantic names for the two airships, but Lord Thomson vetoed the idea of naming them.[30]

Just as the *Titanic* achieved far greater fame than her more successful sisters, the *R.101* tragedy is far more well known than the success of the *R.100*. It is not the intention here to discuss *R.101* in any detail, as she was not the work of Wallis, but it is interesting to compare her design with Wallis's *R.100* (as both were built to the same general specification and requirements) and see how the different design decisions on the two ships contributed to their relative success. Various facets of the designs will be examined in turn.

The shape

In support of the Imperial Airship Scheme, wind tunnel tests at the NPL were used to develop the most aerodynamically efficient envelope shape for the two ships, which meant that the teardrop shape of the two ships was very similar. The most aerodynamic fineness ratio (i.e. the length relative to the diameter) was found to be between 4.5:1 and 5:1, with the widest part of the hull about two diameters back from the bow. The final shape of both airships was derived from profile U721 produced by the NPL.[31]

The section of *R.100* forward of the maximum diameter was in fact an oblate spheroid,[32] the envelope profile in this region being a semi-ellipse; the profile of the rear section was of a circular section. In cross-section, she was a 16-sided polygon (rather than purely circular) but tests showed the difference in drag between these shapes to be negligible. She had only three power cars, each with two engines in tandem, and a small control car external to the envelope, the control car being the only protuberance in the forward section, which was known to be more sensitive to turbulence caused by such protrusions.[33] The three power cars accounted for 18 per cent of the overall drag of the airship[34] compared to 13 per cent for the fins and the remaining 69 per cent for the envelope; the overall drag coefficient was found to be less than *R.33* or *R.38*[35]. *R.101* had two of her five power cars in the forward section, and her control car in a similar location to *R.100*; this (and her greater weight) may have contributed to her lower top speed (71mph) compared to *R.100* (80mph) – although *R.100*'s engines were more powerful. Another advantage of not having large accommodation cars external to the envelope was that the envelope size that could be constructed inside a shed of a given size was maximised, as no clearance for the external cars was required.

Framework

Both *R.100* and *R.101* were largely conventional in the general arrangement of their frameworks and structure, based on three-dimensional Warren trusses (an efficient truss of triangular sections) forming light but rigid girders. *R.101* was 15-sided with 15 bays (later 16); transverse frame girders were triangular with the point inwards and longitudinals were also triangular with the point outwards, being attached to the outside of the transverse

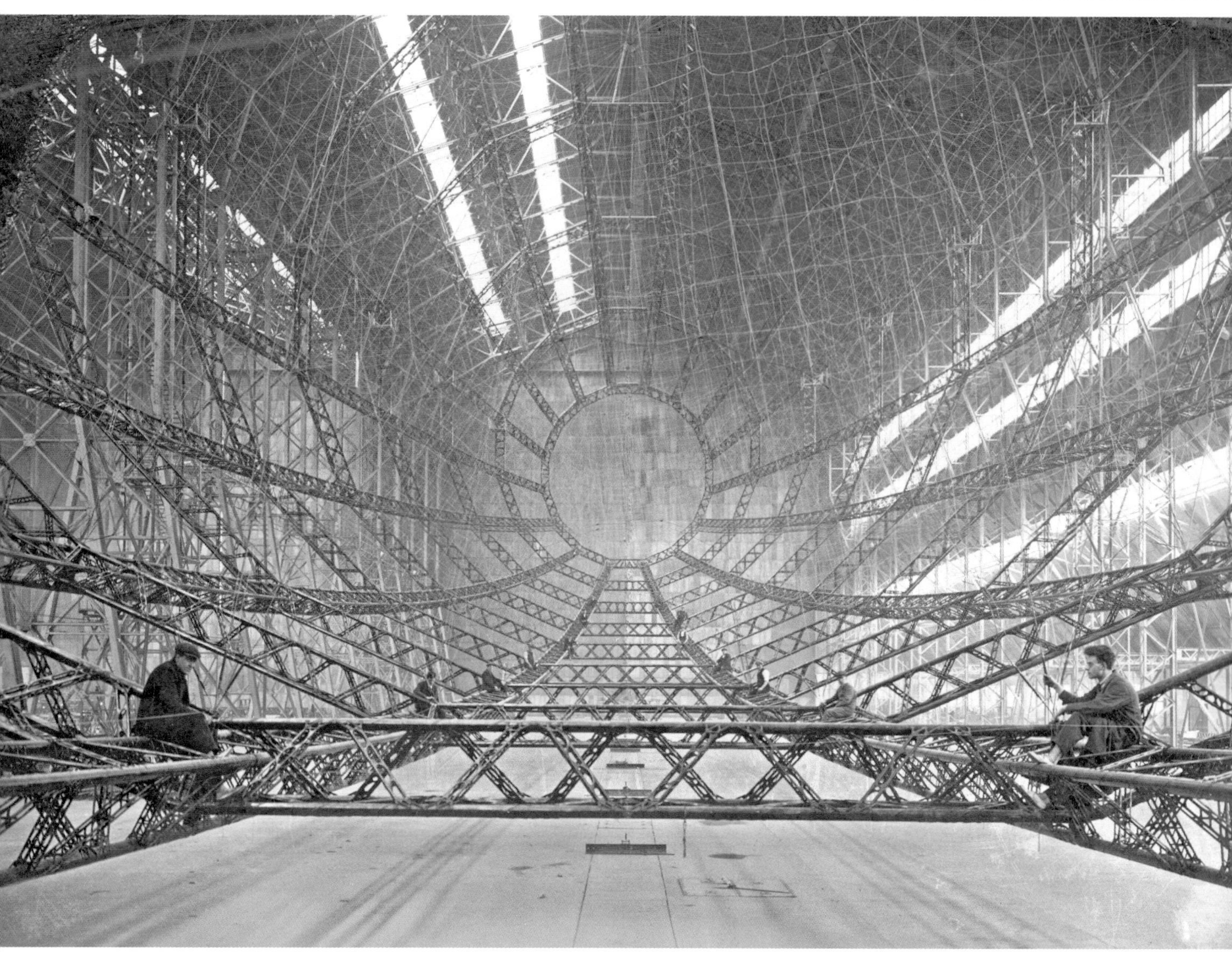

A fine view of the framework of *R.100*, almost complete and hanging from the roof of the shed. *(BAE SYSTEMS via the Science Museum)*

frames. *R.100* was 16-sided with 15 bays, the transverse frames also being triangular with the point inwards; Wallis had originally planned to use the space within these girders for ventilation and as passageways for moving around inside the ship.[36] One novelty in *R.100* would have been the use of a triangular bracing girder within each transverse frame (instead of traditional bracing wires running across the frame); however, this idea was dropped.[37] *R.101* did dispense with bracing wires by using a very deep section for the transverse frames – 10.5ft compared to the 2.5ft of *R.100*'s transverse frames. *R.100*'s framework was designed to cope with updraughts of 4,000ft/s; these exert a shear force on the structure, and it had been estimated that an updraught of 2,000ft/s had caused the failure of the structure of the first American-built rigid airship, ***Shenandoah***, leading to her loss in a storm in September 1925.

The design and manufacture of the *R.100* girders showed a series of Wallis innovations, and is an excellent demonstration of Wallis's penchant for production engineering. Continuing the idea he began with *R.80*, he fashioned the main framework from a series of only seven different parts, allowing these to be economically mass-produced (some in their millions); the entire structure was made from only 42 different types of part.[38] Simple construction meant that unskilled labour could be used, which was in ready supply from the surrounding farm workers (although Shute reported alarming levels of promiscuity among the workforce!) and Hull trawlermen (whom Wallis found had no fear of heights).[39] The whole assembly was accomplished by 20 to 30 men within a 12-month period,[40] this helping to keep costs down.

The main longitudinal girders required tubes longer than were available, so Wallis devised a machine (built to his design by Messrs Charles Churchill) to make tubes of the required length by winding a long strip of duralumin into a spiral and riveting the edges together, both the tubes and the machine being the subject of patents.[41] The length of the tubes was thus limited only by the length of the duralumin strips available. The Wallis tubes were also cheaper – the duralumin strip was one-third of the price (per lb) of the tubing in the lengths available[42] and in tests by the Royal Aircraft Establishment (RAE) it was found that the spiral tubes and a girder made from it 'compares favourably as regards stress carrying capacity with other forms of duralumin construction'.[43] During construction, the damp conditions in the Howden shed were found to be corroding the framework, and Wallis elected to have the whole framework varnished to halt the corrosion, despite the weight penalty of doing so.

The ship's transverse frames were assembled on the floor of the shed, and then hung from the roof in the correct position, the longitudinal girders then being hoisted into position to join each transverse frame to its neighbours. The whole framework remained hanging from the roof until the gasbags were inflated.

Unusually for an airship, the *R.101* main structural members were made of stainless steel (with bracing parts made from duralumin), designed and fabricated by the Boulton & Paul aircraft company's skilled labour force in Norwich, then transported to Cardington for final assembly.[44] A measure of the success of Wallis's framework design can be seen in the fact that the final structure of *R.100* was its intended weight, whereas the largest part of the overweight problem experienced by *R.101* was due to her structure.[45]

The main solution to *R.101*'s weight problem was to insert an extra bay into the centre of the ship; this added very little to the structure weight, but added substantially to the lift. This technique had been used previously on Zeppelins, and the technique continues to be used on ships to cure deadweight problems or to increase carrying capacity.

Wallis's tube machine – flat strip enters on the right and is formed into a spiral, being pneumatically riveted before emerging as a tube on the left. *(BAE SYSTEMS via the Science Museum)*

The extreme tail cone of *R.100* collapsed during her sixth test flight on 22 May 1930; the cause was believed to be air pressure differences in the slipstream. The tail was rebuilt in heavier-gauge materials and with a blunt end, making the ship about 12ft shorter – much to Wallis's annoyance. Wallis gave consideration to all-moving tail fins for directional control[46] but did not carry this through to the final design.

The gasbags

Lifting gas

The enduring image of the airship era is the *Hindenburg* disaster which, together with the images of the burned-out wreckage of *R.101*, highlights the flammability of hydrogen as a lifting gas. However, this impression hides two underlying truths – first that prior to these accidents, nearly all airship accidents were due to structural failure (rather than fire), and that hydrogen was actually reasonably safe as a lifting gas. Wallis himself argued for the benefits of hydrogen in a 1926 paper:[47]

1. Hydrogen is very light, so any leaking gas tends to rush upwards and away from the ship, and not to accumulate around the leak.[48]
2. Helium, although non-flammable, is not quite as light as hydrogen, so using helium reduces the ship's disposable lift by about 16 per cent compared to using hydrogen.
3. Helium cost about 30 times as much as hydrogen, and is only available from the USA (and hence was expensive to transport in pressurised cylinders).
4. The ability to 'recycle' the hydrogen. As fuel and ballast is used up during its journey, an airship becomes lighter, and hydrogen must be deliberately vented to keep its lift constant. It was planned to add hydrogen to the engine fuel mix (see section on engines below), the hydrogen being that which would otherwise be vented from the gasbags.

While these arguments find much in favour of hydrogen over helium, the discussion was rather academic, as helium was only available in large quantities from the USA (it was found in two natural vents in Texas and Kansas) and the Americans embargoed the export of helium, thus effectively preventing its use in Europe.

The lift generated by the gasbags also varies inversely with the temperatures of the gas in the bag and outside the ship. For this reason, the Imperial Airship Service schedules were designed with take-offs and landings occurring at times away from the hottest part of the day, thus maximising the available lift of the ship as it manoeuvred.

As a safety consideration, Wallis ensured that there was ventilation space between the gasbags and the outer cover, and between the gasbags and the passenger accommodation. One of his patents[49] describes a gasbag fitted with a double outer layer, which would have been filled with nitrogen or similarly inert gas, but it appears this form of bag was not implemented on *R.100*. The hydrogen for *R.100* was generated by special plant installed at the Howden site, using the silicol process to generate up to 60,000cu ft per hour.[50] This was piped beneath the floor to connections under each bag. Great care had to be taken with the filling to prevent tearing the bags, or getting them in the wrong position.[51]

Suspension wiring

The gasbags containing the lifting gas were of lower diameter than the outer skin of the airship, usually within the internal diameter of the supporting framework. The gasbag volume was thus not the full volume of the visible external envelope (the gaps between the bags and framework allowed for working or cargo spaces, and also allowed any escaping lift gas to circulate away from the ship). The general arrangement was to use a series of bags, usually one within each bay (framework section) of the airship. The bags were cylindrical in shape; in the early straight-sided ships they were all the same size, but in the later streamlined ships they were different sizes, although usually still cylindrical (in the sections where the hull was tapering, there was thus an uneven gap between the gasbags and the outer cover).

The gasbag attachments were made from steel cables and had to provide two services – holding up the bag when empty, and when full, transmitting the generated lift to the surrounding structure. While the lift was at right angles to the length of the airship in level flight, if the ship was climbing or diving, then the buoyancy of the bags led to longitudinal forces being generated (a forward pull when the ship was climbing and vice versa), which the gasbag wiring also had to contain. Due to the buoyancy of the gas, more lift force was exerted towards the top of the bags (zero at the bottom rising by 0.068lb/sq ft per foot in height,[52] thus around 8lb/sq ft at the top of the largest bags in *R.100* and *R.101*).

The Zeppelin method of gasbag containment at the time was to use a series of wire hoops around the circumference of the bag, in order to transmit the lift from the bag to the longitudinal keel beam at the bottom of the envelope. In *No.9* and *R.80*, the bags were allowed to press upon the longitudinal girders at the top of the frame (the bag was contained within a net to prevent bulging between the girders), and the lift was then carried down to the keel by lift wires running from top to bottom of each transverse frame (in addition to the radial stressing wires within these frames).

However, for the new airships, the Air Worthiness Panel specified that the gasbags were to exert no force upon the longitudinal members whatsoever. This ruling (intended to make testing of the forces in the cables and frames easier to perform) meant in effect that the gasbag cables could only be attached to the transverse frames. Solutions to this new problem were derived uniquely and independently by Wallis for *R.100* and by Richmond and Rope for *R.101*, and the different solutions are worthy of comparison.

In *R.101*, the solution adopted was to hold each bag with two harnesses similar to a parachute, one over the forward part of the bag with its cables anchored to the frame behind and one over the rear part of the bag with its cables anchored to the frame in front. The harnesses were anchored directly to the lowest point on each transverse frame (where the tension could be measured if required), thus avoiding the longitudinal frames, and the fore-and-aft pairing meant that longitudinal lift forces were also adequately dealt with. A full-scale bay of the *R.101* framework had been built to undergo stress testing, and the new suspension method was tested by inflating a gasbag within this test section.[53] Although this appeared satisfactory, this innovation in *R.101* caused considerable problems. The bags were found to rub in places on the girderwork, and sharp protuberances on the frame made many holes – after her initial test flights, all but one of the gasbags were found to be holed, one with a remarkable 103 holes. The overweight problem of the ship was initially dealt with by 'letting out' the gasbag harnesses to increase the capacity of the bags (and thus lift), but this led to further rubbing (despite over 4,000 pads being put in place to cover protuberances on the frame). It is certain that the main cause of the *R.101* crash was loss of hydrogen from the fore part of the ship, and it is probable that damage to the gasbags (possibly from wear but exacerbated by the rough weather) was a major contributing factor to this loss of gas.

For *R.100*, Wallis sought his own method of containing the gasbags in accordance with the given constraints. His initial idea was that of the 'parallel helix', a series of wires stretched tightly from one transverse frame to the next, though not connecting corresponding joints between frames, but the next joint around the frame. The problem with this method was that volume contained by wires arranged this way was slightly smaller than the full volume available within the bay, this being enough to reduce the overall lift by 4–5 tons,[54] and he sought a more economical method. Wallis knew of the idea of 'great circle' routes, a concept from terrestrial navigation which allowed calculation of the shortest route between two points on the spherical surface of the Earth.[55] Thus inspired, he realised that if he wrapped a series of cables helically around the cylindrical gasbags, the cables should naturally form great circle segments; these would be anchored to the transverse frames, and hence the tension in each would be easily measurable. By using a 'right-handed' and a 'left-handed' series of cables, he would have a mesh of cables to contain the whole bag; as each wire would be stable (as they already sat in the position of shortest distance over the surface), they would not move out of position, and this would remain true even if there were longitudinal forces in play, such as when the ship was climbing or diving. Wallis's mathematics was good enough to confirm that his idea appeared sound, but for maximum gas volume he wished to use tapering gasbags within the streamlined shape of the envelope, and he was less confident of his solution when he applied the idea to non-cylindrical bags. He thus enlisted the help of a professor at University College, London,[56] who confirmed that the calculations were valid on the tapering bags too, and noted that the cables would follow geodesic lines around the surface.[57] Thus geodesy and aeronautics came together for the first time in the elegant gasbag wiring of *R.100*, although its golden age would not come until the next stage of Wallis's life.[58] Importantly, the outer surface of the gasbags would thus occupy the maximum available volume within the framework (95 per cent of the envelope volume was filled with gas), maximising the lift available.

It appears that Rope's parachute harness was not the subject of a patent application, but Wallis did patent his geodetic harness, although the word does not make an appearance in the applications.[59] Due to the greater lift force to be contained at the top of the bags, the cables were pitched more closely at the top, fanning out towards the bottom; the cables were free to move into the 'great circle' positions and as there were no connections between the wires, they were all 'isotenic', i.e. with equal tension in every part, which could be quite easily measured at either end of the wire. Additional horizontal wires were strung between the transverse frames to support the main wires when the gasbags were not fully inflated, but these were not attached to the main wires.

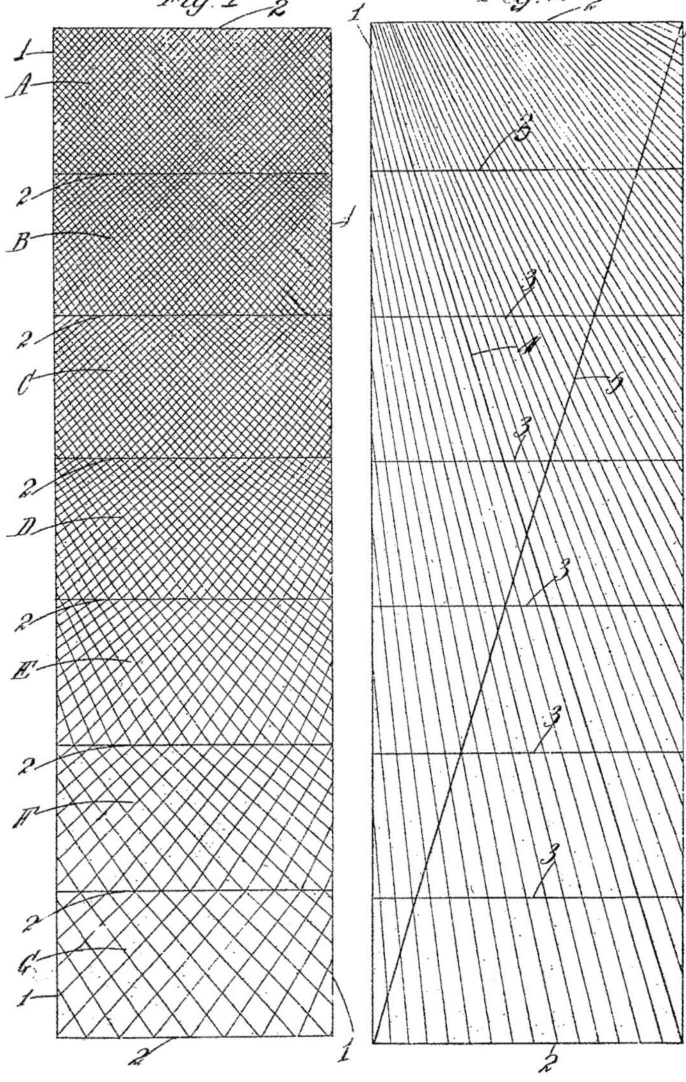

The geodetic wiring for the gasbags on *R.100*. The panels with more densely packed wiring would be towards the top of the bag where hydrogen pressure was greatest (Patent GB233020). *(BAE SYSTEMS)*

Material

Throughout the development of airships, a number of materials had been used to make the gasbags, which had to be flexible, strong, tear-resistant and gas-tight. Most commonly, a permutation of rubber-coated canvas was employed, often supplemented by doping or covering in a material known as 'gold-beater's skin', a thin membrane from the outer part of an ox's intestine which had excellent gas-tight properties (this was first used in the bags for *No.9*). However, an airship of the *R.23* class required around 350,000 intestines[60] to make her gasbags, so it was not surprising that there were sometimes shortages. The Germans were the experts in the manufacture of this material, and despite British efforts at making an alternative, the German version remained the best. Both *R.100* and *R.101* thus used gasbags made in Germany (by a subsidiary of the Zeppelin company[61] and these were of standard fabrication – cotton fabric with two layers of 'gold-beater's skin' glued to the inside; then varnished on the inside and (with the addition of beeswax and aluminium powder) on the outside.

Richmond formulated a rubber-based gasbag material[62] and Major Phil Teed on Wallis's team developed 'an excellent substitute' material, but despite Wallis's assertion[63] that 'first-class bags from synthetic materials' were practical, these appear not to have been adopted. Reflecting in 1970, he noted that 'GB's skin is probably as good as anything that can be made but nylon and polyurethane may be better'.

Valves

As an airship rises, the atmospheric pressure outside it falls, thus leading to an increase in volume of the gasbags. To prevent too large a pressure differential being set up (which might lead to rupture of the bags, or their enlarged size causing them to come into contact with the structure) the bags contained large valves, held closed by a spring, and when the pressure outside the bag fell sufficiently (compared to the internal pressure), these valves opened to bleed out some hydrogen and stabilise the pressure (loss of gas is thus proportional to the change in altitude required), and airships tended to fly relatively low and avoid repeated changes in altitude for this reason.[64] Traditionally, the gasbags each had one of these relief valves at the bottom (as hydrogen would not leak downwards), and they functioned entirely automatically. The valves were quite large – up to 4ft across – due to the volume of hydrogen that might need to be discharged in a short time, and fed into a fabric trunking which was led up within the transverse frames to the top of the ship where the gas could safely escape. Wallis patents describe the operation of these vents and trunks.[65] Most of the bags had an additional valve at the top; this was controlled manually by the crew for venting gas to make the ship descend under pilot control, such as when coming in to land. Note that any gas lost by venting (either automatic or manual) could not be replaced during the flight, and this effectively limited the range of the commercial airship (and meant that the base facilities had to include hydrogen generators to top-up visiting airships).[66]

In respect of the gas valves, *R.100* was in fact completely conventional, using valves of a standard design and in the conventional locations at the top (manoeuvring valves) and bottom (relief valves) of the gasbags. *R.101*, however, used a novel method of gas valving. The valves were conventional in construction, but had two unique characteristics – they were designed to function as both relief and vent valves, and were positioned halfway up the sides of the bag.[67] This positioning meant that they were easier to inspect than conventional manoeuvring valves, but also that any leak in the valves would allow hydrogen (at least from the bottom half of the bag) to escape, with an attendant loss of lift. During *R.101*'s test flights, some accidental operation of these valves was observed, especially when rolling during rough weather, leading to loss of hydrogen from the bags. It is likely that this also occurred during her final flight due to the stormy conditions encountered over France, and may have contributed to the loss of lift which brought the ship down.

Covering

The cover was described by Wallis as 'perhaps the least satisfactory part of a modern rigid',[68] noting that a poorly fitted cover could reduce performance more than any other factor. The conventional covering for the outer envelope of airships consisted of a layer of canvas painted with cellulose dope – this made the canvas smoother, stiffer and also airtight; metal powder was often mixed with the dope to increase the reflectivity of the cover and hence reduce heating of the gas by the sun. Some measure of insulation and internal ventilation was provided by an annular air space between the gasbags and the cover.

The canvas was usually stitched into position between the frames and then doped, as this also tightened the covering, and this was done on *R.100*. For *R.101*, however, it was initially decided (for reasons of speed) to pre-dope the sections, and then stitch them on.[69] Unfortunately this plan proved unsuccessful as the dope-hardened covering tended to split when fitted, and the original cover had to be entirely replaced by one doped in situ as per the normal practice.

To keep the cover smooth and flat in flight, it needed to be tensioned to minimise 'flutter' which both increased drag and damaged the cover. This was usually done by fitting a mesh on the inside of the longitudinal girders (the cover was on the outside) then lacing the cover down on to the mesh, so that the cover formed a slightly concave outer panel. *R.101* used reefing booms to push out the cover midway between the panel edges, giving her a more circular appearance in section. Patents by T.R. Cave-Browne-Cave on the *R.101* team[70] and Wallis[71] both described improvements to this system, a Wallis alternative[72] using air scooped in from forward motion to inflate the cover and keep it taut seems to have been found impractical and was not actually used.

The *R.100* cover was satisfactory, although there was some 'flutter' when travelling at high speed, leading to standing wave patterns being observed in the cover. The ship flew over Farnborough on one test flight so that the effect could be photographed from an aircraft. Part of the cover on the upper fin split during rough weather in the later stages of the ship's voyage to Canada, but repairs were made in flight.

Engines

Airships were powered by diesel or petrol engines carried in 'power cars' protruding below the main gas envelope. These drove standard or variable-pitch propellers, either in fixed positions or via a swivelling mechanism for additional control. Reversing was achieved either by stopping and reversing the engines,[73] requiring some care to avoid overheating if the radiator was out of the propeller slipstream, or by having a separate reversing engine (although not initially intended, this was the scheme used on *R.101*).

Part of the Imperial Airship specification was that the ship had to use 'fuel that could be safely used in tropical climates' and the implication of this was that petrol was not to be used, as it was more volatile and burned at a higher temperature than heavier oils, and was hence seen as more of a hazard in tropical climates.

Research in 1920 by a Mr Ricardo had shown that adding hydrogen gas to an engine burning kerosene would increase its smoothness, economy and lower its running temperature. It was planned to develop such engines for the airships; the hydrogen for the fuel additive would be that which would otherwise be vented from the gasbags during normal flight to compensate for the weight of other fuel burned.[74]

Development of the engines proved extremely difficult, with vibration problems prompting a major redesign, which left the engines underpowered and seriously overweight. For the maiden flight to Canada, Wallis obtained permission to fit *R.100* with petrol engines (factory reconditioned Rolls-Royce Condor V-12s each developing 650hp). These engines were only half as heavy as *R.101*'s, but as petrol is about four times as heavy as diesel, *R.100* would have required about 30 per cent more weight of fuel for the same range as diesel engines. *R.100* carried around 30 tons of petrol held in tanks spread throughout the length of the ship,[75] and used nearly all of it on her voyage to Canada.[76]

A further Wallis innovation in the *R.100* power cars[77] was a layout with the hull attachments in the centre of the car, and the engines at the ends – this permitted the simplest attachment possible to the engine itself, hence facilitating engine replacement (the radiator was fitted to the centre section, and served both engines).

Success – and failure

The construction of *R.100* and *R.101* continued very much in parallel, sometimes one team appearing to be in the lead, sometimes the other, though the media tended to favour the 'Government ship', *R.101*. *R.101* was first taken from her shed on 12 October 1929, with her first test flight two days later; *R.100* was only slightly behind, taking her first flight on 16 December to the Cardington mast, some 'panting' of parts of the cover being investigated on a trial flight the following day, resulting in some of the cover bracing wires being tightened. It had already been decided that *R.100* would open the service to the Canadian city of Montreal, and *R.101* the service to Karachi in India (now in Pakistan) with a stop at Ismailia in Egypt. The base facilities at all three places were ready to receive their charges.

Early trial flights showed that *R.101* exhibited slow rolling at high wind speeds (leading to unwanted operation of her gas valves), and chafing of her gasbags on the structure.

R.100, after initial trials including a 53-hour endurance flight, was undergoing some modifications in June 1930, and pending successful further trials, it was decided not to cut *R.101* to insert the new bay in case she would have to undertake the Canadian flight in her place – but *R.100* was ready for her maiden flight to Canada departing on 29 July 1930.[78] This she undertook successfully, although Wallis was not on board, having been forbidden by his new boss, Sir Robert McLean, from going on the trip, and the design team was represented by Nevil Shute Norway.[79] The airship performed entirely as expected and as she had done on her trials (maximum speed was 81mph, but there was no financial bonus for this above-specification speed), with only one incident where a thunderstorm over the St Lawrence river led to some tearing of the cover on her fins; this was detected and temporary patching was put in place during the flight, and she arrived safely at the Montreal mast after a flight time of just under 79 hours. After a flight around the area for the benefit of the press, the return trip began on 14 August and was even less eventful, the ship being back at the mast at Cardington after just 59 hours.

With the commercial airship programme showing its first major success, it was the turn of *R.101* to undertake her maiden voyage to India. As the summer was climactically disadvantageous to an airship, it was decided to postpone this flight to the autumn (also allowing time for her extra bay to be inserted). After just a single 16-hour trial flight in her lengthened condition, she embarked on her flight to India with 54 people, including Lord Thomson, on board; it seems likely that he exerted some pressure

R.100 moored to the St Hubert mast at the end of her transatlantic flight. Note the truncated tail cone. *(BAE SYSTEMS)*

for the flight to take place in time for him to attend a conference in India. Crossing the Channel and over northern France, she experienced the roughest weather she had encountered, and travelling at about 2,000ft near Beauvais suffered a sudden loss of lift in the fore part of the ship. The helm managed to level her out from the resulting dive using up-elevator, but no sooner had they done so than she went nose-down again and struck the ground, bursting immediately into flames.

All of the senior crew, design staff and the six passengers died in the inferno; only eight on board survived, two more succumbing to their injuries within days.

The effect on the British public was not unlike that following the *Titanic* disaster – deep shock that a technologically advanced flagship had been destroyed apparently by a simple natural occurrence, with a heavy loss of life of those on board. A memorial service was held at St Paul's on 11 October.

The public inquiry which was conducted immediately after the disaster[80] found that the ship was brought down by a loss of lifting gas from the forward part of the ship, but did not give any strong indication as to the reason for the loss of gas. Nor did it point any fingers of blame to any individuals, although this may have been partly out of respect, as her political master Lord Thomson and all of her principal designers had been on board. It is notable that Dr Hugo Eckener of the Zeppelin Company was invited to give evidence to the inquiry, but neither Wallis nor any of his *R.100* design colleagues were called. Later reconsideration of the circumstances of the crash[81] has suggested the cause as storm damage to the forward gasbags, with primary blame on the shoulders of Lord Thomson who effectively pressed ahead with the flight schedule despite misgivings and lack of time for trials of the modified ship.

Although of completely separate design, the *R.101* disaster spelt the end for *R.100* as surely as if she had crashed herself, but research by the Airship Heritage Trust suggests that her fate was not sealed as quickly as is often thought.[82] She was deflated in the Cardington shed in December 1930, and her fate was discussed by Parliament during 1931.

Some contemporary papers[83] continued to discuss (almost as if *R.101* had never crashed) a future programme for *R.100*, reiterating the original intention that the programme would continue even if one of the airships should fail, even suggesting that a continued flying programme would restore public confidence in airships (and noting the ongoing programmes in Germany and the USA). This correspondence also notes the excellent condition that the airship was in, apart from the outer cover for which a replacement was required. It was also proposed to add a bay to *R.100* to increase her fuel capacity and hence range (as originally built, she could reach Egypt without refuelling, but not India).

A helium vent discovered in Canada offered the possibility of selling the ship to Canada for refilling with helium, but with the continuing depression the funds were not available. The ship was broken up between November 1931 and February 1932, the framework being sold for scrap for just £427;[84] a few fragments of the structure can be seen in museums. One bay of the structure was initially retained and used for structural deflection tests. Hung on the wall of the Cardington shed, the 3½-ton section was loaded with weights attached to the joints, and after a settling period, the deflections of the structure noted. Quantitative results were recorded although no qualitative assessment was presented, and the report gives no indication of the reasons for performing the test.[85]

Even before *R.100* flew, plans had been prepared for a larger *R.102*, costing about £500,000 and built to carry 160 passengers for 6,000 miles at 95kts.[86] This design of ship was to be the basis of the main phase of the Imperial Airship Scheme, but these plans were all shelved following the crash. *R.100* had flown for just under 300 hours, nearly three times that of *R.101* up to her crash.

Although he did not work on *R.100*, Herbert Jeffree (who joined Vickers in 1934 and would later become one of the main figures of Wallis's design team) learned that when the *R.100* was scrapped, parts of the structure were showing signs of impending failure.[87] Official tests on sections of girder, removed from the airship even before she was broken up, confirm this, noting corrosion of the duralumin up to 40 per cent of the depth of the metal in places, blaming this 'low condition' on poor heat treatment procedures by the duralumin manufacturer.[88] Although the structure which was tested still met its design strength, it does call into question how much life was left in the *R.100*. Sir Peter Masefield remained convinced that *R.101* was 'one of the best airships ever designed and constructed' and as good if not better that *R.100*, noting that neither design would have had a very long life.[89] However, Wallis (long after he had any vested interest) called it 'the crudest piece of design', suggesting *R.101*'s framework was inferior in some respects even to that of *HMA No.1*.[90]

	HMA.9	*R.23 class*	*R.80*	*R.100*	*R.101(mod)*
Volume (cu ft)	846,000	942,000	1,200,000	5,156,000	4,900,000
Length (ft)	526	535	535	720	731
Diameter (ft)	53	53	70	134	131
Speed (mph)	43	52	60*	81	70
Range (miles)	–	–	1,000	4,095	2,585

* some sources say 70mph

Table 2.1: Comparative data for the Wallis airships and *R.101*.

With hindsight

Although many other early airships came to premature ends, the reasons were varied in nature and there was no common failing of the airship concept itself – indeed, given the small number of airships built, they could legitimately be regarded as 'teething troubles', which even heavier-than-air craft suffered from. Both *R.100* and *R.101* were designed to be experimental ships and had incorporated many important innovations into their designs, but it is possible that the *R.101*'s innovations, such as her gas valves and gasbag harnesses, may have contributed directly to her crash, while her generally overweight structure made it more difficult for her to recover when things went wrong.

Despite the end of the airship programme, Wallis personally had benefited greatly from the *R.100* experience. He had been the main designer and project manager on a large cutting-edge technology project, and had produced a design to specification, within time and on budget, in contrast to the benchmark of another team working in parallel to the same guidelines. He had already proven his loyalty to Vickers, with whom he would stay for the remainder of his working life, and he would provide the company with one of its most outstanding designers, working alongside Rex Pierson and rivalling Hawker's Sydney Camm, Avro's Roy Chadwick, and even Supermarine's Reginald Mitchell. As he crossed over to the Vickers Aircraft, he would carry his wealth of skills with light alloys and some of the innovations that had been born in the demolished frame of *R.100*.

Airship revivals

With airships firmly off the UK agenda, Wallis remained (rather by default) Britain's foremost rigid airship designer for the rest of his life. This meant that he was still consulted from time to time about possible revivals of airships, although he 'continued to express the view that in view of the great developments in heavier-than-air transport, there is no future whatever for the airship'.[91] A magazine article on this topic in 1968 was one such occasion.[92] It proposed to use airships for cargo transportation, noting the ability of the airship to go almost anywhere and the availability of helium (including from North Sea gas) and lightweight gasbag materials, but the basics of this particular proposal were quickly shot through by Wallis in correspondence with the editor.[93] A more practical proposition arose in 1971,[94] when he (recently retired) was engaged as a consultant by Shell International Gas to consider an application to use airships for the transport of gas itself – specifically methane from wells in North Africa to the UK, although routes in the Far East and between Nigeria and the USA were also under consideration.[95] The gas wells were remote in the desert, so access to power for liquification plant was difficult and pipelines would be required to transport the liquefied gas to ports for shipping – hence the concept of using airships was seen as an option worth considering. The suggested size was around 1,280ft in length and 266ft in diameter with a gas volume of 28 million cu ft – far larger even than *R.100*. Wallis expressed 'grave apprehension' about various aspects of the scheme, including the idea that the methane should be stored in an axial gasbag surrounded by helium for additional lift (and to lift the airship when no methane cargo was being carried).[96] However, he approached the task with typical thoroughness, and calculated costs for an airship fleet and supporting ground plant, also calculating comparative costs for liquefying the gas and transporting by sea, the latter appearing to be the better option. Wallis discussed the engine requirements with Robin Jamison at Rolls-Royce,[97] who reminded him that public acceptance of a scheme involving large airships filled with methane might be hard to achieve. Wallis even proposed two further alternatives, one a rigid airship but using hot air as the lifting gas (which gave an airship volume saving of around 30 per cent compared to the helium ship) and the other using a large transport aircraft to carry liquefied gas, having an aircraft design in mind suitable for large tankage. It appears that the technical obstacles were large, and the economics (including the cost of the massive shed that would have been needed to build the giant ship) were against the scheme, and it was not proceeded with.

Summary – *R.100*

R.100 remains Britain's finest ever rigid airship, and her success cemented Wallis's reputation as both a designer of quality and an innovator of considerable merit. The technical expertise gained by Wallis during her construction, especially production engineering and the use of light alloy structures, would serve him well as he moved on to work with aircraft. The seed of the concept of geodetic structures was also planted during the construction of *R.100*, and its timely germination in the early spring of rearmament would be momentous both to Wallis and to Britain.

Chapter 3

Geodetic Aircraft

Chance favours only the prepared mind.
(Louis Pasteur)

From airships to aeroplanes

Having achieved some measure of fame as designer of *R.100*, Wallis regularly hosted visitors at Howden to see the construction. One such visitor was Jack Rennie of the Blackburn Aeroplane Company at nearby Brough.[1] Rennie was working on a large metal seaplane, and the two men got on well together. Wallis became an increasingly frequent visitor to Brough, both fascinated by the potential of aeroplanes and astonished by the crudeness of their structure against the elegance of his *R.100*. This led to some Wallis experiments for the seaplane wing.[2] He was also visited by Sir Robert McLean, Chairman of Vickers (Aviation) Ltd, who was impressed with Wallis and his work. McLean suggested that the Vickers Chief Designer, Rex Pierson (see biography in Appendix 1), take his son to visit Wallis and *R.100*. Pierson was the man responsible for all Vickers aircraft designs from the First World War and the years since, including the Vimy bomber that Alcock and Brown had flown across the Atlantic in 1919. Pierson arranged a return visit to the Weybridge works for Wallis in October 1928, and the easy friendship apparent at their first meeting was rekindled. McLean 'believed it was the task of a leader to discover subordinates of originality and thereafter to give them free rein and his full support'[3] and he saw Wallis's potential immediately. Eager to embrace Wallis's skills and delighted at the blossoming relationship with Pierson, McLean offered Wallis the post of Chief Designer (Structures) alongside Pierson himself. Wallis accepted, realising that he could apply his knowledge to make aircraft fly as far as airships, but much faster. However, it was agreed that he would stay at Howden at least until *R.100* was inflated in her shed (scheduled for spring 1929) and remain available should any major problems arise with the airship, his actual appointment being on 1 January 1930.[4]

Vickers first posted him to its recently acquired subsidiary, Supermarine at Southampton, where they were experiencing difficulties with an air yacht for the Guinness company executives;[5] bending of the large wings under load was causing aileron reversal.[6] The yacht had been designed by R.J. Mitchell, designer of the Schneider Trophy-winning S-6B seaplane, and later to design the Spitfire. Both he and Wallis were 'prima donna' designers intent on delivering the best possible aircraft for their customers,[7] but being both powerful and of like polarity, they soon found that they could barely stay in the same room together, and Wallis was hastily transferred back to Weybridge.[8] Here Wallis was paired up with Pierson (with whom he did get along), and the two men would together develop all of Vickers' main aircraft designs for the next 15 years, Pierson concentrating on overall design and Wallis on their structures.[9]

When he arrived at Weybridge, one of Wallis's 'first tasks was to design a special wing structure for the Viastra',[10] a colonial airliner, following a suggestion from an Australian customer.[11] His new wing was tested at RAE Farnborough, and reports were prepared comparing the old and new structures.[12] It is very notable that the construction method is referred to in the reports as 'Vickers-Wallis construction', showing that Wallis had established himself as a brand within the company very quickly.[13] He also worked on 'Wallis experimental wings' for the Vickers Vivid[14] and a redesigned rear fuselage section for the Vickers Jockey fighter.[15]

Vickers was already convinced of the benefits of all-metal aircraft, and had largely adopted it while many other manufacturers continued with all-wooden or hybrid construction – compare the all-metal Spitfire and the part-wooden Hurricane. Although the metal aircraft structures of Vickers in the 1920s were among the best in the world, Wallis knew he could do better.

Wallis's first complete aircraft structure design was on the Vickers Type 207, a tender to Air Ministry specification M.1/30 for a carrier-based torpedo bomber, released in March 1930. Pierson had already begun the design of the Vickers submission when Wallis joined the company, basing it on the form of its earlier Vildebeest torpedo bomber. However, Wallis's skills in fabrication of duralumin structures were used to create a novel design for its wing spars. This used a double tube for the main spar, with a series of inter-connecting diagonal spacing struts.[16]

The aircraft first flew on 11 January 1933, but in a high-speed dive during a test flight on 23 November, it broke up in mid-air. Vickers' Chief Test Pilot Joseph 'Mutt' Summers (see biography in Appendix 1) was in control, and together with his observer John Radcliffe, managed to parachute to safety, although Radcliffe had a heart-stopping moment when he initially snagged on the structure during his exit. The fault was later traced to structural overload in a tailplane incidence jack, which had led to a distortion of the structure. The tailplane design was within the guidelines given by

Wallis's first complete aircraft structure design was the ill-fated M.1/30 biplane. *(BAE SYSTEMS)*

the Air Ministry (thus Wallis's design was not directly to blame for the crash), and following investigation by the RAE at Farnborough, the stress formulae requirements were changed. Wallis himself noted that the break-up appeared to indicate that several parts of the structure had reached their failing stress all at the same time:

> *Unfortunately, this indirect tribute to my skills as a designer did not remove the impression from the minds of Summers and Radcliffe that the break-up was entirely my fault. It was entirely due to my fanatical notions about structures, based of course on my successful experience in designing R.100, and for several weeks, Summers refused to speak to me, believing that I had, through carelessness and lack of judgement, endangered their lives.*[17]

A concept is born

In July 1931, the G.4/31 specification was released for a single-engined general-purpose aircraft with good load-carrying capability, reliability, short take-off characteristics and able to be used as a night or day bomber, dive bomber, torpedo carrier and in other roles. As a successful design for such a flexible type of aircraft was likely to be purchased in significant numbers, the specification led to design submissions from no fewer than nine manufacturers.[18]

For the Vickers design, Wallis hit upon the stroke of genius that was to make his name as an aircraft designer:

> *I remember being particularly struck with the great loss of useful volume involved in the fuselage of the [Vickers] Victoria, in which the simple braced wire rectangular structure of the Vimy had been given a streamlined form by the simple device of adding a complex structure of light wooden frames to the rectangular base. It was, I think, when looking at the structure in the shop that I got the idea of applying geodesic mathematics which I had used when designing the retaining mesh wires for the R.100 gas bags to produce a curvilinear structure in metal which nevertheless possessed a rigidity usually associated with straight ties and struts.*[19]

Wallis's idea was to call upon geodesic mathematics once again, and with it describe a series of helical structural members following geodesic lines which followed the required curved aerodynamic outer shape of the fuselage – this would be more complex than the *R.100* gasbag wiring, but the principle remained the same.[20] He reasoned that if (as on *R.100*) two series of helices were used, one right-handed and one left-handed, and that these were joined at each intersection, then he would have a framework of great strength (as the geodesic lines already followed the shortest path between intersections and thus would not readily change in shape). As this load-bearing framework would all reside immediately beneath the outer skin, the geodetic construction[21] would also mean that the internal volume was one large space, uncluttered by parts of the framework. The main benefit which Wallis was aiming for was a substantial reduction in structural weight, which in practical terms meant an increase in payload capacity, and together with the uncluttered internal spaces able to accommodate large loads and fuel tanks, this offered a massive potential increase in capability and range. Yet a further benefit was that breaks in the geodetic framework (such as caused by enemy fire) would mean that the load from missing members would simply transfer to those around it, so the overall integrity of the airframe would only be compromised if a very substantial section was removed, a feature that was to save many an aircraft

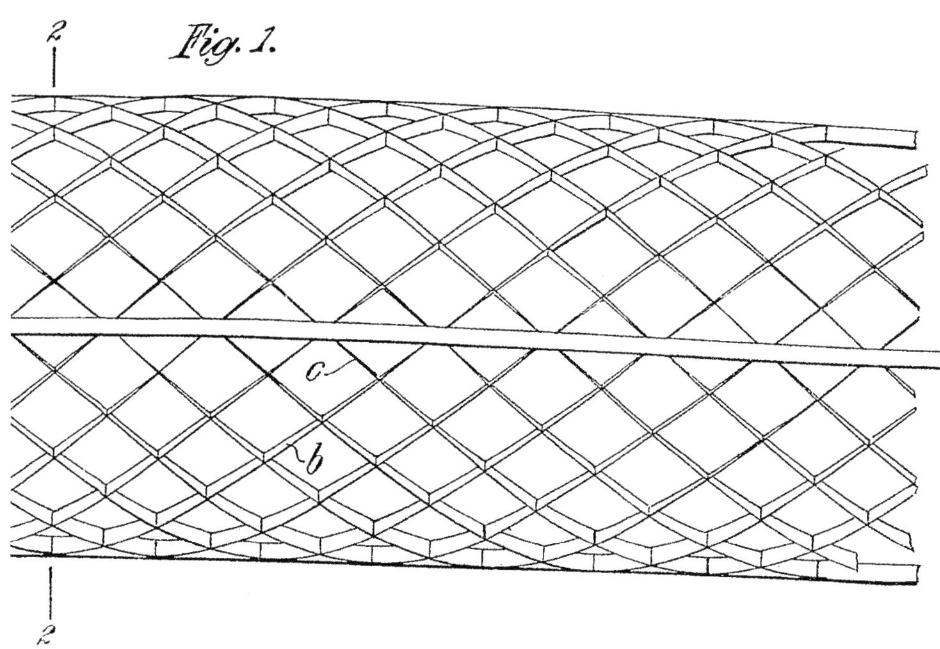

The basic form of geodetic fuselage. (Patent GB452726). *(BAE SYSTEMS)*

and airman in the years ahead. A desire for higher speed suggested the adoption of a monoplane design, and to further enhance range, Wallis wanted to use a relatively thin wing with an aspect ratio of around 9 or 10.[22] Using conventional structural practices, a wing of AR 9 would weigh about three times that of one with AR 6. However, using geodetics, Wallis was able to design a wing with the AR he sought but with lower weight than a conventional wing.

Faced with this totally new design concept, the company was initially somewhat sceptical, but Wallis's persuasiveness about the multiple benefits of geodetic construction won Vickers round so effectively that it decided to proceed with three designs to meet the specification. One was a biplane (to meet the expectation of the Air Ministry), but the others were low-wing monoplanes of similar airframe design but with different engines (one radial, one inline as on the M.1/30). Predictably, the Air Ministry selected the biplane design (Vickers Type 253), and a prototype contract was signed in April 1932.

The Vickers biplane used standard wing construction and a partial implementation of the new geodetic principles in the fuselage. Despite this, it was the first of all the G.4/31 prototypes to fly, on 16 August 1934, and after an initial test programme at Brooklands and the RAE at Farnborough (which included fitting of an uprated engine), it went to the A&AEE at Martlesham Heath in Suffolk on 13 April 1935 for official trials. A report on the trial results with the nine G.4/31 contenders (seven biplanes and two monoplanes) was prepared by the end of May, with (surprisingly) a monoplane submission, the Westland PV-7, being recommended by Air Vice-Marshal (later Lord) Dowding. This prototype crashed[23] due to insufficient torsional strength in its wings; consequently, the Air Staff selected the Vickers Type 253 as their first choice and an order for 150 aircraft was the result.

Even as Vickers proceeded with full development of the Type 253, it had not lost faith in the Type 246, which featured full geodetic implementation in both fuselage and wings, and on 12 April 1932, the Board had agreed to proceed with the development of the monoplane designs (together designated Vickers Type 246, although the inline-engined version was dropped in favour of the radial-engine version) in parallel as a private venture. This was a considerable commercial gamble (the prototype cost over £30,200), which indicates McLean's faith in Wallis and his arguments in favour of geodetics.

The Type 246 was first flown on 19 June 1935 from Brooklands, with Mutt Summers again at the controls – Wallis flew with him the following day. On subsequent trials at the RAE, it was compared with the 'conventional articulated' Vickers Vincent, these aircraft having almost identical requirement specifications and very similar all-up weight (AUW). It was noted that the structure weight of the Type 246 was only two-thirds that of the Vincent, but the Type 246 fuselage was more than twice as strong in flexure (bending) and nearly twice as stiff in torsion (twisting). The fuselage was required to demonstrate a safety factor of 7 (i.e. to withstand seven times the loading expected in normal operation), but the test report[24] showed that the fuselage sustained a load factor of 11.5, and as it was not showing signs of failure or deformation, the planned testing to destruction was not performed. A later test of the wing[25] demonstrated a load factor of 7.7, 10 per cent above the requirement.[26]

In tests against its biplane stablemate (which used the same engine), the monoplane showed dramatically better all-round performance at a higher AUW and had greater disposable load[27] – around double that of its competitors – due to its lighter structure weight.

The Air Ministry ordered 150 of the biplane in the summer of 1935. However, unable to accept their conservatism in light of the dramatic difference in performance between the biplane and the monoplane, McLean wrote to Air Marshal Hugh Dowding on 5 July 1935 saying of the biplane, 'In my view it is not a modern machine' and unilaterally proceeded to build monoplanes instead – by such means McLean did not make any friends, but his methods would ensure that Britain would have the aircraft it needed for the years ahead. Faced with such corporate arrogance (albeit justified by the figures), the Air Ministry acquiesced and on 10 September Vickers was formally instructed to change the biplane order to one for monoplanes (79 initially with later orders for 17 then another 80).[28] The aircraft was to be developed as a long-range medium bomber, some

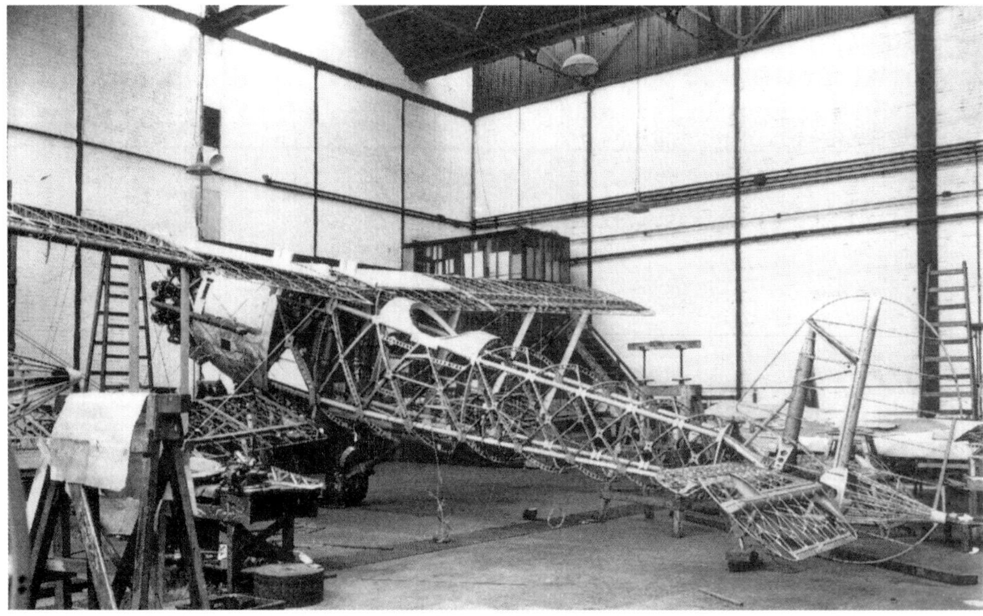

The G.4/31 biplane under construction. Note the geodetic fuselage but standard wing structure. *(BAE SYSTEMS)*

requirements of the original specification having been dropped. With the contract came the name Wellesley after the family name of the Duke of Wellington, beginning a tradition of names beginning with 'W' for Vickers' geodetic aircraft. One Air Staff officer commented, 'It will encourage that fellow Wallis to go on with geodetic structure' which of course it did![29]

The theory of geodetic construction

The basic theory of geodetics is summarised by Wallis in a 1935 paper.[30] Consider a string wrapped around a curved body; if the string is pulled tight between two points on the surface, it will assume the minimum distance between them around the surface – a geodesic line.[31] The tension in the string causes an inward force against the surface, normal to the surface at every point and proportional to the curvature of the surface at that point. If the string is now replaced by a rigid strut of the same shape, the forces acting remain the same, and the enclosed cylinder can be removed 'but its comfortable presence may be adequately represented by designing each geodetic bar with a high second moment about the bi-normal axis' – in practice, this could be done by using a strut slightly elongated in the direction radial to the original (and now non-existent) cylinder. Further calculation showed that other secondary forces were much smaller, and could be disregarded if the bi-normal forces were handled adequately, particularly when in compression.

If a geodetic strut is pulled or pushed axially, or twisted, then the principal effect is to move the centre point of the strut in (typically) a direction tangential to the cylindrical surface. To restrict and oppose this movement, the centre point needs to be propped up at this point and 'the equivalent of a prop can be provided in actual design by arranging that the geodetic bars which are loaded in opposite sign shall cross each other' at the centre point. Thus a right-handed geodetic spiral could be adequately propped by another left-handed spiral, with each crossover connected by a rigid junction (in practice, by a pair of fishplates).[32]

Theory showed that the magnitude of the secondary forces handled by the geodetic strut was principally dependent on the (arbitrary) distance between the ends of the strut. Crucially, for any length of strut, making the strut half as long reduced the bi-normal moment 'to a small fraction of its original value' – in fact, about one-twelfth of its magnitude. In practice, this meant that any desired strength could be achieved 'within very wide limits by tracing on the given surface any suitable number of opposite-handed geodesics' and hence controlling the length of each geodetic member to within the limits required.

Thus we arrive at the final geodetic structure – a series of interconnected right-handed and left-handed spirals whose spacing can be increased or decreased as the designer requires in order to carry any desired load. The radial depth of the geodetic struts is small compared to the radius of the enclosed (imaginary) cylinder, leaving a large internal volume which (crucially) is wholly uncluttered by any form of strut or bulkhead, all the load-bearing structure being in the outer surface.[33] The only exception to this was where 'local inputs . . . of any serious magnitude' occurred, such as wing-fuselage connections or large openings for hatches, in which case 'distribution by other means such as hoop-frames' would need to be provided. One notable example of this was the wing of the Wellesley – the thickness/chord ratio of the wing was insufficient to handle the vertical shear forces caused by the lift generated by the wing, requiring conventional spanwise spars to be included in the wing structure[34] and lengthwise longerons to be included in the fuselage structure; 'these take the bending loads and the geodetic or diagonal members look after torsion'.[35] In the Wellesley, these were arranged so that the fuselage was, in effect, made up of a chain of self-stabilising sections. In the Wellington, these longerons effectively split the fuselage into four panels of geodetics (two flat sides, curved top and curved bottom sections around the bomb bay) which were independent of one another for manufacturing purposes.[36] The covering of the geodetic framework could not sustain any stresses so had to be flexible – consequently, it was covered in fabric, hand-stitched to the geodetic members, then doped and painted to form a smooth skin.

The Structure Sub-committee of the Aeronautical Research Committee studied the Wallis paper, and was initially somewhat critical of the content, especially the claimed novelty of geodetics.[37] They argued that ribs in some conventional structures follow geodesics, nor is the curvature inherent in the geodetic members novel; however, many of the technical objections raised by the report were disproven by later tests.

Due to the mutually propping geodesic spirals, geodetic structure is highly redundant by its nature, each connection transmitting away a proportion of the propping forces, the transmitted forces being further distributed via further connections to other parts of the structure. Loss of any strut (due to combat damage, for example) would lead to 'very rapid equalisation of forces in all the similar members' of the structure, and with a suitable safety margin in the structural members, the redistributed loads would be easily handled. This was confirmed by a gunfire test carried out on a Wellesley wing at the Shoeburyness range on 12 April 1937.[38] Seven shells from a two-pounder gun were fired at the wing; two shells passed right through, having missed all the structural members. Structural tests carried out later at Weybridge found that the safety factor was reduced to approximately half of its original value, but the aircraft would still have been able to get home safely from a combat mission. The aileron mechanism was also hit, but continued to function. It was concluded that only a hit on the wing spar near the root would have crippled the aircraft, also noting that the Wellington and Warwick (which were in development at that time, the latter still unnamed) had two and three wing spars respectively (in fact both had three), thus making catastrophic damage less likely.

One problem that Wallis had not solved in the Wellesley structure was that of large openings in the geodetic framework. Where such openings were required, such as the cockpits, Wallis used heavier framing around the opening to carry the extra load from the deleted members. A bomb bay was thus difficult to include and as a result the Wellesley carried its 2,000lb bomb load in two aerodynamic pods slung beneath the wings – the first use of aerodynamic fairings over externally slung bombs. These were initially fully enclosed but the bomb doors were found to cause excessive vibration when dive-bombing, and the doors were later removed (although this had no appreciable effect on drag). These pods were first fitted to the pre-production Wellesley (Type 281), this aircraft being the result of extensive rebuilding of the prototype – other changes including the addition of perspex cockpit hoods (the prototype was found to be a bit draughty), hydraulically-operated landing gear (both state-of-the-art features at the time), a larger rudder and a more powerful engine. Various other details of the Wellesley, including the cockpit windscreens and gun mountings, were the subjects of further patents.

A contemporary article compared various methods of aircraft structure, describing geodetics as 'in a class by itself', noting that the method lies 'between the monocoque and the girder'[39], meaning that the forces are not handled fully within a stressed skin nor fully within an internal framework, but lie somewhere between the two.

BACKGROUND

RANGE OF AN AIRCRAFT

The range of an aircraft can be calculated in many ways, but is often seen in the form of the Breguet Range Equation:

Range = Lift/Drag × specific fuel consumption × $\log_e$ (take-off weight/landing weight) × Cruise speed

Consider the four parts of this equation in turn:

Lift/Drag The 'lift/drag ratio' is a measure of the aerodynamic efficiency of the airframe (how easy it is to push a certain weight of vehicle through the air). In level flight at a steady speed, the drag on the airframe equals the thrust of the engines, and the lift from the airframe equals its weight.

Specific fuel consumption (SFC) is the weight of fuel used per unit weight of payload carried over a unit distance. This property is a measure of the efficiency of the engines (and thus largely down to the skills of the engine designer).

Weight This property is essentially a measure of the fuel-carrying efficiency of the airframe (a larger amount of fuel carried by a lighter structure will increase range).

Speed Finally, and most simply, the range is directly proportional to the cruise speed, so for greatest range, we wish to fly as *fast* as possible (if that does not adversely affect the specific fuel consumption).

If we assume the SFC to be fixed, then for a given fuel load, the range achievable is directly proportional to the L/D and inversely proportional to the empty weight of the aircraft. A good structure will thus be light, offering high lift with low drag.

The drag on an airframe absorbs energy from the airframe and dissipates it into the surrounding air, so it must be compensated for by the thrust of the engines (or loss of height), otherwise the aircraft's speed will constantly decrease. Drag can be split up into three principal components:

Parasitic drag, itself made up from: *form drag* (or *profile drag*), caused by the shape of the object, a more streamlined form having lower drag; *friction drag,* caused by air rubbing against the skin (the so-called 'wetted area' of the airframe); and *interference drag*, caused by the creation of turbulence around and behind the airframe as it flies.

(Lift-) induced drag, caused by the creation of lift.

Wave drag, caused by the creation of supersonic shock waves, and thus only relevant to transonic and supersonic flight.

The complex task for the designer of a long-range aircraft is thus to create a balanced design for an airframe which generates as much lift and as little drag as possible, while carrying a large fuel load and powerful engines.

Fabricating the geodetics

Deriving the most efficient pitch (spacing) for the geodetic members involved substantial calculation, but a method was found to give a good approximation of the answer within a more workable timescale.[40] This translated into the practical problem of production of a large number of differently curving geodetic members – 1,650 in total for the Wellington, each with a unique curvature – a problem which critics of geodetics (including the Air Ministry) said would make the technique unfeasible for mass production. However, a power-operated machine was devised which allowed flat strip metal to be formed into the W-section members quickly and easily, and the required curvature added as defined by three points in space; these machines were still in use at Weybridge in the 1980s.[41] Four such members met at each intersection, where typically two were partly overlapped and riveted together on simple jigs, and the other two were joined by riveting fishplates on the outside (the fishplates were standard and so could be mass-produced in great numbers). Patents were awarded for methods of holding the members together for riveting.[42] Norman Boorer gives credit for the production success of the Wellington to Trevor Westbrook, the General Manager at Weybridge,[43] who said 'I will make geodetics a success, providing that Wallis keeps out of my way!'[44]

Thus equipped, Vickers was able to build around ten Wellesley aircraft per month (initially Type 287, later the revised Type 294 when a wing strength problem was found with the first eight production aircraft, which were strengthened to meet the same specification).[45] They produced a total of 176 aircraft between January 1937 and May 1938.

Long Range Development Unit

For a subsonic aircraft, the amount of lift generated is proportional to the volume of the cylinder of air through which the aircraft flies. The diameter of this cylinder is the wingspan of the aircraft, so increased wingspan increases lift, and hence range. Long narrow wings are thus desirable, but these are a problem for the aircraft designer, as wings of this shape are difficult to make sufficiently stiff to resist aileron reversal and similar effects. However, the geodetic structure offered excellent torsional stiffness characteristics, allowing Wallis to design a wing of high aspect ratio (8.8) for the Wellesley.

Presented with a light, lean design with the capacity for a large fuel load, the RAF recognised the Wellesley's possibilities as a long-range aircraft. They had established a Long Range Development Unit (LRDU) as early as 1933, and its leader, Wg Cdr O.R. Gayford, took the world distance record (5,309 miles) in February that year in the custom-built Fairey Long Range Monoplane, flying from Cranwell to Walvis Bay, Namibia. Five Wellesleys were assigned to the LRDU at RAF Upper Heyford in January 1938. In addition to the long-term goal of recovering the world distance record (which had since been captured by France and then Russia),[46] the LRDU also undertook research work associated with long-distance flight. This included evaluating the new technique of fuel jettisoning – required if an aircraft carrying a large load of fuel needed to land early (before much of the fuel had been burned off). The techniques developed with the Wellesley were successful, and were widely adopted for later aircraft – and are still in use today in military and civil aircraft.

The LRDU Wellesleys underwent substantial modifications for their record attempt. The structure was unaltered, but the more powerful Bristol Pegasus XXII engine (with a more aerodynamic fairing behind it), an improved variable-pitch propeller and an automatic pilot were fitted, all military equipment was removed, and the oil and fuel capacity was extended – fuel from the standard 485 gallons to an incredible 1,290 gallons, making up just over half of the gross weight at take-off.

During testing of the modifications, a bizarre situation arose. Bob Handasyde was flying as observer with Mutt Summers, and he noticed disturbing bending of the wings. The problem was traced to the new perspex canopy designed by Wallis – it was, in fact, the canopy which was flexing and creating the illusion to Handasyde that it was the wings that were bending!

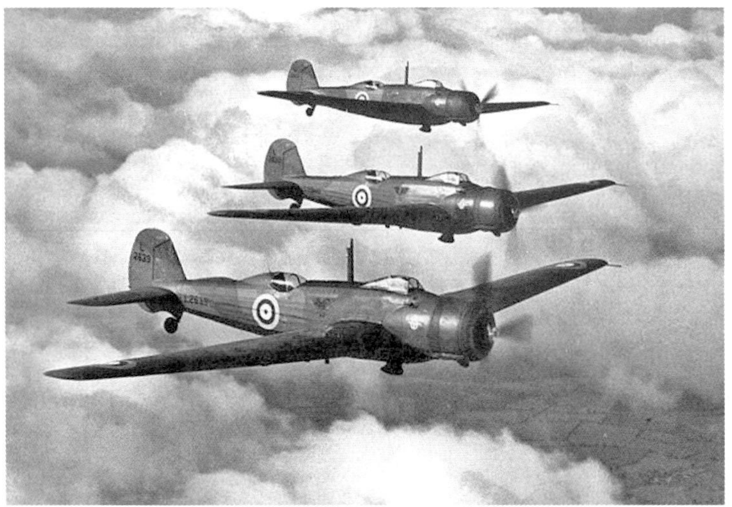

Three Wellesleys of the Long Range Development Unit. These aircraft broke the world distance record in 1938 and held it until 1946. *(BAE SYSTEMS)*

On 7 July 1938 four Wellesleys led by Sqn Ldr R. Kellett flew from Cranwell to Ismailia in Egypt via the Persian Gulf in 32 hours, a distance of 4,300 miles and the longest formation flight up to that time. After further training back in Britain, the aircraft returned to Ismailia on 25 October 1938 to make final preparations for the record attempt.

Three aircraft, again led by Kellett, took off at 0355 on 5 November to fly (approximately) a great circle route, aiming for Australia.[47] This route was chosen as it mostly lay over Commonwealth and other friendly territories; three naval vessels were stationed along the route to deal with communications. Despite less than ideal weather conditions and unfavourable winds en route at the planned height of 10,000ft, the flight went largely according to plan, the main excitement en route being at the pilot changeovers – this necessitated the pilot folding down the back of his seat and sliding out backwards, his replacement then sliding in and folding the seat back up behind him, and required prompt action if the autopilot was not functioning. All three crewmen took turns at piloting, in stages of three to four hours each, the first pilot taking the largest share.[48]

One aircraft was forced to land in West Timor due to shortage of fuel, and it (officially) held the distance record for the few hours until the other two aircraft landed at Darwin in Australia at 0400 on 7 November. The aircraft had flown 7,158 miles (almost exactly double the distance from London to New York). This record was to stand until November 1945 when it

		Fairey LRM	Bleriot 110	ANT-25	Wellesley	Boeing B-29
	PRIMARY DATA					
i	Length m	14.8	14.6	13.9	12.0	30.2
ii	Span m	25.0	26.5	34.9	22.7	43.1
iii	Wing area m2	79.0	81.0	87.9	58.5	161.3
iv	Empty weight kg	3056	2680	4200	2889	33795
v	Gross weight kg	7938	8790	11500	8346	61240
vi	Power kW	425	447	560	753	6560
vii	Fuel litres	3849	6600	7940	5863	25752
viii	Fuel weight kg	3079	5280	6369	4690	20602
ix	Aspect ratio	7.9	8.7	13.9	8.8	11.5
x	Speed km/h	151	220	210	240	357
xi	Crew	2	2	3	3	10
	DERIVED DATA					
v/iii	Wing load kg/m2	100.5	108.5	130.8	142.7	379.7
vi/v	Power/mass kW/kg	0.054	0.051	0.049	0.090	0.107
v/iv	Gross/Empty	2.6	3.3	2.7	2.9	1.8
viii/v	Fuel fraction	0.39	0.60	0.55	0.56	0.34
	OTHER DATA					
	LD record date	8 Feb 1933	7 Aug 1933	14 Jul 1937	7 Nov 1938	20 Nov 1945
	LD record km	8544	9105	10149	11520	12740
	LD record hours	57.4	55	62.3	48	n/k
	Type	Custom built	Custom built	Custom built	Modified service	Service

Table 3.1: Aircraft holding the World Flight Distance Record, 1933–46.

was broken by a four-engined Boeing B-29 Superfortress, which flew 11,236 miles from Guam to Washington D.C. Although the absolute distance record has been broken, the Wellesley's distance record has not been bettered by any other single piston-engined aircraft (although this is not a recognised FAI record category).

Following the record flight, the unit made a publicity tour of Australia, but two of the three LRDU Wellesleys were written off when engine failures caused forced landings; LR.1 came down in a ploughed field following take-off from Sydney, and LR.2 came down in the bush in the north-west of the country.

It is informative to compare the Wellesley with the aircraft which had earlier held the long-distance record; comparative figures are given in Table 3.1.[49]

It can be seen that the Wellesley is the smallest of the four record holders, but not particularly exceptional otherwise. Where the Wellesley scores is in its substantially greater power/weight ratio, which meant that it was able to fly the fastest and hence cover the ground at a higher rate to claim the record. The fact that it is the only type not to have been custom-built for an attempt at the distance record is also notable.

The Wellesley in RAF service

The first production Wellesley flew on 30 January 1937, and went to Martlesham in March for tests initially, with the third aircraft going directly to 76 (Bomber) Squadron at RAF Finningley in Yorkshire. The aircraft ultimately equipped five UK-based squadrons plus four in the Middle East, although during a reassessment in mid-1939 it was decided to post all of this type of aircraft to the Middle East as they were replaced in the UK by new twin-engined types; it was also decided to add a third crew member as navigator, who sat between the other two near the side windows. Consequently, no Wellesleys saw operational service from the UK during the Second World War although the type did see extensive service in North Africa, especially in Egypt, Sudan and Ethiopia against the Italians, before being finally withdrawn from RAF service in 1943.

There were very few special types of Wellesleys (particularly compared to the later Wellington), most being just single aircraft used for experimental purposes. Like its biplane half-sister, Wellesley K7772 was used by the Bristol Aircraft Company, as an engine test bed for the sleeve-valve Bristol HE15 engine, and K7740 was given an extended cockpit canopy linking the pilot and gunner positions, and giving more window area to the navigator. The latter aircraft was also used for tests as a torpedo bomber (part of the original G.4/31 specification) in December 1940, but this was for torpedo testing rather than trials for service adoption in this role.

In 1937 Vickers (Aviation) was absorbed into Vickers-Armstrongs with Sir Charles Craven as Chairman, and Wallis became Assistant Chief Designer to the whole department. This meant that he was also responsible for aerodynamics as well as structures, and that he was able to concern himself 'in the aerodynamic design of our aircraft with access to the staff who dealt with that side'.[50]

The Vickers Wellington

In response to the October 1932 Air Ministry specification B.9/32 for a twin-engined bomber capable of carrying a 1,000lb bomb load for 720 miles, Pierson produced a high-wing monoplane design. However, confident of progress with G.4/31, this design was dropped in October 1933 in favour of a totally new design using entirely geodetic construction. Pierson and Wallis thought that the specified weight of 6,500lb (originally 6,300lb) was far too restrictive and their design studies effectively ignored this, producing an aircraft capable of carrying 4,500lb for over 2,500 miles – but weighing over 19,000lb. The Air Ministry, which normally rigidly enforced the specified weight, was able to see sense in the design, and their weight restriction was lifted.

The prototype B.9/32 emerged as a mid-wing monoplane with full geodetic construction, apart from the fin which had been taken from a Supermarine Stranraer to save design time. K4049 first flew on 15 June 1936, piloted by Mutt Summers with Wallis and Trevor Westbrook aboard. Subsequent testing showed that it had some exceptional possibilities as a service aircraft, including excellent stability, and the first production order for 180 was placed in August 1936 at a cost of £10,000 each;[51] originally given the name Crécy, this was changed to Wellington in September.

The Wellington prototype broke up during a high-speed diving trial near Martlesham Heath in April 1937; the pilot escaped, but the flight engineer was killed. The problem was traced to over-balancing of the elevator and, as the flight test programme had been largely completed, the crash did not affect delivery of the production aircraft (some elevator balance problems remained, but these were resolved early in the production process).

In 1935 Wallis was asked by the ARC to comment on the suitability of geodetics for use in a large flying boat;[52] he noted there would be 'a decided saving in weight' with the use of a geodetic wing, and that geodetics might also be used for the upper hull and the tail (but not for the lower hull, which would need a solid outer skin). This application of geodetics was not proceeded with.

In spring 1935 the Air Ministry issued specification B.1/35 for a heavy bomber of 100ft span; Vickers submitted a tender in

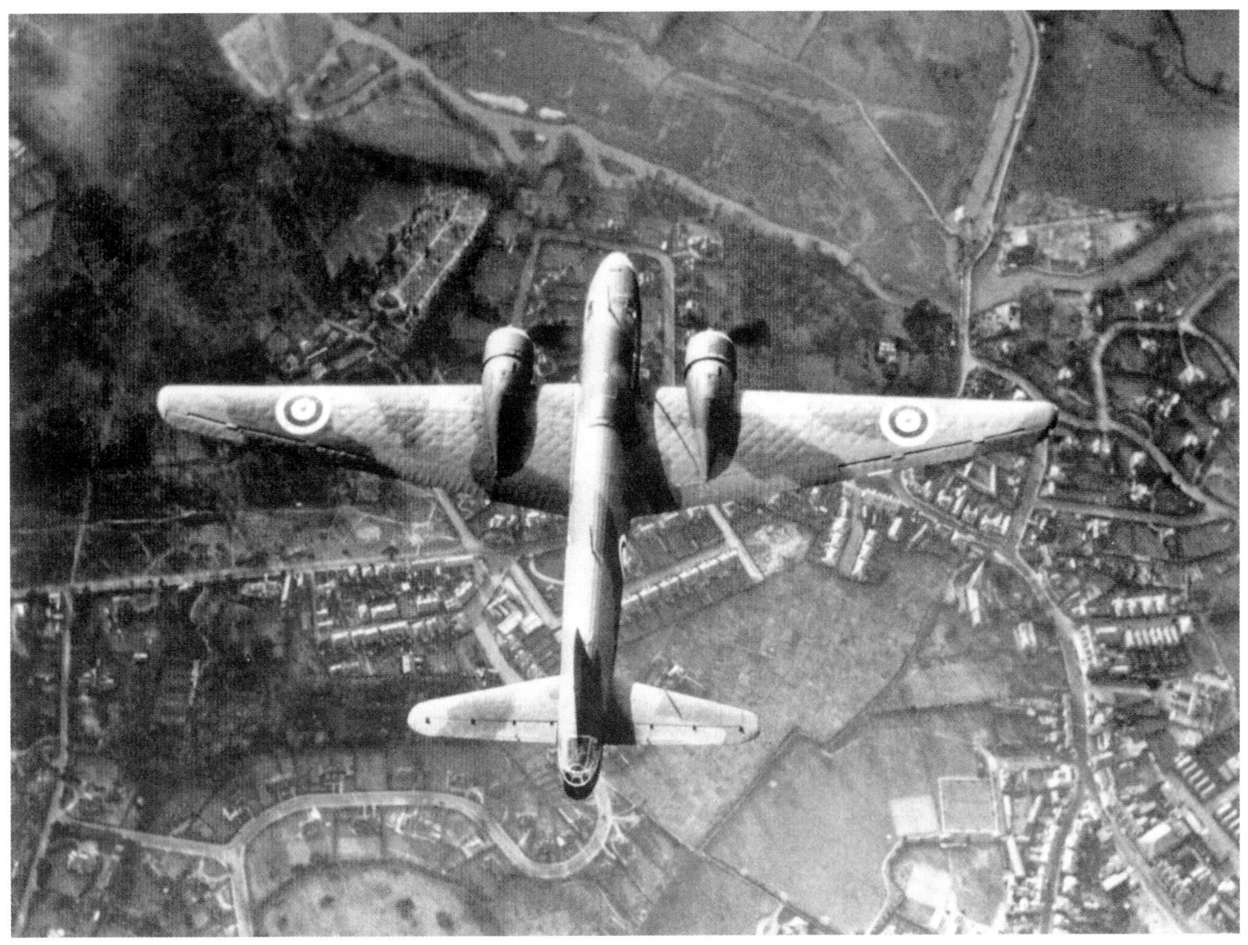

An early Wellington in flight. Note the high aspect ratio wings and the geodetic structure, which can be made out through the fabric covering. *(BAE SYSTEMS)*

The internal volume of the Wellington's wings was divided only by the main spar, allowing the fitting of large fuel tanks. The tanks were in three parts to allow flexing of the wing. *(BAE SYSTEMS)*

July, and was awarded a prototype contract in October. With both the B.9/32 and B.1/35 on the drawing board at the same time, the opportunity was taken to combine the detailed design, resulting in two aircraft (the Wellington and the Warwick) that shared 60 per cent of their parts, thus greatly assisting production. The linked ancestry of the two aircraft can be seen in the fact that the internal frame numbers were taken from the Warwick, with several being omitted in the Wellington, and also that the original Warwick was allocated Type 284 and the redesigned Wellington as the later Type 285. The redesign also meant that the production Wellington differed substantially from the prototype aircraft. The fuselage section was deeper than the prototype's circular section, and the four longerons were placed at the top and bottom of the side panels (on the prototype, there were two lateral longerons with others on the top and bottom of the aircraft). The deeper rear fuselage gave room for a retractable tail wheel, and the nose, fin and horizontal stabiliser were also new designs.

The Mark I had nose, tail and retractable ventral gun turrets of Vickers design, but these were replaced by two Fraser-Nash turrets in later marks (the ventral turret was deleted in favour of beam guns). Most marks were powered by Bristol Pegasus rotary engines driving Rotol propellers, though the Mark II used Rolls-Royce Merlins. The bomb bay was divided lengthways into three sections, the vertical members between the sections being used to strengthen the bay, this being capable of carrying a wide variety of bomb loads, including two 18in torpedoes;

however, some aircraft were converted to carry a single 4,000lb HC 'Cookie' bomb, for which Wallis had to design a new bomb bay structure (the Wellington was the first aircraft to carry this bomb).[53]

The wing was strengthened by three spanwise spars, the fore and aft ones being attached to the fuselage to transmit lifting forces, the central spar handling the wing bending loads and passing through the fuselage without being attached to it directly. Design of the wing petrol tanks caused some difficulty, due to the potential size of the tanks (the wings had two massive internal spaces running the length of the wing, one behind and one ahead of the main spar) and the fact that structural forces could not be transmitted to the tanks. Consequently, the tanks were split into three lengthwise sections, interconnected by external flexible pipes, the whole tank arrangement being inserted into the inboard end of the wing as a single unit. As a test for maintenance of the tanks, an exercise was carried out whereby a wing was removed, the tanks taken out and changed, inspected and the wing reattached all within three hours. Initially the tanks were not self-sealing, but this was quickly rectified following early combat experience. Some early structure problems were found in the wing spars due to the use of steel fishplates joining duralumin members, and there were instances of outer mainplanes breaking away; as late as May 1942 Vickers and RAE were looking at a new design of the main spar, which was found to be prone to fatigue cracks.[54]

The Weybridge and Southampton works of Vickers-Armstrongs were bombed on consecutive days in September 1940, and it was decided to relocate the design offices. Wallis moved with his staff to nearby Burhill Golf Club, Rex Pierson went to Brooklands College, and George Edwards set up an Experimental Department in new buildings at Foxwarren, about 3 miles from Weybridge.[55] Aircraft construction was already dispersed – having foreseen the possibility of attacks on aircraft factories, the government had set up a number of 'shadow factories' around the country. These were tasked with large-scale production of military hardware, leaving the original factory to perform any research and design work and to resolve initial production problems. Thus it was that about 80 per cent of the Wellingtons were built at Hawarden near Chester (opened 1939) or at Squire's Gate, Blackpool (opened 1940), the remainder being built at Weybridge. With the production problems for geodetics sorted out, mass production was comparatively straightforward for the semi-skilled work force of the shadow factories, as demonstrated by an exercise (shown in newsreels of the time) whereby an entire Wellington was constructed within a period of 24 hours. The critics of geodetics as a practical means of construction were well and truly silenced.

The Wellington in service

As the Wellington design was reasonably mature at the start of the war, and it continued to be produced throughout, the aircraft naturally took place in a number of significant actions. These included the first daylight raids against German naval targets. They were unsuccessful and resulted in the loss of many bombers,[56] proving the fallacy of the self-defending bomber force, and it was this result that led to the cessation of unescorted daylight raids and adoption of a night bombing policy. Also notable is the first of the '1,000 bomber' raids in May 1942 by 'Bomber' Harris, the Air Officer Commander-in-Chief of Bomber Command – more than half of the aircraft taking part were Wellingtons.

The Wellington built up an excellent reputation among aircrews for its ruggedness in service and its ability to make it home even after sustaining appalling damage, a reputation enhanced by many photographs showing the fabric covering burned away, although the structure beneath may be

The nature of the Wellington's geodetic construction allowed the airframe to survive even after substantial damage. *(BAE SYSTEMS)*

relatively intact. This legendary reputation is substantiated by combat statistics: despite being in service right through the war (including the early days of grievous losses), less than 18 per cent of all Wellingtons were lost on operations, compared to nearly 30 per cent for the Whitley, and over 50 per cent for the Hampden. The Wellington has the lowest rate of combat losses of any twin-engined British bomber apart from the Mosquito (due to its higher speed, later entry into the war, and the fact that many Mosquitoes were not bomber variants) and the later Warwick (which was mainly used on less dangerous Coastal Command duties). The Wellington's reputation for combat survivability is most commonly put down to the rugged and redundant properties of the geodetic construction.[57] The geodetic structure was also relatively simple to repair – any damaged members could easily be cut out and replaced, and re-covered with fabric, all without specialist spares or technicians.

The Wellington was an extremely adaptable aircraft, and served with all RAF Commands (except Fighter Command). As the four-engined bombers started in service from 1941, many Wellingtons were used on other duties, including coastal reconnaissance, transport and training. Many of the marks (assigned by the Air Ministry, as opposed to the Type numbers assigned by Vickers) signified different engine or defensive armament combinations. The Wellington was also used as a test-bed aircraft, one-off versions including dorsal mounting of a 40mm cannon (in single fin and twin fin variants), tail mounting of a Whittle jet engine, and (post-war) an aircraft fitted with Dart turboprop engines.

Design office effort was thus taken up in producing these special-purpose variations of the bomber, and although Rex Pierson and his staff were well suited for this work, Wallis recalled later[58] that it 'held no interest' for him (for most, the basic structure of the aircraft was unaltered) and he was 'free to work on whatever problems interested me', although it seems unlikely that he was twiddling his thumbs at this time. Two versions of the aircraft, built at Foxwarren under the guidance of Edwards, but to which Wallis did have substantial input are worthy of further discussion:

Mine-sweeping from the air

In late 1939, the Germans began laying air-dropped magnetic mines[59] which were claiming ships in the Thames estuary and elsewhere, and a solution needed to be found quickly – pressure to do so came directly from Churchill, who wanted progress reports every 24 hours. Fortuitously, one of the mines was accidentally dropped on a beach, and successfully defuzed by bomb disposal experts; the magnetic trigger was recovered intact, allowing its operation to be studied. Sweeping these mines was problematic from surface vessels, and the idea arose of sweeping from the air, if an aircraft could

project a large enough magnetic field. Dr Hudson at the RAE calculated that, if underwater detonation was achieved, the aircraft would be moving quickly enough to be clear of the resulting explosion.

After initial calculations by Wallis, a small group led by Edwards was charged with fabricating the apparatus, and they worked tirelessly on this for several weeks (including the Christmas period of 1939), designing the DWI ('Directional Wireless Installation') Wellington – this designation was a cover for its real purpose, 'detonation without impact'.[60] A 51ft-diameter coil was wound on a large jig of Edwards's devising,[61] using 2in aluminium strip, separated by paper, and this was fitted inside an alloy aerodynamic fairing; a small inlet at the front scooped in air to circulate around the coil and keep it cool. The coil was mounted beneath the aircraft, attached to the nose, wings, and tail, this location having been derived from wind tunnel tests. The Mark I Wellington with the coil first took to the air on 21 December 1939, flown by Summers with Wallis on board (Edwards was watching from the ground), less than a month from the start of the project.[62] The aircraft was flown to A&AEE, where a Ford V8 engine driving a 35kW electric generator was installed; the current (a massive 310amps) from this circling in the coil generated the magnetic field. Test flights at A&AEE repeatedly flew over the captured mechanism from the mine at different heights and off-centre tracks, and on each run, whether the aircraft was able to trigger the mechanism was plotted on a diagram. Three more new Wellington Mark Is were fitted with the coil and began operations very quickly, the first DWI-swept mine being detonated on 8 January 1940.

A further 11 Wellington Is were taken off operations to be converted for DWI work by a sub-contractor. To permit flights at slightly greater heights (up to 110ft), these were

The DWI's magnetic coil was contained within a 51ft-diameter ring mounted under the wings of a Wellington I. *(BAE SYSTEMS)*

fitted with a Gypsy Six aero engine and 90kW generator, the original four aircraft being refitted with the uprated equipment.

The RAE conducted experiments into performing sweeps with several aircraft in echelon and V-formation,[63] this being found to give a more effective and thorough sweeping than using a single aircraft performing multiple passes. Twenty-four mines were swept from the Thames alone using the DWI aircraft,[64] and many of their pilots received decorations due to the dangerous nature of their work (though there was no instance of a DWI being blown up by one of the mines that it swept). Meanwhile, degaussing of ships had become standard practice so that magnetic mines no longer posed a significant threat, although the 15 DWIs (plus some additional conversions performed in the field) did go on to see service overseas in North African harbours, the Suez Canal and elsewhere.

The technical and managerial success of DWI saw Edwards promoted out of the drawing office in spring 1940 to become Experimental Manager at Foxwarren.[65]

High-altitude Wellingtons

As early as 1938, the Air Ministry had requested that experiments be done on a high-altitude bomber, capable of delivering a 1,000lb bomb load from 35–40,000ft, as this was beyond the capability of known enemy fighters and flak. The Wellington was the obvious choice to meet this requirement, due to its already good ceiling, although there were several unknowns in the design of the required pressure cabin (novel at that time) and fitting this to the geodetic airframe. Two prototypes, one with Bristol Hercules and one with Rolls-Royce Merlin engines, were ordered in May 1939. A cabin for three men with an operating pressure of 7lb/in^2 was designed,[66] and fitted on to the structure in place of the existing cockpit and forward gun position. The pressure vessel, 18ft 3in long and 65in in diameter, had a perspex dome on top for the pilot (slightly offset to port), optically flat windows beneath the nose for the prone bomb aimer, and small windows on the top and sides for navigational sighting. Access was by a 3ft 2in circular door in the hemispherical rear dome; this could be opened at altitudes up to 15,000ft and a safety valve was fitted to preclude a reverse pressure gradient (as might occur during an emergency descent). Riveted seams were then sealed internally, so that internal pressure would force the sealing compound into any crevices. The pressure vessel was lagged internally with fibre material to reduce heat loss, and was proof tested to 15lb/in^2, particular attention being paid to the windows, which were tested to 50lb/in^2 under harsh temperature conditions. Initially a conventional rear turret was to be provided, but the conditions for the gunner would have been terrible and it was decided to lock the turret in position dead astern, to be operated remotely from the pressure cabin, presumably by the navigator.

Progress with engines was not so swift, the original Hercules VIII being substituted by the less powerful Hercules III in June 1940, allowing completion of the aircraft by the end of August (although the exact date of its first flight is not recorded). The air raid on Weybridge in early September saw the prototype R3298 transferred to Blackpool later in the month. A height of 20,000ft was reached on a test flight from there on 21 October, curtailed by icing on the windows, and modifications were made to blow warm air over these, allowing 30,000ft to be reached ten days later. Hercules VIII engines were fitted to the second prototype R3299, but these did not give the expected power and the required ceiling was not reached. Only one more aircraft was completed before effort was switched to the Mark VI. The Mark V featured in Wallis's 'Note' (see Chapters 4 and 7), his hope being that bomb-aiming experience gained when 'high altitude squadrons of Wellington Vs are in operation' following the 'recent introduction of the stabilised bomb sight' would contribute to acceptance of his big bomb plans; as a sampler, he suggested that 'a few squadrons' of the aircraft could 'bring the French and German coal industry to a standstill in the course of two or three months' using 4,000lb deep-penetration bombs.[67]

To circumvent the problems with the Hercules, it was decided to concentrate on the Merlin-powered Mark VI aircraft, which it was expected would give the required performance, although it was not until a year later that the type was ready. Other changes from the Mark V included the addition of a wireless operator, the intention to use a pressurised rear turret (although delays meant that a fixed conventional turret was actually used), and the fitting of perspex 'double glazing' to all windows, warm air being passed between inner and outer panes to prevent icing. New hydraulic fluid was found to be necessary, as conventional fluid became too viscous at the low temperatures experienced at altitude. The prototype W5795 was built at Foxwarren and reached 40,000ft; this aircraft and W5800 had an extra 6ft added to each wing for altitude tests, but it conferred no advantage and was removed again.

By the time the Mark VI flew, the de Havilland Mosquito was available with its comparable bomb load and excellent height performance (albeit with no pressure cabin for the crew), and less importance was being placed on high-altitude bombing by the Air Ministry. As a result, interest in the Mark IV waned, although a total of 64 aircraft were completed (18 of which had started as Mark Vs), many at the 'Extension Factory' in Windsor. Most were used for experimental

The high-altitude Wellington had a 65in-diameter pressure cabin mated to the geodetic structure. *(BAE SYSTEMS)*

purposes on the effects of high-altitude flight, although at least one aircraft did undertake a small number of combat operations. Escape from the pressure cabin in an emergency had always caused concern, and this may have contributed to the loss of the crew of W5795 near Derby on 12 July 1942. At 32,500ft, a propeller blade sheared and punctured the pressure cabin; the decompression may have incapacitated the crew (four plus a civilian flight test observer), none of whom escaped as the aircraft broke up and fell to earth.[68]

The Americans were also interested in high-altitude bombing, and had been supplied with details of the Wellington's pressure cabin design. They provided some of their latest Sperry bombsights, which were fitted in the aircraft for high-altitude trials. The experience gained with the pressure cabin was useful in developing the high-altitude Spitfire and the F.7/41, and also at the end of the war when the pressure-cabin airliners were in development.

Wellington in retrospect

With Weybridge and the two shadow factories in production, a peak of 45 Wellingtons per week were being built and a total of 11,460 Wellingtons were produced,[69] a number still unsurpassed by any other British multi-engined aircraft.[70] Overall, Wellingtons are estimated to have undertaken over 47,000 sorties with Bomber Command, dropping over 40,000 tons of bombs; more details of these are described in the many books about the Wellington in squadron service.[71]

Comparing the early Wellington with its main contemporaries, the Handley-Page Hampden (also designed to meet B.9/32) and the Armstrong-Whitworth Whitley (designed to the later B.3/34), the Wellington impresses; both it and the Hampden had a nominal bomb load of 4,000lb but the Wellington could carry it nearly twice as far. The Whitley fared better as a load carrier, but had a poorer rate of climb, lower ceiling and lower top speed than the Wellington.

As thoughts turned to commercial aircraft towards the end of the war, Vickers gave consideration to three commercial types based on its three main types: the Windsor Empire, the Warwick Continental and the Wellington Continental.[72] Of these, the latter appeared of the greatest utility, and able to compete with the Douglas DC-3. As Vickers found itself with factories tooled-up to make the (now redundant) geodetics, and to economise on design time, the first Vickers post-war design, the Viking VC1[73] utilised the geodetic wings of a Wellington married to a new pressure cabin fuselage, and 19 of these aircraft were built before the stressed-skin wing was ready, which was then used for production aircraft.

Vickers Warwick

As has been seen, the Warwick was designed at the same time as the Wellington and had a high degree of shared parts (the Warwick had five more rows of geodetic members in the nose, twelve more in the forward fuselage and seven more in each wing). Externally, they remained very similar but could be distinguished by some details: the Warwick's longer fuselage meant that the cockpit was now ahead of the propellers, the longer engine nacelles extended past the trailing edge of the wing, the fin was a slightly different shape (and several Warwick versions had a dorsal turret).[74] It would thus be expected that the Warwick should have come along shortly after the Wellington and taken over from it as the principal design. However, although their structures were similar, the greater weight of the Warwick required more powerful engines, and it was here that problems arose. Originally to have used Bristol Hercules engines, in January 1937 the new Rolls-Royce Vulture was specified instead and in November it was decided to fit the second prototype with Napier Sabre engines; the following month, the Bristol Centaurus was added to the mix, further complicated (or simplified) by the

Air Ministry adding the 'power egg' concept, whereby all the engines had to fit on to the same mountings, allowing interchangeability without modifying the airframe.

In the event, all of these engines experienced problems which delayed the programme, and the first Vulture-engined prototype K8178 did not fly until August 1939, just before the start of the war (the Wellington had been flying for three years by this time). It was found to be underpowered, and the first flight of the Centaurus-powered prototype L9704 in December was a marked improvement (the poor performance of the Vulture also affected development of the Avro Manchester). With Sabre supplies for fighters taking priority and delays in the production of the Centaurus, consideration was even given to reverting to Hercules or Merlin engines, but these would have compromised range and bomb load. In July 1940, Pratt & Whitney Double Wasps became available, and these were trialled in L9704. In January 1941 a contract for 250 production machines was finally placed (and the aircraft received its official name). Still hedging its bets, the Air Ministry split the order into 150 aircraft with Double Wasps and 100 with the Centaurus.

The first production machine was not completed until April 1942, by which time the once impressive performance of the Warwick was looking rather tame compared to the four-engined heavies already entering service. The Warwick (and the continuing production of Wellingtons) was thus assigned to other duties, notably air-sea rescue, long-range anti-submarine work and transport, where its capacious fuselage and long range could be used to best advantage. There were a number of notable accidents (many due to rudder balance problems), including to most of the Vickers test pilots – both 'Mutt' and Maurice Summers, 'Tommy' Lucke, Bob Handasyde and 'Shorty' Longbottom (the latter fatal). Although generally very impressed with the aircraft, Lucke observed that it was 'not to be until February 1945, when the Warwick was produced in its final form . . . [with] a dorsal fin, that the aircraft could be described as satisfactory'.[75] He noted

Overshadowed by the success of its smaller twin, the Warwick saw greatest success in the anti-submarine and air-sea rescue roles. *(BAE SYSTEMS)*

that, following Longbottom's accident, Wallis designed a test rig to see how much rudder force a pilot could exert, and it was found that much depended on the pilot's seating position, which may have contributed to the survivability of some of the accidents.

Thus beset with problems, only 846 Warwicks were built (all at Weybridge), at a total cost of £14.5 million (just over £17,000 per aircraft).[76] Although production continued into 1946, all were withdrawn from service by the end of 1947 (the Wellington remained in service until 1953).

Intermission: the 'Tin Mosquito'

In 1941, as Wallis worked on the high-altitude Wellington, there was no British fighter that could reach the same altitudes. There arose a perceived threat that high-altitude German bombers might be able to penetrate British airspace, resulting in the Air Ministry issuing specification F.7/41 for a twin-engined high-altitude fighter. Wallis and Pierson set about producing a design, with a pressurised crew compartment and, in the lower-mid fuselage, a formidable armament of four 20mm cannon. This would be Wallis's only fighter built, and the last fighter to be built by Vickers. Lightness of structure was needed to reach the height required, but the high speed requirement meant that use of geodetic construction was not appropriate. Pierson produced a bold design with elliptical wings, and to produce this form, Wallis invented an entirely new form of wing structure, the first true stressed-skin design in a Vickers aircraft – although it had done some early work on stressed-skin construction, its technique had not been well developed (indeed, the use of geodetic structures meant that Vickers had continued to use fabric coverings longer than most other manufacturers).

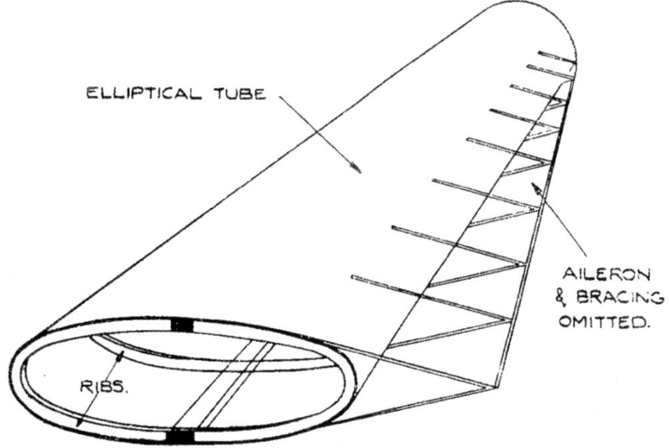

The F.7/41's wing consisted of stressed-skin elliptical tube with trailing edge structure attached externally. *(BAE SYSTEMS via The National Archives)*

The wing structure consisted of a series of elliptical ribs which were covered in a heavy-gauge skin, the whole being in effect a flattened cylinder with constant thickness/chord ratio from root to tip; the complexity of this shape led to a row between Wallis and Edwards (who 'got lumbered' with building it at Foxwarren).[77] The top and bottom were manufactured separately, each with a central spar, the two halves being joined at the front and rear by a screw toggle arrangement to form a single torsion box.[78] A preliminary report on the new aircraft from the RAE[79] was very positive and noted that the design was 'specially notable for the absence of any web plating or bracing between the top and bottom booms and for the absence of stringers running spanwise under the metal skin'. It also noted that 'average conventional' structure at the prototype stage is typically 15.5 per cent of AUW, but that this design achieved 12 per cent, 'comparable to the very best achievements to date', half of the saving being due to good spreading of weight along the span and a further quarter to the high thickness in the outer part of the wing.

The shape of the structure gave rise to its nicknames of 'peapod' and 'lobster claw' construction, the unobstructed internal volume being used for large fuel tanks as on the geodetic aircraft. The trailing edge structure, including ailerons, was attached to the rear of the main torsion box and covered with fabric. The fuselage was of circular section, with a pressurised cabin for the pilot, who looked out through a bubble canopy as on the high-altitude Wellingtons. The overall form of the aircraft was similar to the de Havilland Mosquito, leading to the aircraft being dubbed the 'Tin Mossie'.

One-thirteenth-scale model tests on the initial design by Vickers-Armstrongs and NPL, and confirmed by the RAE, showed some undesirable aerodynamic performance, especially at high incidences.[80] However, this was quickly traced to the leading edge planform, and the shape was modified by extending the leading edge forward slightly and this proved satisfactory.

During a high-speed taxi run at Farnborough on 24 December 1942, the prototype DZ217 became airborne, rather to the surprise of the test pilot, D.W. 'Tommy' Lucke, who decided to remain in the air for a brief test flight – it thus became the only Wallis design, and probably the only Vickers design of the era, whose first flight was not made by Mutt Summers.

Twenty-eight experimental flights were made in the prototype,[81] revealing a good overall performance marred by poor ailerons and spinning characteristics; the Rolls-Royce Merlins also gave some trouble at higher altitudes, which remained unresolved. By mid-1943, the threat from the German bombers had not materialised, and the programme (including the nearly-completed second prototype) was cancelled. Several dozen of a competing design from Westland (the Welkin) were completed, but did not see service for the same reason; these had inferior performance to the Vickers aircraft.

Vickers Windsor

The Vickers submission for the B.12/36 specification, for a four-engined long-range bomber, was a high aspect ratio aircraft that would have used geodetic construction, but the contract was awarded to the Short Stirling. Vickers was also unsuccessful with its submission for B.1/39, but tried again with B.5/41 for a high-altitude heavy bomber capable of 345mph at 31,000ft.[82] The submission was based on the Warwick, with the span lengthened by 20ft and the fuselage by 4ft, with a pressure cabin as on the Wellington Mark VI and either four Centaurus or Merlins. The design used an elliptical planform wing, as on the F.7/41 but with higher aspect ratio. Two Merlin-engined prototypes were ordered, and the type given the name Windsor.[83]

In late 1942 the Air Ministry revised the specification to B.3/42. In this, the pressure cabin had been removed (a conventional oxygen system was to be retained) and rearward-firing 20mm cannon added, these being mounted on the after end of the

The inside of the 'lobster claw' wing shows the skin tensioning toggles fore and aft and the large unobstructed internal volume. *(BAE SYSTEMS via Brooklands Museum)*

outer engine nacelles and controlled from a sighting position in the tail of the aircraft. The cannon installation was incorporated because the machine guns in service aircraft of the time were seen as inadequate, especially for the rear from where most attacks came; design of the cannon installation was done at the Vickers Crayford and Dartford works. To test out the novel configuration, Warwick L9704 had prototype barbettes fitted to its nacelles, and was subjected to ground and air firing trials. These proved satisfactory, and the test mechanism was transferred to the Windsor. One concern was how the flexibility of the wing and fuselage would affect the aiming of the cannon, but tests with the second prototype showed that this was not a major problem. AUW was increased to 68,000lb, including 12,000lb of bombs (to the range of bomb loads considered at the time,[84] the Windsor would later have added Wallis's Tallboy and Grand Slam). A further unusual feature of the Windsor was the undercarriage, which had four main wheels, each based on the Wellington's gear, one wheel retracting into each engine nacelle.

The Windsor prototypes were built by the Experimental Department at Foxwarren, the first, DW506, being flown for the first time from Farnborough (where final assembly had taken place) by Mutt Summers on 23 October 1943; no armament was included, ballast being carried instead. Handling was found to be satisfactory, with AUW up to 54,000lb. The second prototype DW512, with Merlin 85 engines, flew from Wisley on 15 February 1944 (piloted by Maurice Summers, Mutt's brother), giving a very

The Vickers Windsor was an imposing presence on the ground, with its four main undercarriage wheels. Note the slightly sagging outer wings, which would have become straight in flight. *(BAE SYSTEMS)*

similar performance to DW506. On 2 March 1944, a problem with one of the propellers caused DW506 to make a forced landing at Grove airfield, and the aircraft broke its back. It was dismantled, and the outer wings used for gunfire tests, other parts being salvaged for reuse, notably the tail unit which was used on DW512. A third prototype, NK136, flew on 11 July.

While the geodetic structure of the Warwick was similar to that of the Wellington – indeed much was deliberately the same – the structure of the Windsor incorporated a number of technical improvements. The fuselage incorporated only three longerons (one along the top and one at each side), but the third prototype reverted to the four -longeron model used on the Wellington and Warwick. More revolutionary was the wing, which was one continuous geodetic structure carried right through the fuselage from wingtip-to-wingtip, and it had no separate wing spars as on the earlier aircraft, 'the geodesics at any point being disposed in relation to the generator at the angle at which they will most effectively resist the combined axial, torsional and shear loads at that point'.[85] At the wing root, members were laid at 16 degrees to spanwise direction to handle the heavy bending loads, but the angle increased gradually towards the tip, the members reverting back to the conventional 45-degree angle for torsional stiffness. Ideally, the geodesics should have continued around the leading and trailing edges, but as the small radii required were unfeasible, the members in the top and bottom halves (which could be fabricated separately) were arranged to meet at the edges, being joined by brackets. Member thickness also reduced towards the tip. This meant, however, that every joint in the wing was different and consequently industrial fabrication would have been 'a production engineer's nightmare'.[86] Unusually too, for improved aerodynamics, the wing was constructed with a built-in droop, being designed to become straight in flight. As a consequence, the covering had to be fitted tighter on top, so that in flight the tension was the same top and bottom. The RAE's test pilot, Capt Eric Brown, remembers particularly this flexing of the wings, and thought the Windsor 'did not handle quite as well as a Lanc'.[87]

One aspect of geodetics which became increasingly unsatisfactory as aircraft speeds rose was the fabric covering, and Wallis's concerns were realised when both DW506 and DW512 exhibited a 'ballooning' of the covering, especially when diving, this getting worse over time due to stretching of the covering and leading to an appreciable loss of performance. His solution was to replace the fabric panels with a surface woven from flat ribbons, the ribbons either being thin metal or a series of high tensile steel wires woven

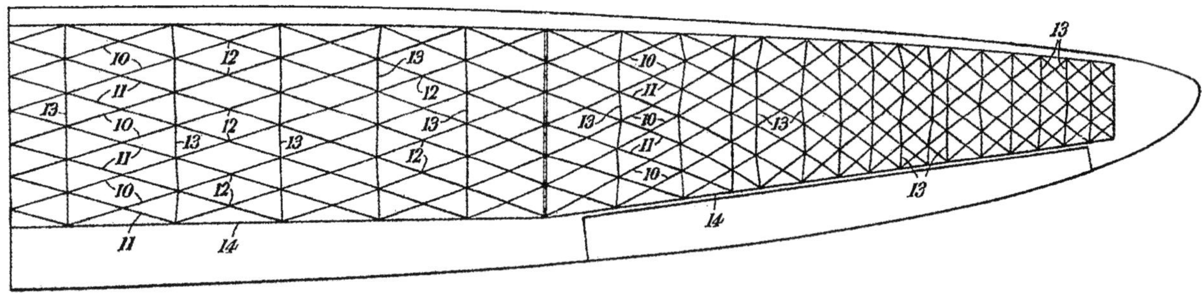

The Windsor wing structure was more complex than the Wellington's, with the members at different angles along the length of the wing (Patent GB575392). *(BAE SYSTEMS)*

together with textile thread and the whole coated in plastic. The ends of the ribbons were anchored to the airframe and tensioned as required (using a tuning fork to set the tension correctly!), and the finished weave oversprayed with PVC or similar material to give a smooth outer surface.[88] Wallis experimented with various forms of the wire-and-textile ribbon,[89] and this was used for the covering on NK136. Despite 'considerable success', he was concerned about 'some psychological reactions which tend to make people reluctant

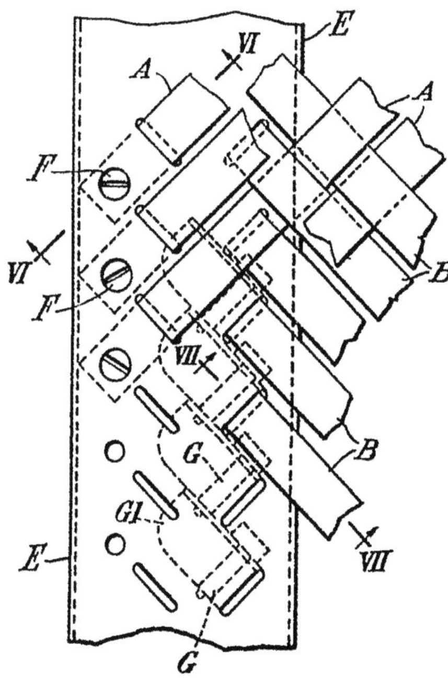

Tensioned flat metal ribbons were Wallis's solution for the covering of the Windsor to cope with its higher speed (Patent GB580574). *(BAE SYSTEMS)*

to commit themselves to the use of aircraft covered with a material which, in spite of all my efforts, continues to be described as fabric' and enquired of Bruntons, the wire manufacturers, if they could supply him metal ribbons of high tensile strength in lengths of 30–40ft.[90] This 'Geosteel' weave using stainless steel ribbon 1/1000th of an inch thick was proposed for the later variants of the aircraft.[91]

Although orders for 300 Windsors were placed as early as 2 June 1943, by the time the aircraft was ready, the Lancaster was already offering a performance similar to the Windsor's theoretical performance and, as the war came to an end, the Windsor orders were first reduced then cancelled altogether (even the fourth prototype, NN670, which was 95 per cent complete, never flew), as were the Rolls-Royce Clyde turboprop engines which were to have been one of the powerplant options.

Plans to develop civil versions had been in development since late 1943, including a non-pressurised variant with up to 40 seats (or 18 beds), and pressurised variants for transatlantic routes with up to 24 seats. The pressurised aircraft, with a range of up to 4,000 miles at 225mph,[92] would have used either a stressed-skin fuselage or a flexible bag within the geodetic fuselage. To maximise the internal volume of the cabin, the flexible bag which Wallis proposed to use would have been non-circular; the varying pressures within the unevenly-shaped bag would have been balanced (as in the *R.100* gasbags) by using geodesic wires within the covering, the spacing of which would have been proportional to the pressure forces at that point – a geodetic pressure cabin within a geodetic fuselage structure.[93] However, all of these were dropped with the military variant, although some of the design experience gained was used on the later Viscount airliner. Nevertheless, the Windsor remains the largest and most complex aircraft of geodetic construction ever built – it would have been beaten by the six-engined Victory bomber, but he never got to build it (see Chapter 4).

The end of geodetics?

Although some thought geodetics to be 'a dreadful aberration',[94] the Wellington was a highly successful aircraft, but it was of its time, and geodetics was unable to survive as aircraft speeds increased. Even Wallis's son has described the Windsor as the 'dying gasp of superseded technology'.[95]

With the covering and internal pressure cabin problems solved, and with factories tooled up for manufacture, Wallis hoped that geodetic production would continue after the war, and was working on a 'new geodetic wing' as late as July 1945.[96] However, George Edwards (by now Chief Designer) had seen the promise of stressed skin in his work with the F.7/41 and in the Lancaster, and knew that it was the way ahead. As Experimental Manager, he had already tried to talk Wallis out of geodetics for the design of the Windsor,[97] but failed, and after many heated discussions with Wallis on the matter, Edwards brought the debate to an end.[98] Wallis, in his heart-of-hearts, must have appreciated the wisdom of Edwards's arguments (if not the authority of the speaker), for even as he was hearing them, he had supersonic aircraft on his drawing board.

Although there have been no more geodetic aircraft, the concept of geodetics as an efficient structure remains. The Dome of Discovery for the 1951 Festival of Britain was a geodesic dome segment 365ft diameter and about 50ft high fabricated from aluminium; like the famous Skylon nearby, it was scrapped at the close of the festival.[99] The

Brooklands Museum holds this wind tunnel model of the six-engined Victory bomber – it was never built. *(Author)*

This unlabelled image from the Science Museum papers shows an elevated railway bridge fabricated as a pair of geodetic tubes. *(BAE SYSTEMS via the Science Museum)*

person most associated with the geodesic dome for architectural use is Richard Buckminster Fuller, and although many of his dome structures remain, his patent on the dome also dates from 1951[100] despite earlier evidence for earlier geodesic buildings, including patents.[101] There is no evidence that Fuller ever met Wallis or was influenced by his structural ideas.

In 1958, Wallis was himself engaged in design calculations for bridges using geodetic tubes. These suggested that a span of up to 125ft was possible, with a structure weight of 200lb per foot; the tube was to be fabricated from steel. Diagrams show single and double geotubes erected on pillars, but there is no information on specific application of the idea.[102]

Recently there has been a resurgence of interest in the geodetic tube for bridge construction. The design of the Greenside Place Bridge in Edinburgh[103] was driven by a requirement to have the footway unobstructed by any structure, and use of an external geotube was the natural result of the design study (the designers had no previous knowledge of geodetic structures). A similar, but longer, geotube was installed as a pedestrian bridge over the M8 motorway between Edinburgh and Glasgow in 2008.

Summary – geodetic structure

Inspired by his experience with light alloy structures and geodesic wiring in *R.100*, Wallis developed a series of new structure concepts for aircraft, summarised in Table 3.2.

Key among these was the use of geodetics in aircraft, a new concept which offered a lighter yet stronger structure than contemporary alternatives, permitting construction of more efficient aircraft shapes with greater load-carrying capability, and hence greater range. Geodetics were implemented in several aircraft including the Wellesley, which held the world long-distance flight record for eight years, and the iconic Wellington, which was in production throughout the war and built in greater numbers than any other British multi-engined aircraft. The ultimate use of geodetics was in the Windsor, but it came too late to see war service. Geodetic structure was not suited for use at high speeds or with pressure cabins, and so it was superseded by stressed-skin aircraft shortly after the war.

	M.1/30	Wellesley	Wellington	Warwick	Windsor	F.7/41
Original Specification	M.1/30–Mar 1930	G.4/31–Jul 1931	B.9/32–28 Oct 1932	B.1/35	B.5/41–B.3/42	F.7/41
Prototype Contract	1930	Apr 1932 (biplane)	Sep 1933 (Goshawk engines)	7 Oct 1935	1941	1941
1st flight (prototype)	11 Jan 1933	16 Aug 1934 (biplane) 19 Jun 1935 (monoplane)	15 Jun 1936 (Mk I) 3 Mar 1939 (Mk II)	Aug 1939 (Vulture engines) 5 Apr 1940 (Centaurus engines)	DW506 23 Oct 1943 DW512 5 Feb 1944 NK136 11 Jul 1944	24 Dec 1942
Named		10 Sep 1935	5 Jun 1936 ('Crécy') 8 Sep 1936 ('Wellington')	Jan 1941	1941	
Original production contract		May 1935 (150 biplanes), changed 10 Sep 1935 (79 monoplanes to B.22/35)	15 Aug 1936 (180 to B.29/36)	28 Dec 1940 *or* 3 Jan 1941 (250 bombers; 150 Double Wasp + 100 Centaurus)	2 Jun 1943 (300 bombers)	
1st flight (prod. model)		30 Jan 1937	23 Dec 1937	1 May 1942		
Service delivery		Apr 1937 to 76 Squadron	Oct 1938 to 9 Squadron	15 Dec 1942 to 33 MU		
Last production	Only 1 prototype	May 1938 (176 built)	13 Oct 1945 (11,461 built)	3 Jun 1946 (846 built)	Only 3 prototypes; 4th cancelled before completion	Only 1 prototype; 2nd cancelled before completion
Service withdrawal		1943	1953	Nov 1947		
Construction	Conventional, with novel wing structure	Geodetic with fabric panel covering	Geodetic with fabric panel covering	Geodetic with fabric panel covering	Geodetic with woven ribbon covering	Stressed skin with 'peapod' wing
Notable crashes	23 Nov 1933: tail structure collapse; total loss, crew escaped	25 Jul 1935: prototype undercarriage failure; belly landing, little damage	Apr 1937 (B.9/32 prototype): elevator balance problem; total loss; pilot escaped, flight engineer killed	28 Aug 1942 (1st prod. aircraft): loose fabric panel; total loss 18 Feb 1943 (2nd prod. aircraft): ground fire at RAE; total loss	2 Mar 1944 (DW506): jammed propeller, forced landing at Grove Airfield, broke back; total loss	

Table 3.2: Vickers Aircraft incorporating Wallis innovations, 1930–45.

Chapter 4

Towards the 'Bouncing Bombs'

Success is the ability to go from one failure to another with no loss of enthusiasm.
(Winston Churchill)

Grand plans

In 1939, on the day that war was declared, Wallis set himself the personal goal of finding 'an engineer's way of stopping the war'.[1] While many debate the size of his contribution, it would take a harsh critic indeed to say that he did not succeed in contributing significantly to this goal.

As always, he approached the problem methodically, and found himself following this train of thought: war can most effectively be won by destroying the enemy's ability to wage war, such as by destroying military targets and the means to manufacture and transport munitions – crucially, it is *more efficient* to attack the infrastructure supporting the military than attacking military targets directly. But most targets are generally dispersed (aircraft around an airfield, factories around the country, power stations connected by grid), and it is thus difficult to find and destroy a significant part of the enemy's capability in any one area. However certain important resources – fuel (coal, oil), water (for consumption, industry and canal transport), electricity (from coal or hydro-electric) – tend to be concentrated in small areas, and have the additional advantage of being in known, immovable, locations (mines, power stations, reservoirs), as are features such as bridges and canals.

Targets such as dams, oil storage tanks and coal mines immediately posed a significant problem – their massive nature made them invulnerable to small explosives, and in 1939 the RAF's largest bombs were a mere 250lb (many had been in storage since the First World War) with even 500lb bombs still in development. Further, Wallis knew that even if 250lb bombs did hit their target, they did very little damage (one British factory which had been hit by seven such German bombs was back in operation within days and had only one of its machines rendered unrepairable), so it was clear that attacking massive targets with them would be completely ineffectual.

A plan is formed

Wallis knew of the power of shockwaves transmitted through the ground, and began his own programme of research into the behaviour of explosives and the shockwaves they created.[2] Two important conclusions came out of this work, which occupied a good deal of his time during 1940:[3]

1. The volume disrupted by an explosion was proportional to the cube of the charge weight (so, for example, 1000lb of explosive would have four times the combined effect of two charges of 500lb detonated separately).
2. The pressure wave from an explosion was transmitted further and more effectively through earth than through air.

Thus was born the idea of the 'earthquake bomb' – to create an explosion that was both massive and deep underground, where the power of the explosion would be effectively transmitted outwards through the surrounding earth, causing far more damage and over a wider area (so a direct hit would not be necessary) than the blast from a similar-sized bomb exploding in air. In addition, a 'camouflet' effect might be achieved, the explosion of such a large charge creating an underground cavern, into which the target above would then collapse.

From July 1940, Wallis put his ideas down in a paper entitled 'A Note on a Method of

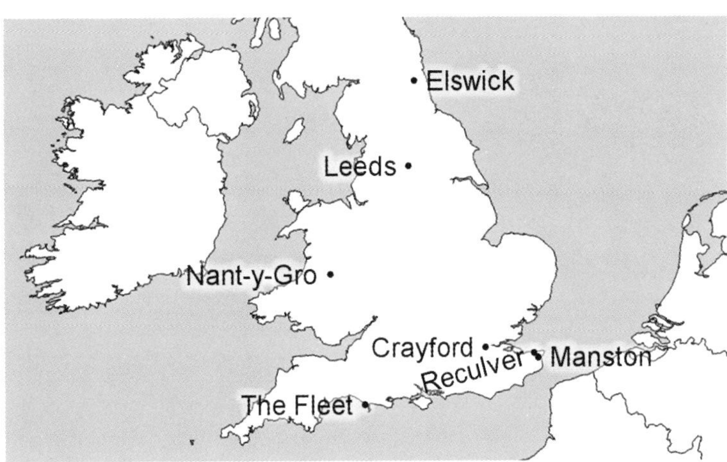

Locations associated with Wallis's early work on the 'bouncing bombs'. *(Author)*

BACKGROUND

EXPLOSIVES FOR BOMBS

Normal combustion requires fuel to combine with oxygen, releasing heat, but contact between the fuel and the air limits the speed of combustion. In explosive compounds, the fuel and oxygen are within the same chemical molecules and, on initiation (by heat or shock), the molecules break down, releasing their energy very rapidly. In addition to the liberation of heat, the production of combustion gases produces an expanding pressure wave (typically travelling faster than sound), which is the main destructive agent; the rate of expansion (known as the 'brisance' of the explosive) depends on the explosive mixture and together with the overall charge size is the main determinant of the force of an explosive. At the moment of detonation, a detonator fuze (or pistol) is triggered (by a time delay, air pressure, hydrostatic pressure, etc.) producing a small detonation which initiates the main charge. Some explosives are sensitive to shock, making them liable to premature detonation, and this effect (undesirable for a delayed-action weapon) can be controlled by mixing different explosive compounds or by adding stabilisers into the mixture. At the start of the Second World War, Amatol (a mixture of >60% TNT (trinitrotoluene) and ammonium nitrate, the latter being added as it was much cheaper than TNT but overall the destructive power remained largely unchanged) was still the standard filling for General Purpose (GP) bombs, as it had been since the First World War. Use of Amatol gave way to other explosives in critical applications, notably Torpex – 'Torpedo Explosive' – (a mixture of 40% TNT, 42% RDX (cyclotrimethylene-trinitramine) and 18% aluminium powder) which had a greater destructive power (but was more expensive) than Amatol. Beeswax was also added to Torpex in some applications (such as Wallis's earthquake bombs) to reduce shock sensitivity and hence prevent premature detonation.

Attacking the Axis Powers' (the 'Note' running to more than 50 pages, plus an appendix and figures).[4] He circulated about 100 copies of this in March 1941 to those whom he thought might take the idea forward.

The 'Note' is based on three axioms: that warfare depends on industry, that industry depends on power, and that power depends on stores of energy. He noted that most of the energy stores were impossible to disperse but also invulnerable to conventional means of attack, proposing as the solution his 'new technique of air attack' based on large earth-penetrating bombs dropped from great height.

The 'Note' sets out a well-constructed argument for the new technique, supported by careful reasoning about the likely benefits of the new scheme. It included sufficient theory and discussion of possible secondary problems (such as bomb aiming), and proposed solutions to these, to be compelling overall.

Having shown the theoretical arguments for using as large a bomb as possible, he settled on 10 tons as the largest practical size for carrying by aircraft (2 ton and 4 ton intermediate versions also being proposed for development). The bomb was to be dropped from 40,000ft in order to achieve the maximum ground penetration, and the bomb had to be robust enough to withstand striking the ground at high speed and penetrate to a useful depth.

Variations in performance due to bombing errors and other operational variables were discussed, including problems of bomb aiming from 40,000ft (he expected that experience would be gained when 'high altitude squadrons of Wellington Vs are in operation'), an accuracy as high as 40yds being suggested (the reader of one copy of the report has scribbled 'Tosh' against this claim, correctly as events would prove). Additional benefits to the scheme are also proposed – greater immunity from fighters at height and the fact that the structural strength required of such a large bomber would also give it greater immunity from serious damage if attacked (he cites the gunfire tests on the Wellesley structure at Shoeburyness in 1938 as evidence for this claim, see Chapter 3).

He then goes on to describe the main types of targets proposed. These include petrol/oil storage tanks, coal and oil fields, dams, dock/lock gates and 'surface transport' (disruption of railways or canals by cratering of cuttings and embankments) and the likely effect on each of a hit or near miss by the deep-penetration bombs. It is notable that the discussion of destroying dams is focused on removal of hydro-electric generating capacity; side effects such as secondary destruction caused by floodwaters, flooding of mines and loss of water for industry or drinking, are not mentioned, although these would assume greater significance later on.

Although Wallis had consulted widely with relevant experts in constructing the 'Note', he had deliberately omitted all references to maintain the confidentiality of these experts. However, some readers found some of the figures and claims to be somewhat fanciful, and many criticisms centred on these details, rather than on the main thrust of the report. Wallis thus wrote an addendum to the 'Note', which he circulated in June 1941.[5] This cited some of his sources, in order to give credibility to some of the figures, and also clarified some of the misconceptions evident, most notably that the volume of material affected by an explosion is more important than the surface area affected.

The Air Ministry was highly sceptical of the proposal, seeing the timescale for the development of the large bomber as too long (the RAF had only just begun using four-engined bombers), though its main objection to the idea, which was not stated to Wallis at the time, was the perceived difficulty of hitting a target from the great height required, this being well beyond the scope of the bombsights then available (although strange in light of the work being conducted on the high-altitude Wellington at the same time).

However, the Ministry of Aircraft Production (MAP) was sufficiently interested to set up a special 'Air Attack on Dams' committee specifically to consider the proposal as it related to dams, which first met on 11 April 1941,[6] and granted Wallis £1,000 to work further on the idea.[7]

The dams

The identification of dams as lucrative targets was not unique to Wallis, nor was his the only effort giving consideration to how to breach them. In pre-war planning, including the Western Air Plans drawn up by the Air Staff in 1937,[8] the dams were placed among a range of significant targets within Germany. Some schemes had been proposed for destroying them, beginning even before the war with an RAE plan for a pilotless aircraft packed with explosives to be crashed into the Möhne Dam, followed by a 1941 plan by Wg Cdr Finch-Noyes (Chief Superintendent of the Research Department at Woolwich) to use an air-dropped hydroplane skimming missile of 3,000lb. Also notable was the 'Toraplane', an air-launched glider carrying a standard 18in torpedo proposed by Wallis's former colleagues Sir Dennistoun Burney and Nevil Shute Norway originally for Coastal Command as an anti-ship weapon. Although full-scale trials were conducted from Fairey Swordfish aircraft, the device was abandoned in 1942 as it was not accurate enough for operational use.[9] It is unclear when, if at all, Wallis was made aware of these earlier proposals.

One attack on a dam had even been carried out, by the Royal Navy's Force H based in Gibraltar – Operation Picket – which was described as a 'full scale experiment to confirm the opinion of the Bombing Committee' which had, in July 1938, considered that torpedoes were likely to be more suited to attacking dams than GP bombs.[10] On 2 February 1941, eight Fairey Swordfish of 810 Squadron took off from HMS *Ark Royal* to attack, with conventional torpedoes, the Tirso Dam in Sardinia, a massive arch dam opened in 1922. The attack was unsuccessful, even though it was believed that two or three torpedoes had hit the dam; the aircrews thought silting in the lake had prevented all the torpedoes from reaching the dam.[11] Indeed, the raid had a negative effect as it highlighted dams as potential targets, and led directly to anti-torpedo nets being fitted to a number of the Axis dams, including the Möhne.

The dams remained as particularly attractive targets for a number of reasons:

1. They would be (relatively) easy to find.
2. The flooding and damage caused by breaching a dam could be significant due to the proximity of coal mines, factories and other industrial targets on the river beneath the dam.
3. Loss of water would create problems for the population, canal transport and steelmaking (the Ruhr steelworks and other industries used substantial quantities of water for its steelmaking),[12] as well as depriving hydro-electric stations of their raw material.
4. Any rebuilding effort would have to be substantial and thus cause further disruption to the enemy.

In the 'Note', Wallis specifically mentioned the features of the Möhne Dam, although the Sorpe and several other smaller ones in the Ruhr catchment area were also identified as potential targets, as well as the Eder further to the east, which had a larger reservoir than the Möhne and was important for the canal network.

Determining the charge size

Masonry is very strong when in compression, but weak in tension.[13] The construction of a gravity dam is such that the pressure of the water and the weight of the masonry combine to keep every part of the structure

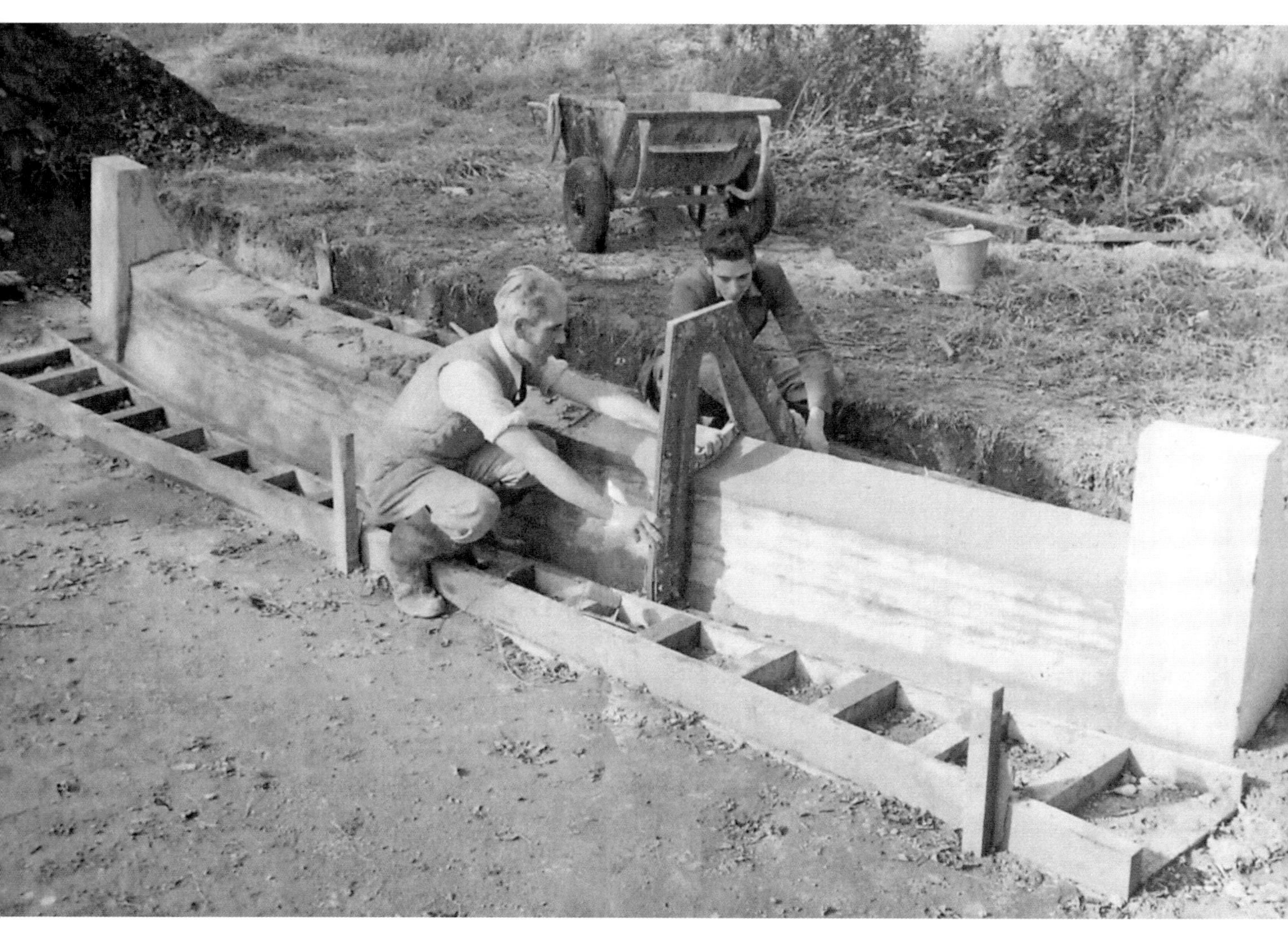

One of the Möhne Dam models under construction. Note the layers of concrete and the movable former for shaping the next layer. *(Author's collection)*

in compression; even if cracks appear in the wall, the compression forces keep the wall together. Substantial forces must thus be brought to bear to break the wall. When an explosion hits the water side of a dam, the masonry is further compressed, and the compression wave travels through to the air face; with nowhere to go, the wave energy is reflected back into the wall where it is now a tension wave – if the magnitude of this tension wave is enough to overcome the compressive forces already existing in the wall, then the dam will be damaged.[14] It was quickly realised that creating this tension wave required a charge of sufficient size to be delivered to the vicinity of the dam.

Disappointed by the lukewarm reception to the 'Note', Wallis asked the AAD committee to sanction research to investigate the minimum size of charge that would be needed to break a dam. This they did, asking Dr Glanville of the Road Research Laboratory (RRL) at Harmondsworth[15], who was a member of the committee, to undertake the work – they already had considerable experience in predicting the effect of explosions on buildings using models.[16] Under the guidance of Dr Collins, the RRL built a series of accurate one-fiftieth scale model dams at Harmondsworth and also at the Building Research Station (BRS) at Garston, near Watford[17]. To retain scale behaviour, the models were built up in a similar way to the original dam by Dr Norman Davey and Mr A.J. Newman of the BRS, plus two assistants. The first Möhne model contained thousands of tiny blocks of masonry bedded in concrete on the outer faces around a solid concrete centre, the sections beyond the two towers being solid concrete for easier construction, later models being all concrete, cast in layers.[18] Davey dates the construction request to Christmas 1940.[19]

Collins was slightly more conservative in his estimates than Wallis, reckoning that a 20,000lb bomb (around 9 tons) containing a 15,000lb charge would be the largest that could reasonably be carried by an aircraft of the foreseeable future, so the initial experiments used a scaled charge equivalent to this – the charge ratios varied according to a cubic relationship; as the model was one-fiftieth the size of the real dam, the charges used were 1/(50×50×50) as large, around 56g in this case.[20] The results were disappointing – four explosions at distances equivalent to 45m, three at 30m and two at 15m produced cracking and leakage of the model dam, but no catastrophic failure. The depth of the charge was also found to be an important variable in the effect of the explosion.

Late in 1940, another member of the AAD committee, Dr Stradling (formerly head of the BRS and by then Chief Scientific Adviser to the Ministry of Home Security), who had been making discreet enquiries about suitable dams, obtained permission from Birmingham Corporation to use a dam at Nant-y-Gro, near Rhayader in Wales, 'for experimental purposes' which might result in its destruction. This dam was no longer needed following construction of a larger one in the valley below, and was itself around one-fifth the size of the Möhne – it would thus allow a useful check on the scale effects to be performed. At least four one-tenth scale models of this dam (hence of similar size to the Möhne models) were also constructed at the RRL[21] during 1941, and test explosions were carried out at set distances from the real and model dams. Measuring equipment on the dams recorded the movement of the masonry, but again no breach could be obtained in the model and, allowing for the scaling, prediction suggested that the real dam should be suffering more damage than it was actually showing. The ultimate test was on 1 May 1942, when a charge equivalent to 30,000lb was detonated a short distance from the Nant-y-Gro dam. Wallis and his wife were in the small crowd of spectators, and although the waterspout was impressive, it made only a few cracks in the dam – just as Collins's calculations had predicted.

However, the solution was already being formed – although the idea of placing charges in contact with the masonry had been considered early on, this had not been tried on the models until Collins decided 'off his own bat' to try one around the beginning of March (so informal was the test, that the actual date was not recorded). The results were remarkable, with even the smallest charge producing a spectacular destruction of the models. Some scaling differences were worrying, and in re-examining the data, Dr Glanville recognised that the displacement of the masonry appeared to vary according to a linear relationship (rather than a cubic one, as in the case of the charge weight), and if this was correct (reworking the calculations for the destroyed models suggested that it was), it would account for the discrepancies observed. To prove the theory, it was decided to mount a further test at the Nant-y-Gro dam which, if predictions were correct, should breach it. A charge of 112kg was required, and the charge in a 224kg anti-submarine mine was found to be sufficiently close to this. The mine was hung 3m down the face of the dam by the Royal Engineers, and on 24 July 1942 high-speed cameras from the RAE at Farnborough and observers (including Wallis) witnessed the explosion – and the creation of a breach in the dam very close to the predicted size.

The final result of these tests was the prediction that a charge of just 3,600kg, detonated 9m beneath the water, would be capable of breaching the Möhne and Eder dams, but only if it was in contact with the dam wall. This was both good and bad news – a practical bomb to break a dam could be much

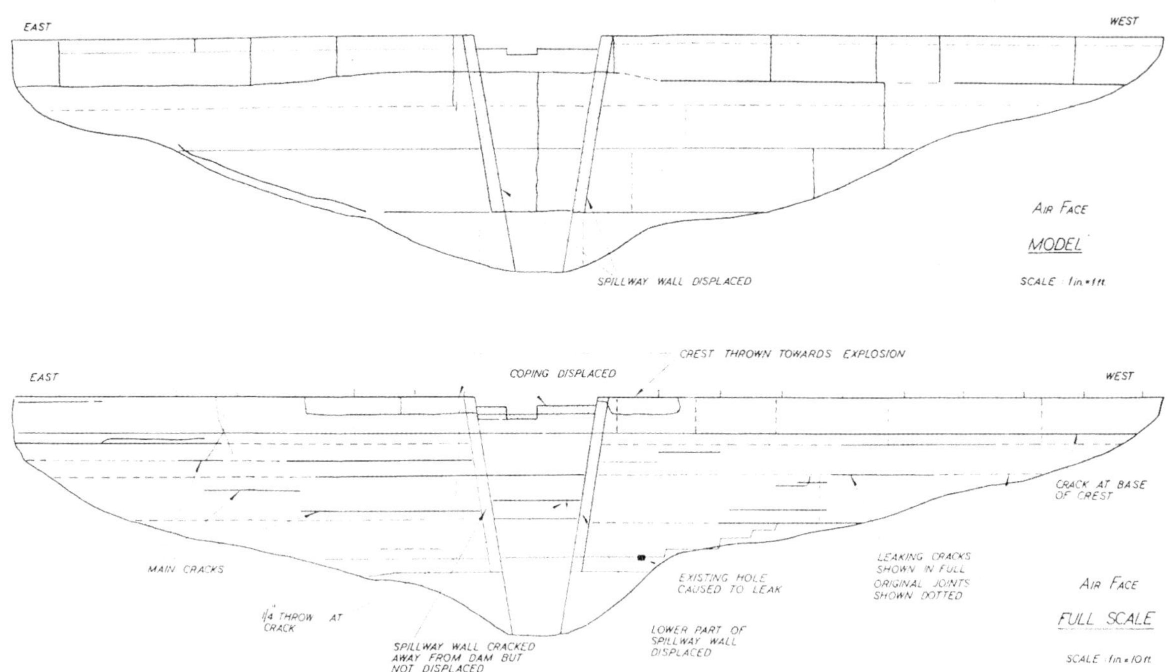

Diagrams showing the explosion damage to the test model of the Nant-y-Gro dam (top) and to the real dam following the first non-contact explosion; the correlation between scales is remarkable. *(Crown Copyright via The National Archives)*

lighter than had earlier been thought, but for it to work at all, the bomb had to be placed right against the dam wall, an accuracy undreamt of.

The 'bouncing bomb'

Now that the science had revealed a plausible weight of explosive, Wallis simply regarded the in-contact placement as a new requirement and set his mind to solving this as an engineering problem (he later credited Collins's demonstration work as being the real genesis of the weapon). In the early spring of 1942, he had the idea of 'a missile' which would be dropped some distance from a dam and ricochet over the water in a series of bounces to strike the dam. This offered two significant advantages: it would jump over any anti-torpedo nets placed ahead of the dam wall, and (as the water slowed its speed) it would arrive at the dam travelling very slowly, so there was a good chance that it would sink close to the wall.

Some initial tests made on 1 April[22] using a bathtub of water in his garden, helped by his children, confirmed that marbles could be skipped over water with some degree of repeatability, and Wallis believed that the same would be true if the idea was scaled up to a bomb-sized missile. Later that month, further tests by Wallis on nearby Silvermere Lake were made from a rowing boat crewed (she would say captained) by Wallis's secretary, Amy Gentry, who was a ladies rowing champion; these tests were also encouraging. Thus was born the 'bouncing bomb', which would become the most famous of Wallis's inventions.[23]

Wallis knew that naval gunners had on occasion extended the range of cannon balls by deliberately skipping them over the water, and this may have been the seed of the idea.[24] This was certainly mentioned in the document in which Wallis set out his idea in detail, 'Spherical bomb, surface torpedo', which appeared originally dated 29 April,[25] with a further section dated 14 May[26] (subsequently, Nelson was mentioned as the originator of this practice, but the research cited by Wallis refers to its use in the 16th and 17th centuries). His paper emphasised the advantages of the missile being spherical (including uniform detonation of the large explosive charge, and stability of the flight path in the turbulent region around the carrier aircraft immediately after release). It also referenced some theoretical justification of the bouncing theory in work performed by, paradoxically, a German scientist.[27] This work had shown that if a missile struck the water with an angle of incidence of less than 7 degrees, then it would ricochet, rather than sink; the missile would emerge with a lower incidence, and so should skip again, at the next bounce, and so on. Wallis's paper also noted the importance of the density of the missile, as this would determine how far it would tend to sink into the water before ricocheting.[28] He proposed to control the density using a double skin, an inner canister containing the charge and a spherical outer casing containing the charge canister plus a surrounding airspace, being held proud of the canister by a series of welded or wooden spacers. It was noted that the predicted range (three-quarters of a mile) would allow an attacking aircraft to drop the missile and turn away before reaching the target, be it a dam or a moored ship. To achieve the low angle of impact required (he initially aimed for 5 degrees), he suggested the aircraft fly at 470ft/sec (320mph) at a height of just 26ft! A further benefit of a spherical missile over a cylinder (realised later but not mentioned in this paper) was that spheres would experience lesser impact forces on hitting the water than a cylinder, as a sphere made contact more gradually.

Curiously, an *unwanted* ricochet effect had previously been tested by the Marine Aircraft Experimental Establishment (MAEE) on Mark VII depth charges. These were generally dropped on U-boats from a height of around 100ft from Sunderlands, but had been found to ricochet rather than sinking immediately (hence missing their targets). The experiment, conducted in August 1942, dropped six dummy stores, and found that even though they were not the ideal shape (the charges were cylindrical, dropped end-on), four of the stores made one bounce before sinking, and the other two also had some residual bounce which, although the store never left the water, was believed to alter the underwater path of the store. This behaviour was highly undesirable from an aiming point of view, as it altered the final position of the explosion, but the report makes no recommendation as to how to practically prevent the ricochets.[29]

The second section of Wallis's paper set out a series of model experiments to test the theory scientifically. He proposed to observe and record the performance of the test spheres manually, avoiding 'the elaboration and expense

A scene well known to viewers of *The Dam Busters* film, this photo shows the real marbles experiment on 1 April 1942 with Wallis at the catapult and his family as research assistants. *(© Mary Stopes-Roe)*

of photographic records if simpler means will suffice' – no films of the tests survive in the archives, so it is possible that none were made. The tests began in June 1942 at the NPL's experimental ship tanks at Teddington, continuing on a total of 22 days until September (Wallis did not have sole use of the tanks). These experiments verified the basic bouncing theory, and Wallis began to develop an understanding of the interplay between the speed and height of release on the range and consistency of performance. A variety of sphere densities and surface finishes were also tested – smooth, round dimples, angular dimples, grooves etc. – these choices perhaps being influenced by some wind tunnel work done by Wallis in the mid-1930s on the flight of golf balls;[30] cylindrical shapes were tested as well. Penetration of the various spheres into the water was measured by placing metal plates at the bounce locations and moving these up and down just beneath the surface – if the sphere penetrated far enough to hit the plate, a thud was heard.

In June 1942, Cdr Lane of the Admiralty's Department of Miscellaneous Weapons Development (DMWD) went to see Wallis to discuss the latter's earlier idea for a smoke-laying glider.[31] Wallis introduced the 'bouncing bomb' into the discussion, and this led directly to Rear Adm Renouf (the Admiralty's Director of Special Weapons) paying a visit to Teddington to see the tank experiments.

The mystery of backspin

Missing from his 'Spherical Bomb' paper is the application of backspin to the missile (i.e. a spin about a horizontal transverse axis in the opposite direction to the rotation of the undercarriage wheels) yet this would turn out to be a critical feature of the weapon. It is believed that the idea of adding backspin came from George Edwards,[32] the Vickers Experimental Manager and later Chairman of BAC, who was a keen cricketer of note (and continued to turn out for the works team's annual match against the Air Staff until his retirement from BAC in 1975). Edwards knew that backspin on a cricket ball makes it bounce higher on the pitch, and was sure the same would be true on water. Wallis was not so sure, so another demonstration was set up at Silvermere Lake by Edwards[33] using a catapult that could apply forward or backspin, as desired. An unspun missile was found to make 4 or 5 bounces, a forward spun one the same but more quickly, and finally a backspun one made around 15 bounces! Wallis reluctantly conceded, later rather grudgingly giving credit for the idea to an anonymous 'cricketer of my acquaintance', and Edwards himself believed that Wallis would have added the spin in due course anyway. This is probably true, for a number of compelling reasons. Although not mentioned in the 'Spherical Bomb' paper, Sweetman[34] believes that Wallis was already planning on using backspin, suggesting that Collins thought this was probably for reasons of stability. Certainly, the catapult used at Teddington[35] made use of a blade inserted into a slot on the top of the holder for the projectile. This retarded the release of the upper surface of the test spheres, thus adding a degree of backspin.

The practical reasons for including backspin are clearly laid out in the main patent application for the weapon which was initially submitted on 11 August 1942.[36] The primary reason given in the patent for backspin is the aerodynamic lift that is generated from the spinning motion – an effect known (though not named or described in the patent) as the Magnus effect, after the (again German) physicist who first described it in the mid-19th century. The spinning causes air close to the surface to be carried around, causing the airflow above and below the missile to be uneven, in fact lengthening the path of the air passing over the sphere. This has the same effect as an aerofoil wing (which is bulged on top and straight on the bottom, hence airflow over the top also takes a longer path), and generates lift in the same way. The added lift meant that the missile fell more slowly towards the water, hence increasing the range to first contact and (more importantly) reducing the crucial

These test spheres at the RAF Museum, Hendon, are typical of those used by Wallis for his experiments at Silvermere Lake and at the Teddington ship tanks. The similarity of some to golf balls may account for the codename 'golf mine' applied to the 'bouncing bomb' concept. *(Author)*

angle of incidence. It also had the beneficial side effects of reducing the vertical impact speed, aiding the ricochet effect off the water (as Edwards had initially predicted) again due to the lift generated, and stabilising the travel of the missile (this was thought to be the main reason, by both Collins and the Germans, for adding backspin), although this latter feature was not mentioned explicitly in the patent.

Calculation of the magnitude of the lift force generated by the backspin is set out in a formula in Wallis's notes.[37] Calculating this for the Upkeep store gives a lift force of 23.4kN, although later analysis[38] notes that this is a theoretical maximum, and actual lift being typically about half of this value, suggesting an actual lift of 12.3kN.

This can be compared to the gravitational force[39] pulling the store downwards of 41.1kN, so the lift generated by the spin in effect reduces the pull of gravity by about 30 percent. Dropping from 60ft, this prolongs the first impact by 0.4s to 2.3s,[40] and reduces the impact angle by 1.6 degrees to 8.6 degrees. Note that this is still greater than the maximum 7 degrees permissible for a bounce to take place, but the backspin again comes to the rescue, reducing the apparent impact angle below the limit allowable for bouncing to occur. Due to the backspin, the bottom of the store is moving forward (due just to rotation) at a speed equivalent to the circumference of the store multiplied by the rotation speed, which for the 130cm diameter store at 500rpm is about 34m/s. This figure can effectively be added to the forward speed of the aircraft (232mph = 104m/s), and so the backspin effectively reduces the impact angle to 6.6 degrees, and hence a bounce will occur. As the angle at which the store emerges from the bounce is always less than the impact angle[41] due to

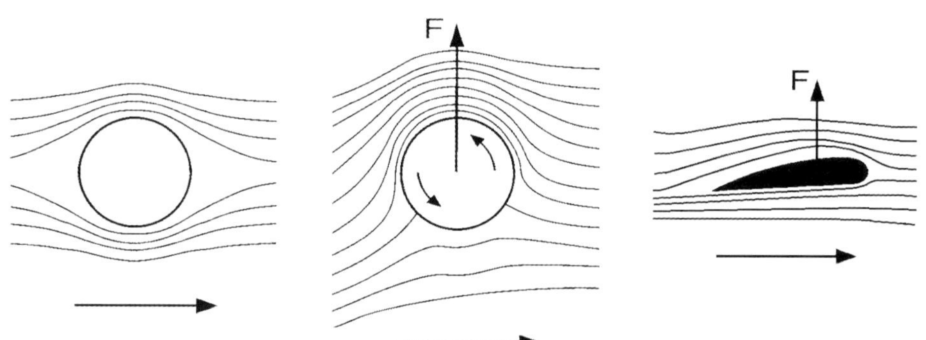

Generation of lift – an unspun cylinder (left) has an even airflow so there is no lift, but if the sphere has backspin (centre) the longer top path generates a lifting force F in the same way as an aerofoil section wing (right). *(Author)*

The prototype carrying, spinning and release gear for the golf mines (most similar to Highball). Note the drive belt (51) and the outward-swinging arms (34) to carry the store (Patent GB937959). *(BAE SYSTEMS)*

energy lost in the splash, and the emerging angle is approximately the same as the next impact angle (due to symmetry), then multiple bounces will occur – until so much kinetic energy is lost from the store that it can no longer break contact with the water and it then sinks. Faster backspin would further decrease the effective impact angle, but would result in greater stresses on the structure of the store itself and on its mountings.

Backspin was an important feature for a further very crucial reason – as the missile sank, the backspin would tend to drive it forward in the direction in which it had been dropped. If the target was a dam, then if either the missile undershot slightly or overshot slightly (striking the dam and bouncing back away from the face), the spin effect would push the missile forward towards the dam and hence it was more likely to sink while in contact with the masonry – the ideal position, of course. If the target was a ship, the same effect would carry the bomb forward beneath the vessel, again an ideal location for detonation being away from the armour belts around the waterline. This effect is mentioned in the 1942 patent document, but it is unclear whether the effect was predicted by calculation or derived from experimental observations.

Fig. 5.

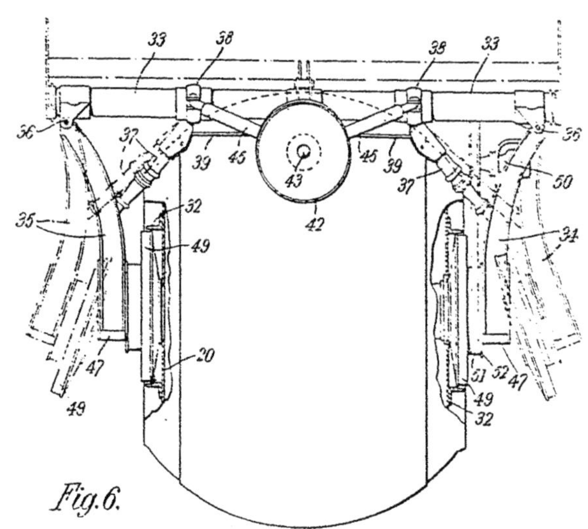

On the other hand, if the target was a canal or lock and the bomb was to be dropped on land, it was to be given forward spin to increase the range as it rolled along the ground to drop into the water at the end of its trajectory – this application was also included in the text and figures of the 1942 patent.

Backspin thus offered a host of benefits, but no disadvantages – other than the problem of actually mounting, spinning and releasing a large store. The system employed is again described in the 1942 patent, and in a very slightly modified form in a follow-up patent applied for in July 1943.[42] Figures in both patent documents clearly show the Highball mechanism, although the text is deliberately vague about a specific weapon. Both patents note that the missile would need to be balanced to minimise vibration to the carrying aircraft.

Prototypes

As the tank tests continued at Teddington, AM John Linnell[43] from the MAP was encouraged enough by the results to suggest a full-scale test, although his colleague Dr David Pye was less enthusiastic, partly because he had one eye on the aircraft work that Wallis might be neglecting due to his 'bombing project'. However, Vickers-Armstrongs was given permission to convert a Wellington and the Oxley Engineering Company in Leeds was approached to produce prototypes of

Prototype 'bouncing bomb' of the 'central disc type' showing the central charge cylinder and the hollow end pieces to make the bomb spherical. Bombs of this type were test dropped from the Wellington into The Fleet. *(BAE SYSTEMS via Nuffield College, Oxford (Cherwell Archives))*

the bombs, some with smooth surfaces, some dimpled. Wallis chose a diameter of 46in for the prototypes as a good compromise between the 2in test spheres and the expected full size. Admiralty visitors to Teddington included Lane and Renouf and other senior officers, who were also very impressed, Wallis putting a model battleship in place of the target dam for their benefit. Admiralty interest was crucial at this time, as MAP interest was waning,[44] Lane even recalling 'the whole initiation of action has been Naval in consultation with the inventor'.[45]

Some of the inter-service and technical detail proved slow to resolve, but the prototype bombs were both tested for balance on a static rig and in the Wellington between the end of October and the start of December. On 2 December, 'Mutt' Summers and Wallis flew the Wellington carrying four spheres over Queen Mary Reservoir at Staines for a spinning test. Wallis operated the rotation gear, and Summers was unaware that the spinning was in progress. Two days later, with Handasyde in the co-pilot's seat and Wallis acting as bomb aimer, Summers flew the Wellington (now altered to carry only two spheres) from Weybridge to the south coast, their destination being The Fleet, the long narrow lagoon that separates Chesil Beach from the mainland. The two weapons were released, but both burst on hitting the water – Wallis decided he needed to reinforce the casings. The drops were filmed using a theodolite camera, the moment of release being signalled by a flash from a light positioned in the cockpit window – see Appendix 4 for a full list of test drops.

After a short delay due to bad weather, the next two drops (one smooth sphere, one dimpled) took place on 15 December, the Wellington now flying from nearby RAF Warmwell. One again shattered, and the other was found to be badly dented on recovery. To minimise delays to future tests, two solid wooden bombs were to be manufactured. There were early tests of dropping 'golf mines' on land against a wall target at Porton, but it is unclear what the specific purpose of these tests was. The cost of the project thus far had been around £15,000[46] (slightly less

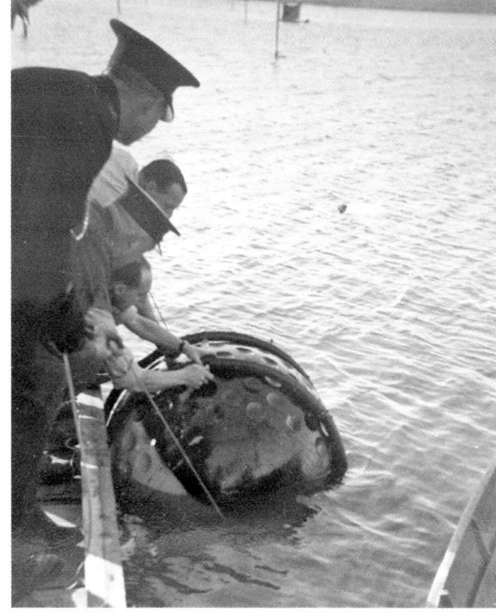

Prototype 'bouncing bomb' about to be recovered from The Fleet. The bombs were made light enough to float to aid recovery and hence assessment of impact damage. *(BAE SYSTEMS via The National Archives)*

than the cost of a Wellington bomber), each of the stores costing around £1,000.

The third trial on 9 January was not much better, one again breaking on impact, and one dropping on to land due to a release gear problem. Next day a smooth sphere was dropped from 100ft, and although a good bounce was recorded, the sphere again broke apart. On 23 January, a wooden sphere dropped from 42ft bounced successfully 13 times, and two more dropped next day did even better.

Wallis had brought all of his ideas, results and aspirations for the weapon together in a further paper entitled 'Air Attack on Dams' over Christmas, and circulated this to a few key people in January. In addition to the dams bomb, now with a planned diameter of 79in and a total weight of 11,474lb, Wallis proposed a smaller version of the bomb purely for anti-ship purposes of 35in diameter weighing 850lb,[47] which would be carried by Mosquitoes in pairs (originally Beauforts had been proposed). The weapons had acquired the codenames Upkeep and Highball respectively around the turn of the year.[48] (Further variations on the 'golf mine' theme are discussed in a later chapter.) Even at this stage, he had not evolved a final internal design, and while at Weymouth to watch some test drops, calculated the relative volumes of three designs. In addition to a plain cylinder, there was also the 'central disc type' (a flattened sphere with the explosive in a disc around the widest part of the sphere (5in wide in the original drawings, but around 15in wide in the prototype store)) and the 'baked apple type' (a flattened sphere with the explosive in a cylinder running the whole width of the store).[49] As well as Upkeep and the Mosquito Highball (1,000lb), there was also a proposal for a 'heavy type' Highball to be carried by Wellingtons (in fours) and Warwicks (in sixes), targets suggested for both types including dams, merchant ships and locks.[50]

Wallis showed films of the test drops to Vickers staff, the Admiralty and MAP staff on 28 January; the Navy staff were very impressed (Renouf had seen the 'Air Attack' paper) and MAP ordered 250 Highballs, which were to be manufactured at the Vickers-Armstrongs works at Crayford. RAF support was not so forthcoming, and in a letter to Cherwell[51] at the Cabinet Office, Wallis was very upbeat about recent progress, pressing him to support the dams weapon also, stressing the importance of using the two weapons simultaneously to avoid one giving away the secret of the other. He also emphasised that Lancasters modified for the dams weapon could be returned to normal 'in a few days'.

A further series of drops at Chesil Beach on 5 February also gave encouraging results, one travelling more than 1300yds. Early in February, further tests at Teddington[52] were undertaken in order to record the underwater behaviour of the stores, these being filmed from a glass-fronted tank lowered into the

Comparison of 'bouncing bomb' internal structures (not to scale) – the prototype 'central disc type', Highball 'baked apple type' padded cylinder and Upkeep plain cylinder. *(Author)*

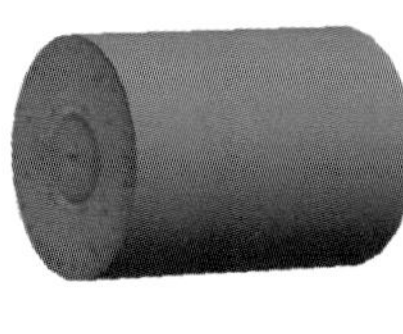

water, and Wallis was able to confirm that they would 'develop horizontal force directing it towards the target' in another letter to Cherwell on 20 February, in which he offered to come to London to show him the films.

Arthur 'Bomber' Harris, recently appointed C-in-C of Bomber Command, was shown the plans on 14 February,[53] but thought it 'tripe of the wildest description'. He did mellow considerably when shown the Chesil Beach films by Wallis and Summers. The next day, a meeting at the Air Ministry concluded that an operation against the Möhne Dam was tactically feasible, as was modification of aircraft within the timescale dictated by the water level (mid-May).[54] It had also been realised that the raid would not be without cost – it was reckoned that Wallis's work on the Highball project had put the B.3/42 back by four to six weeks, and that work on Upkeep would increase this to several months; there was also a knock-on effect at Avros, as some of its designers would be working on the carriage gear for the Lancaster.

The pressure which Wallis was trying to bring to bear on Whitehall to accept his weapon came to a head on 23 February, when he met with Craven, the Managing Director of Vickers-Armstrongs. He was distressed that Wallis appeared to have been making a nuisance of himself, and told him to cease his efforts with the weapon. Wallis was furious, and offered to resign on the spot, prompting cries of 'Mutiny!' from Craven (Wallis's other war work for Vickers meant that a resignation was not a serious possibility). However, Wallis's persuasion had already done the trick, and on 26 February in a meeting in Linnell's office, he was given the go-ahead for the dams operation. Thirty new Lancasters were to be converted to carry the store, of which 150 were ordered.

Bluff called

Wallis's first reaction was barely-contained panic. After all the preparatory work and 'sales pitch' to the ministries, he now had just 80 days to prepare everything for the actual raid. Alongside this, he also had Highball to work on for the Navy.

On 8 March the Chiefs of Staff agreed to set up an ad hoc committee[55] to monitor the progress of both Operation Highball and Operation Upkeep.[56] The Admiralty attempted to get Renouf to chair the committee, but the RAF's AVM Bottomley was appointed instead. Following revision of the original orders in the light of manufacturing limitations, 23 modified Lancasters were to be built, as well as 120 Upkeeps from Elswick and Barrow, half of which were to be HE filled, the remainder inert filled for trials.

As the work on the two bombs, although simultaneous, was now effectively for two separate 'weapons systems' (to use the modern expression), the two weapons will be described separately in the next two chapters.

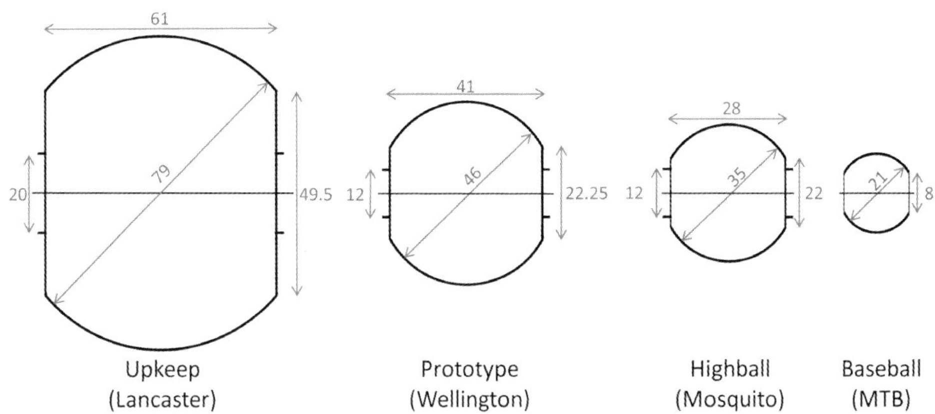

Comparative dimensions (in inches) of the principal proposed variants of the 'golf mine'. *(Author)*

Chapter 5

Upkeep – The Anti-Dam Bomb

Experience is as to INTENSITY, not as to duration.
(Thomas Hardy from Tess of the D'Urbervilles, 1891, quoted by Barnes Wallis on the frontispiece of his 'Note on a Method of Attacking the Axis Powers', 1941)

Upkeep: the dams bomb

Wallis's first reaction to the decision to go ahead with the dams operation was not one of elation, but of dread. He was now committed to making his wild theories a reality, and there were just 80 days until the best time to strike the dams. The task remained considerable – despite all the testing already done, the final form of the bomb was still undecided, as were the details of the mechanism required to attach it to the aircraft.

Norman Boorer of Wallis's drawing office staff 'and lots of others'[1] set to work drawing the 'final' form of Upkeep between lunchtime on 27 February and teatime the following day. This was a sphere of 79in diameter, with flattened poles each fitted with a 20in diameter flange to support and spin the weapon. At the core of the sphere was a cylinder for the charge, 51in (originally 49in) diameter and 60in long, made from 3/8in sheet steel. Around the core cylinder were arranged a series of wooden staves made from white pine, extending the solid shape of the metal cylinder out to that of a sphere of the required diameter.[2] Each stave was bolted to its neighbour using six screws, then steel straps[3] were fitted around the circumference of the store running in shallow grooves, each strap secured by two bolts, giving the weapon the appearance of a whisky barrel. Wallis initially planned for the outer spherical shape to be made of steel, but the resources required to make such large spherical shells were not available. However, Oxley Engineering in Leeds confirmed in early March that they had steel in stock to produce 100 cylinders to the required dimensions.[4]

Set into tubular pockets in one end of the mine were four pistols to initiate detonation of the weapon. Three were standard Mark XIV hydrostatic pistols as used in naval depth charges, and one a 90-second delayed-action fuze, also of a pre-existing design. As depth charges were designed to be dropped from aircraft and fired from the deck of destroyers, the pistols were designed to withstand impact forces of over 400*g* and so were perfectly suitable for this new application. The

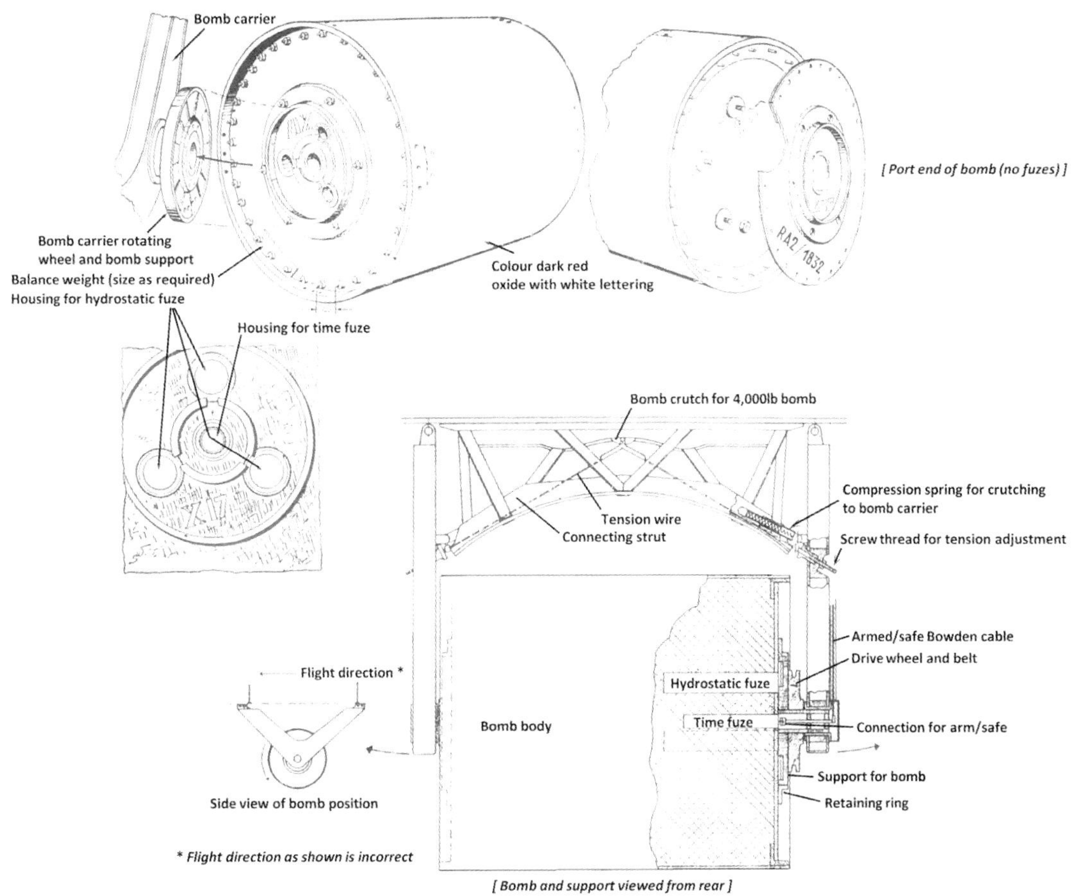

The German technical drawings made following analysis of Barlow's Upkeep are the best contemporary drawings that survive (labels have been translated). *(Author's collection)*

hydrostatic pistols were in triplicate purely for mechanical redundancy, and were reliable enough to be armed prior to the loading of the store into the aircraft, being preset to operate at a depth of 30ft.[5] The fourth pistol was intended as a self-destruct mechanism should the other pistols not fire, being set to detonate the store 90 seconds after leaving the aircraft. It was armed by pulling out a pin, and for this reason had to be mounted in the centre of the mine – the pin was attached to a fuzing unit on the forward starboard calliper arm, and so was pulled out as the arms opened at the moment of release.[6]

Torpex explosive was chosen as the filling for the bombs, as it was believed to have the best properties for an underwater detonation. For the test weapons, the place of the explosive filling was taken by a mix of concrete and cork which was formulated to give a similar density to the explosive.

The detailed design of the supporting callipers, and other aspects of the release gear, was done at Avros under Roy Chadwick.[7]

Flight trials

Due to spring lowering of the water level in The Fleet, it was now unsuitable for trials, and after checking alternative coastal test venues, including Shoeburyness (where there was an explosives test facility) and Orfordness (where there was a bombing range), Reculver on the north Kent coast, between Herne Bay and Margate, was selected – it had a wide, flat beach which would allow the bombs to be recovered at low tide. Nearby RAF Manston would host the trials aircraft.

The first Upkeep Lancaster ED765, known as the 'Provisioning Lancaster' and bearing the Vickers Type 464,[8] was delivered to the RAE at Farnborough for initial testing on

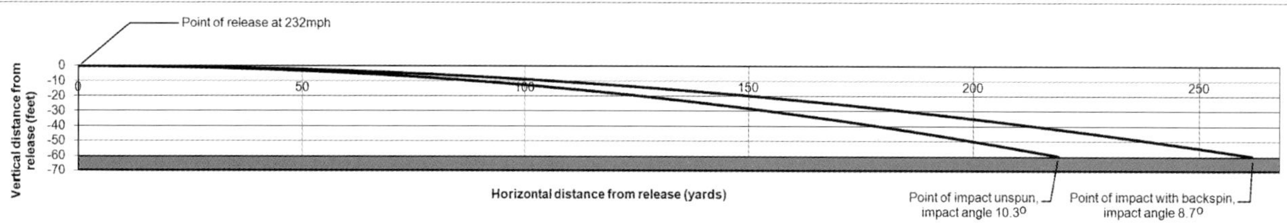

The path of Upkeep from release to first impact (to scale); the effect of backspin is to increase the range and reduce the impact angle. *(Author)*

8 April, flying to Manston two days later.[9] Spinning trials were done on the ground at Manston, and on 13 April the first two drops were made, the Lancaster being flown by Bob Handasyde, one of the Vickers-Armstrongs test pilots, with Wallis, Wg Cdr Guy Gibson and his Bombing Leader, Flt Lt Bob Hay, watching from the shore. These initial tests were 'essentially directed towards determining the range and trajectory of the large store'[10] – see Appendix 4 for a full list of test drops.

The first drop was from 250ft, but the store disintegrated, so the height of the second drop was lowered to 50ft.[11] Again, the straps snapped and the wooden slats broke off, one of them damaging the elevator on the Lancaster, but more remarkably, the bare cylinder bounced over the water as originally intended. After a delay due to poor weather, two more drops were made on 18 April, in both cases the casing breaking off and the store sinking immediately. While the third bomb to be dropped also shed its casing, the bare cylinder bounced along successfully for 700yds – the expected range of the store. Presented with a *fait accompli*, Wallis relented (despite reluctance bred from earlier tests which showed a cylinder to perform less satisfactorily than a sphere) and ordered the casings to be removed from the remaining stores. Speaking after the war, Norman Boorer reckoned that the problem of keeping the slats attached to the cylinder might never have been solved, but as it turned out 'it was one of these problems that we didn't have to solve'.

However, not all the problems were so easy – the first drops of the bare cylinder on 21 and 22 April both sank straightaway. Wallis reviewed his calculations, and decided on a lower release height, just 60ft, which was accepted by Gibson at a conference to discuss the issue on 26 April. A drop from 50ft[12] on 29 April proved satisfactory, as did another on the following day from 65ft, though there was a tendency for the store to veer to the left at the end of the run.[13] By the end of April, 120 Upkeeps had been delivered, 58 HE filled and 58 inert (plus 4 spares).[14]

All of the trial drops were filmed. For most trials two cameras were used, one a high-speed cine-theodolite side-on to the flight path which panned to follow the path of the store, plus a second mounted behind the aiming point which thus recorded any errors of line (though the latter were rare and the second camera was discontinued after a few tests). A light in the cockpit was set to flash to indicate the moment of release. Herbert Jeffree of Wallis's staff proved expert at analysing the films and deriving tables and plots of the trajectories achieved, including the heights and distances of the bounces.[15] Another recording instrument (probably also designed by Jeffree) allowed the path of the bomb, tracked via a peephole, to be drawn on to a cylindrical perspex sheet. The path could then be traced on to paper and the perspex cleaned ready for the next drop.[16]

The test drops continued into May with mostly satisfactory results, it being noted that range appeared related to release speed – variations in height and rotational speed had little effect on range. Confidence in Upkeep's performance was high enough to allow 617 Squadron to make their first three practice drops with the weapon on 11 May. Some test drops did continue after this, although the bulk were now training drops by 617 crews.

All of these ballistic tests and training drops used inert-filled stores. Following spin tests with live stores, which showed that the charge and detonators could be safely spun at 600rpm,[17] two test drops of HE-filled Upkeeps were made. One fully operational weapon was dropped off Broadstairs on 15 May, giving perfect performance above water, and detonating at an estimated 30ft underwater.[18] The column of water thrown up reached around 1,500ft, well above the level of a chase Lancaster carrying Gibson and other observers (the weight of the water column falling back down probably contributed to the forces pushing at the dams on the night of the raid). A second drop was made of an unspun Upkeep from 500ft – this weapon contained fuzes but was not armed, the intention being to prove that it could survive a severe impact with the water without detonating, which it did successfully.

Mounting, spinning and releasing

Originally, Wallis had planned to mount the bomb on an axle with ropes wound around it, and when the bomb was released, the ropes would impart backspin as it fell (rather like a yo-yo), but this idea was abandoned even before testing began.[19] Instead, to carry an Upkeep, the Lancaster's bomb bay underwent some rather dramatic surgery. The bomb bay doors were removed, and fairings were inserted at the forward and aft ends to smooth the airflow over the bomb and through the rear of the bay. The Upkeep was suspended across the bay, with its centre of gravity beneath that of the aircraft. The bomb was suspended from two V-shaped calliper arms, one on each side of the fuselage, attached through the fuselage sides to the roof structure of the bomb bay, and pivoted at the top on a fore-and-aft axis. At its lowest point, each calliper carried a metal disc 20in

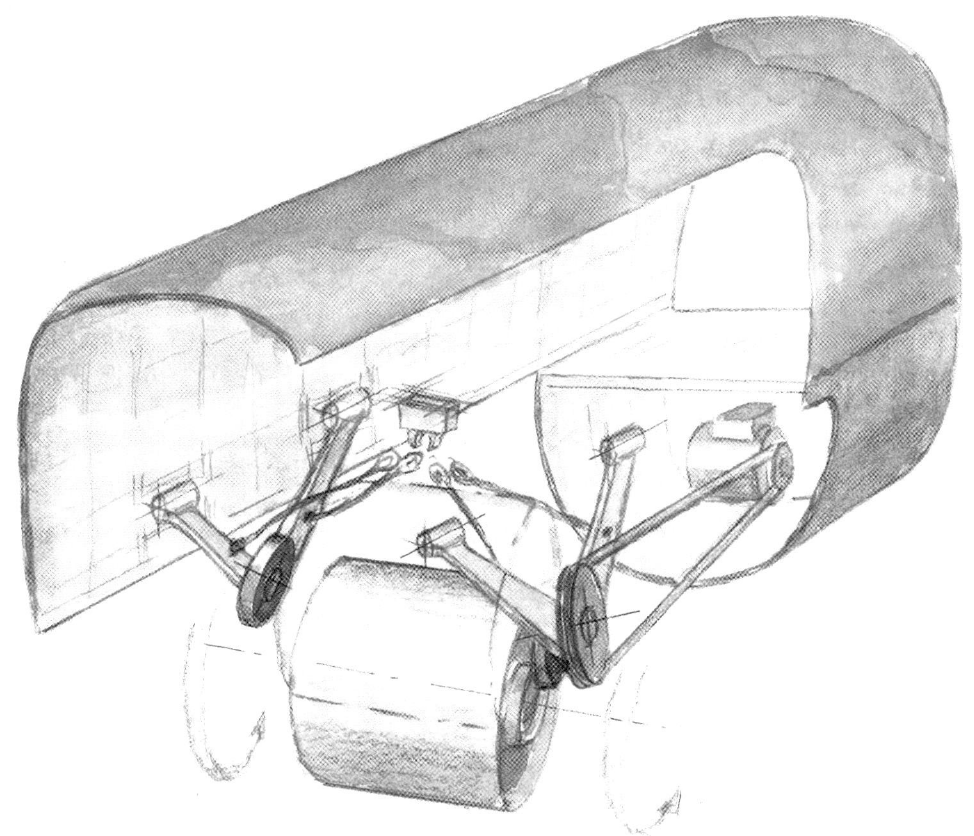

A modern drawing by Norman Boorer of the Upkeep spin and release mechanism in the Lancaster. *(Author's collection)*

in diameter which was free to rotate on a ball race; a circular flange was attached to each end of the bomb and the discs engaged with these rings. The callipers were sprung outwards by the compression in four strong springs; once the bomb was fitted between the discs, the callipers were pulled in and held closed by cables attached to a bracket fitted into a standard bombslip.[20] When the bomb release was pressed, the slip would release the cables and the springs would force the calliper arms apart and the bomb would drop away.

No detailed contemporary engineering drawings of the calliper mechanism are known to have survived. The detail work on the calliper was done by Avro, probably by Chadwick (the Chief Designer and designer of the Lancaster) himself, to guidelines given by Wallis. Nor does any drawing of the Upkeep mine itself survive; Norman Boorer, who drew the plans of the weapon, put much effort into tracking down a copy of his drawings after the war with the hope of presenting it to the Brooklands Museum, but he was unable to do so from any archive sources.

The bomb was spun by a hydraulic motor on the forward starboard side of the fuselage (driven by the hydraulic connection usually used to power the bomb bay doors).[21] The motor was connected to the disc on that side of the bomb via a rubber drive belt (Norman Boorer's recollection that the belt was toothed does not seem to be confirmed by any other

BACKGROUND

THE DAM BUSTERS FILM (1955)

Wallis and 617 Squadron achieved lasting fame through *The Dam Busters* film, which premiered over the two nights on 16–17 May 1955 (the raid's 12th anniversary) at the Empire Leicester Square. The film was based on Paul Brickhill's book of the same name[i] and also drew on Guy Gibson's autobiographical account [ii] published after his death. It was a great critical and popular success, and did much to bring Wallis to public attention through his portrayal by Michael Redgrave (both were later knighted, Redgrave nine years before Wallis himself). While the film does present a simplified and slightly idealised view of the events leading up to the raid (partly due to the Wallis weapons still being secret at the time), on the whole it is a substantially accurate documentary on the operation and Wallis's contribution to it (though the role of several other scientists and engineers appear to be collapsed into Wallis's character).

The portrayal of Wallis himself is largely fair, although Redgrave spoke more quickly than Wallis;[iii] Redgrave sat in on talks and meetings with Wallis to pick up some of his mannerisms (and used to walk behind him mimicking his walk when he visited the set),[iv] but told him 'I'm not going to mimic you, you know' to which Wallis replied, 'No, of course. Your problem is not to imitate a person, but to create him'![v] Molly was played by Ursula Jeans, Harris by Basil Sydney and Gibson by Richard Todd in his most famous role.

The story of the making of the film is told by Jonathan Falconer,[vi] and a detailed critique of the movie covering its historical accuracy and context is given by John Ramsden.[vii]

[i] Brickhill, Paul, *The Dam Busters* (Evans Brothers, 1951).
[ii] Gibson, Guy P., *Enemy Coast Ahead* (Michael Joseph, 1946).
[iii] Richard Todd, speaking at a meeting of the Barnes Wallis Memorial Trust, June 2008.
[iv] Richard Thorp, actor who played Henry Maudslay (private communication).
[v] Redgrave, Michael, *In My Mind's I* (Viking, 1983), 196, and Prins, Francois, 'Dam Busters – the film' (*FlyPast*, October 1985), 34–8.
[vi] Falconer, Jonathan, *Filming The Dam Busters* (Sutton, 2005).
[vii] Ramsden, John, *The Dam Busters: A British Film Guide* (I.B. Tauris, 2003).

sources). The motion of the powered metal disc was transferred to the bomb simply by friction between the disc and the end of the bomb, the lack of any further friction devices aiding a clean separation when the moment of release came. In action, the bombs were spun up by the wireless operator to about 500rpm some five minutes or so before dropping, the speed being regulated as required via a valve and a tachometer gauge.

Wallis was unsure about the effect of waves created by the explosions on following attacks. He consulted Professor Bullard who offered a brief analysis and was 'confident that after five minutes, the height of the waves will be measured in inches rather than in feet'.[22]

In addition to taking part in the drop tests, the third prototype Lancaster ED825 went to A&AEE at Boscombe Down at the end of April for a series of handling trials, including climbing, diving and stall tests with the Upkeep store fitted, aimed at establishing performance limits for the modified aircraft.[23] Maximum level speed with Upkeep (in its spherical form) carried was found to be 233mph and the maximum all-up weight of 63,000lb allowed for 1,774 gallons of fuel, giving a maximum range estimated at 1,720 miles (assuming that the store did not make the return journey). Following damage to two of the 617 Lancasters during practice drops at Reculver, there were no spare aircraft on the squadron, so ED825 was flown to Scampton on the day of the raid and quickly readied for action (fortuitously, as Flt Lt Joe McCarthy's usual aircraft developed a problem during pre-flight checks, so ED825 was available to take him to the Sorpe that night).

Setting the release height

Having thought so long about his 'surface torpedoes', it is remarkable that Wallis had not mentally devised a solution to two important problems of placing the weapons, namely how to find the correct height and the correct distance for their release (as accuracy in both was imperative) – more remarkable still since the problems are essentially the same, and were eventually solved by simple triangulation. Finding the height accurately was seen as 'the major problem in the proposed attacks'.[24]

The Dam Busters film romantically shows Gibson himself conceiving the height spotlights idea during a visit to the theatre, but this is entirely fictitious, nor was it Wallis's idea, nor even a new one. The idea came from Benjamin Lockspeiser at the Ministry of Supply, having been previously tried by Coastal Command for low flying over the sea; it had been found an unsatisfactory technique in this case, purportedly due to the rough surface of the sea. However, it appeared to be a reasonable solution for the dams mission, and one of the Lancasters was fitted with two Aldis lamps set to converge at 150ft (as the required height was at that time). One of the lamps was in the aerodynamic fairing at the rear of the bomb bay (on the aircraft centreline), and the other in the bomb aimer's camera position in the nose (a foot or so to port of the aircraft centreline). Again the film is inaccurate in this respect, showing the forward lamp just behind the bomb aimer's bubble, and the rear lamp too far back.

It is a common misrepresentation, perpetuated by many artworks showing the attack in progress, that the lights shone down on the centreline of the aircraft, but had this been the case then they could not have been seen from the cockpit; nor did they converge to a single spot as some images suggest, as if they diverged again, it would be impossible to tell whether the aircraft was now too high or too low. In fact, the forward light shone directly to starboard, at 30 degrees from the vertical, and the aft light (located 20ft astern) shone 7.5 degrees forwards and 40 degrees from the vertical; this arrangement also meant that if the height was changed, then only one lamp needed to be moved and in only one

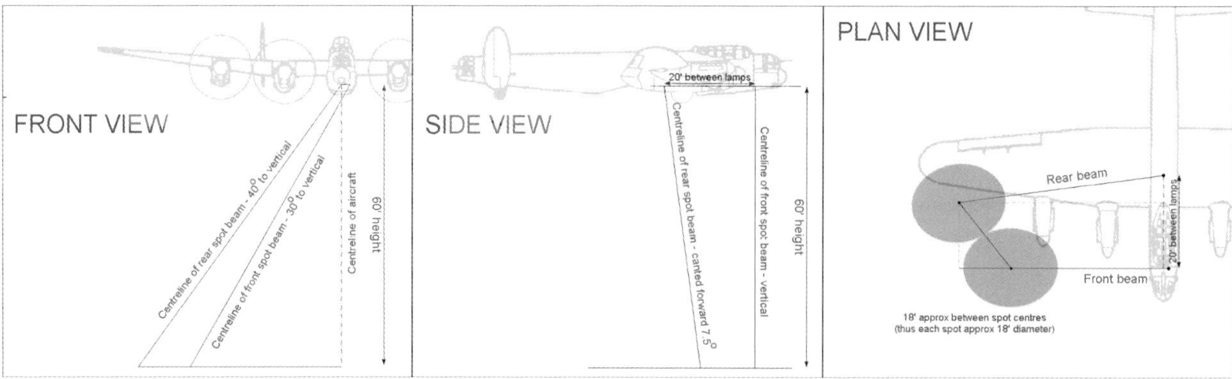

The set-up of the height spotlights (to scale) in the Lancaster. *(Author)*

dimension.[25] The light spots, each about 18ft in diameter, thus formed a diagonal figure of eight when the aircraft was at the correct height, and this arrangement also meant that the observer (who would be the aircraft navigator) could easily tell if the aircraft was too high or too low by the relative positions of the light spots (as the aircraft height varied, the forward spot would move sideways, while the rear spot would move diagonally).

To check the accuracy of the spotlamps, trials were conducted over the airfield using a theodolite, and the ability to hold a steady height over water was also checked.

Setting the release distance

The release distance problem was solved pretty much as depicted in the film (and again not by Wallis). Wg Cdr Dann at MAP was an expert on sighting, and had been set to work on the problem. His solution was made possible by the realisation that the main target dams had two sluice towers, and as these were a known distance apart, the problem was again reduced to one of triangulation, though it seems the height triangulation solution was arrived at independently. Dann's sight consisted of a triangular piece of wood, with an eyepiece at one corner and two nails at the other corners. The triangle formed by these three elements formed a geometrically similar triangle to that formed by the two towers of the target dam and the correct release point. The bomb aimer thus looked through his eyepiece during the approach, and when the nails coincided with the two towers, he would press the release.

During practice, some of the bomb aimers found the Dann sight very awkward. They lay prone on the floor of their compartment and needed to prop themselves up on their elbows in order to see forward, with the sight in one hand and the release in the other – the buffeting of the aircraft made sighting difficult in this position. Some bomb aimers used a variation on the same idea, which had also been proposed by Dann – they tied a string loosely between two screws at opposite sides of their clear view panel, then looped the string round a nail, which they pulled to their eye. This put their eye at a set distance from the panel, on to which they drew lines corresponding to the width of the sluice towers using a chinagraph pencil. The bomb aimers were free to use their preferred method, and no record was kept of which bomb aimers

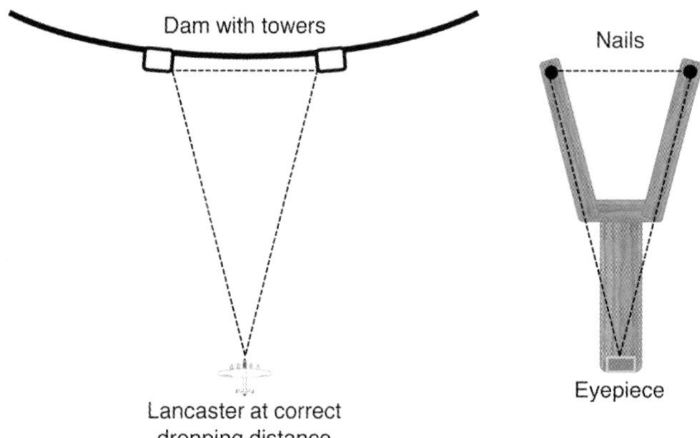

The principle of similar triangles was used to find the range to the dam; when the nails on the sight coincided with the towers on the dam, the bomb was released. *(Author)*

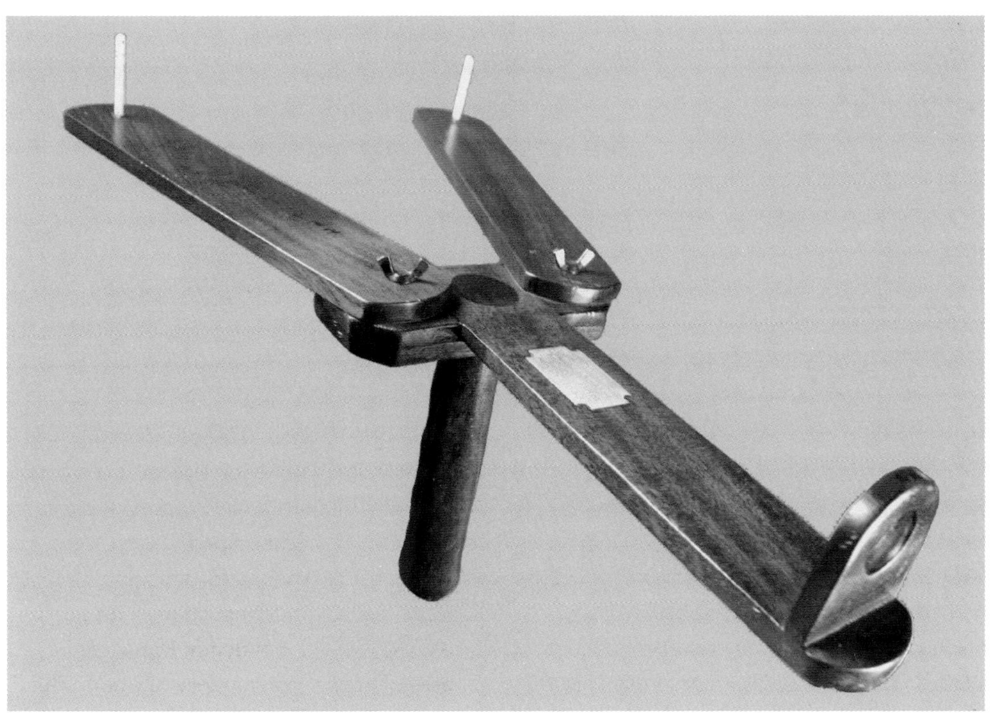

An original Dann sight. This example was given by David Maltby to his father as a souvenir of the raid. *(© David Worrow)*

used which method, but it is probable that at least half used the latter method. Flt Lt John Hopgood's bomb aimer (Flt Sgt John Fraser) used the Dann sight[26] and Gibson's bomb aimer (Plt Off Frederick 'Spam' Spafford) probably did so too, but Plt Off Les Knight's bomb aimer (Fg Off Edward 'Johnny' Johnson) definitely (and accurately) used the nail-and-string method at the Eder;[27] Sqn Ldr Melvyn 'Dinghy' Young's bomb aimer, who made the initial breach at the Möhne, did not make it home so his method is not recorded, but Flt Lt David Maltby (who enlarged the breach) gave his aircraft's Dann sight to his father as a souvenir, so presumably it was used in the attack.

Defences on the dams

The Möhne Dam was protected by two anti-torpedo nets which spanned the full width of the dam. These were positioned about 25m from the water face by two timber booms. Flak guns were located in the two towers, and there were several more in nearby fields. Photo reconnaissance interpreters were puzzled by the appearance, in the days before the raid, of 'structures' along the crest of the dam. Their observations caused some concern, but the structures turned out to be fake pine trees (made from wooden frames covered in camouflage netting) intended to camouflage the dam – something which they wholly failed to do.

All of the other target dams were undefended by either guns or passive defences (nets or barrage balloons); the surrounding hills would prove enough of an obstacle to the attacking aircraft.

Wallis knew from his early research that the Möhne was the most important target, and the next most important in the Ruhr area was the Sorpe (although quite close, the Eder was not part of the Ruhr river system). The Sorpe had a completely different construction, with a concrete wall at its core with wide buttressing banks of earth on both sides, the water side having a brick lining. He knew, therefore, that an Upkeep attack on this dam would have a lower chance of success, and the first meeting of the CoS ad hoc committee, while recognising its importance, decided that it should be 'ruled out as being unsuitable for attack, for tactical and technical reasons'.[28] However, the priority of the Sorpe as a target meant that it was still listed for attack, it being estimated that six Upkeeps might be sufficient to crack the central core and cause sufficient damage to cause some leakage which might lead to failure of the dam.[29] Hence a different method of attack was devised – Upkeep would be unspun and dropped while flying *along* the crest of the dam, the expectation being that the bomb would roll down into the water where the self-destruct fuze would detonate it. There is some conjecture as to whether Wallis actually counselled against attacking the Sorpe, but was overruled by the Air Staff because of the importance of the target. In either case, Wallis must have been less confident of success than at the walled dams, although he reported that this type of attack 'offered very good prospects of damaging Z [the Sorpe] to an extent which would bring about its destruction', noting that damage 'would not be immediately apparent to the crews'.[30]

Final preparations

A total of 23 Lancasters (3 for trials and 20 for the operation) were modified to carry the Upkeep mine, and 617 Squadron under Wg Cdr Guy Gibson was specially formed to perform the mission (Gibson had recently completed his second 'tour' on bombers with 106 Squadron, having had another tour on night-fighters in between).[31]

The photo reconnaissance unit at RAF Medmenham built three scale models of the primary targets for crew briefing purposes.[32] The Eder offered the most troublesome terrain, but for some reason the Eder model was not ordered until 11 May, and was not delivered until 18 May, by which time it was redundant.[33]

As well as using Wallis's novel weapon, the dams raid also introduced new control procedures. Normally, aircraft maintained only wireless telegraphy contact with their operation controller in Britain (at Grantham in the case of 5 Group), and there was no aircraft-to-aircraft communication, other than by Aldis lamp. For the dams raid, where the situation could change rapidly, this was deemed insufficient, and radio contact by voice over the target was to be used. Tests showed that the standard radios gave poor reception among hills, so VHF sets were acquired from Fighter Command and fitted instead, and these were found to work well. This arrangement allowed Gibson to keep in close contact with all his pilots, and it was copied subsequently for Main Force bombing raids as the 'Master Bomber' technique. Morse messages by wireless telegraphy continued to be used for communication with Grantham.

As the full moon period approached, all of the parts of the operational jigsaw were coming together. Upkeep trials at Reculver were giving consistent performances, and these moved into a training phase on 11 May, with the aim of giving each of the 617 crews two practice drops. Three drops were made on this date, including one by Gibson, and several more took place the next day, again with mostly satisfactory results. Some of these drops did give some hair-raising moments, with water splashes causing damage to Lancasters flown by Flt Lt Les Munro on 12 May and Sqn Ldr Henry Maudslay the following day, the latter losing an elevator and being lucky to stay in the air. Munro's ED921 was repaired, but Maudslay's ED933 was too badly damaged, despite round-the-clock work by the ground crews at Scampton. More drops took place on 14 May, Wallis being most heartened by the consistency achieved.

So the weapon was ready, the height and range problems were solved, and in addition to the test drops at Reculver, much aerial navigation practice was undertaken around the UK to practise for the long flight at low level. This culminated in a full 'dress rehearsal' on the night of 14 May, involving a long cross-country flight and practice attacks on Colchester Reservoir and Uppingham Lake; with this too Gibson was satisfied.

One final hiccup was to come from the unlikely source of Upkeep's smaller brother, Highball. Trials of the anti-ship version of the weapon were still proving problematic, and it had been an often-stated objective throughout that both weapons should be used simultaneously to avoid one giving away the principle of the other to the enemy, as it was recognised that effective countermeasures would be able to be deployed quite quickly following the initial use of either weapon. However, the time constraint enforced by the water levels in the reservoirs persuaded the Chiefs of Staff to allow the attack on the dams to go ahead on its own.

Operation Chastise:[34] Wallis's Grand Experiment

On 16 May 1943, the night of a full moon, 19 Lancasters of 617 Squadron took off from RAF Scampton (Lincolnshire) in three waves to attack the primary targets of the Möhne, Eder and Sorpe Dams. Of the 19 aircraft which set off, two returned early, one returned without attacking, and five crashed or were shot down outbound, so only eleven aircraft succeeded in dropping their Upkeeps (of which three were brought down after delivering their weapon) – five at the Möhne, three at the Eder, two at the Sorpe and one other. The full story of the preparations for the attack and the squadron's outward flight have been told many times (see Further Reading) so only a summary of the actual attacks and results will be given here.

Möhne Dam

After a dummy run over the dam to check out the approach and defences, Gibson dropped the first Upkeep, but his mine went off to port and detonated 50ft from the dam. Hopgood then attacked, but was hit by flak during his approach, and the mine was dropped late. It bounced right over the dam, and detonated on the power station on the other side. Hopgood managed to get his aircraft to gain some height before it exploded, and this allowed two of the crew to escape by parachute, although they were both seriously injured and became POWs. Flt Lt Harold 'Micky' Martin then attacked, but his Upkeep veered sharply to port and exploded some distance from the dam (an occurrence Wallis had feared if the aircraft was not flying level, causing the cylinder to 'dig in' at one side). 'Dinghy' Young then attacked, and after three bounces, his Upkeep mine exploded in contact with the wall. Maltby then came in to attack, but as his Upkeep was dropped, it was realised that

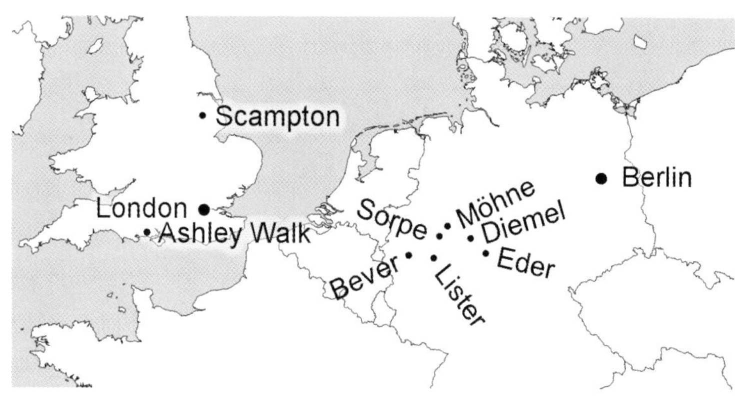

Locations of the target dams. *(Author)*

Plot of bombs dropped at the Möhne Dam. *(Crown Copyright/ Author)*

the dam was already crumbling. His mine also exploded in contact with the wall, and together with Young's, a breach 76m wide was created. Young was unfortunately shot down on his way home (the third time he had come down in the sea, hence his nickname, but he did not survive this time).

Eder Dam

Gibson and Young flew on to the Eder with the three aircraft that still had their mines, while Martin and Maltby headed for home. After locating the dam, Flt Lt David Shannon made four passes over it, the steep dive and turn required to line up with the target proving difficult (the mine was not to be dropped unless the bomb aimer was completely happy with the approach). Maudslay tried twice, then Shannon twice more before releasing his mine, which exploded close to the dam towards one end. Maudslay attacked again, this time releasing his mine, but it hit the parapet of the dam and exploded immediately; it seems probable that the explosion damaged the aircraft, as there was no further radio communication from Maudslay and his aircraft crashed near the Dutch border on its way home. Knight made one dummy run, releasing his mine on the second attempt; it bounced three times before hitting the dam, the rear gunner seeing clearly in the moonlight a 10m hole punched through the masonry, although the flow of water quickly washed away the masonry above the hole and widened the breach to around 70m.

Plot of bombs dropped at the Eder Dam. *(Crown Copyright/ Author)*

Sorpe Dam

Unlike the Möhne and Eder Dams which were walled dams, the Sorpe was constructed of a concrete core flanked by earth banking on both sides. Different tactics were thus employed against the dam, which was to be attacked by flying along its crest, and the mine dropped without spin at the centre of the dam. McCarthy (flying the trials Lancaster ED825 which was the reserve aircraft, as his own had developed a fault immediately before take-off) made the first attack, making nine dummy runs as the target was covered in mist; on the tenth run, the mine was dropped and exploded on the dam crest. Flt Sgt Ken Brown arrived at the dam over an hour later, dropping his mine in the same fashion on the sixth run; it also exploded on target.[35] Although the crest and the stone facing on the waterside were damaged, the dam was not breached and no seepage through the core, as hoped for, resulted (despite initial aerial reconnaissance photos which showed discoloration in the compensating basin below the dam; this was probably due to water raised by the explosions cascading down the air side). Albert Speer, the German Minister of Armaments and War Production, inspected the dam and found the bomb crater just above water level: 'Just a few inches lower – a small brook would have been transformed into a raging river which would have swept away the stone and earthen dam.'[36] The damage to the crown of the dam required the Germans to half empty the reservoir to effect repairs, so there was some (albeit controlled) water loss, at a time when it could be ill-afforded, as a result of the attack. Wallis asked Harris to consider a high-level follow-up raid in an attempt to accelerate any leakage, but the bombs available were not really suitable (Tallboy was still a year away); Harris even approached the Americans to do the job, but they felt it was too far to penetrate into Germany at that time.[37]

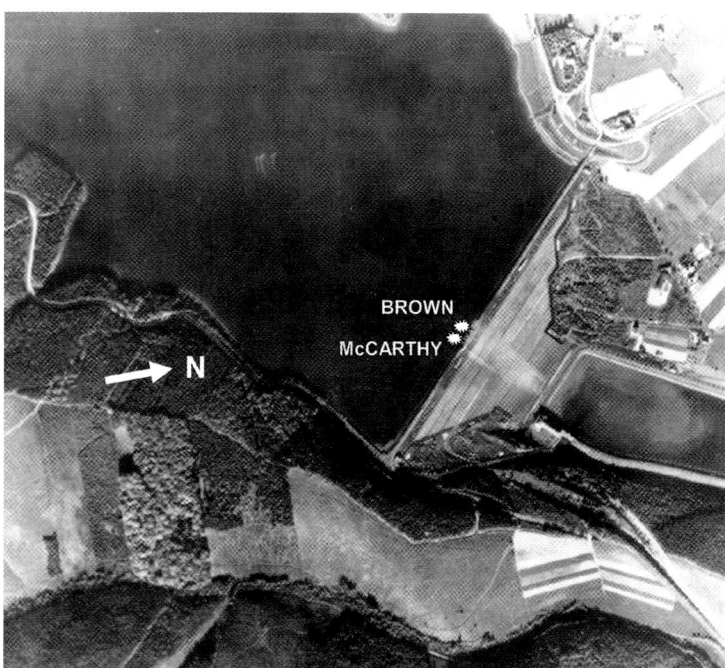

Plot of bombs dropped at the Sorpe Dam. Note the discoloration of the water in the compensating basin (right). *(Crown Copyright/Author)*

Other dams

The Lister,[38] Ennepe and Diemel dams in the Ruhr area were reserve targets for the raid, to be attacked by remaining aircraft if the main targets were destroyed (the Henne was also on the target list, but deleted a few days before the raid, due to a concentration of flak in a nearby town). After the Eder breach, Flt Sgt Bill Townsend was ordered to attack the Ennepe Dam; on his fourth run, the Upkeep was dropped, but it exploded short of the dam. It was subsequently established that it was the Bever Dam which had been attacked. The Bever reservoir was a similar shape to the Ennepe and was only 5 miles away, but as the aiming sights were set for the Ennepe, a hit would have been impossible (also, the Bever dam was an earth-bank dam like the Sorpe, rather than a walled gravity dam).[39] These other dams had at most one sluice tower, so it is not clear how the correct dropping distance was to be ascertained for these dams.

Other aircraft

The Lancasters flown by Astell, Byers, Ottley, Burpee and Barlow were all brought down en route to the Ruhr by flak or by hitting ground hazards. In addition, Munro turned back after suffering severe flak damage crossing the Dutch islands (which disabled his intercom and thus made vital inter-crew communication impossible), and in the same area Rice flew too low and his mine was torn off by the sea; he managed to regain height and return safely to Scampton with a somewhat shaken (and wet) crew. Finally, Anderson made it to the Ruhr, but was unable to locate any targets (allegedly due to the build-up of mist in the valleys), and returned home with his mine. Gibson was somewhat displeased with this result, partly as there were orders against landing with an Upkeep still on board, and saw to it that this crew was immediately posted from his squadron.[40]

Results

Debriefing

The primary eyewitnesses to the attacks were the aircrews themselves, the rear gunners having the best seats in the house. The first information to reach the 5 Group Ops Room at Grantham was a coded message made by each aircraft after its attack. In case the aircraft failed to return, this message was designed to give a brief summary of the outcome of its attack and consisted of the aircraft's identity, the word

'Goner' (to indicate a successful drop), then a number indicating the position of the explosion (ranging from 1, no explosion, to 7, explosion in contact with the dam), a number indicating the size of breach (8, none; 9, small; or 10, large), and finally the code letter of the target (A for the Möhne, B for the Eder, and C for the Sorpe). In addition, there was a series of special control codewords, including the now infamous 'Nigger' which meant the Möhne had been breached and the Eder was now the primary target, and 'Dinghy' which meant the Eder was breached and the Sorpe was next to be attacked. The transmissions received were as shown in Table 5.1.

Sent by	Message	Time of message/attack	Meaning of message
Gibson	Goner 68A	0037 / 0028	Exploded 5 yards from Möhne, no apparent breach
Martin	Goner 58A	0053 / 0038	Exploded 50 yards from Möhne, no apparent breach
Young	Goner 78A	0050 / 0044	Exploded in contact with Möhne, no apparent breach
Maltby	Goner 78A	0050 / 0049	Exploded in contact with Möhne, no apparent breach
Gibson	Nigger	0056	Möhne breached, Eder now primary target
Shannon	Goner 79B	0206 / 0137	Exploded in contact with Eder, small breach
Maudslay	Goner 28B	0146*/ 0145	Overshot Eder, no apparent breach
Gibson	Dinghy	0154	Eder breached, Sorpe now primary target
Knight	Goner 710B	0200 / 0151	Exploded in contact with Eder, large breach

*0156 was actually recorded, but it is believed this should have read 0146

Table 5.1: Wireless telegraph messages received from the attacking aircraft.

The aircraft transmissions were not received in quite the same order as the attacks took place, which caused some confusion at Grantham, but the 'Nigger' and 'Dinghy' codewords were the cause of great celebration when they were received. Wallis was congratulated by all present, including Harris whose hard-won support had been justified. These simple messages do give a good sketch of the placement and effect of the bombs, with only two minor exceptions – the detail that Young's bomb did cause the dam to fail just as Maltby dropped his bomb (and hence Maltby's Wireless Operator should have sent Goner 710A), and that Shannon claimed a small breach in the Eder which was not witnessed by the other crews.

After landing, all crews were debriefed more thoroughly than was usual for a raid, and were required to complete a special questionnaire about some details of the mission and Upkeep performance, including number of bounces made, number of runs made at the target, and the damage seen. The reports are summarised in Table 5.2.

Dam	Pilot	Bounces	Spun?	Runs	Results
Möhne	Gibson	3 bounces	500rpm	One run	Two holes in dam*
Möhne	Martin	Not seen	480rpm	One run	None visible
Möhne	Maltby	3 bounces	Yes	One run	Breach before attacking
Eder	Shannon	2 bounces	Yes	Three runs	Gap 9ft wide east side
Eder	Knight	3 bounces	Yes	Two runs	Large breach 30ft below top of dam
Sorpe	McCarthy	N/A	N/A	Ten runs	Crown crumbled 15–20ft
Sorpe	Brown	N/A	N/A	Ten runs	Crown crumbled 300ft
Bever	Townsend	1 bounce	Yes	Three runs	No damage

* evidently refers to raid, rather than result of his own mine

Table 5.2: Summary of Operation

Reconnaissance photographs taken on the morning of 17 May showed the huge breaches in the two dams, and the flooded landscape in the valleys below. Some discoloration of the basin beneath the Sorpe gave some hope that the dam was leaking, but it is more likely to have been caused by water from the explosion splashes washing down the air face of the dam. Gibson was still clearly hopeful of success, telling Wallis to 'wait for the Sorpe' in his letter of congratulation of 20 May.[41]

On the ground

Over the 24 hours following the raid, most of the water from the two ruptured reservoirs poured down the valleys beneath the dams – 116 million m^3 from the Möhne (88 per cent of capacity) and 154 million m^3 from the Eder (76 per cent of capacity). A summary report by Dr Prüss (Superintendent of the Ruhr Valley Dam Association) was prepared by the end of September, and this gives a detailed analysis of the prosecution of the raid (mostly on the Möhne and Sorpe, as the Eder was outside his jurisdiction), as well as a summary of the damage.[42] Some of the detail, such as the number of aircraft involved and the number of attacks made, is inaccurate, but understandable from eyewitnesses to a combat action.

Some of the best scientific evidence of the exact timing and effectiveness of the Upkeep detonations is included in this report,[43] being logged by the seismographs of the Geophysical Institute at the University of Göttingen, which is around 45 miles from the Eder Dam and 80 miles from the Möhne. Allowing for the transit time of the pressure waves, accurate timings for the explosions of the mines of Gibson, Martin, Young, Maltby, Shannon, Knight and (possibly) Townsend can be noted from the recordings (the other four mines detonated in air, and did not produce enough ground shock to register).

Other evidence in this report includes explosion damage to the west fender supporting the anti-torpedo nets, suggesting that one of the mines (most probably Gibson's) detonated very close to it. The second mine (Martin's) is placed 80–100m from the dam on the west side, the third clearing the dam and exploding below it (Hopgood's) – these two in fact occurred in the reverse order – and the fourth (Young's) is credited with making the breach. It is remarkable that this report emphasises the fact, underlined in the original, that 'the last mine which exploded close to the centre of the wall was able to cause the breach without previous serious damage having been sustained by the wall as a whole', that is, the Germans appreciated the fact that the breach was in effect caused by a single mine. The fifth attack by Maltby seems to have gone unnoticed as the breach had already occurred.

The attacks on the Sorpe, by McCarthy and Brown, are then described in good detail and largely accurately (except for exaggeration of the numbers of aircraft involved). The attack on the Bever is also described (this by Townsend thinking he was attacking the Ennepe as ordered).

Details of the damage to the wall of the Möhne beyond the breach, and the steps taken to repair it, are then given: 12,500m^3 of masonry was washed away by the water, and an additional 6,800m^3 was so severely cracked that it had to be removed and replaced also. Less severely cracked parts were repaired by pumping in cement, at the same time as the breach itself was repaired with new stone.

Beneath the dams, the water caused devastation – reports are full of superlatives, and although some later commentators have disputed the magnitude of the damage caused, it was clearly massive in scale and area. Sweetman et al.[44] quote German reports of the attack including:

Möhne

2 power stations at the dam destroyed, 1 other flooded and others affected
11 factories and an iron foundry destroyed, 114 factories damaged
25 road and rail bridges destroyed, 21 damaged[45]
Many pumping stations and waterworks damaged

Eder

2 power stations disabled (the power stations beneath the Eder were at the ends of the dam, so they were damaged but not washed away by the floodwater)
50 hectares arable land washed away
Fritzlar airfield partially flooded
30,000m^3 of silt had to be dredged from the Fulda, plus 5,000m^3 from the Weser
5.5km of Fulda banks to be rebuilt

Sorpe

2 craters 30m apart, 3m below water level, 12m deep (or 4.5m deep x 8m wide); repair of the craters required around half of the water in the reservoir to be emptied, so this water was also lost, although in a controlled manner

An estimated 87 per cent of the 132 million m^3 in the Möhne reservoir was released within 12 hours of the breach, sweeping a 10m wave down the valley. West of Essen, one of three lakes on the Rhine had been drained to deny its use as a landmark to aircraft and, in advance of the floodwaters, the other two were quickly emptied into the river – when the flood arrived, the now empty lakes were able to absorb around 15 million m^3 of the water. Around 75 per cent of the Eder reservoir's 202 million m^3 was released, although the smaller breach made by Knight's mine meant that the flow went on for longer than at the Möhne, and the wider valley meant that the flood spread out more quickly. Speer said that it was the loss of water for the coking plants used for steel production that did the greatest harm.[46]

The human toll was also large, with 47 casualties recorded in the Eder floods and 1,294 at the Möhne – of these, more than half were foreign workers, many of whom were housed in a camp a short distance from the Möhne Dam; the camp was completely washed away by the flood.

Aftermath

The result of Operation Chastise, its impact on the war (in both the short and long terms) and its cost in lost aircraft and men has been the subject of much controversy. Out of 19 aircraft dispatched, 8 were lost and 53 of the 56 crew in those aircraft were killed. Three baled out of Hopgood's aircraft, but only Fraser and Burcher survived, and Tees survived the crash of Ottley's aircraft; all three became prisoners of war. Typical Bomber Command raids of the time were experiencing losses around 5 per cent of aircraft dispatched (though often not hitting their targets), and Operation Chastise was well above this average. It should be noted that the high losses were not directly attributable to Upkeep nor to its method of delivery (only one aircraft was lost in the actual dam attacks, and was due to flak), but more to the low-level flight to the targets (two of the crashed aircraft had hit electricity pylons) and a bit of bad luck. Had a Chastise-type operation been mounted again, it is probable that a height of 1,000–3,000ft would have been used for the inward flight (above ground hazards but lower than normal bombing heights where nightfighters would be hunting) despite a greater risk from flak.

The Upkeep weapons themselves performed to expectation, with those placed accurately causing damage very close to the experimental estimates. The carrying and release apparatus in the aircraft worked well, although some crews reported vibration from their spinning store, this being 'quite alarming' according to one pilot,[47] but presumably this was due to an imbalance in the individual store.

One benefit of the raid, which was probably unappreciated beforehand, was the massive propaganda value of the reconnaissance photos, which were a clear sign of a major strike against the enemy.[48] The corresponding damage to morale in Germany was also substantial.

What was unexpected was the speed with

which the broken dams and other damage was repaired – most coalmines and bridges were operational again within weeks or months, and remarkably the broken dams were both rebuilt during 1943 (the Möhne in an incredible 19 weeks), in time to catch the winter rains (though neither was used to full capacity until after the war). This massive rebuilding effort in turn caused a large diversion of manpower from other work, including Hitler's Atlantic Wall (and was the only time the Nazi slave labour force, the Organisation Todt, was used within Germany itself). Indeed on the balance sheet of war, the 53 men lost on the raid were probably paid back many times over in Allied lives *not* lost on the Normandy beaches, due to the uncompleted defences there.

Wallis had always expected (as did some senior Germans, including Speer)[49] that the dams would have been attacked with incendiaries to destroy the wooden scaffolding and delay the rebuilding work,[50] but such a mission never appears to have even been planned, probably due to the improved defences around the dams. A low-level attack would not have been required, but incendiaries are impossible to aim with any accuracy, so a high-level attack would have needed good luck to hit the scaffolding.

In a classic case of closing the stable door after the horse has bolted, barrage balloons were in place at all the main German dams, including the breached ones, within 24 hours of the raid, and searchlights, smoke apparatus and extra flak guns were soon in place too. This had a further benefit in the diversion of manpower, as these active defences required manning, and both men (more than 1,000 at some of the dams) and the guns were thus diverted away from other installations. When the dams were rebuilt, novel defences were also created against further Upkeep or similar low-level attacks, including floats against the dam wall to prevent Upkeep-type bombs from sinking there, netting over the air side, and cables strung out above the approach to the dam.[51] Powerful searchlights were placed on the dams to dazzle oncoming pilots, and the Germans also tested mines laid in the water which could have been remotely detonated as aircraft passed overhead. Similar defences were also installed at other dams. The roofs of the sluice towers on the Möhne and Eder dams were dismantled to prevent their use for rangefinding; the flak positions were initially left intact, although later in the war when the guns were more urgently needed elsewhere, they were replaced by wooden dummies.

If Chastise woke the Germans up to the vulnerability of their dams, it also caused genuine fears that British dams might be attacked,[52] Churchill asking for steps to be taken on the day of the raid itself.[53] By 3 June, when a meeting was held to discuss possible reprisal attacks, it was stated that 'it is known that the enemy have some information about 'Upkeep'[54] and by August it was 'clear from a recent Intelligence Report that the enemy is probably in possession of a specimen Upkeep and has considerable information' on its technical specification.[55] By October, it was known that agents were looking for information on a 'rotary mine'; it was suggested that the weapon codenames be changed, and a standard mine be renamed as the 'Rotary Mine' in order to divert any attention in the wrong direction.[56] Minefields, barrage balloons, floating or suspended barriers, floating masts, smoke, cables hung from pylons, and searchlights were all considered as countermeasures, Wallis favouring the latter solution. Five dams near Sheffield were seen as the most vulnerable, as well as two reservoirs near London. It was thought by Wallis that the German intelligence must have come from Rice's mine lost on hitting the sea off Holland, but it was actually Barlow's, which had stayed attached to its support arms when his aircraft crashed after hitting an electricity pylon, so the pin of the self-destruct fuze had not been pulled out. From this example (and some operational details acquired by interrogating their aircrew prisoners) they quickly developed a full technical specification for the weapon. Drawings dated ten days after the raid[57] show details of the construction and operation of the 'rotating depth charge'; paradoxically, these German drawings are the ones most often seen in modern publications, as the originals were spirited away and have not come to light again since the war. Despite being presented with a working weapon, the Germans reverse-engineered the concept of the 'bouncing bomb' (in fact, none of the eyewitnesses to the attacks had observed that the bomb skipped over the water) and decided to go back to basics and develop their own spherical weapon from scratch. Their research led eventually to their own bouncing bomb, codenamed Kurt, but this was actually similar to Highball (so it will be further discussed in the next chapter). It is not known what happened to Barlow's Upkeep after the German assessment was concluded.

The main scientific result of Chastise was that Wallis and his theories were vindicated and his hypothesis proven unequivocally – Upkeep had been able to destroy the huge dams, and (although five mines were dropped against the Möhne, and three against the Eder) there is clear evidence that it was the first mine to be dropped in the right place that had broken the dam wall in each case. The letters of congratulation[58] that he received after the raid, while acknowledging the success as a team effort, also recognised that the victory was in the most part down to Wallis. Lockspeiser called it a 'magnificent personal achievement', Tizard had 'no hesitation in saying that yours is the finest individual technical achievement of the war' and Glanville said that 'without his great effort and inventive genius, it would never have succeeded'. Gibson himself recognised that the raid had been 'the last great experiment which has proved [sic] all your theories'. David Pye (who had been involved in the early preparations but had by then moved on from his Air Ministry post and so was not aware of the later work leading up to the raid) acknowledged the rigour with which Wallis dealt with the problem and was 'full of admiration for the way it was tackled, the scientific approach *in excelsis*'.

By whatever benchmark is used, it is clear that the raid was a magnificent feat of arms, a great technical success, and it achieved its principal aims. One Tornado pilot of 617 Squadron has said, 'If someone was asked to do it again today and managed to achieve a hit, then you'd still consider it to be a remarkable achievement.'[59]

Further 'dam busting' operations

After being proven so dramatically in Operation Chastise, it is perhaps surprising that Upkeep was never used again operationally, despite numerous possibilities, several of which were given serious consideration. All of 617's remaining Upkeep Lancasters were retained by the Squadron pending a decision on more operations, but no further aircraft were ordered, although the special jigs and tools were kept in case further production was required.[60]

Even before the German dams were attacked, potential new targets were being considered. An Air Ministry report[61] of early April considered the possibility of disrupting the Italian electric rail network by attacking hydro-electric power stations with Upkeep or Highball. However, of 45 power stations considered, of which 21 had reservoirs, only two (Ampollino in Calabria in the south, and Suviana in Bologna in the north) were thought to be vulnerable to this form of attack, and the grid network was reckoned to be 'highly-developed' and able to prevent disruption even if these dams were destroyed.

AVM Robert Saundby, AVM The Hon. Ralph Cochrane[62] and Wallis discussed possible further targets for Upkeep before the end of May, including canals and the Rothensee Ship Lift,[63] and Wallis attended a meeting at the Air Ministry on 11 June 1943[64] to formally consider future targets. The results of two overland trial drops conducted on 4 June at the Ashley Walk bombing range in the New Forest, using forward spin, had shown that 'the performance of the store over average open ground was entirely satisfactory' running for around 1,000yds when dropped from heights of 80ft and 100ft, but that stones thrown up by the impact had damaged the release aircraft, especially at the lower height. It was noted that 'the store was undamaged by the drop and was fit for use again' in both cases. Further test drops from 150ft and 200ft were suggested to determine a maximum acceptable release height, and two more drops (from 200ft and 250ft) were performed on 9 June.[65] Runs of only 500–600yds were noted, as well as craters 3½ft deep at the first impact point in both cases, these results being described as 'markedly inferior' to the earlier ones.[66] At the 11 June meeting there was a suggestion to acquire further Upkeep-capable Lancasters, but this decision was deferred pending further investigation of the range of viable targets, although 30 sets of the necessary parts were ordered while the jigs were still available. Wallis was asked about producing a smaller Upkeep variant to permit a greater fuel load and thus larger operational radius, but this was ruled out as it would require new trials and the charge in a smaller weapon would be less effective.

Another similar meeting was held on 1 July 1943 to further discuss future use of Upkeep and also potential targets for the 'deep penetration' bomb, which was now being prepared but had not yet acquired its codename. These included canals (noting recent trials, with such targets in mind, of the standard 12,000lb HC blast bomb into water), river barrages, railway viaducts (especially those on the three remaining main routes out of the Ruhr, a fourth having already been cut by Chastise) and, for the penetration weapon, the Rothensee Ship Lift. Upkeep was also being considered for attacking beach defences in August.[67] Test explosions of the standard 12,000lb bomb and Upkeep were suggested to compare the cratering effects, and for use against canals; Upkeep was test dropped into shallow water with forward spin and experimental work on models of canal embankments was also carried out.[68]

Access to three redundant viaducts for trials purposes had been obtained, but advice from Wallis was that an Upkeep would have to be placed right against a pier (certainly within 3ft) for it to have any chance of doing serious damage. Trials of the 8,000lb and 12,000lb HC bombs dropped against similar targets had given very unpredictable results, and although the Upkeep trials had also given mixed results, a summary reported on 2 August was very upbeat, stating that 'the overland performance of the Upkeep weapon with forward spin is entirely satisfactory and there are excellent prospects of employing this weapon successfully against the viaducts'.[69] Hence it was suggested to drop inert-filled Upkeeps against dummy viaduct piers set up at Ashley Walk; 617 carried out the first of these trials on 4 August,[70] making five successful forward-spun drops

Locations of other targets considered for attack using Upkeep. *(Author)*

(a sixth aircraft had its weapon 'hang up') from 150ft and in one case just under 100ft. The weapons were found to run straight, with a range over the flat ground of around 1,100yds, the detonators firing successfully about 50 seconds after release. The exercise was repeated the next day, this time aimed at one of the range's wall targets from 600yds, with the aim of seeing if the store would remain in contact with the wall until the detonators fired. One store hit the corner of the wall and carried on, a further four missing the wall altogether. Unfortunately, turbulence at low level caused the sixth Lancaster (ED765, the first prototype) to clip the ground and crash, the aircraft actually rolling on the store for some distance; Flt Lt W.H. Kellaway and his crew were lucky to escape with their lives, although the pilot and bomb aimer were so seriously injured that they never flew again. Despite this, a further trial was carried out on the 12th; however, it was found that the paths of the Upkeeps were too unpredictable, and so it was deemed unlikely that they could be placed accurately against a ground target when delivered in this fashion. An 'instantaneous fuze' was proposed to detonate the bomb on first strike with the target, but this was considered to pose too great a risk to the dropping aircraft.[71]

Towards the end of July, Wallis was furnished with details of the Janiskoski Dam in the Petsamo region of north-east Finland on the Russian border, for urgent assessment of its vulnerability to Upkeep.[72] The dam had a complex construction consisting of two walled sections which met at an angle, with a power station at the junction, and outer sections of earth-bank construction. Although the region was remote, there was considerable German presence in the area (Finland was in alliance with Germany at this time), due to the proximity of nickel mines (which the Germans were exploiting) and the Russian port of Murmansk (which the Germans were trying to capture), and the destruction of the dam was being considered to disable the power station which had been built to power the nickel smelters.[73] Replying 'at a few hour's notice', Wallis was very confident of Upkeep's capability to destroy the power station if it was attacked directly; the wide approach to the dam meant that an attack would have been straightforward and, due to its large catchment area, the water level of Lake Inari was relatively constant. A night attack was preferable to avoid fighters known to be stationed in the area, but at the high latitude, such an attack was not possible before mid-September, and from the end of October the lake was frozen over. Operationally, the distance to reach this target would have been problematic – Janiskoski was 1,150 miles from the nearest UK base at Sumburgh (1,250 miles from the nearest bomber base at Lossiemouth) and the maximum range of a Lancaster carrying Upkeep was estimated at 1,300 miles. The alternative was to fly to Russia and carry out the raid from there, with the inherent security problems and risk of attack when on the ground. This was the option preferred by Bufton, Director of Bomber Operations at the Air Ministry, in his report of 30 July,[74] though his principal recommendation was to try to persuade the Russians to bomb the power station themselves. No attack was carried out,[75] though the idea of using a Russian airfield as a forward base would surface again when the *Tirpitz* was in 617's sights in 1944.

There were also plans to use Upkeep against the Bissorte Dam in south-east France, about 5 miles from the town of Modane (between Lyon and Turin) and during his period as acting commander of the squadron in September 1943, 'Micky' Martin carried out some test runs in Wales, where the topography was similar; bizarrely, Cochrane used an attack on the *Tirpitz* as a cover story[76] for the purpose of this training.[77] It was at this time that the squadron mounted its first attack (with 1,000lb bombs) against the Anthéor Viaduct on the Cote d'Azur, in an attempt to break this rail link between France and Italy. The Bissorte attack was planned with the same objective, to sweep away the rail and road links in the valley below the dam. The dam sits at around 7,000ft in an Alpine hanging valley, and a successful approach along the relatively short reservoir would have required great flying skill to achieve; despite the small size of the reservoir compared to the German targets, the results of a breach would have been spectacular, the water falling down a steep slope over 2,500ft to the village of La Praz directly below, and undoubtedly the village, and the road and railway through it, would have been erased by the water. A model test was carried out at RRL at Wallis's suggestion, but was inconclusive due to problems with the model, but from experience it was estimated that eight Upkeeps had a 'reasonable chance of causing a breach', even if the lake was frozen over, as the first mine would shatter the ice.[78] The Ministry recommended that the Upkeeps be kept in storage, but that the Lancasters be converted back for normal use. Five months later, it was asking that Upkeep aircraft be kept serviceable in case a raid was required,[79] and although a briefing model of the area was made[80] the raid did not go ahead. Wallis was also asked to examine information about the Assuan Dam in Egypt to assess its vulnerability to Upkeep attack, his assessment being that in essence, it was very similar to the Möhne, but it is not known why this target was under consideration or how such an operation would have been mounted.[81]

In July 1943 Wallis was asked for his opinion on the vulnerability to Upkeep attack of the Suviana, Moncenisio, Salto and Posticciola dams in Italy; he was confident that the Suviana could be attacked immediately, but in the others the water level was unsuitable.[82] At the start of 1944 the Salto and Posticciola dams (both north of Rome, the latter on the Turano river) were again being considered as Upkeep targets to disrupt Axis communications in support of the forthcoming Allied landing at Anzio.[83] These dams were again located in difficult terrain, and required an even sharper drop and pullout than at the Eder – trials were done over the airfield (617 Squadron was by now stationed at Woodhall Spa), and it was shown that the aircraft could drop 1,800ft over a ground distance of less than 3,000yds (again a theodolite was used to check heights). Wallis was also concerned about the greater curvature of these two dams, and suggested that the RRL carry out a model trial to test this.[84] However, it was eventually decided the raid would cause more harm than good to the advancing forces, as well as causing substantial civilian casualties, and it was cancelled on 20 January 1944, the day that one of 617's remaining Upkeep Lancasters crashed at Snettisham on the Wash during the low-flying training, killing Flt Lt Thomas O'Shaughnessy and all but two of his crew.

By October 1944 'dam busting' attempts were back on the agenda, but Upkeep had now been superseded by its more elegant offspring, Tallboy. There were fears that the low Kembs Barrage on the Rhine would be used to flood out approaching Allied troops, and on 7 October 617 uniquely dropped Tallboys from low level to achieve accurate placement against the sluice gates, one of which was successfully destroyed, releasing the stored water. On 15 October 9 Squadron hit the Sorpe Dam with several Tallboys, including two perfectly placed along the crest, but the massive construction of the dam defeated this weapon too.[85] In December the Urft Dam, a conventional walled dam near the Belgian border, was also causing concern as Allied troops approached. Upkeep was considered for this attack,[86] but the terrain around the approach to the dam was too high for practical release of Upkeep (110ft high at the ideal release point 660yds from the dam) and, following Operation Chastise, a cable had been strung across the approach deliberately to deter a low-level attack. Instead, Tallboys were used in combined raids by both squadrons on 8 and 15 December; these were again unsuccessful, but the Germans lowered the water level, so the aim was achieved, and further attacks on this target were cancelled.

As early as 1 June 1943 the Russians were asking for the specification of the weapon that had breached the dams.[87] The Chiefs of Staff agreed to supply details of the weapon by a secure route, as long as the British Mission in Russia could 'make greatest possible capital out of our handing over this important and highly secret information', although physical problems sending it are noted, and it is possible that it was never received.

The Chastise Lancasters

Considering their fame, it is difficult to track with absolute accuracy the subsequent history of the 23 Type 464 Lancasters that were fitted out to carry Upkeep. Following the losses of the raid, there remained 15 of the aircraft. Flower[88] states that ten were retained in Type 464 spec after the raid, but as eight were used on further operations (see below) this figure is not possible. At least six different aircraft were used in Upkeep trials at Ashley Walk in August 1943[89] (including ED765 which crashed during the trials), and the crash of ED918 at Snettisham meant that no more than 13 of the aircraft remained at end of January 1944.

The 617 ORB shows (possibly erroneously) that eight were used on further operations (ED932, ED906, ED912, ED825, ED886 by November 1943, ED817 by April 1944, ED933 and ED909 by June 1944) suggesting that they might have been converted back to standard specification (ED825 and ED886 both FTR from missions to drop arms for the SOE in December 1943). Thus no more than five Type 464s remained at end of June 1944 – the four which flew on Operation Chastise but did not fly on any further 617 operations (ED929, ED921, ED936, ED924) plus ED915. The ORB also shows that ED909 and ED933 flew (carrying 1,000lb bombs) on the Saumur raid in June 1944 (possibly with no bomb doors) – if the ORB is correct (and it is not totally accurate on such details), then this is the only time when ex-Chastise aircraft flew alongside aircraft carrying Tallboys.

Thirty-nine HE-filled Upkeeps remained in storage, but by early 1945 their condition was deteriorating, two dangerously so. The Chastise Lancasters were all in storage at Lossiemouth, so ED933 was flown down to Woodhall Spa to uplift the two stores and dump them into the North Sea in early April. By August 1946 there were concerns for the condition of more stores plus the Lancasters themselves, so ED909, ED906, and Gibson's ED932 were selected to perform Operation Guzzle – the disposal of the remaining stores far out into the Atlantic. The route from Woodhall Spa was chosen to be away from built-up areas, and after a brief search of the dropping zone, the stores were released (initially from 4,000ft but increased to 10,000ft after a store exploded on hitting the water); in this way, the remaining Upkeeps were disposed of between September and December 1946.[90]

These three aircraft remained at Scampton as the 'station flight' bearing new registrations, but all of the surviving Chastise aircraft were victims of the post-war reduction in arms, being struck off charge and unceremoniously broken up in 1946 and 1947.

Summary – Wallis's 'finest hour'

Even as the last of the waters of the Möhne and Eder reservoirs flowed over the broken dams, Wallis himself recognised that his 'finest hour' was upon him. He wrote to Chadwick on 25 May[91] thanking him for his outstanding efforts in supporting the raid and rushing through the conversion of the Lancasters, and while eager to co-operate on 'another terrific adventure', noted that 'no such spectacular target remains to be brought down'. Despite his substantial later work, history has proven this theory too and ensured that the name of Wallis is synonymous with the 'Dam Busters' and the 'bouncing bomb'.

And it truly was a remarkable technical achievement. A wholly novel weapon had been conceived and delivered with incredible accuracy (this had been the first air raid in history in which absolute accuracy was essential to success), and in two cases had performed as intended and very close to what had been predicted, with results that were far out of proportion to the amount of explosive or the size of the attacking force.

Just as *R.100* had enhanced Wallis's reputation as a designer, so Operation Chastise proved his credentials as a designer of weapons. 'Bomber' Harris was famously heard to tell Wallis 'you could sell me a pink elephant', an unlikely comment from the once deeply sceptical C-in-C – yet one which is absolutely true. Crucially, the results of the raid also verified the 'earthquake' theory, namely that a relatively small quantity of explosive placed correctly could created shockwaves of sufficient magnitude to destroy massive structures. And so, as work continued on Upkeep's little brother, Highball, Wallis turned his attention back to the idea from whence it had all come – the 10-ton bomb.

Chapter 6

Highball – The Anti-Ship Bomb

Even a fool knows we can't reach the stars, but that doesn't stop the wise from trying.
(Anonymous)

Highball – to sink the *Tirpitz*

The early development history of Highball was shared with that of Upkeep, though by early in 1943 they had developed into separate weapons. The Royal Navy was principally interested in Highball as a means to destroy the German battleship *Tirpitz*, which had been based in Norway since early 1942, from where she posed a threat to Russia-bound convoys which thus required heavy naval escort. The substantial defences around the ship's anchorage and the mountainous terrain surrounding the deep fjords both posed major difficulties for any aerial attack. Small bombs were unlikely to have any serious effect on the battleship's armour, and double anti-torpedo nets around the ship meant that torpedoes would probably not get through. Highball offered a number of potential advantages:

1. It could be launched at greater range than a torpedo, allowing the attacking aircraft to turn away sooner and hence minimise exposure to the defences.
2. Its faster travel meant that sighting would be more accurate.
3. Its above-water path would leap over the anti-torpedo nets.
4. As its point of detonation would be under the ship (due to the travel imparted by the spin on the store), rather than on the armour belts, a Highball hit was likely to be much more effective than a bomb or torpedo.

The Chiefs of Staff ad hoc committee, in addition to a desire to use Highball simultaneously with Upkeep, initially proposed carrying out several strikes with Highball itself, the Italian fleet being a favoured secondary target to the *Tirpitz* and her consorts in Norway.[1] However, it was recognised that a large force of Highball aircraft would require to be built up before attacks in such force could be contemplated, and this might delay use of Upkeep. By the time of Operation Chastise, it was felt that the difference in shape of the two bombs and the low likelihood of the bomb's bouncing behaviour being observed 'would not suggest surface attack against ships' even if an Upkeep was recovered intact;[2] this effectively cleared Upkeep for use in advance of a Highball attack.

In addition to shipping, other potential Highball targets identified included the Brest U-boat pens (the pens at other ports were deemed unsuitable for attack using Highball), lock gates, floating docks and the Rothensee Ship Lift. Of these, the U-boat pens seem to have been given most consideration, but it was thought that they would be difficult to hit (partly due to heavy defences) and serious damage was unlikely (unless a U-boat happened to be in the pen attacked),[3] and significant preparations for attacking the pens were never made.

As with Upkeep, a special squadron was formed to deliver Highball, number 618.[4] The initial 20 crews were drawn from Mosquito crews from Bomber Command and Beaufighter crews from Coastal Command, in roughly equal numbers.[5] Delivery of the aircraft was slow compared to the Upkeep Lancasters, the first of the modified Mosquitoes not being ready until early April, and only 16 available by mid-May. In parallel with the development trials at Reculver, 618 Squadron was to begin operational training at RAF Skitten, north of Wick (RAF Sumburgh on Shetland being the base from which it was expected an attack on *Tirpitz* would be launched). Renouf arranged for the veteran French battleship *Courbet*,[6] which had been in use as an anti-aircraft battery at Portsmouth, to be towed to Loch Striven[7] to act as a target ship.[8] Loch Striven is an off-shoot on the west side of the Firth of Clyde, and the surrounding terrain was similar to that where the *Tirpitz* was being kept in Norway.[9] Initial tests were to determine 'optimum range and trajectory' of the store[10] – see Appendix 7 for a full list of test drops.

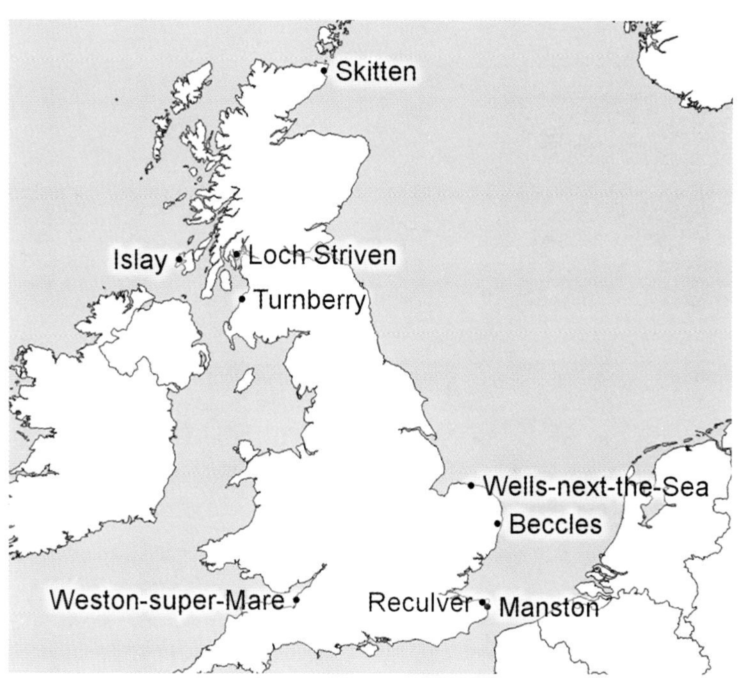

Locations associated with the development of Highball. *(Author)*

During the early drop tests at Reculver, it was found that the outer wooden casing had a tendency to break, although not as badly as with Upkeep. After tests on 18 April, when the three Highballs dropped, all shed parts of their casings (found to be due to the crushing of the wood on first impact and tension failure in the bands), it was decided

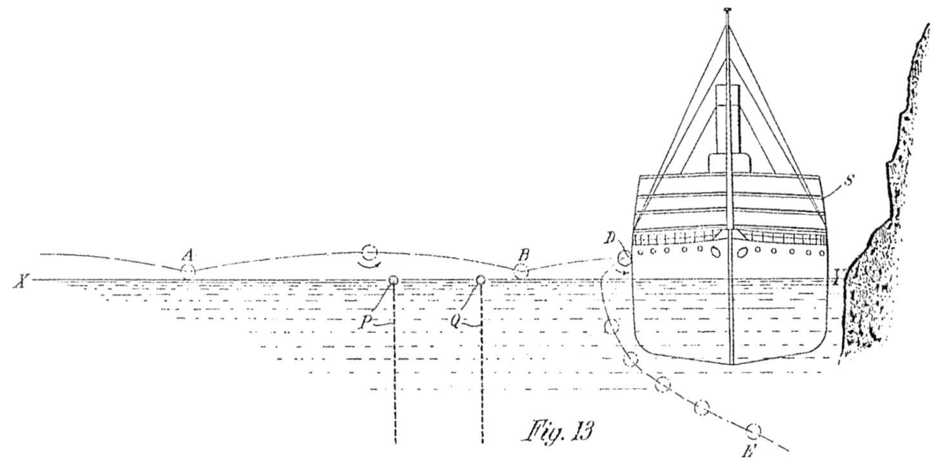

The path of Highball to its target, skipping anti-torpedo nets P and Q. On sinking, the backspin carries the store forwards beneath the unarmoured part of the hull before exploding at E (Patent GB937959). *(BAE SYSTEMS)*

to add a steel plate 18in wide and 5/32in thick around the stores to hold the wood in place,[11] and good results from stores dropped on 28 and 29 April led to this form being adopted. Plastic moulded casings were also considered, but this was not proceeded with,[12] and by the end of April, more than 150 Highballs had been delivered, with 74 inert filled and 79 HE filled.

At Skitten, 618 Squadron was initially kept busy with navigation exercises, including over Loch Cairnbawn, where HMS *Bonaventure*, the mother ship for the X-craft submarines, was stationed and, combined with smaller craft, posed as the *Tirpitz* for dummy attacks – over 125 sorties were made. The squadron had only 19 modified aircraft by 27 June, and these still required minor modification to be operational;[13] nevertheless, a second order of 30 aircraft was in progress,[14] with the intention that these would form the second squadron for operations in the Mediterranean.

To evaluate the effectiveness of possible defences against Highball/Upkeep attack, the Boom Defence Department[15] of the Admiralty designed two net defences, and these were laid in Loch Striven; the net consisted of numerous chain-link panels of net suspended between posts, and were designed to 'carry away' when hit by a bomb, the drag of the net bringing the store to a halt.[16] Between 19 and 21 March the Wellington, flown by 'Shorty' Longbottom, made seven drops against these nets using three buoyant wooden spheres, two smooth and one dimpled – the spheres were recovered for reuse, though were found to be slightly damaged and so were sent back to Weybridge for examination and rebalancing. The nets were hit on three of the drops, twice letting the bombs through (though slowed down substantially), and on the third being pulled from its supports as intended and sinking with the bomb (which was recovered after 90 minutes rather waterlogged).[17]

The Loch Striven trials were organised and controlled by MAEE at Helensburgh, and flown from RAF Turnberry,[18] the Wellington being flown by a Vickers crew and the Mosquitoes by 618 Squadron. Ground crews from MAEE were supervised by Vickers staff, including Jim Rogerson, who later went to Skitten;[19] lochside recording and photography was done by MAEE[20] in conjunction with RAE staff. Local wind conditions were telephoned from the *Courbet* to Turnberry when a take-off was due, the aircraft flying north up the Clyde, passing Craigmore on Bute and turning into the mouth of Loch Striven while in a shallow dive; after release,[21] the aircraft turned to port over the hill, down into Loch Riddon and south back to Turnberry. When stores were recovered, they were loaded on to a lorry on a landing craft of the Boom Defence Department, and this sailed over to Wemyss Bay on the east side of the Firth. Once the craft was beached, the lorry drove off and away to Turnberry[22] for examination of the store, the craft laying off ready to pick up the empty lorry again.

The first dropping trials against the *Courbet* took place on 9 and 10 May 1943 from which it was noted that the striking velocity was a 'critical factor' due to the fragility of the depth pistols. Highball's performance was deemed to be 'not satisfactory' largely due to problems with the release,[23] which manifest itself in premature release of the stores or lop-sided release caused by a hang-up on one side, leading to a 'wobble' on the store. This had not been apparent in the earlier Reculver trials, and Wallis initially reported that the failures had been traced to 'variations in dimensions of stores after filling, and incorrectly dimensioned jigs for setting up the calliper arms, and that modifications in hand should overcome the problem, to be confirmed by further drops at Reculver before the aircraft returned to Scotland.[24] Later, the fault was attributed to the use of steel-hearted cables in part of the release gear,[25] which stretched – these were replaced by rods by mid-June, subsequent tests involving violent manoeuvres being satisfactory.[26] 'Whip' in the fuselage was also regarded as a factor,[27] as was the high rate of spin of the stores[28] (if not perfectly balanced), and even the 'bumpy air' encountered over the loch.[29] Looking back at the problem, Boorer recalled that 'it took us a long time in developing the release mechanism to get rid of that', saying that the cancellation of the *Tirpitz* operation was 'because we didn't get it going in time'.[30]

Setting the distance

As the striking velocity was dependent on the distance travelled, accurate ranging was important and Wallis designed a special sight for use with Highball, which rather artfully exploits the similar triangles rule seen previously in the Dann sight used by 617 Squadron, though it is embodied in a more complex arrangement involving two small pivoted glass panes.[31] A light attached to the pilot's helmet produced a reflected vertical line on each pane, the angles of which varied according to the settings of the device. When the two lines were observed to coincide with the ends of the target ship, the store would be released. The sight was preset with the known length of the target ship, the angle of attack (as angles less than a right angle would shorten the apparent length of the target), the speed of the aircraft (as that would affect the range of the store), and even the sea conditions (as that would affect the run, and hence also the range, of the store).

Early tests of the sight were very satisfactory, the average range error being 'well under 100 yards', and the whole squadron was quickly equipped with the device by the start of July.[32]

As Highball was not intended for use in night attacks, there was no need for a spotlight altimeter, and the pilots judged the drop height by eye throughout the trials. It was found that range did not vary significantly for minor variations in drop height – additional speed gained from a higher drop was offset by greater depth of impact (and hence a bigger splash). There was also considerable variation between drops, as demonstrated by one archive film shot which shows a double drop on Loch

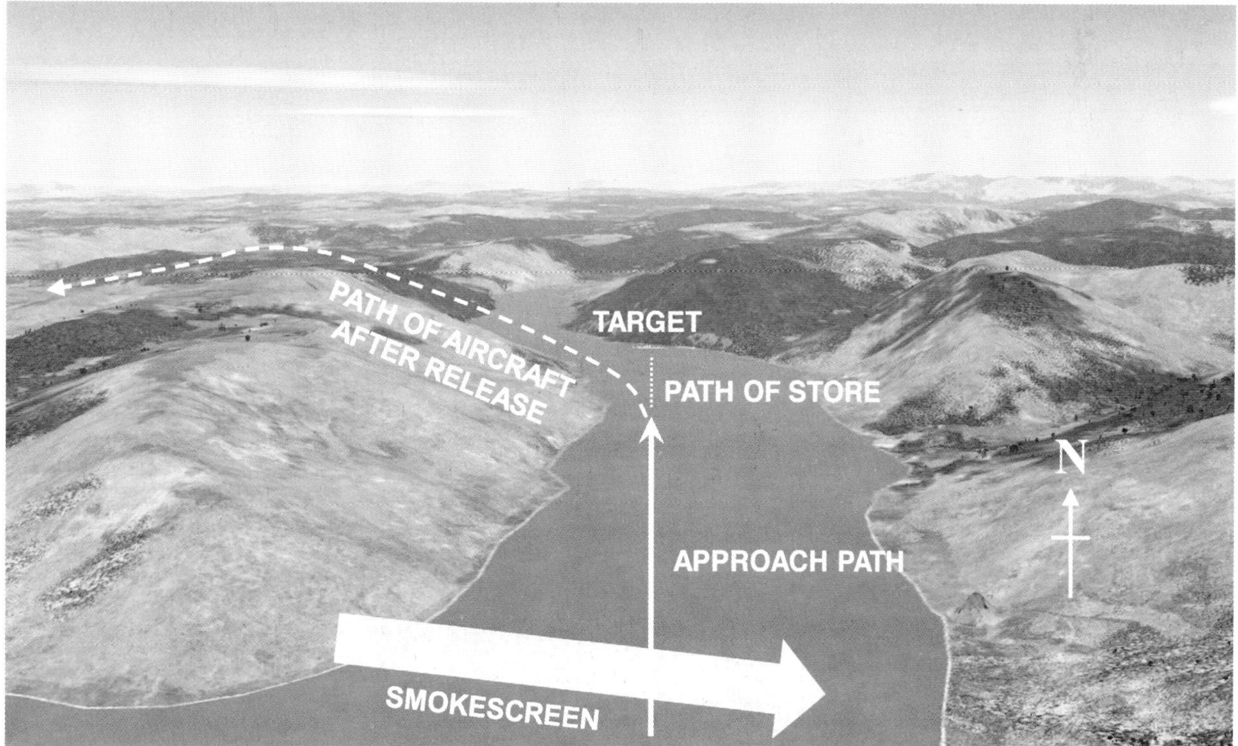

Loch Striven showing the *Courbet*'s position and path taken by aircraft. *(Author)*

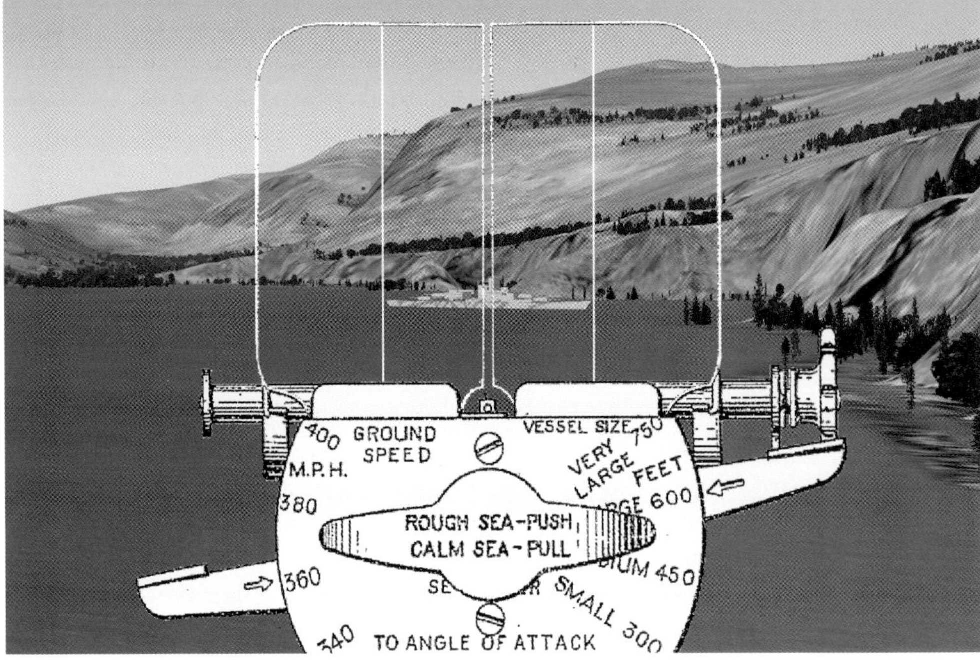

Wallis's range-finding bombsight, as it would have appeared in use attacking the *Tirpitz*, the two vertical lines on the glass marking the ends of the ship at release; in reality, the *Tirpitz* was not moored at such a convenient angle. *(Author)*

Striven in which the two stores are dropped a fraction of a second apart onto very calm water and one bounces up to nearly double the height of the other.

Operation Servant

The codename assigned for the first use of Highball was Operation Servant. As the range of potential targets was narrowed down, this codeword became synonymous with the planned attack on *Tirpitz*. The German battleship had been moored in the Norwegian fjords, ready to strike at convoys heading round the North Cape to Russia. Originally, she had been in Trondheim Fjord, but by the end of March had been moved north to Kaa Fjord, a narrow inlet right at the head of Alten Fjord. This was 860 miles from the nearest UK base, and initial estimates suggested that this was just within the range limit of the Mosquito. More detailed investigation[33] showed that this was not the case (even with long-range tanks), and considerable effort was devoted to exploring schemes to enable the aircraft to make an attack and reach Allied territory with an adequate margin of fuel. These schemes included towing the Mosquitoes with Liberators or Lancasters, flying to a forward base in Russia from where to make the attack, making the attack from the UK and abandoning the aircraft over Sweden (or the sea) afterwards, and launching the operation from a carrier (though no aircraft as large as a Mosquito had flown from a British carrier at that time). Approaching the target at low level, the 20 aircraft would have attacked in waves of four or five aircraft roughly abreast, releasing their stores almost simultaneously before turning away for the safety of the mountains; one archive film[34] shows three Mosquitoes making simultaneous drops in training for a formation release.

For several reasons, following detailed calculations of ranges and operational logistics, the most practicable option was thought to be the Russian plan, although the politics would have been formidable and secrecy of the weapon compromised.[35] By the start of July, AVM Bottomley wrote that the operation had a 'very remote chance of success whilst the ships are based in . . . Alten Fjord' and the Chiefs of Staff advised Churchill that the chances of hitting *Tirpitz* with Highball were 'negligible' as she could only be approached at a fine angle (rather than broadside on).[36] Plans to attack Mediterranean harbours with Highball at the same time were thus also put on hold, as it was undesirable to carry out that operation first and risk compromising the main prize in the north.[37] At Skitten, 618 continued its navigation practice and 'sat for hours at the model of Kaa Fjord, flying our hands around, and the problem just got bigger and bigger'.[38]

Highball was not the only weapon being ranged against the *Tirpitz* – beneath the waters of Loch Striven, unseen by the crews of 618 Squadron,[39] a fleet of X-craft midget submarines was also training to attack the battleship. By the end of June, the Admiralty and Air Ministry had agreed, with Churchill's backing, that Operation Source (the X-craft operation) should take priority over Operation Servant, as it was deemed that Source had a 'greater chance of success'[40] and an unsuccessful Highball mission 'might result in altered dispositions by the enemy to the detriment of Source'.[41] This and the continuing technical problems with Highball led to a decision to reduce the squadron to a cadre, with crews being released for other duties.

This may have prompted the suggestion from Coastal Command to deploy the squadron to northern waters for anti-submarine patrols; the weapon was to be forward spun (to prevent it bouncing and hence giving away the nature of the device, and also because the low profile of a U-boat meant that a bouncing attack might simply go right over the target vessel), and would act simply as a depth charge. Technical trials were completed quickly, and the squadron was declared ready for anti-submarine duties on 28 July;[42] the stores had been stripped back to the bare cylinder and were to be dropped from 150ft at not less than 218 knots.[43] It seems that some patrols were flown carrying the modified stores;[44] Curtis recalls attempting to drop a live Highball near Skitten in August 1943, but the store hung up and he had to make a very careful landing back at Skitten, dropping it on to the grass after it had been 'safed' by an armourer.

During further training of 618 Squadron crews with the cylindrical store, it was found that the store still bounced on numerous occasions and, fearful of observation of this behaviour by U-boat crews, it was 'considered inadvisable' to continue the anti-submarine duties, and the earlier proposal to disperse most of the squadron was put in hand,[45] the majority having left by the end of September. Most of the Highball Mosquitoes were sent to Maintenance Units for storage;[46] 26 were ordered to be converted back to standard bombers at the end of October.[47] Some of the 618 crews returned to Coastal Command, but a 'Special Detachment' of 618 Squadron was re-armed with Mk XVIII 'Tsetse' Mosquitoes fitted with six-pounder guns and, operating from RAF Predannack in Cornwall, achieved some success against U-boats in the Bay of Biscay. Sqn Ldr Rose, who commanded the squadron, became part of this detachment, but in November 1943 he and his navigator were killed in the Bay of Biscay after being shot down by an armed trawler.

Technical trials continue

Early in July, two double drops had been attempted at Reculver with mixed results,[48] and further tests were undertaken from 12 to 15 July, dropping the front and rear stores separately to see if the problem was due to the mechanism or to interference between the stores, a total of eight Highballs being dropped with good results, although some minor problems with the mechanism were still noted.[49] Still trying to cure the 'wobble' and variability in performance, the quality of the wooden casing came under scrutiny, and reconstruction of the wooden portion using seasoned ash was begun. A design was also prepared for the revised type of store in which the wood, tensioning bands and partial steel outer casing would be replaced with a

A close-up of the Mosquito's bomb bay with two Highball stores in position. *(BAE SYSTEMS via The National Archives)*

stouter half-inch metal casing with no wood.[50] Development of a new hydrostatic pistol capable of surviving greater impact forces (1,850*g*[51] compared to 600*g* in the original) was also put in hand, and this was tested to 2,000*g* by early August and found to function satisfactorily; a revised version of the Mark XIV depth charge pistol had also become available, and following pistol trials as part of the next series of impact trials, the new Mark XIV was adopted.

Drops of two ash and two steel stores on 30 July at Reculver were inconclusive – one of the ash stores was slightly dented on first striking the water and the second dropped prematurely and was severely damaged. One steel store also dented on first impact, the other hitting the beach after several bounces (though being largely undamaged); inspection revealed that the welding on the stores (and others still to be used) was of poor quality. Further tests of properly welded stores (which were found to be easier to balance) took place on 23 August,[52] and these were found to be satisfactory both with and without additional internal stiffening of the casing. Further trials to test robustness against the *Courbet* took place on 7–8 September, reusing some of the Reculver stores. The stores all 'ran with perfect steadiness and entire absence of wobble', but none of the stores were caught in the nets around the target ship, so it was impossible to check how well they had stood up to the impact (observers reckoned that several had split on striking the ship).[53] To prevent a repetition on future trials, the Admiralty moved the *Courbet* into shallower water, and the nets were extended. Wallis was consulted about conducting the impact tests against the wall target at Ashley Walk instead of the battleship, and he was 'satisfied' that the results would be satisfactory,[54] the tests being carried out there on 27 September. These showed that the internal cylinder was distorted by the impact, and it was decided to thicken the steel from which it was made. Tests of the new store against the *Courbet* resumed on 26 November, 33 being dropped over the next two weeks, at various angles between 45 and 90 degrees to the ship; 17 stores hit the ship,[55] 9 sank short and 4 missed (all oblique), the others being jettisoned due to hang-ups.[56] It was found that the outer casing was damaged by the impact, and there were concerns that this deformation was severe enough to have affected the underwater travel of the store, hence potentially reducing the effectiveness of the explosion. Suggested remedies included strengthening of the outer plating and filling the gap between the outer and inner cylinder with a shock absorber such as cork. The Air Staff were becoming impatient with progress and, while agreeing to further modifications, said that these 'should be regarded as its last chance'[57] (although in the event, this was rather over-dramatic).

By November, 50 of the redesigned stores were on order for trials (plus another 200 for operational use), the inner cylinder now being 5/16in steel and the outer casing 3/8in, this store offering 'full promise of being satisfactory';[58] 50 of the older type were to be upgraded with the thicker outer shell.[59]

All of these problems and their protracted solutions meant that secondary trials to determine the underwater path of the store, the optimum depth setting for the hydrostatic fuze, and the likely ranges achievable in smooth water and open sea, originally postponed from June[60] still had not taken place. A programme for these was now drawn up,[61] the main trials to take place in Loch Striven[62] and the rough water trials in Saligo Bay off the west coast of Islay (although 618 had already carried out some informal rough-water trials, dropping Highballs towards a beach between Wick and John O'Groats).[63] The latter took place on 4 January 1944, four drops being made at 25, 45 and 90 degrees to the prevailing waves, with one drop along the sea (which was running a 4–6ft swell). The drops were made directly towards, or away from, a movie camera on Coul Point which recorded any line errors, with cameras at Kilchiaran (365yds to the south) and at Saligo (365yds to the northeast) also recording. The range achieved on all four runs was within the usual limits encountered with smooth-water drops (though there was more irregularity

The *Courbet* in position in Loch Striven, with a Highball about to strike. *(BAE SYSTEMS via The National Archives)*

towards the end of the runs), and the line errors were all less than 10yds. The conclusion of the experiment was that moderately rough seas did not greatly affect range or line.[64]

Another trial which had been put off for some time was determination of the underwater path of the stores, codenamed Operation Substance. In order to obtain the position of detonation in three dimensions, a series of hydrophones and piezoelectric pressure gauges were hung at various depths from booms extending from the target ship, their output being recorded on two galvanometers synchronised with each other and with a 500Hz tuning fork supplying a time base. By comparing the precise timings of the sounds of the pistol detonation to reach each sensor, the detonation position could be accurately triangulated. For more detailed analysis, it was proposed to include six small 'cracker fuzes' within the store, timed to go off at two-second intervals; however, due to the severity of the impact damage on the stores, it was decided to postpone this aspect of the trial, although further trials with standard stores were made in December, using a variety of impact angles to minimise forces on the pistols (Wallis calculated that hitting at 45 degrees reduced the impact force to about one-quarter of the force when hitting at right angles).[65]

Two of these drops had shown that the stores had sunk vertically after impact, indicating a lack of spin on the store.[66] A small number of drops took place during January and February 1944 until the new 'shock absorbing stores' were available; these were tested at Reculver in March, followed by impact trials at Ashley Walk and finally back to Loch Striven, 20 being dropped during May to test the underwater performance.[67] The stores used three types of shock-absorbing outer filling – wooden shells, paper shells and shells made from aerated Catacol resin. The paper ones were seen as problematic for use in tropical climates, and the Catacol ones were considered the best – it was also the easiest to manufacture as the resin could be simply squeezed into the gap between the cylinder and the already welded outer shell.[68] The ship target was now HMS *Malaya*,[69] the *Courbet* having been returned to the south coast in preparation for the Normandy landings.[70]

During these trials (and despite substantial use earlier), shortcomings with the range-finding sight were reported, and it was decided to redesign it for use by the observer rather than the pilot. This was due to the mounting of the sight, which meant that the aircraft had to be pointing directly at the target, so allowance for drift could result in a sudden change in direction of the aircraft at the moment of release, leading to less reliable running of the store. With the new set-up, the pilot could allow for drift during his approach (pointing ahead or astern of the target if necessary), the observer performing the ranging and telling the pilot when to release.[71] The new arrangement was found to give 'complete satisfaction'. This batch of trials included double drops of two Highballs, and some experimentation was done to arrive at the best release interval to use. A practical problem was that of countermining, i.e. the detonation of one store prematurely triggering the detonation of the other, and a release interval of 0.3 seconds was selected as this should place the stores an estimated 8ft apart at the moment of first detonation, but if the

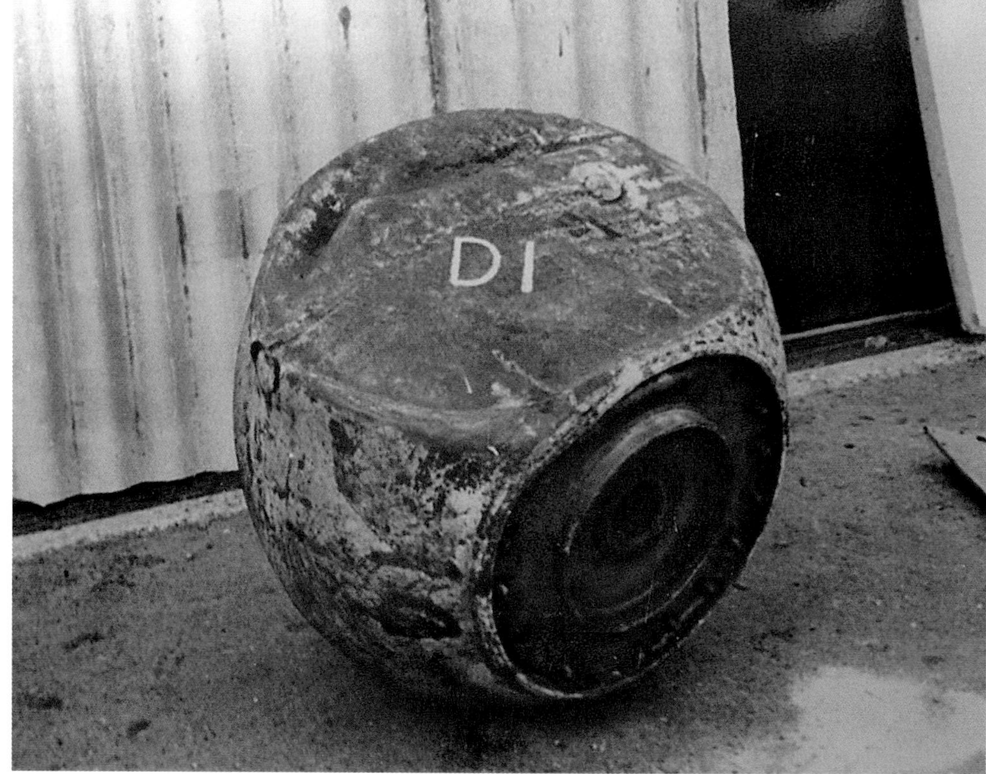

The ongoing problem with Highball was deformation caused by impact with the ship target – this would have stopped the spin and impaired the store's underwater path beneath the ship. *(BAE SYSTEMS via Brooklands Museum)*

During the Highball practices in 1944, HMS *Malaya*'s hull was punctured by three dummy stores. Although Highball was not intended to puncture the hull, the self-destruct timer would have detonated a live store and severe damage would have been caused. *(BAE SYSTEMS via The National Archives)*

second should explode at the same time, this short distance would mean that it would still contribute usefully to damaging the target.[72]

Highball against the Japanese – Operation Oxtail

In a review of Highball progress up to March 1944, the CoS ad hoc committee stated that the store was 'fit for operational use against ships in harbour or in a moderate sea with specially modified aircraft flown by properly trained crews' with the store likely to achieve a range of 1,000yds and survive impact well enough to function as intended. By that time, 25 aircraft were available, though 618 Squadron consisted of just four aircrews and other personnel. The ad hoc committee felt that its work was done, and that it should be dissolved; however, the Chiefs of Staff saw possible deployment of Highball in the Far East and decided that it should remain in being *pro tem*.

By June 1944, the details of the plan to use Highball against Japanese capital ships had been worked out, codenamed Operation Oxtail. Mosquito ranges from land bases in Indonesia had been calculated,[73] but the main plan would involve flying the Mosquitoes from a fleet carrier. To this end, the Royal Navy's foremost expert in carrier operations, Eric Brown, had made the first landing of a Mosquito on an aircraft carrier on 25 March; the Mosquito had been fitted with an arrestor hook and had its fuselage strengthened to take the forces involved.[74] Take-off was also a worrying time, the Mosquito being a large aircraft with no catapult capability, and with a known tendency to swing during the take-off run (for which there was little room on the narrow flight deck). However, the trials were deemed a success, and the operation was on.

The main practical problem was the rundown of 618 Squadron itself, so it was necessary to inject some new manpower into the squadron and train the crews up in the art of dropping Highball. In addition, they needed to gain experience in deck landing, which was new to all of them. Training began at RNAS Crail using Fairey Barracuda aircraft, later making deck landings on HMS *Rajah* in the Firth of Forth. This aircraft had acquired a poor reputation among the Fleet Air Arm pilots, and although it was considerably easier to land-on than a Mosquito, the squadron ditched five Barracudas during this phase of training. Eric Brown was called upon again to offer his expertise, and with the outline of a carrier painted on to the runway at RAF Beccles in Suffolk, he instructed the 618 crews in the skills needed for carrier landing,[75] during which two Mosquitoes were written off. The PR crews all made successful carrier landings on HMS *Implacable* and on 6 September DZ537 became the only Highball Mosquito ever to do it.[76] During this phase, over 100 practice Highball drops were made at the MAP bombing range off Wells-next-the-Sea on the north Norfolk coast, with a further 78 drops against the *Malaya* in Loch Striven.[77] These revealed a number of minor practical problems, for which small modifications were made.[78] On 11 October a crew was killed when their Mosquito flew into a hill in Yorkshire en route to Turnberry from Beccles, sparking a security operation to recover the Highballs from the wreckage.[79]

In late October, 25 Highball and 3 photo reconnaissance Mosquitoes[80] were flown to Abbotsinch (now Glasgow Airport) and transported by road to the Glasgow docks to be embarked on HMS *Fencer* and HMS *Striker*[81] with 150 Highballs; around 400 RAF air and ground crew also boarded, and on 31 October, the two ships left for Australia, arriving in Melbourne on 23 December. Crews went to a holding unit (on paper No.1 Personnel Depot, in reality billeted at Melbourne Cricket Ground) and the aircraft were transported to Fisherman's Bend airfield for servicing after having their transport 'cocoons' removed. They were flown to an RAAF base at Narromine, north-west of Sydney, during February and March 1945.[82] To maintain secrecy, 12 standard Mosquitoes were also shipped to Narromine to be used for flying and navigation practice, and although some unarmed training flights were undertaken (resulting in at least three fatal crashes) the squadron was idle for much of the time. Knowing that the Special Detachment was seeing action on the other side of the world was bad for the morale of the squadron, one of whom recalled feeling 'very guilty going out to Australia because out there we did nothing that was dangerous apart from drinking to excess',[83] and this deepened as it became apparent that the squadron would not be used operationally.[84] The Commander of the British Pacific Fleet visited Narromine on 29 June to deliver a signal from the Air Staff in London saying that 618 was to be disbanded, the axe falling officially on 21 July (even before the war against Japan was over). The HE-filled Highballs were destroyed in a static explosion, and the Mosquitoes sold or broken up. Highball gear was stripped out and dumped at sea, other squadron equipment was left on site or shipped to Singapore.[85]

Tunnel attacks

The suggestion of using Highball against railway tunnels had been made quite early in the project and, under the codename 'Grouse Shooting', a disused tunnel at Maenclochog in Wales had been identified as a possible test site,[86] the trials being undertaken on 7 October 1943, observers including Wallis himself.[87] Flying from RAF Angle, Sqn Ldr Longbottom dropped a total of 12 forward-spun stores from between 50ft and 100ft; Wallis wanted the first bounce to be in or near the mouth of the tunnel to obviate any effect of curvature of the railway line. Seven stores hit the face of the tunnel, but two entered the tunnel with sufficient speed that they went right through (the tunnel was only 100yds long). From the results, it was estimated that nine out the twelve would have gone in had it been a double-track tunnel. The Highballs themselves were satisfactory, both the wood-covered and all-steel stores standing up to the impact, the latter performing best. The self-destruct pistols also functioned according to expectations. With satisfactory delivery performance established, it was also necessary to test the likely effectiveness of the explosive when delivered in this way; there were concerns that, as the explosion would be untamped, actual damage might be too light to be worthwhile.[88] To this end, the 'Grouse Shooting 2' test consisted of a series of four explosions carried out in an old tunnel of the Great Western Railway (GWR) in Denbighshire, near Wrexham, using 250lb depth charges, each containing 70lb of explosive. Substantial damage to the tunnel was sustained (although it was recognised that the tunnel was in poor condition beforehand) and both the Chief Engineer of the GWR and an expert from the RRL were of the opinion that a stoppage of traffic of at least a month would have resulted had it been a modern tunnel, it being estimated that penetration by eight Highballs would be 'desirable' for similar results on a target tunnel.[89] An earlier test had been undertaken near Newquay, Cornwall, on a granite-lined tunnel, 500lb of gelignite placed on the roof bringing down an estimated 300 tons of debris.[90] Despite this double demonstration of the possibilities, and preliminary examination of 19 railway tunnels (mainly in northern Italy), most of which were reckoned to be suitable for attack at one or both ends,[91] it was not considered worthwhile to maintain a Highball unit specifically for tunnel attacks, both placement and likely damage being seen as 'uncertain' under operational conditions,[92] and a March 1944 review concluded that use of Highball against tunnels was 'very unpromising'.

Highball in the Grumman Avenger (codename Tammany Hall)

Carriage of Highball in a Grumman Avenger,[93] given the codename Tammany Hall,[94] was under consideration as early as mid-August 1943[95] – although single-engined and not as fast as the Mosquito, it was designed for carrier operation and had the performance to carry two Highballs. Longbottom undertook air tests in Avenger FN795 at this time with different bomb bay door configurations, presumably to assess the suitability of the aircraft.[96] Preliminary discussions between MAP and Pierson and Wallis indicated no material difficulty in using the store in this aircraft 'but practical trials by the prototype [Avenger] are not expected before February 1944'.[97] Maj Hew Kilner noted that work on this project would set back work on the third Windsor prototype, but this delay was accepted by MAP.[98] The Highball installation was fitted into a 'crate' which was then bolted into the bomb bay of the Avenger, thus minimising mechanical alterations to the basic aircraft. The first installation of stores took place in mid-February 1944[99] and test drops were under way by mid-April. Some stores, including the first, fell prematurely from the aircraft, and this was found to be due to twisting of the crate because of inadequate stiffness – it was attached by only two bolts, one at the forward end and one at the rear. The installation was modified by adding side attachments, and in later tests violent manoeuvres were unable to dislodge the stores;[100] otherwise, there were minimal teething troubles with the installation, such as the air turbine to spin the stores. Films of test drops from the Avenger show performance similar to Mosquito-dropped

In a film still, a Grumman Avenger drops a Tammany Hall (Highball) store at Reculver.
(BAE SYSTEMS via the RAF Museum)

stores,[101] the trials programme continuing at least until December.[102]

As the Avenger was designed as a carrier-based aircraft, and the trials seemed to be satisfactory, it is surprising that the decision to deploy Highball operationally went in favour of the Mosquito. In May 1945 MAP advised that it was cancelling the requirement for Highball Avengers, indicating that the three trials aircraft (FN795, FN766 and JZ317) were to be returned to standard configuration and then transferred to the Royal Navy.[103]

Highball in the Douglas A-26 Invader (codename Speedee)

Even before Operation Chastise took place, consideration was being given to fitting Highball to Douglas Invaders or Martin Marauders[104] due to limited availability of Mosquitoes, and the Americans were informed about Highball on 15 April 1943[105] for 'operational reasons as well as political'.[106] After Chastise, the Americans were very interested in the 'bouncing bomb' technology (particularly the range of the weapon and the comparatively short time it took to reach the target),[107] and it was agreed that a trial Highball installation would be fitted to an A-26 Invader, which had a similar specification to the Mosquito. An aircraft was flown into Wisley and modified at Foxwarren in January 1945, the installation being ready for testing in February. These tests (probably flown from the USAAF technical site at RAF Bovingdon), which consisted of two unrecorded drops to test the mechanism plus two recorded drops on the range at Wells-next-the-Sea on 17 February 1945, were satisfactory with both stores bouncing for over 1,100yds, although a shut-off had to be fitted to the air turbine to stop it overspeeding after release of the stores. As in the Mosquito, the stores were dropped without opening the bomb doors, though the A-26's larger bomb bay allowed the stores to fit flush with the line of the fuselage.

The dropping gear was removed from the aircraft and shipped to the USA, together with 25 inert Speedee stores (as with Tammany Hall, the different codename disguised the fact that they were 'standard' Highball stores). The gear was fitted into another Invader, and trials commenced in Choctawhatchee Bay near to Eglin AFB in Florida on 13 April. A number of successful drops were carried out, ranges of 1,300–1,600yds being achieved with dropping speeds of 360–400mph and release height of nominally 30ft.[108] Results very similar to the Highball performance were recorded from the start of the tests, with slightly longer ranges due to the faster release speeds, although there were variations in drop height down to 15ft, resulting in some splash damage to the bomb doors on 24 April. On the 37th drop,[109] the first bounce hit the tail and carried it away; the aircraft nose-dived into the water and broke up immediately, killing Lt Anderson and his crew of three. Subsequent analysis showed that the drop had been made from a height of just 9–10ft. Films of the tests were not being developed due to problems with the developing plant, and it is possible that the danger of the gradually reducing drop height might have been noticed had the pilot been able to see the films of his earlier drops (on one drop, the store bounces up to well over double the height of the dropping aircraft). A.D. Grant of Wallis's staff had travelled to Florida with the test aircraft to monitor installation of the dropping gear and the stores, and had already started his journey home by the time of the crash, but he returned to Eglin for a time to assist with the investigation.

In May, Ira Eaker, Deputy Commander of the USAAF, consequently advised the British Joint Staff Mission in Washington that they had no requirement for the weapon though planned to 'keep in mind' the weapon pending further British progress; co-operation with the RAF was commended, and Eaker expressed his thanks to ACM Sir Charles Portal, Chief of the Air Staff, in particular.[110] However, when he returned from the USA, Grant felt there was still the chance of a US Highball force being used in the Pacific, and he felt the Theatre Commander had neglected the RAF Mosquitoes already available 'in favour of the American force'.[111] Edwards suggests that the US did convert a squadron of Grumman Avengers,[112] but there is no evidence that this actually took place.

Baseball

Following initial Admiralty interest in Highball, in December 1942 DMWD proposed a variant for MTBs embodying the same principles, codenamed Baseball.[113] This would be smaller than Highball, just 300lb (of which half would be explosive) and would be tube launched as a potential replacement for 18in torpedo tubes, with an anticipated range of 1,000–2,000yds. It had the additional advantages that more rounds could be carried in the same space and 'that it is a weapon which needs no accurate estimation of range . . . with the added advantage that its time of travel to the target is comparatively small', thus giving a better chance of a hit. While the benefits of spin were already known, it was noted that it would be more difficult to add spin than in an aircraft installation.[114]

The DMWD at HMS *Birkbeck* (a requisitioned pier at the north end of Weston-super-Mare) conducted a series of small-scale experiments on rotation, size, density, moment of inertia, speed and launch height, 66 half-scale models fabricated in either aluminium or steel having been fired by October 1943.[115] In the air-dropped golf mines, the aircraft's forward motion gave the store the required horizontal velocity, but in ship launching at comparatively low speed, a rocket catapult was to be used, and this was tested at Brean Down, a peninsula south of the town. This consisted of a short track upon which ran a rocket-propelled carriage with two upward-pointing arms with fittings to take the axle of the store; spin was added manually using an electric buff wheel rubbing on the store; during acceleration, the axle was pressed back into its supports then, when the rockets were expended and the carriage slowed, the store would separate and continue on its way. Attempts to arrest the launch carriage initially proved more problematic than the weapon, and on later tests at Middle Hope, north-east of Weston, the projector carriage was not arrested, although the tests (using many dozens of test stores of sizes varying from 12in to 21in) continued to cause frustration for a variety of reasons, most notably attempts to keep the thrust on the launcher within the limits which the wooden deck of an MTB could bear. An alternative using a tube launcher with a cordite propellant charge was made at Elswick and tests of this conducted at ROF Woolwich,[116] but the results are not known. In the final assessment, it was decided that replacing a standard 20ft torpedo tube with a Baseball projector 'would have little or no operational value, despite the fact that, weight for weight, seven balls could be carried in lieu of one Mark XV torpedo'.[117]

DMWD also tested a similar weapon, codenamed Bullseye, which had been proposed by a Norwegian, Kommander Bull, in August 1942. This was a saucer-shaped skipping bomb, spun on a vertical axis, also projected from the launching ship by rocket. Trials were undertaken at Middle Hope in autumn of 1943, but again the final report in February 1944 was not favourable.[118]

Kurt – the German Highball

It was known from intelligence by August 1943 that the Germans had recovered an Upkeep from Operation Chastise, and knew its technical specification; although there was confidence that the secrets of backspin and possible anti-ship use were safe, it was thought 'reasonable to assume that they will experiment with the weapon and investigate its possible applications'.[119] This turned out to be correct, though there are surprisingly major differences between the German weapon (codenamed Kurt) and Upkeep. Application as an anti-ship weapon clearly *was* appreciated and, in fact, the Germans seem to have had no 'dam busting' ambitions for their weapon (despite British fears of a Chastise-like reprisal).

The stores were manufactured by armaments company Rheinmetall-Borsig in Berlin, and one of their employees was interrogated shortly after the end of the war by British experts, including Lane of DMWD.[120] One surprise from the interrogations was that the Germans had considered their own 'bouncing bomb' *before* the war, following research by Professor Wagner of the Henschel Works in Berlin, but this was not taken forward until after Chastise by the Graf Zeppelin Research Institute in Stuttgart and the TAL in Berlin, which performed some model evaluations on cylindrical and spherical bombs fired across a swimming pool, also including 'step-disc' shapes (cylindrical but with multiple flat faces). Wallis was sent a copy of some of the experimental documents but he was unimpressed, commenting that 'German technicians have not carried the analysis of the whole phenomenon anything like as far as has been done in England' and, because they had not attempted to predict full-size performance 'from this point of view the present report is valueless'.[121] The Germans were aware of the Magnus effect and also knew that the angle of impact had to be less than 7 degrees, with 1.5 degrees said to give the best results; such a shallow angle required either a dangerously low drop height or a faster horizontal speed, and the latter was achieved using rocket assistance. Kurt weighed 750kg and comprised a 12mm spherical steel shell, 75cm diameter, weighing 150kg and filled with 300kg of HE (an explosive formula developed specially for the weapon). The fuze pockets were very similar to those in Highball, with two hydrostatic pistols and a time fuze. The sphere was attached to a Venturi rocket pack weighing about 300kg, giving an all-burned velocity of approximately 250m/s. The rocket was ignited 0.7 seconds after release, and 2.5 seconds after release (just before hitting the water), a separation charge caused the rocket to drop away. The store was not spun (a major difference from the British weapons) as the German model experiments had suggested that spin actually *caused* instability, the range-enhancing effect of spin being compensated for by the higher impact velocity imparted by the rocket motor. Some of the full-scale drops used the basic unspun sphere without the rocket, and archive films show a bouncing trajectory similar to Highball, roll stabilisation being achieved using an internal gyroscope wheel. The original version had a tail consisting of four fins, later versions having a box-type biplane tail surrounding the rocket motor.

Kurt was primarily intended to be dropped operationally from a Me.262, carried externally in special fairings, but experimental drops were made from a FW.190 and a Me.410 Hornisse. It was dropped from a height of around 30m (controlled by a radio altimeter) at an aircraft speed of 150m/s, at test ranges at Leba and Travemünde. At the end of the war, it was estimated that there were 800 stores available (probably more than the total number of Highballs manufactured!), the expected use being for long-range attacks on merchant shipping.[122]

It is rather surprising that, having been inspired by the recovery of an Upkeep, the German weapon should bear closer resemblance to Highball. Perhaps even more surprising is that there was a proposal for adding rocket propulsion to Highball in a manner very similar to Kurt.

An MAEE report of August 1943[123] noted that the ranges achieved with Highball (a theoretical maximum of about 2,000yds) were attributable to its low lift/drag ratio and poor shape. It went on to suggest a possible range of 5,000yds if a shape similar to a flying boat hull was adopted, or if a rocket-propelled version was developed, the accompanying drawings bearing much resemblance to Kurt. Presumably only one store could then be carried, and the practical matter of decreased aiming accuracy due to the longer range appears not to have been considered.

Highball bounces on

Despite never being used in anger, and some early misgivings in certain circles, technical developments of Highball itself continued throughout the war, although the store as carried by 618 to Australia could be considered as the definitive Type I version of the store (a steel cylinder carrying 600lb of Torpex, with a pressed steel spherical outer shell, the gap between being filled with Catacol aerated resin).

More extensive rough-water trials were conducted in the autumn of 1945, again off Islay, by an MAEE detachment of three Mosquitoes led by Lane and based at RAF Port Ellen on the island. On 25 October Flt Lt Scargill had made seven successful drops and Sqn Ldr Jacques six. On his seventh run in DZ579, Jacques dived from 4,000ft and levelled off as planned to drop the store at around 30–40ft. However, the store must have caught a wave badly, as it created a larger splash than usual, and this caught the tail of the Mosquito, ripping off the port side of the tailplane, causing the aircraft to bank violently to port, whereupon the wingtip hit the water and the aircraft cartwheeled into the sea.[124] Sqn Ldr Jacques and his flight observer Flt Lt Savill were killed instantly. Another Mosquito was over the area within a few minutes, but an air sea rescue launch had to turn back due to the roughness of the weather. The bodies of the aircrew were eventually recovered, and both are buried in Bowmore Cemetery on Islay;[125] many parts of the aircraft were also recovered, but very few were larger than 3ft across. Despite the many drop tests conducted, this appears to have been the only time that a Mosquito suffered any damage during the delivery of a Highball.

The greatest ongoing concern regarding the use of Highball continued to be the denting of the outer casing on impact with the target, thus reducing the spin-induced forward motion during the sinking phase. To improve this performance, Wallis in the autumn of 1944 proposed a completely new version of the store to be manufactured from magnesium alloy, this new Type II store being given the codename Card.[126] The redesigned store would have a thick outer shell allowing the internal cylinder to be dispensed with. He consulted with Dr Aitcheson of Birmingham, who was an expert on this material – he described making a magnesium forging the size of Highball as 'an adventure'. Wallis thus proposed making the store in two parts with an equatorial weld, but Aitcheson then had concerns about making such large welds in this alloy; the materials problems were thus significant, and it was June 1945 before the first test specimens were ready. These emerged as castings – believed to be the largest magnesium alloy castings made anywhere, by a factor of about three (a zirconium-magnesium alloy forged version was also in development). Even so, the new

A simulation of the rocket-propelled Highball proposed by MAEE in 1943. *(Author)*

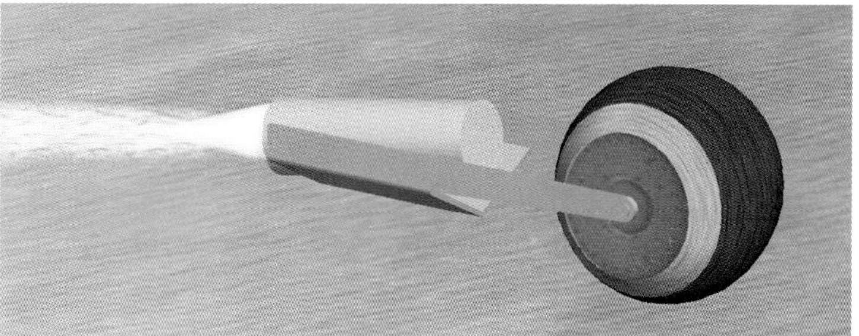

Three film stills show the final moments of DZ579; the Highball's splash breaks off the port tail-plane causing the pilot to lose control and crash into the sea. *(Crown Copyright via The National Archives)*

store was slightly smaller than Highball Mark I (warhead size was reduced by about 10 per cent), which meant that a different aircraft installation was required and any given aircraft could carry only one type of the store.

At the end of the war, a review of the requirements for Highball was carried out, but the Admiralty remained keen on Highball as it was potentially 'an even more effective anti-ship weapon than the torpedo', having the advantages of a higher charge/weight ratio, simpler sighting due to its faster travel to the target, and greater range of release (up to 2,500yds, depending on speed of release aircraft).[127] From the various aircraft options considered, firm requirements for using the new store in Sea Mosquitoes (codename Black Cat) and in Sea Hornets (codename Hot Dog) were stated[128] although an order for 50 Mosquitoes had just been cancelled (presumably due to VE Day) with just three new aircraft to be obtained for further development work.

For fitting in naval aircraft, the Admiralty insisted that the new weapon should not require dedicated aircraft as had the previous version – it was to be capable of installation (or removal) within 24 hours, and to comply with this, a box fitting known as a 'crate' was developed (based on experience with the Avenger installation) which could be attached into the bomb bay with just four bolts; after removal, the bomb doors could be refitted, and the Mosquito was back to standard specification. The same crate could be used in both the Mosquito and the Hornet.

Tests of the magnesium store at Ashley Walk at the end of May 1946[129] were initially disappointing, with impact causing failure of some of the castings; trials were also conducted at Wainfleet using Mosquitoes and Sea Hornets based at RAF Coningsby 20 miles away.[130] An installation for the Sea Hornet was also in progress in the autumn of 1946, though only one store was carried and spun electrically at 2,000rpm to give an estimated range of 4,000yds.[131] A revised version of the store was then produced incorporating a central diaphragm as part of the casing (and thus effectively dividing the charge into two halves). In a trial on 16 April 1947, a forged store split badly, but an example of the new store with the diaphragm was only slightly flattened by impact, and Wallis was 'reasonably certain that the casting form of diaphragm store is a great success'.[132] The conclusion from

five further test drops in November was that substantial distortions 'as to make its subsequent satisfactory underwater functioning distinctly doubtful' were still occurring, suggesting returning to a steel casing but with the same casting shape as the magnesium store.[133]

With a casing far stronger than that previously available came the possibility of using much greater rates of spin than had been practical before, and further research by Wallis in an experiment at the NPL testing tanks using 12in-diameter spheres had shown that very high rates of spin might also offer substantial increases in range. For the spin proposed – 6,000rpm – the air turbine and electric spin systems were not powerful enough, so Wallis proposed 'treating the Highball itself as a kind of turbine' modified by milling a series of cups into the circumference of the widest part of the store. Thrust from a bank of cordite rockets was then fed to a single nozzle, which was directed at the ring of cups, and these rapidly spun up the store.[134] However, despite detailed plans being drawn up, it appears that the rocket-spun Highball was never actually tested.

The curtain was finally coming down on the Highball project, the Admiralty (in light of guided missile developments) now being 'concerned only with the development of weapons released at very long range, of the order of 20,000yds or more'. There was some suggestion that Vickers continue the development work for export as a private venture,[135] but that seems not to have been taken up; Ministry permission to dispose of the remaining Highball and Card stores was requested in January 1948.[136]

Summary – Highball

Intended primarily as an anti-ship weapon, Highball was in continual development from 1943 until 1947, including two periods of operational deployment (although it was never used in action). It was also tested as an overland weapon, particularly for attacking tunnels. Mainly carried in the Mosquito, it was also tested in the Avenger, A-26 Invader and Sea Hornet. A magnesium alloy version was developed to replace the original steel version, but proposals for rocket-spun and rocket-propelled versions were not proceeded with. Overshadowed by the fame of Upkeep, its larger brother, Highball remains one of the most-tested secret weapons never to have seen action.

Chapter 7

The Earthquake Bombs

Research serves to make building stones out of stumbling blocks.
(Arthur D. Little)

An idea revisited

Operation Chastise was particularly significant for Wallis because it demonstrated that his shockwave theory was valid, the dams having been breached by a relatively small explosive charge placed so as to maximise the earthquake effect that was at the heart of his thesis. This led to his earthquake bomb idea being re-examined. Wallis recalled:

> *After the dams had been burst, Sir Wilfred Freeman, the Chief Executive at the Ministry of Aircraft Production, asked me if I remembered my mad idea of a 10-ton bomb . . . I said 'Yes, indeed, Sir Wilfred, I do.' 'Well,' he said, 'how soon could you let me have one?'*[1]

Wallis also noted that the bombs 'were produced solely on the authority and owing to the foresight of Sir Wilfrid Freeman and that no Air Force authority was given for the production of this bomb until a year after Sir Wilfrid Freeman had decided on the manufacture', praising Freeman's 'foresight and courage' in supporting their development.[2]

The theory of the weapon was presented in his 'Note'.[3] He demonstrated that the expanding gas bubble generated by an explosive was destructive but of comparatively small volume, while the pressure pulse radiating outwards also had substantial destructive power but affected a much greater volume (and far more so if transmitted through a solid, rather than air). The pressure wave created an overpressure (compression force), but this was followed by an underpressure (tension force) and this 'rebound' could be more destructive than the compression, especially on masonry and other brittle materials. He also disputed the generally-held opinion 'that no advantage is to be gained by increasing the size of the charge beyond a weight of 1,500lb', showing that all of the principal destructive characteristics of bombs vary in proportion to charge weight.

Taken together, 'it is necessary to inject the largest possible charge to the greatest possible depth in the medium (earth or water) that surrounds or is in contact with the target', the resulting pressure pulse having maximum destructive capability and effective radius, compared to a bomb with the same charge weight detonated in air. In order to deliver these characteristics, the fundamental properties of the penetration bomb were thus:

1. To have an aerodynamic shape for maximum speed gain, accurate aiming and smooth penetration.
2. To be as heavy as possible, while still practicable for carriage in available aircraft.
3. To have a casing strong enough to remain intact during ground penetration, but as light as possible to allow the explosive content to be as large as possible.

These indicated research requirements in aerodynamics, casing shape, casing materials and explosive performance, all of which were put in hand immediately.

The casing

The 'Note' included general arrangement drawings for the 10-ton bomb, and the heritage of the bomb as it emerged in 1943 is clear; main differences from the original are the external suspension lugs and the internal longitudinal stiffening ribs, and fins of slightly different shape. Also presented is a second 'water penetration' type, with a blunt-nosed casing covered by a thin Bakelite nosepiece to the original aerodynamic profile; this would fracture on water impact, leaving the blunt casing which would give better stability when travelling through the water.[4]

The external casing shape was straightforward, Wallis adopting the conventional ogival nose as used on shells and generally held to give the best trade-off between explosive content and aerodynamic performance.[5] Less apparent was the thickness of casing to use, requiring the minimum thickness (to allow maximum charge weight) but also enough strength to survive impact with the ground at supersonic speed, and this had to be established experimentally. Wallis had made a series of 2in-casing models, carefully turned down to give a range of casing thicknesses, and he had these fired from a mortar into earth.[6] Those that were too thin split longitudinally (a tensile hoop failure) and mushroomed into a Chinese lantern shape, and of those that did

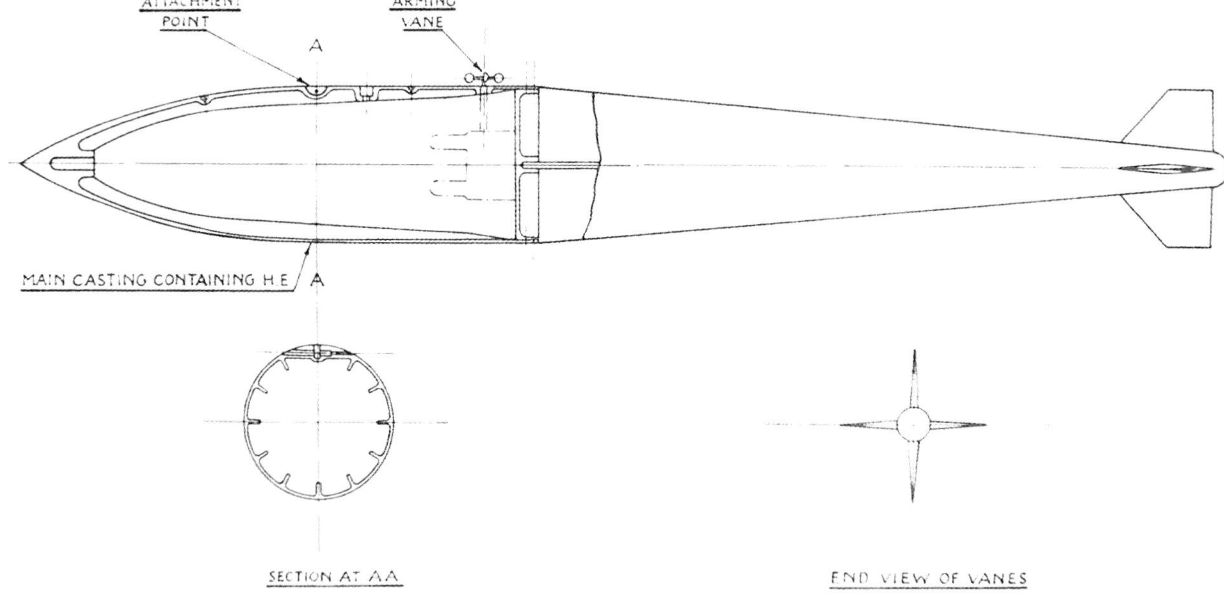

Wallis's 'Note' of 1941 includes this drawing of his proposed 10-ton bomb, although the design adopted differs in a number of details. *(BAE SYSTEMS via The National Archives)*

not deform, the one of minimum thickness was the shape to be adopted.[7]

Three sizes of bomb were envisaged: in addition to the 10-ton (22,000lb) bomb, a 6-ton (12,000lb) bomb was to be developed, and for aerodynamic tests a 4,000lb bomb was to be used.[8] With the official Ministry go-ahead for the project[9] in mid-July 1943 came the weapon's codename: Tallboy[10] (with suffixes Large, Medium and Small respectively); orders were placed for 100 Tallboy Large, 100 Medium and 18 Small.[11] The bombs were identical shapes, merely different sizes, and it is virtually impossible to tell them apart in photographs unless there is a visual size reference in the photo.[12]

For Tallboy Large, the casing was 46in diameter and 12ft 6in long from an overall bomb length of 25ft 5in; Medium was 38in diameter and 10ft 4in long from an overall length of 21ft (see Appendix 5 for details of sizes and weights). Wallis wrote to Chadwick in August 1943 to advise him of the details of the upcoming stores;[13] Chadwick saw no substantial problem in carrying the bombs in the Lancaster.[14]

To avoid a perceived risk of pre-detonation by friction between the casing and the HE, the casing internal surfaces were required to be reasonably smooth with any projections or rough areas removed by grinding (a task given to the apprentices, who had to crawl inside the casings),[15] the internal surfaces then being further smoothed with a hardened coating of varnish or shellac.[16] The casings were machined to take the rear plate, then the nose was drilled to accept a nose piece which was cast separately and 'cemented in' or attached via a 3.5in screw thread.[17] The whole bomb was then 'dressed' on a lathe to give a smooth external finish. Twenty bolts attached the rear plate, which carried three fuze pockets containing the detonating pistols spaced 120 degrees apart. A shallow recess 2in in diameter was milled on one side of the casing; this marked the centre of gravity of the store, and also engaged a pin on the roof of the bomb bay to prevent the store from rotating or moving fore/aft during carriage.

The tails were made of light alloy, fabricated by Short Brothers at Rochester, and attached to the rear of the main casing using turnbuckles; the first were delivered to 16 Maintenance Unit in February 1944.[18] Modifications were needed to add removable circular plates to permit hand access to the pistols, and holes for the arming wires connecting the pistols to the aircraft. The bombs were usually stored without the tails, these being attached just before loading into the aircraft. The ROF

To derive the lightest-but-strongest casing design for Tallboy, 2in model casings of various thicknesses were fired from a mortar into the ground; those to the left are too thin and deformed on impact, those to the right performed better. *(© Brooklands Museum)*

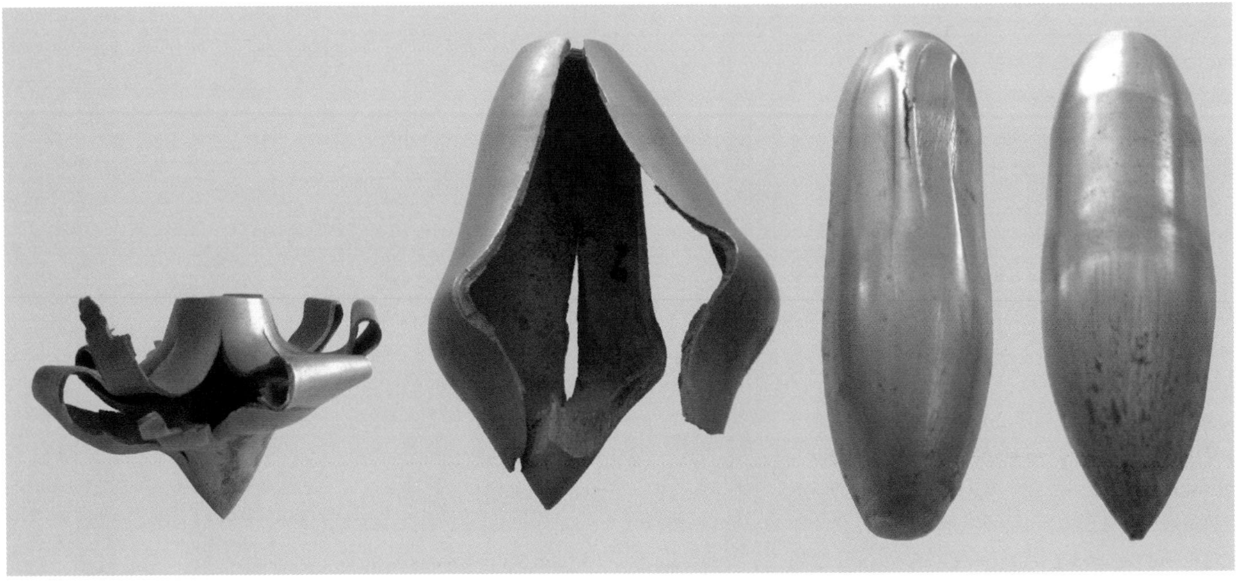

Woolwich was to fill inert stores, ROF Risley to fill the live stores.

Manufacture

The casing strength was limited by the tensile strength of the material, which thus needed to be as high as possible. Major Teed was Vickers' resident metallurgist, but was unavailable,[19] so Wallis sought the expertise of the steelmakers in Sheffield; the various steelworks had slightly different proficiency, in terms of both manufacturing processes and materials. The bomb casings were a substantial production challenge, due to both their size and fine tolerances.

From the initial order, 50 Large were to be made by ESC (Sheffield) and 50 by Firth-Brown (Scunthorpe); 50 Medium were to be made by David Brown at Penistone (near Sheffield) and 50 by Clyde Alloy Steel in Motherwell (near Glasgow). Of the 18 Small casings, 12 were to be forged by Vickers-Armstrongs at Elswick and six cast by Firth-Brown (three in manganese-molybdenum steel and three in pearlitic manganese steel); six additional casings in chromium-molybdenum steel were added later, to be cast by ESC.[20]

The chromium-molybdenum steel (also known as Hykro) offered a much higher yield point than the pearlitic manganese steel, which reduced the effect of 'mushrooming' on striking the ground, and was hence more satisfactory.[21] However, as Firth-Brown was equipped for manufacture of the pearlitic manganese steel, this continued in order not to reduce the total output, although the 'number of bombs in this steel was considerably less than that of the chromium-molybdenum steel'. It was hoped that reports on the comparative behaviour of the two steels would be forthcoming, but it transpired that the two types could not be kept separate by the RAF, so no assessment as to the relative measurements of the two steels was obtained.

Finish machining was required and this could take up to a week of lathe time per bomb, so manufacturing and finishing shop capacity was also an issue. Sub-contracting the machining was seen as a practical way to better utilise available capacity, and several sub-contractors were sought for each of the foundries. Firth-Brown (Scunthorpe) sub-contracted to Firth-Brown (Sheffield), David Brown (Sheffield) to Craven Bros, English Electric and Vickers-Armstrongs, Clyde Alloy to Mirrlees-Watson (Glasgow), James Potts (Motherwell) and Nairn's linoleum factory (Kirkcaldy).[22] Enquiries were also made of Duncan Stuart, Fullarton, Hodgard and Barclay, Beardmore's, and John Brown of Clydebank about machining Tallboy casings,[23] but it is unknown whether any of these companies undertook this work. Internal finishing was to be carried out at the foundry, with fitting of the nose pieces performed by the machinists.

By the end of August, ESC had made two castings of Tallboy Large, the first being unsuccessful. It was anticipated that two per week could be produced until the end of the year, whereupon 15 per month could be produced. Firth-Brown could manage a similar production rate from early 1944 in manganese-molybdenum steel. Hadfields could produce one per week from November 1943.[24] The first casting from Clyde Alloy emerged too large so that, when turned down to the correct external diameter, it was too thin – it was thus marked up for aerodynamic testing only.[25]

Due to problems of concurrently manufacturing the Medium and Large bombs, the Chief of Air Staff (with prime-ministerial approval) cancelled the order for the Large bombs on 30 September after nine had been made (the need for specialised carrier aircraft being cited as another reason).[26] At the same time, the Medium order was increased to 325, with 125 to be made in the USA.

The order for American Tallboys (known officially as M109 or T-10) was placed with Scullin Steel in St Louis, and these were cast conventionally. A.O. Smith in Milwaukee, which was a specialist in pressure vessel manufacture and had gone over to arms manufacture, was also asked to make the bombs; however, it was unable to make castings of the size required, so proposed fabricating Tallboy casings from two castings, for the nose and rear portions, with the straight cylindrical section being made from two or three sections of rolled sheet steel, the five sections being welded together. This arrangement was expected to be 'at least as satisfactory as casting'.[27] Although MAP ordered 25 of these Tallboys, Hurd asked Babcock & Wilcox (Britain's leading experts in welding) to look over the A.O. Smith proposals. It expressed concern about the longitudinal welds in the main body of the bomb, as these would be subject to double the stress at impact of the circumferential welds which attached the end castings, and proposed a new manufacturing option – similar to the Smith proposal, but also casting the central section, hence the finished casing would have only two welds, both circumferential.[28] However, this proposal seems not to have been taken up.

Scullin had cast 36 Tallboys by March 1944 and tests on the first store to be received by Vickers-Armstrongs showed that it was 'satisfactory and . . . has been made within drawing tolerances'.[29] There were noticeable surface undulations, and Wallis was concerned that any thickness variations would lead to instability as the store started to spin; he thus asked for future casings to be machined (although evidence suggests that this was not done).

The American and British casings appeared very similar, although as the American cast casings were not machined externally, they had a slightly rougher finish (nor were they finished internally). They were shipped to the UK unfilled,[30] joining the British castings for filling and the fitting of the tails, the latter sometimes causing problems due to the roughness (and hence slightly varying size) of the outside of the casing; in some cases, special tail units had to be manufactured.[31] Some loading problems with the stores at Woodhall Spa were checked out by Edwards who found that 'USA bombs are smaller than the British bombs'[32] by up to 2in in circumference.

Although Whitworth taps and gauges for fitting the rear plate and fuze pockets were to be sent to the US by air,[33] it appears that the US casings used UNC bolts, and hence different bolts and tools were needed from the Whitworth bolts used on the British backplates.[34] Curiously, 9 Squadron aircrews were told that the Tallboy was an American weapon, and that *all* the casings came from the USA (allegedly due to steel shortages in the UK).[35]

Tests and trials

To test penetration of the bombs into various types of surface, the 2in mortar technique was used in a number of trials from September 1943 through to May 1945. Most were conducted at RRL, but Wallis organised some of them himself, including firings into concrete at 750mph in November 1943;[36] RRL target materials included chalk, clay, concrete, and armour plate.[37] The chalk tests (September 1943) were done at the Chinnor Cement Works in Princes Risborough, Buckinghamshire, and also at Crichel Down (for later comparison with drops of the full-size stores, when 'good agreement' with the model predictions was found). Clay tests (October 1943) were made at Richmond Park (London clay) and Stewartby, Bedford (Oxford clay). In January 1945, sandstone tests were done at Bewdley (soft) and Caple Hill, Ross-on-Wye (intermediate). Concrete slabs were tested in March 1944, later tests (November) being performed to check the minimum angle for ricochet on concrete. A series of tests on armour plate in a variety of steels were conducted between November 1944 and February 1945.

A&AEE dropped the first of the Tallboy Small stores at Orfordness in December 1943, the stores showing 'considerable oscillation' after the bombs had fallen around 15,000ft,[38] this also being noted in further tests from 20–22,000ft[39] in January 1944 at Crichel Down, one of the three bombs becoming so unstable that the tail broke off. One of the others was carefully excavated to trace its underground path.[40] The casings were found to have failed, and these were returned to ESC for analysis.

To cure the instability, it was proposed to twist the tailfins by 5 degrees, thus imparting a spin to the bomb as it fell (an idea derived from the fletcher's art of twisting the feathers on arrows). Some worries were expressed about gyroscopic precession from spinning the store, and the consequent reduction in aiming accuracy. Wallis sought the advice of Relf at the NPL, and he raised no objection to the fin twisting, so it was agreed to try this right away,[41] ballistics tests on two stores being undertaken at Orfordness.[42] The offset fins gave a rotational speed of around 300rpm by the time of impact.[43]

The trials of six revised stores were conducted in March 1944, each dropped individually from a Lancaster at 18,000ft. High-speed cine cameras were used to record the trajectory in two planes for calculation of impact velocity, with a further camera in the Lancaster to measure initial yaw. The new stores proved to be stable and performed consistently, achieving an average striking velocity of 1100fps, though a consistent drift to port of around 90ft was also noted (this may have been due to the gyroscopic precession from the spin), and it was suggested that this should be allowed for in the sighting.[44]

A Tallboy M was first fitted to Lancaster DV405 on 28 February 1944 at A&AEE,[45] guidelines for future installation including ensuring equal oleo and tyre pressures to keep the aircraft level, and to have the bomb placed on the trolley in such a way that the roof bolt could easily locate the indent in the bomb.[46] This bomb was dropped from 16,000ft at Crichel Down on 20 March, achieving 'good stability' in flight, and penetrating 33ft into the chalk.

Wallis viewed the two drops conducted on 7–8 April 1944 at Ashley Walk, which are recorded as 'terminal velocity' tests[47] but which were significant in being the first drops of live Tallboys, both bombs making craters over 92ft in diameter. Another was dropped at Crichel Down on 10 April, Wallis even taking Molly along this time. Analysis of the films showed that the bombs were stable in flight, Wallis being congratulated by MAP and expressing 'feelings of intense satisfaction at having accomplished a task with unknown pitfalls',[48] though in his diary he simply noted 'bombs OK'.[49]

With the trajectory sorted and casings apparently performing adequately, the remaining unknown was the best HE filling for the bombs. Torpex with 5 per cent beeswax (as a desensitiser) was the initial recommendation as the HE filling. Six bombs with this filling were dropped on the Ministry of Home Security target[50] at Ashley Walk on 24–25 April, but the

The Lancaster bomb bay fitted for carriage of Tallboy or Grand Slam. Note the peg in the roof (centre) which engaged with a hollow in the side of the bomb, the attachments for the carrying strop (right and left), the ropes for pulling up the strop ends after release, and the crutches at each corner to hold the bomb steady. *(USAF)*

small size of craters produced suggested that the HE was not being completely detonated.[51] Fuzes used on most land targets had an 11-second delay, but 30 - and 60-minute fuzing was also common to avoid obscuring targets with smoke from the first few bombs to go down. 0.5 second fuzes were used on a small number of the U-boat pen attacks, with 0.07 - or 0.5-second fuzes used for capital ships.

During March and April 1945, five Tallboys were statically detonated at Shoeburyness to test the blast pressure developed from a range of explosive fillings; it was found that bombs containing Torpex D1 gave impulse values about 15 per cent greater than those containing 60/40 RDX/TNT.[52]

BACKGROUND

BOMB AIMING

The task of bomb aiming is a well-defined theory, greatly complicated by a substantial number of real-world factors. A bomb dropped in a vacuum will follow a known parabolic path to the surface, but in the atmosphere, the aim can be upset by such factors as: height and speed of the aircraft; air pressure differences (varying the speed of the bomb); wind (causing the bomb to drift); the bomb reaching terminal velocity (causing its path to become straight); and imperfect release (such as the aircraft climbing due to enemy fire). All of these possible errors increase with the altitude of release, which also makes the target smaller to the bomb aimer.

To aid the bomb aimer, mechanical sights were introduced, the Mk IX Course Setting Bombsight being the main one used by Bomber Command early in the war. This was superseded in 1942 by the Mk XIV sight developed by Professor Patrick Blackett, Director of Naval Operational Research, and Henry Braddick of the RAE. This was a far more sophisticated sight,[i] which used an electro-mechanical computer to calculate, in real time, the impact point of a bomb. It displayed this as a cross-hair in a sighting head mounted in the nose of the bomber, and the bomb aimer then had to guide the pilot towards the target, pressing the release at the moment the cross-hair fell across the target. Preset inputs included the bomb's terminal velocity, height of the target and wind speed/direction (calculated by wind-finding aircraft flying ahead of the main bomber force), with 'live' inputs of altitude and airspeed coming from the bomber. Two gyroscopes stabilised the sight against changes in attitude of the bomber, which in theory meant that only a very short straight run up to the target was required; however, in practice 'you had to fly extremely accurately . . . in theory you could do a turn and come on [to the target] but it didn't work out – you had to be absolutely stable, everything stable and then it wasn't too bad' and a run-up of 'six miles or something like that' was desirable.[ii] If the sighting computer failed, the bomb aimer could perform the main calculations manually using a simple 'emergency computer', but in practice this was very rarely required.[iii]

The Mk XIV (and its American-manufactured replica, the T-1) were in widespread use in Bomber Command from 1943 to 1945, its accuracy (probably) exceeding that of the Americans' own Norden sight. Uniquely, 617 Squadron were later equipped with an improved version known as the Stabilising Automatic Bomb Sight (SABS) which achieved greater accuracy but required a longer run-up; it also released the bombs automatically.[iv]

[i] Blackett, P.M.S. and Braddick, H.J.J., Patent GB581970, *Improvements in or relating to bombsights for aircraft*, applied for 31 December 1941.
[ii] Don MacIntosh, 9 Squadron Pilot (private communication).
[iii] Jim Brookbank, 9 Squadron Bomb Aimer (private communication).
[iv] Mk XIV / T-1 sights are not unusual in museums, but Brooklands Museum is believed to be unique in having a SABS on display.

Operational deployment

Due to the size of Tallboy, special bulged or 'blown' bomb bay doors were required for the Lancasters; some of 617's aircraft had these already to permit carriage of the 12,000lb HC bombs. Conventional bombs had lugs that engaged a bomb carrier, which was then winched up to be attached to the roof of the bay. The aerodynamic Tallboys had no lugs, so a special chain-link strop was looped round the bomb and held closed by an electro-mechanical bombslip.[53] Extra links were added for carrying Grand Slams. One problem that was encountered on early missions was the strops hanging down after release, and they damaged the edges of the bomb doors as they closed. Using rubber bungees to pull them up automatically was unsatisfactory, so ropes were attached to allow them to be pulled up manually, the ropes being held in place by 'Wallis wedges'.[54]

Once Tallboy operations were in progress, the bombs were stored in a bomb dump on the side of a road (closed to the public) between 617 Squadron's base at Woodhall Spa and 9 Squadron's base at Bardney.[55] The tails were fitted on to the casings by the armourers, a task requiring accuracy to maintain the balance of the bomb – one 9 Squadron armourer cut a profile template from a tail packing case, and placed this around the bomb to check there was no eccentricity.[56]

The bombs were carried on 'Type H' bomb trolleys, and once positioned under the aircraft (the trolley could be steered at both ends), four manual winches were used to lift the bomb up to meet the aircraft; it was the bomb aimer's job to check that the pin in the roof engaged the hollow in the bomb correctly. The bombs were usually carried with the tailfins at 45 degrees to the vertical, although some photos show them with the fins in the horizontal/vertical position.

During the second half of 1943, 617 Squadron (still a special operations squadron, now under the leadership of Wg Cdr Leonard Cheshire) were becoming experts in precision bombing from high level, but paradoxically were finding that the key problem was in marking targets effectively at low level. Various techniques were tried, eventually leading to the successful idea of dive-bombing markers into place, initially using Lancasters and later Mosquitoes and ultimately Mustangs. The 4,000lb HC 'Cookie' blast bombs and the 8,000lb HC 'Super Cookie' had been used by Bomber Command for some time, and 617 were the first squadron to use the 12,000lb HC version.[57]

Dropping trials of this bomb into shallow water to test its effectiveness on canal banks had been satisfactory,[58] and use against viaducts was also proposed; Upkeep was also mooted

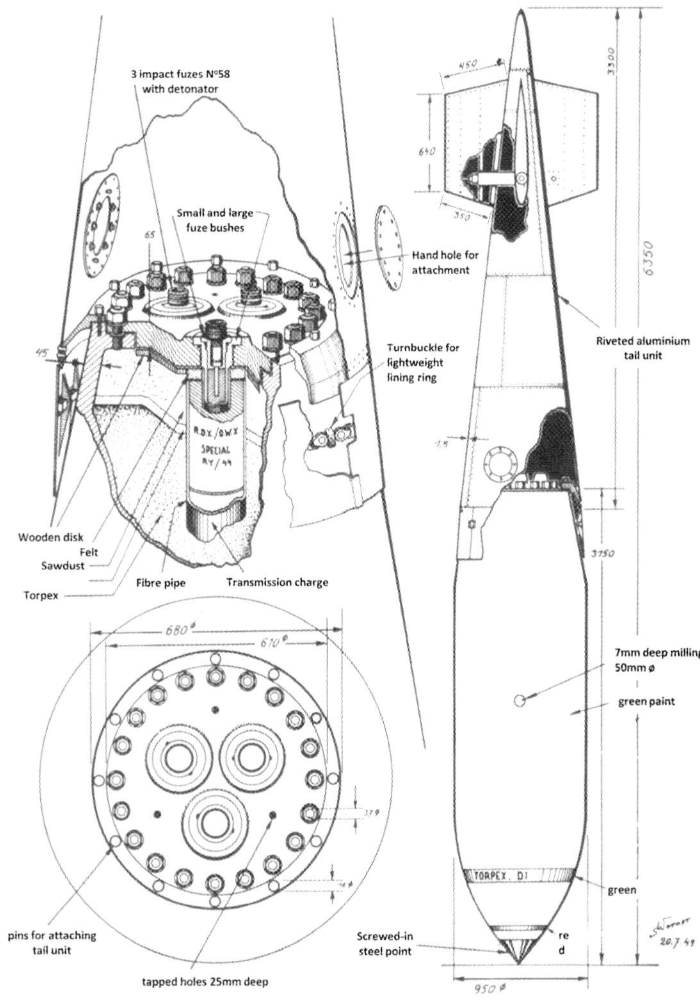

As with Upkeep, one of the best contemporary Tallboy diagrams is a German one dated July 1944, which is believed to have been drawn from one defuzed at Wizernes (labels have been translated). *(Author's collection)*

for both types of targets, hence the overland trials in August (see Chapter 5). However, Wallis noted that the German viaduct targets were of substantial reinforced concrete construction, and that for any bomb to be effective, detonation would need to be in contact with the masonry.

On 15 September 1943 the Dortmund–Ems Canal was attacked with 12,000lb HC bombs, bad weather preventing the bombs landing in the canal and the raid was unsuccessful. The Anthéor viaduct in southern France was attacked by 617 in three separate low-level raids on 16 September and 11 November 1943 and 12 February 1944, the last placing 12,000lb HC bombs within 5 yds... yet the viaduct was not seriously damaged. This showed that blast power alone was insufficient for this type of structure, and confirmed the need for Wallis's earthquake bomb.

As with Upkeep, the Germans successfully defuzed an unexploded Tallboy (probably from one of the V-weapon site attacks), and had the full technical detail laid out in a drawing dated 20 July 1944.

By October 1944, an apparent problem with the release slips had been identified, with as many as 30 per cent failing to release instantaneously, the hold-ups resulting in overshoots of many hundreds of yards.[59] Wallis's initial examination of this 'genuinely disturbing' problem found some corrosion due to water penetration in the slips,[60] and further investigation by A&AEE was put in hand. They tested 12 slips, 9 of which had been used operationally with one brand new, these being fitted into Lancaster PD198 and dropping a Tallboy on to a bomb trolley (three drops per slip). The average delay was found to be just 25.9ms, which would be insignificant on operations;[61] it was suggested that the timing chronograph equipment be fitted into operational aircraft for trials under real conditions, but this does not seem to have been done.

Grand Slam

The successful operational use of Tallboy from June 1944 led to MAP giving the go-ahead on 12 July 1944 for the production to restart on Tallboy Large, now known as Grand Slam,[62] for delivery in early 1945. A scaled copy of Tallboy M, all of the British-made Grand Slams were made from the chromium-molybdenum steel used for the bulk of the Tallboys.[63]

Although on paper well above the maximum load for a Lancaster, modifications to the 'B.1 Specials', including more powerful engines and

Three attacks (two using 12,000lb HC bombs) on the viaduct at Anthéor on the Côte d'Azur failed to break it, despite near misses, and demonstrated the requirement for the earthquake bombs. The difficult approach was made down the valley seen through the arches. *(Author)*

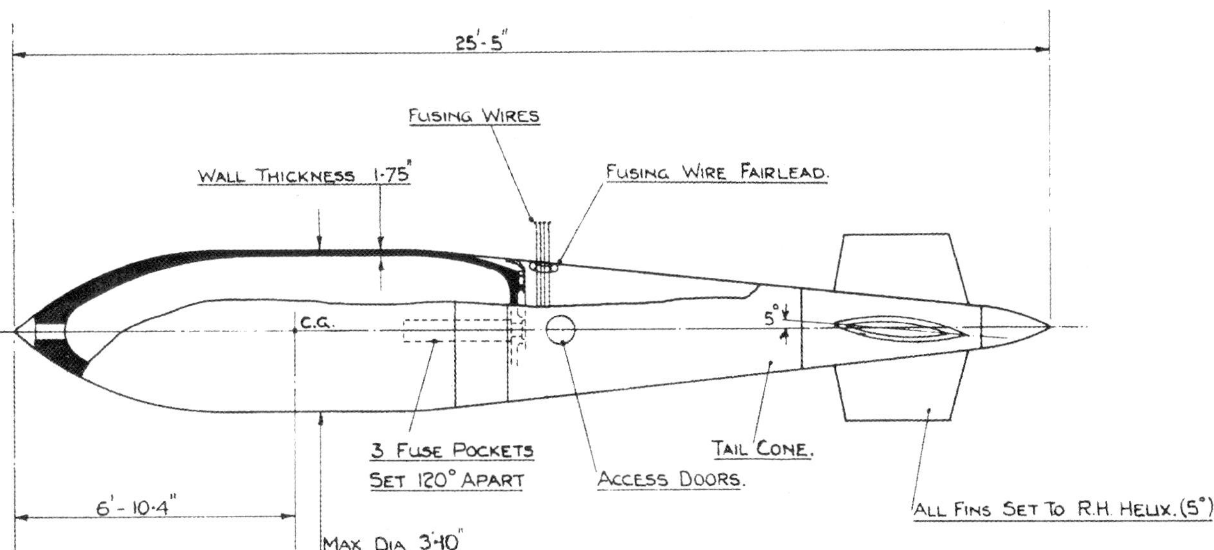

Grand Slam was an enlarged copy of Tallboy. Note the 5-degree offset fins, a detail missed on the German drawing. *(USAF)*

the removal of nose and dorsal gun turrets and bomb bay doors (the ends of the bomb bay were faired over), allowed the aircraft to carry Grand Slam up to the required dropping height. A total of 33 of this variant were built, although only 22 saw operational service with 617 Squadron.

Wallis was at Ashley Walk for the only test drop of a Grand Slam, from 16,000ft at 1030 on 13 March 1945. Aimed (probably) at the submarine pen, it missed by 350ft, but made a crater about 130ft across and up to 70ft deep. Given the successful detonation of this 'earthquake bomb', a record on seismograph equipment might have been expected (as had occurred with Upkeep strikes on the Dams Raid). However, the nearest equipment, about 90 miles away at Kew in SW London, registered only three small events on this date, and none of these were around the time of the trial.[65]

American Grand Slams (officially designated M110 or T-14) were also produced in cast and welded forms; it is not known if any US-made examples were dropped by the RAF. The backplates for these bombs had the three fuze pockets in a line, rather than the triangular layout used in the British version.

Operational results

Wallis was keen to see how the actual results of the Tallboys dropped in action matched up to the experimental tests, and he was granted permission to visit many of the target sites shortly after their liberation.

> *I had the unique privilege of landing in Normandy in early July 1944 and living in the American 'lines', to see the heavy concrete underground buildings that had been captured, as a consequence of which I had recommended (and succeeded) in getting the 10-ton bomb restarted; entering Brest the day after it fell to the Americans, to see the damage done to the submarine pens by Tallboy in September 1944.*[66]

At the suggestion of an MAP official, he spent a week from 19 October 1944 touring the Pas-de-Calais sites of Wizernes, Éperlecques (Watten), Siracourt, Marquise-Mimoyecques and 'Saint Leu d'Esserent where are the great caves or caverns wherein Tallboy is supposed to have caused a great subsidence'.[67] He revisited Wizernes and Marquise, plus the Sangatte gun batteries,[68] during a day trip on 3 April 1945, spent five days in the Paderborn area from 20 April touring the dams and other targets, and made another day trip to Germany on 19 July to view V-2 rockets at Cuxhaven.[69] Some of the sites were also visited by a team from the RRL.[70]

A Grand Slam (vertical) and Tallboy (horizontal) in Nairn's workshop, one of the machinist sub-contractors. Note the centre of gravity mark on the Tallboy, and the end plate in the foreground which has three fuze pockets in a line, more typical of an American-made store. *(© Fife Council Museums: Kirkcaldy Museum & Art Gallery)*

Subterranean collapse	103 Tallboys/12 per cent:[72]	
Saumur Tunnel	19 Tallboys	Tunnel roof collapsed by direct hit, railway tracks cut by craters; tunnel not used again before liberation
Marquise-Mimoyecques (V-3)	14 Tallboys	Concrete slab damaged, underground tunnels collapsed; site never completed
V-1 storage at St Leu-d'Esserent/Creil	11 Tallboys	Entrance and caves collapsed; site abandoned
V-1 storage at Rilly la Montagne	12 Tallboys	Entrance and caves collapsed; site abandoned
V-2 site at Wizernes	32 Tallboys	Underground tunnels collapsed and concrete dome displaced; site never completed[73]
Underground oil storage facility at Farge	15 Tallboys	Results not known

Table 7.1: Subterranean targets upon which earthquake bombs were dropped. All of these targets were built beneath limestone or chalk – this material is very soft, making site excavation easier but also allowing greater depth of bomb penetration.

The targets upon which the earthquake bombs were dropped were chosen according to operational requirements pertaining at the time. Details of the individual raids can be found in several primary and secondary sources;[71] however, in considering their success as weapons, it is more useful to consider the different *types* of targets together.

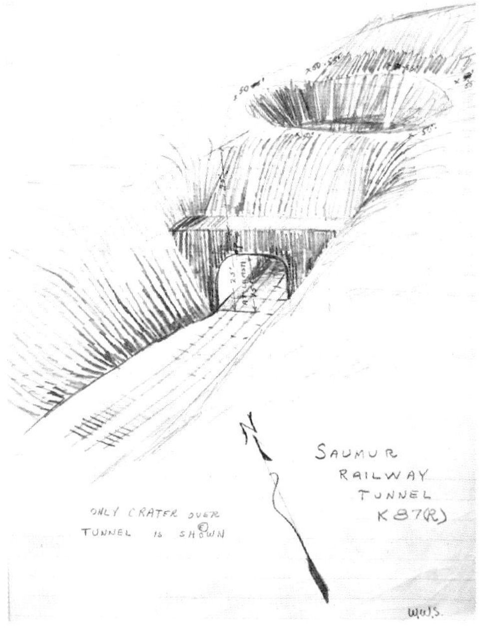

This contemporary sketch of the Saumur Tunnel dramatically shows the hit on the roof which completely blocked the tunnel and vindicated the 'earthquake bomb' theory on its first operation. *(Crown Copyright via The National Archives)*

Subterranean Collapse

The first operational Tallboys were dropped on 8 June 1944 on the Saumur railway tunnel in the Loire Valley. The railway track was cratered and the tunnel roof was caved in by a direct hit just behind one entrance, blocking this resupply route to the German front line against the Normandy invasion. One bomb was 680yds from the aiming point, for the other 18, an average error of 115yds was achieved. This was such an impressive debut that 'the Air Staff are satisfied that the present order for 375 Tallboys should now be increased to a total of 2,000' at a rate of 240 a month.[74]

At St Leu d'Esserent there was a series of caves and tunnels approximately 20–40ft underground; these were used for storage of V-1s. The Tallboys (plus 1,000lb bombs) created a series of roof falls and damaged the large doors at the entrances. Rilly la Montagne was a similar site and comparable results were achieved.

Work in excavating the V-2 facility beneath the dome at Wizernes was not complete when the site was attacked, the dome being slightly displaced by a Tallboy near miss, and several of the tunnels beneath the structure also collapsed due to the bombing; the site was never completed.[75]

Possibly the most significant, certainly the

Concrete structures	269 Tallboys /32 per cent, 15 Grand Slams/37 per cent:	
E-boat pens, Le Havre	22 Tallboys	At least 3 hits on roof, 1 penetration
E-boat pens, Boulogne	11 Tallboys	No hits, but damage from near misses and over 100 E-boats sunk
U-boats pens, Brest	27 Tallboys	9 hits on roof, 5 penetrations and 4 large craters, blockship sunk
U-boats pens, Lorient	11 Tallboys	3 hits on roof, no penetrations but substantial damage
U-boats pens, La Pallice	18 Tallboys	6 hits on roof, no penetrations but substantial damage
U-boats pens, Bergen	24 Tallboys	2 hits on roof plus hits on shipping
E/R-boat pens, Ijmuiden	53 Tallboys	4 or 5 hits on roof, at least 1 penetration, substantial damage
U-boat pens, Hamburg	15 Tallboys, 2 Grand Slams	6 hits on roof by Tallboys, 4 penetrations
E-boat pens, Waalhaven/ Rotterdam	16 Tallboys	3 hits on roof, part of roof over entrance collapsed
Midget submarine pens, Poortershaven	18 Tallboys	Target destroyed
V-1 launch bunker, Siracourt	16 Tallboys	Roof damaged
V-2 launch bunker, Éperlecques (Watten)	33 Tallboys	Roof damaged
U-boat factory, Farge	5 Tallboys, 13 Grand Slams	2 penetrations by Grand Slams

Table 7.2: Concrete structures upon which Tallboys and Grand Slams were dropped. Wallis's bombs were not intended for concrete penetration, but these structures were important to the German war machine, and Tallboy was the only weapon with any chance of success against them.

most underrated, of the V-weapon sites was the V-3 at Marquise-Mimoyecques. On the surface, this consisted simply of a concrete slab with three openings, and Allied intelligence did not know what was beneath. In fact, the openings were each for a multi-barrelled long-range gun which, had it become operational (and a prototype in Germany had demonstrated the efficacy of the weapon),[76] would have been able to rain tons of shells on to London each day. Impregnable to conventional bombs other than by a direct hit on one of the openings, Tallboys managed to damage the concrete slab and, more importantly, collapse the underground tunnels leading to the guns, ensuring that they would never be used. Had the works been completed, it would have posed a far greater threat to London than the V-1s and V-2s, and the Marquise weapon's relative obscurity is attributable to its obliteration by Tallboys.[77]

The oil storage facility at Farge, buried beneath a forest near the U-boat factory, was the only such target attacked, although this type was specifically mentioned in Wallis's original 'Note'; unfortunately neither contemporary reports nor modern sources give any indication of the amount of damage caused to the site.

In summary, these underground targets were Tallboy's bread and butter, and the bombs performed exceptionally well, literally causing earthquakes that collapsed the underground chambers and made the sites unusable.

Concrete Structures

The first pens to be attacked were at Le Havre on 15 June 1944 and the next day at Boulogne – these ports operated fleets of E-boats which were harassing the Normandy invasion forces in night attacks. These two raids resulted in 100 vessels being destroyed, some flung up on to the quayside. On 16 June, V-1 'flying bombs' began falling on London, and bombing efforts switched to the launch sites of these weapons.

At Siracourt, a Tallboy hit on the roof produced a 30ft-diameter crater and created 'severe bending' of the inside of the roof. The two attacks on the blockhouse at Éperlecques had resulted in only one Tallboy hit on the edge of the roof (plus some near misses), and repair work was under way when the site was liberated.

After all of the main V-weapon installations had been attacked (the smaller launch sites were being bombed by Main Force aircraft), attention switched back to the submarine pens and during August 1944, five of the pens were attacked.

A team of seven, including two scientists from RRL, performed a detailed survey of the Brest pens in October 1944, in collaboration with the US Strategic Bombing Survey.[78] This looked in detail at the effect of the nine individual bombs which hit the structure, noting the thickness and composition of the concrete at the point of impact, as well as the effect of any bomb traps or other defensive devices. Ballistic penetration by Tallboy into the concrete was estimated at 6–8ft although, in addition to cratering the top surface

Railway bridges	160 Tallboys/19 per cent, 20 Grand Slams/49 per cent:	
Bielefeld	31 Tallboys, 1 Grand Slam	3 spans of 1 viaduct initially broken by Tallboys, several spans of double viaduct broken by Grand Slam
Arnsberg	34 Tallboys, 7 Grand Slams	2 spans broken, tunnel mouth collapsed, line blocked by crater
Altenbeken	16 Tallboys	1 span broken
Vlotho	15 Tallboys	Bridge damaged
Arbergen/Dreys	17 Tallboys, 2 Grand Slams	2 spans broken, other spans displaced
Nienburg	12 Tallboys, 5 Grand Slams	All 3 spans broken
Bremen	25 Tallboys, 5 Grand Slams	1 span broken
Bad Oeynhausen	10 Tallboys	2 sections broken

Table 7.3: Railway bridges upon which Tallboys and Grand Slams were dropped. Although the 'Note' suggested use of the earthquake bombs for disruption of transportation, it was by way of cratering effects rather than by destroying bridges, although subsequent analysis suggested that these offered better targets (as they could not be repaired as quickly as a crater).

Ships and naval installations	133 Tallboys/16 per cent:	
Tirpitz	76 Tallboys	At least 3 hits and several near misses caused severe damage and she turned over
Lützow and *Prinz Eugen*	13 Tallboys	*Lützow* sunk by near misses
Other shipping/naval installations	44 Tallboys	No damage recorded

Table 7.4: Ships and naval installations upon which Tallboys were dropped.

('knock out'), bombs which had not penetrated the roof were able to cause substantial 'spalling' or 'scabbing' of the underside of the roof, this causing a large amount of concrete to fall from the inside of the roof. Where perforation had occurred, it was noted that in all cases detonation had taken place within the roof, i.e. the bomb had not perforated the roof entirely prior to exploding. The findings were found to be 'in reasonable agreement' with the experiments done previously on models at the RRL. Following his visit, Wallis noted the problem of 'premature detonation of which there was considerable evidence at Brest'.[79]

The *Valentin* U-boat facility at Farge, near Bremen, was a unique and substantial target; it was a covered production line for assembly of prefabricated Type XXI U-boats, including a wet dock from which completed submarines could embark directly into the River Weser. It had a reinforced concrete roof up to 23ft thick, and was nearly completed when attacked. Two Grand Slams succeeded in penetrating the roof, and the plant was not operational by the time of its capture by ground forces.

Despite not being designed for penetration of hardened concrete structures, about one-third of the earthquake bombs were dropped on this type of target, with reasonable results. Some were destroyed completely, others suffering damage which reduced or stopped their contribution to the German war effort.

Railway Bridges

The primary rail route from the Ruhr to eastern Germany passed over the double multiple-arch viaduct at Bielefeld, and by February 1945, over 3,000 tons of bombs had been dropped on it by the RAF and USAAF with little result, although one Tallboy attack had brought down a short section of one of the viaducts. Following the successful test drop of Grand Slam on 13 March, Sqn Ldr C.C. 'Jock' Calder of 617 Squadron dropped the first operational bomb the next day at Bielefeld. The single Grand Slam brought down several spans of both viaducts. Harris wrote to 617:

> *I have just seen a stereo pair of the Bielefeld Viaduct taken after your visit yesterday, my congratulations on your accurate bombing. You have certainly made a proper mess of it this time and incidentally added another page to your history by being the first Squadron to drop the biggest bomb on Germany so far, good work. Keep up the training. We can't afford to put these new little pets in the wrong place.*[80]

The 'little pets' and their little brother were dropped on a further seven bridges over the next two weeks, bringing down all of them with a combination of hits and near misses on the spans and piers – at Bad Oeynhausen, a near miss of 50–60ft caused a collapse.[81]

Ships and naval installations

The stories of the attacks on the *Tirpitz* have achieved a legendary status within the RAF second only to the Dams Raid.[82] After being damaged in Kaa Fjord by the X-craft submarine attack in September 1943, she was further damaged by air attacks from Royal Navy carriers in a series of raids in spring 1944. By September, Tallboy had already proven its worth, and it was seen as a new possibility to dispose of this menace to the Arctic shipping routes. However, Kaa Fjord was too far north to reach from the UK, so agreement was reached with the Russians to use Yagodnik on the Kola Peninsula as a forward base. Twenty Lancasters of 617 Squadron and 14 of 9 Squadron (carrying Tallboys and JW mines), plus support aircraft, took off on 11 September for the flight to Russia, but deteriorating weather meant that several crash-landed, some being written off. Consequently, only 17 Lancasters of 617 Squadron and 10 of 9 Squadron were serviceable when the weather cleared on 15 September and Operation Paravane was on. However, smoke-laying apparatus on the ship and around the fjord was very effective, and the aim of most aircraft was spoiled as the smoke cloaked the target. One Tallboy hit her on the fo'c'sle and passed through and out her starboard side before exploding, effectively finishing her as a seagoing warship (although this was not appreciated by the Allies at the time).

She was then taken under her own steam to Tromsø Fjord, where it was intended to use her as a gun battery against a possible invasion of Norway. This meant that she was now within range of Britain, and a second attack (Operation Obviate) saw 39 Lancasters take off from forward bases at Lossiemouth, Milltown and Kinloss in the north of Scotland on 29 October, flying up the Norwegian coast, then dog-legging through a gap in radar coverage to Sweden and on to Tromsø. Although the smokescreen apparatus had not yet been set up at Tromsø, the clear weather en route came to an end during the bombing run, as a sheet of cloud swept in between the Lancasters and their target. Many aircraft managed to bomb, but only near misses were achieved.

This mission was thus rerun (as Operation Catechism) on 12 November with 31 aircraft, and this time the weather remained clear. Three of the Tallboys found their mark, and there were many near misses. One hit caused one of *Tirpitz*'s magazines to explode after a few minutes, and the ship turned over and sank (as far as the shallow water would let her).[83] A total of 92 Tallboys (including those jettisoned or left in Russia), more than 10 per cent of the wartime total, was expended in achieving this result, a measure of the importance placed on this target. While acknowledging the efforts of the X-craft crews, RAF airmen and the Norwegian Resistance, Murpurgo notes that 'ultimately her destruction can be set to the account of the ingenuity of Barnes Wallis'.[84]

A report 'to appreciate the relative merits of Tallboy Medium and the 2,000lb AP bomb' noted that Tallboy would not penetrate the *Tirpitz*'s armour deck and that the ship could not be sunk without this, hence concluding that the '2,000lb AP bomb is more effective than Tallboy for attacking the *Tirpitz*'.[85] Most remarkable is the date of this report – 17 November 1944 – by which time *Tirpitz* had already lain on the bottom for five days.

The heavy cruiser *Lützow* was also sunk by Tallboys, on 16 April 1945; although no direct hits were achieved, it appears that a near miss around 60ft away was enough to damage her hull sufficiently to cause sinking. A vessel at Ijmuiden was also sunk by Tallboys to prevent the Germans using her as a blockship.

Tallboy was thus highly effective as an anti-ship weapon – the large number of bombs used against the *Tirpitz* representing aiming limitations against such a small target, rather than an ineffective weapon.

Dams

In May 1944 there was renewed interest in attacking the Sorpe Dam and Wallis wrote what Gp Capt Bufton described as 'an excellent technical appreciation of the vulnerability of the Sorpe Dam to attack by Tallboy aircraft'[86] also noting that 'no attempt on this dam should be made with Upkeep as it is not really a suitable target for this form of attack'. Although a Tallboy attack was deemed practical, there was insufficient tactical justification for an attack, and it was not until September that a raid, which 'would have as one of its primary objects the destruction of main rail routes which are some 4 miles due north of the dam',[87] was contemplated. Wallis suggested 'that 4 or 6 hits

Dams	65 Tallboys/8 per cent:	
Sorpe Dam	16 Tallboys	Several direct hits on crest and elsewhere, no breach
Urft Dam	38 Tallboys	Several near misses, no breach
Kembs Barrage	11 Tallboys	Sluice gate breached by Tallboy dropped at low level

Table 7.5: Dams upon which Tallboys were dropped.

reasonably close to the crest of the dam, that is within 50 or 60 feet of the crest, should be satisfactory', noting that the approach should be perpendicular to the dam and from the air side to give a better penetration angle.[88]

9 Squadron duly delivered during a raid on 15 October,[89] making a number of direct hits on the dam, including two on the crest. The reduced autumn water level meant that the craters were not deep enough to reach down to the water, and the dam stood – had the water been higher, the resulting outflow through the craters would have eroded the dam further and could have caused significant flooding. One Tallboy was found in the mud when the reservoir was partially drained in 1958, and it was successfully defuzed.

The Kembs Barrage in Alsace (a low sluice-type structure, part of the Rhine canal system) was successfully breached on 7 October 1944, thus preventing the Germans using it to flood US troops approaching from Belfort. Uniquely on this raid, the Tallboys were dropped at low level for accurate positioning, in addition to a second force of Lancasters approaching at mid-height to split the defences. Use of Upkeep had been considered for this raid, but there were no more than eight Upkeep-equipped Lancasters remaining and there was insufficient time to train the new crews for delivery of the weapon.

During December, three raids were also mounted against the curved gravity dam at Urft, 30 miles south-west of Cologne, again to prevent it being used to flood troops; despite numerous near misses (and German demolition charges), the dam was only damaged, and the Germans prevented further harm by lowering the water level. Partial repairs were made shortly after the war, but complete repairs took several years, due to access difficulties caused by the dam being in the Vogelsang Training Area.[90]

The performance of Tallboy against dams was thus very disappointing, and presents a paradox: Upkeep came about from Wallis's initial plan to destroy dams with penetration bombs, which themselves were only produced following the successful use of Upkeep, but Tallboy proved to be ineffective against dams. It remains open to conjecture if the use of Grand Slam would have made any difference to this.

Other targets

Having failed to breach the banks of the Dortmund-Ems Canal with the 12,000lb HC bombs in September 1943, a Main Force raid a year later near Ladbergen was successful, despite only six Tallboys being dropped due to chaotic communications aided by German jamming. Although aqueducts had been the target, two Tallboys created deep breaches in the canal embankments, draining the canals (the canal split into two branches at this point) for 6 miles. The damage was repaired, but the attack was repeated by 9 Squadron in March 1945 with similar results.

The Sorpe Dam following the raid by 9 Squadron in October 1944. Despite accurate placement of several bombs, the dam was not breached. *(Crown Copyright)*

Other targets	103 Tallboys/12 per cent, 6 Grand Slams/15 per cent:	
Dortmund-Ems Canal	24 Tallboys	Embankments breached, canal drained on two occasions
Heligoland gun emplacements	27 Tallboys, 6 Grand Slams	2 direct hits
Synthetic oil plant	27 Tallboys	Mostly superficial damage
Berchtesgaden	25 Tallboys	Damage to Berghof and SS barracks

Table 7.6: Other targets on which Tallboys and Grand Slams were dropped.

Summary of results of the earthquake bomb operations

The 833 Tallboys and 41 Grand Slams thus dropped on targets, plus approximately a further 5 per cent of both bombs lost due to hang-ups or emergency jettisoning, make a total of 872 Tallboys and 43 Grand Slams expended on operations. The massive levels of destruction inflicted meant that they were highly successful, and Wallis's original idea (using a large underground explosion to create an earthquake effect) was again vindicated in practice. The bombs' successful use against the underground targets and the V-weapon blockhouses was particularly significant.

Overall, the point of impact of about 85 per cent of Tallboys could be traced on post-raid photographs, and from these, it was possible to calculate the average radial aiming errors, which were as follows:[91]

June–August 1944	Using SABS Mk IIa	170yds
December 1944–March 1945	Using SABS Mk IIa	125yds
February–March 1945	Using Mk XIV	195yds

Table 7.7: Average radial aiming errors of Tallboys.

During a post-war interview, Leonard Cheshire claimed average aiming errors of 60yds from 10,000ft and 80–90yds from 20,000ft.[92] Aiming errors tended to be spread in all directions, slightly greater in the direction of attack due to the forward speed of the aircraft – at 250mph, pressing the button one second late would result in an overshoot of over 100yds.

The average crater diameter in soil was found to be 97ft with a depth of 25ft; comparing with the original estimate for the 10-ton bomb presented in the 'Note' in 1941 (and correcting for the smaller charge size of Tallboy), the actual crater size is within 10 per cent of the estimate.

German countermeasures

Having relied, with good cause but for Wallis's inventiveness, on thick concrete roofs to halt Allied bombs, the Germans realised that they needed to become even more creative with their concrete. After the severe damage wrought at the Éperlecques V-2 site by USAAF bombing while the concrete was wet, a new method of building massive structures while keeping them relatively invulnerable during construction was needed. Variously called *Verbunkerung* ('sheltering') and *Erdschalung* ('earth formwork'), the idea was to build the concrete roof of a structure directly *on the ground* (shaped accordingly), and once it was able to withstand bombing, a protected working space could be excavated underneath. The Siracourt V-1 site and the Wizernes V-2 site were both constructed using variations on these principles.

With the appearance of the penetration bombs, it was recognised that further work was needed on the existing structures, and the Brest U-boat pens saw no less than five different methods being tried. Key among these was *Fangrost* ('rust catcher') which was a double layer of pre-cast 'burster girder' concrete beams laid on the roof; the top layer had a bevelled top and was laid perpendicular to the one beneath. The hope was that many bombs would strike the bevelled tops and be deflected, hence not striking the main roof at a useful angle and thus not penetrating very deeply into the roof. Although installation of *Fangrost* had begun on all of the main U-boat pens (Brest,

St Nazaire, Lorient, La Pallice and Bordeaux), none had been completed at liberation and it was never put to the test as none of the Tallboys dropped hit the sections of the roof with *Fangrost* on them – although it seems likely that it could have been very effective.

Rothensee Ship Lift – the one that got away

The target which received the greatest level of investigation, but which was never attacked, was the Rothensee Ship Lift near Magdeburg. Completed in 1938 as part of a larger canal project, it was used to lift barges over 18m from the River Elbe to join the Mittelland Canal, and all canal traffic between the Ruhr and Berlin had to pass through the lift. The main section was a trough 85m long and 12m wide, supported by two cylindrical floats 38m long and 10m in diameter, positioned vertically within 60m-deep shafts beneath the trough. By pumping water into and out of the shafts, the floats raised or lowered the trough. The lift was surrounded by a concrete apron believed to be up to 50ft thick.

The lift was considered at various times as a possible target for all four Wallis weapons. Wallis's 'preliminary investigations indicated that the Mosquito weapon aimed along the canal would be able to put the ship lift out of action' but was less confident of an overland attack using Upkeep.[93] It was 'also agreed to investigate the general vulnerability of the Rothensee Ship Lift to high and low-level attack with 4,000lb HC or MC bombs' and Glanville at the RRL was 'requested to undertake trials with model structures to determine [the] effective radius'.[94] These tests appear to have focused on the use of Tallboy

Stage 1: mound created on surface

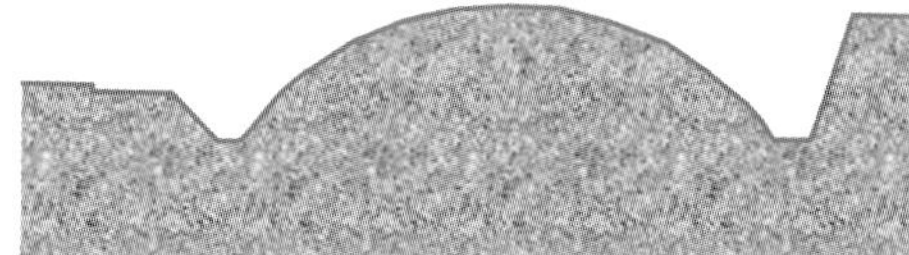

Stage 2: reinforced concrete laid on top within formers

Stage 3: dome complete, earth beneath is dug away

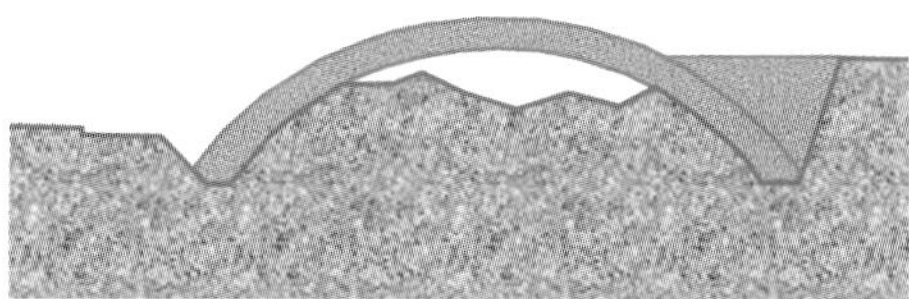

To prevent bomb damage to works in progress, the Germans developed the technique of *Erdschalung*, building a roof on the ground then excavating a working space beneath. This technique was used at Wizernes, but Tallboy near misses caused the tunnels to collapse and the site was never used. *(Author)*

Fangrost was designed to limit the effectiveness of 'earthquake bombs', consisting of a series of concrete beams in a cruciform pattern on the roofs of U-boat pens (this is St Nazaire); installation of *Fangrost* was incomplete, and no Tallboys struck the completed sections. *(© Holger Forstemann)*

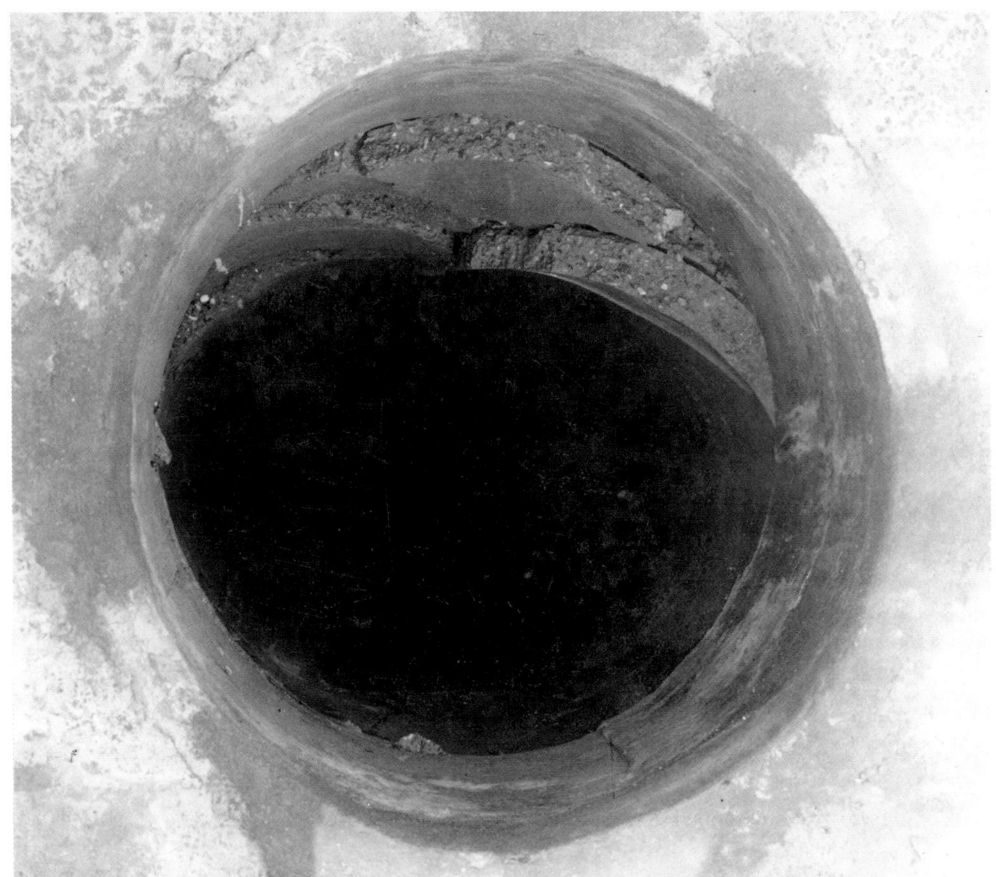

One of the models of the float shafts of the Rothensee Ship Lift that was tested at the Road Research Laboratory. The scaled charge has deformed the circular shaft, so a Tallboy near miss would almost certainly have disabled the lift, but an attack was never carried out. *(BAE SYSTEMS via the Science Museum)*

variants, it being reported to the Air Ministry that Tallboy Medium would need to detonate within 30–40ft at a depth of 100ft, or Tallboy Large within 40–50ft, and the cancellation of Tallboy Large on 30 September 1943 by the Chief of the Air Staff resulted in the Air Ministry losing interest in this target.[95]

In March 1944, Wallis and Glanville discussed the target in detail, with Wallis agreeing that Vickers would manufacture two one-twentieth scale steel models of the shafts for testing at the RRL.[96] These tests took place in July using scaled charges equivalent to Tallboy Medium detonating 80ft underground, it being reported[97] that a model with steel-lined shafts suffered little damage, while an unlined model gave 'severe shattering and movement'. The actual shafts were lined with cast iron, whose properties were thought to lie somewhere between the two conditions tested, and overall it was thought that 'the full-scale damage would be severe enough to cause the structure to be put out of action, provided the charges were placed in a position corresponding to that in the model tests'. Wallis reported these favourable findings to the Ministry, noting that Tallboy Large (which was again on order) would not be available before November, and suggesting that an 'attempt be made without waiting for the larger bomb' citing results of Tallboy hits on the U-boat pens;[98] he also had new information that the apron was no thicker than 12ft at any point. Their reply suggested that they had been planning on destroying the upper works of the lift, rather than the shafts, and were eager for more estimates of likely success against the target.[99]

Despite the favourable predictions, and some further correspondence discussing Rothensee in the archives, no final decision is recorded. It was located around 100 miles further east than any of the other German transportation targets, so it may be that the range was too great for a Lancaster carrying a Grand Slam, but it remains unclear why an attack was never actually carried out.

Post-war developments

As the Allies marched eastwards for Berlin, many of the earthquake bomb targets were overrun, allowing a detailed inspection to be made of the sites and the damage which had been inflicted on them.

The presence of the remaining structures[100] offered the opportunity for more scientific testing of the weapons on them. The first site selected was the blockhouse at Éperlecques. It had been hit on the edge of the roof by a Tallboy in July 1944, and repairs to this damage were already in hand when the site was captured two months later. The Americans decided to use it for tests of the Disney bombs,[101] two being dropped unsuccessfully in January 1945, with a further 18 in March. Of these, only two hits were made on the structure (described as 'excellent bombing accuracy' in an American report). A 'series of tests with Tallboy' was scheduled by the RAF, particularly to test case strength and explosive sensitivity,[102] and although HQ Bomber Command gave permission for the tests and preparations were made for them to start at the end of May[103] it appears that these tests never took place, presumably due to the end of the war in Europe.

The task of ongoing testing was assigned to 15 Squadron at RAF Mildenhall, under the codename Project Ruby, part of the larger show of strength codenamed Operation Front Line. At the end of May, 'C' Flight was formed, mainly from a nucleus of aircraft (five Lancaster B.1 Specials) and aircrew (44 officers and 20 NCOs) from 617 Squadron, with three new B.1s delivered directly to the squadron. Wg Cdr 'Jock' Calder, who had dropped the first Grand Slam with 617 Squadron, was in command.[104] Four American B-17s and three B-29s were based at Marham alongside 15 Squadron for participation in Ruby during 1946. The target selected for penetration testing was the *Valentin* U-boat factory at Farge, sand-filled bombs being used for the trials as the factory was close to housing. On 28 March one 15 Squadron aircraft went to Farge, but it missed; the Americans hit it with a Grand Slam on the same day. On 23 May two aircraft scored one direct hit, and on 29 June three aircraft scored two direct hits with Tallboys. Further tests were made (including with Disney bombs and a 1,650lb bomb which was intended as a trials model of a 12,000lb successor to Disney)[105] and the Farge trials were formally concluded on 31 August.[106] Explosive sensitivity trials took place in parallel at the Heligoland U-boat pens.[107]

Only the Amazon bombs (see below) were able to penetrate the 23ft-thick roof at Farge, most Tallboys breaking up due to the impact; some of the Amazon casings were able to be reused. The American welded bombs tended to fail at the circumferential weld holding on the rear casting, even when reinforced with extra internal welding, but were generally thought to be superior to the British cast bombs. Both British and American pistols were able to survive the impact.[108]

The Americans followed up Ruby with the Harken Project, dropping 35 25,000lb Samson and Amazon II bombs (see below) at Farge in 1947. The 'British Phase' of Harken was to test the strength and penetration qualities of 'the British 1,650lb model bomb' as used on Ruby, five hits being made on the roof with the 13 bombs supplied. These were dropped from B-29s and not by the RAF, and no Wallis-designed bombs were dropped during Harken.[109]

American developments

The Americans had taken a keen interest in the results of the Tallboy and Grand Slam attacks, but had initially favoured deployment of the 4,500lb Disney bomb to achieve greater penetration with rocket assistance rather than by gravity alone. However, by April 1945 the Large Bomb Mission was recommending that

Disney bombs not be used operationally if 12,000lb or 22,000lb bombs were available, due to the small warhead in the Disneys.

Work began on integrating Tallboys and Grand Slams with the Boeing B-29 Superfortress in late 1944, and the Tallboy installation was ready for testing in March 1945.[110] The required modifications were more extensive than those required in the Lancaster, due to the B-29's two-part bomb bay and mid-wing layout; raising the wing would have been too complicated, so the Tallboy was carried semi-recessed, protruding some 15in from the belly. This caused 4 per cent additional drag on the aircraft, rising to 10.5 per cent after dropping. An alternative layout also tested (and preferred for several reasons) used bombs carried externally on wing pylons between the fuselage and inner engines; with two Tallboys, the B-29's range was estimated at 2,100 miles, falling to 300 miles if two Grand Slams were carried. After early tests, an order for 50 modified B-29s was placed in the summer of 1945, but the end of the war led to cancellation, and it appears that as few as three aircraft were actually converted.[111] Grand Slams would not fit beneath a B-29 so, for loading, the bomb had to be placed in a hole and the aircraft rolled over the top.

The Americans used steel tails for their Tallboys 'to facilitate shipping and handling', this weighing an extra 75–100lb; the design was copied from a small number of British tail units shipped to the USA.[112] Plans to permit carriage by B-32 Dominator aircraft required Grand Slam tails to be shortened by 18in.

The Americans produced a different 22,000lb deep-penetration bomb, known as the Amazon (T-28). Similar in general layout and construction to the welded Grand Slams, it had a longer and narrower casing to improve target penetration. Four Amazon bombs were tested alongside Grand Slams during Project Ruby. Based on Ruby experience, the Americans produced revised casing shapes known as Amazon II (T-28E1), the longer and thinner Samson (T-28E2) and the T-28E4. These were all 25,000lb and were tested in the Harken trials in 1947.[113]

A 44,000lb version of the earthquake bomb (T-12) was also developed – this was tested using a B-29, but it was struggling to get off the ground with it (even with a light fuel load), although six were dropped in 1948. The T-12 would mainly have been carried by the giant Convair B-36, from which test drops were made in 1949.[114]

During the war, the Massachusetts Institute of Technology had been engaged in developing the 2,000lb Razon bomb, whose range and azimuth could be remotely controlled by the bombardier after dropping. The bomb was too light to be effective against massive targets, and in 1946 the control idea was transferred to a Tallboy-based bomb known as Tarzon, which used a standard Tallboy casing with the addition of a new radio-controlled octagonal tail (made by Bell Aircraft) and an annular fin around the casing. Three B-29s were modified to carry it, and it was used with limited success in Korea, mostly against bridges, from late 1950 to autumn 1951. Tarzon was the smallest of an intended family of Large Controlled Bombs for deep penetration, with ten different weights up to an incredible 100,000lb.[115]

Engineering studies were funded to examine the use of Tallboys and Grand Slams on the Northrop XB-35 and YB-49 flying wings. Although designed with eight bomb bays within the wing, none were large enough to take a Tallboy, but Northrop 'furnished a proposal of semi-external suspension for two 12,000lb bombs or two 22,000lb bombs';[116] however, control difficulties with the aircraft meant that it never entered service and so the configuration was not tested.

Back in Britain

Although the Tarzon appears to have been an American idea and developed without

Wallis's (or other British) involvement, there was some British interest in the concept of a guided bomb. MAP wrote to Wallis in February 1945 on the possibility of modifying Tallboy to allow lateral control during dropping, requesting that he investigate the possibilities.[117] Development of a Tallboy Mark III was in progress in the second half of 1945, but the ESC reported 'having serious difficulties in the casting'.[118] Penetration tests with models were continuing, with 2in models tested against armour plate at Shoeburyness in July 1947. 'Scalability trials' were also conducted 'to determine whether the results of dynamic impacts follow a linear law and, if not, what is the smallest size of model which may be used to forecast full-scale results', using a series of 2in, 6in, 12in and 18in trial rounds.[119] The shells were made at Elswick, and some stores were spun (at up to 4400rpm) for the tests. High-speed cameras operated by the RRL's expert were used to measure the deceleration of the stores as they passed through plate. There was also 'consideration of hollow-type charge fitted to nose of Tallboy-type bomb to improve penetrative performance, particularly against concrete targets' in which the Ministry was 'greatly interested'.[120]

The Avro Lincoln (follow-up design from the Lancaster) could and did carry Tallboys, but the later V-bombers had no requirement to do so (although they did have bomb bays big enough and the capacity to carry them). Some sources suggest that the Handley-Page Victor could carry a Grand Slam or two Tallboys, but there appears to be no evidence that it ever carried either bomb.

One remarkable footnote about the earthquake bombs is that it was the one major Wallis project that generated no patents at all. It may be that, technically, there was nothing novel in them – despite the special development work behind them, they were in essence just armour-piercing bombs of unprecedented size.

Summary – earthquake bombs

The wartime summary of Tallboy performance[121] concludes that its use is justified in any theatre where the number and importance of suitable targets justifies withdrawal of one or more squadrons from the Main Force to drop it, and that 'in Western Europe this policy has paid'. A broader, more modern view[122] says that, despite their cost, their ability to destroy targets that other weapons could not meant that 'some would say they were worth their weight in gold' and with certainty 'atom bombs apart, the Tallboy and Grand Slam were the most effective air-dropped weapons deployed' during the war.

If we consider his aircraft and bomb work as another experiment, and Wallis's desire to make a positive contribution to the war as his hypothesis, then he clearly proved it. He had not designed the greatest British bomber of the war, but he had designed the one made in the largest numbers. He had designed three new weapons which, while they were for specialist use, were used on important targets that could not be effectively attacked in any other way.

As the nation celebrated the victory to which Wallis had contributed more than most, and prepared to rebuild the shattered landscape, Wallis already had his eye set on the future – he wanted to fly faster than sound.

Chapter 8

Early Supersonics and Wild Goose

A student who can weave his technology into the fabric of society can claim to have a liberal education; a student who cannot weave his technology into the fabric of society cannot claim even to be a good technologist.
(Lord Ashby, Technology and the Academics, 1958)

To the sound barrier and beyond

By the end of the war, the idea of the 'sound barrier' had been clearly established. Aircraft that had approached the speed of sound (either deliberately or accidentally) had experienced severe shuddering and loss of control effectiveness. Some had been broken up by the vibration and lost, and this would continue to happen until 'compressibility' and its effects were better understood. Yet it was known that the barrier was not unbreakable – bullets and shells flew faster than sound, V-2 rockets had managed over Mach 2 at impact, and even Wallis's own 'earthquake bombs' had reached in excess of Mach 1 in their fall to Earth.[1]

The Germans were well advanced with supersonic aerodynamics, especially in the use of swept wings to delay the onset of compressibility, and this knowledge would be exploited after the war by the British, Americans and Russians, both from captured aircraft and from German scientists 'persuaded' to join a new team.

Meanwhile, changes were afoot at Vickers. Wallis had been discussing his post-war aspirations with Maj Hew Kilner, by now Managing Director, as early as 1944, and he met him on 27 January 1945 to finalise details of his appointment as Chief of Research and Design in a newly created Research & Development Department.[2] The R&D Department was to be independent of the main works (where Edwards was promoted to Chief Designer to work with Pierson as Chief Engineer), and had no specific terms of reference, allowing Wallis to pursue such projects as interested him – looking retrospectively from 1960, it was stated: 'The aim of this Department is, and always has been, to discover a form of aircraft that shall be capable of operating economically and, in the case of civil aircraft, properly, over still air ranges of 10,000nm.'[3]

This 'anomalous role' was also without 'any clarity in the relationship between Wallis and his colleagues at Weybridge, and in the looseness of the arrangement Wallis saw his advantage',[4] but although initially favourable to all parties, it would lead in time to him becoming somewhat isolated from the rest of the company. Vacating his wartime offices at Burhill Golf Club, Wallis and his team moved into 'The Paddock', the central buildings of the Brooklands racetrack, his new office being in the old clubhouse itself.[5] Key figures in his new department were 'old faces' from previous projects – Major Phil Teed was (in effect) his deputy, Norman Boorer his Chief Designer, Elsa Hoare his Chief Calculator (with her team of four mathematicians, all from Holloway College for women), Cecil Hayes and Alec Grant as General Manager of the department.

One legacy of the war was Wallis's attitude to test pilots. Shortly after the Dams Raid, he had told his elder son, 'I am never going to kill another pilot', which the latter understood not as a desire, but as a firm decision which informed Wallis's thinking regarding future piloted aircraft.[6] One reason for this was the radical change in design which Wallis was proposing: 'When I introduced the very revolutionary change in structural form brought about by putting the wings at the back and having no tail at all, I didn't want to kill pilots so we developed this method of making large flying models almost as big as a Spitfire and controlling them by radio.'[7] However, the very pilots whose lives he did not want to risk were actually opposed to the idea – Leonard Cheshire expressed his disagreement with Wallis's idea 'that you don't put a pilot in a new project if you possibly can avoid it . . . The Americans are quite different – they've got no hesitation in putting a pilot in, so you go ahead much faster. And pilots expect it. I mean, if you become a pilot, you accept a risk.'[8] Another disadvantage of the Wallis approach was the requirement for extra systems which a test pilot would have circumvented – telemetry, radio controls, launching trolleys and so on – which ideally would have been bought in, but as they were so specialised, R&D had to design, build and test all of these themselves, which inevitably added to the lead time. Today, when a radio-controlled model aircraft can be purchased for little more than pocket money prices, it is hard to appreciate that Wallis had to develop his own from scratch – admitting this in the 1960s he said, 'You know, it took longer to work out the radio control than it did to make the invention of the swing wing.'[9]

Locations associated with Wallis's early supersonic work. *(Author)*

The Miles M.52 and the Vickers Transonic Rocket

In Britain, the Ministry of Aircraft Production had commissioned a supersonic research aircraft as early as 1943 and (allegedly for reasons of secrecy) it was to be developed by the relatively small Miles Aircraft Limited, a company better known for its trainers and other light wooden aircraft.[10] The specification (E.24/43) called for a speed of 1,000mph at 36,000ft – ambitious, as the world speed record at the time was barely half this figure. The Miles M.52 was light (about 6,000lb) with short stub wings, and was to be powered by a Power Jets W.2/700 turbojet engine of 2,000lb thrust (later increased to 4,000lb with an early afterburner). The engine was located immediately behind the pilot with a long jetpipe to the rear of the aircraft, around which were annular fuel tanks. The pilot sat semi-reclined in the small nose cone (which could be detached in an emergency) in front of the annular engine intake. It had retractable undercarriage for standard take-off and landing, although its small laminar-flow wings would have meant a high approach speed. The thin wings and elevators were tested on a Miles M.3B trainer (first flown in August 1944) and found to be satisfactory for low-speed handling, the engine being tested in the rear of Wellington W5518/G. Wind tunnel tests were conducted using models, and a wooden cockpit mock-up created, before work commenced on the prototype alloy airframe itself.

Work was well advanced on the prototype, and test pilots lined up for the test programme (including Eric 'Winkle' Brown) when, in February 1946, the aircraft was cancelled, a decision made by Benjamin Lockspeiser, Director General of Scientific Research at the Ministry of Aircraft Production. A number of factors contributed to this decision, one being Wallis's presence at the meeting when the aircraft's fate was decided, and his strong opinion that radical new designs should first be tested using radio-controlled models in order not to endanger the lives of test pilots.[11] However, Sweetman[12] says that the programme was in trouble as early as late 1943, and that the RAE had concluded by July 1944 that the M.52 could not reach supersonic speed in level flight, and that further work would be unable to overcome the difficulties. Whatever the reasons for it, the cancellation continues to attract criticism, as do the circumstances in which it was made, and also the decision to subsequently pass technical details of the aircraft on to the Americans;[13] although Derek Wood[14] lays the main blame on Lockspeiser himself, Reginald Turnill[15] accuses Wallis of losing Britain the supersonic race by his influence on the decision.

Miles suggested converting the near-complete M.52 airframe into an unmanned rocket aircraft (using a Walther motor taken from a captured Me.163 Komet), and dropping this from a Lancaster, but the

A Vickers Transonic Rocket shortly after release from the carrier Mosquito. This achieved Mach 1.38 in October 1948, but Wallis's input to the project is unclear. *(BAE SYSTEMS via Brooklands Museum)*

Ministry was not keen on this plan, perhaps because of the known volatile properties of the fuel used. Instead, a £500,000 contract was awarded to Vickers for a test programme based around 24 models.[16] The first six of these were effectively one-third scale models of the M.52, while later ones would have trialled various swept wing forms (one effect of the acquisition of the German aerodynamics work was that the British actually slowed down their own research to evaluate and assimilate the German work, including swept wing).[17] The date of the decision to use models is unclear – Brown places the decision *after* the cancellation of the M.52,[18] but in the same journal, D.S. Bancroft (Chief Aerodynamicist at Miles) states that the model contract was placed a few months *before* the cancellation.[19]

The models were powered by 'hot' hydrogen peroxide rockets[20] developed at the RAE (which also did the telemetry) and were designed to be expendable, hence requiring no landing gear. Instead, they were to be dropped from a converted Mosquito Mk XVI (PF604), after which they were controlled by radio. The Transonic Rocket programme, known as Operation Neptune, operated from St Eval in Cornwall, launches taking place heading west out into the Atlantic, and a ground station was set up in the Scilly Isles to receive the telemetry data from the aircraft. The first flight did not take place until 30 May 1947 when bad weather caused the Mosquito to lose control and the model was torn away during the recovery. On the second flight in October, the rocket did not ignite properly, and over the next year a further five (wingless) models were expended in trying to get the RAE rocket to perform satisfactorily.

On 10 October 1948 (almost a year after Chuck Yeager's first supersonic flight), the third TR was launched successfully, the rocket firing six seconds after dropping, and propelling the model to 930mph (Mach 1.38) in level flight. The only failure was that the nose-down command at the end of the trial appeared not to function, and the aircraft flew on until contact was lost some 70 miles distant. Despite this success, no further test flights were made.[21]

While Wallis and his fledgling Research & Development Department definitely worked on this project,[22] it is unclear how much effort Wallis himself put into it as, remarkably, there is no direct reference to it whatsoever in his archived scientific papers (even retrospectively in the context of later projects), nor is it mentioned in either of his biographies.

Fundamentals of Supersonic Flight

A review of the supersonic prototypes in development around the world in the 1940s and 1950s shows 'numerous varieties' of aircraft designs, which illustrate the fact that there was 'no common agreement among aircraft designers' at the time regarding the fundamental principles underlying the problem of supersonic flight, nor about the best solution to it.

Reviewing this situation in 1958,[23] Wallis proceeded to 'examine with anxious care' a series of seven important characteristics of supersonic aircraft and thence to discuss (with around a page devoted to each) how the desirable values of these characteristics relate to derived properties such as range, speed, rate of climb, ceiling, manoeuvrability, payload and take-off performance. In conclusion, he summarises these features for four areas of performance, as shown in Table 8.1.

Due to the 'contradictory conditions' apparent from the table, he notes that 'no conventional aircraft' can possibly be designed to meet them all – thus the ultimate requirement becomes one for an aircraft with low AUW, low wing loading, low stalling speed, low thickness chord ratio, but with *variable span* (and hence aspect ratio and L/D ratio). Boldly, he states that 'we arrive at the inescapable conclusion that the only possible solution lies in an aircraft of variable geometry' with 'no alternative interpretation... possible'.

Further theory in support of variable geometry (VG) is given in a 1953 paper[24] in which he notes that (in subsonic flight) increasing the span is the most effective way of reducing L/D, followed by thickness/chord (which should not be less than 10–12 per cent) with a rounded leading edge, but in supersonic flight the span and frontal area should be small, thickness/chord not exceeding 2–3 per cent with a sharp leading edge; wing area can also be smaller, as the fuselage itself generates lift (though this is negligible at subsonic speeds). His argument is that these conflicting requirements mean that if supersonic flight is not to be abandoned, then VG *must* be embraced (as sweepback effectively alters the leading edge sharpness, decreases the span and increases the chord).

The wing-controlled aerodyne

Even prior to his involvement in the rocket project, Wallis (in common with most other aircraft designers at this time), recognised that supersonics was the way ahead, and his ideas for the future of aircraft were enshrined in the wing-controlled aerodyne (WCA) in 1944. He discussed the concept with Sir Wilfred Freeman[25] at the MAP and, as he had with the earthquake bombs, Freeman encouraged him to develop the ideas further. They were fully set out in his longest (and most mathematical) paper – 'The Application of the Aerodynamic Properties of Three-dimensional Bodies to the Stabilization and Control of Aerodynes' completed in 1947,[26] although the first patent application relating to the work was submitted as early as March 1945.[27]

In the introduction, he noted the incremental nature of aircraft development over the previous 40 years and that the early open frameworks had become closed in... and while this was done for streamlining reasons, it incidentally meant that fuselages had become solid bodies and thus possessed many of the aerodynamic properties of an airship. However, the success of aeroplanes had meant that 'the knowledge and experience gained in the design of airships has not been used' in their ongoing development, and the belief that a tail was indispensable for control and stable flight had become firmly established.

Thus, although airship designers were familiar with the aerodynamic forces produced by solid bodies in flight, and their effects on stability and control were well known (though only partially understood), there had been little crossover of this

	Long range & Supersonic Speed	High ceiling & Rate of Climb	Manoeuvrability	Take-off & Landing
Lift/Drag	High (9–10+)	Low	Low	Low
Thrust/Weight	Low	High	High	High
Sweep	Large	N/A	N/A	N/A
Thickness/Chord	Low	N/A	N/A	N/A
Wing Loading	Low	Low	Low	N/A*
Aspect ratio	Small	Large	N/A	Large
Span	Small	N/A	N/A	Large
Stall speed	N/A	N/A	Low	Low
All up weight	N/A	N/A	N/A	Low

* although not mentioned explicitly in this paper, low wing loading is usually also correlated with short take-off performance
In addition, *all wetted surfaces* to generate lift.

Table 8.1: Ideal characteristics for supersonic aircraft.

knowledge into aeroplane design (the first RAeS paper in this area not being until 1936) and one of the effects of the collapse of airship building programmes had been a 'cessation of interest in work upon the motion of solids in real fluids'. Wallis had the knowledge, however, that an icthyoid body, even in its simplest form, had the property of producing powerful *moments* at small angles of incidence with the unusual but most valuable characteristic that these moments did not produce large resultant *forces* in any direction. He also knew that conventional aeroplane forms were not well adapted aerodynamically for speeds approaching the speed of sound, either in wing or tail form.

His conclusion was, therefore, that 'the time is right for a big change in the anatomy of aircraft', the way forward being 'in the application of the aerodynamic characteristics of solids to the stabilisation and control of aerodynes[28] with an accompanying revolutionary change in anatomy and technique'. This was a proposal which his paper demonstrated was practicable and would additionally remove some of the aerodynamic difficulties being faced, such as coping with the change in the CP position as the aircraft passed through the transonic region.[29]

The shape which arose from his investigations consisted of only three parts – a body and two wings, with the wings able to be moved relative to the body (in incidence and azimuth), this movement being used to both control and stabilise the body – he thus referred to this as a wing-controlled aerodyne. The basic principle is described in the patent document:

> *The body . . . is mounted on the wing in such a position that the centre of gravity of the aircraft is located forward of the centre of pressure of the wing, and means are provided whereby the pitching . . . moments developed on the body by air pressures due to small disturbances in pitch . . . are counteracted by pitching . . . moments due to the wing of opposite sign and of such magnitude as to give the requisite stability to the aircraft in normal flight, such means being adjustable for the purpose of giving control.*[30]

The basic shape, though simple, was thus inherently stable, and offered a number of other stability advantages – for example, he showed that dihedral, while helpful for manoeuvrability, could also lead to directional instability such as 'Dutch rolling',[31] but on a WCA, the dihedral and directional stability were directly coupled so that it was naturally stable. In the standard (and delta) aircraft planforms, there was a positive pressure forward on the top of the fuselage and a negative pressure below and to the rear of the fuselage, giving a tendency for fore and aft instability. He demonstrated that, when the wings were placed at the back of the fuselage, the positive pressure area on the top of the wing and the negative pressure area under the rear end of the fuselage cancelled themselves out because they were one above the other.

He recognised that although 'the classic stability equations are perfectly general and may be applied to any rigid flying body', it was only practical to calculate performance at a finite number of wing positions, extrapolating where necessary for positions in between. The remainder of the aerodynes paper is devoted to proofs of the aerodynamics.

The aerodyne concept relied on three key ideas – variable wing sweep, tailless design and laminar flow:

Variable wing sweep[32]

It was already known that swept wings were advantageous for transonic flight (as the sweep delayed the onset of the compressibility effect which gave the control

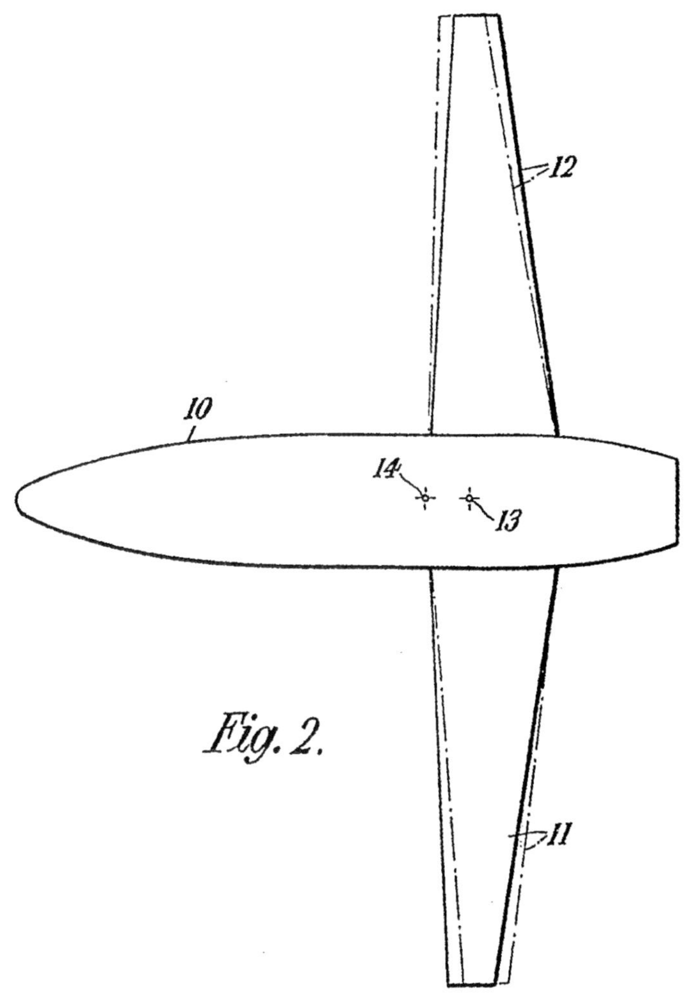

The basic layout of Wild Goose – just a body and two wings with independent variable sweep (Patent GB595464). *(BAE SYSTEMS)*

problems during early flights into this region), and so Wallis wished to use a high angle of sweep. While good for high-speed flight, highly swept wings are problematic at low speeds, giving rise to control instability in the crucial landing and take-off phases. Wallis's ingenious solution was to introduce wings with variable sweep (now generally referred to as variable geometry) – that is, they would be unswept for take-off, but could be swept back for supersonic flight, before being swept forward again for landing.[33] This would give an unprecedented speed range, i.e. the ratio of landing speed to maximum speed: 'Conventional aircraft have a ratio of high speed to low speed of about 3.5; the [aerodyne] would have a ratio of about 10 or 12, which means that we can attain a Mach number of about 2 in combination with a landing speed of about 100mph.'[34] He also noted that a swept forward wing flexes on take-off in such a way as to increase the angle of incidence, enabling the aircraft to take off sooner (and conversely a swept back wing loses incidence when taking off) – another reason for having unswept wings at take-off.[35]

A fundamental problem with variable-geometry wings is that, as the wings are swept, the centre of lift/centre of pressure (CP) moves aft with the wings, while (because the wings are relatively light) the aircraft's centre of gravity (CG) moves aft only slightly. As an aircraft's stability depends crucially on the relationship between these two points, the wing sweeping motion can thus lead to control instability, and the ideal situation – that the pilot would not have to make any control inputs as the wing position was altered – is difficult to achieve. Wallis not only had a solution to this problem, but wanted his aircraft to be inherently stable throughout the sweep range, with no control action required from the pilot.

Tailless design

As conventional aircraft increased in size and adopted multi-engine installations, the additional control forces required led to a corresponding increase in tail sizes. However, tail drag may be as much as 20 per cent of an aircraft's profile drag and the weight of the tail is typically 3–5 per cent of the AUW of the aeroplane, yet it produces no useful lift, its function being solely control and stability. Wallis thus proposed to completely delete the tail from the aircraft, the control solution being in his variable-sweep wings. He proposed using differential operation of the VG wings, swinging the wings *together* for pitch control, and *independently* for roll control (one wing being advanced (thus generating slightly more lift), the other moved backward (generating slightly less), the aircraft hence rolling away from the advanced wing.

It is notable that conventional wing control

surfaces (ailerons for roll and flaps for additional lift during take-off and landing) were also to be deleted, *all* lift and control being derived through wing movement alone. This simplified the structure and made the wings lighter, resulting in less movement of the CG as the wing sweep angle was altered.

There were other contemporary tailless designs, such as the Northrop XB-35/YF-49, the Armstrong-Whitworth AW.52 and various Horten designs from Germany, but these were also attempting to be fuselage-less designs, with everything contained within the wing, which created their own control and stabilisation difficulties.

Laminar flow

The aerodyne's fuselage shape was driven by the desire to achieve laminar flow over the length of the body. Ideal flow over a surface (such as an aircraft wing) is laminar (i.e. layered), with successive layers of air moving smoothly past each other and the surface; the air behind the aircraft is thus left undisturbed by the passage of the aircraft, and the only drag encountered by the aircraft is that necessary to part the air enough to let the aircraft slip through and the friction drag over the 'wetted' surface. In practice, the drag on the layer closest to the surface causes it to break away from the surface and become turbulent (aided by the reduced pressure over the wing caused by the aerofoil, and by any discontinuities in the surface). The cost to the aircraft of creating this turbulent wake is an additional induced drag component (earlier onset of turbulent flow means greater drag), and it was this component which Wallis sought to remove by maintaining laminar flow over more of, or preferably the whole, aircraft surface (wings and fuselage). Laminar flow research was ongoing at the RAE and other aircraft companies, including Folland and Handley-Page, and continued over the following decade or so.[36]

Wallis found in a 'brilliant' 1928 paper by Professor Melville Jones[37] such 'scientific insight into the fundamental nature of the [low-drag] problem' that it 'would be hard to equal'.[38] His suggestions for delaying the onset of turbulent flow included maintaining a falling pressure gradient as far aft over the surface as possible – practically, this meant that the body needed to fatten slowly from the bow to a maximum diameter near the stern, with the thickest section at about 60 per cent chord rather than the 25 per cent chord of a conventional aerofoil.[39] Jones also suggested sucking the boundary layer into the surface, at the point just before the turbulence began, to further delay the onset – this 'boundary layer control' thus reduces drag, but the suction process itself requires energy so is not without cost.

Heyday – the low-drag torpedo

Wallis realised that, in developing the ideal shape for a body for high-speed flight, the work would be equally applicable to bodies travelling through water, and as early as August 1945 had the approval of senior management to develop marine applications[40] – Sir Frederick Yapp, Chairman of Vickers-Armstrongs, forming a Torpedo Sub-Committee consisting of representatives from Barrow, the Whitehead Torpedo Works and Vickers Armaments Technical Department, with Wallis as Chairman.[41] Wallis consulted right away with two academics at Cambridge on underwater turbulence at sea (on which no data was available), laminar flow, boundary layer control and effects of marine growth.[42] The low-drag torpedo was given the codename Heyday.

A model of the Heyday torpedo. To sustain laminar flow as long as possible the fattest part of the body is more than halfway along its length. *(© Brooklands Museum)*

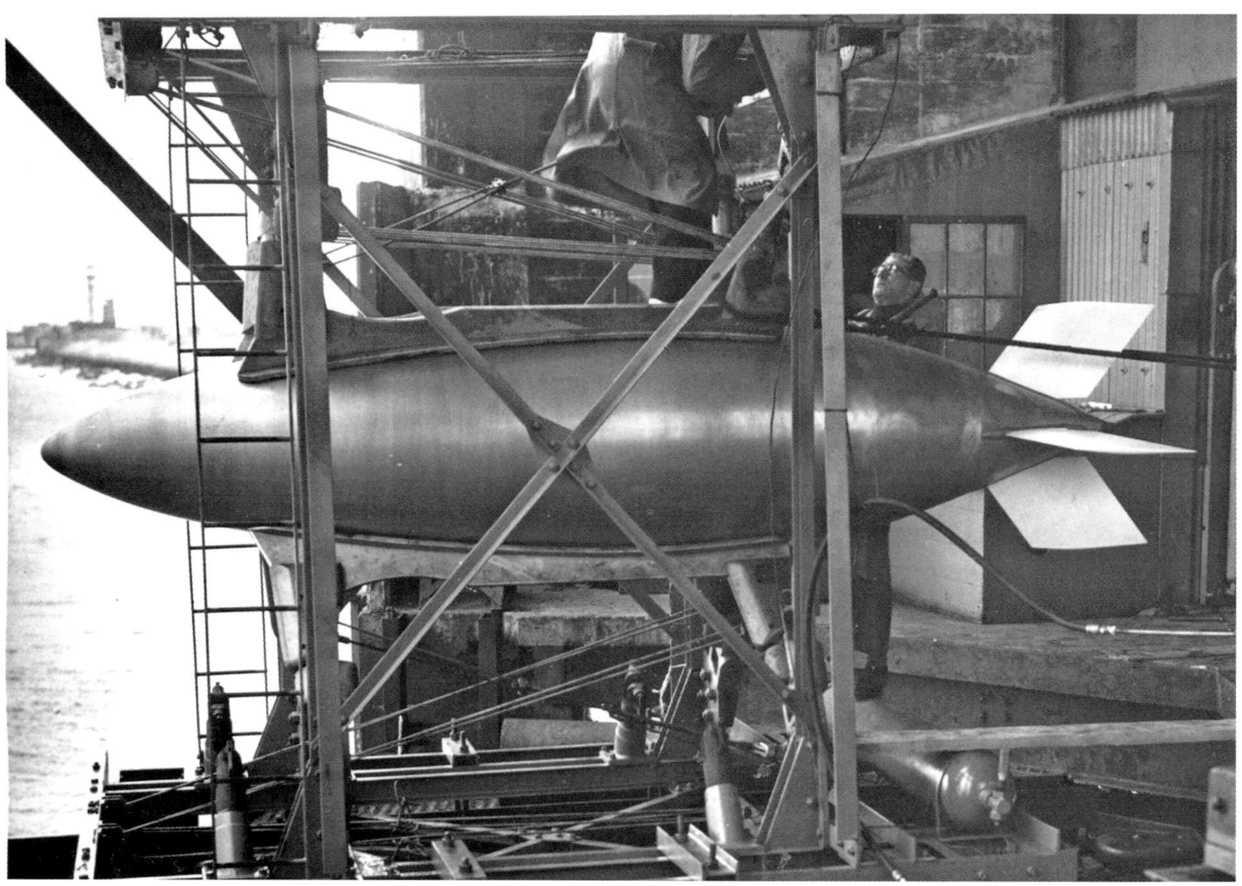

The full-size Heyday in its handling cradle at Weymouth. *(BAE SYSTEMS via Brooklands Museum)*

Compared to a standard torpedo (which has turbulent flow over nearly its full length), it was estimated that a torpedo of the same displacement (3,000lb), with the icthyoid shape and laminar flow over its full length, would experience only 6.5 per cent of the frictional resistance, meaning a potential tripling of top speed to 100kt and with that, a tripling of range – an attractive prospect indeed. A potential problem was the new shape, which would be shorter than existing torpedoes, but fatter (though still circular in section). However, early consultation with the Admiralty suggested that neither change 'within reason', nor even a modest increase in weight, would be a problem for the Navy.

Research on some detailed questions remained – including refining the shape (especially the part aft of maximum diameter, and its interaction with an engine tailpipe) and the degree of smoothness required from the surface of the body. The two critical factors were the Reynolds number (which 'determines the behaviour of the fluid in its passage over the model') and the realistic nature of the turbulence encountered in the fluid. Wallis realised that together these practically ruled out water tunnel or water tank experiments, requiring the use of free-running self-propelled models in the open sea.

Initially some basic water tank experimentation was done at the William Froude Tank at the NPL (site of the 'bouncing bomb' experiments). This used a half-scale test body (with only moderately smooth surface finish) on a tail-mounted spike, attached to a moving carriage. Pressure measurements were taken at 78 points in a plane over the upper and lower surfaces of the body, employing specially devised apparatus consisting of manometers and dye extrusion. The sediment in the tank proved problematic, clogging the small holes used for measurement, and only one good set of data was recorded – this suggested that laminar flow was being achieved over about 50 per cent of the length, which was deemed very promising. Further tank work was undertaken to record lift, drag and pitching moments to assist with the design of the control surfaces to be used on the sea-going model, and launching gear for the model was built. Heyday's fins were pivoted on a single hinge, such that the fin rotation varied according to the angle made with the stream, hence maintaining stable control.

To prevent early initiation of turbulent flow, an outer casing with a high surface finish was needed – under 1/1000in variation per 3in length[43] – and together with the curvilinear shape, this posed a considerable machining challenge; thin castings in light alloy were seen as the best way to produce these. Messrs J. Stone & Co. were approached to manufacture them, and following some preliminary tests, declared themselves able to produce the required castings by the end of 1947. Admiralty interest remained high, and a research contract with Vickers-Armstrongs was signed in April 1948, producing a firm contract with Stone's in June, the first castings being delivered to Vickers at Elswick in January 1949 for machining.

Despite all these preparations, and encouraging preliminary results from the aerodynamic work, the experiments conducted in Weymouth Bay during 1951 showed that laminar flow could only be achieved over 28 per cent of the torpedo at best, and although Heyday exhibited less drag than a standard 21in torpedo, it was not by a significant amount.[44] Adding suction to pull in the boundary layer to delay the onset of turbulent flow was shown, by calculation, not to offer a practical solution in this case, as it would take too much power. The Americans also experimented with the possibilities of boundary layer control, on their research submarine USS *Albacore*, but achieved disappointing results.

Green Lizard – missile with variable wing sweep

While Heyday and its development did give some valuable information on laminar flow, the project can also be seen as Wallis hedging his bets with a naval application of his aeronautical ideas. A second project which fulfilled a similar double purpose was Wallis's idea for an early surface-to-air guided missile,[45] given the codename Green Lizard.[46] The aim was interception of incoming Soviet bombers, Air Staff requirements suggesting a capability of launching 2,000 weapons within a 15-minute window.[47] However, missile systems were still embryonic, with matters of propulsion, guidance and homing still not resolved.

The Wallis contribution to the solution was to simplify the launch requirements by using a cordite charge to fire the missile from a large tube (the tube gun being

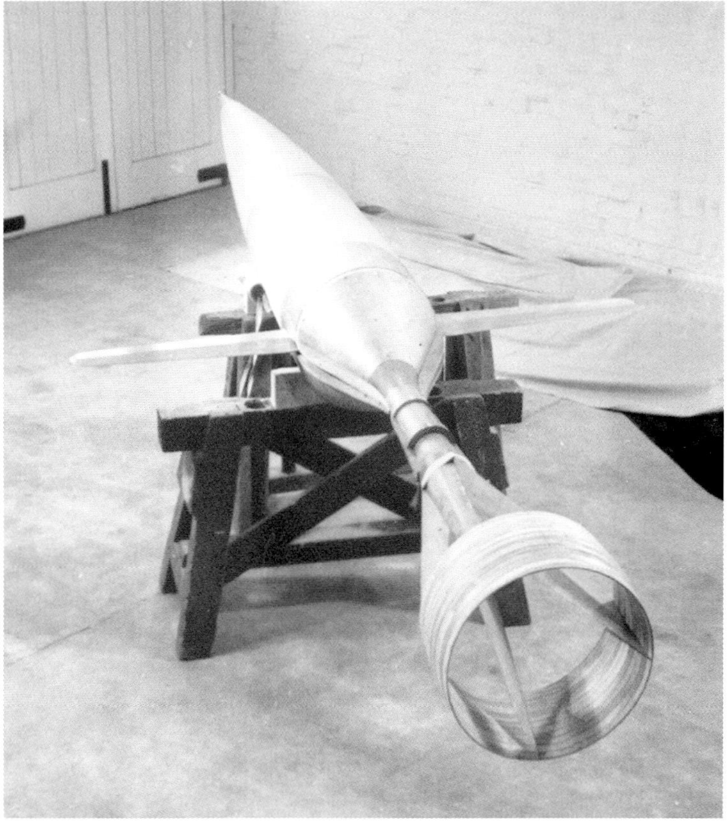

Prototype Green Lizard missile. After emerging from the launch tube, the wings would fold out to the position shown, and the 'tail' obturator would fall away. *(BAE SYSTEMS via Brooklands Museum)*

in a ground installation[48] or on a mobile launch vehicle) and to add variable-sweep wings to the missile in order to extend its range. Gun launching offered advantages 'of economy of propellant, of avoiding the difficulty of jettisoning boosts over friendly country, and of allowing the missile to be more readily handled in the feeding and loading stages' against the 'problems of having a long and heavy gun which could be trained and elevated, or of designing guided weapons capable of withstanding very high firing accelerations'.[49]

The main function of Green Lizard's variable wing sweep was to allow the wings to be folded flush into the sides of the missile for launching, flipping out to a straight attitude on clearing the launch tube in order to increase the range compared to a wingless missile,[50] though they were also to be used for directional control. The missile was built around a central tubular spine transmitting the launching impulse from an 'obturator' in the tail, annular fuel tanks and warhead being disposed around this spine;[51] propulsion was by a turbojet with (in the original version) air intakes formed in the gap between a circular rear body and elliptical forward body.[52] Laminar flow was not assumed in the performance calculations. Terminal guidance would have been by radar, a proximity fuze detonating the warhead.[53]

Later drawings show two interchangeable versions:[54] 'Type A' with four separate retractable air intakes around the rear fuselage feeding a rear-mounted turbojet, and 'Type B' with an annular intake in the nose feeding the engine which exhausts via a long central jetpipe extending to the rear.[55] In these versions the explosive warhead was replaced by an annulus of 91lb grenades.[56] Shortly before reaching the target, the missile would have started a 'violent rolling action' before releasing the grenades by centrifugal force to form a lethal cone whereby the 'probability of a hit can be substantially

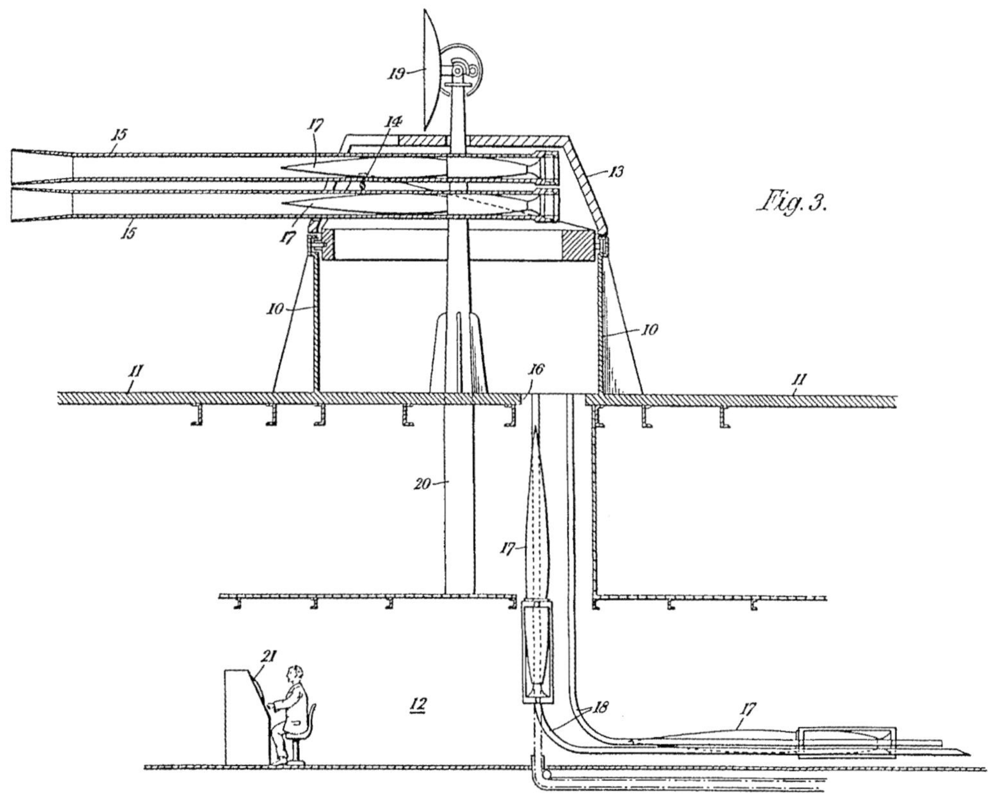

A proposed gun emplacement to fire Green Lizard missiles *(Patent GB692140). (BAE SYSTEMS)*

enhanced'.[57] The warhead release mechanism was tested satisfactorily over a sandpit[58] and tests with different types of explosives were also conducted.[59]

The prototype gun was 32ft long (later 48ft) and fabricated at Elswick, being trained by means of lowering the rear end into a pit to an angle of up to 30 degrees. A series of 48 test firings of 256lb and 500lb dummy missiles took place at the Ridsdale range in Northumberland between July 1950 and May 1952,[60] achieving muzzle velocities of up to 1267fps (860mph, about Mach 1.1). This was slightly less than the Mach 1.3 predicted and which it was hoped would give useful data on the design of the air intakes.[61] Wallis had been in discussion with Dr A.A. Griffith at Rolls-Royce regarding the turbojet engine, and it was the design of the intakes which appeared to concern them most (although the engine itself was not ready before the termination of the project).[62] Photos show a Green Lizard model on the rail trolley (see below) at Weybridge, and it was planned to launch it when the turbojet installation was ready, but there is no record of it actually having been tested on the trolley; it appears that planned supersonic firings at Larkhill did not take place either. Further Ministry funding of £140,000 was awarded in April 1952 for the project which should 'concentrate . . . on developing gun launching as an alternative to boost launching', but by August support for gun launching had evaporated, although funding for the 'variable sweepback concept . . . in aid of both aircraft and guided missiles' was to be continued.[63] Support for variable sweep on guided missiles was also withdrawn shortly thereafter,[64] and the project was cancelled altogether in September 1952,[65] together with the competing Green Water interceptor.

While the Heyday project did not generate any patentable material, Green Lizard made up for this with a total of at least nine – covering the basic layout of the missile, operation of the wings, the launcher and the warhead itself.

Variable geometry in the US

The Americans had experimented with variable sweep as early as 1946, performing wind tunnel tests with a model of a modified Bell X-1 with sweep angles between 0 and 45 degrees – these tests 'left little doubt that sweep variation about a fixed pivot located within the fuselage is not acceptable'.[66] There was interest in the Messerschmitt P.1101, a captured prototype of a swept-wing fighter, which allowed its wing sweep to be varied (on the ground) between 35 and 45 degrees for aerodynamic research purposes. The Bell X-5 was a copy of the P.1101 layout, with the added ability to vary sweep *in flight* between 20 and 60 degrees. The wing pivot was mounted on a rail and, as the wings were swept, the whole wing assembly was translated forward inside the fuselage, hence attempting to keep the CP forward and maintain aerodynamic balance throughout the sweep range. This was a heavy and mechanically complicated solution, and took up substantial space inside the fuselage. The X-5 also exhibited 'vicious spinning tendencies', which led to the loss of one of the two aircraft and its pilot in October 1953.[67]

A similar wing mechanism was used in the Grumman X10F Jaguar naval fighter, although development problems (mostly associated with the engine) plagued the project, which was cancelled in April 1953 – the introduction of the steam catapult and the angled flight deck had also reduced the margin of advantage offered by a variable-sweep aircraft. So, as far as the Americans were concerned, variable wing sweep was a dead end by the early 50s.

Wild Goose

Heyday and Green Lizard were supporting acts for the main player in the Wallis ensemble, the wing-controlled aerodyne. Wallis saw this as the key to the development

Early experiments with the wing-controlled aerodyne were made at Brooklands using models. This model is ready for launch on the catapult used for the bouncing bomb tests. *(BAE SYSTEMS via The Flambards Experience)*

of his long-term goal, a long-range supersonic airliner, but development funding was only available from military sources, and so the latter had to be emphasised. However, the volume and weight of the wing pivot mechanism is far more significant in a military aircraft than in a large airliner, and so offered less advantage in the military application; this catch-22 was to bedevil his variable-sweep work for years to come.

In support of the civil side, Wg Cdr F.W. Winterbotham[68] arranged for Wallis to spend a couple of weeks in the summer of 1948 with the flamboyant American motor racing driver turned RAF fighter pilot Whitney Straight, who was by then the Chairman of BOAC. During the meeting, in the tranquil surroundings of Taormina, Sicily, Wallis laid out all the advantages of his vision for civil aviation, and although Straight was an eager listener to his ideas, no financial support was forthcoming.[69]

As already seen, the laminar flow fuselage meant that the fattest part of the fuselage was towards the rear. For reasons of aerodynamics, weight distribution and to leave the forward fuselage clean to help the laminar flow, the wings were positioned further aft also. This gave rise to a rather unconventional planform for an aircraft, but one familiar in nature – that of a goose – so the new Wallis concept aircraft was christened Wild Goose. The fuselage was

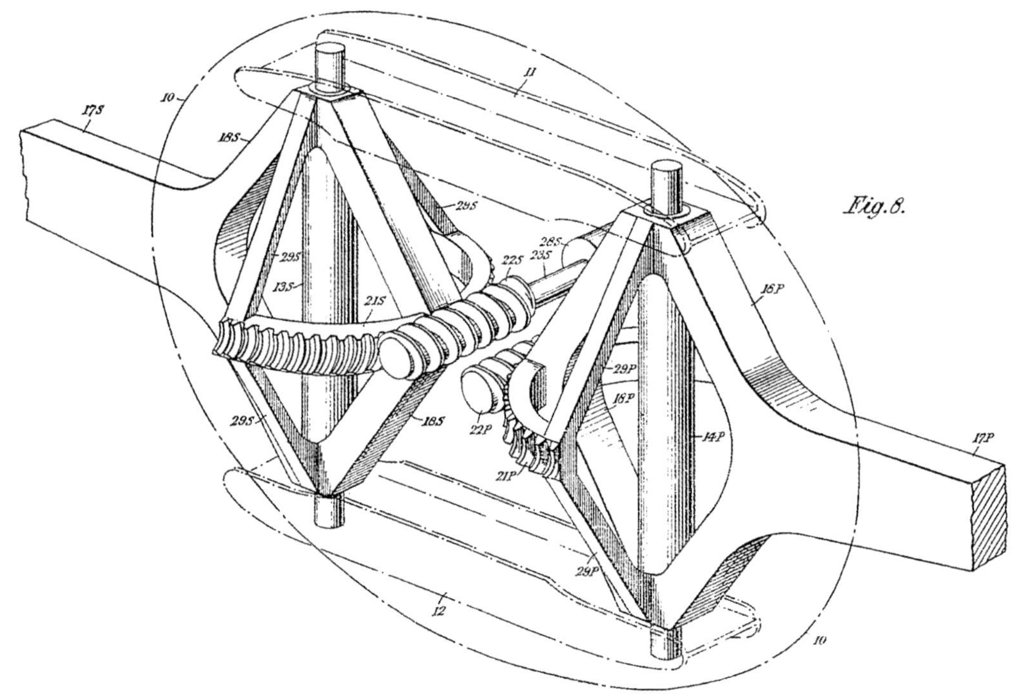

The basic Wild Goose wing pivot (Patent GB741719). *(BAE SYSTEMS)*

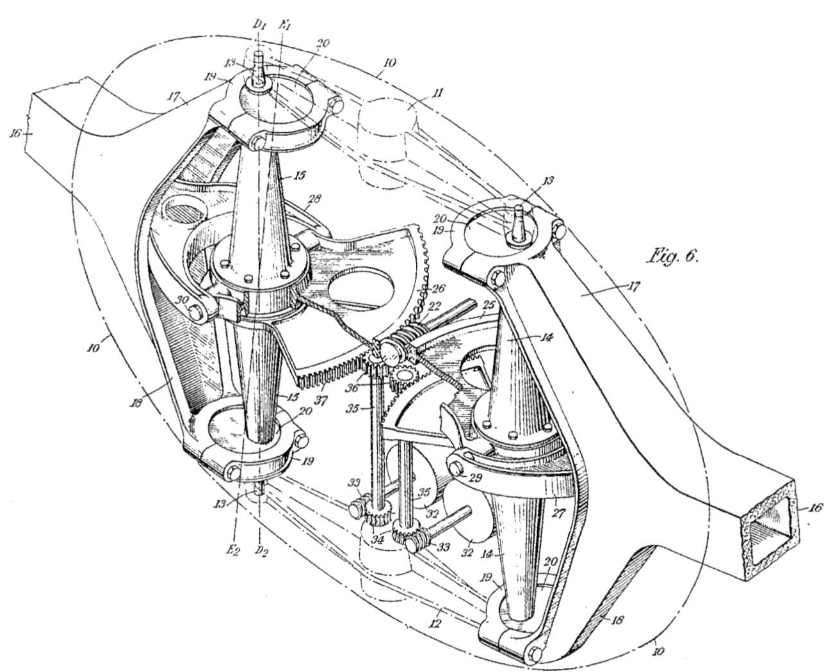

The improved Wild Goose wing pivot with variable dihedral (Patent GB756019). *(BAE SYSTEMS)*

flattened slightly to enhance the pitching moment (which was four times as large as the yawing moment), and the aim was to 'balance the body pitching moment and control the aircraft only by moving wings'.[70]

Wallis worked on the details of his design throughout 1945 and 1946, and his aerodynes report was well received by his wartime associates Lockspeiser and Tizard at the Ministry of Supply, and funds were made available for experimental work.[71] To prove that the radical Wild Goose shape and its variable geometry were practical, Wallis built a series of small wooden model aircraft, and these were flown at Brooklands from 1947.[72] Some were hand- or catapult-launched,[73] others had rubber-powered propellers at the rear of the fuselage. Some had adjustable wings, and some had wings that could be set to change their geometry in flight, even sweeping right back parallel with the fuselage.[74]

A tilting wind tunnel was also built in the Jackson Shed at Brooklands, the model flying free (apart from a light cable carrying control instructions), with the tunnel being tilted nose-down to give the effect of powered flight – 'when the wind speed and angle are correct, the model stays stationary in space'.[75] The model was controlled from beneath by a pilot using a conventional control yolk, his head stuck up into a perspex bubble in the floor of the tunnel allowing him to fly the model from a 'chase' position. Conventional wind tunnel tests were also done, including a series at the NPL in the latter half of 1949;[76] one surviving film[77] shows Wild Goose on a gimbal support, hanging under its own weight with the airflow off (as the CG was above the support), then when the airflow is started, it immediately assumes a stable flight position.

From these calculations emerged the detailed design of the 'full size' Wild Goose model[78] which, following the Wallis doctrine of not risking test pilots, was to be controlled via radio by a pilot on the ground, the model size being 'determined by choosing the smallest aircraft in which it is possible to install the necessary radio apparatus for pilotless testing'.[79] It consisted of an icthyoid fuselage fabricated from steel tubing, covered by a removable 'aeroshell' made largely from balsa wood. The wings (fabricated from balsa

Detail of the Wild Goose wing pivot and wheel. Note the bolt for holding different dihedral angles (centre). *(BAE SYSTEMS via Brooklands Museum)*

plywood) were positioned at approximately the widest part of the fuselage, each on a separate vertical pivot placed within the fuselage, but mounted on the pivot with a dihedral[80] – the dihedral had the effect of additionally changing the incidence of the wing as it was swept.[81] Some models also had modified pivots which used eccentrics within the pivot mechanism[82] to allow the dihedral to be varied independently of the sweep.[83] The control signals (which were recorded on a rolling chart at Wallis's insistence) operated two rack-driven commutators working both in the same direction for pitch control and in opposite direction for lateral control. It was decided to retain a vertical stabiliser on the models initially, although this was a fixed fin with no rudder. Power was by one or two throttleable 'cold' rocket motors of Wallis's own design – compressed air forced high-test peroxide (HTP) at 350–500psi over a silver gauze catalyst which broke down the peroxide, generating high-pressure steam which provided the thrust via a Venturi nozzle.[84] The aircraft were fitted with a semi-recessed sprung main landing wheel between the wings, with a skid further forward. Another practical requirement was 'the development of an "infallible" servo-motor system' which had to be developed alongside the other systems.[85]

In order to achieve flying speed, Wallis proposed to mount the model on a trolley, and this emerged, following experiments with pram wheels and wind tunnel models,[86] as a vehicle with four (faired) wheels and the model mounted on a vertical spigot whose height and incidence could be varied. The model was free to pivot on top of this, so that it would always be facing into wind, even if the trolley was not. The model was attached via a conventional bombslip, which was released to launch the model; originally, this was going to be within the model, but it was fitted instead on to the trolley. Like Wild Goose itself, the trolley was rocket-propelled and radio-controlled.

Preliminary trials of the completed aerodyne and trolley were conducted at Brooklands in the first ten days of June 1949.[87] These consisted of static tests of the propulsion systems of both aerodyne and trolley, free runs of the trolley to test its radio control, steering and braking systems, and free runs of both together; satisfactory performance of all aspects was demonstrated.

Wild Goose tests at Thurleigh

The location chosen for the full test programme was the runway at the former RAF Thurleigh[88] and the Wild Goose models tested there acquired the name 'Thurleighdyne'. A total of 12 were built.[89] The launching trolley was ferried to Thurleigh by road on 22 June, the runway was marked out,[90] and a control tower erected on a Queen Mary trailer.[91] Three runs were made before the end of the month, and the first incident took place on 25 July when the brakes failed to function, and the trolley was damaged when it hit a tree. Twenty-six runs had been made by 8 September, including two with a release of the model – both of which resulted in an immediate stall and a broken model.[92] This was attributed to turbulence around the trolley, and led Wallis to develop the 'jump-start' technique, in which the take-off was effected entirely automatically at a 'pre-determined value of lift force, thus enabling the aircraft itself to decide the instant at which it will leave the trolley'.[93] When released, the model then leapt upwards, quickly clearing the disturbed air around the trolley.[94] The mechanics of the attachment was the subject of a patent.[95]

Through the cold winter, Wallis went every week to Thurleigh, living in a hut alongside the airfield and typically working 17-hour days. A locked-on run was made on 17 January 1950, the trolley planned to accelerate to 90mph then slow again; however, the speed continued to rise to 120mph, any disappointment in the misbehaviour of the trolley being outweighed by the fact that the trolley instruments had recorded a lifting force on the model of three times its weight.[96] On a second run two days later, the trolley rockets burned out too soon. Another attempt with more fuel was successful, and in the afternoon, they tried a release with Wild Goose unpowered. The jump-start worked perfectly, and the plane climbed smoothly before being levelled out by the pilot (Alan Nash) at 50ft, followed by a crash into the ground. The control input recorder upon which Wallis had insisted showed that the crash was due to the pilot's slow reactions

A Wild Goose 'Thurleighdyne' being prepared for a run at Thurleigh. Note the two rocket nozzles on the trolley and the gash on the fuselage to permit wing sweep. *(BAE SYSTEMS via Brooklands Museum)*

(understandable given that it was the first flight of a new type of aircraft), but the brief flight had shown that Wild Goose could fly – Wallis made no mention of the crash, writing 'LAUS DEO' in red letters in his diary.[97] After further gliding flights, the red pen next came out on 22 February for 'FIRST POWERED TAKE OFF' followed by 'magnificent success. . . speed up to 110mph. . . Nash started a very sweet turn. . . turned too fast. . . went into a flat spin and landed heavily'.

Wallis was so enthused by these automatic take-offs and successful flights that he could:

> *. . . now foresee the bomber station of the future as consisting of an airstrip no larger than about 800 × 1000yds from which something like 30,000 tons of high explosive can be launched on a target 10,000nm away every 24 hours of the year, aided by a ground crew consisting perhaps of 100 or 200 men at most, provided of course that such a volume of attack lies within the economic capacity of ourselves and our allies.*[98]

Although he recognised that he was being 'more than usually uppity' in his letter, he continued boldly:

> *To my mind, there would now be no undue risk involved in scrapping every prototype that is on the stocks in this country (retaining perhaps one of the best of them) and diverting the tremendous expenditure and manpower thus freed to the intensive development of this new scheme.*

At Thurleigh, 'over 100 runs were made without any mishaps whatsoever' according to Wallis,[99] although a report by the ARC for the Ministry of Supply on the status of the Wallis work in December 1951 notes that 'no completely satisfactory flight was made' there.[100]

From June 1950, building work for the RAE commencing at Thurleigh would have compromised security and safety, and 'a thorough investigation of British aerodromes has shown Predannack in Cornwall to be the most satisfactory alternative to Thurleigh'.[101]

The pilots

Originally it had been planned that a member of the Vickers technical staff would be capable of flying the models. While 'we were able to demonstrate easily enough that this was true in a wind tunnel . . . it turns out to be untrue on an aerodrome when the undulating character of the horizon makes it impossible for the pilot to judge what motion the aircraft is undergoing until it is too late to rectify'[102] and it quickly became clear that 'a skilled pilot was necessary for this task'.[103] One suggestion to Wallis was to recruit 'Queen Bee' pilots,[104] but he had already considered this option and found their skills 'elementary in comparison with our requirements'. One of the pilots engaged was Leonard Cheshire VC, who had commanded 617 Squadron during the crucial period when the earthquake bomb tactics were being developed. After a brief period at Weybridge, he moved to Predannack in October 1950,[105] taking administrative charge of the flying unit in addition to his ground controller duties.[106]

Originally controlled from a single pilot station on the Queen Mary trailer, this was found to be unsatisfactory due to the pilot's difficulty in judging distance accurately, and so two pilots were used to fly the circuit – a 'pitch pilot' (or 'height pilot') was positioned to one side halfway down the runway, the 'roll pilot' (or 'axis pilot') beyond the end of the runway. The first pilot flew the aircraft from take-off and around the circuit, a switch then being thrown to allow the second to take over roll control on 'finals' to line up the aircraft with the runway before it was brought down to land.[107] The two pilots were 'in constant telephonic communication', and the dual control method was known as 'twist and steer'.[108]

Early models were controlled via a push-button board, but Cheshire quickly expressed a desire for a 'stick' adaptation with proportional control, and this was implemented, although it required additional radio channels. A governor was added to the stick to prevent it being moved more quickly than the wing motors could follow.

The 'pitch pilot' operated a joystick with a forward/back motion, the control position being rotated by an assistant to keep the pilot pointing towards the model. The 'roll pilot' sat rather precariously in a 'high chair' 40ft up at the end of the runway, observing the model through binoculars (as he was usually much further away from the model) and controlling via a normal yolk. Wallis noted that 'the gliding angle of this low-drag anatomy is so fine that it is possible to fly the aircraft straight into the ground without flaps' although it also required 'lining the aircraft up at a distance of 2,000yds from the desired point of contact and within such height limit as will enable it to land on the fairway within the boundary of the aerodrome'.[109]

Even so, 'this form of controller proved unsatisfactory as it is impossible for a ground-based pilot to appreciate the nature of the disturbances experienced by the aircraft while in flight sufficiently quickly to apply the necessary corrections' and this 'made it necessary to embark at once on the production of an autopilot working in conjunction with servo motors for moving the wings',[110] which was completed in autumn 1951.

Wild Goose tests at Predannack

Situated close to Lizard Point, Predannack was a satellite field to RNAS Culdrose, and had been host to the Special Detachment of 618 Squadron during the war. Reconnoitred in February, Wallis was working the following month[111] on the specification for a straight section of railway track 750yds long which was built alongside the main south-west – north-east runway (this included cutting a channel across one of the secondary runways), with a concrete emplacement at the south-west end for preparation of the models for flight, and to allow the trolley to be loaded on to a road trailer for transport to covered storage or off-site. The railway cost £21,000, with a further £4,000 spent on refurbishing old airfield buildings for a staff of 30,[112] and building a new fence.[113] The work was completed by the autumn of 1950. A new rocket-powered launching trolley was designed and built for the railway, enabling it to reach 100mph in about 400yds,[114] with the model free to rotate into wind on a spigot as on the tyred trolley. The weight of the trolley was 'only a fraction of that of the aircraft which it carries' and release of the aircraft automatically brought the trolley braking system into operation. The features of the trolley were the subject of a further patent.[115] In late 1952 the trolley was modified so that it could be turned around within 30 minutes to run in the opposite direction (if the wind direction changed).[116]

The 'high chair' used by the roll pilot was positioned at one end of the runway – it was not for the faint-hearted. *(BAE SYSTEMS via Brooklands Museum)*

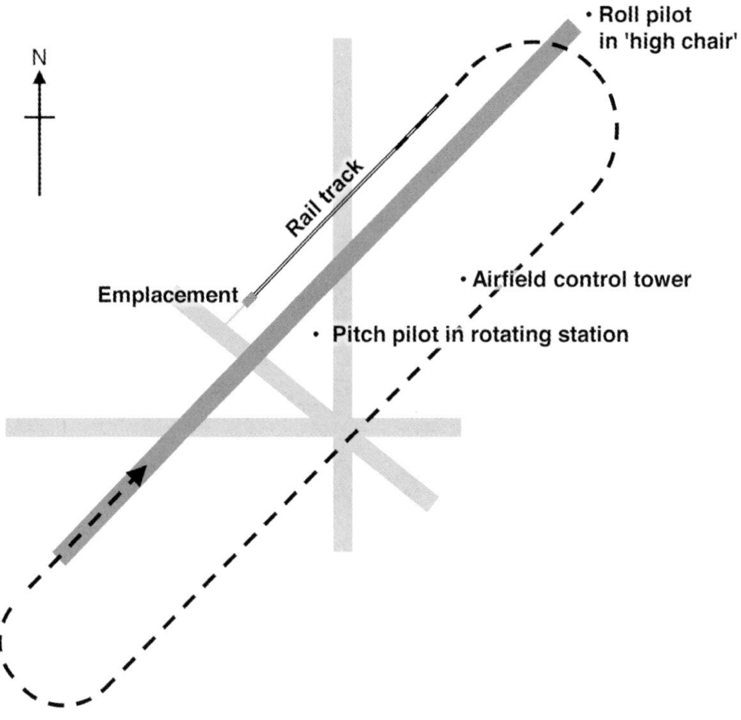

The layout of Predannack airfield during the WCA test flights. *(Author)*

A progress report in April 1951[117] showed numerous 'housekeeping' functions occupying the staff, including testing the radio control gear in a Spitfire and grinding of the rail surfaces, with the first trial run anticipated in July. Locked-on runs in late 1951 showed lifting forces far less than predicted by wind tunnel work at the NPL. With the new auto-pilot and other equipment, the weight of the model had now risen to over 800lb,[118] so Wallis stripped this back to 350lb for a demonstration flight in February 1952,[119] which had been organised for officials including Cochrane who had recently become Vice Chief of the Air Staff. The model flew successfully, but this was no more than had been achieved at Thurleigh more than 18 months earlier. He elected to refit all equipment and attempt a 'heavy' launch on 29 April. Despite non-ideal weather, the launch went ahead, and Wild Goose soared perfectly around the circuit. But, on bringing her in to land, Nash misjudged the distance and at 150mph, flew her into the side of one of the airfield's concrete sheds – the 'solution to the problem of landing her without disaster'[120] being the subsequent adoption of the two-pilot control system to prevent incidents such as this. However, the model's performance had been perfect, and Wallis was delighted – a delight which cost him £37 in the pub that night!

Further gliding and powered tests were suspended after an 'unexplained cut in the jets' caused aircraft 3A to crash on 26 July, prompting more ground tests throughout the autumn (the cause of the crash was never found, although radio signal distortion was suspected).[121] Locked-on runs resumed in November[122] with aircraft 3B, partly to convince detractors from the RAE who thought that no useful data could be obtained from ground trials. Following runs at various heights above the trolley and different incidence angles, it was concluded that the 'locked-on technique can yield satisfactory aerodynamic data, provided sufficient tests are carried out. . . but. . . little reliance [can be placed] on spot tests'.[123]

By the summer of 1953, Thurleighdynes 3B,

Wild Goose thunders down the Predannack track ready for launch. This photograph appears to show a NE–SW run, which is unusual – most were SW–NE. *(BAE SYSTEMS via The Flambards Experience)*

3C and 3D were all close to flying condition, and undergoing rocket and mechanical tests.[124] During the latter, it was noted that substantial wing sweep torque was lost if there was not accurate alignment between the motors and the gearbox with the worm shaft (which engaged the gear rack on the wing), although ample power was available if alignment was correct. A procedural change was thus made to check both the radio and the wing torque immediately before take-off, although primary testing was still to be done in the hangar. The new roll pilot position was also ready – use of the old Thurleigh tower was deemed 'unsatisfactory', hence the adoption of the 'high chair' which had been built from a tower-ladder found in a hangar, following some modifications.

Thirty-one powered Wild Goose flights were recorded between July 1952 and October 1954[125] with occasional crashes[126] (the later flights even as its successor was in parallel development).[127] These tests showed that 'Wild Goose had achieved a lift coefficient at gs up to 0.7', despite NPL's prediction that nothing would be achieved above 0.3.[128] One of the most spectacular of the Predannack films is from a camera which was mounted on the Wild Goose fuselage to give a 'pilot's eye view' as it took off and performed a complete circuit.[129]

The mysterious Heston JC.9

Despite the very great efforts made to perfect the ground-based control systems, a subsonic manned prototype based on Wild Goose was ordered, although the reason for doing this so early in the project is not clear, nor is it clear who decided to do so, given Wallis's desire not to risk test pilots flying in the aircraft. Construction was sub-contracted to the Heston Aircraft Company, which designated it the JC.9.

In late 1951 when Cochrane assumed his new role, Wallis wrote to him with 'the briefest outline' of work in hand or in prospect in the R&D Department . . . his outline running to nine pages! This included details of the specification of the JC.9:

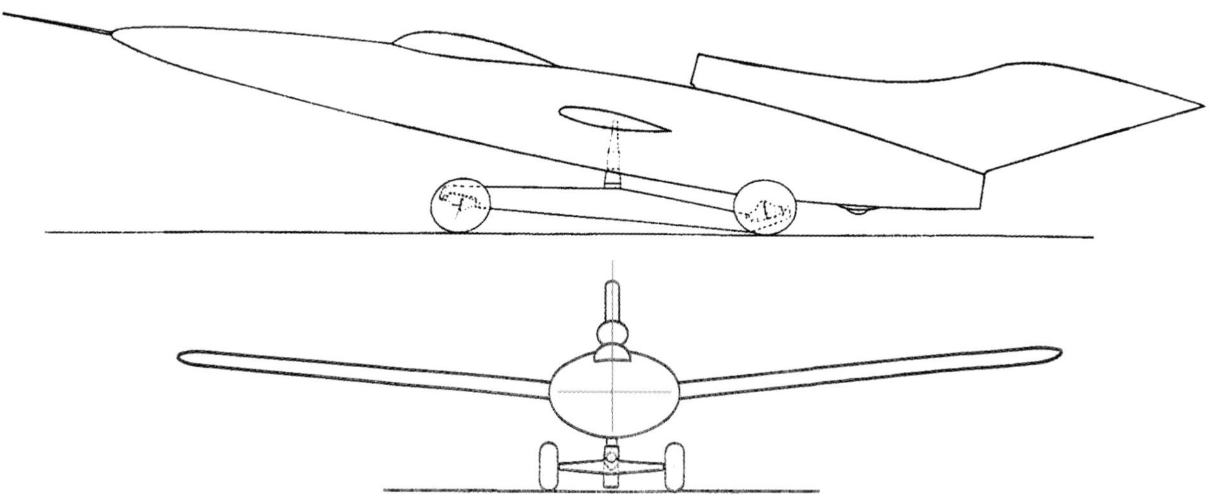

The Heston JC.9 shown on an unpowered take-off bogie. Note the fin-mounted air intake and the wing dihedral. Overall length was 46.5ft with an unswept span of 38ft. *(BAE SYSTEMS via Brooklands Museum)*

We have already placed a sub-contract with Heston Aircraft for the design and manufacture of a single-seater manned aircraft capable of 1 or 2 hours flight duration. The structure has been stressed to take 7g in subsonic flight and the AUW is coming out at about 5,500lb when fully loaded. The following development programme has been arranged for this aircraft:

Static structure tests *The design of the fuselage offers no unusual features but the wings are, of course, entirely novel. We have therefore arranged for test specimens to be made incorporating the pivot bearings and these will be tested to destruction under static loading combined with motion and sweep. The final design of the servo motors and reduction gears is held up pending the completion of our own short-term research programme . . .*

Half-mass model *In order to avoid any risk on a first flight, the Heston Aircraft Company are designing and making a model of half the AUW of the full-size aircraft. At a weight of 2,750lb, this model will use the same structure as has been developed for our short-term research programme and Heston have therefore only to provide the fuselage and wing outer covering. The weight is low enough for the half-mass model to be launched from the Predannack trolley, and by the time this model is ready, we should have gained sufficient experience at Predannack to fly it with confidence by means of the ground-based pilot.*[130]

Full size test *On completion of the test with the half-size model, it should be possible for the full-size aircraft to be taken up by a test pilot without undue risk.*[131]

A report for the Ministry of Supply at this time[132] noted that Heston JC.9 construction was 'well advanced' but 'proceeding slowly', and that the aircraft was as small as feasible for propulsion by an Adder jet engine; the engine was mounted in the tail, different plans showing air intakes on the upper sides of the rear fuselage or built into the front of the vertical stabiliser. The aircraft was shipped in sections to Weybridge for final assembly.

By May 1952 the contract had been terminated, this decision being criticised in a letter to the Ministry,[133] which was told 'that the programme would be very unhealthy without this item' also remarking that 'it was very difficult to persuade Mr Wallis to work in a systematic

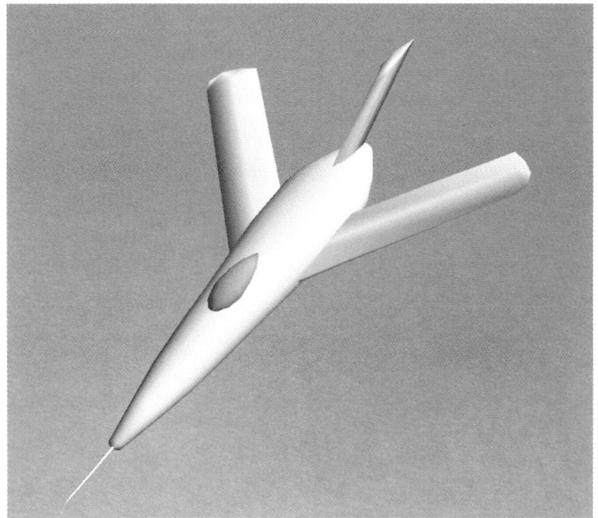

A simulation of the Heston JC.9 in flight, with wings in the low-speed configuration (left) and swept for high speed (right). *(Author)*

manner'.[134] The reasons for the cancellation, as with the order itself, are unknown,[135] and it was certainly unfortunate in view of the later struggle to validate the variable geometry concept by building a manned research aircraft.

Practical applications of Wild Goose

Beyond the model tests, Wallis was naturally looking ahead to practical applications of Wild Goose – and he had many. In June 1950 he was instructed by Kilner to direct a design study for a photo reconnaissance aircraft at Heston, even though this would 'delay the production of the one-man flying models', i.e. the JC.9. It is unclear what became of this design, though it may have evolved into the later photo reconnaissance (PR) aircraft (see below).

In his 1951 exposition to Cochrane,[136] Wallis describes a 750lb 'supersonic defence missile', a 15–20,000lb 'long-range reconnaissance aircraft' with 7,000-mile range, a 30,000lb 'pilotless bomber aircraft', a 60,000lb 'piloted bomber aircraft', a 70,000lb 'military transport aircraft' and a civil aircraft (all with 10,000-mile range) plus a 'high-speed fighter aircraft' (not described in detail).

The full treatise on Wild Goose had to wait for his 1953 paper, 'The Air Defence of Great Britain: A New Approach'.[137] Very much a sales pitch in the mould of his wartime 'Note', Wallis first provided an in-depth analysis of the air defence situation, only later presenting his aircraft ideas as the ideal solution to the problems faced. He took his cue from a 1951 statement by Lord Trenchard, the founder of the RAF:

> *'. . . the key to the whole situation – the vital, overriding defensive measure to prevent war, and in the event of war, to win it . . . is an overwhelming, unchallengeable air force of long-range machines.'*[138]

Wallis went on to note that Britain also needed long-range aircraft to reach its empire without landing on foreign soil, or offensively to reach the main Russian industrial targets. Defensively, fighters or SAMs with short range required many weapons at many bases, whereas a long-range fighter could offer 'defence in depth' and attack incoming bombers long before they reached British airspace (500 miles at least). To meet the varying requirements of these long-range aircraft, he proposed three similar variants of the Wild Goose concept, a communications (transport) aircraft, an attack (bomber) aircraft and a fighter (see specifications in Table 8.2), though he noted that it could also perform the functions of a PR aircraft,

	Type 1 Communication	Type 2 Attack	Type 3 Fighter
Non-stop range	10,000nm	10,000nm	4,000nm
Cruising speed	1,350kt	1,350kt	1,350kt
Cruising height	78,000ft	78,000ft	78,000ft
Cruising height for max endurance	40,000ft	40,000ft	40,000ft
All up weight	50,000lb	25-35,000lb	15,000lb
Payload/armament/special equipment	4,000lb	Up to 10,000lb	4,000lb
Fuel fraction	50 per cent	50 per cent	30 per cent
Endurance at 385kt	12 hours	12 hours	8 hours
Crew (+ passengers)	2 + 30	2	2

Table 8.2: Basic specifications for Wild Goose variants.

radar reconnaissance aircraft, early warning patrol aircraft and other duties.

Wallis went on to describe the theory of Wild Goose and variable geometry 'to remove the incredulity that the performance figures quoted above, not unnaturally, raise at first sight', concluding by noting that the WCA offered two performance maxima: maximum range (achieved by flying at fastest practical supersonic speed) and maximum endurance (at any desired subsonic speed, but 174–485kt is suggested, depending on engine characteristics).

Arnold Hall, Director of RAE, was recorded as saying that Wallis was 'entirely right' in thinking that UK air defence should rely on manned supersonic fighters and offensive power on long-range supersonic bombers. Furthermore, Hall was confident that Wallis could produce such an aircraft for both requirements, although he thought that Wallis's range and weight estimates were both too optimistic.[139]

In October 1952 Wallis submitted a brochure for a PR aircraft of 52ft span, based on the Wild Goose concept, with some novel additional features.[140] Wings could be swept from straight right back to 90 degrees (parallel with the fuselage); pitch was to be controlled by via a lateral pivot joining the forebody and afterbody, and for roll, the afterbody was to be split vertically along its centreline, each half carrying a wing.[141] The estimated performance was 6,000 miles at 50,000ft at M 0.9 plus 15 minutes at 5,000ft at M 1.5 plus 30 minutes at M 2.7 at 50,000ft, carrying a crew of two plus cameras in an AUW of 20,000lb.

The RAE's assessment of the aircraft was highly critical:[142] structure weight was estimated around 5 per cent heavier than the brochure, 'the performance claimed is not substantiated' and although 'no detailed calculations on stability and control have been done in view of the results of the performance estimates', the 'method of control presents serious problems'. The control concerns were centred on various aspects of the novel configuration, estimated wing pivot loadings and the absence of a fin. High levels of laminar flow were also claimed, which the RAE thought unsubstantiated. In trying to find something worthwhile in the brochure, they were 'most attracted by the idea of using variable sweepback as a means of reconciling the conflicting aerodynamic and structural requirements involved in a possible reconnaissance aircraft designed to fly for a great distance at high subsonic speed and to do a short burst at supersonic speed', although a previous design study is cited which showed that 'variable sweepback conferred little or no advantage'.

One further feature of these Wild Goose designs was the use of the prone position for the pilot, lying flat on his front. This allowed for a smaller, more aerodynamic cockpit and helped with high *g* manoeuvres, but was tiring for the pilot and giving the pilot a forward view caused problems. The prone position had been tested by the Germans before and during the war, the Americans had converted a Lockheed XF.80C Shooting Star, and in Britain, the RAE had converted a Desford trainer for experiments relating to their Transonic Research Aircraft (TRA).[143] In the PRU aircraft, the cockpit was amidships with the two crew prone, looking through windows in the 'floor', with a periscope arrangement to the nose of the aircraft for a forward view. The TRA was abandoned as it had 'too many unknown factors, of which pilot fatigue in the prone position was found to be an important one',[144] so presumably this would have been a black mark against Wild Goose also.

In the summer of 1953 Wallis was asked by George Edwards to conduct a design study for a Valiant replacement, based on Wild Goose – but he was given just four weeks to produce proof of the concept or face cancellation of the Predannack experiments. Wallis 'argued his way out of his definitive damnation',[145] but this was the first sign that even his own company was not fully supportive of his work.

Summary – Wild Goose

In the Wild Goose work, Wallis had developed (out of his airship experience) a new anatomy for aircraft, and by 1954 had shown by extensive experiments that this was a practical proposition. Along the way, he had built up the equipment and expertise to conduct flight trials of large rocket-powered models controlled by radio.

Boorer suggested with hindsight that Wild Goose tried to do too much too fast, simultaneously introducing many new and unproven technologies – laminar flow, tailless design, variable geometry and differential control.[146] The expected benefits of laminar flow were eventually discounted[147] and consequently the 'high levels in the ratio of lift to drag for which he had hoped' from Wild Goose had not been achieved.[148] However, Wallis had lost no faith in the other main features of its design, the tailless shape and swing-wings for lift and control at all speeds.

In his own words, Wallis 'wasn't getting quite the high aerodynamic efficiency that I wanted in order to develop very long ranges, so I decided to turn the fuselage into a small delta-wing aircraft and put the wings at each corner of the base',[149] a change that would turn Wild Goose into a Swallow.

A simulation of the Wild Goose PRU aircraft (based on a plan in the Brooklands Museum). The vertically-split rear fuselage is pivoted at the broad band amidships to give roll control (the aircraft is rolling left here) and the dark area ahead of the pivot are the windows for the two prone pilots. *(Author)*

Chapter 9

Swallow

Remember that all models are wrong; the practical question is how wrong do they have to be to not be useful?
(George E.P. Box and Norman R. Draper, Empirical Model-Building, *1987)*

A new shape

From the various planforms proposed for supersonic flight by the early 1950s, the slender delta was showing the greatest promise. The nose of an aircraft creates a cone-shaped shock wave at supersonic speed (becoming more pointed as the speed increases), and the delta shape emerged as it was found advantageous to keep all other parts of the aircraft within this cone to minimise overall drag. Research work showed that most of the lift from a delta wing is developed near the leading edge,[1] so Wallis decided to adopt a new 'arrowhead' planform, taking the delta then cutting away the *drag-inducing* but *non-lifting* rear part of the delta, leaving wings which were essentially *all* leading edge.[2] By cutting the base out of the delta, he was left with a smaller delta forebody and wings trailing behind – thus, if the undercarriage was on the forebody, any amount of nose-up pitch on landing or take-off would have seen the wingtips contact the ground. The solution to this problem was immediately at hand – where the forebody met the wings, he would place a pivot to sweep the wings forward, the variable geometry conferring a usable landing configuration upon the new design while retaining all of the aerodynamic benefits of variable sweep already demonstrated by Wild Goose. The double pointed 'tails' immediately suggested a name for the new shape – Swallow.[3]

Further aerodynamic improvement was through 'the development of an all-lifting form'[4] with the fuselage blending into the forebody which then contributed to lift (unlike the Wild Goose fuselage). This meant that for a given wing loading there would be the minimum possible wetted surface and therefore minimum friction drag. The resulting low wing loading ensured that the optimum altitude was high enough so that the engine specific fuel consumption was a minimum for given speeds, hence further assisting with long range.[5] The uniform distribution of weight offered by the all-lifting form helped reduce structure weight,[6] yet another contributor to long range. The low wing loading also offered advantages in manoeuvrability and in take-off and landing performance.

The new form and its attendant features formed the basis of a batch of patents,[7] Wallis's patent agents noting that 'the broad conception of an aerodyne comprising a forewing of delta-shaped plan formation with two main wings respectively attached to the ends of the base of the forewings so as to be adjustable in sweep between an outspread position for subsonic speeds and a swept aft position for supersonic speeds appears to be completely novel' and that the 'configuration of a delta-shaped forewing and pivotable main wings arranged so that in a swept aft position for supersonic speeds, the high drag low lift areas have been removed, would also appear to constitute a novel and patentable invention'.[8]

In Wild Goose, the airflow around the ovoid fuselage had created a pitching moment which was balanced by the lift from the wings, making the whole stable. In Swallow, the former was replaced by the lift produced by the forewing:

> *When such an aerodyne is in uniform horizontal flight, the pitching moment due to the lifting forces exerted upon the forewing acts in the opposite sense to that due to the lift forces exerted upon the main wings to obtain equilibrium. Pitch stability can be maintained because the pitching moment due to lift on the main wings changes with change of angle of incidence more rapidly than does the pitching moment due to lift on the delta-shaped forewing and in the opposite sense.*[9]

Wallis also suggested[10] that 'the time is right for a fresh examination of the square-cube law' which states that, if all the linear dimensions of an aircraft are multiplied by n then the AUW will be multiplied by n^2 but the weight of the essential structure of the aeroplane will be multiplied by n^3; thus the weight of the structure expressed as a percentage of the AUW must be multiplied by n and it follows that aircraft must become progressively less structurally efficient as their size increases.[11]

A multi-exposure photograph of a Swallow model demonstrates the arrowhead planform operation of the variable wing sweep and pivoted engines. This model is now held by the RAF Museum. *(BAE SYSTEMS via The Flambards Experience)*

It appears that one of the primary goals of one of the earliest variants of Swallow was to be, in modern parlance, a stealth aircraft. With the merging of the wing and fuselage, 'radar returns less than those for a normal aircraft doing similar duty seem almost certain',[12] leading very quickly to a patent submission,[13] with optical experiments using light in place of radar to 'proceed as rapidly as possible' on the shape. The preliminary design, known as 'Pancake', laid out the basic shape of Swallow (see image in Chapter 12), with long thin wings attached by pivots to the rounded delta forebody. Although there was no tail, small wingtip finlets made from 'a non-conducting material permeable to electro-magnetic waves' were to be used as rudders, and ailerons and flaps appear on the trailing edge of the wings. Four engines were placed side-by-side beneath the rear fuselage. Another novel feature which would appear on many later variants of Swallow was the 'rising and falling' cockpit (also referred to as the 'pilot's turret'); Swallow would assume a nose-up attitude on landing, giving pilot view problems, and a raised cockpit was undesirable for drag reasons. Wallis's solution was to put the pilot in a cylindrical cockpit which could be raised up hydraulically out of the top of the fuselage when landing or taking off;[14] presumably he would have flown on instruments when the cockpit was retracted.

Swallow experiments at Predannack

Wallis had the first subsonic model completed 'within three months of the moment when the idea for Swallow had first struck him'[15] which won him a bet and a bottle of rum! Experience gained with the Thurleighdyne paid off, and by the end of September 1954, 25 locked-on runs to gain aerodynamical data had been completed on the trolley, although on the last of these, Swallow broke away (unplanned) from the trolley and was damaged,[16] requiring a couple of weeks for repairs. Design of an 'all metal sub/supersonic Swallow powered by a [Rolls-Royce] Soar turbojet' was in progress for expected flight within a year, and two wooden backup aircraft were also to be built as test-beds for the flying controls and autopilot (the autopilot also being tested on the Wild Goose models already flying). A total of ten serial numbers were assigned to Swallow,[17] although none were visible on the models which flew.

As early as October 1954 it was decided that Swallow would not actually be launched from the trolley, instead taking off conventionally from a runway.[18] There was some discussion as to whether it should be flown by 'direct control' or with an autopilot, although the latter would

BACKGROUND

SWALLOW MODEL VARIANTS

The following list of variants is based, with additions, on a summary report by Major Phil Teed, November 1955 (Brooklands Museum SWG-INF-002). No Type 004 was listed.

Type 001 Mark 1 A wooden model with wings fixed in the subsonic position, 30ft span and weight of 800lb, powered by hydrogen peroxide rocket motors giving a top speed of about 100mph and three minutes' endurance, it was controlled by six-channel radio. This type was used for the locked-on runs, taxiing trials, and the first of the powered free flights.

Type 001 Mark 2 A modification of the Mark 1, with a larger aspect ratio and chemical jet engine. Four of this type were planned, two for direct radio control, two with autopilots. Its most noticeable difference from the Mark 1 was its circular wingtip fins. One of this type made the final free flight, crashing into the sea.

Type 002 A 'fully equipped military machine which will meet the requirements of Specification No R.156T' with an AUW of 45,000lb.

Type 003 To be fabricated in light alloy and have pivoted wings of 33ft span (subsonic configuration) and weight of about 2,500lb; power would be from two Rolls-Royce Soar turbojets giving an endurance of 30 minutes ending in an unpowered landing at around 65mph. This variant was expected to be able to reach Mach 2 at 50,000ft, carrying telemetering equipment to transmit basic flight data; six of this type were to be built.

Type 005 Similar to Type 001 Mark 2, but powered by a Palas jet engine, giving 15–20 minutes duration, control by radio-controlled autopilot; four aircraft of this type were anticipated.

Type 006 Manned research aircraft, proposed 1957.

incur several months delay. It was decided to use direct control, at least initially, following investigation of aerodynamic data from the locked-on runs and some ground runs. By mid-November the model had been repaired and made a further 14 lock-on runs, with another 20 in prospect. In total, 82 trolley runs were made.[19] The RAE was also to undertake supersonic wind tunnel tests, although progress was initially slow due to difficulties in manufacturing the test models.[20]

By March 1955 preparations for ground steering trials of the Type 001 were being made.[21] These were to cover all CG positions from tanks full to tanks empty and, with elevons fully down, were to involve power burns of increasing duration up to 100mph. If all went well on these tests, a fixed elevon position to lift the nose was to be tried. The undercarriage was to be given temporary strengthening in case of the aircraft running off the runway, and it was planned that several pilots would steer the model to get a feel for the handling. Four taxiing burns of 4, 8, 12 and 16 seconds duration took place on 25 April.[22]

These tests continued during the summer, with six Type 001 Swallows in various states of construction by May.[23] As with the trolley launches, it was hoped to make the take-off as automatically as possible, and although there was a desire to avoid a prolonged rotation with only the main wheels on the ground, it was found from the trials that the anticipated steering problems in this attitude did not arise.[24] To find the take-off speed, run durations were increased gradually, a wing lift being noted at 98mph, a small bounce at 102mph and at 107mph a second in the air was achieved. For run #373 on 30 August, a burn of 24 seconds was tried 'to get genuinely airborne', but drift prior to take-off meant that one wheel left the runway first and, when the roll control system

The Type 001 Swallow model on the rail trolley at Predannack. Although it made many locked-on runs to gather data, the actual flights took place from a runway. *(BAE SYSTEMS via The Flambards Experience)*

tried to correct this, the drift increased, leading to a wingtip contacting the runway, and the model rolled heavily to starboard and cartwheeled on to its nose – all of this occurring in less than 5 seconds.

The first full flight took place on 18 November 1955,[25] the film of the flight showing the graceful craft making a clean take-off and performing a complete circuit, and although the landing was 'a bit jerky and a bit violent, no damage was done'.[26] Just three more flights were made over the following 18 months, one crashing into the ground shortly after a bumpy take-off run.[27] On the last of these, on 29 June 1957, the Mark 2 autopilot model was lost in the sea off Predannack, this being put down to 'an unfortunate accident at the ground control end as the actual flight and take-off had been a remarkably good one'[28] – pilot error! Despite 'strenuous efforts' by the Predannack team,[29] the wind and weather prevented a recovery before night fell, and the craft sank during the night. Stanley Hooker, Chief Engineer of Bristol Aero Engines, wrote to Wallis in 1958 to say that he was 'stimulated by seeing the films of the Swallow' and 'had no idea that you were so advanced with the aerodynamic tests'; confessing to some initial scepticism, he concludes that 'you can regard me as completely converted, and anything that we can do to further this project we will do with all our hearts'.[30]

The original lease agreement said that Predannack was to be vacated by June 1957 (although this was actually postponed to September),[31] and the plan for the final six months of work had been to test fly the second Swallow and remove equipment from the site, with a view to finishing by mid-July and vacating by September, but it appears that the loss of the Swallow brought the test programme to a slightly premature conclusion. With the end of the test flights and the departure of the trials team, the rail track was sold for scrap for £560.[32]

Tests at Larkhill and Aberporth – but *not* Woomera

To confirm the basic aerodynamics of the Swallow shape at supersonic speeds, and to augment their wind tunnel tests (which predicted an L/D for Swallow of between 8.9 and 9.8 in supersonic flight at 70,000ft),[33] it was arranged with the RAE to fire one-tenth scale models of Swallow at the Larkhill rocket range on Salisbury Plain (this was the largest that could be fired with available boosters). These non-lifting, uncontrolled 'gash' models about 8ft long were largely fabricated from steel in the main Vickers-Armstrongs factory and finished in the R&D Department. They had a fattened square-section 'fuselage' containing telemetering equipment;[34] engines were not simulated. Launched on the nose of a rocket at a shallow angle, for about 20 seconds of powered boost after which the rocket fell away, the model achieved free flight for a further 20 seconds or so, the nose then being blown off in order to destabilise the model and bring it down within the bounds of the range. In March 1955 the first firing of a Swallow model took place, achieving a speed of Mach 2.46,[35] and the second 'up to the full 2.5' as planned.[36] Intended to be expendable, the damage suffered by the two models was 'surprisingly slight', and a third model was constructed from parts salvaged from them,[37] this reaching Mach 2.65 on 29 July. A total of ten launches were made up to October 1957.[38]

A similar series of rocket-launched models were flown from Aberporth[39] from March 1957 into 1959,[40] to measure the key parameters of the flying body, most notably drag-due-to-lift.[41] A 'barrel roll' technique was tried to generate lift, but this was unsuccessful and a second technique using 'spoiler-induced oscillations' was tried, also unsuccessfully. The supersonic test programme had been undertaken as 'it was thought that techniques would rapidly be developed for the measurement of all fundamental aerodynamic data at transonic and supersonic speeds, thus filling the vacancy in experimental aerodynamics caused by the lack of suitable wind tunnels' but 'these hopes have not been realised and the trials under review serve as a final confirmation of this'.[42] Reliance was thus put back on to wind tunnel models, which were continuing to produce successful data.

Following an April 1955 proposal (under the banner of CUKAC, the Combined United Kingdom Australian long-range weapon Committee) to carry out further Swallow trials (with the 003 type) in Australia, Major Teed (accompanied by the Director General of Development at the Ministry of Supply) visited Woomera during November to check it over.[43] Woomera was a wide expanse of semi-desert used for aircraft and rocket testing, and at that time work was proceeding there on the Jindivik.[44] The Australian officials offered 'no hostility whatever' to the use of the site, but Teed came away with 'a very poor impression of it' – although the site had adequate facilities (most of Vickers-Armstrongs's requirements could be easily met), it was remote (requiring a 300-mile flight from Adelaide followed by two hours by road in temperatures typically over 38°C). One refinement from the Jindivik program was suggested – using a third pilot for primary control during the main part of the flight, with the other two fulfilling take-off and landing duties as at Predannack (it appears that ground control only would have been used, even for the supersonic flights). However, Teed's final recommendation from the visit was that the use of Woomera should be avoided if possible, despite a Ministry of Supply undertaking to make use of the site.

Despite the advances being made with the models and ever-increasing proof that the WCA concept was a viable one, which led to grudgingly increasing interest from the ministries, there was an unexpected obstacle in the way of the project – Vickers own senior management – which tempered the official interest shown in the concept. One official wrote: 'I wish I could tell you that we have made great advances since then but unfortunately the fact is that we have come up against a difficult situation within the firm', continuing:

> *The unfortunate fact is that George Edwards, who is really the head of the Aeronautical side of Vickers, clearly does not believe in the Swallow project. I know this because I have talked with him and in his present mood he will not agree to any major re-deployment of effort within the firm because he thinks it can be more profitably employed on other projects. His main doubts are that Wallis cannot achieve the structure weights which he claims.*[45]

He concluded with the opinion that Swallow could not be developed further 'unless we have the main might and strength of Vickers, that is either the George Edwards team at Weybridge or at Supermarine, deployed on it'.

Operational requirement OR.330

In August 1954 specification R.156T/ OR.330 was issued for a high-altitude reconnaissance aircraft to support the V-bomber force, and in April 1955 this was expanded to include a bomber role as a future replacement for the V-bombers.[46] In January 1956 the Defence Research Policy Committee endorsed the completion of a Swallow design study at an estimated cost of £10,000, but this design study was superseded by preparation of a detailed brochure for a Swallow variant to meet OR.330. On a visit to Weybridge on 8 May 1956, Wallis outlined to Ministry officials the work on Wild Goose and Swallow and the wing pivots which were undergoing rig testing. Wallis proposed to carry the single nuclear bomb in the rear of the fuselage, which protruded from the rear of the aircraft, but this concerned the Ministry men due to the underbody engines – the bomb would pass through the jet efflux when dropped.[47]

As with Wild Goose, it was planned that Swallow would be principally controlled by differential wing sweep, a patent describing a double sweep system with a main sweep system operated by a motorised worm gear, and a secondary hydraulic system for small but rapid movements for control purposes.[48] Despite proof of the concept by the Thurleighdynes, 'control by differential sweep was not believed in' in certain circles and 'it was felt that the use of trailing edge flaps with sweep in the wing for trim would be better'[49] but this was not an ideal solution either, as adding flaps complicated the otherwise simple (and hence light) wing structure.

Due to potential problems with having the engines beneath the fuselage,[50] Wallis looked for an alternative location for them.[51] They could not be built into the wing root (as on the V-bombers) due to the position of the wing pivot, nor into the main wings due to their variable sweep. Placing them within the forebody or above the rear of the forebody gave aerodynamic difficulties. The only location left was thus a podded mounting on the wings themselves 'subject to the big objection that the axes of the engines must remain substantially parallel to the stream in all positions of the wing' and the asymmetry problems that 'may be encountered in the event of a power failure at take-off and subsequently in flight'. There was also the substantial issue of the gimbal itself and of the servo motors needed to move the engines.[52]

Countering these caveats were several substantial advantages of this configuration: as the mass of the engines (and the CG) would sweep with the wings (and the CP) 'mass balance' was obtained automatically, stiffness of the wing would be assisted by the engine mass reducing the potential for flutter, and 'bending moment at the wing root is greatly reduced and a lighter wing capable of higher speeds is the result'. With fuel tanks in the wings, it also removed the problem of piping the fuel around the wing pivot.[53] Most significantly of all, the engine pivoting required to cope with variable sweep could also be used to vary the engine thrust direction in pitch, roll, and yaw for control purposes, thus removing the requirement for any control surfaces, hence simplifying the wing. With the engines podded in pairs, one above and one below the wing for symmetry, each pair mounted on a single gimbal, Wallis thus arrived at the rather elegant configuration which was submitted for OR.330.

A detailed assessment of the brochure was conducted by the RAE, its report being largely positive.[54] The RAE's 'best guestimate' of L/D was 8–9 compared to Wallis's expectation of 10, and a further programme of free flight and wind tunnel experiments was proposed to get a better idea of the actual figure. Structure weight was estimated at 26–30 per cent (Wallis estimated 24 per cent), but any figure below 36 per cent was deemed worthwhile, the Wallis concept offering the possibility of an OR.330 aircraft with an AUW half that of a conventional aircraft. It was noted that 'the shapes which were best for high speeds were very awkward for landing' and the two possibilities for overcoming this were Wallis's variable sweep and vertical take-off and landing (VTOL), the latter as embodied in a competing proposal by Dr Griffith at Rolls-Royce. An Air Staff summary[55] echoed these findings, noting that the project showed 'outstanding promise' and that 'nothing so far had proved that the Wallis theory was wrong', also stating Viscount Knollys's[56] claim 'that Vickers were wholeheartedly behind the work'.

The Air Staff assessment[57] noted recent 'changes in design which are thought to be a considerable advance' and that Wallis was 'now satisfied with the design for his hinge, and it is generally agreed – I understand

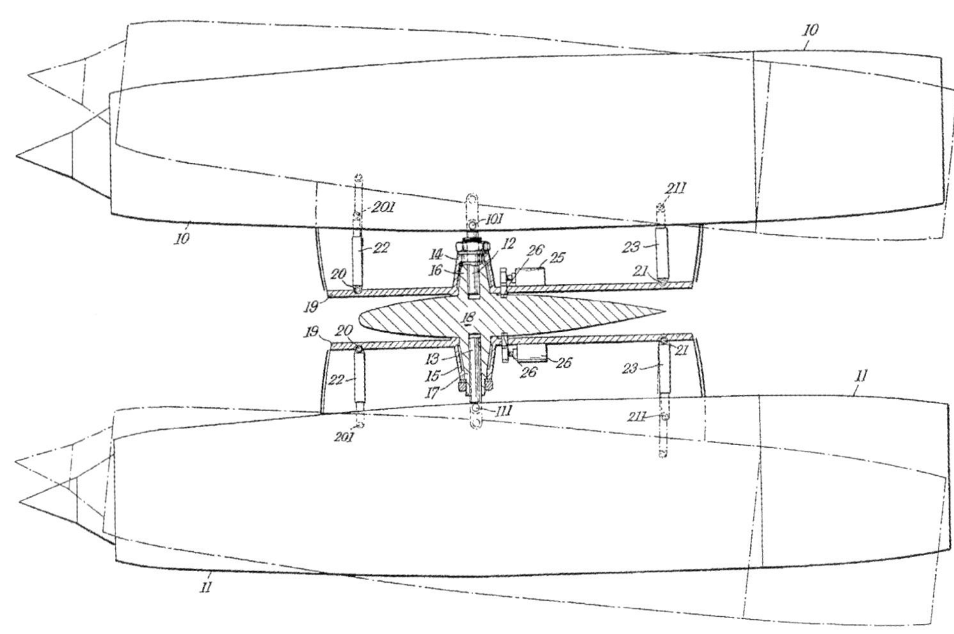

The operation of the gimbal mounting for the wingtip engines (Patent GB870739). The engines here are mounted separately, but in other schemes the engine pair was mounted on a single gimbal. *(BAE SYSTEMS)*

even by Mr George Edwards who has considerable doubt about the project – that the engineering of this is satisfactory and that it would stand up to the loading required'. Wallis hoped that the new engine configuration, 'controllable in such a way that the thrust line is kept correct for the different sweepback positions' and 'used for lateral and longitudinal control' would also 'silence critics who think a fin is needed'. In describing how the wings would be controlled, Wallis said 'I fancy that in the fully developed design, sweepback of the wings will be controlled entirely by a combination of Mach meter and apparatus for measuring density, as it will be on these two factors that optimum position of the wings will depend'[58] – a situation described as 'such that the aircraft would probably chase its [critical Mach number] as the value rose with increasing sweepback'.[59]

Wallis was asked[60] to produce a brochure for a subsonic research aircraft 'of the same linear dimensions as a recce/bomber to O.R.330'. Wallis expected to produce the brochure by mid-January 1957 (this was held up by a month due to illness),[61] with the Ministry of Supply assessment by March and a decision by April. If the Ministry's decision was favourable, a 30,000lb subsonic research aircraft was to be developed over three years at a cost of £1 million, but if unfavourable it would lead to cancellation of the whole project. A second report[62] suggested that a research aircraft design study be started 'sooner rather than later' to save time 'in getting the Swallow into the air', recording that 'Dr Wallis's own staff and resources are lamentably small and he is receiving little worthwhile help from the main Vickers organisation' and that 'I believe George Edwards is the main stumbling block and anything CAS can do to influence him to support Wallis's work would be to the RAF's ultimate benefit'. These opinions were still prevalent years later, Tuttle commenting that 'personally I believe one of the reasons variable sweep has taken so long is that we left it with Wallis too long, although his ideas are very, very bright still'.[63]

The 'great hydraulic wing pivot'[64]

One inconvenience of the mathematical theory behind Swallow was that it had shown that the ideal location for the wing pivot was very close to the leading edge of the wing. As the wing was thin there, a small pivot mechanism was needed, so Wallis dispensed with the geared pivots in favour of a single ball joint which could ingeniously be operated hydraulically to vary sweep and/or incidence, the patent document showing the mechanical complexity of the pivot and its hydraulic control system.[65] For an aircraft of AUW 70,000lb (as proposed for OR.330), the pivots would weigh just 60lb each;[66] even so, they could not be shrunk sufficiently to hide entirely within the wing, and this and many of the other Swallow variants have a 'pimple' on the leading edge to enclose the pivot. However, as the pivot was central to the structure and safety of the aircraft, this mechanism was thought too complex and potentially unreliable by some.

Wallis liked the idea of the ball pivot, and designed a simpler mechanism on this concept, using polytetrafluoroethylene (PTFE)[67] as a dry lubricant for the joint. In order to prove that PTFE was a practical and reliable material for the wing pivot, a trial half-pivot was manufactured and a test programme commenced. The trial pivot consisted of one half of a hard anodised duralumin ball 9in in diameter and a duralumin outer case lined with petals made from tinned steel backing strip coated on one side with porous bronze, the bronze being impregnated with PTFE. After curing, the parts were cleaned and mounted in a test rig. A load fluctuating from 13 to 25 tons was applied to the bearing surfaces which were oscillated through an angle of 60 degrees to simulate wing sweep and through 1 degree in a plane perpendicular to the wing sweep to represent wing spar deflection. In a progress report in March 1958,[68] Wallis noted that 8 million alternations had been successfully completed to date, while sweeping back and forth through the full range of sweep, the bearing surfaces being inspected at regular intervals. By November '1,566,491 load fluctuations, 75,477 wing sweep movements and 319,478 wing spar deflection

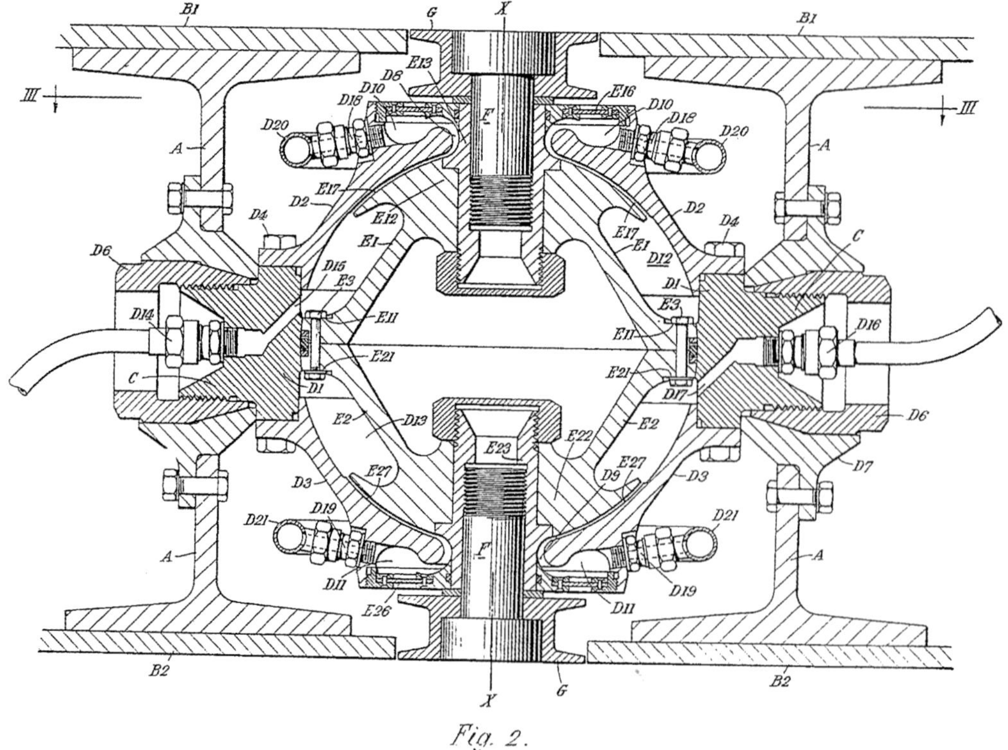

The hydraulic wing pivot. By pumping hydraulic fluid into the various chambers, the sweep and incidence could be altered (Patent GB860823). *(BAE SYSTEMS)*

movements' had been performed.[69] In a subsequent test, after 80 hours at a constant load of 25 tons, 8,600 wing sweep movements and 24,847 wing spar deflection movements' had been attained. Incredibly, there was hardly any wear on the PTFE pivot.

The 1957 Defence White Paper

By 1957 Britain had her own atom bombs and a V-bomber force to deliver them, and the hydrogen bomb was nearing completion. The vast cost of these weapon systems and of maintaining defence of her empire meant that Britain was living well beyond her means and budget changes, especially to the armed forces, were essential. These were enshrined in a Defence White Paper delivered by the new Minister of Defence, Duncan Sandys, in April. This introduced radical reform of all the armed forces (including halving the size of the Army, scrapping the Navy's last remaining battleships and the removal of National Service),[70] but the most profound effect was felt by the Royal Air Force and the aircraft industry which depended upon it. Key proposals were the replacement of manned aircraft by guided missiles in both the defensive and nuclear offensive roles. This meant a reduction in the number of aircraft projects to be funded, and the forced merger of some of the aircraft companies if they were to be awarded the few contracts that would remain. The Lightning and Buccaneer, which were nearing service delivery, survived, but the only new aircraft contract to be awarded was for a short take-off and landing (STOL) tactical strike aircraft (which would become TSR.2). Virtually all other aircraft projects and supporting research contracts were terminated, and this included the Swallow research work and the tenders for the supersonic bomber of OR.330 (the Swallow variant and the Avro 730).

Following publication of the White Paper, Sandys received a glowing endorsement of the Wallis Swallow work from Louis Rosenhead of the University of Liverpool.[71]

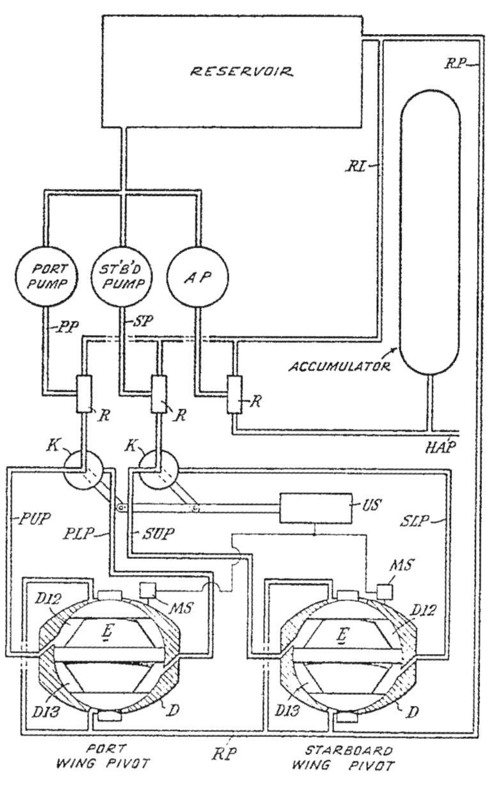

Part of the hydraulic system for the wing pivot (Patent GB860823). *(BAE SYSTEMS)*

Calling Wallis 'one of our really original thinkers in the field of aircraft design', he noted the results already achieved and the fact that Swallow was revolutionary but practical, inviting Sandys to continue funding the project as he did not think that 'the money involved is excessive' and 'he may be able to give us a five-year lead in the international race'. The Swallow project was already well known to Sandys from his time as Minister of Supply, but Rosenhead's letter gave him cause to ask Sir Frederick Brundrett to review the project, his report being completed by mid-July.[72] Brundrett's opinion was that Swallow still required lengthy and expensive development for military application, and that the defence decision to cancel was correct. He did, however, back civil application of the ideas though added cagily that it was 'a matter of very close examination to decide whether the civil airlines could afford it'. He concluded by offering no objection to

Wallis seeking American funding for the project, and Sandys passed a summary of the report's conclusions back to Rosenhead. It is notable that as early as October 1960, Sandys's successor, Harold Watkinson, was beginning to rue any American involvement, noting the Ministry's earlier lack of objection to US funding but that 'it would be a very sad thing if the Americans were able to succeed with a British invention which we, in fact, have rejected'.[73]

The Air Staff were also 'disturbed' at the decision to cancel Swallow,[74] suggesting that it was 'wrong for the Minister of Defence to delete one item unilaterally from the research programme' and that 'we have only just received the Swallow brochure and this is being assessed now . . . the Swallow is the outstanding item in the research programme. It would represent a complete breakthrough in aerodynamics and would radically alter the manned aircraft versus missile picture . . . I therefore most strongly urge you to ask the Minister of Defence to withdraw his decision on the Swallow and to withhold judgement until the brochure has been properly assessed.'

In an Air Staff review of the situation in light of the cutbacks,[75] Swallow was again spoken of highly, the project being seen as promising due to its 'variety of applications' and being assessed as 'the most promising single project . . .', concluding that emphasis should be given to 'projects which show promise of . . . a marked increase in performance. In particular, the Air Staff is attracted by the potential gains to be expected from the successful development of the Swallow.'

Sir Charles Dunphie, Chairman of Vickers-Armstrongs Ltd, and Knollys met with Sandys on 19 March,[76] and he confirmed the project's cancellation, but two months later he met with the Board of Vickers,[77] and Knollys argued the case for continuation of the work focusing on 'two possible versions of a smaller aircraft', both capable of Mach 2.5, one a research aircraft of 10,000lb AUW, and the other a very long-range strike aircraft of 25,500lb AUW, estimated costs being £217,000 and £319,000 respectively.

A further Ministry endorsement of continuing support for Swallow came in August 1957.[78] Noting Wallis's ability to 'overcome what were previously felt to be insuperable difficulties', it suggested that concentrating most of the money outwith the missile projects on to Swallow could revolutionise flight, and 'far from withdrawing completely from the front rank of aeronautical powers as a result, we should emerge away out in front'; however, the Ministry of Supply publicly announced withdrawal of support for Swallow on 26 August.[79]

After Sandys

A brief revised programme of Swallow research[80] prepared in April 1957 noted that the demonstration of long range depended on having a wide speed range, but the converse was not true. Wide speed range required proof via piloted flight, an aircraft of AUW 10,000lb being the smallest possible, although the pilot would have to be contained within an aerodynamic contour (no cockpit blister) to permit high lift/drag (L/D) in supersonic flight. Wind tunnel work was required on this shape, as well as on the 'rising and falling cockpit' and thermal insulation.

Plans for a single-seat manned research aircraft, designated Swallow Type 006, were in hand by August 1957,[81] to be powered (and controlled) by four outboard engines or one under the fuselage.[82] This would have been capable of reaching Mach 1.4 at 36,000ft in 8 minutes, then flying for 25 minutes at Mach 1.4 before descent and landing. An RAE report on the aircraft,[83] while noting that the benefits of variable geometry were 'unassailable', was unenthusiastic about the swivelling engines, saying this feature was 'unjustifiable at this stage'. Although 'wing-mounted engines will simplify the balancing of the aircraft in the two wing positions

Simulation of the Swallow version to meet OR.339 (based on a drawing in SM Arch BNW I2/6). This design could have been adopted for TSR.2. *(Author)*

and may ease the aero-elastic properties', they would 'pose difficulties in maintaining control if an engine cuts immediately after take-off',[84] this being exacerbated by the large distance of the engines from the centreline when the wings were fully forward. L.F. Nicholson, Head of Aerodynamics at the RAE[85] reported that Wallis 'now accepts that control by moving engines need not be regarded as an essential in any research aircraft', although he certainly had not given up on it, and devised a practical solution to the engine-out performance.[86] This was based on automatic mechanical detection of the unequal thrust caused by loss of an engine on one side, and rebalancing this by asymmetric vectoring of the engine pods. The mechanism would cause the engines on the unfailed side to swing 'toe-in', thus decreasing the moment arm of those engines while also increasing the drag from the more sideways presentation of the nacelles to the airflow, thus restoring equal forces overall. It was claimed that this 'simple device can be made to take corrective action well in advance of the time it takes a human pilot to decide what is wrong'.

A further report in September reiterated the problem of R&D's isolation from the rest of the company, noting that it

> *is well known that Wallis does not receive the backing from the rest of the firm which he would require if he were to undertake the design and building of a research aircraft. It has been proposed (by Lord Weeks) that some other firm might be brought in to provide that backing, but I do not believe such a course is practicable in the light of our previous experience. As I have stated before, I would recommend that we proceed no further with Vickers in this matter, unless the detailed design and construction of any proposed research aircraft is passed from Wallis's Research Department to the main part of the firm.*[87]

The one new military aircraft requirement to survive the Sandys bloodbath was GOR.339 for a strike aircraft, capable of delivering nuclear weapons via a high-level or low-level mission. It was to be capable of

Mach 2 and of STOL from a grass strip – a formidable package of requirements indeed.[88] The specification was issued just before the Sandys report, with submissions invited by January 1958. With this now the only bait available, the aircraft companies went into a feeding frenzy over it, submissions being made from companies including English Electric, Avro, Hawker, Shorts and (Vickers) Supermarine. Wallis got hold of the specification and produced a Swallow variant to suit – this was very similar to the OR.330 Swallow, with a modified forebody shape around and ahead of the cockpit. He estimated that producing two aircraft would cost about £3.6 million over three years.[89] However, in a direct comparison of the Wallis and main Vickers proposals, the latter was favoured as

> *the Wallis proposal for OR.339 does not offer any significant advantage over the Vickers design – in fact its range performance on the specified sortie is considerably worse . . . largely due to . . . poor performance of Orpheus engine . . . if an engine of the size required with the characteristics of the RB.142 were available the Wallis design would show to advantage, having an operational radius on the OR.339 sortie some 10 per cent greater than the Vickers, allied to a much greater operational flexibility.*[90]

The Government's preferred solution was effectively to force English Electric and Vickers-Armstrongs to merge (forming the British Aircraft Corporation on 1 January 1960) to work on a development of English Electric's P.17A proposal, which emerged as the TSR.2.

Asking the Americans for money

After Ministry of Supply funding of Swallow was stopped in the wake of the Sandys report, Vickers had been continuing to fund the project itself, but was planning to stop this funding in 1958. Consequently, the Wallis team sought a new funding source and found a possibility in the Mutual Weapons Development Programme (MWDP), an early attempt to set up collaborative military programmes, with the US as its main driver (although the MWDP offices were in Paris).

Major Harry Legge-Bourke MP expressed some concern at this scenario, saying that 'if Britain were to hand over lock, stock and

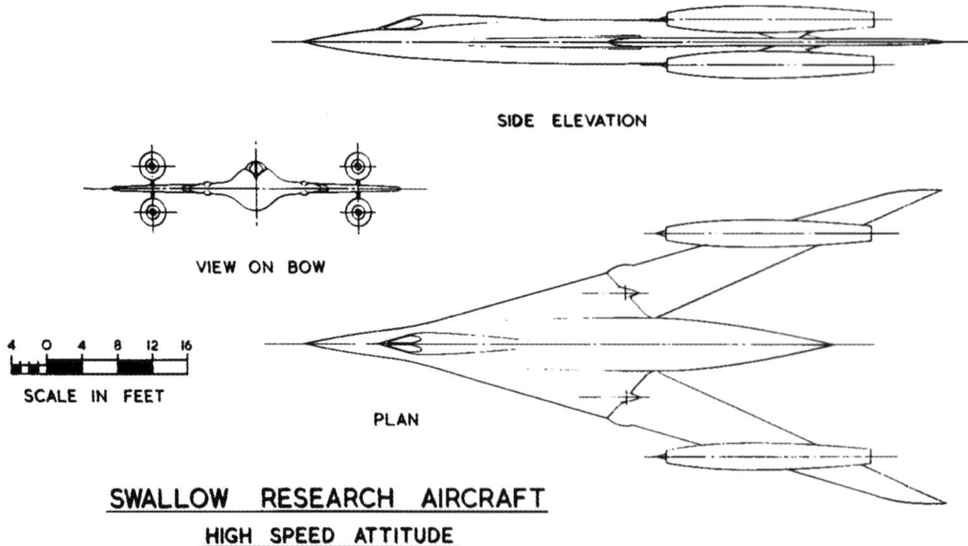

Three-view drawing of the research aircraft in the proposal for MWDP funding in April 1958. *(BAE SYSTEMS via Brooklands Museum)*

barrel to the United States one of the most original ideas since the Wright Brothers . . . she would not only slight a man who had served her well but would throw away one of the greatest geniuses ever produced'.[91] He also thanked the Minister of Defence for supporting Swallow as long as he did, noting that Wallis 'was not entirely helped by some people very close to [him] during that period'.[92]

A brochure giving the definitive description of the Swallow aircraft and the theory behind it was submitted to the MWDP office in April 1958.[93] It included plans for the proposed Swallow research aircraft, for which the MWDP funds were primarily sought; this was an update to the earlier Type 006 proposal, featuring wings fitted with detachable leading and trailing edges, allowing different profiles to be tested without altering the main structure of the aircraft. A detailed table of information for the research aircraft, supersonic fighter, supersonic military transport and high- and low-level bomber and strike naval aircraft was presented, together with detailed weights and project costings, and the report concluded with an appendix giving a full specification for the research aircraft.

The brochure submission resulted in visits to Weybridge by MWDP staff led by John Stack, on 9 May[94] and 6 August.[95] The visitors were 'very favourably impressed' with the Swallow concept, Stack describing it as a 'good engineering solution' to the problem of flight across the wide speed range. One of the MWDP team thought the concept most applicable to carrier-based aircraft, little in the way of performance enhancement of naval aircraft having occurred in the previous ten years, noting Swallow's ability to loiter efficiently at subsonic speed. The outcome of the meeting was a recommendation to develop a full-scale military demonstrator version of Swallow of about 40,000lb AUW – the brochure to be prepared about this aircraft being the basis of MWDP representation in Washington for funding support – as well as an invitation for the Vickers-Armstrongs

Wallis and his team at Langley in November 1958. Front row: Elsa Hoare, Phil Teed, Barnes Wallis, John Stack (NASA) and Herbert Jeffree; back row: Norman Boorer, Cecil Hayes, John Christie (MoS), Philip Hufton (RAE) and Lindsey Turner (NASA). *(NASA)*

team to visit the NASA Research Center at Langley Field later in the year. This visit (Wallis was accompanied by Major Phil Teed, Norman Boorer, Cecil Hayes and Elsa Hoare, plus two Ministry men) went ahead in November, with the aim of preparing a work programme for the military demonstrator.

The programme of research which was agreed at the 1958 visit to Langley was for the UK (Vickers and RAE) to perform sub-, trans- and supersonic wind tunnel tests on Swallow with no power simulation, and for the USA to perform power simulation tests on Swallow and further wind tunnel tests on three other VG layouts derived at Langley. Supporting research would cover pressure distribution, control forces, and induced drag, the Vickers team agreeing to do further engineering design study following on from the results of the wind tunnel tests. The Langley team had models in their wind tunnel within two weeks, and concluded around 500 hours of tests by April 1959, communicating their results to the UK by July 1959. Even before these began, the Americans were so concerned about lack of control from the gimballing engines that they added fins to each nacelle. The results of these tests were given in two substantial NASA reports,[96] and showed 'longitudinal instability' (notably a tendency to pitch-up at low speeds). The addition of the fins helped control slightly, but the gimballed nacelles were found 'ineffective for longitudinal control' due to the short moment arm in the unswept position. They were, however, found to be sufficiently effective for directional and lateral control, although 40 per cent of the turning moment came from nacelle drag. Simulated engine-out tests showed little effect on longitudinal stability, and directional stability could be maintained by nacelle deflection.

The results of the Vickers-Armstrongs research are contained in a series of internal reports.[97] These describe lift, pitching moment and drag coefficient experiments on a number of models with different sweepback of forewing and afterwings, using various incidence settings and varying

A Swallow model in the wind tunnel at Langley. *(NASA)*

amounts of camber and twist, the final tests also including a fuselage within the forewing. The experiments were performed in Vickers-Armstrongs's low-speed tunnel at South Marston, and showed that greater camber and twist resulted in reductions in the tendency to pitch up, although this was not removed altogether. It was concluded that 'pitch-up is due partly to flow separation from the trailing edge of the afterwings, and partly to leading edge separation from the forewing' with the further possibility that 'interference between the forewing and afterwings contributes to the pitch-up'. Additional wind tunnel work was performed at Imperial College in 1958–9, including investigation of interference between the wing and the engine pods.[98]

The Langley and South Marston results substantiated the Swallow's pitch-up tendencies, and this led to an apparent loss of interest in the Swallow concept. Stack noted that the Langley work had shown that 'the original basic aerodynamic design of the Swallow was unsound, although the mechanical principles and engineering of the moving wings and hinges were quite excellent', encouraging NASA designers to rework the aerodynamics while retaining the original mechanics, leading to a 50,000lb carrier- or land-based aircraft design. Stack expressed his opinion that the original Wallis direction was 'on the wrong lines' and that Vickers should pursue a 'detailed technical argument' for its VG ideas while his team investigated using VG with the Hawker light strike fighter.[99]

The Vickers-Armstrongs team were not the only British designers looking to the US to fund innovative aircraft research. Ralph Hooper and Bob Marsh of Hawker also visited Langley in 1959, seeking support for their P.1127 (forerunner to the Harrier). During a tour of the facility, they were surprised to see a wind tunnel model of Swallow, and the Americans were surprised (Britain being 'only a small country') that the Hawker men had never heard of it![100] Some MWDP funding was awarded to Bristols for the Pegasus engine for the

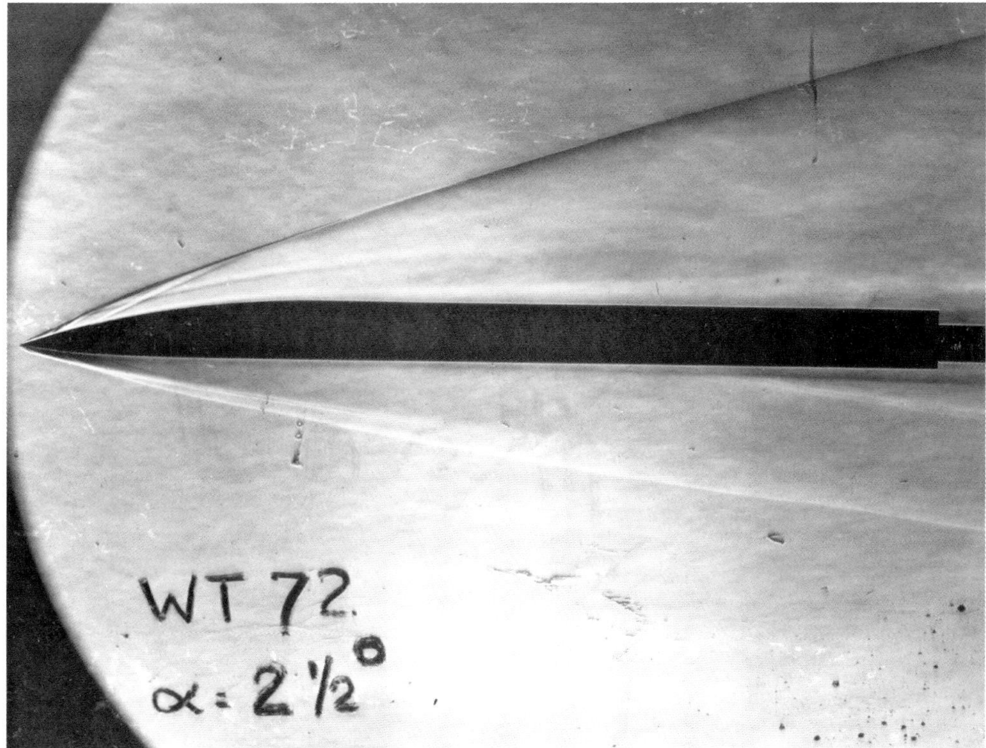

Schlieren photograph of Swallow wing section in the supersonic wind tunnel. Note the shock waves. *(BAE SYSTEMS via the Science Museum)*

P.1127, but the structures men at Hawker got nothing.

The failure to secure MWDP funds for Swallow effectively killed the project. However, at this time, three notable things happened in the story of Wallis and variable geometry – the concept finally began to catch on for practical use in aircraft, others emerged to claim that they, and not Wallis, had been the origin of the concept, and Wallis realised that the Mach 2.5 top speed of Swallow was no longer high enough, so he moved on to faster and more radical designs. The latter will be the subject of the next chapter, but it is interesting to follow the other two threads here.

Variable geometry takes off in the USA – the TFX / F-111

The Langley interest in Swallow did make it clear to the Americans that the key to successful VG was the use of an outboard wing pivot, and their wind tunnel experiments (with three other layouts in addition to the Swallow) found that a model with fuselage-mounted engines and an outboard pivot gave the most promising performance. This resulted in a patent application;[101] although this cites some earlier patents, none of Wallis's are included.

This layout was adopted for the General Dynamics TFX (later F-111). A NASA paper[102] detailing the chronology of the development of the F-111 boldly claims that 'not only was the variable-sweep concept born at . . . Langley' but that it was their 'research breakthrough' in late 1958 which provided the key to the stability issue, but the evidence suggests that this breakthrough was the one handed to them by the Vickers-Armstrongs team. The paper summarises the F-111 as 'an example of how these research and development investments eventually pay substantial dividends'. While the use of variable geometry in Swallow was mainly to achieve safe landing performance from an efficient supersonic aircraft, the NASA paper noted that the increased operational flexibility inherent in VG aircraft meant that a single aircraft type for multiple roles was a practical use of the concept; this would help achieve a secondary aim, that of reducing the number of aircraft types in service. The F-111 was conceived primarily for the USAF tactical bomber role, but its flexibility meant that it was also seen as a candidate for a US naval requirement.[103]

In December 1962, following publication of some details of TFX in the media, including an article in *Newsweek*, a New York lawyer friend of Wallis's patent agent wrote to suggest that 'it may be worthwhile to review these patents with a view to possible infringement by the TFX variable wing geometry'.[104] The agent passed this on, although Wallis's initial thought was that the work had been done under the MWDP programme 'so that the question of infringement hardly arises'. A further article in the aviation press in April 1963 included 'a diagram which looked familiar' and Grant noted that 'we have ample evidence that a similar planform was shown in the brochures handed to the Americans in 1958'; however, the brochures had been 'classified "Secret" and it is doubtful therefore if this can be claimed as prior publication' (which would be needed to invalidate the patent). He also noted 'that the US patentees descend to a quite lengthy denigration of the Swallow, something which would not be allowed by the British Patent Office', and suggested they seek the opinion of both the Ministry and their American patent agents.

Wallis wrote a short report on the released General Dynamics information, remarking of the revelation that each wing had to have its own pivot that 'it is surprising to be told that it took 22,000 hours of wind tunnel testing and more than 25 million man hours of design and development to discover this obvious necessity, even after it had been pointed out to the technologists at NASA during our visit in 1958'! He was satisfied, however, 'that the infringement of our patent lies in the use of pivots which are separated laterally at the base of a delta-shaped forebody'.[105]

In 1963 the Commercial Director at Weybridge asked Boorer to go with him to the States 'to try and get some money out of them' and they worked for about six months on litigation for patent infringement. Eventually it was decided that the patent was so general that there was little chance of a successful outcome, and the claim was dropped 'but it's true to say that they went on with their development because of the Wallis interest'.[106]

The discussion continued in the press, Wallis saying that 'it would be perfectly safe to say that the TFX has had its genesis in this country'.[107] Asked at the roll-out whether the aircraft owed anything to Wallis, Edward Heinemann, Vice-President of General Dynamics, said that it was hard to say that anyone was the inventor, although Wallis deserved 'a lot of credit'.[108] However, at a later press demonstration of the F-111, General Dynamics President Frank Davis said that their system 'owed nothing' to Wallis.[109] A 1981 NASA review of variable geometry omits entirely British VG research prior to 1958, and describes the Wallis work as 'a low level effort'.[110]

In 1965, in the wake of the cancellation of BAC's potentially world-beating TSR.2 on cost grounds, it was announced that the UK was to purchase F-111s instead – Wallis was not a swearing man, but if he ever came close, it would have been that day. There was probably little consolation in 1968 when the cancellation of the F-111 order was announced.[111]

The main wing structure in the F-111 was a carry-through box fabricated from steel with simple vertical wing pivots outboard. Although the structure itself was adequate, what was not realised at the time was the susceptibility of the steel to fatigue failure, and this contributed to a number of early crashes. Once the susceptibility of this material was identified, every F-111 in service had to undergo proof load testing on its wing structures every three years or so (this was expensive, but less so than replacing the wing pivot structures in every aircraft). Some of the other early F-111 crashes were traced to faulty welds in the wing or tail structure.

Claims and counterclaims

In December 1959, Wallis gave a Christmas Lecture at the Institute of Civil Engineers[112] at which he showed publicly, for the first time, photos of Wild Goose and a model of Swallow, leading to criticism from the aeronautical press for allowing this 'revolutionary principle of aeronautical research' to be revealed by leaks and 'full exposition before an audience of schoolboys'.[113] Some details of Swallow, however, had been leaked to the press in May 1958[114] in the wake of the withdrawal of funding for the project. This leak was described as a 'breach of security' by the Minister of Supply, but it contained enough detail for the RAF Review of July 1958 to include a short article on Swallow with an outline plan and, incredibly, a spectacular painting of Swallow on the cover with a nuclear explosion in the background.

Thus began a continual trickle of articles in the press about Swallow, focused on the loss of funding despite the promise shown from the experimental work, but also sparking a debate about who thought of variable geometry first.

One of the claimants was Leslie E. Baynes, who conducted a long discussion on the topic with Major Oliver Stewart, a regular aviation correspondent in *The Times*.[115] Baynes was Chairman and Technical Director of the Baynes Engineering Company, and had been a project designer at Shorts, also working pre-war with gliders (including the commercially available *Scud* recreational glider) and designing the *Baynes Bat* during the war, a flying-wing glider which was designed to carry an underslung tank to the battlefield; although tested by the RAE, it did not see action. He had also undeniably created one of the first aircraft with a wing pivot, although it was simply a mechanism to allow the wing on his *Baynes Bee* light aircraft to be rotated parallel to the fuselage for easier storage.[116] Post-war, he proposed a fighter with variable wing sweep in 1947, performing wind tunnel tests in 1948 and patenting the idea in 1949. However, the Air Ministry seems to have discouraged him, and his correspondence with Stewart shows a degree of bitterness about this in light of the American TFX and SST work potentially overtaking the British pioneering of VG, and also about Wallis getting 'all the credit' for it in the press. He noted that the early Wallis VG patents were specifically for tailless layouts with the VG mostly related to control 'rather than a means for increasing the speed range to embrace supersonic flight'. This was a legitimate claim, as supersonic speed is not mentioned in the early Wallis patents (even though it is certain from other documentation that this was his aim), and it is quite possible to patent a new application of an existing technology. Baynes's patents did also cover control by differential sweep. Stewart picked up Baynes's torch, stating: 'To him belongs the credit for seizing upon the essentials of comprehensive, in-flight variable sweep; for undertaking mathematical studies and wind tunnel trials and for completing the first design for a high-speed variable sweep naval fighter.'[117]

This was followed by a further article[118] prompting Wallis's daughter Mary to write briefly to *The Times* a few days later pointing out that her father's work predated that of Baynes. Stewart's reply to her crossed in the post with a letter from Wallis to Stewart (also in response to this article) noting a 'large amount of written evidence . . . showing that the original idea came to me in the year 1944', noting his patent claim of March 1945.[119] Wallis also makes the points that he had not heard of Baynes or his patent prior to *The Times* article, that neither Baynes nor the Americans appreciated the importance of having no tail, and that the dispute with the Americans over royalties was ongoing. Curiously, he also mentions that Wild Goose is 'a far better attempt' than Swallow. Baynes's next letter to Stewart again emphasises the different 'objects' of his and Wallis's patents (Baynes for supersonic speed, Wallis for efficiency and control), noting that his own patents would not have been granted had there been prior art. Several other journalists picked up on the discussion, although Baynes was careful to be even handed throughout and not to play down Wallis's own contribution to the field, eschewing the implication by one journalist that Wallis was getting credit for ideas originating with Baynes. He also demonstrated the same views as Wallis as to the practicality of VG for the SST, describing Concorde and the Lockheed SST as 'two more aeronautical white elephants', and expressing similar concerns about the 'eventual extinction' of the British aircraft industry by the Americans.

Another contributor to the debate was Harald Penrose, former Chief Test Pilot of Westland, who had flown the *Pterodactyl* tailless aircraft designed by Geoffrey Hill in 1930.[120] This featured minor variable sweepback for longitudinal trim variation, cranked by hand.[121] Penrose noted that Hill 'did envisage greater sweep-back for high speeds' and also upheld the claim of Baynes who 'while the last war was raging, sent us drawings of a fighter with variable sweep wings'.[122] Hill also had a 1948 patent[123] on a supersonic delta-wing aircraft, but the forward part of the delta could be swept forward until the leading edges were unswept, the aim being 'speeds well into the sonic range . . . without involving dangerously high take-off and landing

Simulation of an airliner using the Swallow configuration, in high subsonic attitude (based on a plan in the Barnes Wallis Memorial Trust collection). The fuselage is a 'double bubble' with 100 passengers on each deck and it has the 'rising and falling' cockpit. *(Author)*

speeds'. The aircraft demonstrated an outboard wing pivot (at a time when Wallis's were still inboard), and also claimed novelty for the 'cuff' which faired the leading edge of the wing into the fuselage in a manner similar to Tornado and other later aircraft.

Wallis noted the 'dispute over our claims and the American refutal of them' was still ongoing in 1965, and that 'my firm consider that they are entitled to claim some royalties on all machines made with variable sweep, whether they carry tails or not'.[124] The arguments about the origins of VG and which configuration was the best 'provided the air correspondents of the 1960s and 1970s with many a readable story'.[125]

Theme and variations – and the SST

Regarding Swallow, Boorer noted that 'we did quite a number of studies based on this configuration' and many variations on the main theme of Swallow can be found in the various archives, and although some can be positively correlated with various reports, there are many whose provenance, date or place in the chronological sequence has been lost.

Despite Wallis's main goal being a long-range civil airliner, there is very little material regarding designs for civil applications. One civil application was illustrated in his 1959 Christmas Lecture,[126] showing a Swallow airliner with 100 (rear-facing) seats. Other plans for eight-engined aircraft[127] show an elliptical-fuselage 60-seater and a double-bubble fuselage with 100 passengers on each deck; both variants feature the 'rising and falling' cockpit.

A brief 1960 report[128] summarised the performance of Swallow in the carrier-based interceptor role, but this was just a reworking of old figures. Swallow's real final fling was probably in the form of the 'Flat Model'[129] which underwent wind tunnel testing in 1959, but by then the engines had come back to the fuselage and a tail fin had appeared, so already the purity of the Swallow's true aerodynamic form was being eroded.

As the 1960s began, design studies on both sides of the Atlantic were looking for the most efficient shape for the SST, in Britain under the guidance of the Supersonic Transport Aircraft Committee, which had been formed in 1956. A 1961 study[130] for the SST project investigating the efficacy of variable geometry for this application found no 'clear cut decision to be made between the variable sweep and the fixed geometry configurations considered' although 'the variable sweep aircraft has performance comparable with the best fixed geometry aircraft, has possibly more potential development, and can offer a considerable amount of gain in terms of handling characteristics, approach speeds, noise and off-design performance'. Despite 'gaps in our knowledge', the report suggested that enough research had been done to allow 'a variable sweep aircraft to be started immediately', concluding with the warning of 'real danger of this country falling behind in this field as operational aircraft are being designed in the US incorporating variable sweep'. Despite these conclusions, there does not seem to have been any serious consideration of variable geometry options for the Concorde, which was finalised as a slender delta in 1962. There is no record of Wallis having made any formal (or indeed, informal) contribution to the Concorde design.

In 1961 President Kennedy announced a national competition to develop an American SST. In 1963 Boeing was reported as considering VG for a supersonic airliner, and the company had 'been working on variable geometry for four or five years' according to senior executive Wellwood Beall who 'had only just heard of Dr Wallis's work' at this time.[131] In 1964 deltas from North American and Lockheed, and the Boeing VG proposal were selected as finalists. North American was eliminated from the race in 1966, the delta Lockheed L-2000 being finally beaten in 1967 by the Boeing 2707, which incorporated variable geometry wings to give a 4,000-mile range with 350 passengers; top speed was to be Mach 2.7. Further design work suggested that the VG design would be heavier than a non-VG design by 7 per cent, and as this was deemed insufficient to justify the low-speed benefits given by variable sweep, a revised design, 2707-300, was produced without VG.[132] Due to budgetary and environmental considerations (and possibly the progress being made by Concorde), Congress cancelled the American SST project in March 1971.[133]

Had Concorde been based on the Swallow form, presumably it would have performed at least as well as the delta form, and with longer range, might have had better commercial prospects and even seen service on routes other than just transatlantic. However, it would also have suffered from the same environmental complaints levelled at Concorde regarding pollution and noise and been hit by the early 1970s' leap in the oil price, all factors which were ultimately to spell commercial disaster for Concorde.[134]

Variable geometry takes off in the UK . . . eventually

As in the US, Wallis's arguments promoting variable geometry had gained substantial support in the UK by 1960, and although VG would contribute to Wilson's technological 'white heat', it would not be Wallis who was fanning the flames. Having finally been persuaded of the benefits of VG, the Ministry was not convinced that Wallis and his R&D Department could deliver an actual aircraft – or, as Norman Boorer put it, 'we'll fund it, providing it's taken away from Wallis, because if we leave it with him, he'll only go and squander it on lots of funny new ideas and not get on with what we want him to do'.[135]

One option for quick production of a VG research aircraft would have been to add swing wings to an existing type, and design studies were undertaken for VG versions of both the Supermarine Swift[136] and the English Electric Lightning.[137] The Lightning study was seen as the 'first practical step to put variable sweep into the air'. It was proposed to build only one as an experimental type, which could be flying in summer 1963, and although the engineering design work was not done in great depth, a brochure for a naval application of the aircraft was produced.[138] A diagram of the aircraft shows wing pivots similar to Swallow.

Although variable geometry had been turned down for use in TSR.2, largely because the development work needed meant that the in-service target of 1965 could not be met, there was a suggestion that, if the ongoing development of a naval VG aircraft proceeded satisfactorily, and the size and structure of TSR.2 could remain relatively unaltered, then VG might be added to later TSR.2 models.[139] Outline plans for a TSR.2 with swing wings were incorporated into an (undated) BAC brochure[140] featuring a variety of VG concept aircraft.

In 1959, a new Military Projects Office was formed at Weybridge under George Edwards, the main staff being Maurice Brennan (who formerly had been at Saunders-Roe) and Norman Boorer (who had been Chief Designer under Wallis). Their first task was to design a fighter/ bomber, to the Joint Naval/Air Staff OR.346, of under 50,000lb (this was the heaviest that could land on a carrier), which would have performance slightly better than the TSR.2 (AUW 80,000lb).[141] 'To see how aircraft carriers worked', Boorer and three others spent a week as honorary officers on board HMS *Centaur* telling them about the new aircraft, though he later admitted 'it was only a reason to have a week's holiday on an aircraft carrier'! Initial ideas for a smaller form of TSR.2 gave way to the Type 581, which had swing wings, two engines in the rear fuselage, a fin (but no horizontal stabiliser, wingtip elevons being used for control) and a droop nose for improved landing view; this was submitted under ER.206 in 1960. With further changes in service requirement, this in turn became the Type 583 in 1962, which was similar but with the addition of a horizontal stabiliser, outboard wing pivots and no droop nose. This aircraft was superseded by the Hawker P.1154 VTOL aircraft, but the cancellation of the planned *Queen Elizabeth*-class carriers in February 1966 meant the cancellation of the new aircraft too; existing carriers were refurbished instead, taking the new Blackburn Buccaneers augmented by an order for American Phantoms.[142]

In 1964, all of the VG work was transferred from Weybridge to Warton,[143] Boorer spending six months in Lancashire handing over the baton. The first VG project to emerge from Warton was for a STOL fighter and trainer dubbed the P.45, the detailed brochure[144] showing an aircraft similar to the later Hawk, but with swing wings (and also a new wing pivot test rig built at Warton). The P.45 lost out to the French-led Jaguar project, but VG work was to proceed in another (UK-led) collaboration for a multi-role aircraft known as AFVG (Anglo-French Variable Geometry) in July 1965.[145] Warton built a full-scale mock-up, but in June 1967, the French pulled out claiming 'we haven't got enough money to put into variable wing sweep in France',[146] and the UK government had to concoct a new unilateral holding project (UKVG) to keep the concept ticking over. It was claimed that 'in light of extensive research already completed, and more recently two years' specific design attention', all of the main design problems for swing-wing aircraft could be resolved via 'conventional means'.[147] At this time, as well as on several previous occasions, BAC pressed the government to build a VG demonstrator, but permission was again refused.

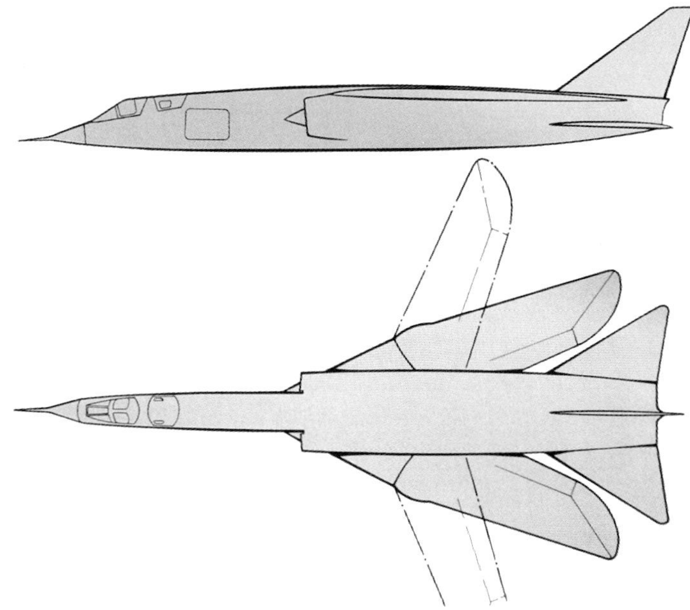

Variable sweep was an obvious solution to the short field take-off requirement of TSR.2, and the second generation of the aircraft could have incorporated VG as shown in this early 1960s BAC brochure image. *(BAE SYSTEMS via Brooklands Museum)*

The Navy's Phantoms were to have Rolls-Royce Spey engines, and Boorer and former Vickers test pilot Jeffrey Quill[148] were of the opinion that the Dassault Mirage would offer far better performance if fitted with these engines:

So we went over to Paris to talk to Dassault on this, and while we were walking round the shops, being engineers like we are, there in a corner we could see them building a variable wing sweep Mirage – so they got everything from us and said they couldn't afford it, then went back and built their own! We took a dim view of that.[149]

Meanwhile, UKVG was being promoted by BAC as a replacement for the F.104 Starfighters used by several European air forces, in competition with projects including the short-lived Advanced Vertical Strike, a West German/US collaboration on a swing-wing aircraft with retractable vertical lift fans.[150] By the end of 1968, UKVG was at the centre of discussions between West Germany, Italy, the Netherlands, Belgium and Canada. The latter two dropped out, leaving the others to form Panavia to develop what was now called the Multi-Role Combat Aircraft (MRCA) project, later named Tornado; the Netherlands withdrew a year later, leaving BAC, MBB (Germany) and Fiat (Italy) as partners. Ollie Heath noted that the MRCA project was not specifically set up to exploit VG, but rather that it turned out to be the best solution for the complex requirements.[151]

Two full-size wing pivot test rigs were built at Warton in support of Tornado work. One tested bearing designs, and showed that PTFE-lined bearings were satisfactory (confirming Wallis's work a decade earlier), but that lubricated metal bearings were not. The other rig was to test the pivot support structure, but this failed almost immediately showing that welded stainless steel in the pivot area was not acceptable (confirming the earlier F-111 experience). Tornado's carry-through box structure was consequently fabricated in welded titanium and the wing pivots are PTFE-coated pins mounted just outboard of the main fuselage.[152] On AFVG, Warton had initially wanted to position the pivot inboard, but Dassault wanted it outboard. The pivot location was investigated again for Tornado and retained outboard, giving rise to the short fairing ahead of the wing root known as the 'nib' (the remnant of the delta forebody) also seen on the F-111. The division of work meant that the wings were actually in a German-built section of the aircraft, but BAC passed on all the relevant research to MBB.

Evolving from the earlier design studies (a single-seat version being dropped), Tornado emerged as a two-seater variable-geometry aircraft with a large fin and tailerons. Twin RB.199 engines were mounted inside the rear fuselage. There was very little feedback from the Americans' F-111 experience into Tornado, with the exception of the direction of operation of the wing sweep lever.[153]

The Tornado made its first flight at Manching in Germany in August 1974. Initially conceived for low-level attack missions, the UK initiated further development to produce a lengthened variant for air defence. Nearly 1,000 aircraft (including 120 of both types for export to Saudi Arabia) had been built by 1998 when production ceased. The UK had its variable-geometry aircraft at last (albeit produced in partnership).

After Britain's early massive lead in the VG race, Tornado came a disappointing eighth out of the ten variable-geometry aircraft to enter military service around the world[154] (there have been no VG civil aircraft). Tornado was also a more conventional implementation than Wallis's original Swallow tailless concept – practical requirements meant that it was also fitted with leading edge slats and double-slotted flaps, further increasing the structural complexity. Indeed, the aircraft's Wallis pedigree became so distant that some argue his contribution to Tornado was nil in practice, although Boorer said that 'the real engineers up there [at Warton] always credit Wallis for having brought variable wing sweep in'.[155] No Tornado wing structure failures have been recorded, and the service performance of pivots has also been

The Tornado wing pivot is a simple pin, rotating in one dimension only. Note the hydraulic pipes which must bend around the pivot. *(Author)*

'remarkably trouble free',[156] although some suggest that use of the more complex Wallis pivots would have been more problematic.

In combat situations, manoeuvrability is often key to survival, and relying on wing sweep alone for control would be considerably less efficient than the tailerons used on the Tornado – the wing flaps and spoilers can even be used asymmetrically to assist in high-speed manoeuvres.[157]

Summary – Swallow

Accelerated to flight status by the earlier work on Wild Goose, Swallow showed that an arrowhead aircraft consisting of a lifting delta forebody with engines mounted on trailing VG wings was a practical proposition for producing a long-range supersonic aircraft. However, as the project reached maturity in 1957, the Defence White Paper saw Government funding for most aircraft projects withdrawn. Wallis took the project to the Americans for funding, but succeeded only in rekindling their interest in variable geometry, leading directly to the F-111. In Britain, the use of VG was also in the ascendancy, leading (after a number of false starts) to the Panavia Tornado, although there was no direct Wallis contribution to this aircraft, the detailed design having been taken away from him. Much to his annoyance, both the F-111 and Tornado had moved away from the tailless concept that was his original justification for VG.

By 1960 Wallis himself had lost interest in conventional VG, as he wanted to fly much faster than the Swallow would allow. An exponent of lateral thinking long before de Bono coined the phrase, Wallis now used *orthogonal* thinking, rotating the primary pivot axis for his variable geometry through 90 degrees to produce yet another aircraft concept.

Chapter 10

Towards the Universal Aircraft

Things turn out best for the people who make the best of the way things turn out.
(John Wooden)

Death of the delta

The elation of the Vickers-Armstrongs team after their visit to the Langley Research Center in November 1958 evaporated very quickly in the New Year as it became apparent that no MWDP funding would be appearing for UK Swallow development work, and the results of the latest round of wind tunnel tests confirmed its problems at low speeds. More crucially, they had shown 'that even with the superior values of L/D then realised, the desired performance could not be obtained with an aircraft of this type since, by this time, the inescapable relation between range, speed, height and temperature was also becoming clear'. Ultimately, despite the results from Predannack and the Swallow flights at Larkhill to over Mach 2.5, Wallis realised that Swallow was simply *too slow*. The Americans had announced their intention to have a Mach 3–4 civil airliner in service by 1967, a target which seemed not unreasonable in 1959, and so Wallis concluded that Britain needed to match that, or to have a Mach 3 airliner flying earlier,[1] if the commercial supersonic race was not to be lost to the Americans.

This target effectively ruled out Swallow, or any other delta aircraft, on aerodynamic grounds – the Mach cone created by a supersonic aircraft, behind which all parts of the aircraft must lie, grows increasingly pointed as Mach number increases, and as Mach 3 is approached, the cone becomes so narrow that there is no space for a practical wing, even a delta, to fit within it. On the economics, Wallis repeatedly cited figures that the cost of developing any new supersonic aircraft form would be of the order of £100 million,[2] and argued that hence Britain should be using those funds to develop a Mach 3 aircraft, rather than spending £100 million on a Mach 2 airliner then having to spend the same again later to reach Mach 3. He also observed that any *conventional* form of SST would, for transatlantic range, require an AUW of at least 300,000lb, far greater than the AUW of the types that he had been designing.[3]

At supersonic speeds, wave drag becomes increasingly significant until it is the dominant drag factor, and coupled with the inability to use a delta above Mach 3, this meant that another new aircraft shape was required. Wallis's solution[4] was to use a wing of very high chord, which allowed the drag-inducing thickness/chord ratio to be kept small while allowing a wing thick enough for manufacture, and the wave drag of the fuselage was kept 'to a very low value by hiding the payload and fuel behind the air intake'. This led to a design where the whole frontal area of the fuselage was an air intake (ducted to rear-mounted engines), and the wings were short but extending over almost the whole length of the fuselage. While efficient for high-speed cruise, this new form would have had very poor low-speed characteristics, so Wallis also proposed a new form of variable geometry to cope with this. Rather than build the wing in one piece, it would be composed of a series of winglets or blades, each pivoted transversely at its centre. When 'closed' the blades would meet to form the continuous long-chord wing for high-speed flight, but at lower levels, the blades would all rotate leading edge up (in the fashion of a Venetian blind) to form a series of flaps, and thus generate a large amount of lift, enough even to give STOL performance. This new form was christened Cascade, although it is also referred to as the 'all speed aircraft'.

The blades could be rotated up to 45 degrees for maximum lift, with pitch control at all speeds 'by using the leading flap of the leading blade and the trailing flap of the trailing blade as bow and stern elevators respectively, in-phase as regards port and starboard bow, out-of-phase as regards bow and stern' and in roll 'out-of-phase as regards port and starboard but in-phase as regards bow and stern'.[5] The Cascade wing gave no yaw capability, so yaw control was by conventional fin and rudder. Pitch stability was achieved 'by so arranging that the forward portion of high speed surface stalls before the rear portion' and at low speed 'a system of differential opening

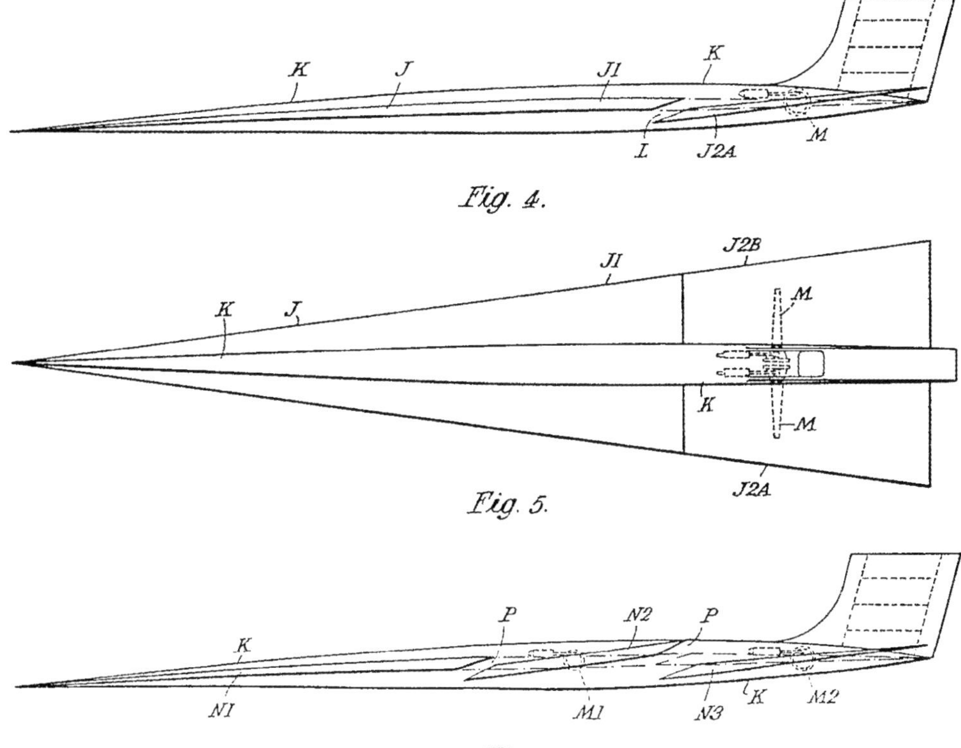

The 'compound delta' shows the origin of the Cascade concept; the vertical tail would have housed a mixture of turbojets and ramjets (Patent GB894365). *(BAE SYSTEMS)*

of blades so that the forward blades stall before the rear blades'. The large frontal intake fed into a high-pressure trunking running along the fuselage, and tappings were to be taken from this to feed slots on the blades which would 'greatly augment' lift at low speeds.

The Cascade idea appears to have originated in Wallis's final fling with laminar flow. In a 1959 patent,[6] he describes a delta wing with one or two large rotating blades forming the rear part of the delta. By rotating the forward edge of the blades *downwards*, some of the airflow was diverted up over the blade, thus creating a greater pressure on the top which would help maintain the laminar flow. This patent is notable, as it was the last of Wallis's patent applications which would be published. He applied for a further dozen UK patents between 1959 and 1965 (including two for the full Cascade concept under the name 'Casca'), but all of these applications were abandoned, many of them in 1962; it is unclear why all of these later patents were not proceeded with (although patent documents become public record, materials relating to UK applications which do *not* proceed to publication are only kept for seven years).

Documents[7] show a version of the Cascade aircraft with a square-section fuselage, full-frontal intake with ducting diverging around a rear-hinged 'pop-up' cockpit for two crew in tandem and a delta-shaped Cascade wing. This version has two sets of four angled lift jets within the fuselage, probably the only time that Wallis dabbled with engine-powered STOL. Given the already good STOL performance of the Cascade, it is unclear why he would permit the extra weight penalty of eight additional engines to shorten take-off further. This point is queried in a report by Morien Morgan of the RAE,[8] who otherwise found the aircraft concept 'quite fascinating', suggesting that a 'proper study is undertaken by an experienced aircraft design office'. He noted that Wallis's own team was too small to do it and that 'this is the basic reason for the Swallow idea being stuck for years; a tragic situation which – as an old friend of Wallis – I watched with increasing disquiet'.

Initial free-flight wind tunnel tests with three versions of Cascade had been conducted by November 1959 and appeared very favourable,[9] the aircraft being statically stable in pitch. This allowed Wallis to outline his new concept to Sir Solly Zuckerman (then Chief Scientific Adviser to the Air Ministry) at a private meeting at the end of January 1960.[10] Wallis stated that the Cascade aircraft could ultimately achieve Mach 4.5 at 93,000ft, this being invulnerable

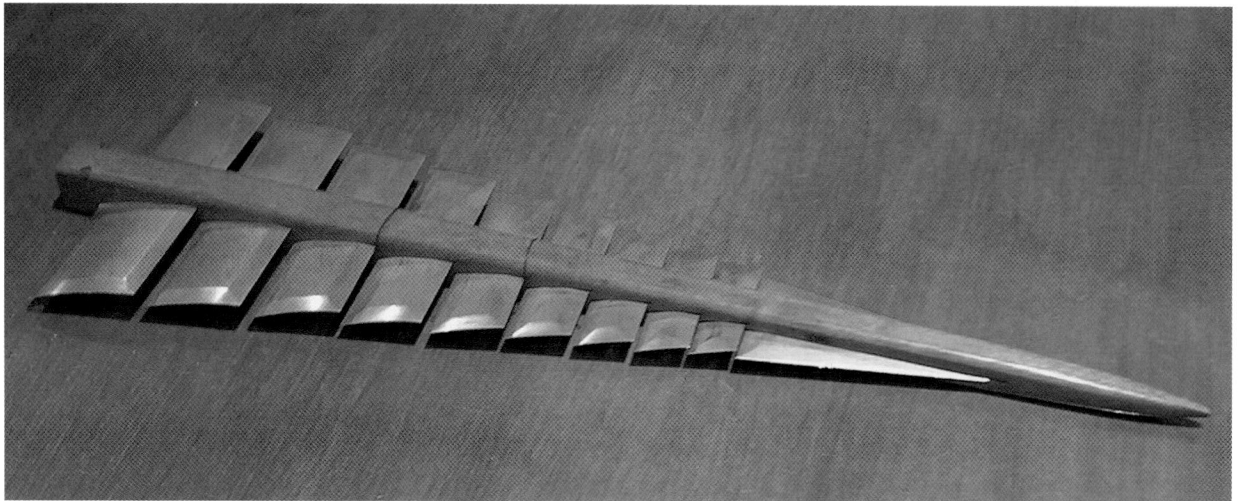

A simple wind tunnel model of Cascade. *(Author)*

to attack by either surface- or air-launched Soviet missiles, and thus offering a 'fluid deterrent,' playing to contemporary fears that the UK's static deterrent was no longer effective due to increasing accuracy of Russian ICBMs. This was backed up with the STOL characteristics which offered the ability for dispersed operation from short unsurfaced airstrips.[11] He also stated that the mechanical construction of Cascade was simpler than Swallow (there were no three-dimensional wing pivots to worry about), and its flight characteristics were inherently stable, volunteering that a single seat turbojet-propelled prototype capable of Mach 2.5–3 could be in the air within three years, a 50,000lb nuclear-capable bomber taking a further two years. Zuckerman was so excited about taking the details to Mountbatten (Chief of the Defence Staff), that he persuaded Wallis to part with the only copy of some of his calculations.

On seeing information on Cascade, AVM Bufton requested a full brochure for Air Staff consideration by Easter 1960, for a bomber capable of carrying a 6,000lb payload (including a 3,000lb bomb), with a radius of action of 2,000 miles at Mach 3 at 100,000ft. It was to operate 'from any reasonable runway' and ideally to offer VTOL 'but not at the expense of performance or time'. A reconnaissance aircraft of similar characteristics was also requested. Wallis's team obliged within a week, preparing specifications of a Cascade aircraft[12] of just 45,000lb AUW, with a take-off run of 300yds; range would be an immense 6,500 miles at around 75,000ft.

Wallis was pressed to complete his Cascade study 'in time for the Government decision on Supersonic Transport and Civil Airliner orders',[13] but Edwards told Wallis 'that he is not going to let BNW ruin all the work on supersonic airliner project that Bristol Aircraft have done'. An internal Vickers appraisal with comments from Edwards and his Chief Designer was passed

Simulation of a Cascade airliner for 96 passengers (based on drawings in SM Arch BNW I3/6). The winglets are slightly tilted for low-speed flight. *(Author)*

to the Ministry in July 1960 expressing concern about the 'complexity and weight' of the new wing and that efficiency when flying below cruising speed was less than ideal.[14] It concluded that Cascade offers 'no clear advantage over orthodox solutions, although considerably increased mechanical complexity'. Whether this was a fair appraisal, or one biased to favour conventional options is unclear, but it may have been the fatal blow for Cascade.

Isothermal flight

In addition to the wave drag and engine problems posed by flight above Mach 3, there was the problem of kinetic heating. As speeds increase, the friction caused by the air rubbing past the airframe causes the skin temperature to increase, potentially enough to cause permanent damage to the aircraft – the crucial factor being the equilibrium (or 'soak') temperature reached in steady flight at a particular height (the effect decreases with height due to the thinning atmosphere).

In another of his grand visions entitled 'The Command of the Air'[15] in February 1961, Wallis observed 'that it is neither stability, control nor propulsion but kinetic heating that bars the way to further rapid progress in the design of aircraft'. His approach to the problem was from an unusual direction, and suggested a solution which was not obvious. The usual method was to 'treat the equilibrium temperature of the supersonic aircraft as a function of speed in which height forms a parameter held constant at selected levels while speed varies', in other words, for a given height, how fast can an aircraft travel without exceeding a particular temperature? He noted that the impression given by this sort of analysis was that 'we should construct aeroplanes from materials that would withstand the highest possible temperatures'. However, he realised that 'the idea of using the soaking temperature of an airframe as the principal parameter with height as the independent and speed as the dependent variable does not seem to have been developed' – i.e. can height and speed be controlled together in order to stay below a given temperature? This was the founding principle of isothermal flight.

Conventional thinking thus dictated that fast aircraft had to be made of materials able to withstand the high soak temperatures – light (aluminium) alloy had to be kept below 150°C, titanium alloy was good up to 300°C, ferrous alloys being able to withstand 600°C. This was undesirable as these other materials were heavier and harder to work than light alloy (and in the case of titanium, far more expensive).[16] Another disadvantage of a high soak temperature was with the fuel. At low temperatures, the vapour pressure of aviation fuel is low (just 7.5psi at 150°C) and irregularly-shaped fuel tanks can be used; at higher temperatures, the vapour pressure increases dramatically (100psi at 300°C), meaning that stronger cylindrical or spherical tanks must be used, which increase weight and reduce capacity within the aircraft structure. Despite these disadvantages, all contemporary high-speed aircraft seem to have followed the route of using special materials for the airframe, and ignored the substantial advantages to be had in keeping the soak temperature below 150°C. The idea of isothermal flight was to treat this temperature as a fixed limit, then develop a flight regime which managed the speed according to height, only allowing the speed to rise once sufficient height had been gained, thus keeping the temperature within the envelope. Isothermal flight was thus not an 'invention' in the conventional sense, nor (as some commentators pointed out) was it originally Wallis's idea, but it seems that Wallis was the first to press its advantages seriously – although when opening a materials exhibition in February 1960, Wallis referred to an 'immediate need for a new material which will maintain its strength and elasticity' at 300°C for the next generation of airliners.[17]

Predating the isothermal idea, Wallis had recognised the limits posed by kinetic heating, and had investigated possibilities for using vacuum-filled panels for insulation purposes in aircraft,[18] no doubt exploiting the thermodynamics he had learned during the design of the stratosphere chamber (see Chapter 11). The vacuum-insulated skin is described in a patent,[19] and would have used an inner skin of light alloy and an outer skin 'capable of tolerating high temperatures without serious deterioration of its functional characteristics, such as resin-bonded glass fabric'. The panels were kept apart by spacers of low thermal conductivity and the space between them was evacuated to a degree 'sufficiently good for practical purposes'. Results of the initial experiments suggested better insulation properties than contemporary alternatives using insulating materials (rather than vacuum) and suggested 'it is surely possible to proceed with confidence on the production of a test cabin', which was to be a simplified cylindrical fuselage section 6ft long and 5ft diameter with the vacuum insulation around the curved surface. This was fabricated, and drawings show the cylinder set up for tests in the stratosphere chamber,[20] but the results are not available. Boorer indicated that later developments used insulating granules within the panels (still partially evacuated), and that the idea was the basis for later developments in insulating panels.[21]

Limited jet lift

Cascade had a very short shelf life. By October 1960 Wallis's thinking was centred on a wholly new design concept, and although Cascade would contribute its wing pivot to this, it was reduced to having just *one* larger pivoted wing.

As already stated, with increasing supersonic speeds, the wave drag from the wings increases and becomes the dominant drag force. Thus the designer would like to make the wings smaller (to reduce the wave drag) if only the lost lift could be replaced somehow. To achieve this, Wallis hit upon the idea (in addition to minimising the AUW) of using some of the engine thrust, directed slightly downwards, to augment lift – his calculations showed that this improved overall range, even though there was a slight loss of forward thrust due to the deflected jet.

Surprisingly, Wallis originally *thought* that he got this idea from the Germans – he was one of the few who were told the intelligence secrets of the V-2 rockets in 1944, and when he heard about the graphite control fins which were situated in the rocket efflux,[22] it was his assumption that the rocket was flown horizontally under power, with the fins used to deflect the rocket thrust downwards, hence creating lift. Using this effect, he calculated that the V-2 would have had a horizontal range of some 1,000 miles, and he reported this to ACM Sir Wilfred Freeman. On 7 August 1944, the first bank holiday taken in the Vickers works since the start of the war, Wallis commandeered the whole compressed air supply in the factory to augment the flow in the 6ft wind tunnel, and proceeded to demonstrate (using a model V-2) that it could be stable at all angles of incidence from 0 to nearly 90 degrees.[23] In fact, the V-2 used a simple ballistic trajectory, giving it a range of only 200 miles, so this impressive demonstration only confirmed that Wallis had, almost accidentally, discovered a new principle of flight, one which would not come into its own until 20 years later.

Wallis remarked in 1961:

> *Since the war, limited jet lift has, however, been openly discussed from time to time, apparently with no other end in view than a relatively small economy in fuel. It is only recently that I have realised that a small amount of jet lift, when applied to a long range aircraft, can be used to bring about a spectacular reduction in the AUW that would otherwise be required, as well as a reduction in wing loading. For example, to satisfy the following spec. – lumped military load 10,000lb, range (all fuel burnt) 8,300nm – it is probable that most aircraft designers would estimate an AUW of about 500,000lb, whereas with limited jet lift it appears that this weight can be reduced by a factor of about five, while still giving the required performance.*[24]

The actual implementation of the jet lift idea could be done by permanently mounting the engines at a slightly downward angle, but also lent itself to yet another variable geometry – pivoting the fuselage ahead of the engines on a transverse axis, in one or two places, so that the engines would be fore-and-aft for take-off and landing but hinged downward slightly for limited jet lift at high speed.[25] A sketch of a two-pivot fuselage appears in Wallis's diary for 15 December 1960.[26] Some variants are shown with Swallow-type swing wings,[27] and crews vary from a lone pilot to a crew of five.[28]

Another idea arrived on the Wallis drawing board at the same time as jet lift, the variable-camber wing, and both are often seen together in drawings from this period. The conventional way to stabilise an aircraft was via the empennage, the transfer of fuel being used in Concorde when passing through the transonic region in order to balance the rearward shift of the CP by changing the position of the CG and hence minimise trim drag at any speed. Wallis noted that there had been no previous attempts to use changes in wing camber for stabilisation – camber can change the moment centre of an aircraft – and he proposed to use these variations for control purposes:

> *It is readily shown that at high supersonic speeds, the equivalent of two-dimensional flow, i.e. infinite aspect ratio, can be developed with wings of low aspect ratio and hence of long chord and that such wings when fitted with both leading- and trailing-edge flaps, can be varied in camber to such an extent as readily to balance movements of the aerodynamic centre of the wings.*[29]

The resulting aircraft combining both new features also used the square-section fuselage with internally integrated engines seen in Cascade (this shape was believed to reduce fuselage wave drag) with a vertical stabiliser and (in effect) a single Cascade-type pivoted winglet, the latter endowed with large leading-edge and trailing-edge flaps for modifying the camber to give 'synthetic stability'. The aircraft would have flown an isothermal flight profile. Construction would have been straightforward, only one pivot being required, and the fuselage of 'elementary shapes and general simplicity' was designed in two symmetrical halves

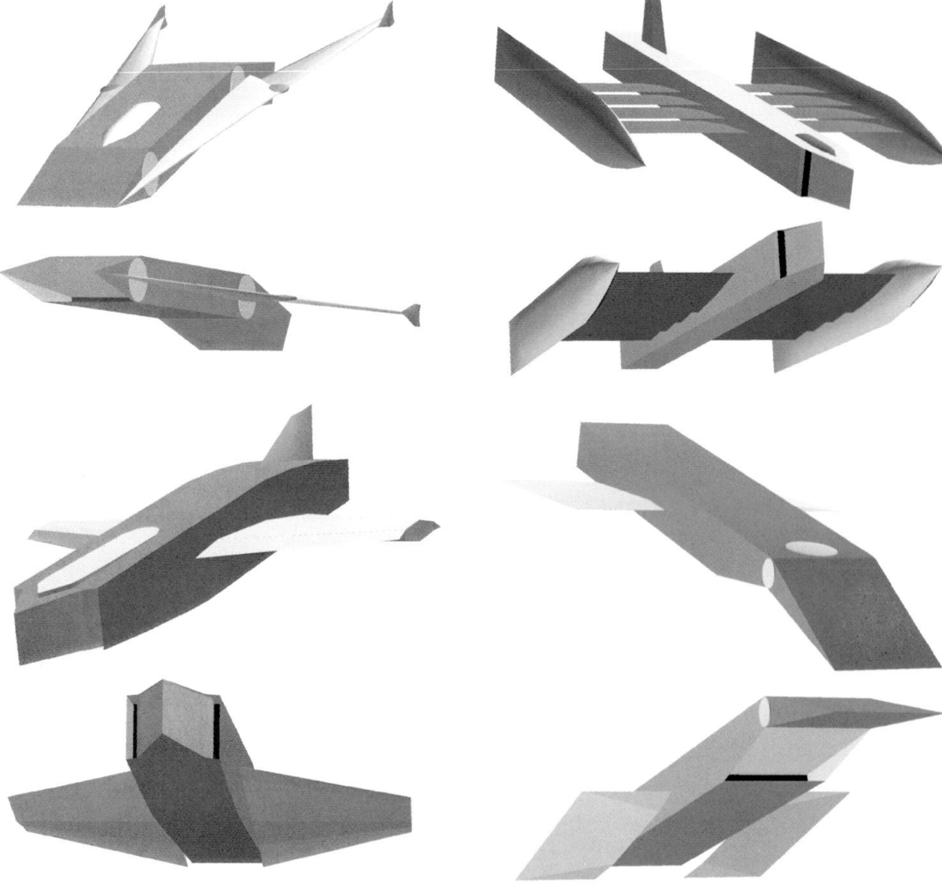

A selection of four simple 3-D models based on archive drawings. Top left: variable-camber fuselage with Swallow-type wings. Top right: Cascade aircraft with wingtip pods containing fuel tanks. Bottom left: cambered duct aircraft with fixed engines and variable-camber wings. Bottom right: variable-camber fuselage and variable-camber wings. All feature the square-section fuselage and 'pilot's turret' cockpit. *(Author)*

for ease of tooling; hence Wallis was able to propose 'two light alloy prototypes being completed in . . . three years' with 'high pressure effort'.[30] The novelty of these ideas was described in seven patent applications between 1960 and 1962, three entitled 'variable camber aircraft' and two 'counterpitch'. However, these were all abandoned around the end of 1962, and while correspondence relating to the applications remains,[31] there are no clear reasons given for deserting the applications.

In a note which appears to have been circulated at the same time as 'The Command of the Air', Wallis emphasises some of the key points in his report, especially 'the factor which decides whether the proposal to carry out all military functions by means of manned aircraft is feasible is clearly the AUW of the aircraft'.[32]

He concludes that this work has 'at present proceeded far enough to show the possibility of rearming and equipping the RAF with an all-purpose, one-design supersonic aircraft that need be no larger in AUW than a Lancaster bomber in the last war, and may in fact be actually somewhat less'.

After receiving 'The Command of the Air', Air Ministry officials discussed it with Wallis who 'confidently answered all the outstanding questions but he did so in a manner generally beyond the limits of our knowledge'[33] and they set up an independent assessment of the project by Dr Archibald Russell of Bristols and Sir Alfred Pugsley, Professor of Civil Engineering at Bristol University. These reviewers also found the paper 'difficult to follow' but noted the advantages, for various reasons, of an aircraft of less than 100,000lb AUW for the intended roles.

Another reviewer[34] thought that 'his theory appears to be excellent as far as it goes', but queried the multi-role flexibility claimed for the design, especially its 'very limited low-level performance because of its very low wing loading, excessively high friction drag which can be disregarded at high level but is all important at low levels, and from the apparently large radar echoing area and poor gust response of this design', which meant that 'the aircraft would be of no use to us in the tactical or close support roles'. While the design was optimised for flight at great height, it was noted that this 'would make the aircraft unacceptable in the defensive role where the heights and speeds necessary would be dictated by the enemy's height and speed band'. Commenting on several positive features of the design, this reviewer concluded by asking if the aircraft could be developed as a supersonic civil transport or a reconnaissance bomber capable of operating at 125,000ft, seeing 'little chance of Dr Wallis's ideas obtaining much official support' unless it could do at least one of these roles well.

The ducted wing

The variable-camber wing (for control) and the variable-camber fuselage (for limited jet lift) gradually came together over the following years. Some drawings show an aircraft with two wings one above the other, each on its own transverse pivot, and thus enclosing a channel of air between them whose direction could be altered by tilting the wings in unison.

The ultimate expression of this idea was the 'ducted wing' which consisted of a hollow box wing structure, through which the airstream could flow chordwise without restriction, but by tilting the whole box, the airflow was diverted downwards to provide a substitute for jet lift. Versions of this underwent wind tunnel tests[35] in 1964 and a patent[36] was applied for in 1965, but it was never awarded – the application was allowed to lapse in 1968 following a Wallis decision 'that in view of the very great improvement that we have made on

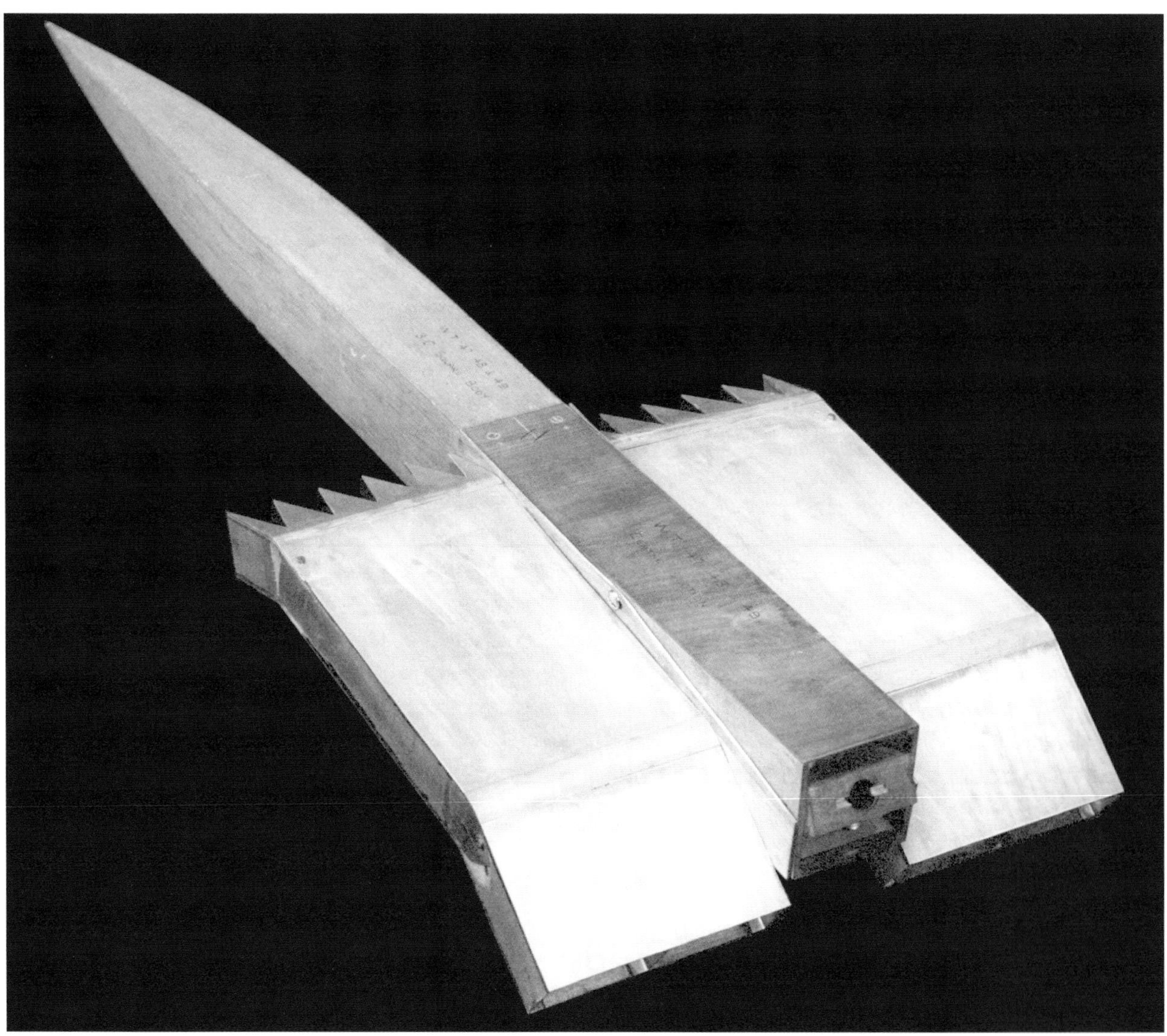

A wind tunnel model of the ducted wing aircraft. *(BAE SYSTEMS via the Science Museum)*

the original invention, it would be wiser to avoid publication in every case of the wing under discussion'.[37]

A note on engines

A further complication of attempting to fly very high and fast was that the efficiency of turbojet engines drops off above about 60,000ft due to the thin air, and they cannot be used much above Mach 2.5 as it becomes too difficult to design an intake to slow down the incoming air (as the airflow must be subsonic before reaching the engine compressor). Ramjets (which use the forward speed of the aircraft, rather than a turbine compressor, to compress the incoming air for combustion) were seen as the powerplant of choice above the turbojet limits and could be used up to around Mach 5. However, they could not be started below Mach 1.5, so turbojet engines were needed for the early stages of flight. To minimise the weight penalty imposed by carrying two sets of engines, combination engines were in early development – these embodied the features of both turbo- and ramjet engines, and could switch between the two methods of operation as required.[38]

Ramjet research was ongoing at Bristols[39] throughout the 1950s and 1960s, and 'the essential parts of a ramjet' had been tested there by 1970, with 'design of the complete engine . . . already finished'.[40] Robin Jamison had led this research, and he was in frequent correspondence with Wallis regarding the latter's queries about engines declaring 'that we shall always be able to find the time to do some figuring on your behalf'.[41] They were still in discussion of suitable engines for a Mach 5 aircraft in 1970,[42] principal findings being summarised by Wallis.[43]

Wallis also discussed engines with John Stack when he met him again in 1971, Stack saying that he was investigating Mach 8–12 flight using rocket engines powered by liquid hydrogen. Wallis asked Jamison about this, who replied that they had 'from time to time' considered hydrogen as a fuel, but its 'volume is an embarrassment' because of the large tanks required due to its low density[44] and the need to carry oxygen for use at high altitudes. Wallis thought that the Americans were 'wasting their time' in aiming for these speeds, considering that Mach 5 was fast enough for semi-global travel, and if 135,000ft could be achieved via low wing loading, then the heating effects 'should not be serious'.

Hall, a colleague of Jamison's, stated that 'the whole project really depends upon the engine development'[45] and a modern discussion of the issues agreed that it was (lack of) engine development which prevented some of Wallis's ideas coming to fruition.[46]

The aircraft of the future

All of these various ideas crystallised around 1964 into Wallis's derivation of the 'ideal aircraft size'. Due to the square-cube law, aircraft become structurally less efficient as size increases, but aeronautical engineers had been (and continue to be) saved from the full effect of this law by developments in power and fuel efficiency of engines and by improvements in materials such as composites. Wallis complained that they failed 'to meet this increase in any other way than by building larger, heavier and proportionally more costly aircraft'[47] which required progressively longer (and stronger) runways. He noted that this went against common sense as witnessed in rail or sea transportation, where multiple platforms or docks are available to allow many simultaneous arrivals and departures – it would be much more efficient to have an airport with a larger number of shorter runways, which in turn required smaller aircraft capable of using them. Having aircraft of low AUW (100–200,000lb was needed, the optimum probably towards the bottom end of that range) meant that STOL performance was a possibility, potentially resulting in fewer accidents (and fewer casualties should an accident occur). Having a greater number of smaller aircraft, each capable of short- or long-haul flights, offered the huge economic advantage that large numbers of any given aircraft type would be built, thus reducing the unit cost and spreading the cost of jigs and tooling. More frequent departures would also bring benefits to passengers.

Wallis's arguments have fallen on deaf ears, and the trend for increasing aircraft size continues today, with the A380 'super jumbo' entering service recently and constant pressures for more long runways at major airports.

The Universal aircraft

Having developed the idea of the 'all-speed aircraft', by the mid-1960s, Wallis was extending his thinking to an aircraft equally flexible in application, but of standard design, which he called the 'Universal aircraft'. This had also changed the aims of the R&D Department, which were now 'to develop new and more efficient aerodynamic forms capable of attaining higher speeds than the swing wing type of variable geometry aircraft can reach [and] to develop forms whereby the costs of design materials jigs and tools and development may all be reduced to a minimum for new types'.[48] He noted the rising cost of aircraft design, due to ever-increasing range and payload, with airframe materials and labour accounting for nearly 60 per cent of the total price. New types and models were customised for a particular customer and flight profile and hence were effectively different aircraft, requiring separate certification and expensive new jigs and tools for manufacture, thus raising the break-even point for the manufacturer. As 'no attempt has been made to assess the immense savings that could be made in the cost of air transport if satisfactory performance in each section could be attained by producing a single type of aircraft that could efficiently operate over the following wide range of performance', he saw the economic potential for the Universal aircraft.

In addition to the now-standard features of a Wallis design (10,000nm range, AUW below 150,000lb,[49] capable of operation from 500yds runways, and the ability to work on short-haul routes economically), he specified ease of maintenance, the ability to carry passengers or freight (interchangeably), the ability to carry one or two ISO containers[50] of up to 10 tons

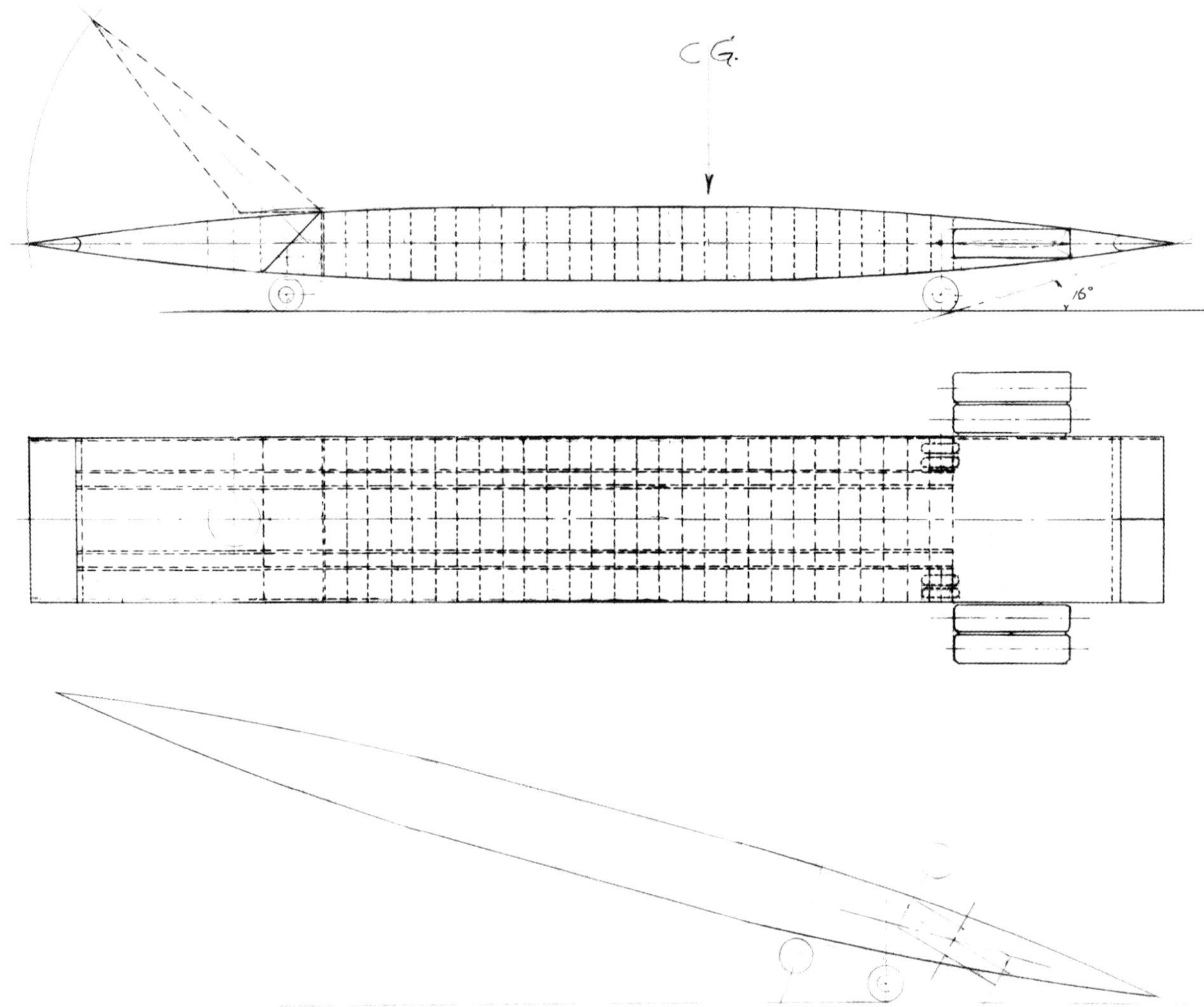

One version of the Universal aircraft. Note the rear-mounted engines which can swivel on a transverse axis *(BAE SYSTEMS via the Science Museum)*

each, and fully automatic flight controls.[51] His one concession to variability was in the engines which would be interchangeable for sub-, super- and hypersonic operation, together with some flexibility in fuel tankage.[52] This would enable a single aircraft to be 'equally efficient when operating over routes varying from . . . 100 miles at low altitude at relatively low speeds to very long ranges of . . . 10,000nm at great altitudes of above 150,000ft and at hypersonic speeds up to . . . Mach 7 or 8'.[53]

The square aeroplane

Seeing the wide adoption of the ISO container for freight, Wallis wanted to exploit their numerous economic advantages in air transport also. Accepting that containers had not originally been planned for air use and did not fit efficiently into aerodynamic circular-section fuselages, he found it 'a fortunate circumstance that the advent of the ISC [International Standard Container] coincided with the introduction of the slender body theory of lift by Gersten', citing other research by the aircraft company SAAB and the RAE on rectangular-section fuselages.[54] Together, these led to 'the inevitable conclusion that a parallel rectangular fuselage is the correct answer and we are thus faced with the problem of designing a flat-sided body that can withstand internal pressurisation without incurring undue weight or distortion' and could also be opened to permit insertion and removal of the containers; passengers were to be accommodated by substituting pallets of seats in place of the cargo containers.[55] Any engineer knows that 'you can't build a square boiler',[56] and the bending moments at the corners caused by pressurisation inevitably meant a heavier structure, but as a square-section fuselage to fit around a container had only two-thirds of the cross-sectional area of a circular fuselage to take the same container, there were some immediate aerodynamic advantages to offset the increased weight.

The answer to the structural problem was to make the side panels from 'a series of semi-circular arcs placed thwartships across the rectangular fuselage', the depth thus created in the corrugated panels (about 9in), augmented by transverse frames every 3ft or so, giving the strength to withstand the pressure difference (which would be limited by safety valves). If two containers were to be accommodated side-by-side, then tie bars running vertically between them would allow the outward pressures at the top and bottom to balance each other out.[57] These structural methods were also appropriate where the external pressure was greater, and as such appear in his submarine designs (see Chapter 11), which he was working on at the same time.

Having produced an efficient solution to the cross-section problems, there remained the problem of fore-and-aft streamlining around the container. This was 'accomplished by bringing the leading and trailing top and bottom surfaces to a knife edge, both having the full span, thus leaving the fuselage rectangular in plan', and thus being equally applicable to one or two containers.[58] This shape also meant that no spherical curvatures were required (only cylindrical), so that the whole structure could be made from flat plate with minimal forming required. The symmetrical double wedge thus formed could be shown to have the minimum possible drag coefficient, and thus the highest L/D possible in supersonic flight. However, for subsonic flight, some camber was advantageous, and thus some form of variable-camber fuselage was called for.

One method for adding camber[59] was by 'providing large chord flaps across the full width of fuselage and wings at both bow and stern' (this aircraft was 150ft long and 23ft wide to suit two containers abreast), another being the fitting of a transverse

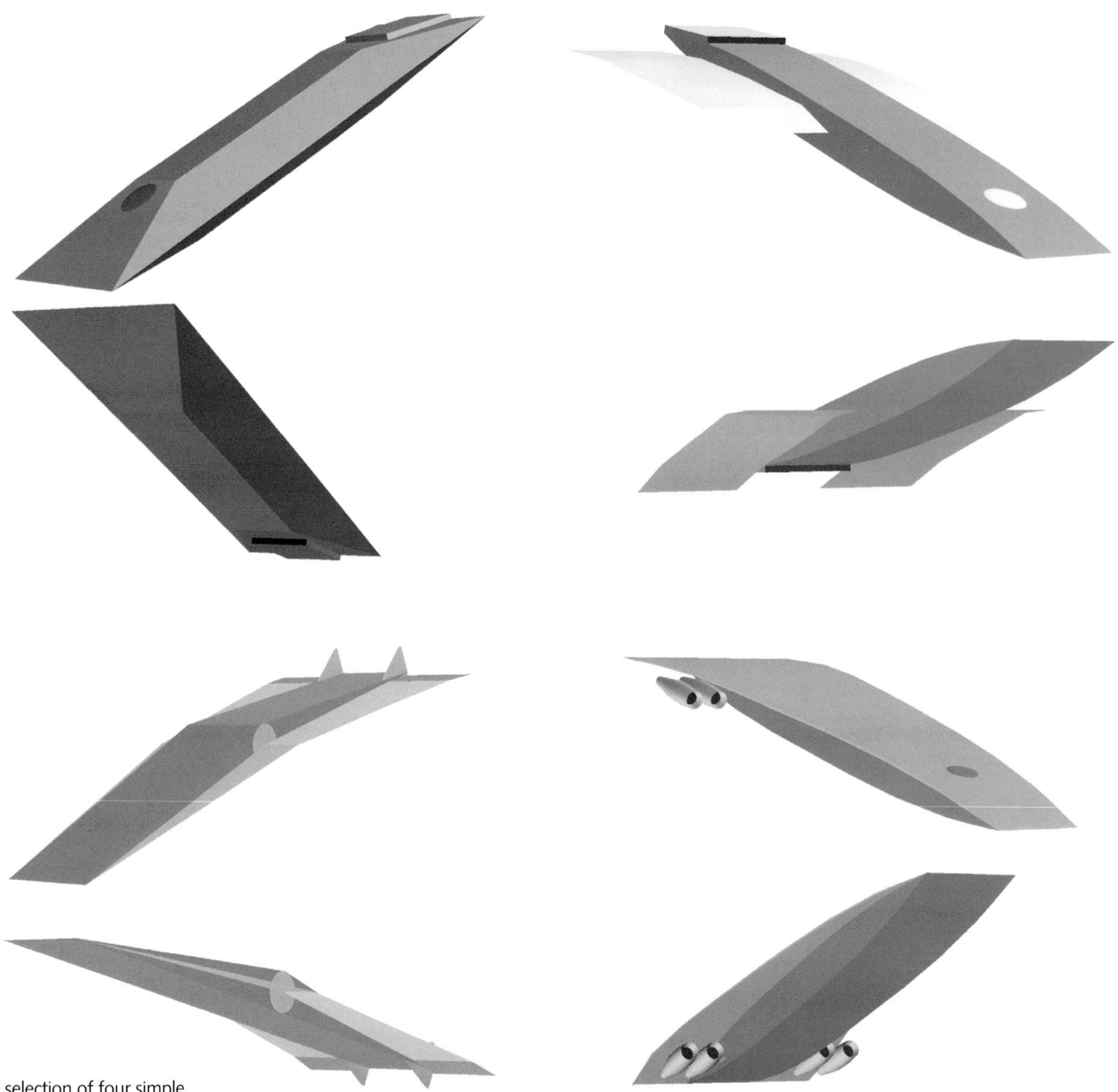

A selection of four simple 3-D models of Universal aircraft based on archive drawings. Top left: wedge fuselage with internal rear engines. Top right: slender body with internal rear engines and variable-camber wings. Bottom left: variable-camber fuselage with fixed wings (engines unknown). Bottom right: slender body fuselage with delta wing and pivotable external rear engines. *(Author)*

pivot at the midpoint of the fuselage.[60] Yet another version[61] has the fuselage tapering to a point at the sides also, and the archives contain numerous other variations on the square-section form, which was known colloquially as the 'flying shoebox', at least within the Wallis family.[62] While the variants of Wild Goose were all variations on a central theme, as were the variants of Swallow, the archive plans from this time show a 'pick-and-mix' set of features, with Swallow-type wings, variable-camber wings, variable-camber fuselages, slender fuselages, square fuselages and so on used in a wide variety of configurations.

The parameters of the Universal aircraft were restated in a 1970 report,[63] with the additional observation that 'the airframe required to meet this complex specification offers an almost identical challenge to the hull frame of a large rigid airship' and that 'in its own field, the airship programme of 1920 presented as many difficult technical problems as the SST programme presents to us today'. The main difference was the number of sides (only four in the case of the aircraft), and 'the principle of construction is thus closely analogous to that of the rigid airship *R.100* but on a much smaller scale'. The report concludes with an appendix giving comparative data on *R.100* and the Universal aircraft, with the ultimate conclusion that the aircraft is 43.8 times as efficient as the airship!

The future

Even after his retiral, Wallis was 'still working on the new type of aircraft',[64] and a banker friend set up a company for him to exploit the idea – Aircraft (BNW) Ltd.[65] However, this was done more out of friendship than with any realistic prospect of putting the aircraft into production (he had, after all, failed to persuade Britain's biggest aircraft company to back the idea).

Wallis remained a firm believer in the concept of low AUW being applied to civil aircraft. Writing to *The Times* in 1971, he predicted 'that the existing type of airport and very long runways will be unnecessary, and will be replaced by small airports and short runways situated in the environs of every major city'.[66] He continued with a list of 'four great objectives' for the future of air transport:

1. The perfection of the civil V/STOL SST aircraft.
2. The silencing of jet engines, for both vertical and horizontal thrust.
3. The planning of the ideal type of small airport with runways suitable for vertical and short take-off and landing – that is runways that do not exceed some 500 or 600m in length.
4. The automatic control of all aircraft from or by means of ground radio beacons operating on small computers that will be carried in all aircraft, the controls of which will be so adjusted thereby as to bring them to the desired haven.

One of his reasons was environmental – he wanted to avoid the destruction of villages and historic places by covering them with unnecessary runways, a point still valid at Heathrow and elsewhere. In a follow-up letter a few weeks later,[67] he added his belief that air freight would rise even more quickly than passenger traffic, citing his work designing an aircraft to carry international standard containers. This list is also the first reference in Wallis literature to refer to silencing of jets – not a serious consideration during his working life, the environmental lobby put it on to the agenda with Concorde, and considerable research work continues in this area.

Summary – later supersonics

Having shown that Swallow did not have the full capability that was hoped for, Wallis continued to develop ideas for new aircraft throughout the 1960s and on into his retirement. Although still fundamentally practical aircraft, both aerodynamically and economically (for manufacture and operation), they were more unorthodox even than his earlier supersonic ideas, and with the British aircraft industry virtually imploding at the time, and the lack of suitable engines, there was never any realistic prospect of these aircraft being built.

However, some of the concepts which he explored, such as isothermal flight and the 'square aeroplane' remain theoretically justified, so it is just possible that they may yet see the light of day if supersonic transport becomes viable again.

Chapter 11

Wallis's Miscellaneous Projects

It was engineering – much more than science – that accomplished the Moon landing, and ... an engineer, not a scientist, was the first to set foot on another world.

(James Hansen, First Man: the Life of Neil Armstrong, 2006)

In addition to the main projects on which Wallis was engaged, he regularly applied his intellect to a range of other tasks that took his fancy. A selection of these is presented here.

The smoke-laying glider (1941)

In January 1941 the Ministry of Supply issued a request for a glider capable of being rocket-launched from a ship in large numbers for the laying of a smokescreen. In response to this, and with the blessing of Craven,[1] Wallis submitted a paper containing several designs in February.[2] The requirement was for the glider to carry a standard smoke canister, fly for a quarter of a mile before initiating the canister, then fly on for the same distance again laying the smoke. From the weight of the rockets necessary to fly this distance at a reasonable speed, plus the weight of the smoke canister itself, Wallis calculated the span of aircraft required at about 11ft – perfectly reasonable for stowing on board a ship. His designs included a tailless 'pterodactyl' type which would have been simple to produce, but he had doubts about the performance of this version compared to the other more conventional designs.

As there were no data available on the performance of rockets, he acquired some signal rockets through the Ministry of Supply for initial experiments, and as no suitable thrust measuring apparatus was available either, he designed and built his own device at Weybridge. The performance of these small rockets was rather erratic, and it was reckoned that scaling up the figures to full scale would be unreliable. A small model glider (21in span) was made, but results were inconsistent (largely due to the performance of the rocket) and a larger model (30in span) with double the wing area was then tested, and it made 'some fairly promising flights' but was rather prone to damage. A third model was designed to cope with rougher handling, and tests were again promising, wind tunnel experiments being used to refine the tail design, and consistent flight performance was then obtained. The experimental report concluded that the scheme showed potential, but depended on consistent rocket performance.

Evaluation by the Admiralty's DMWD suggested that the glider would fly too high to lay a screen by gravity, proposing a torpedo-based alternative laying smoke from the surface of the water. Model tests with a similar glider intended for use as a gunnery target were conducted by a model aircraft company in 1942, but it was felt they were unsuitable to undertake a larger project. By the summer Wallis was too busy with other projects to continue work on the glider, and the plans were shelved in September.

While discussing the glider with Cdr Leo Lane of the DMWD in June 1942, Wallis also mentioned his early 'bouncing bomb' ideas to him, and this led directly to the Admiralty interest in Highball and Baseball (see Chapter 6) which sustained these projects during the latter half of 1942.

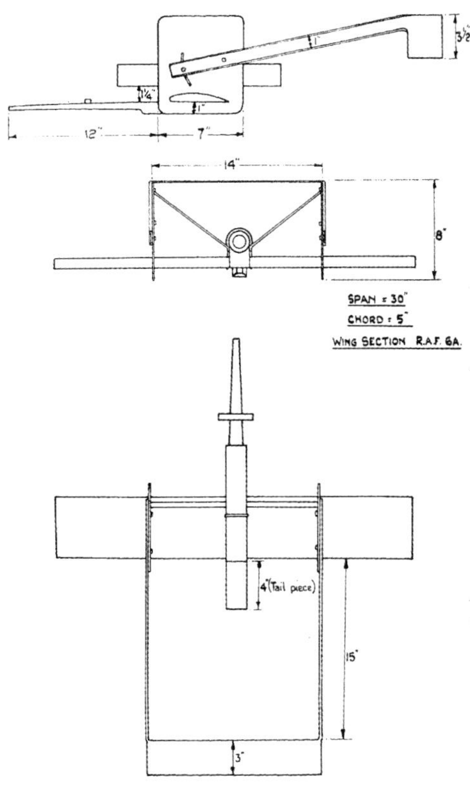

Three-view drawing of the final smoke-laying glider.
(BAE SYSTEMS via The National Archives)

Boom Patrol Boats (1945)

One of the most bizarre of exploits concerned the Royal Marines and their Boom Patrol Boats. Before the war, the Italians had developed explosive motorboats based on recreational craft, with the addition of explosive heads, for attacking ships at sea. These single-man vessels were to be manually steered towards their target, the pilot abandoning ship shortly before the charge exploded. Two of these boats succeeded in crippling the cruiser HMS *York* off Crete in March 1941, and nine attacked the Grand Harbour in Malta in July 1941.[3] Although little damage was done at Malta (a bridge over the harbour entrance was destroyed by the second boat, and the others were blocked by the wreckage), one of the boats was captured intact and the potential of this sort of attack was noted by the British.

A British version (codenamed 'Skylark') was designed and built by Vosper for possible operations against enemy shipping, as well as docks, lock gates and boom defences,[4] to be operated by the Royal Marines Boom Patrol Detachment (later becoming the Special Boat Squadron),[5] from which the famous 'Cockleshell Heroes' came. Initial trials in Autumn 1942 parachuted 4,000lb bombs from a Lancaster (this being the same weight as the boat) and the boats appear to have been ready by May 1943, although the first live drop (with a Royal Marine aboard) did not take place until June 1944 off Harwich.

On 17 January 1945, four Lancasters of 617 Squadron took off from Woodhall Spa to take part in Operation Skyhook, each dropping a Boom Patrol Boat off the harbour at Teignmouth, Devon, from a height of 2,000ft. The four landed within a radius of 100yds, a result which the Navy described as 'very good indeed';[6] the boats then started their engines and proceeded to the pier, two of the aircraft returning to Woodhall to

Lancaster dropping a Boom Patrol Boat. *(BAE SYSTEMS via The National Archives)*

load two more boats for a further drop, the other two proceeding to Exeter to have the boat apparatus removed. Although the trials seem to have been completed successfully, and a plan was mooted to attack shipping in Bergen harbour in February 1945, the Boom Patrol Boats were never used in action.

One of the 617 Squadron fitters who was tasked with maintenance of the boat dropping apparatus, Bill Hilder, flew in one of the aircraft, and recalls the scream of the Royal Marine as the boat dropped away.[7] Hilder claims that Wallis was involved in the briefing for the operation, although the archive materials pertaining to the trial do not record the nature and amount of his involvement in the project, nor the reason for 617 Squadron being involved in the test. The long gestation of the project suggests that Wallis was a relative latecomer.

The Stratosphere Chamber (1945–79)

By early 1945, it was apparent to Wallis that the conditions which future aircraft would encounter, in terms of atmospheric variation, were far greater than common experience hitherto, and any experimentation in real conditions at high altitude would be difficult and expensive. He thus proposed to build a test facility to simulate conditions at high altitude (which meant low pressure and low temperature) and also tropical conditions. His design for this was known as the Stratosphere Chamber, and was essentially a giant pressure vessel into which large aircraft components could be placed and subjected to realistic conditions of low pressure and low or high temperature, all without leaving the ground. He discussed his ideas for the chamber with Kilner in April 1945,[8] was working on preliminary calculations and sketches in May,[9] and construction began in the autumn.[10]

As the likely height of operation of supersonic aircraft was to be 60,000ft, the chamber was required to simulate the conditions at this height – an ambient pressure of less than one twentieth of sea-level atmospheric pressure. Atmosphere temperature falls with altitude, reaching a steady –56°C above 35,000ft, so this temperature became a requirement of operation; for tropical testing, temperatures up to 60°C were also required.[11] The working section of the chamber was designed to house a reasonable length of a large 'double bubble' airliner fuselage, which translated into a vessel 50ft long and 25ft in diameter. This was surrounded by four air circulation ducts of 6ft 9in diameter. Main access to the chamber was via the 'great door' weighing 65 tons; personnel access was possible via an airlock, and other ports could be fitted with windows or sensor equipment as required. The cooling plant, similar to that used in large refrigeration units of the time, used liquid ammonia as primary coolant, cooling methanol within the chamber's heat exchangers; up to 20,000 gallons per hour could be circulated.[12] Heat insulation was carefully calculated to maximise efficiency of the plant, and mostly consisted of 12in thick lagging, constructed so that no metal parts passed all the way through. The addition of water spraying gear allowed blizzard and severe icing conditions to be created.

As such a large pressure vessel was similar to the hull of a submarine, the Vickers Naval Yard at Barrow-in-Furness was contracted to construct the chambers from ½in steel plate, and it was delivered to Brooklands by road in sections. Over a year from autumn 1946, it was assembled on a site adjacent to the clubhouse where the R&D Department was based, before being 'launched' onto the special insulated foundations a few yards away. After a period of fitting out and plan testing, the 'great door' was closed for the first time on 17 January 1950; within a week it had been tested to 1,000ft and within another month, it was up to 65,000ft.

In addition to work on Vickers aircraft, such as the Viscount, Vanguard and VC10, the chamber was also rented out commercially to other aircraft companies, such as de Havilland, and it was used by many other companies to test their products in extremes of temperature and pressure. These included vehicles, tanks, ship components, high-voltage electrical components, radar systems and cold-weather clothing. 'The worst weather in the world occurs right here at WEYBRIDGE' was the marketing slogan.[13]

A later use for the chamber was to support a supersonic wind tunnel. This was created by using the 'vacuum reservoir' in the chamber to suck air at atmospheric pressure through a working section at up to Mach 4. It worked very successfully, although the test times were only of the order of 10–40 seconds before the pressure in the chamber had risen sufficiently to reduce the speed of the flow. The tunnel was operational from 1958 until 1975.

The chamber itself remained in use up until shortly before the sale of the Brooklands site by British Aerospace in the early 1980s. A BAE study had shown that the chamber would cost around £250,000 to demolish, so it was left in situ and now forms part of the Brooklands Museum site.[14]

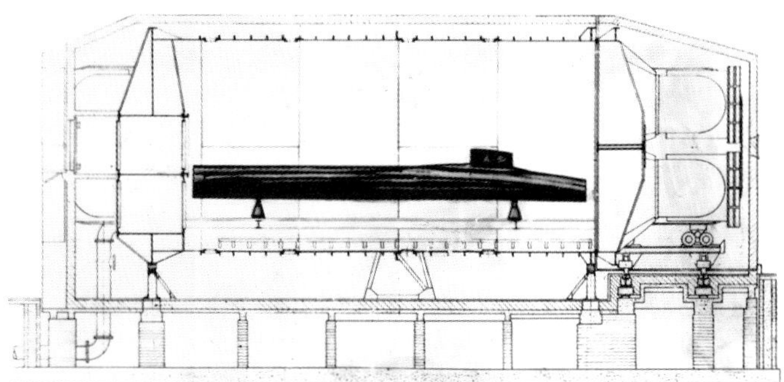

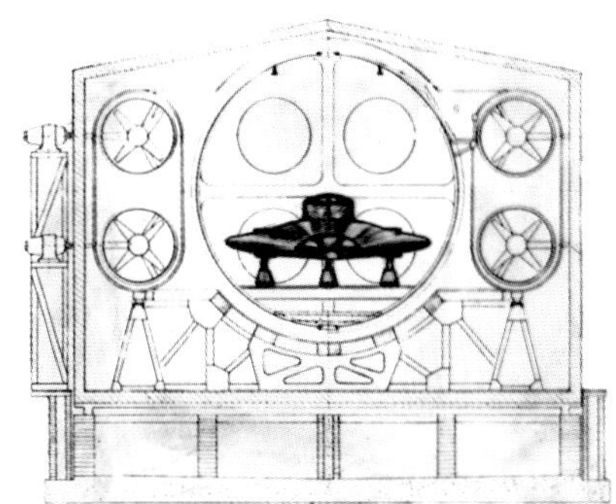

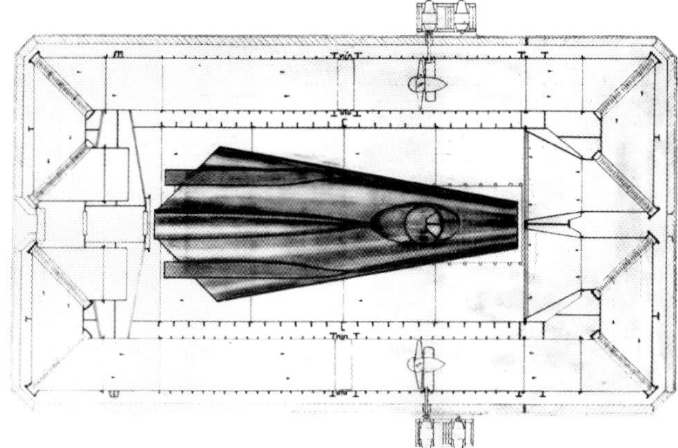

INSTALLATION IN VICKERS-ARMSTRONGS STRATOSPHERE CHAMBER FOR HIGH ALTITUDE & CLIMATIC TESTS ON THE FORE-WING & PILOT'S TURRET.

FORE-WING TEST SPECIMEN

A Swallow fuselage test specimen in the Stratosphere Chamber; Swallow was cancelled before it made it this far. *(BAE SYSTEMS via Brooklands Museum)*

Trawler icing experiments (1955)

One occasion when Wallis used the Stratosphere Chamber for his own research purposes was during an investigation into trawler icing. Two Hull trawlers, the *Lorella* and *Roderigo*, had been lost off Iceland in January 1955 with 40 men. The official inquiry accepted that the losses were due to excessive icing of the upperworks leading to capsizing.[15] Hot water, structure heaters and de-icing paste had been tried by the trawlermen, but all had been found ineffective at preventing ice build-up.

Wallis set out to investigate the problem on behalf of the British Shipbuilding Research Association, building a pond within the Stratosphere Chamber to hold 60 tons of water, and blowing icy spray over specially constructed 18ft models of trawlers.[16] The models were built by Vickers and had been tested for stability in waves at a ship tank at St Albans. They also did some full-scale tests on ropes, lifeboats and other paraphernalia to measure the rate of ice build-up. Several trawler captains visited the site and were impressed with the work.[17] Wallis's tests showed that up to 140 tons of ice could accumulate on the masts and superstructure, more than enough to cause a capsize. His report suggested making the ships more streamlined to give fewer places for the ice to collect – removal of all unnecessary details on the upperworks such as handrails and rigging, simplification of mast structures and replacement of lifeboats with inflatable dinghies.

When more trawlers were lost during the winter of 1967–8, Wallis angrily told the BBC that no action had been taken following his earlier research, although this was refuted by a correspondent to *The Times*, who cited improvements in design that had been made since the earlier tragedies.[18] Wallis also helped to develop a dinghy for use in trawlers, which would launch itself automatically if the ship sank.[19]

Telescope mountings (1952–61)

In the period after the war, the Royal Greenwich Observatory was evaluating designs for the proposed Isaac Newton Optical Telescope for its observatory at Herstmonceaux in East Sussex. In 1952 the Astronomer Royal, Harold Spencer Jones, invited Wallis to join the design team and contribute a design for the drive mechanism. Wallis produced plans not just for the mounting, but some which included the whole telescope building.[20] In 1955 a new Astronomer Royal was appointed and he decided to restart the design process from scratch, and Wallis was not invited to join the new committee; his designs were thus not taken up.[21]

In September 1954 Wallis was approached privately in connection with a proposed large radio telescope to be built in Australia (at Parkes in New South Wales, although the location had not been selected at the start of the project), and still somewhat bitter at his ideas having been ignored by the UK's astronomers, he took up this new challenge.[22] In addition to revising his ideas for the mounting, he was also able to apply his structural expertise to the 64m-diameter dish itself.

The dish

Wallis first concentrated on the dish – this large structure must be light enough to be movable, yet rigid in order to keep its shape as it is moved and gravity and wind pull it in different directions. He proposed to mount the dish on a central support for ease of movement (cf. the contemporary Jodrell Bank telescope, whose dish was attached at the sides, imparting greater variations in stress on the structure during movement).

Considering the general specification, Wallis was quick to see the application of many of the basic airship principles to the design, including making the dish as large as possible (constrained only by cost) and using a minimal number of parts to increase the homogeneity of the structure and keep the manufacturing costs down.[23]

For an earlier bridge project, Wallis had conceived a structural element which was dynamically self-compensating for changes in structural strain – this used the deflection of a loaded structure to generate a change in hydraulic pressure which created a force to offset the deflection, hence restoring the original shape.[24] He had planned to use these elements in the Isaac Newton Telescope, and now suggested using them within the dish structure, as well as 'servo motor mechanisms' to maintain its shape under varying loads. However, the design study carried out by consulting engineers Freeman, Fox and Partners showed that, while the self-compensating feature would work, it would actually be heavier than a rigid dish if the diameter was less than 300ft, so the feature was dropped.

Structural rigidity with lightness was Wallis's forte, of course, and he dusted off some of the ideas of geodetics to propose a dish structure comprising 'two intersecting sets of opposite-handed equiangular spiral frames' which would carry the mesh (or solid) dish surface (for homogeneity of the surface, conventional radial and circumferential members could not be used).[25] Making the frames equiangular meant that all of the frame intersections were at the same angle, so that a single design of junction bracket could be used throughout (light alloy die-castings were proposed to minimise the machining required at each junction); assembly of the whole dish using a single movable scaffold, spiralling outwards from the centre, would also be possible.

This form of structure lent itself to support at a single point (rather than a distributed form of support, such as at Jodrell Bank), suggesting that this point also be the centre of the axes about which the dish would move. A further idea for rotating the whole dish 'at a suitable speed when the dish is in use' for gyroscopic and thermal stability was not proceeded with.

The Parkes Radio Telescope. Note the geodetics in the structure of the dish. *(© Michael Dahlem)*

The mounting

The mount of a telescope performs two functions: it must allow accurate aiming of the attached instrument to any desired point in the sky and, once aimed, it must hold the target against the rotation of the Earth (preferably automatically). The two standard mounting types are:

The alt-azimuth mount which (like the gun turret on a tank) consists of a base rotating on an axis normal to the local surface, carrying the instrument via another axis which can vary the altitude in the vertical plane, and;

The equatorial mount which consists of an axis set parallel to the polar axis of the Earth, upon which the whole telescope is mounted; the polar axis can be mechanically rotated backwards at a constant speed to compensate for the Earth's rotation.

The alt-azimuth mount has the advantage of being mechanically simpler, but tracking is more difficult as two rotation axes must be varied simultaneously. The equatorial mount, once aimed, needs only to rotate in one axis (at a constant speed) to hold its aim, but the mechanism is more complex and, significantly, becomes increasingly cumbersome as the size of the telescope is increased (alt-azimuth had been chosen for Jodrell Bank for this reason).

The conventional solution was to combine the best features of both types – alt-azimuth for the mounting of the large dish, and an equatorial mount as the heart of a control mechanism – with the master unit in a building alongside the main telescope. Wallis, however, quickly realised that the ideal place for the equatorial master telescope was at the same pivot point as the main dish. The master telescope was used to track the target, and any difference in parallelism between it and the main dish (detected by an arrangement of light beams and light sensitive cells) was used to change the position of the main dish – which could thus be accurately controlled with *no computation being required*, but simply acting as a slave following the master equatorial system.

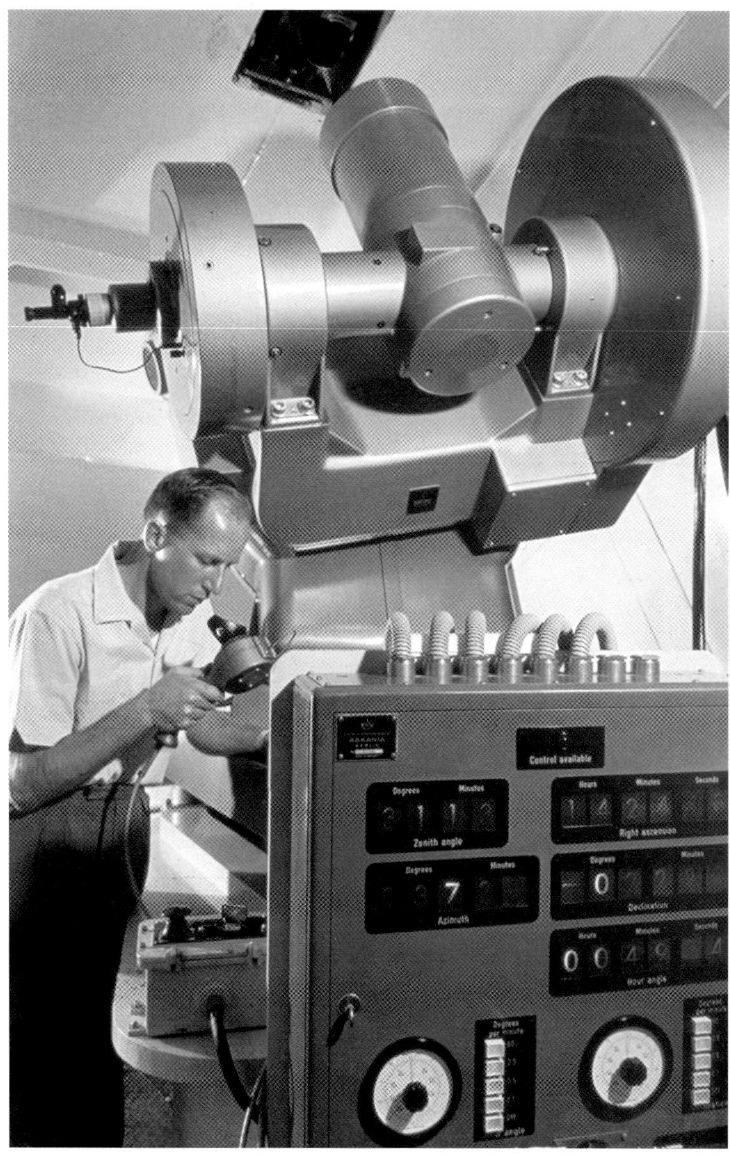

The master equatorial unit within the Parkes Radio Telescope, designed by Wallis; astronomer Jim Roberts is in attendance. *(CSIRO)*

The telescope plans next went to a design study. Vickers-Armstrongs was considered for this due to the Wallis connection, but the best offer came from Freeman, Fox & Partners, the UK-based engineering firm which had built Sydney Harbour Bridge (although Wallis was retained as a consultant on the project). It took some time to complete, being submitted in November 1957, and a site was selected at Parkes in New South Wales, north-west of Sydney, the site having good meteorological conditions all year long. The telescope was opened on 31 October 1961, and the pointing accuracy achievable with the master equatorial system was found to be typically better than one minute of arc.[26]

Wallis was to have been paid a consultancy fee of £1,000 for his work at Parkes, which he was going to donate to the RAF Foundation at Christ's Hospital, but following a disagreement with the Telescope Advisory Committee, he left the project early and refused to accept the fee, even though his ideas were incorporated in the final design.

Parkes's 'finest hour' came in 1969, when the telescope was used to pick up most of the TV transmission from Apollo 11 as astronauts Armstrong and Aldrin made the first moonwalk. Uncharacteristically windy conditions at the time put the dish under abnormal strain – the design limit wind speed for operation of the dish was 50km/hr, but gusts up to 100km/hr were being experienced – but given the importance of the operation, the decision was made to keep tracking and the mounting was undamaged.[27]

The Parkes telescope continues in service today – much of the radio astronomy gear and the surface of the telescope have been upgraded in that time, but the basic dish structure and its mounting are still the original; the Wallis mounting[28] has also been used in 'several other large dishes'.[29]

Momentum bombing (1957)

A problem for all bombers, especially those dropping nuclear weapons, is that of incurring damage from the detonation of their own bombs. Originally designed to drop nuclear weapons from high altitude, the V-bombers were seen as too vulnerable to radar-guided SAMs and fighters by the late 1950s, and were switched to penetrating at low level (to minimise early radar detection). The final stages of the flight, however, still required either a 'pop up' to a safe bombing height for a conventional level approach to the target, or use of a 'toss bombing' technique where the aircraft pulled up into a steep climb ahead of the target to release its weapon which continued upwards in a parabola, giving the bomber time to reverse direction and escape to a safe distance before the weapon exploded. However, either technique resulted in the bomber making itself visible during the weapon release stage where undisturbed flight was most desirable and where ground defences were at their heaviest.

Wallis devised a wholly original solution to this problem in 1957, one which made it possible for the attacking aircraft to avoid passing over its target at all. It came to be known as 'momentum bombing'.[30] Its novelty lay in the use of a small unpowered winged aircraft carrying the weapon, this being carried piggy-back on the bomber aircraft, and capable of being raised clear of the carrying aircraft just prior to release. The wings of the missile were

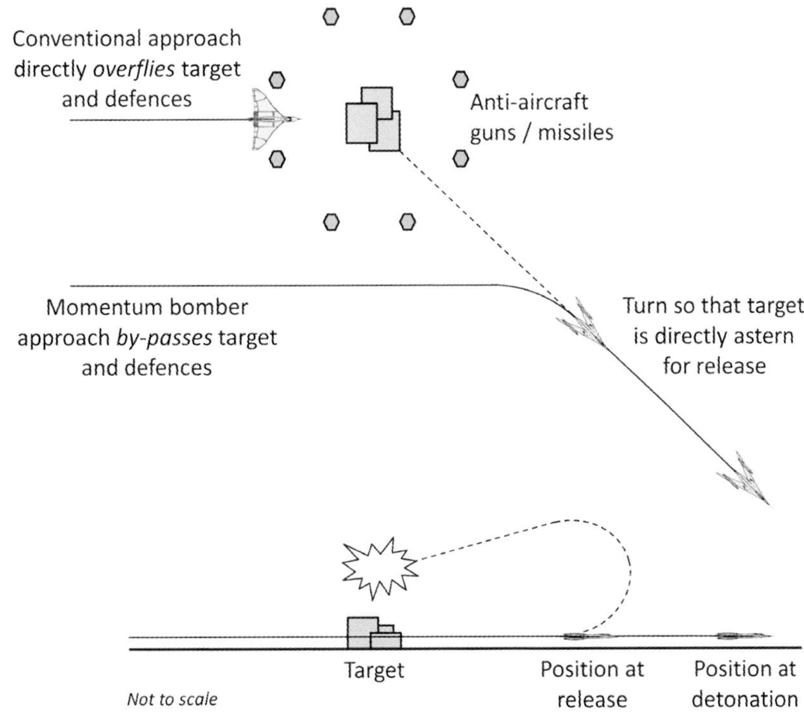

The technique of momentum bombing. *(Author)*

A wooden wind tunnel model of a Swallow momentum bomber. The bomb is the bulge on the rear of the fuselage. (© RAF Museum)

symmetrical in cross-section, either lenticular or wedge-shaped in section, and these assumed a dihedral attitude when the missile was raised into position for launch. Following a low-level penetration, the bomber continued at low level and at supersonic speed, passing over or abeam the target, in the latter case then turning so that the target lay directly behind. The missile was then released, the momentum from its speed causing it to pull up from the carrier aircraft into a half-loop, at which point a timer caused the now-drooping wings to resume a dihedral, allowing the unpowered aircraft to fly straight back towards the target, another timer then detonating the warhead. During the whole flight of the missile, the carrier aircraft had been speeding away from the target at supersonic speed, so it would be well clear of the danger zone by the time detonation occurred. The behaviour of the missile in flight was reflected in the concept's codename – 'Apple Turnover'.[31]

Assuming that the bomber would be a Swallow, Wallis even noted that the increased risk from striking barrage balloon cables, due to the completely low-level attack profile, was mitigated by the relatively low effective impact velocity on the Swallow wing due to it being so highly swept, and to the absence of any leading edge slats (and presumably that the cable did not catch on the wingtip engines).

Wallis proved the mechanics of the concept in typical fashion – a model of the missile was fitted on to a car driven round the Brooklands track and released at an appropriate speed, performing a perfect half loop and coming to rest on the road behind the car.[32]

The beauty of the momentum bombing concept was its simplicity – the missile itself was quite uncomplicated and the support mechanism on the carrier aircraft was not sophisticated. A rocket motor could have been included to give the missile additional range, but this was not an essential part of the design. Carrying the bomb externally would have increased drag on the bomber, but not by much as the missile would have been tucked down into a recess on the top of the fuselage. Plans and a wind tunnel model of a Swallow momentum bomber were prepared, though any contemporary bomber could have been converted to carry the weapon.

Wallis remarked to Lord Weeks in September 1957 that 'the accuracy of the manoeuvre depends on the ability to measure the lateral range of the target on the instant that it is directly on the beam, and a good deal of work will be required on the design of a lateral sight to give this information', and that such a sight was already being worked on which, though novel, 'shouldn't present any great difficulty'.[33]

A technical assessment of two types of momentum bomb was undertaken by the RAE, although these were to be dropped from the bomb bay of TSR.2, rather than carried piggy-back, and had both control surfaces and an autopilot. The report[34] concluded that the claimed advantages of the concept 'are possible', although it makes no mention of Wallis or Vickers, and the idea does not seem to have been taken any further.

Sub-orbital aircraft (1962)

In the wake of the first manned spaceflights in 1961, Wallis realised that it might be possible to produce a 'manned recoverable orbital vehicle' based on his existing work, and he produced a design for a sub-orbital aircraft (also referred to as an 'intermediate spaceplane') though there seems to be no documentation giving its full specification.[35] Julian Amery, Secretary of State for Air, invited Wallis to outline the scheme to the Air Staff, and he and George Edwards visited the Air Ministry on 31 May 1962.[36] Amery also noted 'intensive studies' on a similar scheme proposed independently by the RAE and was sufficiently impressed to write to Peter Thorneycroft, Minister of Aviation, suggesting that funds be made available for a feasibility study. An 'orbital fighter' variant was also suggested.[37] However, in answer to a Parliamentary question in November, Amery (by now Minister of Aviation) seems to have backed away from the idea, noting that 'before the industry can be invited to submit design studies for spacecraft, preliminary research studies will be required', although this basic research was still continuing on both the RAE and Wallis designs.[38]

High-pressure submarines (1965)

In 1965, Wallis turned his attention to a new design for submarines. His design was based on the premise that detection of submarines by aircraft (using sonobuoys) was limited to a depth of about 1,000ft, so he wanted to sail at double this depth, while also achieving long range, high speed and a high degree of silent operation. The main challenges were thus constructing a pressure hull to cope with the great depth, and machinery for high speed, yet quiet, operation. Wallis had novel ideas for both of these areas, which he spelt out in a detailed report.[39]

For the hull, his calculations showed that an arc of small radius was stronger under external pressure than a large one, so he proposed replacing the conventional large circular hull section with a new horizontally elongated cross-section consisting of several smaller circular segments linked together; internal pillars would give additional support 'in a manner reminiscent of the pillars forming the arcades on the north and south sides of the nave of a medieval church'. This

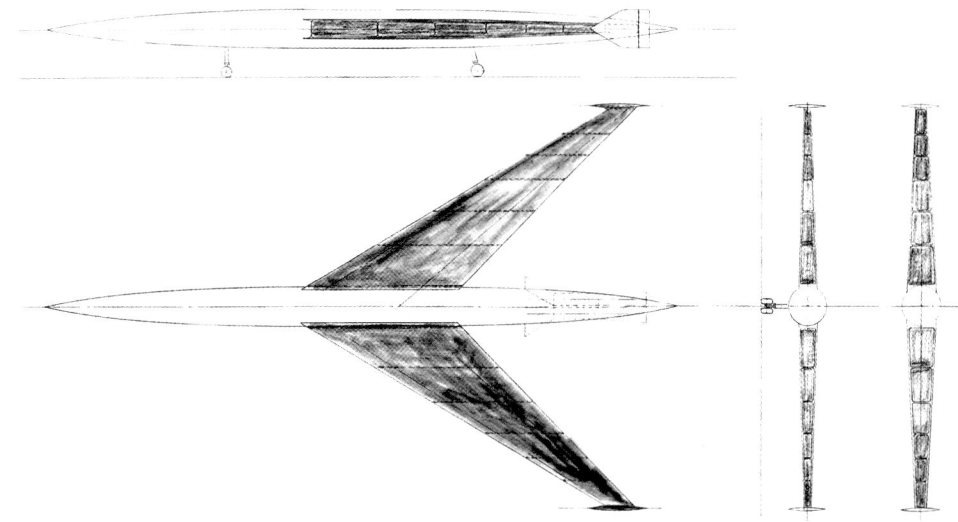

Drawing of Wallis's sub-orbital aircraft; its specification is unknown. *(BAE SYSTEMS via the Science Museum)*

pressure hull would be finished with a light streamlined external shell, to be made from aluminium or fibreglass, with some of the space between being used for fuel tanks (which did not need to be pressurised). The outer hull would be shaped to promote laminar flow over as much of its length as possible, reducing both friction and noise. The Chief Naval Architect at Barrow, once shown the theory supporting the new shape, was surprised that such a simple solution to achieving great depth had not been thought of before.

The desire for high speed would normally promote cavitation from the propellers, but operation at the depths envisaged would mean that the pressure of water would limit the cavitation effect, again keeping the noise down, and Wallis expected that the vessel would be 'practically silent' even at full speed – which was anticipated to be as high as 60 knots (about double that of existing submarines).

To achieve this speed, Wallis was proposing to dispense with the steam turbines typically used in nuclear submarines and use instead a marine gas turbine, which he expected would be no noisier than conventional machinery despite being more powerful. Wallis had already had some preliminary correspondence regarding marine gas turbines with Jamison.[40] However, although common in surface warships, to use a gas turbine in a submarine was unheard of, and Wallis used some novel thermodynamics to make this possible (it was also made clear that the novel hull form and the novel power plant were independent ideas, and did not need to be used together).

First, he noted that while the large nitrogen content of air constitutes part of the mass flow through a gas turbine, it does not contribute chemically to the operation of the engine; consequently, an alternative 'inert passenger' gas could be used without affecting performance, and what he proposed to use instead was carbon dioxide – drawn from the exhaust of the turbine itself – meaning that the engine need be supplied with only fuel and oxygen. The oxygen would be stored as a liquid in tanks inside the pressure hull,[41] passing through a heat exchanger on its way to the engine, the heat coming from the cooling of the engine exhaust gases. As the external water pressure was so high, the exhaust could not be pumped overboard, but instead it was to be cooled and compressed, and passed back for storage in the oxygen tanks – the different densities of the liquefied gases meant that the carbon dioxide could be stored back into the tank that was supplying oxygen at the same time.[42] The small amount of water vapour in the exhaust would be condensed out and either tanked or pumped overboard.

After discussing the proposal with Dunphie in May, he thought that 'the time had come' for Vickers to pass the Wallis proposal to the Admiralty,[43] who forwarded it to its submarine experts at Bath for comment. Their initial reply in early September raised a large number of questions on the detail, but did not discuss the overall feasibility of the proposed design, a view seen as 'finding difficulties for every solution' by a rather disconsolate Roy Turner, Chief Naval Architect at Vickers Shipbuilders in Barrow, and echoed by Wallis. Vickers Engineering's own appraisal written in January 1966 was more positive, despite appreciation of several major engineering challenges that it would pose, but their stated opinion was that the Admiralty would not be interested in the scheme as it had only minor potential

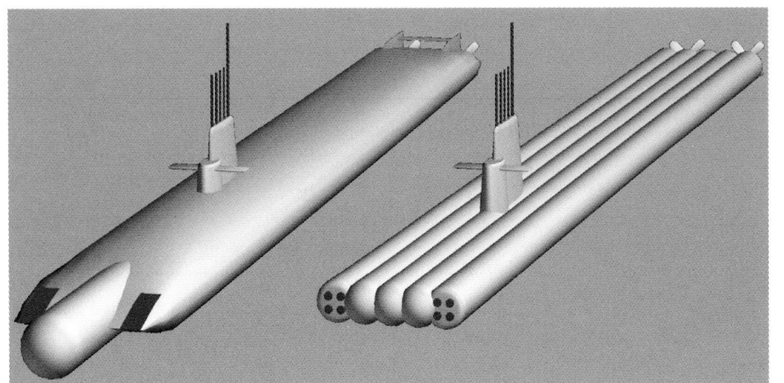

The high pressure submarine, with external shell (left) and bare pressure hull (right); the bulbous nose is a sonar dome. *(Author)*

benefits compared to a nuclear-powered alternative. Detailed answers to the questions raised by Bath were prepared in early February 1966, although it was recognised that some of the figures which Wallis needed were secret, and in March it was agreed to give him permission to see this data as part of an eight-week further study of the proposals. Bristol-Siddeley Engines was to be asked to conduct a prototype evaluation of the closed-circuit gas turbine powerplant, although Director General Ships at Bath commented that the powerplant development would be very expensive.

During 1966 Wallis made slow progress on the submarine figures, which he attributed to his other work on the Ferrybridge cooling towers and his 'new type of aircraft'. Over this period, cracks were detected in the hulls of the *Dreadnought*-class nuclear submarines, and this together with a tightening of Naval budgets, led to formal notification to Vickers in December that 'there is no likelihood in the foreseeable future of any MOD funds being available for the development of this new type of submarine'. This effectively killed the Wallis submarine proposal.

Correspondence[44] shows that he was still working on the submarine ideas in the summer of 1968, and plans in the Brooklands Museum archive (dated 1969) show a version of the submarine with the bow modified for horizontal launching of Poseidon SLBMs. This work proceeded as far as model testing, with archive films showing missiles being ejected horizontally at a scale depth of 100ft and bobbing to the surface.[45] He was also discussing 'the safety-side as seen by the Royal Navy' with Jamison and the British Oxygen Company in August 1970, although claiming to be 'fully occupied with the design of a hypersonic type of aircraft' at the same time.[46]

Archive notes show that the Wallis thermodynamics calculations were reviewed in detail in 1985, possibly related to work on closed-cycle diesel engines,[47] but the concept has not reached production.

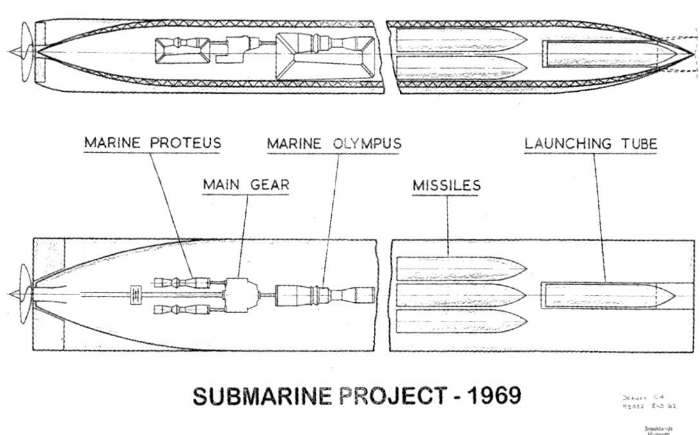

Drawing of a high-pressure submarine designed to launch Poseidon SLBMs horizontally. *(BAE SYSTEMS via Brooklands Museum)*

Cargo submarines (*c.*1965)

During the period when Wallis was doing his 'Strength of England' talks, which focused on exploiting the UK's geographic centrality, he not only emphasised the aviation dimension, but also the need to maintain shipping lanes. As one of the shortest great circle routes from the UK to Australia passed through the North Pole he proposed 'to invent, design and build cheap and reliable merchant submarines'[48] which could exploit direct routes to the antipodes via the North Pole and Bering Strait, and would also keep cargo routes open in the event of war. The idea of cargo-carrying submarines was not new (the Germans used them during the Second World War); however, even using his high-pressure submarine design, there would have been little internal volume available for cargo so the efficacy of such a scheme must be called into question, especially for economic commercial operation.

Cooling towers (1966)

In November 1965, three of the eight cooling towers at the newly-built Ferrybridge 'C' Power Station in Yorkshire collapsed during a gale, the others being severely damaged. As this was a matter involving both structures and aerodynamics, the Central Electricity Generating Board approached Vickers and (with the blessing of the Chairman,

Sir Charles Dunphie, by now the Chairman of Vickers Ltd) Wallis was engaged as a consultant for a three-year period.

Much of the initial correspondence[49] concerned the honorarium to be paid to Wallis; he did not want to accept the fee himself, wishing it to be paid to charity, but this could not be done for tax purposes. Although the archive information is incomplete,[50] it appears that Wallis did undertake some design work himself, as well as being asked to comment on designs produced by others. He probably also visited the Central Electricity Research Laboratory (CERL) which was based at Leatherhead, about 12 miles from Weybridge, which had used the Stratosphere Chamber for tests on electrical equipment.

The size of his overall contribution is unclear, as he is not mentioned in the Committee of Inquiry's report into the collapse, nor in either of two CERL reports which form appendices to it.[51]

Sports projects

In 1936, Wallis carried out a series of wind tunnel tests on golf balls, determining a formula for the distance that a golf ball would carry, and investigating a series of surface finishes including squares, pyramids, dimples and pimples of varying sizes and spacings.[52] There is no explanation of why this work was carried out, but it is likely that it informed his work on the bouncing bombs, both smooth and dimpled versions being tested. He applied his knowledge of spinning spheres to answer a letter on spin bowling in *The Times* in 1947[53] and made further studies into the aerodynamics of cricket and hockey balls.[54]

Wallis also did some work on the skin friction of rowing skulls in 1937, but again the purpose of this work is unclear.[55] In his retirement, he was also frequently pestered by a rather insistent gentleman from Edinburgh who was seeking his advice regarding the design of racing canoes.[56]

Medical projects (1968–71)

When the Bath Institute of Medical Engineering was formed in 1968 to investigate new applications of technology in medicine, it sought out Wallis as its first President. Wallis's daughter Mary is sure that his memories of his father's clanking leg callipers were key to him accepting the post, which he retained until his retiral.

An aspect which Wallis and Herbert Jeffree investigated was three-dimensional mapping of parts of the human body, with a view to fabricating better-fitting prosthetics. One technique tested was projection of an illuminated grid on to the body, and preparation of cross-sections from the data,[57] Jeffree seeking to model the contours of a foot to an accuracy of half a millimetre (having already discounted Wallis's nail grid method, see below).

The Messina Bridge (1971)

In July 1971 Wallis received a letter from Alan Grant, a senior partner in a firm of civil engineering consultants, which had been joint winners of a competition sponsored by the Italian Government for the design of a bridge across the Strait of Messina.[58] Grant had heard of Wallis's recent retiral from BAC, and invited him to collaborate with his company on the detailed design of the bridge.

The geography of the area is challenging – 2 miles wide, the strait (lying between the southern tip of the Italian mainland and the island of Sicily) experiences strong tides, and with Mount Etna less than 50 miles away, earthquakes are a frequent occurrence. To overcome the difficulties associated with a long-span bridge, and the problems that earth movements might cause for a subterranean tunnel, Grant's proposal was to build a floating submerged tunnel, anchored to the seabed approximately 150ft below the surface of the sea.[59] The tunnel would need to be shaped to have minimal resistance to the strong tidal flow, while retaining an internal volume sufficient for traffic. In principle, the tunnel structure was thus similar to a wing, and it was for this reason that Wallis was an appropriate choice to be engaged as a consultant.

Wallis undertook a number of calculations relating to many aspects of the structure and produced some design drawings showing two railway tracks and four lanes for vehicular traffic.[60] However, Wallis casually mentioned his involvement in the project to a journalist, leading to an article in the *Daily Mail* on 27 September 1971 about the tunnel and his part in the design. Grant was extremely unhappy about this apparent breach of confidence and, despite an apology from Wallis, terminated the consultancy, though Grant was 'very sorry that matters have developed in the way they have'.[61]

Other structure projects

Morpurgo hints at some other projects which Wallis undertook, but does not give much detail. He noted that there was correspondence between Wallis and the Ministry of Supply during the war regarding applying light alloy geodetics to pontoons.[62] Also during the war, Wallis produced a design for a new London Bridge and, in the 1950s, a design for a Thames bridge at Charing Cross, in response to the 'slightest hint' from the Chairman of London County Council, Helen Bentwich.[63] The latter would have been a 'tour de force' of light alloy construction, using his hydraulically-compensated 'rigid structure',[64] but his solution would have been costly and susceptibility to corrosion may have been a problem.[65]

Wallis – the artist

As a fully apprenticed engineer, Wallis was good with his hands, and was an excellent draughtsman.[66] He did not get the chance to show his artistic side as perhaps he might have liked (although few could have denied the aesthetic appeal of many of his work projects, such as *R.100* and Swallow). One early example of his handiwork was a multi-drawer shell cabinet made for his stepmother.[67] He also produced a number of fine carvings,[68] including one of his wife's face, its conventional appearance belying the technicalities of its fabrication. Wallis placed a frame with a grid of holes over Molly's face, then placed a probe into each hole in turn and measured the depth to her face (in the manner of a pin sculpture, but done one pin at a time). He then drilled a block of wood with the same grid to the same depth in each case, smoothing over the drilled block to produce the finished sculpture.

Wallis designed the badge for members of the RAF Foundation at Christ's Hospital; this was based on the 617 Squadron badge, also featuring a broken dam, with an angel flying above it.[69] The motto on the badge, '*Virtus spernit humum fugiente penna*'[70] is drawn from the Odes of Horace, and is similar to that used on his own family Coat of Arms, which he designed in the late 1960s.[71]

Wallis and Molly admire his carving of Molly. *(© Mary Stopes-Roe)*

Chapter 12

Wallis with Hindsight

The secret of science is to ask the right question, and it is the choice of problem more than anything else that marks the man of genius in the scientific world.
Sir Henry Tizard

The efficacy of Wallis's aircraft and weapons was well proven during the war, and although Wild Goose and Swallow made many flights as models, these (and his other post-war designs) never flew as full-size aircraft. Consequently, in analysing his later designs, we must rely on a combination of contemporary analysis and modern conjecture, and the author is indebted to the many aerodynamicists and others who have reviewed the Wallis post-war designs at his request and made comments upon them.

Modern analysis of Wallis's variable geometry

Although the volume taken up by wing pivots (particularly the complex designs of Wallis) is more easily accommodated in an airliner than in a military aircraft, the high loading of the wing pivot in such a large aircraft meant that a fail-safe design was regarded as unfeasible, consequently making VG unsuitable for civil aviation.[1]

The use of variable wing sweep for control is still regarded with scepticism by modern designers, the long time taken to alter the wing position (cf. moving a smaller tail surface with a longer moment arm) resulting in low manoeuvrability – not so much of a problem in civil aircraft, but a serious issue for military aircraft. Although removal of the tail was seen by Wallis as a central and immutable feature of his designs, a tail offers a 'practical solution to balance and control problems'[2] which is often a greater advantage than the savings made by not having a tail.

All variable-geometry aircraft that have flown have used single-axis wing pivots, rather than the sophisticated three-dimensional pivots proposed by Wallis. It would have been a challenge to provide a root seal for such a wing pivot. Although Wallis had given consideration to this as early as 1948, and included a solution as part of one of the patents relating to Wild Goose,[3] later Tornado experience showed that 'it was really quite tricky enough to seal it in only two movements'.[4] The design of the 'nib' (the static part ahead of the wing root, and the vestigial remains of the Swallow forebody) and the seal between it and the wing was one of the major challenges on Tornado.

The use of gimballed engines for control is also criticised for the same reasons – slow speed of operation and the fact that movement of a small tailplane may simply be more efficient than moving a heavy engine mounting (despite the weight and drag penalty of adding the tail).

The size of engines shown on some of the Swallow variants is questioned by some contemporary engineers, the large intakes required for operation at supersonic speeds not being depicted adequately. The strength of the wings to cope with aero-elastic problems due to their high aspect ratio is also questioned, especially with outboard engines (although the RAE was satisfied with this aspect of the design at the time).

A major criticism of the location of the Swallow engines is for the 'engine out' case, especially in the unswept position when the engine position is far outboard of the aircraft centreline, and hence an engine out will have a greater effect on yaw of the aircraft.[5] However, Wallis had designed an automatic compensation system to deal with this situation, as described in Chapter 9. How well this automatic system would have worked in practice is a matter for conjecture.

But what finally killed Swallow? Morpurgo makes the following judgement:

> *In analysing such evidence as is available it does appear that the decision to abandon Swallow was not taken by one man, not even by an organisation, and that it was not engendered by any logical series of considerations. There was, instead, a skein of judgements, personal, economic, military and political, so tangled as to be beyond unravelling but together strong enough to strangle the project.*[6]

Ultimately, comments by Wallis himself confirm that the aerodynamics of Swallow were not quite as good as anticipated, so although it would have worked well, it would not have been so far ahead of its contemporaries as had been hoped. So Swallow was not killed, it died of natural causes.

One contributing factor was the attitude to Wallis by his own company. It is certain that the Vickers management were less keen on Swallow than many at the Ministries. Wallis 'was convinced that there was still technological development in the civil aircraft market' to be had, but that Edwards was happier to just trim the percentages to produce the next aircraft.[7] Wallis himself continued to 'laugh like a coot' whenever he saw the F-111[8] as he knew the tail was unnecessary.

Boorer added that Wallis made things harder for himself by 'putting too many eggs in one basket',[9] trying too many untried technologies in one aircraft, and then further complicating things by deliberately eschewing manned test flights. He was also hampered by the fact that his design concepts were all aimed at long-range civil aircraft, with their low manoeuvrability requirements and greater volume within which the variable-sweep mechanism could be more readily accommodated, but available development funding was primarily for military applications, for which the concepts were less well suited.

Important also was the fact that the late 1950s and 1960s was simply a bad time to be an aircraft designer – the costs of development were spiralling, budgets were contracting and, in a shrinking market, there were designs on offer that were safer bets than Swallow. The Wellington had been the right design at the right time – even if Swallow had been the right design, it came at the wrong time. Nevertheless, it was a most elegant aircraft, even in comparison with Concorde.

Modern analysis of Cascade

The Cascade concept was so far from the norm that many engineers can see little value in it at all. Potential problems envisaged include unpredictable interactions between the winglets, especially due to turbulence generated by the forward winglets spilling over the rearward ones. There would also have been strange effects between the winglets and the fuselage sides. With the large air scoop at the front and engines at the rear, much internal space is taken up with the intake, and as the intake would get hot, this heat would have to be sunk internally. Some of the Cascade variants seem to have very little volume available for fuel (although one design shows vertical 'outriggers' outboard of the winglets, which contained fuel tanks), or for cabin pressurisation plant. Structural efficiency of square-section fuselages is questioned by some modern engineers, although Wallis had shown that they were practical; sharp corners also cause increased drag at high speeds, which he may not have appreciated (indeed, Wallis thought at the time that they reduced wave drag).[10]

In the event, Cascade was superseded by the single-wing variable-camber designs, although some of the same concerns (such as the interface between the fuselage sides and inboard edge of the moving wing) would still apply.

Modern analysis of the high-pressure submarine

Many aspects of Cold War submarine construction and operation remain secret, but it has been possible to obtain some modern analysis of Wallis's high-pressure submarine proposals based on unclassified material.[11]

Diving to the 2,000ft depths proposed by Wallis would indeed have conferred the detection difficulties that he sought, but would also have made several aspects of submarine operation problematic, such as communication and weapon release. Detection of surface (or other submarine) targets would also have been impaired, so the submarine would have been 'invulnerable but impotent'.

The gas turbine powerplant proposal has some merit, but some problems too. A large amount of liquid oxygen (LOX) would have been required, making the submarine large and expensive. However, the proposed use of LOX was novel at the time, when high test peroxide (HTP) was more common (and more dangerous – the *Kursk* disaster was attributed to problems with HTP). Another inert 'buffer gas' would have been needed for thermodynamic reasons, requiring storage and processing, and the waste heat from the gas turbine would have required disposal via heat exchangers, operation of which would have been problematic at great depth. Finally, experience with surface vessels powered by gas turbines has shown significant acoustic signatures, so submarines propelled in this way may have been more easily detected than Wallis had hoped.

The multi-cylinder structural form proposed by Wallis, though novel, may not have led to a thinner hull or lighter overall structure than a conventional single cylinder for the same internal volume. Stiffening ring frames would probably still have been required, reducing internal volume, and the vertical bracing pillars between the cylindrical sections would have needed great strength to cope with the compressive forces involved (up to 2,000 tonnes per metre length). Overall, use of conventional hull forms made from stronger materials (such as titanium alloy, as used on the deep-diving Russian *Alfa* class) may have been more efficient.

The proposed horizontal method of missile launch is also fraught with practical difficulties, due to issues relating to buoyancy of the missiles themselves (they are denser than water) and the fact that they need to be clear of the sea before igniting their rocket motors. Loading the missiles via a single launch tube would also have been problematic, particularly if the vessel was afloat.

In summary, Wallis's ideas relating to submarines further demonstrated his ingenuity and showed initial promise, but longer-term investigation reveals practical difficulties which make alternative solutions more attractive, and this is why his concepts have not been adopted.

TSR.2 and Concorde

As the 1950s turned into the 1960s, the great prizes in British aviation were the supersonic bomber and the supersonic transport aircraft, and Wallis must have thought that Swallow (or possibly even Cascade) would have been serious contenders for both (he had designs for both prepared). Although he failed to have his ideas adopted, it is still astonishing that Wallis had no input whatsoever, not even as a consultant, to the TSR.2 and Concorde projects, which were being built by his own company. He never even met the Chief Designer[12] on the Tornado project (who also worked on TSR.2). This promotes the notion that Wallis was seen as a 'mad cousin in the shed' by the main works, with his speculative designs being deliberately kept away from the real aeroplanes. Contemporaries deny that such an attitude existed,[13] but journalists 'believed that the real purpose of his isolation inside BAC's own headquarters was to keep Barnes Wallis and his leisurely ways away from the mainstream activities, and above all away from Sir George Edwards'.[14]

The reason that Wallis hated TSR.2 and Concorde – and he was 'very rude about both'[15] – was not that they were bad designs (TSR.2 continues to be regarded as an aircraft of outstanding potential and Concorde was a technological, if not commercial, masterpiece), but that he knew that he could have designed *so much more* aeroplane for the same money. In comments which he asked not to be published in his lifetime, he said that Concorde was 'wrong from beginning to end' because 'the fuselage is the wrong shape, the wing is fixed . . . and . . . only suitable for the one speed'.[16] Boorer thinks that he must have had some admiration for Concorde 'because it was a beautiful piece of engineering, and of course they achieved the sort of lift/drag ratios that he never thought could be achieved from that sort of wing[17] . . . but he wouldn't have admitted it to anybody!'[18] TSR.2 was cancelled on cost grounds, and had a Swallow-based TSR.2 design originally been adopted instead of the fixed wing, it would have been at least as complex to develop, so it seems likely that it would have been cancelled just the same (though perhaps a VG prototype could have flown before that happened).

Computers – the missing bits

If there is one aspect of the modern world that Wallis would have envied, it would be the availability of computers.[19] Had he had modern computers to handle some of the sophisticated mathematical calculations for structures, modelling airflows and 3-D design aspects, who knows how much more quickly his ideas could have progressed from theory to practice. Calculations for the variable-geometry aircraft would have been done by hand at a finite number of intermediate configurations, but use of a computer would have allowed far more positions to be checked far more quickly. Also, the ability of the computer to act as the centre of a flight control system has enabled designs, which previously would have been considered unflyable, to be flown with impunity – and often giving better performance characteristics than were possible from conventional 'stable' designs.

Some sources have suggested that differential analysers, an early form of mechanical analogue computer,[20] were used to calculate trajectories for Upkeep and explosive behaviour of Tallboy. Arthur Porter, one of the designers of the original differential analyser at the University of Manchester, knew Barnes Wallis[21] and some archive papers from 1944 confirm the use of the device for explosives calculations;[22] however, these papers contain no evidence that this referred to Tallboy or that any Upkeep calculations were performed with it.

Swallow 'Pancake', designed for long-range stealth operation at supersonic speeds. *(Author)*

The future isn't what it used to be

Political difficulties aside, the 1960s were optimistic times for aircraft designers, with the appearance of supersonic and VTOL aircraft for both military and civil applications seen as both inevitable and imminent. Even hypersonic research was promising great things for the next generation of aircraft.

Despite advances made in computing, engines, aerodynamics and materials, most of these predictions did not become reality. The Harrier did give true VTOL, though with very limited payload, and Concorde, rather than being the start of a family of supersonic airliners, has been the only one to see significant commercial service. Critics would say that Concorde was strangled by high fuel prices and environmental concerns (especially noise), but the Wallis solutions to the problem would not have been quite so demanding and with their increased performance margins, might even have given commercial success on more than just transatlantic services.

It appears that what really prevented any of the Wallis (and other) hypersonic designs from coming to fruition was the non-availability of suitable engines.[23] To go above Mach 3 and 80,000ft, ramjets are required (preferably combined turbo/ramjets) and these had not developed far enough to make their adoption a practical possibility by the 1970s, after which their development slowed. Use of rockets was always possible, but inefficiencies caused by the need to carry oxidiser in addition to large quantities of fuel made them impractical for commercial services. Although hypersonic research aircraft have now flown, the technology is still a long way from commercial service.

With no supersonic successor to Concorde heading towards a runway any time soon (despite many design studies),[24] the accent is now primarily on fuel efficiency and with increasing interest in quiet operation.[25] One of the concepts for a 'silent aircraft' is based on work at Boeing on the 'blended wing body', a tailless design which in appearance lies somewhere between the pure 'flying wing' types and the Swallow, and there are some definite similarities between the modern designs and some of the Swallow variants.

Wallis's use of radio-controlled models for flight testing, pioneering in its day, is becoming increasingly common. In the 1950s, the practicalities of model control absorbed as much effort as the design of the aircraft being modelled, but improved radio and computer controls have now made this aspect straightforward. Footage of recent flights of the 21ft-span Boeing X-48B Blended Wing Body test aircraft bears an uncanny resemblance to shots of the similar-sized Swallow model flying at Predannack – 50 years earlier. The military are also making ever-increasing use of UAVs (unmanned aerial vehicles) for reconnaissance and even weapons delivery, allowing the human pilots to remain in the safety of their base – Nash and Cheshire would have been right at home.

Variable wing sweep can be seen as a passing fashion in aircraft design, its benefits (which in practical aircraft were often not much more than marginal, due to the weight of the sweep mechanism) now being bettered by other technologies, such as improved materials and computer flight control systems. As such, we are unlikely to see any future aircraft designs with variable wing sweep as envisioned by Wallis. Witness the Eurofighter Typhoon; although with no greater a top speed nor longer range than the earlier VG Tornado, its empty weight is 20 per cent less which, allied with more powerful engines, gives it four times the rate of climb and (due to greater strength) improved manoeuvrability. However, there is still some research ongoing into aspects of variable geometry. This has included NASA's AD-1 oblique wing research aircraft in the early 1980s and continues with projects such as the 'morphing' aircraft proposed by the University of Bristol – this design features 'elbows' which allow the wingtips to fold up or down together or independently, and has been demonstrated (in the Wallis tradition) via a radio-controlled model.[26]

Nearly 50 years on from Wallis's sub-orbital aircraft, it is even possible that we may be on the verge of a new race for a supersonic transport aircraft, with renewed interest in hypersonic speeds and sub-orbital flight.[27]

One 'concept' of Wallis's that may hold ongoing merit is his Universal aircraft – he deliberately avoided mentioning this in later interviews so that the Americans would not 'pinch the idea in the way they did my variable geometry aircraft'.[28] Although the benefits of containerisation did not, in fact, translate across into air transport, the idea that an aircraft of just 150,000lb AUW could take off from a 500m runway and carry 100 passengers for any distance from short

Silent Aircraft, designed for economic quiet operation at subsonic speeds. *(© Silent Aircraft Initiative, used with permission)*

haul to half-way around the world, remains an intriguing one. This would allow one single aircraft design to cope with nearly all commercial needs, and do away with the need for large airports with long runways – our large airports could instead have shorter runways but more of them, or we could do away with the need for large airports altogether. Larger numbers of smaller aircraft would place additional demands on air traffic control, as well as requiring more pilots, but these expenses could be offset by the lower capital cost of the aircraft (due to larger production runs) and the greater flexibility offered. One driving force behind the Universal idea was the square-cube law, which showed that, as aircraft sizes increase, the structure weight becomes an ever larger percentage of the total. However, developments in materials and engines have meant that we can now build larger structures more efficiently, and so the square-cube law is being evaded. The jury thus remains out on the Universal aircraft.

Many of today's combat aircraft are deliberately aerodynamically unstable for maximum performance, and it is the constant rebalancing of the aircraft by the computerised flight control system that makes them flyable. As some of the Wallis aircraft would have been difficult to fly at certain speeds, it is also possible that the availability of flight control systems could give them a new lease of life. Swallow's summer may be yet to come.

One aspect of aircraft design that has undoubtedly changed radically since Wallis's day is the organisational structure of our aircraft companies. Boorer reckoned that Wallis would have been horrified by the 'disappearance of the chief designer and the appearance of the commercial man as the person who's running the projects'.[29] Wallis had already begun to express concerns about increasing shortcomings in the education system and the aircraft industry in some of his later press interviews.

Wallis's legacy – so much more than 'bouncing bombs'

Wallis could be immensely proud of his contribution to the war effort, through his mainstream aircraft work and the more esoteric 'earthquake' and 'bouncing bombs', for which he has achieved lasting fame. He remains Britain's greatest ever designer of rigid airships, and his radio telescope mounting at Parkes is still in use. As the inspiration for the adoption of swing wing, he would be delighted, 60 years on from his initial work on the concept, that a swing wing aircraft is still in front-line service with the Royal Air Force (even if it *does* have a tail). Artefacts from all stages of his career can be viewed in museums up and down the country, including many bombs recovered from the beach at Reculver and elsewhere (see Appendix 6 for some of them). Craters made by his 'earthquake bombs' can still be seen on the ground and from the air in at least four countries. His fame via *The Dam Busters* film endures and means that his name is still widely recognised – but as this book has hopefully demonstrated, it should be for far more than just the 'bouncing bomb'.

Despite the condition that patents should demonstrate inventiveness (see notes on patents in Chapter 2), most in fact demonstrate only a small, and logical, step forward from what has gone before. It is also notable that, although inventions such as the telephone, television and jet engine made their inventors famous, had those inventors not existed, the invention would *still* have come about, but *someone else* would have been famous for it – their development can be seen as inevitable. Many of Wallis's ideas, however, demonstrate genuine original thought – had he not thought of geodetic structure for aircraft, there would have been no Wellington, had he not thought of the 'earthquake bomb', there would have been no Tallboy and no 'bouncing bomb' and the Dams Raid would never have taken place. Surely this is the mark of a true genius?

RN Wessex recovering a prototype 'bouncing bomb' from The Fleet in March 1983.
(© Crown Copyright/ MOD. Reproduced with the permission of the Controller of Her Majesty's Stationery Office)

Appendix 1

Biographies

The following individuals were close colleagues of Wallis.

Norman William Boorer (1916–2004)

Norman W. Boorer. *(Author)*

Norman Boorer, 'Spud' to his friends, worked in aeronautics for 50 years, much of it alongside Barnes Wallis. At 16 he started an apprenticeship in the Vickers drawing office, becoming a draughtsman and designer on the Wellesley, Wellington and other aircraft. He worked on Wallis's bombs during the war, drawing the original plans of Upkeep, Tallboy and Grand Slam. From 1945 he was Wallis's Chief Designer in the R&D Department, working on the Stratosphere Chamber, Wild Goose and Swallow projects. His four patents relate to the mechanics of variable wing sweep and he spent some time at Warton in 1964 to transfer the Weybridge wing sweep expertise to BAC's later aircraft projects under development there, also spending a week on HMS *Centaur* doing fact-finding for the naval aircraft projects.

After leaving Wallis's department in May 1959, he became Chief Project Engineer on the VC10 and BAC1-11, and from 1967 was Executive Assistant to Sir George Edwards, Chairman of BAC; following the latter's retiral in 1975, he became a Planning Executive. After his own retiral in 1981, 'Spud' became a voluntary consultant at the newly-formed Brooklands Museum where he continued to work as a guide until his death. He was an Honorary Member of the Friends of the RAF Museum at Hendon, a Chartered Engineer, a Fellow of the Royal Aeronautical Society and was awarded the

OBE in 1982. He was unmarried and died in May 2004, having given public lectures on both Wallis and Edwards during the preceding year.

Commander Sir Charles Dennistoun Burney (1888–1968)

Dennistoun Burney was born in 1888, the son of an Admiral of the Fleet. He joined the Royal Navy in 1909, and during the First World War applied his skills in aerodynamics and weaponry to develop the paravane for sweeping sea mines, also being an early supporter of naval aviation. He married Gladys High in 1921, becoming a Conservative MP the following year, and lobbied for the introduction of an airship service across the empire. This led directly to the creation of the Imperial Airship Service, for which the *R.100* and *R.101* airships were built. Burney was appointed Managing Director of the Airship Guarantee Company, which employed Wallis as Chief Designer on the *R.100* (Burney's name also appears on 18 of the AGC's patents) although the relationship between the two men became increasingly frosty during the construction of the ship. In the late 1920s he set up Streamline Cars to develop a rear-engined aerodynamic and technically sophisticated luxury car (also known as the Burney car), although only 13 were built. Wallis appears to have had some input to this vehicle while still at Howden. Some of Burney's ideas were incorporated into the Crossley Motors Streamline in the early 1930s, but this model was not popular either.

He continued to work on armaments during the Second World War, developing the High Explosive Squash Head (HESH) anti-armour shell and the recoilless gun to fire it, and also worked with Nevil Shute on air-launched gliding bombs and torpedoes, but tests on the latter were unsuccessful and they did not see service use. After the war, he applied his paravane experience to stern trawling. He died in November 1968, his son Cecil inheriting the baronetcy which Charles had inherited from his own father in 1929.

Sir George Robert Edwards (1908–2003)

George R. Edwards. (© *Angela Jeffreys*)

George Edwards was born in Essex and, after a period as a structural engineer in industry, he graduated from London University in 1935, the same year joining the Vickers-Armstrongs drawing office and marrying Marjorie Thurgood. He rose quickly through the company, where he successfully (and very quickly) produced the DWI Wellington for aerial sweeping of magnetic mines, becoming Experimental Manager in 1940. A huge cricket fan and skilled player, he recognised that the 'bouncing bomb' needed to have backspin to improve its range, eventually managing to persuade Wallis – who remained shy about where the idea came from, although Edwards maintained that Wallis would have added spin anyway.

Shortly after the war, with Pierson retiring due to ill-health and Wallis heading up the new R&D Department, Edwards became Chief Designer, working on designs including the Viking and Viscount airliners and the Valiant bomber (the latter being the project he would remain most proud of). He became Managing Director in 1953, but also continued to contribute at a technical level, working on the V1000 (until it was cancelled) and the VC10. After the creation of the British Aircraft Corporation in 1960, he continued to contribute to the design of TSR.2 and Concorde, and his astute boardroom expertise saw the company through many troubles, such as cancellation of TSR.2 and ongoing cancellation fears for the VC10 and Concorde.

Like Wallis, he was a staunch supporter of the education system, forging strong links between the company and local education institutions. He and Wallis had a mutual respect for the other (Wallis was on Edwards's list of heroes in a 1979 magazine article), although there were certainly instances when both did not support the other – Wallis wrote to the Vickers MD in 1945 to say that he did not think that Edwards should be Chief Designer, and one of the reasons that Swallow was not taken up was lukewarm support from Edwards, by then MD himself. Edwards was Pro-Chancellor of Surrey University from 1964 to 1979 and, after his retiral in 1977, he took up painting (often of aviation subjects). He was President of the Royal Aeronautical Society and of Surrey County Cricket Club, the latter for ten years. He died in 2003, survived by his daughter, and is fondly remembered as a man with a flair for both leadership and technical details, and with as much interest in his individual workers as the bottom line of the balance sheet.

Herbert Jeffree (1906–2001)

Herbert Jeffree. (© Tony Hadland)

Following the family tradition of an engineering training, Jeffree started his career in aviation at Boulton & Paul in Norwich, where he also met and married his wife Doris. In the early 1930s, Jeffree transferred to a new job at Vickers in Weybridge, and they moved to Blackbird Cottage in Byfleet, never to move house again. Jeffree joined Wallis's team, becoming mainly a stress engineer (he did the stressing calculations on the geodetic aircraft); he made a trip to France to retrieve information about pressure cabins ahead of the advancing Germans, and also attended Wallis's briefing of 617 Squadron prior to Operation Chastise (even though he was not authorised to be there).

Known as 'Jeff' to his colleagues, he was regarded as an expert in many fields (even more so than Wallis). The team often created their own instruments and Jeffree became an expert at grinding his own lenses; of his 15 patents, most are related to lenses and mirrors.

Jeffree succeeded in flying Wild Goose, being able to fly the unorthodox aircraft as well as, or better than, the experienced test pilots. He remained with Wallis's team until his retiral from BAC in the 1960s as Head of Physics.

Jeffree shunned publicity and rarely agreed to be interviewed, often keeping details of his work secret even from his family. He was a keen amateur chorister and for a while sang under the conductor Vernon Handley, for whom he created a customised baton. He died at Ashford Hospital, Middlesex, in 2001, aged 95.

Nevil Shute Norway (1899–1960)

Nevil Shute was born in Ealing in 1899 and showed an early interest in technology. His father was Secretary to the Post Office in Ireland, and the family was in Dublin during the Easter Rising of 1916, Shute earning a gallantry award for his work as a stretcher bearer. He attempted to get into the Royal Flying Corps, but a stutter meant that he failed a medical. He graduated in engineering science from Balliol College, Oxford, in 1922, getting a job with de Havilland Aircraft. In his spare time he learned to fly and wrote short stories. In 1924 he joined the Airship Guarantee Company, working as Chief

Nevil Shute Norway (right) in the navigation hatch of *R.100* with an unknown colleague. *(Published with kind permision of the Headmaster at the Dragon School, Oxford)*

Calculator on *R.100*, later becoming Deputy Chief Engineer under Wallis and making the return flight to Canada in the airship. In 1931, he married Frances Heaton and, with the end of the airship era, he founded Airspeed Ltd. Airspeed designed a number of successful aircraft (such as the Oxford trainer) during the 1930s, and he continued writing and became successful over this period (his pen name being simply Nevil Shute). On the outbreak of war, he joined the RNVR and worked in the DMWD, contributing to many of the 'secret weapons' developed by the Department, including the famous 'Panjandrum'. His fame as a writer saw him sent to Normandy and the Far East as an official correspondent for the Ministry of Information.

He settled in Australia after the war, continuing to write successful stories, many of which, such as *On the Beach*, were made into films. His autobiography *Slide Rule* (1954) describes his time in the aircraft industry, including working on *R.100*. He died from a heart attack in 1960, and was survived by his two daughters.

Reginald Kirshaw Pierson (1891–1948)

Reginald 'Rex' Pierson was educated at Felstead in Essex, and although his father (a vicar) wanted him to work in banking, his interest in engineering saw him apprenticed to Vickers at Erith in 1908, joining the new aircraft section in 1911. He learned to fly at Brooklands, gaining his pilot's licence in 1913, and became Chief Technician of Vickers Aircraft Division from 1914 and then Chief Designer from 1917 to 1945; he was in charge of 500 design staff by 1945.

Over this period he designed 36 basic aircraft types with over 140 variants, including the Vimy in 1917 (design to first flight in six months, and the first aircraft to successfully fly the Atlantic), the Viastra (Vickers's first all-metal aircraft) in 1924, the Vespa (which in 1931 achieved the world altitude record at nearly 44,000ft), all of the Wallis types through the 1930s and 1940s (Pierson producing the overall design and Wallis the structure details), the Viking in 1945 and preliminary work on the Viscount.

He married Dora Mary Llewellyn-Jones at St George's Church, Hanover Square, on 26 April 1917, and they had two children – Michael and Elizabeth. He was awarded the MBE in 1919, OBE in 1941, and the CBE in June 1943. He died on 10 January 1948 after a long illness.

Pierson was renowned as a big man both physically and in spirit, and of absolute integrity. He used a balanced approach between the scientific and the practical, preferring to design incrementally from previous experience. Although he headed a large team, he had no lust for power, and was a talented negotiator, dealing easily with engine manufacturers, ministries and the RAF. The Royal Aeronautical Society's first named lecture was the R.K. Pierson Memorial Lecture in 1952.

Captain Joseph Summers (1904–54)

Joseph 'Mutt' Summers. *(BAE SYSTEMS via Daventry Express)*

Always known as 'Mutt', Joseph Summers is believed to have made more 'first flights' of new aircraft types (at least 40, probably 43) than any other test pilot in history. Joining the RAF on a Short Service Commission in 1920, he very quickly showed himself to have extraordinary skills as a pilot and within three years was working as a test pilot at the A&AEE at Martlesham. He also got married at this time, to Dulcie, and they had a son and two daughters.

In 1929 he joined Vickers as Chief Test Pilot, just in time to fly the first of the Wallis designs, and he would go on to make the first flight in all of them (except the F.7/41) and other notable aircraft, including the Spitfire. Mutt was lucky to escape with his observer when Wallis's first aircraft, the M.1/30, broke up in mid-air, and he experienced a number of other death-defying accidents over the years. He made frequent visits to Germany during the 1930s (Morpurgo states that he spoke fluent German though other sources, including his family, doubt this), where he was eagerly shown their latest developments – though after a visit in 1937 when Vickers reported his concerns to the government, the company was told to 'tell your pilots to mind their own bloody business'!

He lived very close to Wallis, and the two men shared a deep friendship, both inside and outside of work, and together with Pierson, made up the heart of the Vickers aircraft team. He flew the Wellington that dropped the prototype 'bouncing bombs' and also made many of the later test drops; he was in the Operations Room at Grantham on the night of the Dams Raid, giving moral support to Wallis as the night's events unfolded.

Regarded 'by many to be the finest test pilot in England' according to Morpurgo and as 'a shrewd judge of an aeroplane' by Jeffrey Quill, he did not enjoy the drudgery of production testing, leaving this mostly to his juniors, notably Quill and Alex Henshaw. After 22 years as Vickers Chief Test Pilot, his list of 'first flights' concluded with the Vickers Valiant in May 1951. Very much a 'seat of the pants' flyer, he disliked the lack of 'feel' from the new powered controls, and decided it was time to retire from flying, though his daughter believed that it was his failing eyesight which precipitated the decision. After a year working as a Liaison Officer for the company, he retired completely. He was playing golf on his 50th birthday when he was taken ill, and he died a week later, probably from cancer. His Requiem Mass in May 1954 was attended by his colleagues from Vickers and many others.

Summers was awarded the OBE in 1946, the CBE in 1950, and his record time for the flight from London to Paris, set in a Nene-engined Vickers Viking in 1948, still stands. Although one of Britain's greatest test pilots, no full biography of Summers has been published, his complex character and very private nature having defeated at least one author.

Major Philip Litherland Teed (1890–1977)

Like his father Frank, Philip Teed trained as a barrister, but had a more lasting professional interest in chemistry – his father was Public Analyst for the City of London. Philip was educated at Dulwich, Imperial College, and graduated in Criminal Law & Procedure from Oxford's Trinity College in 1912. After service with the RNAS and RFC during the First World War, he completed his final bar exams at Trinity in 1922, joining the AGC in 1924 to work on *R.100*, in particular the hydrogen production plant – his single patent, published in 1926, relates to this work. He also became an expert on metals, authoring many books on their properties and becoming a senior member of the Institute of Metals. He spent the war years working in the USA, then post-war he became Deputy Chief of the R&D Department under Wallis, also becoming a Special Director of Vickers-Armstrongs in 1955, in the same year delivering the RSA's Cantor Lecture, *The Fatigue of Metals*. A close personal friend of Wallis and his family, Teed was a very generous man, after retiral even taking out an advert in *The Times* looking for suggestions on how to spend his money for good causes. He never married and died in 1977, the residue of his estate passing to Churchill College, Cambridge.

Appendix 2

Papers by Wallis

Although much has been written about Wallis and his work, little of Wallis's prodigious own writing was publicly available in his lifetime. As Wallis was most often working on secret projects, he rarely produced papers or reports which were for a general audience, and most of his reports would have been intended purely for internal company consumption, with a small number additionally intended for limited circulation outside the company. However, as many were essentially a sales pitch for a new concept, they are written as if for a non-specialist reader. Document sources are indicated in square brackets.

Published papers

'Some Technical Aspects of the Commercial Airship', *Lloyd's Register Staff Association* (1926): describes some of the technical challenges of *R.100* [RAeS Library]
'Rigid Airship Design and Construction', *Aircraft Engineering* (January 1930), 7–9: technical details of *R.100* [RAFM B3257]
'The Dambusting Weapon' (January 1963): notes written and released by Wallis to accompany the first public release of technical information about the Dams Raid [RAFM B3255 / BWMT]
'The Strength of England', *Advancement of Science* (November 1965), 393–408: Presidential address given to meeting of the British Association for the Advancement of Science in Cambridge [British Library]

Reports for limited circulation

A Brief Note on Geodetic Construction (May 1935): description of the geodetic principle [SM Arch BNW C3/1 / RAFM B3251]
A Note on a Method of Attacking the Axis Powers (March 1941): genesis of the 'earthquake bomb' [TNA ADM 1/11767 / TNA AIR 20/4146 / TNA AIR 20/11994 / SM Arch BNW D1 / RAFM B483 / Churchill Archives Centre WLIS-1]
Spherical Bomb: Surface Torpedo, Part 1 (April 1942) and *Part 2* (May 1942): genesis of the 'bouncing bomb' [SM Arch BNW D4/2]
Air Attack on Dams (January 1943): summary of '*Note on a Method . . .*' and '*Spherical Bomb . . .*' [SM Arch BNW D3/1 / Nuffield College Cherwell papers G375/2]
The Application of the Aerodynamic Properties of Three Dimensional Bodies to the Stabilization and Control of Aerodynes (1947): genesis of Wild Goose [SM Arch BNW

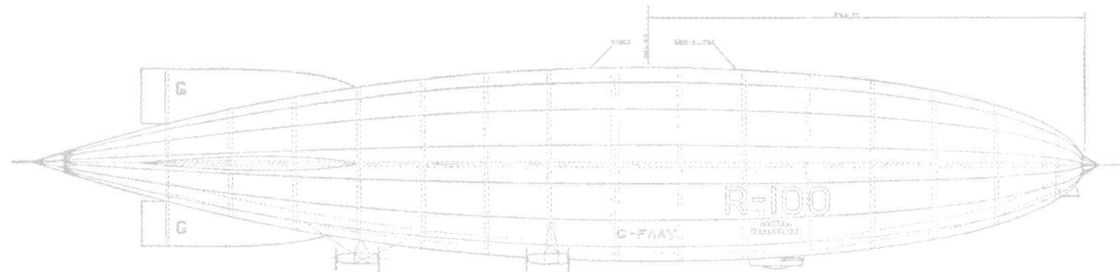

EB1/6 / Churchill Archives Centre WLIS-8]
Research on the Shape of High Speed Bodies (February 1951): Heyday torpedo [Churchill Archives Centre WLIS-7]
The Air Defence of Great Britain: A New Approach (1953): proposals for the application of Wild Goose-type aircraft [TNA AIR 2/14232 / TNA AIR 20/7578 / Churchill Archives Centre WLIS-4]
Giant Radio Telescopes (September 1953) [SM Arch BNW G4/5 / Churchill Archives Centre WLIS-2]
A Note on a Proposed New Type of Aircraft (January 1957): proposals for the application of Swallow-type aircraft [TNA AIR 20/10590 / SM Arch BNW EC6/3 / RAFM B492 / Brooklands Museum / Churchill Archives Centre WLIS-5 and RVJO-E5]
The Fundamental Principles of Long-range Supersonic Flight (March 1958): theory behind the Swallow aircraft [SM Arch BNW EC6/5 / Brooklands Museum]
The Swallow Project: A Variable Geometry Aircraft (April 1958): description of the Swallow aircraft [SM Arch BNW EC6/7 / Churchill Archives Centre WLIS-3 / Brooklands Museum]
The Swallow Project: Proposal for a Research Aircraft Capable of Wide Military Applications (Including Strike Reconnaissance Duties) (October 1958): description of the Swallow aircraft [SM Arch BNW EC6/6 / RAFM B4205]
The Development of Aircraft Capable of Economical Performance at all Speeds: The Philosophy of Cascade (1960): theory of the Cascade aircraft [SM Arch BNW ED1/2]
Cascade Aircraft – Objective and Preferred Aerodynamic Form (July 1960): description of the Cascade aircraft [SM Arch BNW ED1/3]
The Command of the Air, Part I (June 1961): theory of isothermal flight and jet lift aircraft [SM Arch BNW ED6/2 / Brough Heritage Centre]; also *The Command of the Air*, August 1961, which is three-page summary of the June document [within TNA AIR 2/14232]
Manned Aircraft: A Note on Sustained Flight Above 100,000ft and the Possibility of the Subsequent Development of Weightless Flight (May 1962): theory of isothermal flight and jet lift aircraft [SM Arch BNW E6/5 / Brooklands Museum]
The Vickers Limited Proposal for a New Type of High Pressure Submarine (July 1965): theory of new submarine hull shape and submarine use of gas turbine propulsion [SM Arch-BNW F1/2 / Barrow Record Office]
A note on a proposal to create a Universal type of aircraft (undated but *c*.1966): theory of Universal aircraft [SM Arch BNW ED3/10]

Appendix 3

Awards to Wallis

The following awards were made to Wallis during his lifetime. Some of his award certificates are held by the RAF Museum; these are indicated in square brackets:

	1929	Fellow of the Institute of Civil Engineers (FICE)
October	1937	Fellow of the Royal Society of Arts (FRSA) [RAFM X001-2371/003]
March	1938	Fellow of the Royal Aeronautical Society (FRAeS) [RAFM X001-2371/006]
May	1943	Commander of the Most Excellent Order of the British Empire (CBE)
May	1943	RDI (Royal Designer for Industry) 'for aircraft design'
22 March	1945	Fellow of the Royal Society (FRS)
October	1945	Freedom and Livery of the Worshipful Company of Shipwrights
	1947	Freedom of the City of London
March	1951	Royal Commission on Awards to Inventors (£10,000)
May	1952	Honorary Doctor of Science, University of London [RAFM X001-2371/004]
May	1959	Honorary Doctor of Science in Engineering, University of Bristol
	1960	Royal Aeronautical Society (Solent Branch) Reginald Mitchell Memorial Lecture 'Supersonic Communications Throughout the Commonwealth' and Medal
15 May	1963	Air League Founder's Medal (awarded annually for the most meritorious achievement in the whole of British aviation) 'for his great services to British aviation over many years, culminating in his design of the Swallow variable sweep wing principle, which has now been adopted by the United States Government'
	1964	Fellow of the Society of Industrial Artists and Designers [RAFM X001-2371/013]
May–June	1965	Honorary Doctor of Science, University of Cambridge

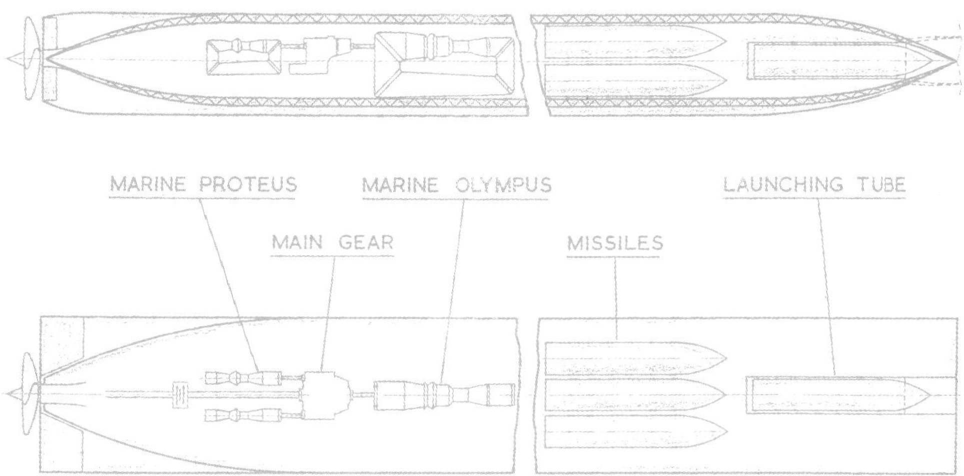

July	1965	Honorary MIMechE [RAFM X001-2371/005]
	1965	Honorary Fellow, Churchill College, Cambridge
	1966	Senior Fellow, Royal College of Art (RCA)
	1966	Honorary Doctor of Science, University of Loughborough
	1966	Honorary Fellow of the Society of Engineers [RAFM X001-2371/015]
May	1967	Honorary Fellow of UMIST; Honorary Life Member of University of Manchester's Students' Union [RAFM X001-2371/022]
June	1967	Honorary Doctor of Science, University of Oxford
December	1967	Honorary Fellow of the Royal Aeronautical Society (FRAeS) [RAFM X001-2371/007]
January	1968	Honorary Life Member and Fellow of the Institute of Patentees and Inventors
26 March	1968	Livery of the Guild of Air Pilots and Navigators
June	1968	Knighthood (Queen's Birthday Honours List)
	1968	Albert Medal of the Royal Society of Arts 'in recognition of his contributions to the development of aeronautical science and engineering'
May	1969	Kelvin Gold Medal of the Institution of Civil Engineers (given triennially for the application of science in engineering)
July	1969	Honorary Doctor of Science, Heriot-Watt University [RAFM X001-2371/016]
December	1975	Royal Medal of the Royal Society 'in recognition of the originality of his ideas and the determination with which he has pursued them' [RAFM X001-2371/002]

The Sir Barnes Wallis Medal is awarded annually by the Guild of Air Pilots and Navigators 'in recognition of an exceptional and innovative contribution to aviation'.
The Barnes Wallis Memorial Trust Book Prize is awarded annually by the University of Hull to a top-performing student of Mechanical Engineering.

Appendix 4

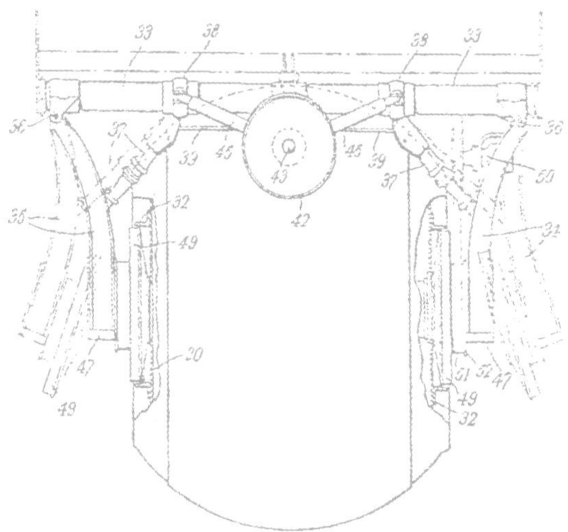

Bomb Experiments and Drop Tests

There are no complete lists of drop tests of the 'bouncing bombs' or 'earthquake bombs' in any of the archive materials, and this appendix attempts to present such lists compiled from the data from all available sources. Different sources give different details about the drops covered, hence there is little consistency between items in the lists; details have not been assumed, and are only given if stated explicitly in the reference(s) cited. Generally, all drop tests referred to in all sources have been listed, although where slightly different references appear to refer to the same test, the most credible details have been presented. Details which are particularly uncertain are indicated by a question mark. There are especially some *date* discrepancies between sources for what are apparently the same tests, and again, the most credible details have been presented; the dates on the IWM films appear especially prone to error. It is likely that there were actually far more drops made (especially Highball training drops by 618 Squadron) than are listed.

Lists of abbreviations used and details of sources are given at the end of this appendix.

'Bouncing Bomb' Experiments and Drop Tests, 1942–8

Date	Aircraft	Flight details/location	Aircraft crew/ observers	Test details - weapon dropped/ drop conditions	Results/outcomes	Sources
1 Apr 1942	n/a	White Hill House	BNW and family	Marble and bathtub experiment	Water skipping is feasible	23, 24
Late Apr 1942	n/a	Silvermere Lake	BNW / Amy Gentry	Various shapes catapulted from rowing boat	Golf ball shape best	24
1 May 1942	n/a	Nant-y-Gro	BNW/Molly/ Collins/others	Non-contact explosion	Dam held (as expected)	24
24 Jul 1942	n/a	Nant-y-Gro	BNW/Collins/ others 'large audience'	Contact explosion with 500lb mine (279lb charge)	Dam breached (as expected)	24
9 Jun–22 Sep 1942	n/a	Teddington No. 2 tank (1 day in No. 1 tank)	BNW and staff	22 days (non-consecutive) of testing using 2in spheres		24
20 Oct 1942 and other dates	W	Weybridge (ground test only)		1-sphere spin test	Further ground tests	24
2 Dec 1942	W	Weybridge – Queen Mary Reservoir	JS/BNW	4-sphere spin test	Pilot unaware of spinning	24, 25
4 Dec 1942	W	Weybridge – Chesil Beach	JS/RCH/BNW as bomb aimer, no camera or observers	'1st Series' – Wellington modified to carry only 2 steel spheres (smooth, 200ft, 224mph, 220rpm and dimpled, 200ft, 233mph, 475rpm)	Both burst on impact – casings to be reinforced with granulated cork and cement	5, 24, 25
15 Dec 1942 (postponed from 13 Dec 1942 by bad weather)	W	RAF Warmwell – Chesil Beach	JS/RCH BNW	'2nd Series' – 2 steel spheres (smooth, 45ft, 255mph, 725 rpm and dimpled, 39ft, 240mph, 860rpm)	Both appeared to shatter, but one recovered was only dented – Vickers to make two wooden bombs as backup for future trials	5, 22(MTE 1016), 24, 25
9 Jan 1943 (postponed from 28 Dec 1942)	W	RAF Warmwell – Chesil Beach		'3rd Series' – 2 steel spheres 'rewelded but not strengthened' (smooth, 80ft, 278mph, 800rpm and dimpled, 50ft, 285mph, 430rpm)	First breaks on impact but ran about 1,400ft, second hangs up then drops late on land due to electrical problem	5, 7, 24
10 Jan 1943	W	RAF Warmwell – Chesil Beach		1 steel sphere 'rewelded but not strengthened' (smooth, 100ft, 289 mph, 980rpm)	Bounces to 55ft but breaks up	5, 7, 24, 25
23 Jan 1943	W	RAF Warmwell – Chesil Beach		'4th Series' – wooden sphere, dimpled, 42ft, 283mph, 485rpm	Bounces 13 times, range not recorded	5, 7, 24, 25

Date	Aircraft	Flight details/location	Aircraft crew/ observers	Test details - weapon dropped/ drop conditions	Results/outcomes	Sources
24 Jan 1943 1033	W			Wooden sphere, dimpled, 48ft, 311mph, 525 rpm	1,200yds, 20–22 bounces	7, 24, 25
24 Jan 1943 1656	W			Wooden sphere, smooth, 108ft, 320mph, 740rpm,	Against boom defence, jumps boom on range	7, 24, 25
28 Jan 1943	n/a		BNW	Trials films shown to Vickers and service staffs	250 Highballs ordered	24, 25
2 Feb 1943 1500	n/a		BNW	Teddington films shown to Cherwell	Cherwell 'less antagonistic'	24
9 Feb 1943	n/a	Teddington		More tank tests	Results show that range is approximately directly proportional to velocity of discharge	5
4 or 5 Feb 1943	W	Chesil Beach		'5th series' – wooden sphere 46in, smooth, 300mph, 425–450rpm – three drops from 80ft, 100ft and 144ft	One travels 1,315yds	7, 24, 25
15 Feb 1943	n/a		BNW	Chesil Beach films shown at Air Ministry		24
19 Feb 1943	n/a		BNW	Chesil Beach and Teddington films shown at Vickers House (Pound/Portal/ Craven)	Portal authorises 3 Lancasters to be converted	24
22 Feb 1943	n/a		BNW / JS	Chesil Beach and Teddington films shown at High Wycombe (Harris)		24
23 Feb 1943	n/a		BNW	Meeting with Craven – 'Mutiny'		24
24 Feb 1943	W	RAF Warmwell – Chesil Beach		3 drops		5, 7
25 Feb 1943	W	Porton (wall target)		2 drops (wooden, 101ft, 114mph, 500rpm and steel, 80ft, 111mph, 505rpm)	Purpose of tests unclear	5
26 Feb 1943 1500	n/a			Meeting at MAP	Conversion of total of 30 Lancasters authorised, 150 Upkeeps ordered	24

Date	Aircraft	Flight details/location	Aircraft crew/ observers	Test details - weapon dropped/ drop conditions	Results/outcomes	Sources
8–9 Mar 1943	W	RAF Warmwell – Chesil Beach		Range test in open sea: 2 46in spheres, high density, one smooth, one dimpled, lap-welded steel; 2 low density 40–50ft, 300mph, 500rpm	Final Chesil Beach trials	5, 7, 22 (MTE 3432), 24, 25
15 Mar 1943	M DZ533		MVL	Flight test of Mosquito at various heights up to 10,000ft		5
24 Mar 1943	M			Highball drop to test mechanism		26
2–7 Apr 1943		Foxwarren		Spin and balance tests		24
9 Apr 1943	W	Manston – Reculver	RCH	Aerial survey of Reculver range		24
11–12 Apr 1943	L ED765/G	Manston		Upkeep spin trials on Lancaster	Rev. counters modified	24
13 Apr 1943 0920 / 0930	W	Manston – Reculver (E-W)	RCH BNW/GPG/Bob Hay	Tests to determine strength of wood covering, and to compare range of high and low density spheres: 0920 – high density, 81ft, 289mph, 520rpm 0930 – low density, 90ft, 286mph, 500rpm	Casing broke but cylinder ran on 'A good average run'	5, 13, 24, 25
13 Apr 1943 1108 / 1907	L ED765/G	Manston – Reculver (E-W)	MVL	1108 – 250ft, 210mph, 300rpm 1907 – 50ft, 252mph, 300rpm	Failed to bounce, but hit seabed and resurfaced, travelling about 40yds on the surface (lower height to be used). Casing disintegrated but cylinder ran on (6 bounces, about 700yds), Lancaster elevator damaged by debris	5, 13, 24, 25
13 Apr 1943 0717 / 0720	M		CFR	0717 – 100ft, 360mph, 700rpm 0720 – 100ft, 360mph, 1000rpm	Cases broke – bands to be tightened and gaps filled with resin	5, 7, 13, 25
16 Apr 1943	W / M	Reculver		2 drops from M 1 drop from W	All shed part or all of casing	5

Date	Aircraft	Flight details/location	Aircraft crew/ observers	Test details - weapon dropped/ drop conditions	Results/outcomes	Sources
18 Apr 1943 1100 (postponed 24 hours)	L	Manston – Reculver	JS	Upkeep Bands tightened and recesses filled with resin	Casing broke, sank	24, 25
18 Apr 1943 1330	L	Manston – Reculver	JS BNW, Prof Taylor	Upkeep Bands tightened and recesses filled with resin	Casing broke, cylinder ran on 700yds – BNW decides to use unpadded cylinder	24, 25
18 Apr 1943	M	Manston – Reculver		Highball, 3 drops Bands tightened and recesses filled with resin	Sections of the casing broke off in all cases and cylinders failed to run. An 18in wide metal band to be fitted over wooden casing	5, 25, 13(3)
19 Apr 1943	M	Ashley Walk No. 3 wall target		Highball, 'strength test'		13 (3), 27
19–21 Apr 1943	W	Turnberry – Loch Striven	MVL	Static spin tests at Turnberry: 3 46in wooden spheres used for 7 drops – net defence trials by MAEE 19 Apr – Smooth, 100ft, 290mph, 500rpm 19 Apr – Dimpled, 100ft, 290mph, 350rpm 19 Apr – Smooth, 100ft, 280mph, 500rpm 20 Apr – Smooth, 100ft, 285mph, 500rpm 20 Apr – Smooth, 100ft, 285mph, 450rpm 21 Apr – Dimpled, 100ft, 285mph, 400rpm 21 Apr – Smooth, 100ft, 280mph, 500rpm	Bombs not damaged by nets Stopped short of net Hit light net; went through 20yds Stopped short of net Hit heavy net and took section out; bomb and net sank Jumped over net, went 200yds Hit light net; went through 20yds Jumped over net, went 300–400yds	5, 20, 22 (MTE 3435–6)
21 Apr 1943	L	Manston – Reculver	SB/RCH	Upkeep, first bare cylinder	Sank immediately	13 (3), 22 (MTE 3437), 24, 25

Date	Aircraft	Flight details/location	Aircraft crew/ observers	Test details - weapon dropped/ drop conditions	Results/outcomes	Sources
22 Apr 1943	L	Manston – Reculver	SB/RCH	Upkeep, 185ft, 260mph, 500rpm, bare cylinder, 'stripped welded'	Sank immediately	12, 25
22 Apr 1943	L	Porton hard target		Upkeep, bare cylinder, 300ft, 130mph, unspun, 'stripped welded'	Cylinder flattened at point of impact, Mk XIV pistols tested and all working	12
24 Apr 1943	n/a	Weybridge		Conference BNW/ GPG/MVL/JS/ Renouf	BNW changes height to 60ft, 232mph, GPG agrees (crews told 26 April)	24, 25
26–27 Apr 1943	L ED825/G	Manston (ground tests only)	MWH	Test programme with Upkeep		
28 Apr 1943	M	Manston – Reculver	CFR / BNW and Renouf	Highball 130ft, 350mph, 700rpm Positive buoyancy, armoured with steel plates	4–5 bounces, 1000yds, slightly damaged	7, 12, 13 (3b), 13 (4), 24, 25,
29 Apr 1943	M		CFR	Highball 60ft, 370mph, 920rpm Positive buoyancy, armoured with steel plates (618 ORB records CFR made 23 drops 13–29 May 1943)	4–5 bounces, 1000–1,200yds, no damage. Decision made to use steel-covered stores.	7, 13 (3b), 13 (4), 22 (MTE 3438), 25
29 Apr 1943 0915	L	Manston – Reculver	MVL GPG ashore	Upkeep 50in, 60ft, 253mph, 510rpm – bare cylinder 'stripped welded', possibly first full-size Upkeep	4–6 bounces, 670yds, 30ft off track to left at end of run, turned left 1.5° at 1st impact, further 1.5° at 2nd impact, then straight	12, 13 (3b), 22 (MTE 3438), 24, 25
30 Apr 1943 1030	L	Manston – Reculver	MVL	Upkeep 65ft, 218mph, 520rpm, flat calm, 'Elswick stripped'	4 bounces, 435yds, 50ft off line to left	12, 24
30 Apr 1943 pm.	n/a	Reculver		Attempt made to retrieve pistols from 29 Apr 1943 Upkeep	Unsuccessful, Upkeep stuck in mud	24
30 Apr 1943	M	Reculver	CFR	Highball, 60ft, 360mph, 700rpm, ash casing	12 bounces, 1,600yds	7, 12
30 Apr 1943	M	Reculver		Highball, 90ft	10 bounces, 1070yds, 50ft off line to left	7, 12
1 May 1943	M	Reculver		Highball, 90ft	7 bounces, 1,000yds, 30ft off line	7, 12, 22 (MTE 1163)
1 May 1943	M	Reculver		Highball, 50ft, 345mph, 700rpm	8 bounces over rough water, some damage to wood and to cylinder	12

Date	Aircraft	Flight details/location	Aircraft crew/ observers	Test details - weapon dropped/ drop conditions	Results/outcomes	Sources
1 May 1943	L	Reculver		Upkeep, 60ft, 213mph, 670rpm 'Elswick stripped'	1 bounce, 40yds	12
2 May 1943 1130	L	Manston – Reculver	MVL	Upkeep, 80ft, 190mph, 680rpm, 2–3ft waves	3 bounces, 360yds, 40ft off track to left	22 (MTE 3427), 24
2 May 1943	M	Reculver	CFR	Highball, 2 steel-cased drops: 60ft, 370mph, 700rpm 60ft, 380mph, 520rpm	Both dented but ran well	7, 22 (MTE 3439)
6 May 1943	L ED765/G L ED817/G	Manston – Reculver (N-S)	MVL/RCH	2 Upkeeps from each aircraft	Only 1 drop 'satisfactory' to BNW	24
9 May 1943	M	Loch Striven/*Courbet* (first use of ship)	CFR	To determine whether Highball would detonate at a given depth, and whether steel sheeting was thick enough. 1 drop from each of 2 aircraft	Both abortive due to technical defect in release mechanism	13 (5), 22 (MTE 3445, 3447), 24
10 May 1943	M	Loch Striven/*Courbet*	MVL	Highball, 2 drops 50ft, 360mph, 700rpm from 1200yds 50ft, 370mph, 800rpm from 1400yds (618 ORB records 10 drops including 5 lost due to premature release)	1st drop hit after 2 bounces at high speed; store recovered from nets, extensively damaged. 2nd drop longer range, hit after 3 bounces, store not recovered. No pistol activation recorded in either drop; believed that pistols not withstanding impact, redesign being considered; marker buoy later found to be in wrong place, hence higher impact velocity (160mph) than desired	7, 13 (5), 22 (MTE 3440, 3445, 3447), 24, 618 ORB
11 May 1943	L (3 from 617 Sqn)	Reculver, towards screens	GPG and others	Upkeep, 60ft	600yds, 'good run' recorded by GPG	24
11 May 1943	L	Manston – Reculver (parallel to beach)	MVL	Upkeep, 75ft, 230mph, 500rpm Upkeep, 50ft, 245mph, 500rpm	75ft: 5 bounces, 430yds 50ft: 6 bounces, 450yds Neither deviates from track	22 (MTE 3441), 24

Date	Aircraft	Flight details/location	Aircraft crew/ observers	Test details - weapon dropped/ drop conditions	Results/outcomes	Sources
12 May 1943	L ED817/G		RCH		'similar results' to 11 May 1943	24
12 May 1943	M	Reculver		Highball, 4 drops, investigating premature release problem		7, 22 (MTE 3442)
12 May 1943	L ED921/G	Reculver	Munro Townsend 2nd pilot	Below 60ft	Lancaster tailplane damaged, repaired	24, 28
12 May 1943	L ED929/G	Reculver	Shannon Barlow 2nd pilot	Dropped 20yds short	Sumpter scolded by GPG	24, 28
12 May 1943	L from 617 Sqn	Reculver	Knight and other 617 Sqn crews			24, 28
12 or 13 May 1943	L ED933/G	Reculver	Maudslay	Below 60ft	Lancaster severely damaged; flew back to Scampton for repairs, not completed before raid	24, 28
13 May 1943	L from 617 Sqn	Reculver	617 Sqn crews			24
13 May 1943	L	SW-NE 5 miles off Broadstairs	MVL/Wynter-Morgan in rear turret RCH/GPG in 2nd L Jeffree in North Foreland lighthouse	Live drop – 75ft, 500rpm	7 bounces, 800yds, sank and detonated successfully, water plume rises to over 1,000ft	24, 25
14 May 1943	L from 617 Sqn	Reculver	617 Sqn crews; includes Martin's 2nd drop			24
14 May 1943 late	L from 617 Sqn	Uppingham Lake and Colchester lake	Whole squadron	Dress rehearsal for Operation Chastise; no bombs dropped	Last flight before operation	24
15 May 1943	L	Off Broadstairs	RCH/Jeffree aboard	Impact test – 500ft, no spin, live but no pistols (last live Upkeep at Manston)	Bomb did not break up or detonate on contact (as expected)	24
15 May 1943	M	Reculver	Visit of Secretary of State for Air	Highball, 4 drops		7, 22 (MTE 3455–6)
16 May 1943	L from 617 Sqn	Scampton – Germany	617 Squadron	Operation Chastise	Möhne and Eder dams breached, Sorpe damaged	
17 May 1943	M	Loch Striven/*Courbet*		Highball		7, 22 (MTE 3442, 3455–6)
18 May 1943	M	Loch Striven/*Courbet*		Highball, 2 drops		7, 22 (MTE 3443, 3456)

Date	Aircraft	Flight details/location	Aircraft crew/ observers	Test details - weapon dropped/ drop conditions	Results/outcomes	Sources
22 May 1943	M	Loch Striven/*Courbet*	BNW on *Courbet*	Highball, miscarriage		23
1-23 May 1943	M	Reculver	CVR	Total of 23 Highball drops at Reculver		618 ORB
22-23 May 1943	M	Loch Striven		More Highball drops		618 ORB
2 Jun 1943	M	Reculver	MVL	Highball, 5 drops		618 ORB
2 Jun 1943	M	Loch Striven/*Courbet*		Highball, 5 drops		7
5 Jun 1943	M	Reculver	CVR	Highball, 6 drops		7, 13 (7), 22 (MTE 3444), 23, 25
6 Jun 1943	M	Reculver	BNW observing	Highball, 2 drops	From 30–50ft, 360mph, range can be expected to be 1000–1400yds	7, 13 (7), 23, 25
10 Jun 1943	M	Loch Striven/*Courbet*		Highball, drops S13–14 plus 2 lost	Bombs fall short	7, 22 (MTE 3446)
10 Jun 1943	M	Reculver	RCH	Highball, 10 drops		618 ORB
13 Jun 1943	M	Reculver		Highball, 3 drops		7, 13 (7)
16 Jun 1943	M	Loch Striven/*Courbet*		Highball, drops S15–16	At least one hits ship	7, 22 (MTE 3447)
16 Jun 1943	M	Reculver	MVL	Highball, 2 drops		618 ORB
22 Jun 1943	M	Loch Striven/*Courbet*		Highball, 1 drop		7, 22 (MTE 3447)
27 Jun 1943	M DZ530 DZ533 DZ471	Reculver		Highball, 5 drops to test balance weights and drive wheels		7, 13 (8), 618 ORB
29 or 30 Jun 1943	M DZ530 DZ533 DZ471	Reculver		Highball, 3 drops to test balance weights and drive wheels		7, 618 ORB
1 Jul 1943	M	Loch Striven/*Courbet*		Highball, possibly drops S17–S19		7, 22 (MTE 3448)
2 Jul 1943	M	Reculver		Highball, possibly drops S20–S27	Some drops hit ship, some miss	7, 22 (MTE 3449)
3 Jul 1943	M	Loch Striven/*Courbet*		Highball, 8 drops		7, 22 (MTE 3450)
5 Jul 1943	M	Loch Striven/*Courbet*		Highball, 2 drops		7, 22 (MTE 3451)
6 Jul 1943	M	Reculver		Highball, 1 single drop plus 1 double drop		7
6 Jul 1943	M	Loch Striven/*Courbet*		Highball, 2 drops		7

Date	Aircraft	Flight details/location	Aircraft crew/ observers	Test details - weapon dropped/ drop conditions	Results/outcomes	Sources
12 Jul 1943	M DZ533	Reculver		Highball, 3 drops: Store AF, front bay, 375mph, 900rpm Store BF, front bay, 375mph, 900rpm Store CF, front bay, 375mph, 900rpm	About 7 bounces About 6 bounces About 8 bounces	5, 7
14 Jul 1943	M DZ533	Reculver		Highball, 3 drops: Store DF, front bay, 375mph, 900rpm Store AR, rear bay, 375mph, 875rpm Store BR, rear bay, 375mph, 800rpm	About 9 bounces 4 or 5 bounces About 10 bounces	5, 7
15 Jul 1943	M DZ533	Reculver		Highball, 2 drops: Store CR, rear bay, 375mph, 700rpm Store DR, rear bay, 370mph, 700rpm	About 12 bounces About 12 bounces	5, 7
30 Jul 1943	M	Reculver		Highball, 4 drops – 2 ash stores and 2 all-steel stores	First ash store slightly damaged, second dropped prematurely	5, 6, 7
Aug 1943	M	Probably Sinclair's Bay		Rough sea Highball trials	Cylindrical form of store cleared for anti-submarine use.	25
4 Aug 1943	L from 617 Sqn			5 Lancasters with Upkeep flew to Boscombe Down 5 Upkeeps dropped, aimed at screens	3 bounces, fuzes detonated 45–55secs after dropping	15, 27
5 Aug 1943	L from 617 Sqn	Boscombe Down – Ashley Walk No. 3 wall target	Kellaway and others Shannon / Rice as ground observers	5 Upkeeps dropped, aimed at concrete wall	Some drops successful; ED765 (Kellaway) crashed and written off; crew survived	15, 27
12 Aug 1943	L from 617 Sqn	Ashley Walk No. 3 wall target		Upkeep land target trial (for use against viaducts) – 5 Upkeeps dropped	Trials declared a failure – Upkeeps failed to maintain straight trajectory and to remain close to piers hit	27
17, 19, 21 Aug 1943	M	Loch Striven		Highball, 13 drops, 130ft, 250-500rpm		618 ORB
18 Aug 1943	Avenger FN795			Flight test of original aircraft only with different door configurations	Highball modifications not ready until spring 1944	6
19 Aug 1943	Avenger FN795	Weybridge?	MVL	Four test flights		25
23 Aug 1943	M	Reculver		Highball, 4 drops – 2 ash stores and 2 all-steel stores	Cylindrical all-steel store is sufficiently strong to withstand water impact, both stiffened and unstiffened	7, 12

Date	Aircraft	Flight details/location	Aircraft crew/ observers	Test details - weapon dropped/ drop conditions	Results/outcomes	Sources
24 Aug 1943	M	Reculver		Highball, 2 drops (steel)		7
24–26 Aug 1943	M	Sinclair's Bay		Highball 24 Aug - 9 drops 25 Aug - 4 drops 26 Aug - 4 drops 5 drops on other dates noted; ORB records 35 drops in total	Approx. 2/3rds noted as 'satisfactory', others 'unsatisfactory'	6, 618 ORB
27 Aug - 1 Sep 1943	M	Sinclair's Bay		"Further releases"	One drop with no spin	618 ORB
Before 31 Aug 1943	n/a	Tunnel near Newquay, Cornwall		500lb charge; static detonations to determine level of damage likely to be done in a Highball attack	30x10ft pile of debris, estimated at 300 tons	3
5-6 Sep 1943		Loch Striven/*Courbet*	BNW on *Courbet*	Weather too rough and no stores available at Turnberry		23
7 Sep 1943	M DZ543 (2 drops) M DZ533 (2 drops)	Loch Striven/*Courbet*	MVL	Highball, 4 drops, all-welded, all 50ft, 360mph, 900rpm, light wind, calm water – test to see if 'all steel type of case is sufficiently robust to stand impact' with *Courbet*; some stores reused from Reculver	All stores lost (consistency of range was achieved)	6, 7, 23, 25
8 Sep 1943	M DZ543 (6 drops) M DZ533 (4 drops)	Loch Striven/*Courbet*	MVL	Highball, 10 drops, all-welded, all 50ft, 360mph, 900rpm, light wind, calm water – test to see if 'all steel type of case is sufficiently robust to stand impact' with *Courbet*; some stores re-used from Reculver	All stores lost (consistency of range was achieved)	5, 7, 12
17 Sep 1943	M	Ashley Walk		Highball, 100ft, 200mph, 900rpm, forward spin	Appears to be related to tunnel attacks	5
27 Sep 1943	M	Ashley Walk		Highball impact trials (as *Courbet* stores were not recovered); Wallis was satisfied that impact data from land trials would be acceptable in lieu of *Courbet* data	Internal cylinder was damaged; thicker metal required	13 (14)

Date	Aircraft	Flight details/location	Aircraft crew/ observers	Test details - weapon dropped/ drop conditions	Results/outcomes	Sources
7 Oct 1943	M	RAF Angle – Maenclochog Tunnel	MVL with BNW, CVR and RCH observing on the ground	'Grouse Shooting 1' Highball, 12 drops, 50–100ft, 10 at 200mph, 2 at 300mph, 900rpm, forward spin, some wood, some all steel	2 stores entered tunnel (618 ORB says 4); estimated 9 would have entered a double tunnel and travelled for 200–250yds; stores stood up well to impacts	13 (16), 25
14–15 Oct 1943	n/a	Railway tunnel between Moss and Summerhill, nr. Wrexham, Denbighshire		'Grouse Shooting 2' 4 x 70lb charges; static detonations to determine level of damage likely to be done in a Highball attack	Estimated that more than one store would be needed to cause significant damage	6
28 Oct 1943	M	Reculver		Highball, 4 drops (1st spherical steel casing)		7
26 Nov 1943	M	Loch Striven/*Courbet*	Hutchinson (2 drops) Stephen (2 drops) Melville-Jackson (1 drop)	Highball, 5 drops, 'low', 375mph, 1,000rpm	3rd drop struck ship after 5 bounces; recovered from 20 fathoms – pistol broken; other stores made 10–15 bounces but fell short of the target by 20–100yds.	7, 12, 19, 22 (MTE 3452), 25
30 Nov 1943	M 'P' and 'J'	Loch Striven/*Courbet*	Melville-Jackson (4 drops)	Highball , 4 drops, 9ft waves 1426 370mph, 1,000rpm 1432 365mph, 1,000rpm 1552 360mph, 1,000rpm 1616 360 mph, 1,000rpm	 8 high bounces, short run Struck ship after 6th bounce – store flattened, pistol OK Struck ship after 9th bounce - no spin at ship, pistol pocket OK Recovered, undamaged	7, 19
1 Dec 1943	M	Loch Striven/*Courbet*	Melville-Jackson (2 drops) Stephen (2 drops) Hutchinson or Melville-Jackson (2 drops)	Highball - 6 drops, different angles of attack, smooth water 1200 370mph, 1,000rpm, 95° 1204 375mph, 1,000rpm ,93° 1258 365mph, 1,000rpm 1307 370mph, 1,000rpm 1431 360mph, 950rpm, 33° (no time) 365mph, 1000rpm, 39°	Two stores caught 4 bounces, hit, recovered, flattened 7 bounces, hit 12 bounces, slight wobble, hit 15 bounces, fell short 8 bounces, hit but missed net 7 bounces, not recovered	7, 19

Date	Aircraft	Flight details/location	Aircraft crew/ observers	Test details - weapon dropped/ drop conditions	Results/outcomes	Sources
2 Dec 1943	M	Loch Striven/*Courbet*	Melville-Jackson (2 drops) Stephen (2 drops)	Highball - 4 drops, different angles of attack 1413 1418 350mph 1,000rpm 85° 1612 370mph 1,000rpm 44° 1618 370mph 1,000rpm 45°	One store caught Store fell out during steep turn 20 bounces, recovered from net, heavily dented, pistol undamaged 5 bounces, recovered, pistol pocket damaged 11 bounces, 10yds short of net	7, 19
9 Dec 1943	M '24' and 'O'	Loch Striven/*Courbet*	Melville-Jackson (2 drops) Stephen (1 drop)	Highball – 3 drops, different angles of attack		7, 19
10 Dec 1943	M 'J' and 'D'	Loch Striven/*Courbet*	Hutchinson (2 drops) Stephen (2 drops)	Highball – 4 drops, different angles of attack	One pistol detonation, detonation location recorded and indicated poor spin after impact	7, 19
11 Dec 1943	M 'P', '24' and 'D'	Loch Striven/*Courbet*	Melville-Jackson (3 drops) Stephen (2 drops) Hutchinson (2 drops)	Highball – 7 drops, different angles of attack	Some hits, some misses. One pistol detonation, detonation location recorded and indicated poor spin after impact	7, 12, 19, 22 (MTE 3453)
4 Jan 1944	M	Saligo Bay, off Coul Point, Islay	Hopwood/ Webster, Hobley, Shaw, Whitfield	Highball, rough sea trials by MAEE – 4 drops, one directly into sea, one along sea, two at 45° into sea	Moderately rough sea does not affect range or line significantly, but does reduce useful range at end of trajectory	6, 7, 12, 20, 22 (MTE 3454)
14 Jan 1944	M 'L', 'U' and '24'	Reculver	Melville-Jackson in 'L', Stephen in 'U', Hopwood in '24'	Highball, 8 drops		7
28 Jan 1944	M 'L' and 'U'	Reculver	Melville-Jackson in 'L' (2 drops), Stephen in 'U' (2 drops)	Highball, 4 drops		7
9 Feb 1944	M	Reculver		Highball, 2 drops, steel spheres		7
22 Feb 1944	M 'U'	Reculver	MVL (2 drops)	Highball, 2 drops		7
24 Feb 1944	M 'U'	Reculver	Melville-Jackson in '24' (4 drops) MVL in 'U' (2 drops)	Highball, 6 drops	One store showed wobble	7

Date	Aircraft	Flight details/location	Aircraft crew/ observers	Test details - weapon dropped/ drop conditions	Results/outcomes	Sources
3 Mar 1944 or later	M	Reculver	MVL (4 drops) and Melville-Jackson (4 drops)	Highball, 8 drops of 'ping pong' stores (no pistols)	3 stores dented by first water impact, one so badly it turned end-over-end	12
11 Mar 1944	M	Reculver	MVL	Highball, 4 drops (C2, A1, A2, B2)	5, 8 and 12 bounces respectively, B2 ended on shingle; 1 store dented	7, 12
15 Mar 1944	M	Ashley Walk	MVL	Highball, 2 drops of 'ping pong' stores (no pistols) as calibration tests for 19 Mar 1944		12
19 Mar 1944	M	Ashley Walk	MVL	Highball, 6 drops (A1, B1, C1, A2 and overcoated wood and B2) to test strength of pistols with different shock-absorbing materials	Slight damage to pistol tubes on some drops	7, 12
8 Apr 1944	Avenger	Reculver		Tammany Hall, 2 drops		7
9 Apr 1944	Avenger	Reculver		Tammany Hall, 2 drops		7
10 Apr 1944	Avenger	Reculver		Tammany Hall, 1 drop, 1 miscarriage		7
14 Apr 1944	Avenger FN795	Reculver		Sight range trials, 8 drops, some with one store fitted, some with two	Average error 25yds	3
21 Apr 1944	M	Ashley Walk		Highball, 6 drops (D1, D2, F1, E2, E1, F2)		7
7 May 1944	M	Ashley Walk		Highball, 4 drops (2 at 90°, 2 at 60°)	Centre weld split, welding at ends burst, endplates damaged	7
15 May 1944	M	Loch Striven/*Malaya*	MVL/Melville-Jackson (Hutchinson sighting for both)	Highball, 8 drops		7, 25
16 May 1944	M	Loch Striven/*Malaya*	MVL/Melville-Jackson (Hutchinson sighting for both)/ BNW observing	Highball, 4 drops, 1 lost (no drops according to BNW diary)		7, 23, 25
17 May 1944 0800-1930	M	Loch Striven/*Malaya*	MVL/Melville-Jackson (Hutchinson sighting for both)/ BNW observing	Highball, 20 drops inc. 6 double (16 runs according to BNW diary)		7, 23, 25
8 Jun 1944 1340–1700	M	Loch Striven/*Malaya*	BNW observing	Highball, 6 drops; first use of range bombsight by observer (previously by pilot)	All hits within 50ft	7, 23

Date	Aircraft	Flight details/location	Aircraft crew/ observers	Test details - weapon dropped/ drop conditions	Results/outcomes	Sources
Jun 1944	M	Loch Striven/*Malaya*		Highball, 32 drops, 600yds or 1,700yds, some at 60°	600yds gives 3 bounces, 1,700yds gives 17 bounces; pistols worked in every case	25
10–12 Jul 1944	M	RAF Beccles -Wells-next-the-Sea	Melville-Jackson/ MVL	Highball, 3 double drops		7
8–10 Aug 1944	M DZ582 'U' M DZ471 Avenger FN795	RAF Beccles -Wells-next-the-Sea	Melville-Jackson/ MVL	6 drops		7, 22(MTE 3457)
18 Aug 1944	Avenger FN795		MVL	Flight test with four dummy 'drops'		6
7 Sep 1944	M	Loch Striven/*Malaya* (listed)	Hutchinson/ Melville-Jackson/ Hopwood/BNW observing	Highball, 2 double drops with 0.3s between releases (5 runs according to BNW diary; 618 ORB records 4, 4 and 2 drops respectively)	"Bad show" recorded by BNW	7, 23, 25, 618 ORB
15 Sep 1943	M	RAF Beccles - Wells-next-the-Sea		618 ORB notes this as the first dropping of stores at Wells	Total of 105 drops at Wells, using 68 stores	618 ORB
17 Sep 1944	M	Ashley Walk		Highball, 100ft, 200mph, 900rpm forward spin	Graph of results is overlaid with outlines of Mont Cenis, St Gotthard and Simplon Tunnels	6
28 Sep 1944	M (5 aircraft)	RAF Dallachy (9 miles E of Elgin) - *Malaya* (15 miles off E coast between Montrose and Dundee)		Highball, 10 drops in 'moderately confused sea conditions'; ORB records 8 attacks in 15ft waves	One hit	25, 618 ORB
Early Oct 1944	M	Loch Striven/ *Malaya*	23 crews	Highball, 4 single drops each totaling 'more than 70'	Two Highballs penetrate hull; 618 Squadron 'fully trained' by end of Oct	29
20 Oct 1944	Avenger FN795	Wells-next-the-Sea	Addison-Scott/ MVL	2 runs each 'to test installation and fuzing'		7
20 Nov–5 Dec 1944	Avenger FN766 / FN795 / JZ317	Wells-next-the-Sea, all W-E	Addison-Scott/ MVL	Tammany Hall ranging trials 20 Nov (2 drops), 2 Dec (2 drops), 4 Dec (4 drops), 5 Dec (4 drops)	6–12 bounces achieved, ranges from 750–1,100yds	7
14 Feb 1945	Douglas A-26 Invader #41-39291	'at sea'	Col Haugen USAAF	Speedee, 2 drops	To test installation; some damage to release gear	7

Date	Aircraft	Flight details/location	Aircraft crew/ observers	Test details - weapon dropped/ drop conditions	Results/outcomes	Sources
17 Feb 1945	Douglas A-26 Invader #41-39291	Wells-next-the-Sea	Col Haugen USAAF	Speedee, 2 drops, 24ft and 31ft	Both stores travelled over 1100yds in 12 bounces; release gear damaged due to overspeeding of turbine after release – shut-off to be fitted	7
Early Apr 1945	L ED933	RAF Woodhall Spa -North Sea (54°30'N 3°30'E)	617 Squadron crew	Two HE-filled Upkeeps in poor condition	Bombs dumped into sea	30
13-28 Apr 1945	Douglas A-26 Invader #43-22644	Eglin AFB – Choctawhatchee Bay, Florida		Speedee trials	10 of first 12 stores running 1,500–1,800yds; 24th drop very low, resulting in splash damage to bomb doors of aircraft	9
28 Apr 1945	Douglas A-26 Invader #43-22644	Eglin AFB - Choctawhatchee Bay, Florida	Lt Anderson + 3 crew	Speedee trials, 37th drop	Speedee bounces into tail of A-26, crashes into sea, crew killed	9
25Oct 1945	M	Machir Bay, off Coul Point, Islay	Jacques (6 drops)/ Scargill (7 drops)	Highball rough sea trials; 40ft, 380mph		12
25 Oct 1945	M DZ579	Machir Bay, off Coul Point, Islay	S/L Jacques/Fl Lt Savill (observer)	Highball rough sea trials, 'Trial 6, Run 6'	Splash breaks off port elevator, Mosquito crashes into sea, crew killed	12, 22(ADM 2542)
15 May 1946	M	?		Highball – details unknown		22(MTE 2100)
1 Jul 1946	M	Wainfleet		Highball – details unknown		22(MTE 2123)
29 Aug 1946	M TW228 / TW230	Wainfleet		Highball acceptance trials, 40ft, 1,000rpm		4
Aug - Dec 1946	L ED906/ ED909/ ED932	RAF Scampton - Atlantic Ocean (280 miles W of Glasgow)	617 Squadron crews	'Operation Guzzle' All remaining HE-filled Upkeeps (probably 37 stores)	Bombs dumped into sea	30
1947?	M	?		Highball - details unknown		22(MTE 3190)
16 Apr 1947	M	Ashley Walk		Card impact trials	Cast store performs well, forged store split badly	8
25–26 Nov 1947	M	Ashley Walk?		Highball/Card? – details unknown		22(MTE 2344)
?	M	?		Highball/Card? – details unknown		22(AMY 613)
13 Jul 1948	Sea Hornet	Wisley		Ground spin trials		8

'Earthquake-Bomb' Experiments and Drop Tests, 1943–6

Date	Aircraft	Flight details/location	Aircraft crew/ observers	Test details - weapon dropped/ drop conditions	Results/outcomes	Sources
Dec 1943	L	A&AEE Boscombe Down – Orfordness range, E. Anglia		4,000lb inert, all penetrated to depth predicted but broke up, oscillations noted after 15,000ft	Hykro steel to be used, tailfins to be offset to give spin	18, 25
w.e. 22 Jan 1944	L	A&AEE – Crichel Down		4,000lb inert, 3 drops, 20–22,000ft	Evidence of instability; one tail fractured during the fall; all casings fractured on impact	2
Not known	L	Orfordness		2 drops, ballistics tests		1
Mar 1944	L			6 drops, 4,000lb inert with offset tailfins, 18,000ft, 190mph	Consistent drift to port 90ft, striking velocity 1,100fps	18
	n/a	Shoeburyness		12,000lb HE, subjected to rough handling, extremes of heat and cold		25
28 Feb 1944	L DV405	A&AEE		Tallboy trial installation in aircraft	Completed successfully	1
20 Mar 1944	L DV405	Crichel Down		12,000lb inert, 16,000ft	33ft penetration, 24ft forwards, 'good stability'	1, 25
7–8 Apr 1944	L	Ashley Walk	Observed by BNW	12,000lb HE, 'terminal velocity' test, first live Tallboy test	Bomb 1 penetrated 8ft of gravel, 20ft of sand and 40ft of clay; crater diameter 92ft, 5ft deep. Bomb 2 penetrated about 1ft of gravel, 30ft of sand and 30ft of laminated sandy clay; crater diameter 90ft, 15ft deep	10
10 Apr 1944	L	Crichel Down	Observed by BNW and Molly	12,000lb	Bomb stable in flight	23
18 Apr 1944 1800	L	Ashley Walk		12,000lb, Torpex (5% beeswax), 18,000ft at 169mph, 11s delay	92ft crater	25
18 Apr 1944 later	L	Ashley Walk		12,000lb, Torpex (5% beeswax)	Similar results	25
24 Apr 1944	L	Ashley Walk, submarine pen target		12,000lb, Torpex (5% beeswax), 0.05s delay, 2 drops		1, 14, 25
25 Apr 1944	L	Ashley Walk, submarine pen target	Richardson	12,000lb, Torpex (5% beeswax), 0.025s delay, 4 drops using SABS		1, 14, 25
11 May 1944	L	Ashley Walk		12,000lb, Torpex, 1 with no delay, 1 with 0.1s delay		25

Date	Aircraft	Flight details/location	Aircraft crew/ observers	Test details - weapon dropped/ drop conditions	Results/outcomes	Sources
8 Jun 1944–24 Apr 1945	L from 9 Sqn and 617 Sqn	Occupied Europe and Germany		Operational use of Tallboy	Many targets destroyed and damaged	
Oct–Nov 1944	L PD198	A&AEE		Static drops to check release delay problems	Delay found to be insignificant	1, 16
9 Mar 1945	L PB592			Handling tests, with and without Grand Slam	Satisfactory, slight vibration of store due to crutches not being strong enough	14
13 Mar 1945	L PB592	Ashley Walk, submarine pen target	Purvis or Hazelden	22,000lb, Torpex, 16,000ft or 18,000ft	Missed sub pen by 350ft, crater 130ft, 70ft deep Crater 124ft, 34ft deep	25, 27
14 Mar–19 Apr 1945	L from 617 Sqn	Germany		Operational use of Grand Slam	Many targets destroyed and damaged	
Mar 1945–Apr 1945	n/a	Shoeburyness		Tallboy blast performance tests – bombs standing on nose on ground; 5 bombs (each different filling) exploded and compared to 4,000lb HC bomb	Estimated damage radii: demolition - 48.5yds, permanent evacuation – 70yds. Torpex DI (desensitised) filling found to give highest impulse intensity	11, 21
28 Mar 1946–Aug 1946	L from 15 Sqn, B-29s from USAAF	Marham – Farge and Heligoland		Project Ruby tests, using Tallboy, Grand Slam, Amazon and Disney bombs – penetration tests at Farge; explosive sensitivity tests at Heligoland	Only Amazon able to penetrate roof at Farge	17

Sources

1 SM Arch BNW D2/17
2 SM Arch BNW D2/19
3 SM Arch BNW D2/20
4 SM Arch BNW D2/22
5 SM Arch BNW D4/2
6 SM Arch BNW D4/3
7 SM Arch BNW D4/5
8 SM Arch BNW D4/6
9 SM Arch BNW D4/7
10 SM Arch BNW D5/2
11 SM Arch BNW D5/3
12 TNA ADM 277/46
13 TNA AIR 8/1237 (with item number)
14 TNA AIR 14/2011
15 TNA AIR 14/2060
16 TNA AIR 14/2189
17 TNA AIR 27/210
18 TNA AVIA 6/13312
19 TNA AVIA 19/704
20 TNA AVIA 19/1269
21 TNA WO 195/8612
22 IWM film (with film reference number)
23 Wallis diaries, RAF Museum, BWMT and Wallis family
24 Sweetman, John, *The Dambusters Raid* (Cassell Military Classics, 1999)
25 Flower, Stephen, *A Hell of a Bomb* (Tempus, 2001)
26 MacBean, John A. and Hogben, Arthur S., *Bombs Gone: The Development and Use of British Air-dropped Weapons from 1912 to the Present Day* (Patrick Stephens Limited, 1990)
27 Pasmore, Anthony and Parker, Norman, *Ashley Walk: Its Bombing Range, Landscape and History* (New Forest Research & Publication Trust, 2002, 2nd edn).
28 Ward, Chris, Lee, Andy, and Wachtel, Andreas, *The Dambusters: The Definitive Story of 617 Squadron at War 1939–1945* (Red Kite, 2003)
29 Curtis, Des, *Most Secret Squadron: the Story of 618 Squadron* (Skitten Books, 1995)
30 *Breaching the German Dams* (RAF Museum, 2008)

Abbreviations: People

BNW Barnes Wallis
CFR Squadron Leader C.F. Rose (618 Squadron)
GPG Wing Commander Guy P. Gibson (617 Squadron)
JS Captain Joseph 'Mutt' Summers (Vickers-Armstrongs Chief Test Pilot)
MVL Squadron Leader M.V. 'Shorty' Longbottom (seconded from RAF)
MWH M.W. Hartford (A&AEE test pilot)
RCH Captain R.C. 'Bob' Handasyde (Vickers-Armstrongs Test Pilot)
SB Captain Sam Brown (Avro Chief Test Pilot)

Abbreviations: Aircraft

L Avro Lancaster (with serial number, if known)
M de Havilland Mosquito (with serial number, if known)
W Vickers Wellington BIII BJ895/G

Appendix 5

Bomb Statistics - Imperial

Bomb	Total weight lb	Explosive lb	Length Imperial	Diameter Imperial	% explosive
Highball/Upkeep (prototype)				46in	
Upkeep (actual)	9,250	6,600	60in	51in	71.4
Upkeep (German estimate)	8,598	6,173	60in	50in	71.8
Highball (original plan)	1,000	545		35in	54.5
Highball (Wellington/Warwick)	1,200	750		48in	62.5
Highball (Mosquito)	1,200	600	28in	35in	50.0
Highball II (Card)	1,200	540	24in	33in	45.0
Baseball	300	150	19in	21in	50.0
Kurt	1,653	661	30in	30in	40.0
Tallboy	12,000	5,200	21ft	38in	43.3
Grand Slam	22,400	9,200	26ft 6in	46in	41.1

Bomb Statistics - Metric

Bomb	Total weight kg	Explosive kg	Length m	Diameter m	% explosive
Highball/Upkeep (prototype)				1.17	
Upkeep (actual)	4,196	2,994	1.53	1.30	71.4
Upkeep (German estimate)	3,900	2,800	1.53	1.27	71.8
Highball (original plan)	454	247		0.89	54.5
Highball (Wellington/Warwick)	544	340		1.22	62.5
Highball (Mosquito)	544	272	0.71	0.89	50.0
Highball II (Card)	544	245	0.61	0.84	45.0
Baseball	136	68	0.48	0.53	50.0
Kurt	750	300	0.75	0.75	40.0
Tallboy	5,443	2,359	6.40	0.97	43.3
Grand Slam	10,160	4,173	7.70	1.17	41.1

Appendix 6

Wallis Bombs on Display

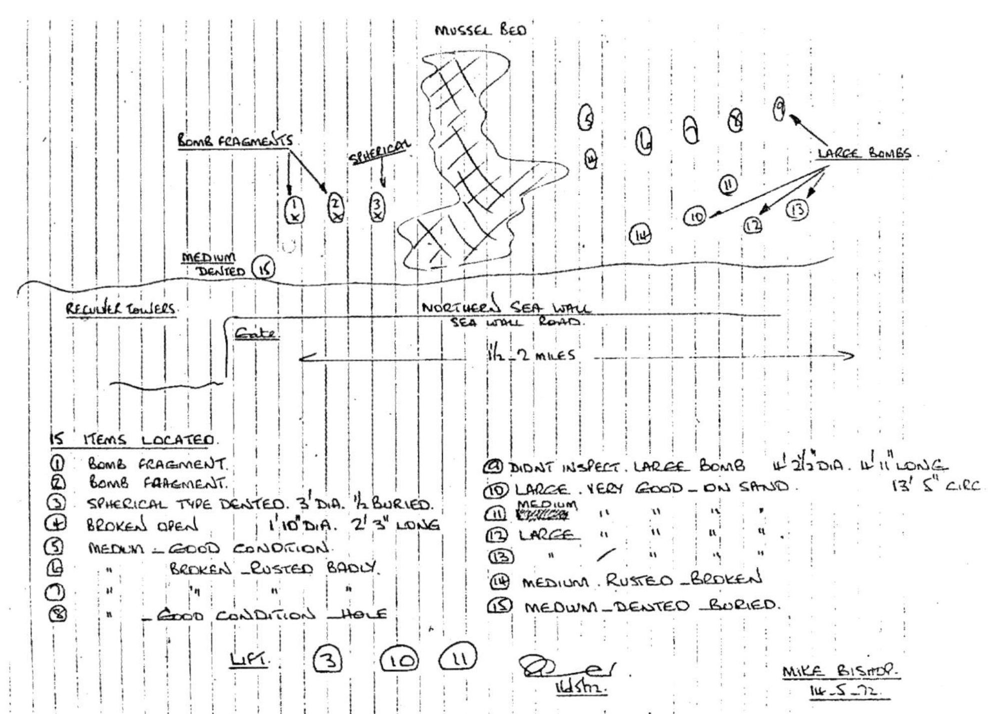

Survey map of Reculver beach showing test bombs. *(Author's collection)*

In May 1972, a survey of the test site at Reculver was conducted by Mike Bishop of the British Sub-Aqua Club – he found a total of 15 bombs or parts thereof, including four Upkeeps. All of these, plus one further Upkeep, have now been recovered from the site, as follows:

'Bouncing Bombs' recovered from Reculver, Kent

Type	Recovered	From	By	Where now
Upkeep (no fuzes)	28 Apr 1975	Reculver foreshore	BSAC/USAF*	Brooklands Museum (on loan from RAF Museum)
Upkeep	29 Apr 1975	Reculver foreshore	BSAC/USAF*	IWM Duxford
Upkeep	29 Apr 1975	Reculver foreshore	BSAC/USAF*	Lincolnshire Aviation Heritage Centre, East Kirkby, Lincs.
Upkeep (3 hydrostatic fuzes)	29 Apr 1975	Reculver foreshore	BSAC/USAF*	Brenzett Aeronautical Museum, Kent
Highball core cylinder	Oct 1977	Reculver	unknown	Spitfire & Hurricane Memorial Museum, Manston
Highball core cylinder	Oct 1977	Reculver	unknown	Scampton Museum (via Blackpool and Amsterdam)
Unknown type	Oct 1977	Reculver	unknown	unknown
Upkeep fragment	Oct 1977	Reculver sea wall	unknown	Petwood Hotel, Woodhall Spa
Upkeep concrete core	Oct 1977	Reculver sea wall	unknown	EOD TIC, Chattenden, Kent
Upkeep end plate	Before 1996	Reculver sea wall	unknown	Grantham Museum
Upkeep fragment	Jun 1996	Reculver sea wall	unknown	Dover Castle (blank end plate and up to 28in of cylinder)
Highball core cylinder	6 Jun 1997	Reculver foreshore	IMPS/EOD**	Herne Bay Museum
Highball complete (dented)	6 Jun 1997	Reculver foreshore	IMPS/EOD**	unknown (not at Mosquito Museum)
Highball core cylinder	7 Jun 1997	Reculver foreshore	IMPS/EOD**	unknown
Upkeep (no fuzes)	8 Jun 1997	Reculver foreshore	IMPS/EOD**	Barnes Wallis Memorial Trust (no fuzes)

* recovery arranged by Malcolm Ilott of Rayleigh Branch of British Sub-Aqua Club, carried out by USAF Sikorsky HH53 'Jolly Green Giant' helicopter

** recovery arranged by Andrew Hemsley of Invicta Military Vehicle Preservation Society, carried out by 101 Engineer Regiment (Explosive Ordnance Disposal) and 222 Field Squadron (Explosive Ordnance Disposal) (Operation Mona Lisa)

'Bouncing Bombs' recovered from other locations

Type	Recovered	From	By	Where now
Prototype	Mar 1983	The Fleet	RN Wessex	Fleet Air Arm Museum
Upkeep	Jul 1984	Ashley Walk	Royal Observer Corps	Part of end section cut up into 617 parts and sold for charity
Upkeep	Jul 1984	Ashley Walk	Royal Observer Corps	617 Squadron at RAF Lossiemouth (previously at RAF Marham)
Upkeep	Jul 1984	Ashley Walk	Royal Observer Corps	Ringwood Town & County Experience, Ringwood, Hampshire
Prototype, poor condition	27 Jan 1989	The Fleet	RN Sea King ZF121	Brooklands Museum (on loan from Holland House Estates, Dorchester)
Prototype, dimpled	30 Sep 1992	The Fleet	Portland Museum / RN Sea King	The Swannery, Abbotsbury, Dorset (previously at Portland Museum)
Highball shell fragment	since 1997	Maenclochog	Pembrokeshire Aviation Group	Haverfordwest (Withybush) Airport
Highball shell fragment	since 1997	Maenclochog	Pembrokeshire Aviation Group	Barnes Wallis Memorial Trust collection

Upkeep Replicas

Type	Made	By	Where now
Upkeep replica, full-size cutaway	1966	Vickers-Armstrongs apprentices	RAF Museum, Hendon
Upkeep replica, half-scale	2003	Thameside Aviation Museum	Thameside Aviation Museum, East Tilbury
Upkeep replica, one third-scale	---	---	Dambusters Inn, Scampton
Upkeep replica	---	---	Lincolnshire Aviation Heritage Centre, East Kirkby, Lincs.
Upkeep replica, full-size	---	---	Eder Dam Museum

All locations given in the tables above were verified during 2008, and supersede those given elsewhere, notably comments by Flower, Stephen, *A Hell of a Bomb* (Tempus, 2001) and Euler, Helmuth, *The Dams Raid: Through the Lens* (After the Battle, 2001).

Examples of the 'earthquake bombs' can be seen at:

- Brooklands Museum, Weybridge (Tallboy, Grand Slam, and Tallboy (Small))
- RAF Museum, Hendon (Grand Slam)
- Yorkshire Air Museum, Elvington (Tallboy and Grand Slam (casing only, no tail))
- 617 Squadron, RAF Lossiemouth (Tallboy and Grand Slam) [*not publicly accessible*]
- BBMF, RAF Coningsby (Tallboy and Grand Slam) [*not publicly accessible*]
- Explosive Ordnance Disposal TIC, Chattenden, Kent (Tallboy and Grand Slam) [*not publicly accessible*]
- Belgian Army base, Meerdaal (Tallboy) [*not publicly accessible*]
- Pakistan Air Force Museum, Karachi (Tallboy)
- Nanton Lancaster Society Air Museum, Canada (Tallboy full-size replica)

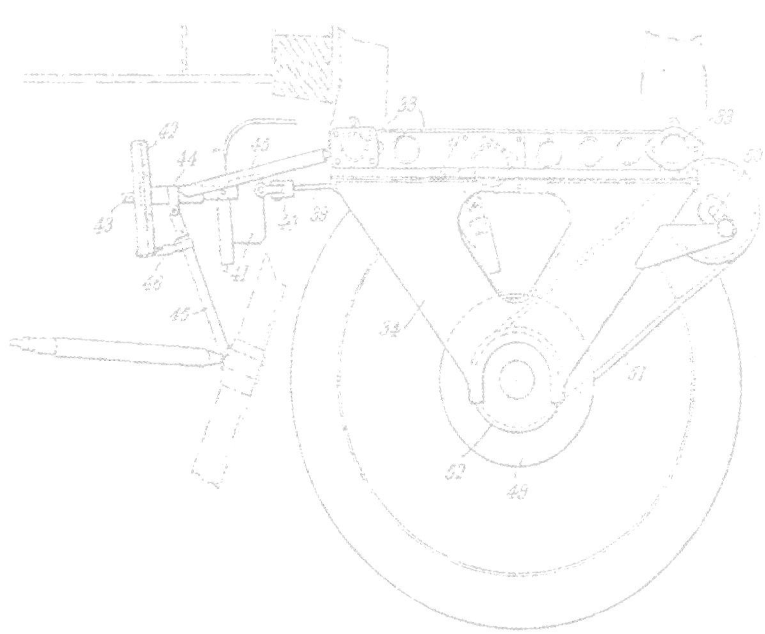

Glossary

Unit conversion table

Length/distance

To convert	**feet**	to	**metres**	divide by	**3.28**
To convert	**nautical miles**	to	**miles**	multiply by	**1.15**
To convert	**miles**	to	**kilometres**	multiply by	**1.61**

Speed

To convert	**feet per second**	to	**miles per hour**	divide by	**1.47**
To convert	**feet per second**	to	**kilometres per hour**	multiply by	**1.10**
To convert	**miles per hour**	to	**knots**	divide by	**1.15**
To convert	**miles per hour**	to	**kilometres per hour**	multiply by	**1.61**
To convert	**miles per hour**	to	**metres per second**	divide by	**2.24**
To convert	**Mach at sea level**	to	**miles per hour**	multiply by	**761***
To convert	**Mach at 35,000ft**	to	**miles per hour**	multiply by	**655***

*varies according to atmospheric conditions, particularly temperature; temperature is virtually constant above 35,000ft

Area

To convert	**square feet**	to	**square metres**	divide by	**10.8**

Volume

To convert	**UK gallons**	to	**litres**	multiply by	**4.55**
To convert	**UK gallons**	to	**US gallons**	multiply by	**1.20**

Mass

To convert	**lb**	to	**kg**	divide by	**2.20**
To convert	**lb**	to	**UK (long) tons**	divide by	**2240**
To convert	**lb**	to	**US (short) tons**	divide by	**2000**

Moment

To convert	**lbft**	to	**kgm**	divide by	**7.23**

Density

1 litre of (pure) water weighs exactly 1kg (2.20lb)
1 litre of Jet A-1 fuel weighs 0.804kg (1.77lb)
1 UK gallon of (pure) water weighs 4.55kg (10.02lb)
1 UK gallon of Jet A-1 fuel weighs 3.65kg (8.05lb)

Terms and acronyms

A&AEE — Aeroplane & Armament Experimental Establishment (responsible for the testing of aircraft and weapons carried by it; based at Boscombe Down, Wiltshire)

AAD — Air Attack on Dams committee (set up by the Ministry of Aircraft Production to investigate ways to breach dams)

ACM — Air Chief Marshal (of the Royal Air Force)

aerodyne	An aircraft which relies on forward motion to generate enough lift to keep it in the air
aerostat	An aircraft which can remain in the air even when static, ie an airship
AGC	Airship Guarantee Company (the wholly-owned subsidiary of Vickers which designed and built *R.100*)
AM	Air Marshal (of the Royal Air Force)
anhedral	Angle of wing which slopes downwards from root to tip
AP	Armour piercing (type of bomb)
Apple Turnover	Codename for momentum bomb
ARC	Aeronautical Research Committee (later Council), a government group charged with overseeing aeronautical research for both civil and military applications
Ashley Walk	An area of the New Forest in Hampshire, site of a bombing range which included concrete areas, wall targets and a dummy submarine pen (now buried); craters can still be seen on the site
aspect ratio	A measure of the proportions of the planform of a wing – longer, narrower wings have a larger aspect ratio; usually calculated as the square of the span divided by the wing area
AUW	All-up Weight, the total weight of an aircraft at the moment it starts to roll down the runway for take-off; now more commonly known as Maximum Take-off Weight (MTOW)
AVM	Air Vice-Marshal (of the Royal Air Force)
BAC	British Aircraft Corporation (formed in 1960 by merger of aircraft interests of Vickers-Armstrongs, English Electric and (later) Hunting; became British Aerospace on privatisation in 1987, whose interests are now part of BAE SYSTEMS)
Baseball	300lb spherical 'bouncing bomb' for use from motor torpedo boats
BBMF	Battle of Britain Memorial Flight, the group within the RAF which maintains and flies its historic aircraft
Black Cat	Codename for Highball when carried by a Sea Mosquito
BNW	Barnes Neville Wallis
BRS	Building Research Station (now the Building Research Establishment) at Garston near Watford, where some of the model dam tests were performed (one of the dam models still exists at the site)
BWMT	Barnes Wallis Memorial Trust
calculator	In the pre-computer era, a person of mathematical ability who was employed to do the numerical calculation work required for engineering projects
camber	Curvature in the profile of a wing; generally more camber generates more lift, but also more drag (flaps and droops on a modern airliner wing are used to increase the camber of the wing for greater lift during landing and take-off)
Card	Codename for Highball Mk II
CAS	Chief of the Air Staff
CG	Centre of gravity (more correctly, centre of mass) – the point at which, for many purposes, all the mass of an aircraft can be said to be concentrated; aircraft stability is often critically related to the relative positions of the CG and CP
chord	The depth of a wing from leading edge to trailing edge, measured in the direction of the airflow
CoS	Chiefs of Staff
CP	Centre of pressure – the point at which, for many purposes, all the aerodynamic forces acting on an aircraft can be said to be concentrated; aircraft stability is often critically related to the relative positions of the CG and CP
DARD	Department of Aeronautical Research & Development at Vickers – Wallis was in charge of this department from its inception in 1945 until his retiral in 1971; often abbreviated to R&D
dihedral	Angle of wing which slopes upwards from root to tip

DMWD — Department of Miscellaneous Weapons Development (a research department of the Admiralty which designed a number of novel weapons, most notably to support the Normandy invasion and the war against U-boats; based at HMS *Birnbeck* near Weston-super-Mare and often known as the 'Wheezers and Dodgers', staff included Wallis's former colleague Nevil Shute Norway)

DNI — Department of Naval Intelligence (at the Admiralty)

drag — The force tending to slow an aircraft down, consisting of parasitic drag (caused by pushing the aircraft through the air), induced drag (caused by generating lift and turbulence) and wave drag (caused by creation of the shock wave in transonic and supersonic flight). In steady flight, the total drag force is exactly balanced by the thrust force.

DRPC — Defence Research Policy Committee

DSR — Department of Scientific Research (at the Admiralty)

DTM — Department of Torpedoes and Mining (at the Admiralty)

ESC — English Steel Corporation, a major steelworks based in Sheffield, which was owned by Vickers; ESC was the main producer of Tallboy/Grand Slam bomb casings

FAA — Fleet Air Arm (aeronautical branch of the Royal Navy)

FAI — Fédération Aéronautique Internationale, the governing body for air sports and keeper of records in aeronautics

flutter — An undesirable and potentially dangerous vibration of part of an aircraft structure, often caused by inadequate stiffness of the part concerned

FTR — Failed To Return

fuze — A detonator used to initiate combustion of the main explosive charge in a bomb, typically triggered by some form of timing mechanism (or air or water pressure); synonymous with pistol

Golf mine — Generic term for all forms of the 'bouncing bomb'

Grand Slam — Codename for 22,000lb MC deep-penetration 'earthquake bomb'

Green Lizard — Codename for a tube-launched surface-to-air missile, which incorporated wings with variable sweep

HC — High capacity, a characteristic of bombs indicating a high proportion of explosive to overall weight (i.e. a light casing)

HE — High explosive

Heyday — Low-drag torpedo design relying on laminar flow over its surface to reduce drag

Highball — Codename for the 1,200lb spherical 'bouncing bomb' for use against capital ships

Hot Dog — Codename for Highball when carried by a Sea Hornet

hypersonic — Travelling at speeds in excess of Mach 5; more generally used to refer to any highly supersonic speeds

IAS — Indicated air speed, the airspeed as indicated by cockpit instruments; differs from TAS, the difference being variable depending on height, wind and other factors

IWM — Imperial War Museum

Kurt — Codename for German 'bouncing bomb' similar to Highball

lift — The force tending to make an aircraft rise; in an airship, lift is generated via buoyancy from the gasbags, in an aircraft it is generated by the shape of the wings moving through the air. In steady flight, the lift force is exactly balanced by the weight force.

MAEE — Marine Aircraft Experimental Establishment (responsible for the testing of aircraft and weapons to be used against maritime targets; pre-war based at Folkestone, moved to Rhu near Helensburgh on the Clyde in 1939)

MAP — Ministry of Aircraft Production, a government department which organised the production of aircraft for the RAF during the Second World War; in 1946, its role was taken over by the Ministry of Supply

MC — Medium capacity, a characteristic of bombs indicating a medium proportion of explosive to overall weight (i.e. a heavy casing)

moment	A force acting on a body which does not act through its centre of mass, hence causing a rotation of the body around its centre of mass
MoS	Ministry of Supply, a government department which existed 1939–59, during which time it organised the supply of equipment to the three armed forces
MTB	Motor torpedo boat – a small, high-speed surface vessel armed with torpedo tubes
MWDP	Mutual Weapons Development Programme (a US-funded programme for assisting international development of military technologies for NATO – Wallis's Swallow and the prototype of the Harrier VTOL aircraft were considered for MWDP funding)
NPL	National Physical Laboratory, the UK's national centre for scientific measurement. NPL owned the ship tanks at Teddington where the model 'bouncing bomb' tests were conducted, as well as wind tunnels and other testing apparatus
oleo	Pneumatic shock absorbers used in aircraft undercarriage struts
ORB	Operations Record Book – a detailed log of the activities of a military unit, especially those involving combat missions
pistol	See fuze
planform	The shape of an aircraft as seen from above; usually relates to wing layout: straight wing, swept wing, delta wing etc.
PR(U)	Photo reconnaissance (unit)
psi	Pounds per square inch, an Imperial unit of pressure
R&D	See DARD
RAE	Royal Aircraft Establishment (responsible for the basic research into aircraft design and testing of prototypes; based at Farnborough, with other stations at Bedford and Thurleigh); the RAE became part of the Defence Research Agency in 1991, since split into QinetiQ and the Defence Science and Technology Laboratory (DSTL)
RAeS	Royal Aeronautical Society, a professional institution that serves all aspects of the aerospace community
RAF	Royal Air Force
RAW	Royal Airship Works (responsible for research into airships; based at Cardington, Bedfordshire)
Reynolds Number	The ratio between viscous and inertial forces in fluid flow, typically used to measure the similarity of flow between two different experimental conditions
RNAS	Royal Naval Air Station
RNVR	Royal Naval Volunteer Reserve
ROF	Royal Ordnance Factory, manufacturers of munitions for UK Armed Forces
RRL	Road Research Laboratory (now the Transport Research Laboratory), where some of the model dam tests and other explosives experiments were performed
SAM	Surface-to-air missile, a ground-launched air defence missile
SFC	Specific fuel consumption, a ratio measure of engine efficiency, indicating how much fuel an engine uses to generate a certain amount of thrust for a set period of time
SHP	Shaft horsepower, a unit of power delivered to a propeller shaft
SLBM	Submarine launched ballistic missile (such as Polaris, Poseidon or Trident)
SOE	Special Operations Executive, a British organisation conducting covert military operations during the Second World War
Speedee	Codename for Highball when carried by a Douglas A-26 Invader
SST	Supersonic transport (aircraft); the UK's SST project developed Concorde
STOL	Short take-off and landing
store	A weapon dropped from an aircraft
Swallow	Codename for a series of aircraft based on the concept of a slender delta shape with the base removed, thus producing a delta forewing with two trailing main wings, these wings incorporating variable wing sweep enabling them to sweep forwards for take-off and landing
sweepback	The angle between the leading edge of the wing and the transverse axis of an aircraft

taileron	A tail-mounted all-moving horizontal stabiliser which combines the features of elevator (for pitch control) and aileron (for roll control)
TAL	Technischen Akademie der Luftwaffe, a staff and technical college for the German Air Force located in Gatow, a suburb of Berlin (roughly equivalent to Cranfield in the UK)
Tallboy	Codename for 12,000lb MC deep penetration 'earthquake bomb'; also referred to as Tallboy Medium, Tallboy Large (22,000lb) being renamed Grand Slam and Tallboy Small (4,000lb) being for trials use only
Tammany Hall	Codename for Highball when carried in a Grumman Avenger/Tarpon
TARZON	'Tallboy Azimuth & Range', a post-war US variant of Tallboy which could be steered remotely after dropping
TAS	True air speed, the absolute speed of an aircraft over the ground
TFX	Tactical Fighter Experimental, the original name for the aircraft which became the F-111 variable-geometry aircraft
thrust	The force tending to push an aircraft forwards. In steady flight, the thrust force is exactly balanced by the drag force
TNA	The National Archives (formerly the Public Records Office); main site is at Kew in London
transonic	Travelling at speeds between Mach 0.8 and 1.2; some of the airflow around a transonic object will be subsonic, and parts will be supersonic, so the transonic region is associated with turbulence and instability
twist	Variation in the amount of camber along the length of a wing
Upkeep	Codename for 9,250lb cylindrical 'bouncing bomb' for use against dams
USAAF	United States Army Air Force
variable geometry	Refers to any part of an aircraft which can change its position during flight; specifically, the term is used to describe wings which can alter their sweepback angle, usually around a vertical pivot
variable (wing) sweep	Another name used for variable geometry
VG	Variable geometry
VTOL	Vertical take-off and landing
weight	The force tending to make an aircraft fall, due to its mass and gravity. In steady flight, the weight force is exactly balanced by the lift force.
wetted area	The external surface area of an aircraft, which contributes to friction drag
Wild Goose	Codename for a series of aircraft based on the concept of building an aircraft consisting of only a laminar flow fuselage and two wings, the wings having variable differential sweep for control
wing loading	A measurement of an aircraft's lift-to-mass ratio, usually calculated as the mass of the aircraft divided by the wing area; an important factor in estimating ceiling, rate of climb, rate of turn and other key performance factors

Notes and Sources

Interviews

During the course of researching this book, I have spoken in person or on the telephone with a number of people connected with Wallis and his work, either directly or indirectly. These include:

Norman Barfield, engineer at Vickers

Norman William 'Spud' Boorer, Wallis's Chief Draughtsman and later Personal Assistant to Sir George Edwards

Des Curtis, Navigator with 618 Squadron

Larry Curtis, Wireless Operator with 617 Squadron 1944–5

Bunty Doherty, sister of Roy Kinnear (Flight Engineer with Astell on Operation Chastise)

William 'Gerry' Gerrard, Pilot with 618 Squadron

B. Oliver Heath, (equivalent of) Chief Designer of the Tornado

George L. Johnson, Bomb Aimer with 617 Squadron 1943–4

Don MacIntosh, Pilot with 9 Squadron 1944–5

Jean Mortimer, daughter of Joseph 'Mutt' Summers

Mary Stopes-Roe, daughter of BNW

Richard Thorp, who played Henry Maudslay in the original *The Dam Busters* movie

Barnes W. Wallis, son of BNW

Primary sources

The Science Museum Library site at Wroughton, Swindon, holds the Barnes Wallis archive, the largest collection of Wallis's own papers which he donated to the Science Museum in 1979, shortly before his death. Films in the collection are now held by the British Film Institute in London. A printed index is available from the Science Museum.

The Brooklands Museum in Weybridge holds a large quantity of materials relating to all the Vickers aircraft built at the site, including those of Wallis. The museum is staffed by knowledgeable volunteers, but there is no detailed index of the collection.

The Barnes Wallis Memorial Trust has a fine collection of artefacts and documents relating to all stages of Wallis's work.

The National Archives at Kew hold many files which relate to Wallis and his projects. An online index is available at http://www.nationalarchives.gov.uk/catalogue/

The RAF Museum, Hendon, holds a number of papers relating to Wallis, including many of his diaries; printed indexes of the films and other items are available from the RAF Museum.

Churchill College, Cambridge, also received a small quantity of the Wallis papers, mostly formal reports and published papers. An online index is available at http://janus.lib.cam.ac.uk (search for WLIS).

Information on patents, including full patent specifications, is available from the UK Intellectual Property Office. An online index is available at http://gb.espacenet.com/

The Imperial War Museum, London, holds many of the films of test drops of bombs and other archive footage, as well as a number of artefacts including letters and the briefing models of the dams.

The Dock Museum at Barrow-in-Furness holds the Vickers Photographic Archive, which includes images of the airships built there, including *R.80*. An online index is available at http://www.dockmuseum.org.uk/archive/index.asp

Tyne & Wear Archive in Newcastle holds information about local industries, which includes materials relating to the Vickers-Armstrongs Works at Elswick. An index is available at http://www.tyneandweararchives.org.uk/pdf/userguide05.pdf

Barrow Records Office holds papers relating to the Vickers works there, including some which relate to Wallis.

The Shell archive in London holds a small amount of information on the gas-carrying airship project.

University of Bristol holds the papers of Robin Ralph Jamison.

Nuffield College, Oxford, holds the papers of Lord Cherwell.

The Times Digital Archive and the *Flight International* Archive have been useful sources of contemporary articles.

Secondary sources

There are many books which cover Wallis, his aircraft, weapons and other projects – see Bibliography. Details cited from secondary souces have been confirmed with primary sources wherever possible.

There is much information (and myth) on Wallis and his work on the Internet. No information from the Internet has been cited without verification from other sources.

Notes

The following abbreviations are used throughout the references and notes:

Boorer lecture	Public Lecture given by Norman W. Boorer (1916–2004) to the Tayside & Fife Branch of the British Association for the Advancement of Science, 21 October 2003.
BWMT	Barnes Wallis Memorial Trust.
CAC	Churchill Archive Centre, Churchill College, Cambridge.
Jamison Papers	papers and correspondence of Robin Ralph Jamison (1912–91), Library of the University of Bristol.
Morpurgo	Morpurgo, Jack E., *Barnes Wallis* (St Martin's, 1972).
Cherwell Archive	papers and correspondence of Lord Cherwell (1886–1957), Library of Nuffield College, Oxford.
RAFM	Royal Air Force Museum, Hendon.
SM Arch BNW	Science Museum Barnes Wallis Archive, Wroughton, Wiltshire; films nominally in the Science Museum collection are held by the British Film Institute in London.
TNA	The National Archives, Kew.
Patent	unless otherwise indicated, Wallis is the applicant and/or inventor on cited patents (although many relating to airships are in the name of the Airship Guarantee Company).

Preface

1. Pat Lucas (Wallis's secretary) to Jamison, 16 October 1968 (Jamison papers D1717–D98).
2. Wallis, Barnes W. (private communication).
3. Ibid.
4. Ibid.
5. Wallis, Barnes N., *A Note on a Method of Attacking the Axis Powers* (March 1941) (TNA ADM 1/11767).

Chapter 1

1. Stopes-Roe, Mary (private communication).
2. What is referred to in England as a 'public school' is a fee-paying school and is usually referred to as a 'private school' elsewhere.
3. Stopes-Roe, Mary (private communication).
4. Morpurgo, 39.
5. Morpurgo, 46–7.
6. Stopes-Roe, Mary, *Mathematics with Love* (Macmillan, 2005).
7. Wallis disposed of many of his papers at this time.
8. Wallis used 'England' as a catch-all term meaning simultaneously England and Wales, Great Britain, the United Kingdom, and even the British Empire/Commonwealth; this usage was common practice in pre-devolution times (Taylor, A.J.P., *Oxford History of England*, 1965).
9. Boorer, Norman W., *Some reflections on work aimed at hypersonic flight in the 1950s, 60s and 70s, with particular regard to Barnes Wallis's contribution* (Brooklands Museum BNW/HYP/001, January 2001).
10. Edwards, George, quoted in Gardner, Robert, *From Bouncing Bombs to Concorde: The Authorised Biography of Sir George Edwards OM* (Sutton Publishing, 2006), 2.
11. Bullard to Morpurgo, 23 May 1968 (CAC BLRD F48).
12. Boorer lecture.
13. Wallis, Barnes N., cited in Boorer lecture.
14. Boorer, Norman W. (private communication).
15. Brickhill, Paul, *The Dam Busters* (Evans Brothers, 1951).
16. Zaidi, Waqar H., 'Barnes Wallis and the "Strength of England"', *Technology and Culture* (January 2008), 62–88.
17. 'Barnes Wallis Talks', *Flight* (8 January 1960), 34–5.
18. Wallis, Barnes N., 'The Strength of England', *Advancement of Science* (November 1965), 393–408 (Presidential Address to Engineering Section of the British Association for the Advancement of Science, Cambridge, 2 September 1965).
19. SM Arch BNW ED6/7.
20. SM Arch BNW H.
21. An unpublished biography by aviation journalist Bernard J. Hurren was written at about the same time, but without Wallis's co-operation. In 1980, following Wallis's death, Hurren sold the manuscript to the Cambridge Archives Centre (CAC HREN). The three-page covering letter that he wrote to accompany his manuscript is so vitriolic to his subject and so laden with factual errors that it is not surprising that he did not find a publisher for his work.
22. His colleague Rex Pierson and Roy Chadwick (designer of the Avro Lancaster) were awarded CBEs on the same date.
23. Confidential note, EEB to Lord Cherwell, 28 May 1943 (Nuffield G375/11).
24. Some cite the publicity that he received following the January 1967 BBC TV documentary *Why not? Why not!* as a contributing factor to the award, e.g. 'Trim and still on wing', *The Times* (20 January 1967), 6.
25. Equivalent to around £250,000 today; paradoxically, he would have received more had he not stated his intention to give his award to charity.
26. Miller, David, *Sir Barnes Wallis, Kt, CBE, FRS and the Christ's Hospital RAF Foundationers' Trust 1951–2003* (Christ's Hospital Club, 2003).
27. Morpurgo, J.E., oration at Wallis's memorial service, St Paul's Cathedral, 27 February 1980.

Chapter 2

1. The R designation stood for 'Rigid', replacing the earlier HMA ('His Majesty's Airship') numbering scheme from *R.26* (which appears with both schemes). The numbers appear variously in the forms *R26*, *R 26*, *R-26* and *R.26*, but the latter form is the most common in texts and is used here (the registrations on the various airships themselves used all of these forms and sometimes just the numerals).
2. Duralumin is an age-hardened alloy of aluminium, containing around 4 per cent copper, 0.8 per cent magnesium, 0.7 per cent manganese and 0.5 per cent silicon. It is about 11 per cent heavier than pure aluminium, but is harder, between two and five times as strong and more resistant to corrosion. It was patented by German metallurgist Alfred Wilm in 1909 (Patents DE244554/GB191006485/CH51312/AT51169B/DK14488C), the name being trademarked in the same year – though it has since become a generic term for aluminium alloys of this type. James Booth & Co. of Birmingham began making duralumin in 1909 (under licence from Wilm). Vickers acquired this company in 1915, largely for access to the alloy which was marketed as 'Vickers Duralumin' – a good investment, as it would be the main material used in airship and aircraft structures for the next 50 years. A 1925 report states that, although many attempts had been made to produce rival alloys, none were 'superior to duralumin' (Meissner, K.L., *Alloys similar to Duralumin made in other countries than Germany*, NACA Technical Memorandum No.314, May 1925).
3. 'Milestones (Airships)', *Flight* (21 August 1919), 1121.
4. Morpurgo, 70.
5. In June 1916, plans to build more *R.23* class ships were modified when more information about the Zeppelins was obtained, further ships being built to a modified design by Constructor-Commander Campbell of the Admiralty, the main difference being the absorption of the external keel into the bottom of the envelope. These ships became known as the *R.23*X class ships, though only two were completed (*R.27* and *R.29*), further developments leading to more advanced classes of ship, including the *R.34*, which successfully carried out a return trip from Britain to New York in July 1919, the first return flight across the Atlantic by any aircraft.
6. SM Arch BNW B5/1.
7. Albert Zahm was an American aerodynamicist who built one of the first wind tunnels and became an authority on airships and aircraft; the 'Zahm shape' which he developed for low drag had a cylindrical centre section with curved bow and stern sections, the length of the bow section being twice the diameter and the length of the stern section being nine times the diameter.
8. This contributed to a rapid uncontrolled rise to 4,000ft when the ship was first cast off, the internal strains causing some frames to be bent, and it took several months to make good the damage before the ship could fly again.
9. To facilitate connections, he colour-coded all of the wiring and pipework; some sources suggest that this was the first time that this technique had been used, but the ship's electrical specification suggests otherwise, stating that 'cables will be painted as usual in HM Service' (SM Arch BNW B5/3).
10. 'H.M. Airship *R.80*: A Description of the New Vickers-Built Rigid Airship', *Flight* (1920), 926–9 and 953–9) gives a contemporary description of the airship including plans and many photographs of the construction; Kender, Martin, '*R80*: The Last British Wartime Rigid Airship', *Dirigible: The Journal of the Airship Heritage Trust*, vol. 12, no. 2 (Summer 2001), 9–19, covers the same ground with a modern perspective.
11. Report on a conference held at Officers Quarters, Walney (20 July 1920) (TNA AIR 11/12).
12. Dawson, Sir Trevor, 'The Commercial Airship – Its Operation and Construction', *Flight* (11 November 1920), 1173–7; it is likely that Wallis and Pratt contributed to the text.
13. *Airships and Balloons* (Vickers Limited Airship Department, 1921), reproduced at http://homepage.ntlworld.com/forgottenfutures/vickers/vickers.htm
14. *R.38*, which the US was buying, was not yet ready and R.34, which was to have been used for the training, had been destroyed in bad weather in January 1921; *Flight* was reporting at this time that *R.80* too was destined for the USA.
15. Mowthorpe, Ces, *Battlebags: British Airships of the First World War* (Sutton Publishing, 1995).
16. Spear, Brian, 'Sir Barnes Wallis, a radical engineer and his patents', *World Patent Information* (28, 2006), 20–33.
17. Patents GB118162, *Improvements in or relating to Riveting Machines*, and GB128968, *Improvements in or relating to Machines for Drilling or Punching Holes for Rivets or the like.*
18. Patent documents describe an invention (a device, process or formula) and stake the applicant's claim to it (what would now be called 'intellectual property'), preventing (in law) another person or organisation from using the invention without the holder's permission. To be awarded, a patent must be practical and demonstrate novelty, and hence its details must not have been previously published; in practice, this means that inventions must be patented before they are seen in public, and consequently many patents describe inventions which do not get used, as they subsequently turn out to be impractical or inefficient.
19. Patents GB131072, *Improvements in or relating to the Mooring of Lighter-than-Air Aircraft*, and GB125003, *Improvements relating to Mooring Devices for Lighter-than-air Air Craft.*
20. Correspondence between Vickers and Masterman (RAFM AC96/46/17).
21. *Airship R.100* (Mr Pye Books, 1983); this is a reproduction of a 1929 publicity booklet.
22. Stopes-Roe, Mary, *Mathematics with Love* (Macmillan, 2005).
23. TNA AIR 2/459.
24. The masts were designed to cope with a 'pull' at the head of 90,000lb; a pull of 33,600lb was recorded when *R.101* was on the Cardington mast in winds gusting over 80mph.
25. Following the loss of *R.38* (the Americans were to purchase the airship, but she broke up in the air near Hull in 1921, killing 44 of the 49 aboard, which included 16 of the American training crew), the Aeronautical Research Committee formed the Airship Stressing Panel and the Airworthiness of Airships Panel, each panel producing a report containing guidelines pertaining to its area of coverage.
26. The gross lift is the total lift given by the lifting gas. Subtracting from this the weight of the structure and engines gives the disposable lift, which is the weight of payload and stores (fuel, cargo, passengers, ballast etc.) that can be carried.
27. Wallis, Barnes N., *A note on aircraft design and manufacture* (1970) (SM Arch BNW ED3/10) states that *R.100* cost £471,113 including the purchase of RNAS Howden, while *R.101* cost £711,592 for the airship alone; movie SM Arch BNW K4 includes a caption stating that *R.100* cost £440,000.
28. Reminiscences by Barnes Wallis (SM Arch BNW A5/5).
29. Reminiscences by Molly Wallis about life and work at Howden, undated (RAFM B3256).
30. Deacon, K., *The Men and Women Who Built and Flew the R.100* (Langrick Publications, 2008).
31. Wallis, Barnes N., 'Rigid Airship Design and Construction', *Aircraft Engineering* (January 1930), 7.
32. Wallis, Barnes N., 'Some Technical Aspects of the Commercial Airship', *Lloyd's Register Staff Association* (1926).
33. Having the power cars far aft gave the additional advantage of having less engine noise in the passenger accommodation.
34. Wallis, Barnes N., 1930, op. cit., 8.
35. Jones, R., and Bell, A.H., *Experiments on a model of the Rigid Airship R.100* (Aeronautical Research Committee report T.2465, June 1927) (DSIR 24/2479).
36. Patent GB233021, *Improvements in or relating to the Framework of Rigid Airships.*
37. Wallis, Barnes N., 1930, op. cit., 8.
38. Wallis, Barnes N., 1930, op. cit., 9.
39. The trawlermen seemed oblivious to the height, working happily on the framework over 150ft above the floor; Wallis did not like heights so when he had to go up into the structure, he got one of the trawlermen to hold on to a safety rope . . . until it was pointed out that he was not *actually* holding the rope, the trawlerman saying, 'Oh, that don't matter, 'e's all right, this 'ere rope's only to give him confidence' (SM Arch BNW K5, Wallis's 1960s audio commentary to contemporary movie footage).
40. Wallis, Barnes N., 'How to build an airship', letter to *The Times* (21 May 1971).
41. Patents GB254782, *Improvements in or relating to the Manufacture of Hollow or Tubular Metal Struts, Spars and other Members of the Framework of Aircraft*, and GB254783, *A New or Improved Machine for Making Hollow or Tubular Metal Members.*
42. Wallis, Barnes N., 1971, op. cit.
43. *Tests of Wallis Patent Spiral Tube* (RAE Report M.T.10331, December 1931) (TNA AVIA 6/6428).
44. Mowthorpe, Ces, op. cit.
45. On first inflation, *R.101*'s gross lift was only 148.6 tons and her disposable lift only 35 tons (24 per cent of gross lift as opposed to the 40 per cent required) – this shortfall was large enough, if not corrected, to preclude her from undertaking flights to India.
46. Patent GB239300, *Improvements in or relating to Controlling and Steering Means for Airships.*
47. Wallis, Barnes N., 1926, op. cit.
48. The fact that there were survivors from both the *R.101* (6 out of 54 aboard) and *Hindenburg* (62 out of 97 aboard) is attributable to these burning properties of hydrogen as well as to the relatively slow speed at which both ships hit the ground when tragedy struck. It is notable that the *R.101* is known to have hit the ground before the fire started (the rear portion of her framework remained largely intact), it was not the fire which brought the ship down (as on *Hindenburg*). The losses of the three American-built rigids – *Shenandoah* (1925), *Akron* (1933) and *Macon* (1935) – resulted in the deaths of over 100 men, despite no fire being involved, the American ships being filled with helium.
49. Patent GB239601, *Improvements in or relating to Airships.*
50. Teed, Major P.L., 'The First Inflation of *R.100*', *Aircraft Engineering* (June 1930), 135–6; the silicol process used silicon, caustic soda and water to produce hydrogen (and sodium disilicate as a by-product).
51. Shute, Nevil, *Slide Rule* (William Heinemann, 1954); the gasbags cost up to £6,000 each and the gas to fill each one cost up to £800.
52. Patent GB233020, *Improvements in or relating to Lighter-Than-Air Craft.*
53. TNA AIR 2/459.
54. Wallis, Barnes N., 1930, op. cit.
55. This can be envisioned by taking a globe of the Earth, drilling two holes at the

two points, feeding a string into the holes, and then pulling it taut from the inside – where the string lies on the surface is a segment of the 'great circle'.
56. Prof. Louis Napoleon George Filon.
57. Geodesic is the scientific name for a 'great circle', deriving from geodesy (the science of Earth measurement).
58. Occasional references are seen to 'geodetic structure' in *R.100* (even in some otherwise respectable sources) – however, the use of geodesics on *R.100* was restricted to the gasbag wiring, the application to structures only coming about when Wallis moved on to aeroplane design.
59. Patents GB233020, *Improvements in or relating to Lighter-Than-Air Craft*, and US1658821, *Lighter-Than-Air Craft.*
60. Whale, George, *British Airships, Past, Present and Future* (Bodley Head, 1919), reproduced at http://www.gutenberg.org/etext/762
61. Fortier, Rénald, *The R.100 in Canada* (National Aviation Museum, 1999), reproduced at http://www.aviation.technomuses.ca/assets/pdf/e_R100.pdf
62. Patent GB154942, *An Improved Composition for Preparing Films for Use as Substitutes for Gold Beaters Skin and the Like.*
63. Wallis, Barnes N., 1926, op. cit.
64. Some German airships were specifically designed to operate at high altitude, but achieved this by having a dangerously light structure.
65. Patents GB281419, *Improvements in or relating to Lighter-Than-Air Aircraft*, and GB283635, *Improvements in or relating to Lighter-Than-Air Aircraft.*
66. It was estimated that *R.100* would lose around 10 per cent of its hydrogen during the flight to Canada, *Flight* (10 April 1930), 426.
67. Patent GB290716, *Improvements in or relating to Aerostats.*
68. Wallis, Barnes N., 1926, op. cit.
69. Patent GB285109, *Improvements in or relating to Airships.*
70. Patent GB299123, *Improvements in Airships.*
71. Patent GB282518, *Improvements in or relating to Rigid Airships.*
72. Patent GB250348, *Improvements in or relating to Lighter-Than-Air Aircraft.*
73. Patent GB271241, *Improvements in or relating to the Valve Mechanism of Internal-Combustion Engines.*
74. 'The Position of the Airship in Aerial Transport', *Flight* (30 April 1925), 262–3.
75. Mr Pye Books, op. cit.
76. For comparison, this is about one-third of the weight of fuel used by Concorde on a typical one-way Atlantic crossing with a similar payload. *R.100* travelled approx. 3,500 miles in 79 hours (outward, against the wind) and the same in 57 hours (inward), an average speed of 50mph for both legs. In November 1929 Wallis had estimated the ship's range as 5,000 miles at this speed (TNA AIR 5/1043).
77. Patent GB282166, *Improvements in or relating to Lighter-Than-Air Aircraft.*
78. The story of the trial flights and the flight to Canada is told by Shute, op. cit.
79. Wallis had already moved to Vickers (Aviation) Ltd at Weybridge, and Sir Robert McLean said that 'Wallis could kill himself if he so wished, but in one of the aeroplanes he was going to build, not in this airship contraption'; Wallis was not disappointed at missing the trip.
80. *R.101: The Airship Disaster, 1930* (Uncovered Editions, The Stationery Office, 1999); this is a reproduction of the Public Inquiry report.
81. Johnston, Ernest, *Airship Navigator* (Airship Heritage Trust, 1995).
82. http://www.aht.ndirect.co.uk/airships/r100/index.html
83. 'Justification for the further flying of Airship R.100' (TNA AIR 2/459).
84. http://www.aht.ndirect.co.uk/airships/r100/index.html; this site notes that the £450 scrap value often quoted elsewhere is incorrect.
85. *Tests on a single bay of R.100 at Cardington* (Aeronautical Research Committee Structure Sub-committee report Strut 253 (1805), 23 May 1935) (TNA DSIR 23/5056).
86. Mr Pye Books, op. cit.
87. Hadland, Tony (private communication); Tony is the son-in-law of Herbert Jeffree.
88. TNA AIR 2/492 contains two reports by the RAE on the condition and strength of *R.100* girders.
89. Masefield, Sir Peter, to *Flight International* (29 November 1980); Masefield wrote *To Ride the Storm* (William Kimber, 1982) about the *R.101* crash.
90. Lord Ventry and Kolešnik, Eugène M., *Jane's Pocket Book 7: Airship Development* (MacDonald and Jane's, 1976).
91. BNW to correspondent regarding airship revival, December 1970 (SM Arch BNW G6/1).
92. 'Bring back the Airship!', *Engineering* (November 1968), 796–9.
93. SM Arch BNW G6/1.
94. SM Arch BNW G6/2–G6/6.
95. Kershaw, Ronald, 'Sir Barnes Wallis to study Shell Airship Plan', *The Times* (13 July 1972).
96. BNW to Jamison, 17 May 1971 (Jamison papers, DM1717–D99); the helium would have accounted for just over one-third of the total gas volume.
97. Jamison to BNW, 27 May 1971 (RAFM B3250).

Chapter 3

1. Now BAE SYSTEMS, Brough; it is about 20 miles from the Howden site.
2. Morpurgo, 155.
3. Morpurgo, 195.
4. Thus, contrary to some sources, it is clear that Wallis had moved on to aircraft design *before* the crash of *R.101* and the subsequent cancellation of *R.100*.
5. Morpurgo, 178.
6. If a wing has insufficient torsional stiffness, movement of the ailerons can lead to the twisting of the wing in the opposite direction and in extreme cases, aircraft motion *opposite* to that intended – so-called aileron reversal, which was a common problem in early aircraft, especially monoplanes.
7. Boorer, Norman W. (private communication).
8. The position at Southampton was presumably intended to have some degree of permanence, as the Wallises had begun to look at houses in the area, before the move back to Weybridge (Stopes-Roe, Mary, private communication).
9. Although geodetics was Wallis's concept, and he alone is commonly credited as 'the designer' of the geodetic aircraft, it should be noted that all of the designs were done in partnership with Pierson – Wallis was principally designer of the internal structure, with Pierson designing the overall form of the aircraft and liaising with the Air Ministry and RAF regarding detailed requirements.
10. Andrews, C.F., and Morgan, E.B., *Vickers Aircraft Since 1908* (Putnam, 1988), 222.
11. Each of Vickers's major designs, and each significant sub-type, was allocated a 'Type number' issued in roughly chronological order; the Viastra project was Type 256. For a full list, see Andrews and Morgan, op. cit.
12. RAE reports M/576A and A.D.1603D; neither report appears to have survived in the archives.
13. Brooklands Museum VIC-VIA.
14. Andrews and Morgan, op. cit., 190.
15. Andrews and Morgan, op. cit., 241.
16. Patent GB376364, *Improvements in or connected with the Construction of Spars or Girders particularly Applicable for Use in Aircraft Construction,* and Patent GB376365, *Improvements in the Method of and Apparatus for Assembling and Securing Strengthening Sleeves to the Ends of Tubular Members.*
17. Wallis, Barnes N., *Notes on Geodetic Construction* (undated but *c.*1935) (SM Arch BNW A3/2).
18. The competing design from Fairey would later lead to their successful Swordfish torpedo bomber, and the Westland submission formed the basis of the Lysander.
19. Wallis, Barnes N., op. cit.; some point to naval architect Sir Robert Seppings as a potential inspiration for the geodetic idea, but his method of diagonal bracing for ships' hull structures was just that, and did not follow any particular geodesic principles. The French aircraft company Latécoère used a form of diagonal grid bracing in some of its early aircraft structures which again bears a superficial similarity to geodetic construction, but it appears that this too is actually just simple bracing.
20. Recall that, although some references suggest that geodetic *structure* was used in *R.100*, the geodesics in *R.100* were only in the gasbag wiring.
21. Wallis referred to his method as *geodetic* construction, to differentiate it from *geodesics* while also indicating its heritage.
22. The aspect ratio (AR) of a wing refers to the ratio of the span to the chord (more precisely, it is calculated by dividing the square of the span by the wing area); as the lift generated by a wing is directly proportional to the volume of a cylinder of air of which the span forms a diameter, longer wings give greater lift and hence confer longer range.
23. The test pilot Harald Penrose parachuted to safety, making one of the first parachute escapes from an enclosed cockpit.
24. RAE Report M.T.11.119, October 1934 (TNA AVIA 6/6511).
25. RAE Report M.T.11.728, December 1938 (TNA AVIA 6/6685).
26. An engineer might argue that the structure was so much stronger than requirements, that it could have been redesigned so that it *just* met the strength requirements, with a corresponding weight saving.
27. In aircraft, disposable load = fuel plus payload (bombs etc.)
28. The biplane prototype K2771 thus did not produce any offspring, although it survived until 1941 as a flying engine test-bed with the Bristol Aeroplane Company at Filton.
29. Boorer, Norman W., 'Barnes Wallis – Designer (1887–1979)', *Aeronautical Journal* (November 1981), 414–29.
30. Wallis, Barnes N., *A Brief Note on Geodetic Construction* (1935) (RAFM B3251 and SM Arch BNW C3/1); the RAFM copy appears to have been originally given by Wallis to Molly as it is inscribed on the cover 'M.F.W. With love from the Author'; although Wallis is the sole author of the report, much of the detailed mathematics for the geodetics was done by Herbert Jeffree.
31. If the surface is that of the Earth, the curve is a segment of a 'great circle' and it represents the shortest possible path between the two points, and is hence important in terrestrial navigation.
32. In the gasbag wiring of *R.100*, the geodesic helices were *not* connected at crossovers.
33. Although the geodetic aircraft were often referred to colloquially as the 'basket weave bombers', the opposing spirals were all formed within a singular structural layer and so did not actually interweave in the manner of basketwork.
34. The Wellesley used a double tube main spar as on the M.1/30; Wallis split this spar towards the wing root to form a Y-spar for additional strength but also to create a triangular cavity in the wing root into which he placed the

retractable main landing gear; both the Y-spar and the landing gear were the subject of patents, GB426134, *Improvements in or connected with Wheel Landing Gear for Aircraft*, and GB426268, *Improvements in and relating to Wings for Aircraft*.
35. Poulsen, C.M., 'Geodetic Construction', *Flight* (16 January 1936), 66–8; the detail of the wing structure is described in Patent GB412232, *Improvements in or connected with the Construction of Wings for Aircraft*, applied for 22 December 1932.
36. 'Geodetics on the Grand Scale', *Flight* (6 July 1939), a–j.
37. *Remarks on Wallis 'Geodetic' Construction*, Aeronautical Research Committee Structure Sub-committee report Strut 255 (1816) (TNA DSIR 23/5067).
38. SM Arch BNW C3/2.
39. Poulsen, C.M., 'Structural Design', *Flight* (1938), 544–9, 552–3.
40. Poulsen, C.M., 'Geodetic Construction', *Flight* (16 January 1936), 66–8.
41. Gardner, Robert, *From Bouncing Bombs to Concorde: The Authorised Biography of Sir George Edwards OM* (Sutton Publishing, 2006), 18; Edwards credits the machine, which was designed by Jack East and implemented by Tony Deedman under Trevor Westbrook's supervision, with being instrumental in the practical fabrication of the geodetic aircraft. It appears that the machine was not patented.
42. Patents GB408674, *A New or Improved Method of and Apparatus for Assembling and Securing Bracing Members on Tubular Members Constituting the Spars of Aircraft or other Structures*, and GB429188, *A New or Improved Method of and Means for Assembling and Connecting Intersecting Bracing Members*.
43. Westbrook had been General Manager at Supermarine, but was 'posted' to Weybridge in late 1936 as Wellington production was being stepped up.
44. Boorer lecture.
45. Andrews and Morgan, E.B., op. cit.
46. Morrison, Robert J., *Russian Shortcut to Fame: A 50-year Hoax Exposed* (Robert Hale, 1990) claims that the Russian flight was faked and did not really break the French record; however, this suggestion is refuted by other writers, such as McCannon, John, *Red Arctic* (Oxford University Press, 1998).
47. Detailed descriptions of the record flight are given by Barfield, Norman, 'Vickers Wellesley variants', *Profile Publications* (No.256), 86–9 and Taylor, H.A., 'The RAF's Long-distance Flights', *Royal Air Force Yearbook* (1983), 46–50.
48. ACM Sir Brian Burnett (private communication); Burnett was navigator and second pilot with Coombe during the record flight.
49. Data on the aircraft has been compiled from a variety of sources; as some data was not directly comparable in its original form, this has been converted by the author.
50. TNA SM Arch BNW A5/5.
51. Lumsden, Alec, *Wellington Special* (Ian Allen, 1974), 42.
52. ARC T.3636.S.228.(1644) (TNA DSIR 23/4895).
53. Ovcacik, Michal, and Susa, Karel, *Vickers-Armstrongs Wellington* (Mark I, 2003), 68.
54. Smith, David J., *Vickers Wellington Crash Log Volume 1 1937–1942*.
55. The remaining buildings at this site now form part of the Cobham Bus Museum.
56. One survivor of these early raids was Sqn Ldr Kellett, who had led the LRDU's record flight.
57. Hawker designer Ralph Hooper suggests that the reputation of the Wellington owed more to its high aspect ratio wing and the 'undistinguished competition' from contemporary aircraft than to the strength of the geodetics (private communication).
58. Post-war reminiscences by Wallis (SM Arch BNW A5/5).
59. The mine lay on the bottom, and when a ship passed over, its magnetic field would interact with a magnet inside the mine, detonating the mine.
60. Gardner, op. cit., 25; DWI was colloquially referred to in the works as 'Down With 'itler'!
61. Boorer, Norman W., *Sir George Edwards, OM, CBE, FRS 1908–2003: Some Personal Reflections* (Brooklands Museum Trust, 2008), 13.
62. Gardner, op. cit., 27.
63. TNA AVIA 6/1111.
64. Gardner, op. cit., 28.
65. Boorer lecture.
66. Equivalent to unpressurised operation at 10,000ft; sea-level atmospheric pressure is about 14lb/in^2.
67. Wallis, Barnes N., *A Note on a Method of Attacking the Axis Powers* (1941) (SM Arch BNW D1 and TNA ADM 1/11767), 43.
68. http://macr.moonfruit.com/
69. Excluding the single prototype; for comparison, the Boeing 737 airliner, which has been in production for over 40 years, has barely achieved half of this number of production aircraft.
70. Holmes, Robin, *One of Our Aircraft: The Story of 'R for Robert' the Loch Ness Wellington* (Quiller Press, 1991), 95.
71. For example: Bowyer, Chaz, *Wellington Bomber* (William Kimber, 1986); Bowman, Martin, *Wellington, The Geodetic Giant* (Airlife Publishing, 1989); Lumsden, op. cit.
72. Andrews and Morgan, op. cit.
73. The VC designation stood for 'Vickers Commercial'.
74. Compared to the Wellington, performance was improved in all areas; bomb load was 50 per cent greater.
75. Lucke, Tommy, 'The Wayward Warwick', *Aircraft Illustrated* (November 1970), 460–5.
76. Barfield, Norman, 'Vickers-Armstrongs Warwick variants', *Profile Publications* (1972), 165.
77. Gardner, op. cit., 37.
78. Patents GB478089, *Improvements in the Construction of Aircraft Wings*, GB565770, *Improvements relating to Aircraft Wings and other Control Surfaces of the Stressed-skin Type*, and GB574090, *Improvements relating to Aircraft Surfaces Intended to Sustain Aerodynamic Pressures* describe various aspects of the invention.
79. Pugsley, A.G., *Special Structural Features of the Wings of the Vickers Pressure Cabin Fighter* (RAE Report No SME 3189, undated but *c*.1942) (TNA AVIA 6/20112).
80. TNA AVIA 6/9583.
81. Jarrett, Philip, 'Nothing Ventured', *Aeroplane Monthly* (March 1992), 26–30.
82. Buttler, Tony, *British Secret Projects: Fighters & Bombers 1935–1950* (Midland Publishing, 2004); Chapter 7 has the background to these projects and details of the competing designs.
83. Andrews, C.F., 'Vickers Windsor', *Air Pictorial*, vol. 28, no. 2 (February 1966), 52–6.
84. Letter regarding B.3/42 bomb loads, Vickers-Armstrongs (Weybridge) to Burhill, 7 October 1942 (SM Arch BNW D4/6).
84. Patent GB575392, *Improvements in Airframe Structures*.
86. Boorer lecture; although fabrication was difficult, he conceded that the Windsor probably had the lightest wing of that size ever made.
87. Brown was impressed by the ability of geodetic construction to handle battle damage, and although acknowledging that geodetics was a technological cul-de-sac, says that it was 'certainly not a waste of time' (Brown, Eric M., private communication).
88. Patent GB580574, *Improvements in Airframe Structures*.
89. Test samples of the woven ribbons are held by the RAF Museum, e.g. X003-8145, X003-8149.
90. Wallis to Bruntons of Musselburgh, undated but *c*.1944 (SM Arch BNW D2/21; this letter is filed with unrelated material on earthquake-bomb targets).
91. Andrews, op. cit., 56.
92. Andrews, op. cit., 56.
93. Patent GB581142, *Improvements in or connected with Pressure Cabins for Aircraft*.
94. Hooper, Ralph (private communication).
95. Wallis, Barnes W. (private communication).
96. Wallis diary for 1945 (RAF Museum X001-2371/087).
97. Boorer, Norman W., 2008, op. cit.
98. Gardner, op. cit., 63–64.
99. Kerensky, O.A., 'Gilbert Roberts', *Biographical Memoirs of Fellows of the Royal Society* (The Royal Society, vol. 25, 1979), 477–503.
100. Patent US2682235, *Building Construction*, applied for 12 December 1951.
101. e.g. Patent DE415395, *Verfahren zur Herstellung von Kuppeln und aehnlichen gekruemmten Flaechen aus Eisenbeton ('Procedure for the production of domes and similar curved surfaces')*, applied for 9 November 1922.
102. SM Arch BNW G7/2; although filed with the Messina Bridge material, the geotube does not appear to be related to that project, being much earlier. Wallis also had aspirations for application of geodetics to shipbuilding (Morpurgo, 246).
103. Fryer, Simon, 'Design and construction of the Greenside Place Bridge Link, Edinburgh', *The Structural Engineer* (1 November 2005), 39–42.

Chapter 4

1. BNW speaking in a post-war documentary, included in DVD *The Dambusters* (History Channel, 2002).
2. Several of the dates in this chapter come from BNW's own recollection of key dates in the story (SM Arch BNW D3/2).
3. SM Arch BNW D5/1 contains much of the background theory and calculation; this was all done over-and-above his 'day job' working on aircraft design.
4. Wallis, Barnes N., *A Note on a Method of Attacking the Axis Powers* (1941) (SM Arch BNW D1 and TNA ADM 1/11767).
5. (Anonymous but by) Wallis, Barnes N., *Addendum to A Note on a Method of Attacking the Axis Powers* (1941) (TNA ADM 1/11767).
6. SM Arch BNW D5/1.
7. TNA ADM 277/46.
8. RAF Bomber Command website: http://www.raf.mod.uk/bombercommand/wap.html
9. Sweetman, John, *The Dambusters Raid* (Cassell Military Classics, 1999).
10. TNA PREM 3/350.
11. Moffat, John, 818 Squadron (Fleet Air Arm) pilot on HMS *Ark Royal* (private communication).
12. The amount of water used to make a ton of steel varies depending on sources (and presumably the steelmaking process used); Michael Redgrave (as Wallis) in

The Dam Busters (1955) says 100 tons, Wallis in a post-war documentary (History Channel, op. cit.) says 150 tons, other sources say up to 260 tons (62,600 gallons according to the US Geographical Survey Water Trivia website – http://ct.water.usgs.gov/education/trivia.htm), although a contemporary report says only 2m^3 (2 tons) is required per ton of pig iron, though more is needed to convert that to steel (SM Arch BNW D3/2).
13. Around one tenth as strong in tension (Kearse, Arthur, QinetiQ, private communication).
14. Kearse, op. cit., suggests that the mine's effect on the dam would be cratering on the water side (over 2.5m deep and 10m diameter), scabbing on the air side and mass shear ahead of the explosion pushing the masonry outwards (the latter was witnessed at the Eder).
15. Still in existence at the same location, now known as the Transport Research Laboratory.
16. Collins, A.R., 'Dam Busting – the uncivil engineering behind the famous wartime raid', *New Civil Engineer* (1972), 48–52 and Department of Scientific and Industrial Research, *Wartime Activities of the Road Research Laboratory* (HMSO, 1949).
17. Still in existence at the same location, now known as the Building Research Establishment.
18. One of the Garston models remains in existence in Bricket Wood in the grounds of the BRE, and it was registered as a 'scheduled monument' by English Heritage in October 2002; as with the other later models, it was cast in layers (not individual bricks) to save time.
19. Davey, Norman, handwritten recollections (RAFM B689, May 1980).
20. Collins, op. cit.
21. Kearse, Arthur, *Technical Aspects of the Dams Raid* (unpublished technical report, QinetiQ, 2006); Euler, Helmut, *Als Deutschlands Dämme Brachen* (Motorbuch-Verlag, 1976), 36, states that 15 models in total were built.
22. Wallis diary for 1942 (RAF Museum X001-2371/081).
23. Although popularly referred to as 'bouncing bombs', the weapons are also referred to as mines (as they were to be detonated in water), although as they were also tested for use on land, 'bomb' is not incorrect. When fitted to an aircraft, the term 'store' is commonly used for all forms of weapons. The German nomenclature (given to the example which was recovered intact) was '*Rotationswasserbombe*' – rotating depth charge – which is the most accurate of all. In British contemporary documents, the generic term covering all versions of the 'bouncing' weapons was the 'golf mine'. It is not clear who first used the phrase 'bouncing bomb', although Sweetman cites use of the term in a letter from Tizard on 30 September 1942.
24. Deliberate skip bombing with conventional bombs dropped at low level, usually against shipping, was also being practised by some aircrews throughout the war (but Wallis probably did not know about this).
25. Prof. Blackett at the Admiralty and Sir Henry Tizard had already seen drafts of the paper, and Tizard was working on getting access for Wallis to the NPL testing tanks at Teddington.
26. SM Arch BNW D4/2.
27. Cranz, C., and Becker, K., *Handbook of Ballistics, Volume I: Exterior Ballistics* (HMSO, 1921), 453; the 7 degrees finding is credited to 1903 experiments by Ramsauer.
28. A more mathematical treatment of the fundamental principles of the 'bouncing bomb', including the effect of Magnus lift, is given in some undated sheets of handwritten calculations headed 'Experimental Spheres' (SM Arch BNW D4/2).
29. MAEE Report H/Arm/RES.7 (TNA AVIA 19/1033).
30. SM Arch BNW G2/1.
31. Pawle, Gerard, *The Secret War 1939–45* (Harrap & Co., 1956), 150.
32. Gardner, op. cit.
33. Gardner, op. cit., 42; he dates this experiment to February 1943, but it must have taken place in the summer of 1942 – every missile tested (from October 1942 onwards) was spun.
34. Sweetman, op. cit., 30.
35. The original catapult was used in the 1955 film, and is now in the collection of the RAF Museum; it is currently on loan to the Barnes Wallis Memorial Trust.
36. Patent GB937959, *Improvements in Explosive Missiles and Means for their Discharge*, applied for 11 August 1942; it is allowable to change the content of a patent up to one year after submission and before the patent is formally examined, so the presence of backspin in the patent document does not necessarily date the backspin idea to the application date of the patent. Indeed, the patent text mentions some results of actual drop tests which were definitely not performed until 1943, so changes were clearly made to the original specification in this case. Unfortunately, the original application document is no longer held by the UK Intellectual Property Office, so it is not possible to compare. Due to military secrecy, this patent specification was not made public until September 1963.
37. *Experimental Spheres* (SM Arch BNW D4/2).
38. Kearse, op. cit.
39. Force due to gravity = 4196kg x 9.81m/s = 41.1kN.
40. This increases the air range to first impact by around 20 per cent, although any range increases offered by adding backspin were really irrelevant, as an unspun bomb could simply be dropped closer to the target; it is not clear if the overall ranges of spun bombs were more consistent than for unspun bombs.
41. In theory – for some of the filmed trajectories, this is clearly not the case due to the stores hitting waves, resulting in the store bouncing up higher than expected.
42. Patent GB937960, *Improvements in Means for Supporting and Releasing Explosive Missiles Carried on Aircraft*; publication of this patent was also held until 1963.
43. Linnell was the Controller of Research and Development at the Ministry of Aircraft Production; Pye was the Director of Scientific Research at MAP.
44. Sweetman, John, 'Barnes Wallis's Other Bouncing Bomb: Part I', *RAF Air Power Review*, vol. 5, no. 2 (Summer 2002).
45. TNA ADM 277/46.
46. Ibid.
47. SM Arch BNW D4/2.
48. Even the weapons' codenames were secret, and remained so for a time even after some technical details of the weapon were made public in 1963. A call to the Vickers drawing office in 1943 was taken by Norman Boorer, who was asked if he knew anything about Upkeep. He said 'No' and the person on the phone thanked him and hung up. He then returned to his drawing board – where sat his drawing of Upkeep! British Scientific Intelligence surmised from its German codename that the Freya navigation system was a single beam system (in mythology, Freya has one eye), and in light of this, it is odd that the codenames Upkeep and Highball were chosen for the 'bouncing bombs'- perhaps it was felt that the concept was sufficiently odd that quite 'obvious' codenames could be used with impunity!
49. *600lb Highball*, 21–22 January 1943 (SM Arch BNW D4/2).
50. SM Arch BNW D4/2.
51. Letter on display at the Ringwood Town & Country Experience; Cherwell was Churchill's scientific adviser, and was not an enthusiastic supporter of Wallis or his ideas.
52. 'Dam Busters ship tank disappearing', *NewsNet: Monthly Newsletter for Staff of the National Physical Laboratory* (December 2007); the Number 2 tank was demolished in 1998, the Number 1 tank in 2007.
53. He may also have seen a copy of *Air Attack on Dams* (January 1943) (SM Arch BNW D3/1), which contained a summary of BNW's *Note* and *Spherical Bomb* papers (also including materials about anti-ship use).
54. Minutes of a meeting at the Air Ministry, 15 February 1943 (TNA ADM 277/46).
55. The minutes of this committee (TNA AIR 8/1237) form a series of progress reports for Operations Upkeep and Highball.
56. These codenames were thus used initially to refer both to the *weapons* themselves and to the *operations* associated with them, though the codenames Operation Servant and Operation Chastise were adopted a little while later for the operations concerning the first use of each store.

Chapter 5

1. Boorer, Norman W. (private communication).
2. It is reported that the staves were manufactured by several woodworking firms, including Morris's Furniture of Glasgow (just one of many war munitions projects on which they worked), though RAFM X001-6488 (written 1966) suggests that the staves were made by shipwrights at Barrow (where the steel cylinders were made).
3. Most diagrams do not show screws, though a contemporary drawing has them; the number of metal straps varies between five and eight, depending on source.
4. SM Arch BNW D2/11.
5. Although most sources (including Wallis's own notes) state 30ft, McCarthy's bomb aimer is sure that the crews were briefed that the pistol was set to detonate at 25ft (Johnson, George L., speaking at Barnes Wallis Memorial Trust meeting, June 2008).
6. Holsgrove, Jack, with Graham, Hugh, *Dambusters Away* (Tessera, 2003). Holsgrove states that the safing mechanisms in the fuzing units were secretly disabled by him under orders, and that the mines were thus fully armed prior to take-off, but there seems to be no practical reason for doing this and his evidence is discredited by historians. He also describes a preliminary experiment in which a concrete dummy Upkeep was carried in a Lancaster, suspended from a conventional bomb slip, but again there is no other evidence confirming that this test took place.
7. *Breaching the German Dams* (RAF Museum, 2008) contains copies of Avro drawings for the Upkeep-equipped Lancaster.
8. All Vickers aircraft designs and variants were allocated a unique Type number.
9. Highball trials were also being conducted between Manston and Reculver during the same period, but as the issues that arose were different for the two weapons, discussion of the Highball trials will be left to the later chapter dealing with that store.
10. *Upkeep and Highball: Proposed programme of trials* (8 April 1943) (SM Arch BNW D4/2).
11. The final drop from a Wellington at Reculver, and the first two Highball drops from a Mosquito also took place on this date, the only day that all three main variants of the golf mine were dropped on the same day.
12. During the daylight test drops, the pilots judged the release height by eye, the actual height being calculated later from analysing the films.
13. Kearse, Arthur, *Technical Aspects of the Dams Raid* (unpublished technical report, QinetiQ, 2006) notes that many stores do appear to adopt a slight left-side-down

attitude during the drop (possibly as the store may have released fractionally later from the right-hand driven disc) and that this attitude becomes more exaggerated as the bouncing progresses; this was one reason why Wallis preferred a spherical weapon, although Highball (which *was* spherical) did not fare much better in this respect.
14. *Notes of a progress meeting 29 April 1943* (TNA AIR 8/1237).
15. *Upkeep – Reculver Trials 13 April–16 May 1943* (MAEE report H/Arm/104, 24 June 1943) (SM Arch BNW D4/2).
16. Sweetman, John, *The Dambusters Raid* (Cassell Military Classics, 1999), 54.
17. SM Arch BNW D2/11.
18. RAFM film FC97-574; shot in profile from the North Foreland, this film confirms that the mine strikes the water directly beneath the Lancaster (which flew straight and level) – some artwork representations of the raid show the mine striking the water *ahead* of the aircraft!
19. Sweetman, op. cit., 31.
20. Holsgrove, op. cit., mentions modifications made to the bombslips, but gives the great weight of the bomb as the reason for these modifications – however, the weight of the bomb was carried by the calliper arms, not by the bombslip itself.
21. Wallis designed a suitable hydraulic motor, but when it was passed for manufacture to the Vickers works, it was found to be very similar to an existing motor produced for operating the hydroplanes in submarines, so the existing submarine motor was used instead.
22. Bullard to BNW, 3 April 1943 (SM Arch BNW D3/2).
23. TNA AVIA 18/715.
24. *Notes on operation with Upkeep* (March 1943) (TNA ADM 277/46).
25. Cooper, Alan, *The Men Who Breached the Dams* (William Kimber, 1982). RAFM DC72/28 confirms this arrangement and gives full detail on how to fit and adjust the spotlamps. However RAE Technical Note Inst.764 (TNA ADM 277/46) states that the rear lamp was *40ft* astern of the forward one, trials conducted on the evening of 8 April yielding excellent results, with height accurate to within 10ft.
26. Euler, Helmuth, *The Dams Raid: Through the Lens* (After the Battle/Battle of Britain International Limited, 2001).
27. Sweetman, op. cit., figures.
28. TNA AIR 8/1237, meeting #1 (18 March 1943)
29. SM Arch BNW D2/21 – The Dale Dyke Dam (also known as the Bradfield Dam) in the hills above Sheffield had been of similar construction. Shortly after its completion in March 1864, it was found to be leaking and, exacerbated by bad weather blowing water over the top of the dam, this quickly led to the failure of the dam. Around 250 people were killed as the lake waters flooded down the valley and into Sheffield. Wallis thought a similar failure could be initiated at the Sorpe by Upkeep (although the Dale Dyke Dam had a clay core and the Sorpe had a concrete core). The Teton Dam in Idaho failed in a similar way in 1976, so Wallis's hopes were not unfounded.
30. *Minutes of a meeting at the Air Ministry to discuss Upkeep, 5 May 1943* (SM Arch BNW D3/2).
31. In his book, Gibson meets the boffins behind the weapon and refers to them as 'Mutt and Jeff' (after characters from the long-running cartoon strip popular at the time) – 'Jeff' was Wallis and 'Mutt' was actually 'Mutt' Summers – something of an in-joke by Gibson!
32. Pearson, Alastair W., 'Allied Military Model Making during World War II', *Cartography and Geographic Information Science* (29(3), 2002), 227–41.
33. All three models are now held by the Imperial War Museum.
34. Operation Chastise was the codeword for the first operational use of Upkeep, and thus became the Dams Raid. In his book, Gibson uses the term 'Downwood' to refer to the operation (the actual operation codename would still have been secret when he was writing).
35. Some references (including Euler, op. cit.) state that Brown attacked at right angles to the dam, but this is incorrect (a diagram by Brown's bomb aimer shows an attack along the crest like McCarthy, and this is confirmed by Heal, Brown's navigator).
36. Speer, Albert, cited by Arthur, Max, *Dambusters: A Landmark Oral History* (Virgin, 2008).
37. Wallis to Bufton at the Air Ministry (6 May 1944) (SM Arch BNW D2/21).
38. Post-war, another dam was built below the Lister, and its reservoir (the Biggesee), which is far larger than the original Lister reservoir, now comes up to the base of the original dam.
39. There remains some controversy about which of these two dams was actually attacked (as there was no damage, there is no evidence at the dam itself); Sweetman makes a powerful case for it being the Bever, but Euler (op. cit.) quotes eyewitnesses that say that a bomb was dropped in the Ennepe reservoir by a Mosquito that night, although this scenario does not seem very credible.
40. This crew had come from 49 Squadron, and were inexperienced compared to most crews on the raid. They returned to 49 Squadron and flew more than a dozen further missions, but were all killed on a raid during September 1943.
41. Letter in the Barnes Wallis Memorial Trust collection.
42. SM Arch BNW D7/1; English translation by British Intelligence, 1945.
43. Seismograph images referred to in the Prüss report are in Euler, op. cit.
44. Sweetman, John, Johnston, Gary and Coward, David, *The Dambusters* (Little, Brown Book Group, 2003), 168.
45. Later in the war on many occasions, a whole squadron carrying Wallis's 'earthquake' bombs would mount a raid to attack a single bridge, so the number of bridges alone destroyed by Chastise is remarkable.
46. Saward, Dudley, *'Bomber' Harris* (Cassell, 1984), 200.
47. David Shannon speaking in *Dambusters: The True Story* (DVD, DD Video/MRA Entertainment, 1993).
48. Lewin, Joseph D., 'German Dams Attacked Successfully', *Engineering News Record* (17 June 1943), 78–82; despite being published just one month after the raid, this article is remarkable for its depth and accuracy, as well as incorporating several reconnaissance photographs and engineering assessments of the destroyed dams and possible future targets.
49. Saward, op. cit.
50. Sweetman, op. cit., 182.
51. SM Arch BNW D7/9 contains a diagram showing some of the defensive measures.
52. SM Arch BNW D2/12.
53. Euler, op. cit.
54. *Meeting held at Gwydyr House to discuss counter measures against the possible enemy use of 'Upkeep', 3 June 1944* (Cherwell Archive G375/13).
55. CoS Committee special report *Upkeep & Highball*, 2 August 1943 (TNA AIR 8/1234).
56. Small note on Highball, 9 October 1943 (TNA ADM 277/46).
57. RAFM L96 contains full German plans of Upkeep, the method of carriage in the Lancaster and details of the fuzes.
58. Letter in the Barnes Wallis Memorial Trust collection.
59. Sqn Ldr P.C. West, speaking in *Dambusters: The True Story* (DVD, DD Video/MRA Entertainment, 1993).
60. CoS Committee report #7 (13 June 1943) and #8 (27 June 1943) (TNA AIR 8/1237).
61. SM Arch BNW D3/2.
62. Air Vice-Marshal (later Sir) Robert H.M.S. Saundby was the Senior Air Staff Officer at HQ Bomber Command; Air Vice-Marshal The Honourable (later Sir) Ralph A. Cochrane was (at the time of Operation Chastise) the Officer Commanding No.5 Group Bomber Command, whose squadrons included 617.
63. Sweetman, op. cit., 187.
64. SM Arch BNW D3/2.
65. TNA AIR 14/2060.
66. Sweetman, op. cit., 188.
67. CoS Committee report #12 (22 August 1943) (TNA AIR 8/1237).
68. Ibid.
69. CoS Committee special report *Upkeep & Highball* (2 August 1943) (TNA AIR 8/1234).
70. TNA AIR 14/2060.
71. CoS Committee report #13 (7 September 1943) (TNA AIR 8/1237).
72. SM Arch BNW D3/2.
73. TNA AIR 9/186.
74. Ibid.
75. The Petsamo region was ceded to Russia in a 1946 peace treaty, and the small Janiskoski area (including the power station) was sold to Russia in 1947.
76. During training for Chastise, when the target was still unknown, the aircrews' greatest worry was that the target actually was the *Tirpitz*.
77. Brickhill, Paul, *The Dam Busters* (Evans Brothers, 1951), 127.
78. Bufton at the Air Ministry to ACAS, December 1943 (TNA AIR 20/164).
79. Bufton at the Air Ministry to AOC-in-C Bomber Command, 7 May 1944 (TNA AIR 20/164).
80. Pearson, op. cit.
81. Wallis to Verity at the Air Ministry, 3 February 1944 (SM Arch BNW D2/21).
82. Wallis to Morley at the Air Ministry, 10 July 1943 (SM Arch BNW D2/21).
83. Brickhill, op. cit.
84. Wallis to Bufton at the Air Ministry, 6 July 1943 (SM Arch BNW D2/14); archive films (and stills from this in Euler, Helmut, *Als Deutschlands Dämme Brachen* (Motorbuch-Verlag, 1976), show a successful explosives test on a highly curved model dam, which could be related to this.
85. Most Tallboy attacks were carried out by 617 Squadron alone or in co-operation with 9 Squadron, but the Sorpe raid was one of a small number involving only 9 Squadron; many attacks were part of a larger Main Force raid involving many other squadrons of bombers and covering fighters.
86. TNA AIR 14/2060.
87. TNA AIR 8/1239.
88. Flower, Stephen, *A Hell of a Bomb* (Tempus, 2002).
89. Pasmore, Anthony, and Parker, Norman, *Ashley Walk: Its Bombing Range, Landscape and History* (New Forest Research & Publication Trust, 2002, 2nd edn).
90. *Breaching the German Dams* (RAF Museum, 2008) has details of the various Operation Guzzle flights.
91. Letter in the Barnes Wallis Memorial Trust collection.

Chapter 6

1. CoS Committee report #1 (18 March 1943) (TNA AIR 8/1237).
2. CoS Committee report #5 (17 May 1943) (TNA AIR 8/1237); this was the day after launching Operation Chastise.
3. TNA ADM 1/14827.

4. Sharp, C.M., and Bowyer, M.J.F., *Mosquito* (Crecy 1995), 373, states that an existing Polish squadron was first mooted to carry Highball.
5. CoS Committee report #2 (3 April 1943) (TNA AIR 8/1237).
6. *Courbet* is referred to by the codename BV7 in some reports.
7. Loch Striven is referred to by the codename HHY in many reports.
8. The loch has a dogleg about halfway along its length, and for most tests the *Courbet* was moored in the knee of this dogleg facing west, such that the ship's crew could see right down the loch from the port side, but could see only hillside from the starboard side; white markings were painted on the side of the ship to improve its visibility. For the first few tests, the *Courbet* was moored in the centre of the loch (Jones, Alan, *Now it can be told*, unpublished notes on his experiences on the *Courbet*, and private communication).
9. The shores of Loch Striven were sparsely populated, and the security services visited the farmers around the loch and instructed them 'not to look' at the activities on the loch. However, the seaside resort of Rothesay is directly south of the mouth of the loch; a smokescreen was laid across the mouth to hide the tests from prying eyes in the town, although this may only have been for the 1944 tests.
10. *Upkeep and Highball: Proposed Programme of Trials* (8 April 1943) (SM Arch BNW D4/2).
11. The same had happened with Upkeep, but on this date it was decided to remove the wood altogether and use the plain cylinder.
12. Notes of a progress report (29 April 1943) (TNA AIR 8/1237).
13. Additional standard Mosquitoes were borrowed from other squadrons for the navigation exercises, and gradually returned to their owners as the Highball Mosquitoes were delivered.
14. CoS Committee report #8 (27 June 1943) (TNA AIR 8/1237).
15. The Boom Defence Department's main duty was tending to the anti-submarine boom across the Clyde between Dunoon and Cloch Point; this kept the large anchorage in the upper firth safe from enemy submarines.
16. *Highball net trials* (MAEE report H/Arm 101d) (TNA AVIA 19/1269).
17. *Wellington Highball trials at Turnberry* (SM Arch BNW D4/2).
18. The original ORB for RAF Turnberry contains no entries between February 1943 and August 1945, so none of the Highball activity is recorded therein (TNA AIR 2/866).
19. Curtis, Des, 618 Squadron (private communication); Rogerson was still on Wallis's staff in the 1950s. George Edwards also occasionally flew on the test flights.
20. Bird, Robin, *Top Secret War Bird of World War Two* (Lord Birdforth, 2004); the author's father was an official MAEE photographer.
21. At least one dummy run was always performed first, the pilot firing a green Verey pistol to indicate that the store would be dropped on his next run.
22. Minutes of a meeting held at RAF Station Manston, 9 April 1943 (SM Arch BNW D4/2); the BDD officer in command of the landing craft knew the destination of the lorry only as 'to an airfield' (Buttery, Tom, BDD, private communication).
23. CoS Committee report #5 (17 May 1943) (TNA AIR 8/1237).
24. Minutes of a meeting held at Weybridge 14 May 1943 (SM Arch BNW D3/2).
25. CoS Committee report #6 (30 May 1943) (TNA AIR 8/1237).
26. CoS Committee report #7 (13 June 1943) (TNA AIR 8/1237); there were still sporadic unplanned releases – one house near Wisley airfield (a satellite of Weybridge) was hit on two separate occasions.
27. CoS Committee report #8 (27 June 1943) (TNA AIR 8/1237).
28. CoS Committee report #9 (12 July 1943) (TNA AIR 8/1237).
29. TNA AIR 8/1234.
30. Boorer, Norman W. (private communication).
31. Patent GB572816, *Improvements in Range-Finding Apparatus*, applied for 10 June 1943.
32. CoS Committee report #8 (27 June 1943) (TNA AIR 8/1237).
33. Notes of a meeting of the Chiefs of Staff 27 June 1943 (TNA AIR 8/1237).
34. RAFM, video cassette '*From reels D4-D14*'.
35. CoS Committee report #8 (27 June 1943) (TNA AIR 8/1237).
36. ACNS and ACAS to First Sea Lord and CAS, 2 July 1943 (TNA AIR 2/8394); also Sweetman, John, 'Barnes Wallis's Other Bouncing Bomb: Part II', *RAF Air Power Review*, vol. 5, no. 3 (Autumn 2002).
37. Report on attacking Italian fleet with Highball (TNA AIR 2/8394).
38. Curtis, Des, 618 Squadron (private communication); with hindsight, he is of the opinion that an attack would have succeeded, if the aircraft could have reached the target area. Although the briefing models of the dams have survived, it appears that the one of Kaa Fjord did not.
39. The submarine crews, however, *did* witness the Highball trials in the loch (John Lorimer, Sub Lt on X-6, private communication); they also used the *Courbet* as a target for their training missions.
40. ACNS and ACAS to First Sea Lord and CAS, 2 July 1943 (TNA AIR 2/8394).
41. Notes of a meeting of the Chiefs of Staff, referring to a meeting of the Admiralty and Air Ministry on 30 June 1943 (TNA AIR 8/1237).
42. Letter from Director of Operations (Torpedo) to CAS, 28 July 1943 (TNA AIR 8/1237).
43. CoS Committee report #11 (8 August 1943) (TNA AIR 8/1237).
44. Curtis, Des, 618 Squadron (private communication).
45. CoS Committee report #13 (September 1943) (TNA AIR 8/1237).
46. CoS Committee report #14 (September 1943) (TNA AIR 8/1237).
47. Curtis, Des, *Most Secret Squadron: The Story of 618 Squadron* (Skitten Books, 1995).
48. Minutes of a meeting held at Burhill, 7 July 1943 (SM Arch BNW D4/5).
49. *Mosquito DZ533 12-15 July 1943* (SM Arch BNW D4/2).
50. CoS Committee report #9 (12 July 1943) (TNA AIR 8/1237) and Minutes of a meeting held at Burhill, 7 July 1943 (SM Arch BNW D4/5).
51. *g* is the force due to gravity, and impact forces are typically quoted as multiples of this.
52. Highball Reculver Trials, 23 August 1943 (SM Arch BNW D4/5).
53. Highball trials at HHY, 7–8 September 1943 (SM Arch BNW D4/5).
54. CoS Committee report #14 (18 September 1943) (TNA AIR 8/1237).
55. When bombs *were* caught in the nets, it is unclear how these were recovered – a few bombs which sank were also recovered. Sandeman, Jess, *Bute's War* (Buteshire Natural History Society, 2006), 40, cites that the divers who manned the chariots and submarines that were tested in Loch Striven were involved in the recovery, but this author notes that these men were especially careful never to speak about their activities, even after the war (private communication).
56. SM Arch BNW D4/5, folder 3.
57. CoS Committee report #20 (14 December 1943) (TNA AIR 8/1237).
58. Minutes of a meeting regarding Highball, 12 November 1943 (SM Arch BNW D4/5).
59. Highball Meeting, 12 November 1943 (TNA ADM 277/46).
60. CoS Committee report #8 (27 June 1943) (TNA AIR 8/1237).
61. Minutes of a meeting regarding Highball, 12 November 1943 (SM Arch BNW D4/5).
62. Trials at HHY, November and December 1943 (SM Arch BNW D4/5).
63. Curtis, Des, 618 Squadron (private communication).
64. MAEE report H/Arm/101.D (TNA AVIA 19/1269); with hindsight, basing this conclusion on only four drops (and only one in each direction) seems rather unsound.
65. Curtis, Des, 618 Squadron (private communication); only broadside-on attacks were considered for the *Tirpitz*, but the geography around her in Kaa Fjord would have made this almost impossible, so it may be that tests of the store's effectiveness when impacting at an acute angle were also being conducted.
66. *Substance Trials* (TNA 277/46).
67. CoS Committee report #31 (21 May 1944) (TNA AIR 8/1237).
68. Minutes of meeting held at MAP on 27 April 1944 regarding Highball Trials and Highball Production (TNA ADM 277/46).
69. *Malaya* was used for bombardment of the French coast in support of the Normandy landings; she must have done so between the 15 May–8 June trials in Loch Striven and later trials beginning 7 September. MacBean & Hogben mentions tests against *Malaya* in September at Invergordon, and Flower mentions tests against the ship off the east coast between Montrose and Dundee on 28 September.
70. Shortly after the D-Day landings, the *Courbet* was sunk as a blockship to form part of the breakwater around the Mulberry harbour off Sword Beach, where her submerged hulk remains in place. Here she was mistaken for an active Allied ship and hit by a torpedo from a German Marder midget submarine – she is thus probably the only vessel to have been attacked by secret weapons of *both* sides during the war.
71. CoS Committee report #32 (4 June 1944) (TNA AIR 8/1237).
72. CoS Committee report #37 (14 August 1944) (TNA AIR 8/1237).
73. TNA AIR 8/1234; the main target was the Japanese naval base at Truk (now Chuuk).
74. Brown, Eric M., *Wings on My Sleeve* (Weidenfeld & Nicolson, 2006, updated edn).
75. Given 618's difficulties landing-on with the relatively docile Barracuda, Brown is of the opinion that the squadron would have suffered greater losses returning their Mosquitoes to the carrier from a Highball mission than during the attack on the target (Captain Eric Brown, private communication).
76. *Flying Review*, vol. 19, no. 4 (1963), 25 (cited by Michael Nelmes, Narromine Aviation Museum).
77. CoS Committee report #42 (23 October 1943) (TNA AIR 8/1237). William 'Gerry' Gerrard of 618 Squadron claimed the longest ever Highball run of around 1800 yards in a drop at Wells; he also annoyed the Admiralty by puncturing the hull of HMS *Malaya* when he released a Highball too late due to the smoke screen (William Gerrard, 618 Squadron, private communication), although Curtis (op. cit.) states that a total of three Highballs punctured the hull (one forward and two aft). RAFM archive films show many Highball drops, including the drop which punctured the bow.
78. TNA ADM 277/46.
79. Parts of this aircraft are now in the Barnes Wallis Memorial Trust collection.
80. Two Highball Mosquitoes remained in the UK for trials purposes.
81. These were small escort carriers and were only for transporting the Mosquitoes, which were lashed on deck as they were too large to go into the hangar; had operations been mounted in the Pacific, the aircraft would have operated from a larger fleet carrier (or shore base).
82. Michael Nelmes, Narromine Aviation Museum (private communication); Narromine was chosen as it was reasonably remote (for security), in a flat area (for low-level flying practice) and close to an RAAF depot at Dubbo.

83. Curtis, Des, 618 Squadron (private communication).
84. A variety of reasons have been given for this, including US opposition, fear of disclosing the secret weapon, lack of suitable fleet carriers and lack of suitable Japanese naval targets within range (many of their large capital ships had already been sunk by 1945).
85. Curtis, Des, op. cit., 136–8.
86. SM Arch BNW D2/14.
87. Goddard, Doris, 'Revealed: Wartime Secret of Rail Tunnel 'Bombing'!', *Western Telegraph* (3 July 1985); the article includes an eyewitness account of the event.
88. CoS Committee report #18 (14 November 1943) (TNA AIR 8/1237).
89. SM Arch BNW D4/3.
90. BNW to Morley at the Air Ministry, 31 August 1943 (SM Arch BNW D2/21).
91. BNW to Bufton at the Air Ministry, 14 August 1943 (SM Arch BNW D2/21); also TNA AIR 14/1221.
92. CoS Committee report #19 (29 November 1943) (TNA AIR 8/1237).
93. Built in the USA as the Avenger, the aircraft was initially known in the UK as the Tarpon, although both names are used in contemporary documents; Avenger is the usual name now in both countries and has been used throughout this section to avoid confusion. The single-engined Avenger's main role was as a carrier-based torpedo bomber.
94. Although just another codename in this context, Tammany Hall was originally the name of a political society in the USA, especially New York.
95. CoS Committee report #12 (22 August 1943) (TNA AIR 8/1237)
96. SM Arch BNW D4/3.
97. TNA AIR 8/1234.
98. SM Arch BNW D2/20. Maj Hew Kilner was the Works Manager at Weybridge during the war.
99. *Tammany Hall: Advanced Instructions for Use* (May 1944) (SM Arch BNW D2/20).
100. Kilner to Wynter-Morgan, 21 August 1944 (SM Arch BNW D4/5).
101. RAFM video WAB 223/H/3.
102. SM Arch BNW D4/5.
103. SM Arch BNW D2/7.
104. Bowyer, Michael J.F., 'To Sink the *Tirpitz*', *Airfix Magazine Annual* (1976), 64–7, states that a Marauder was modified to carry four stores, but there is nothing to support that this actually took place.
105. Sweetman, John, 'Barnes Wallis's Other Bouncing Bomb: Part I', *RAF Air Power Review*, vol. 5, no. 2 (Summer 2002).
106. TNA ADM 1/14827.
107. Johnsen, Frederick A., *Douglas A-26 Invader* (Speciality Press, Warbird Tech Series, vol. 22, 1999).
108. SM Arch BNW D4/7; the RAF Museum and Imperial War Museum hold films of many of the drops.
109. Johnsen, op. cit. Although only 25 stores were supplied, the Americans developed an efficient recovery scheme: a buoy was dropped immediately at the place where the store sank; a diver was then sent down to attach a line to the store, and it was hauled up into a boat (always within 75 minutes of the drop) and readied for reuse.
110. TNA AIR 8/1236. Air Chief Marshal Sir Charles F.A. Portal was Chief of the Air Staff (CAS) at the time of Operation Chastise. Later, he was Chairman of the British Aircraft Corporation from its formation in 1960 until 1963.
111. Memo CRD to ACAS, 12 May 1945 (TNA AIR 2/5879).
112. Gardner, op. cit., 47–8.
113. TNA ADM 116/1050; it appears that Wallis produced initial drawings for the weapon in February 1943, and although he was kept in touch with experimental developments, the later development work was done wholly by DMWD.
114. TNA ADM 116/1050; the Baseball spin problem was not really solved by the time the project was abandoned, as prototypes indicated that spin was not 'really necessary'. Later experiments showed that 1000rpm backspin increased range by about 1/3, but this was not seen as enough to justify the effort required to add the spin.
115. SM Arch BNW D2/9.
116. Ibid.
117. Pawle, Gerald, *The Secret War 1939-45* (Harrap & Co., 1956).
118. TNA ADM 116/1050.
119. TNA AIR 8/1234, CoS Committee special report *Upkeep & Highball*, 2 August 1943.
120. TNA ADM 1/17278 contains notes on the investigations and copies of reports on the German model experiments, though original figures and graphs are not reproduced.
121. BNW to Commander Rodger (DNDP) (TNA ADM 1/17278).
122. TNA ADM 277/46.
123. Shaw, R.A., *The possible range of bouncing bombs* (Report H/Arm/Res.16, MAEE Helensburgh, 5 August 1943) (TNA AVIA 19/1042).
124. *Report on flying accident or forced landing not attributable to enemy action* (25 October 1943) (TNA ADM 277/46); observers initially thought that the Highball had struck the aircraft, but subsequent analysis of trials films showed that it was the splash that crippled the aircraft.
125. Ogilvie, Malcolm, Museum of Islay Life (private communication).
126. SM Arch BNW D2/22.
127. TNA AIR 2/5879.
128. Minutes of a meeting held at Vickers-Armstrongs, 28 June 1945 (SM Arch BNW D2/22).
129. Wallis diary for 1946 (RAFM X001-2371/108).
130. *The Present Position of the Highball Project* (2 September 1946) (TNA AIR 2/5879).
131. Experiment had led to the result that the range of Highball was proportional to the square of the release speed, with a theoretical maximum range of about 4,500yds.
132. BNW to Aitcheson, 17 April 1947 (SM Arch BNW D2/22).
133. *Card Store Mark II* (27 January 1948) (SM Arch BNW D2/24).
134. BNW to Charlesworth at Ministry of Supply, Fort Halstead, 13 January 1946 (SM Arch BNW D2/22); includes blueprint of proposed rocket turbine installation.
135. SM Arch BNW D2/22.
136. Vickers-Armstrongs to Ministry of Supply, 28 January 1948 (SM Arch BNW D2/23).

Chapter 7

1. Website of the Barnes Wallis Memorial Trust – http://www.barneswallistrust.org/dambusters.htm
2. SM Arch BNW D2/14.
3. Wallis, Barnes N., *A Note on a Method of Attacking the Axis Powers* (1941), chapters 3–5 (SM Arch BNW D1 and TNA ADM 1/11767).
4. SM Arch BNW D6/4 includes a report on a 'Bomb Type Y', which is generally similar but with a large spherical charge casing and a contact fuze (thus not a penetration weapon), shown being carried by a Stirling bomber. This report is undated and anonymous, so may not be the work of Wallis.
5. MacBean, John A., and Hogben, Arthur S., *Bombs Gone: The Development and Use of British Air-dropped Weapons from 1912 to the Present Day* (Patrick Stephens Limited, 1990), 140, has a photo of a wind tunnel model of Tallboy; the ogive curve is a segment of a circle, in Tallboy being double the diameter of the casing body.
6. Boorer, Norman W. (private communication).
7. Brooklands Museum holds original examples of the 2in models, exhibiting a variety of levels of deformation.
8. In the 'Note', Wallis also proposed to drop the 4,000lb version operationally from high-altitude Wellingtons, partly to support his case for the 10-ton bomb; Brooklands Museum holds the sole remaining example of the 4,000lb bomb.
9. Communication between the MAP and Vickers-Armstrongs was facilitated by A.H. Hurd, a Vickers-Armstrongs employee who was seconded to the MAP during this time, and he was able 'to dispense with a great deal of red tape which might have created delays and difficulties if the negotiations had been handled by a professional civil servant' (post-war letter in SM Arch BNW D2/14).
10. Although several theories have been mooted for the origin of the Tallboy codename, it came from the Air Ministry, presumably randomly assigned from a master list of codenames.
11. SM Arch BNW D2/14; all three sizes were ordered at the same time – some sources state that the Medium was ordered following cancellation of the Large, but this is incorrect.
12. Boorer, Norman W. (private communication); although he drew the bombs, Boorer never actually saw a Grand Slam until he visited the USAF Museum in Ohio during a visit to the USA in 1967.
13. SM Arch BNW D2/14.
14. Chadwick to Wallis, November 1943 (SM Arch BNW D5/2); Chadwick was also a believer in the 'big bomb' theory, and had designed the large bomb bay in the Manchester/Lancaster accordingly.
15. Shortland, Jim (private communication).
16. SM Arch BNW D2/14.
17. SM Arch BNW D2/19.
18. SM Arch BNW D2/17 Part 3.
19. Teed spent the war years in the USA on unknown business (Stopes-Roe, Mary, and Boorer, Norman W., private communication).
20. SM Arch BNW D2/14; these steels were the main alloys manufactured by the various foundries: pearlitic manganese steel contained 0.26–0.3 per cent carbon and 1.5–1.7 per cent manganese, manganese-molybdenum steel was the same plus 0.3–0.5 per cent molybdenum, and chromium-molybdenum steel (Hykro) contained 0.25 per cent carbon, 3 per cent chromium and 0.6 per cent molybdenum. Stainless steel contains more than 10 per cent chromium, typically 18 per cent.
21. SM Arch BNW D2/14.
22. Mirrlees-Watson and James Potts were light engineering companies, Nairns was a linoleum manufacturer, and all three were engaged in producing war munitions; Nairns's activities are detailed in *Nairns 1939–1945: An Account of the Wartime Activities of Michael Nairn and Company Limited of Kirkcaldy* (Nairns, 1945).
23. SM Arch BNW D2/17 Part 3.
24. SM Arch BNW D2/14.
25. SM Arch BNW D2/17 Part 3.
26. MacBean and Hogben, op. cit.
27. SM Arch BNW D2/14.

28. SM Arch BNW D2/17 Part 3.
29. SM Arch BNW D2/17 Part 2.
30. The Americans did eventually start filling casings for their own use; this was first done on 10 August 1944 by the US Navy's Naval Mine Depot at Yorktown (DEFE 12/2392).
31. HQ Bomber Command to HQ 5 Group, 29 January 1945 (AIR 14/2189).
32. SM Arch BNW D2/17 Part 2.
33. Hurd to Wallis (SM Arch BNW D2/14).
34. Shortland, Jim (private communication).
35. MacIntosh, Don, 9 Squadron Pilot (private communication).
36. Wallis to ESC, 15 November 1943 (SM Arch BNW D2/19).
37. SM Arch BNW D5/3.
38. TNA AVIA 6/13312.
39. In the 'Note', the drop height proposed was 40,000ft, but the Lancaster could not reach this height with a full load, typical operational drops being made from 15–18,000ft with a consequent reduction in penetration. However, despite some initial concerns, the penetration depths achieved in practice were sufficient for successful functioning.
40. SM Arch BNW D2/19.
41. SM Arch BNW D2/17 Part 3.
42. SM Arch BNW D2/17 Part 2.
43. Godwin, John, *The Man-Made Earthquake: A Short History of Very Heavy Conventional Aerial Bombs* (http://members.cox.net/nukeinfo1/)
44. TNA AVIA 6/13312; mention was also made of results being corrected for the rotation of the earth, but it is unclear what this involved. The terminal velocity was estimated at 3,300fps, so the bombs were still accelerating when they struck.
45. SM Arch BNW D2/17 Part 3.
46. Edwards to Wallis, 22 March 1944 (SM Arch BNW D2/17 Part 2).
47. SM Arch BNW D5/2.
48. Wallis to Plowden, 15 April 1944 (SM Arch BNW D2/14).
49. Wallis diary for 1944 (RAF Museum X001-2371/082).
50. This was a reinforced concrete structure meant to resemble a submarine pen.
51. SM Arch BNW D2/17 Part 2.
52. Road Research Laboratory Reports (SM Arch BNW D5/3).
53. The first 30 strops and releases were ordered on 9 December 1943 (SM Arch BNW D2/17 Part 3); no known example of the strop remains (although Flower states that the RAF Museum have one, this is incorrect).
54. 617 Squadron engineer, cited by Shortland, Jim (private communication).
55. MacIntosh, Don, 9 Squadron (private communication).
56. Shortland, Jim (private communication).
57. The blast bombs were formally known as High Capacity (HC) stores as the explosive content was a high proportion of the overall weight (the casing was a simple drum of sheet steel); Tallboy and Grand Slam had comparatively heavy cast casings, and so these were classed as Medium Capacity (MC) stores.
58. Meeting at Air Ministry, 1 July 1943 (SM Arch BNW D3/2).
59. Cochrane to Wallis, 11 October 1944 (SM Arch BNW D2/17 Part 1).
60. Wallis to Cochrane, October 1944 (SM Arch BNW D2/17 Part 1).
61. *Tallboy release units: timing of release delays* (A&AEE report, 20 November 1944) (TNA AIR 14/2189 and TNA AVIA 18/923).
62. Comments, e.g. HQ 5 Group to HQ Bomber Command, 6 April 1945 (TNA AIR 14/2011), suggest that Grand Slam was not an official codename; however, it appears to have been the de facto name 'used by all and sundry'. 'Tallboy Medium' was then generally known simply as 'Tallboy'. From this time, the bombs were to be officially known as '22,000lb MC', with Tallboy as '12,000lb MC'.
63. SM Arch BNW D2/14.
64. Some photos show one of the first aircraft (PB995) in flight carrying a Grand Slam with both nose and dorsal turrets intact.
65. Musson, Roger M.W., British Geological Survey (private communication).
66. Wallis reminiscences (SM Arch BNW A5/5).
67. Boyd at MAP, to Wallis, 16 October 1944 (SM Arch BNW D2/17 Part 1) and Wallis diary for 1944 (RAF Museum X001-2371/082).
68. The Sangatte batteries housed giant guns used to shell the Dover area; they were being considered as possible targets for Tallboy tests (SM Arch BNW D2/17 Part 1).
69. Wallis diaries for 1945 (RAF Museum X001-2371/083 and X001-2371/087).
70. *Note on an Examination of Certain Bombed Targets in France* (DSIR RRL Report to the Ministry of Supply, November 1944).
71. e.g. *617 Squadron Operations Record Book 1943–45* (TNA AIR 27/2128) , Flower, Stephen, *A Hell of a Bomb* (Tempus Publishing, 2001), and Ward, Chris, Lee, Andy, and Wachtel, Andreas, *The Dambusters: The Definitive Story of 617 Squadron at War 1939-1945* (Red Kite, 2003).
72. The numbers of bombs quoted relate to those dropped on or near the targets concerned; not all sources, even primary sources, agree precisely on the numbers and types of bombs used on every raid, and the numbers quoted here are taken from what appears to be the most reliable source in each case, usually *The Results of Attacks with 12,000lb MC (Tallboy) Bombs* (Operational Research Section, Report No. S.218, 2 May 1945) (TNA AIR 14/2011), or the 617 Squadron ORB (TNA AIR 27/2128). Percentages quoted indicate the proportion of the total number of each type of bomb dropped operationally.
73. Although a concrete dome structure, the nature of the destruction at Wizernes was by subterranean collapse, rather than by piercing the concrete, hence its inclusion here.
74. Air Ministry to Freeman at MAP, 12 June 1944 (SM Arch BNW D2/17 Part 2).
75. This site is now La Coupole museum.
76. 'The V3', *After the Battle* (No. 6, 1974), 38–41, and Pallud, John Paul, 'The Secret Weapons: V3 and V4', *After the Battle* (No. 114, 2001), 2–19.
77. Further damage to the Marquise-Mimoyecques site was done during post-war demolition attempts by the Royal Engineers (SM Arch BNW D7/3).
78. *A Second Examination of the Damaged Submarine Pens at Brest* (DSIR RRL Report to the Ministry of Supply, January 1945).
79. *The results of attacks with 12,000lb MC (Tallboy) bombs* (Operational Research Section, Report No. S.218, 2 May 1945) and SM Arch BNW D2/17 Part 1.
80. 617 Squadron ORB (TNA AIR 27/2128).
81. *The results of attacks with 12,000lb MC (Tallboy) bombs* (Operational Research Section, Report No. S.218, 2 May 1945).
82. Brickhill, Paul, *The Dam Busters* (Evans Brothers, 1951); Cooper, Alan, *Beyond the Dams to the Tirpitz* (William Kimber, 1983); Sweetman, John, *Tirpitz: Hunting the Beast* (Sutton, 2000).
83. Post-war investigation of her hull revealed that some of the near misses had also 'dished in' the hull plates by several feet in places, although the welding had stood up to this very well.
84. Morpurgo, 295.
85. *Choice of bombs for the attack on the Tirpitz* (Report from the Air Ministry, 17 November 1944) (SM Arch BNW D2/18).
86. Bufton to Wallis, 17 May 1944 (SM Arch BNW D2/17 Part 2).
Gp Capt S.O. Bufton was an RAF Staff Officer at the Air Ministry.
87. Collier to Wallis, 29 September 1944 (SM Arch BNW D2/17 Part 2).
Wg Cdr J.D. Collier was also an RAF Staff Officer at the Air Ministry.
88. Wallis to Air Ministry, 2 October 1944 (SM Arch BNW D2/17 Part 1 and SM Arch BNW D2/21).
89. This was one of very few Tallboy raids carried out by 9 Squadron without 617 Squadron.
90. TNA FO 1013/910.
91. *The results of attacks with 12,000lb MC (Tallboy) bombs* (Operational Research Section, Report No. S.218, 2 May 1945).
92. Undated note (SM Arch BNW D2/14).
93. Minutes of meeting at the Air Ministry, 1 June 1943 (SM Arch BNW D3/2).
94. Minutes of meeting at the Air Ministry, 1 July 1943 (SM Arch BNW D3/2).
95. Bufton to Collier, 17 March 1944 (SM Arch BNW D2/17 Part 2).
96. SM Arch BNW D2/21.
97. SM Arch BNW D6/2.
98. Wallis to Bufton, 4 August 1944 (SM Arch BNW D2/17 Part 1); Wallis also noted that the USAAF was proposing to carry Tallboy Large on the B-29 so 'it might be better to leave the attack to be carried out by the Americans with Tallboy Large as a successful result would then be certain'. However, the preparation of the B-29 for carrying the big bombs was not completed until summer of 1945.
99. Collier to Wallis, 26 September 1944 (SM Arch BNW D2/17 Part 1).
100. Most of the structures still exist, their massive size making demolition impractical in most cases; earthquake-bomb damage can still be seen on some, e.g. the *Valentin* U-boat factory at Farge.
101. Developed by DMWD, the Disney bomb weighed 4,500lb, and after some time in free fall, a rocket motor ignited to accelerate the bomb towards the target. Although a British weapon, it was not used by the RAF, but the USAAF dropped them in pairs from B-17s and had used them operationally on four occasions by early April 1945. It is believed that 'Disney' was a randomly assigned codeword, as 'Tallboy' had been.
102. Large Bomb Mission to Commanding General, AAF, Washington D.C., 26 April 1945.
103. HQ Bomber Command to HQ 5 Group, 3 May 1945 (TNA AIR 14/2011).
104. Ford-Jones, Martyn R., 15 Squadron official historian (private communication).
105. *Comparative Test of the Effectiveness of Large Bombs against Reinforced Concrete Structures (Anglo-American Bomb Tests – Project Ruby)* (Air Proving Ground Center Eglin AFB, Florida, 31 October 1946).
106. 15 Squadron ORB (TNA AIR 27/210).
107. These pens were obliterated in the 'British Bang', a deliberate massive explosion of discarded munitions, in April 1947.
108. *Comparative Test of the Effectiveness of Large Bombs against Reinforced Concrete Structures (Anglo-American Bomb Tests – Project Ruby)* (Air Proving Ground Center Eglin AFB, Florida, 31 October 1946), 85–7.
109. *Harken Project: Bombing Analysis and Related Subjects, American and British Phase* (USAF, Dec 1947) – it is unclear what this 1,650lb bomb was; TNA AIR 20/6775 says that no British bombs were dropped during the Harken trials
110. *Closeout of EO 552-554, Program for large bombs in aircraft* (AAF Engineering Army Air Forces, Sept 1953); the conversion work was performed by the Bell Aircraft Corporation.
111. Godwin, op. cit., and *Weekly Newsletter* (HQ US Army Strategic Air Forces, Rear Echelon, Washington DC, 28 July 1945); bomb requirements were estimated at 600 Tallboys and 125 Grand Slams per month.
112. *Conference on Large Bomb Program for Very Large Bombing Aircraft* (AAF ATSC, Engineering Division, 19 April 1945).

113. Godwin, op. cit.
114. Ibid.
115. Memo from HQ US Army Strategic Air Forces (Rear Echelon), Washington DC, 18 August 1945.
116. HQ Army Air Forces, Asst Chief of Air Staff, Materiel and Supplies to General Crawford, 7 October 1946, and Northrop Aircraft Inc to Commanding General, Air Materiel Command, Wright Field, Dayton, Ohio, 6 January 1947.
117. Vessey, Director of Scientific Research at MAP, to Vickers-Armstrongs, February 1945 (SM Arch BNW D2/14).
118. SM Arch BNW D5/5.
119. Ibid.
120. Bullock at the Air Ministry to Wallis, 10 May 1951 (SM Arch BNW D2/14).
121. *The results of attacks with 12,000lb MC (Tallboy) bombs* (Operational Research Section, Report No. S.218, 2 May 1945).
122. MacBean and Hogben, op. cit.

Chapter 8

1. The speed of sound in air varies slightly according to atmospheric conditions, most notably local air temperature, so supersonic speeds are usually quoted relative to Mach 1 (the local speed of sound) rather than in absolute units; the unit is named after the Austrian physicist Ernst Mach. At sea level at 15 degrees C, the speed of sound in air is around 340m/s, decreasing gradually to about 295m/s above 35,000ft. As the speed of sound increases with temperature, late 1940s speed record attempts in the high subsonic region took place over the desert so that aircraft could fly faster (in absolute terms) while staying below the potentially dangerous speeds nearer Mach 1. Another side effect of this is that, if an aircraft flies through regions of air at different temperatures, its Machmeter will fluctuate even though its absolute speed stays constant.
2. Wallis diary for 1945 (RAFM X001-2371/087).
3. *A survey of the trend of invention in the Department of Research & Development of Vickers-Armstrongs (Aircraft)* (SM Arch ED3/3).
4. Morpurgo, 305.
5. Motor racing had been abandoned at Brooklands in 1939, and the whole site was purchased by Vickers in 1946. The clubhouse is now the centrepiece of the Brooklands Museum.
6. Wallis, Barnes W., speaking at meeting of the Barnes Wallis Memorial Trust, Howden, June 2007.
7. Wallis speaking in 1960s TV documentary film (SM Arch BNW K17).
8. Cheshire speaking in 1960s TV documentary film (SM Arch BNW K17).
9. Wallis speaking in 1960s TV documentary film (SM Arch BNW K17).
10. Brown, Eric M., 'Miles M.52: the supersonic dream', *Air Enthusiast* (August–November 1980), 35–42.
11. Shortly after the Dams Raid, Wallis told his elder son, 'I am never going to kill another pilot', which the latter understood not as a desire, but as a decision which informed Wallis's thinking regarding future piloted aircraft.
12. Sweetman, Bill, *High Speed Flight* (Jane's Information Group, 1983).
13. The rocket-powered Bell X-1 (in which Charles 'Chuck' Yeager broke the sound barrier on 1 October 1947) bears a remarkable resemblance to the M.52 in many ways, notably in having all-moving tail surfaces.
14. Wood, Derek, *Project Cancelled: British Aircraft That Never Flew* (Bobbs-Merrill Company Inc, 1975), chapter 2.
15. Turnill, Reginald, and Reed, Arthur, *Farnborough: The Story of the RAE* (Robert Hale, 1980).
16. Wood, op. cit., notes that the £500,000 budget represented five times the amount spent on the M.52 project.
17. Turnill and Reed, op. cit.
18. Brown, Eric M., 'M.52, Me 163 and Bell X-1 – the RAE Connection', *Space Chronicle: Journal of the British Interplanetary Society*, vol. 55, Suppl. 2 (2002), 86–7.
19. Bancroft, D.S., 'The Miles M.52 Supersonic Aircraft', *Space Chronicle: Journal of the British Interplanetary Society*, vol. 55, Suppl. 2 (2002), 77–85.
20. Hot rockets used a separate oxidiser to burn the liquid fuel to produce thrust; cold rockets used a catalyst to break down the liquid hydrogen peroxide into steam which produced thrust.
21. *Flight Trials of a Rocket-propelled Transonic Research Rocket: the RAE-Vickers Rocket Model, Parts I–IV* (Ministry of Supply, Aeronautical Research Council Reports and Memoranda No. 2835, 1954).
22. Boorer lecture.
23. Wallis, Barnes N., *The Fundamental Principles of Long-range Supersonic Flight* (Vickers-Armstrongs, 15 March 1958); this report was prepared in support of Wallis's pitch to the MWDP (Brooklands Museum).
24. Wallis, Barnes N., *The Air Defence of Great Britain: A New Approach* (Vickers-Armstrongs, 1953) (TNA AIR 2/14232 and CAC WLIS 4).
25. Wallis to Major Oliver Stewart, 30 April 1965 (RAFM B493).
26. SM Arch BNW EB1/6; this copy is dated 1947, although many sources date this paper to 1946.
27. Patent GB595464, *Improvements in Aeroplanes*, applied for 1 March 1945.
28. An *aerodyne* is simply a vehicle which flies by virtue of its dynamic motion (as opposed to an *aerostat*, i.e. an airship which remains flying even when static); Wallis primarily used *aerodyne* to distinguish his new form from conventional *aeroplanes*.
29. In subsonic flight, the CP is around the ¼ chord point on the wing, but in supersonic flight it moves to around ½ chord – the aircraft designer must manage this change in CP position in the transonic region, e.g. on Concorde, fuel was transferred from the wing tanks into the tail tank in order to move the CG backwards to balance the CP movement.
30. Patent GB595464, op. cit.
31. Dutch rolling caused handling problems on aircraft such as the Northrop flying wing designs and some of NASA's later lifting bodies.
32. 'Variable wing sweep', now synonymous with 'variable geometry' or 'swing wing', was not a term used by Wallis. Buttler, Tony, *British Secret Projects: Jet Fighters since 1950* (Midland Publishing, 2000), 101, notes that the term 'variable geometry' does not appear to have been used *at all* prior to 1952.
33. Wallis did not invent the concept of variable wing sweep, although he probably 'reinvented' it in isolation, as it is unclear what access he had to information on earlier research; certainly the German work was not available to him when he started.
34. Wallis to Cochrane, 12 September 1951 (SM Arch BNW EA2/7).
35. Manuscript notes from a presentation by Wallis at the Imperial Institute, 5 April 1952 (RAFM B493).
36. Lancaster PA474 (now the BBMF Lancaster) was used for flight trials of laminar flow wings, which were mounted vertically on the upper fuselage.
37. Jones, M., *Skin Friction and the Drag of Streamline Bodies* (R&M No. 1199, December 1928).
38. Wallis, Barnes N., *Research on the Shape of High-speed Bodies Undertaken at the Research & Development Department, Vickers-Armstrongs Limited, Weybridge* (Vickers-Armstrongs, 1951) (CAC WLIS 7); this report is almost exclusively about the torpedo application.
39. Boorer, Norman W., 'Barnes Wallis – Designer (1887–1979)', *Aeronautical Journal* (November 1981), 414–29 credits Young and Owen at the RAE with developing this shape.
40. Molly beat her husband to getting a submarine into the water – she launched HMS *Alderney* at Barrow on 25 June 1945!
41. CAC WLIS 7, op. cit.; Sir Frederick Yapp was the Chairman of Vickers-Armstrongs at this time.
42. The academics were Bullard (Dept of Geodesy and Geophysics) and Pantin (Trinity College) (CAC BLRD J154).
43. Boorer lecture.
44. Boorer, 1981, op. cit.
45. 'Wallis was never very interested in guided missiles' despite the Green Lizard project (Boorer lecture).
46. This codename was one of the 'Rainbow Codes' used for secret projects by the Ministry of Supply up to 1958; other examples included Blue Steel (stand-off missile), Red Dean (air-air missile) and Yellow Sun (nuclear bomb).
47. SM Arch BNW EA1/2.
48. Patent GB692140, *Improved Means for Launching Guided Missiles*, applied for 29 April 1949.
49. Clemow to PDGW/ADGW(R), 5 May 1952 (TNA AVIA 54/1780).
50. Patent GB741717, *Improvements in Projectiles and other Flying Bodies*, applied for 25 January 1947.
51. Patents GB759677, GB759678 and GB759679, *Improvements in Guided Missiles*, applied for 29 April 1949.
52. Patents GB759680, *Improvements in Self-propelled Missiles*, applied for 29 April 1949.
53. Patent GB764291, *Improvements in Missiles for Long-range Bomber Interception*, applied for 16 June 1950.
54. SM Arch BNW EA2/8.
55. The latter type is illustrated in Wood, op. cit., 185.
56. 100 in some drawings.
57. Patent GB764292, *Improvements in Missiles for Bomber Interception*, applied for 16 June 1950.
58. Boorer, 1981, op. cit.
59. Silent film in SM Arch BNW K6.
60. The gun was cleaned between firings by lowering a man with a cloth head-first into the barrel, with a rope tied around his ankles (Boorer lecture).
61. SM Arch BNW EB2/4 and SM Arch BNW EA2/8.
62. SM Arch BNW EA1/2.
63. TNA AVIA 54/1780.
64. Mitchell at the Ministry of Supply to Kilner, 13 September 1952 (TNA AVIA 54/1780).
65. Boorer, 1981, op. cit.
66. Polhamus, Edward C., and Toll, Thomas A., *Research related to variable-sweep aircraft development* (NASA Technical Memorandum 83121, May 1981).
67. Jenkins, Dennis R., Landis, Tony, and Miller, Jay, *American X-vehicles: An Inventory X-1 to X-50* (NASA Monographs in Aerospace History No 31, June 2003); despite this loss, the X-5 test programme of 149 flights between June 1951 and October 1955 was generally successful, and it was the first aircraft to demonstrate variable sweep in flight. The final flight of the X-5 was made by a young Neil Armstrong making his first flight as a test pilot, although he does not remember much about the aircraft (Neil A. Armstrong, private communication).
68. Wg Cdr F.W. Winterbotham had been an Air Intelligence Officer and keen supporter of Wallis during the war.

69. Morpurgo, 313–6.
70. Boorer, 1981, op. cit.; the unfortunate Boorer was tasked with drawing the planform of a goose shot at Wisley, and comparing its CG with that of the aircraft.
71. Morpurgo, 313.
72. Wild Goose films (RAFM WG1).
73. The catapult was the one used for the golf ball tests at the NPL tanks in 1942.
74. One late catapult model is described as 'balsa model 1/5th size weighing 2.88lb, fired horizontally 10ft above probable landing area' (SM Arch BNW EB1/4).
75. Caption to animated film of wind tunnel operation (Wild Goose films, RAF Museum).
76. *Summary of subsonic and supersonic free flight and wind tunnel tests of 'Wild Goose' and 'Swallow' Type Models Conducted by the Department of Aeronautical Research & Development During the Period September 1949 to June 1959*, 13 March 1961 (Brooklands Museum); the same information is given in Wood, op. cit., ch. 11.
77. Wild Goose films (RAFM WG1).
78. Overall span (unswept) was 26ft 6in and AUW was 700–800lb (though the structure was designed to handle weights up to 2,500lb); flight endurance was 4–5 minutes.
79. Wallis to Cochrane, 12 September 1951 (SM Arch BNW EA2/7).
80. Different dihedral angles were tested by way of a joint in the pivot which could be adjusted manually on the ground, but 11 degrees is most frequently mentioned.
81. Patent GB756019, *Improvements in the Control of Flying Bodies*, applied for 2 March 1949.
82. Patent GB741719, *Improvements in the Control of Flying Bodies*, applied for 9 August 1948.
83. Wallis to Cochrane, 12 September 1951 (SM Arch BNW EA2/7).
84. Brooklands Museum SWG-FTR-004 includes diagrams of the rocket installation.
85. *A note on the wing-controlled aerodyne* (Vickers-Armstrongs, Weybridge, undated) (TNA DSIR 23/20474).
86. SM Arch BNW EB1/5.
87. SM Arch BNW EB1/4.
88. Thurleigh was taken over by the RAE in 1946 and was situated four miles east of the main RAE site at Bedford, where wind tunnel work was done.
89. http://www.vicflintham.co.uk/post-war-research-aircraft-and-prototypes/Manned.html; the assigned serial numbers were XA197–202 (203–4 were both cancelled) and XA947–52 although many flew without visible markings. 'Project 93020' appears in some papers and also refers to the Thurleighdyne.
90. Brooklands Museum SWG-FTR-004 includes a plan of the airfield.
91. A long low-loader trailer, mainly used by the RAF for recovery of crashed aircraft.
92. SM Arch BNW EB1/4.
93. Wallis to Cochrane, 12 September 1951 (SM Arch BNW EA2/7); the lift force had to reach at least 150 per cent of the weight of the aircraft for release to occur.
94. Morpurgo, 318.
95. Patent GB673551, *Improvements in Releasable Attachments*, applied for 19 October 1949.
96. Morpurgo, 320-1.
97. Wallis diary for 1950 (RAFM X001-2371).
98. Wallis to Goddard, March 1950 (SM Arch BNW EA2/6).
99. SM Arch BNW EB2/3.
100. TNA DSIR 23/20339.
101. Clarke, ARD (Research), 11 April 1950 (TNA AVIA 65/260); the investigation included comparisons of prevailing wind directions and strengths at Culdrose and Mildenhall in addition to Predannack.
102. Wallis to Cochrane, 12 September 1951 (SM Arch BNW EA2/7).
103. TNA AVIA 65/260; Jeffree alleged that he could fly the models better than the test pilots, due to being uncontaminated by flying skills learned on conventional aircraft.
104. Wallis to Goddard, op. cit.; the Queen Bee was an unmanned DH Tiger Moth biplane flown by radio control for use as a target tug, which entered service before the war.
105. Morris, Richard, *Cheshire* (Viking, 2000), 264–5.
106. Ibid; Cheshire resigned from the project in March 1952, to spend more time working on (what became) the Cheshire Homes, one of which he set up in an old building outside the Predannack perimeter.
107. Boorer, Norman W., *Sir Barnes Wallis, CBE, FRS, RDI, FRAeS 1887–1979: Some Personal Reflections* (Brooklands Museum Trust, 2008), 26.
108. Wallis narration to *Wild Goose and Swallow Tests* film (SM Arch BNW K2).
109. Wallis to Cochrane, 12 September 1951 (SM Arch BNW EA2/7).
110. Ibid.
111. Wallis diary for 1950, op. cit.
112. Wallis to Goddard, op. cit.; the R&D staff at the time (most of whom would have been at Weybridge) were listed by Wallis as 3 senior calculators, 3 senior draughtsmen, 3 physicists, 1 electronics expert, 2 electricians, about 12 junior technicians (apprentices and others) and a works staff of about 20–30.
113. TNA AVIA 65/260; £25,000 in 1950 is equivalent to about £700,000 today.
114. Wallis narration to *Wild Goose and Swallow Tests* film (SM Arch BNW K2); a more powerful second trolley was prepared to reach 175mph with the heavier models, initially being used as a reserve in case of damage to the first trolley.
115. Patent GB673550, *Improvements in Means for Launching Aeroplanes and other Flying Bodies*, applied for 19 October 1949.
116. Memo of a meeting at Predannack, 21 November 1952 (Brooklands Museum SWG-FTR-004).
117. *Revised programme of flying trials at Predannack – part 1*, 6 April 1951 (Brooklands Museum SWG-FTR-004).
118. Endurance was limited by the compressed air capacity in the aircraft, and additional air bottles had been fitted; this pumped fuel to the rocket as well as providing hydraulic power for the wings and (when fitted) to the autopilot.
119. A Trials Record Sheet, a pro forma with two pages of details of the parameters of the trolley and aerodyne, was completed for each run; trial #1 is recorded as 21 February 1952 (Brooklands Museum SWG-FTR-001).
120. Morpurgo, 346.
121. Memo of a meeting at Predannack, 21 November 1952 (Brooklands Museum SWG-FTR-004).
122. Trial #89, 10 November 1952 is recorded as the 'first of a series of three locked-on runs with aerodyne at different heights above ground level' (Brooklands Museum SWG-FTR-001).
123. *Locked-on Runs with Aircraft No 3B November–December 1952* (Brooklands Museum SWG-FTR-004).
124. Memo of a visit to Predannack, 24 June 1953 (Brooklands Museum SWG-FTR-004).
125. *Summary of subsonic and supersonic free flight and wind tunnel tests of 'Wild Goose' and 'Swallow' Type Models Conducted by the Department of Aeronautical Research & Development During the Period September 1949 to June 1959*, 13 March 1961 (Brooklands Museum).
126. Wallis narration to *Wild Goose and Swallow Tests* film (SM Arch BNW K2); Wallis remarks that about half a dozen models were crashed altogether.
127. SM Arch BNW EC2/1 Part 1.
128. Morpurgo, 330.
129. *Wild Goose and Swallow Tests* film (SM Arch BNW K2).
130. Work on the half-mass model had begun in April 'in view of the importance which we know the RAF attach to the Heston single-seater type' (Brooklands Museum SWG-FTR-004).
131. Wallis to Cochrane, 12 September 1951 (SM Arch BNW EA2/7).
132. TNA DSIR 23/20339.
133. E.T. Jones to Chief Scientist et al., 9 May 1952 (TNA AVIA 54/1780).
134. Extract from unconfirmed ARC minute on Wallis's work for the Ministry of Supply, 13 February 1952 (TNA AVIA 65/260).
135. Boorer, N.W., 2008, op. cit., notes that the JC.9 cancellation occurred at the same time as Heyday's, suggesting that the two events may be linked and attributable to the laminar flow result; Wood, op. cit., described the cancellation as 'inexplicable'.
136. Wallis to Cochrane, 12 September 1951 (SM Arch BNW EA2/7).
137. Wallis, Barnes N., *The Air Defence of Great Britain: A New Approach* (Vickers-Armstrongs, 1953) (TNA AIR 2/14232 and CAC WLIS 4).
138. Lord Trenchard, 'Long-Range Air Power', letter to *The Times* (12 January 1951), 7.
139. Teed, P.L., *Note on an after-dinner conversation with A.A. Hall*, 7 July 1953 (SM Arch BNW EB2/6).
140. Patent GB832606, *Improvements in Aeroplanes*, applied for 4 February 1954.
141. A drawing of this aircraft in the hand of Norman Boorer is held by Brooklands Museum (SWV4(a), 16 September 1952); plinth-mounted models of the 'Attack' and 'Fighter' variants in Table 8.2 are held by the Barnes Wallis Memorial Trust and IWM Duxford respectively; these appear to show the same 'split fuselage' method of control, although maximum wing sweep is only about 70 degrees.
142. *Proposal for Photographic Reconnaissance Aircraft by Vickers-Armstrongs Ltd.* (RAE Farnborough Tech Memo Aero 236, January 1953) (TNA AIR 2/14232) and *Structure weight estimates for the Vickers-Armstrongs Design Study for a Photographic Reconnaissance Aircraft* (RAE report Structures A/11048/DRL, 3 December 1952) (TNA AVIA 13/1224).
143. Brown, Eric M., *Wings on My Sleeve* (Weidenfeld & Nicolson, 2006, updated edn), 171–3.
144. Brown, op. cit.
145. Morpurgo, 346.
146. Boorer, 1981, op. cit.
147. Wallis to Cochrane, 12 September 1951 (SM Arch BNW EA2/7); although laminar flow had been unworkable in practice, Dr Dryden, Director of NACA, continued to argue that there was 'no limit to the length over which laminar flow may be propagated'.
148. Morpurgo, 348.
149. Wallis narration to *Wild Goose and Swallow Tests* film (SM Arch BNW K2).

Chapter 9

1. Boorer, Norman W. (private communication), stated that omitting the rear part of the delta was an idea which Wallis had picked up from his reading. Wallis himself cites the highly swept arrowhead configuration of Robert T. Jones,

A.E. Puckett and H.J. Stewart (SM Arch BNW EC1/3), but a letter to Wallis from his patent agents in November 1956 (SM Arch BNW EC6/2) noted that Wallis's implementation of this form appeared novel enough to constitute a patentable invention.

2. Remarkably, of production aircraft, only the English Electric Lightning appears to have adopted a similar 'notched delta' planform, although arguably its shape derived from adding sweep to a straight wing, rather than by cutting out the rear portion of a delta.

3. The de Havilland DH.108 was a tail-less swept-wing aircraft built for supersonic flight, and was also called Swallow, but the two projects were unrelated; the three DH.108 prototypes made a total of 480 flights 1946–50, but all three aircraft crashed, killing their pilots, which is testimony to Wallis's fears about using test pilots in radical new designs.

4. Wallis, Barnes N., *Aerodynamic requirement for long-range supersonic aircraft* (13 March 1958) (SM Arch BNW EC3/6).

5. As the specific weight of a jet engine increases at high operational altitudes, a balance had to be found between the cruise and other requirements of the engine.

6. A structure weight of less than 24 per cent of AUW was his goal, compared to, for example, 33 per cent for the VC10.

7. The Patent Survey produced by Brewer & Son for Wallis, 13 March 1958 (in same folder as *The Fundamental Principles of Long-range Supersonic Flight*, op. cit.) summarises his key patents relating to Swallow; all are officially entitled *Improvements in aeroplanes*, so the more helpful titles here are from the Survey: GB832760 (general arrangement), GB832761 (fore-body structure shape), GB832762 (improved fore-body shape), GB842363 (control by pivoting jets), GB854459 (control by differential sweep), GB861230 (Y-spar for effecting sweep), GB870739 (dual-pivot arrangement for engine/wing mounting), GB950400 (main-wing incidence varying with sweep).

8. Brewer & Son to Wallis, 23 November 1956 (SM Arch BNW EC6/2).

9. Patent GB832760, *Improvements in Aeroplanes*, applied for 26 January 1954; not published until 13 April 1960.

10. Wallis, Barnes N., *The influence of size on performance of aircraft* (undated) (SM Arch BNW EC3/14).

11. Some practical issues, such as crewing, mean that the economics of operating aircraft does not follow the same rules (e.g. two smaller aircraft may be more structurally efficient than one larger aircraft, but the single aircraft needs only a single crew).

12. *Radar invisibility* (Vickers-Armstrongs, 11 November 1954) (SM Arch BNW EC2/1 Part 1).

13. Patent GB852881, *Improvements in Aeroplanes and other Flying Bodies*, applied for 10 September 1954.

14. The solution adopted for Concorde was the famous droop snoot, lowering the nose to improve the pilot's view; this was the subject of BAC's first patent, FR1395377.

15. Morpurgo, 349.

16. *Report for quarter ending 30 September 1954* (SM Arch BNW EC2/1 Part 1).

17. XK831-5 and XK850-4 (http://www.vicflintham.co.uk/post-war-research-aircraft-and-prototypes/Manned.html).

18. Minutes of a meeting held at Predannack, 1 October 1954 (Brooklands Museum SWG-FTR-005).

19. *Summary of subsonic and supersonic free flight and wind tunnel tests of Wild Goose and Swallow Type Models Conducted by the Department of Aeronautical Research & Development During the Period September 1949 to June 1959*, 13 March 1961 (Brooklands Museum).

20. *Visit of Hufton and Hamilton of RAE to R&D Department* (4 November 1954) (Brooklands Museum SWG-FTR-005).

21. Minutes of a meeting held at R&D, 3 March 1955 (Brooklands Museum SWG-FTR-005).

22. Wallis diary for 1955 (RAF Museum X001-2371/116).

23. SM Arch BNW EC2/1.

24. *Accident to 001* (30 August 1955) (Brooklands Museum SWG-FTR-005).

25. http://www.vicflintham.co.uk/post-war-research-aircraft-and-prototypes/Manned.html; remarkably, this date does not warrant an entry in Wallis's diary.

26. Wallis narration to *Wild Goose and Swallow Tests* film (SM Arch BNW K2).

27. The RAF Museum has film footage of at least two of these other take-offs.

28. TNA AVIA 65/260.

29. 'Secret Salvage', *Flight* (5 July 1957), 6; this article claims that the Royal Navy recovered the craft.

30. Letter quoted at meeting of the Barnes Wallis Memorial Trust, Howden, June 2007.

31. Notes on a meeting at Weybridge to discuss work at Predannack, 3 May 1957 (TNA AVIA 65/260).

32. TNA AVIA 65/260; the emplacement and much of the concrete bed for the rail track can still be seen at the airfield.

33. Warren at RAE to Mrs Hoare, March 1954 (SM Arch BNW EC2/1 Part 1).

34. The telemetry was done by (later Sir) James Hamilton from the RAE at Farnborough (Boorer, Norman W., private communication); Hamilton would later be Director-General of the Concorde project where he was in charge of the wing design.

35. *Swallow – Aberporth Models* (Brooklands Museum SWG-FTR-005).

36. Wallis narration to *Wild Goose and Swallow Tests* film (SM Arch BNW K2).

37. *Progress report no.9* (19 May 1955) (SM Arch BNW EC2/1 Part 2).

38. *Swallow – Aberporth Models* (Brooklands Museum SWG-FTR-005).

39. Aberporth is on the Welsh coast, and rockets were fired out to sea so that, unlike at Larkhill, there were no practical range limitations.

40. *Programme of free flight models for Aberporth* (Brooklands Museum file *Miscellaneous VS Studies*).

41. *Results from the Supersonic Free-Flight Model L.2 of the Swallow Project*, MoS/RAE to Hayes, 17 May 1957 (TNA AVIA 73/2).

42. Hayes, Cecil W., *Report 62: Supersonic Free Flight Trials of Swallow 1 October 1958 to 30 June 1959* (Brooklands Museum).

43. Brooklands Museum SWG-INF-002.

44. Jindivik was an Australian-built radio-controlled target drone, used extensively by the RAAF, RAF and FAA.

45. DGSR(A)/MOS to Satterly, 28 April 1956 (TNA AIR 2/14232).

46. Buttler, Tony, *British Secret Projects: Jet Bombers since 1949* (Midland Publishing, 2003), chapter 6.

47. TNA AVIA 73/2.

48. Patent GB854459, *Improvements in Aeroplanes*, applied for 10 February 1956; not published until 16 November 1960.

49. *The Swallow Project* (undated but c1957) (SM Arch BNW EC3/5).

50. Boorer, Norman W. (private communication); in addition to the rear-mounted bomb passing through the engine efflux, the potential problems included overheating due to having four engines so close together, risk that damage to one engine might affect those next to it, excess drag, and potential for ingestion of foreign objects being mounted so close to the runway. The Tu-144 prototype had its four engines in a similar layout, but the production models used two separate pairs of engines.

51. *Considerations governing the position of engines on Swallow aircraft*, 2 April 1959 (SM Arch BNW EC3/5).

52. *Swallow aircraft: a note on the use of external engine pods as aircraft controls* (undated but c1956) (SM Arch BNW EC3/5).

53. One of the main maintenance loads with Tornado (and presumably other VG aircraft) is the attention that has to be paid to the fuel lines, control lines and other services where they pass around the wing pivot.

54. *Swallow Project: A Summary of Various Expert Opinions* (RAE Aero/Supersonics Section, 28 July 1956) (TNA AIR 2/14232).

55. Kirkpatrick, A/ACAS(OR) to DCAS, 13 August 1956 (TNA AIR 2/14232).

56. Viscount Knollys was Chairman of Vickers Ltd at this time, the group that included Vickers-Armstrongs Ltd.

57. *Progress Report on the Swallow – Wallis Project,* Satterly (ACAS(OR) to DCAS, 10 October 1956 (TNA AIR 2/14232).

58. Wallis to Cawood at MoS, 22 October 1956 (TNA AVIA 73/2).

59. Stinton, Darrol, *The Anatomy of the Aeroplane* (Granada, 1966), 277.

60. *Progress Report on the Swallow – Wallis Project,* op. cit.

61. TNA AVIA 65/260 and TNA AIR 20/9717.

62. *Second Monthly Progress Report on Swallow,* Satterly (ACAS(OR) to DCAS, October 1956 (TNA AIR 2/14232).

63. Sir Geoffrey Tuttle to Sir Ronald Lees (DCAS), 8 May 1962 (TNA AIR 20/11344); Air Marshal Tuttle was a former DCAS and employed by BAC 1960–1977, being General Manager at Weybridge at this time.

64. Morpurgo, 349; he claims that Wallis described the pivot as 'the last really big thing that I shall be privileged to do'.

65. Patent GB860823, *Improvements in Pivot Bearings*, applied for 26 April 1955, published 8 February 1961.

66. Notes of visit to Vickers (Weybridge) to discuss Swallow proposals for OR.330, 8 May 1956 (TNA AVIA 73/2).

67. Polytetrafluoroethylene, most commonly found in the non-stick surfaces of pots.

68. *Variable Geometry Aircraft: The Swallow Project* (26 March 1958) (SM Arch BNW EC1/3).

69. *PTFE wing pivot test* (11 November 1958) (SM Arch BNW EC3/6).

70. Sandbrook, Dominic, *Never Had It So Good: a History of Britain from Suez to the Beatles* (Little, Brown, 2005).

71. Rosenhead to Sandys, 28 June 1957 (TNA DEFE 13/205).

72. Untitled report on Swallow project, 17 July 1957 (TNA DEFE 13/205).

73. Watkinson to Chief of the Defence Staff/Chief Scientific Adviser, 4 October 1960 (TNA DEFE 13/205).

74. Kirkpatrick, ACAS(OR) to DCAS, March 1957 (TNA AIR 2/14232).

75. *The Research Aircraft Programme: A Review by the Air Staff* (March 1957) (TNA AIR 2/14232); the Handley-Page Boundary Layer Control Scheme was another research project dropped at the same time.

76. TNA AVIA 65/260.

77. Briefing reports for meeting between Minister and Board of Vickers, 28 May 1957 (TNA AIR 2/14232 and TNA AVIA 65/260).

78. *The Manned Aircraft Research Programme (A Note by DDOR6)* (30 August 1957) (TNA AIR 2/14232).

79. 'Support Ended for Aircraft Team', *The Times* (27 August 1957), 11. The total cost of the R&D research programme up to this date was approximately £1.5 million of which MoS had funded £1 million up to withdrawal in April 1957,

the remaining £500,000 coming from Vickers's own funds; this was a tiny sum compared to the cost of other cancelled projects, such as Vickers V1000 transport (£4 million), Fairey Rotodyne (£13 million), Bristol 188 research aircraft (£20 million) and BAC TSR.2 (£195 million); Wood, Derek, *Project Cancelled: British Aircraft That Never Flew* (Bobbs-Merrill Company Inc, 1975). Another source gives the cost of the project between 1948 and 1956 as £2.5 million: Satterly (ACAS(OR)) to DCAS, 10 October 1956). The Langley work on Swallow cost $200,000 (TNA DEFE 13/205).
80. *Swallow development – revised programme* (12 April 1957) (TNA AVIA 73/2).
81. SM Arch BNW EC3/13.
82. Wallis's preferred engines were the Rolls-Royce RB.108s developed for the Shorts SC.1 vertical take-off demonstrator (later revised to Bristol Orpheus B.OR.3s); the belly engine would have been a Bristol Orpheus BOR.12, an option preferred by the CAS (TNA AIR 2/14232).
83. *Variable Geometry Research Aircraft* (RAE Report, 2 September 1957) (TNA AVIA 65/260).
84. The same concerns were voiced by modern aerodynamicists reviewing the Swallow concept.
85. Nicholson to MoS, 3 September 1957 (TNA AVIA 65/260).
86. Patent GB885033, *Improvements in Aeroplanes*, applied for 2 June 1959; the solution is also described in a Wallis handwritten report (SM Arch BNW EC3/5) and, via animation and voiceover, in a film (SM Arch BNW K9).
87. Report by DGSR, 27 September 1957 (TNA AVIA 65/260).
88. In retrospect, it is readily apparent that these requirements (especially the STOL performance) might have been more easily met by incorporation of variable geometry in TSR.2, but VG was 'given only passing thought' (*TSR.2 with Hindsight*, Royal Air Force Historical Society, 1998, 15).
89. Loose minute from OR13b, 28 April 1958 (TNA AIR 2/14232).
90. *Comments on proposals to meet OR.339 by Dr Wallis,* Somerville for RAE Director to MoS, 19 November 1958 (TNA AVIA 13/1224).
91. 'Swallow Jet Decisions', *The Times* (23 May 1958), 10.
92. 'The Aircraft Industry Debate', *Flight* (6 June 1958).
93. *The Swallow Project: a Variable Geometry Aircraft* (Vickers-Armstrongs, April 1958) (Brooklands Museum).
94. SM Arch BNW EC6/7.
95. SM Arch BNW EC2/3 Part 1.
96. Runckel, Jack F., Schmeer, James W., and Cassetti, Marlowe D., *Performance, stability and control investigation at Mach numbers from 0.4 to 0.9 of a model of the Swallow with outer wing panels swept 25° with and without power simulation* (NASA Technical Memorandum SX-296, May 1960) and Schmeer, James W., and Cassetti, Marlowe D., *Performance, stability and control investigation at Mach numbers from 0.6 to 1.05 of a model of the Swallow with outer wing panels swept 75° with and without power simulation* (NASA Technical Memorandum SX-306, June 1960)
97. Harris, R.M., and Hayes, C.M., *Subsonic Wind Tunnel Tests of the Longitudinal Characteristics of Swallow in the Low Speed Configuration, parts I-VI* (Department of Aeronautical Research & Development, Reports 64-69, August – December 1959) (Brooklands Museum); the summary is in Report 67.
98. SM Arch BNW ED2/2, EC4/1 and EC5.
99. Note on a meeting, 2 October 1959 (TNA DEFE 13/205).
100. Hooper, Ralph (private communication).
101. Alford, William J., and Polhamus, Edward C., Patent US3053484, *Variable Sweep Wing Configuration*, applied for 7 July 1960.
102. Staff of Langley Research Centre, *Summary of NACA/NASA variable-sweep research and development leading to the F-111 (TFX)* (Langley Working Paper 285, 22 December 1966); the TFX (Tactical Fighter Experimental) designation was superseded by F-111.
103. The F-111 undertook flight deck trials on USS *Coral Sea* in 1968, but by that time its weight had increased to over 50,000lb which was seen as too heavy for naval operations, and the aircraft was not acquired by the Navy (although they would later use the Grumman F-14 Tomcat which also featured variable geometry).
104. SM Arch BNW EC7/2.
105. This was covered by Patent GB832760, *Improvements in Aeroplanes*, and its US equivalent US2915261.
106. Boorer, Norman W. (private communication), and SM Arch BNW EC7/2.
107. 'Dr Barnes Wallis Foresees Air Supremacy for Britain', *The Times* (12 November 1963), 5.
108. 'Mr Heinemann in Town', *Flight International* (17 December 1964), 1032.
109. 'British Silence on TSR.2 Rival', *The Times* (6 April 1965), 9.
110. Polhamus, Edward C., and Toll, Thomas A., *Research Related to Variable Sweep Aircraft Development* (NASA Technical Memorandum 83121, May 1981).
111. This decision cost around £45 million (Wood, op. cit.).
112. Wallis, Barnes N., *High Speed Communications Link the Commonwealth* (lecture to the Institute of Civil Engineers, 30 December 1959).
113. 'Straight and Level', *Flight* (8 January 1960), 52.
114. 'US May Support Swallow Jet', *The Times* (14 May 1958), 12.
115. Correspondence regarding the origins of VG, 1962–5 (RAF Museum B494).
116. 'An Unorthodox Aeroplane', *The Times* (5 April 1937), 11.
117. Stewart, Oliver, 'British pioneer of variable geometry', *The Times* (10 June 1965), vii.
118. '"First designer of swinging wing" claim', *The Times* (2 July 1965), 6.
119. Patent GB 5954664, *Improvements in Aeroplanes*, applied for 1 March 1945.
120. Hill, Geoffrey T.R., Patent GB352961, *Improvements in Means for Adjusting Wings of Aircraft*, applied for 15 January 1930.
121. 'Early Days of Variable Sweepback', *The Times* (5 March 1965), 14, and Penrose, Harald, letter to *Flight International* (17 June 1965), 970.
122. Harald Penrose to Major Oliver Stewart, 9 March 1965 (RAF Museum B494).
123. Hill, Geoffrey T.R., Patent GB651436, *Improvements in Aircraft*, applied for 4 June 1948.
124. Wallis to Major Oliver Stewart, 8 July 1965 (RAF Museum B494).
125. Turnill, Reginald (private communication).
126. 'Barnes Wallis Talks', *Flight* (8 January 1960), 34–5.
127. Undated plans in the Barnes Wallis Memorial Trust collection.
128. Military Project Office to Clark at the Ministry of Aviation, 4 March 1960 (Brooklands Museum).
129. Storey, R.F.R., *Swallow N (S.N.2 'Flat' Model) low speed static stability measurements with 3 different engine configurations and wing leading edge modifications* (Vickers-Armstrongs, November 1959) (Brooklands Museum).
130. *Variable Sweep and the Supersonic Transport* (Aerodynamics Department, Vickers-Armstrongs, Weybridge, 29 November 1961) (TNA DSIR 29/23195).
131. 'US Aviation Experts to Study the Concord Project', *The Times* (10 June 1963), 10.
132. 'A New Shape for Boeing's SST', *Engineering* (8 November 1968), and Owen, Kenneth, 'How Boeing chose its supersonic shape', *The Times* (26 September 1969), 29.
133. Owen, Kenneth, *Concorde: Story of a Supersonic Pioneer* (Science Museum, 2001); it is estimated that the cost of Concorde to Britain and France was about £1,000 million each, and that the USA also spent £1,000 million on their SST project over the same period, but got nothing to show for it.
134. Sales of at least 200 Concordes were predicted in the 1960s, but in the end only 20 were built (including prototypes); the price of jet fuel more than quadrupled between 1970 and 1975.
135. Boorer, Norman W. (private communication).
136. *Variable Sweep Swift Conversion* (28 June 1961) (Brooklands Museum file *Miscellaneous VS Studies*).
137. *A Note on a Variable Sweep Research Aircraft based on the MkI Lightning* (Vickers-Armstrongs, Weybridge, 29 November 1961) (Brooklands Museum file *Miscellaneous VS Studies*).
138. *Lightning for the Royal Navy* (BAC brochure, undated but *c*1961).
139. *A note on variable sweepback and its possible application to TSR.2* (undated but *c*.1961–2) (TNA DEFE 13/205).
140. *Variable Sweep* (BAC brochure, Report No.1599, Military Project Office, Weybridge, undated but *c*.1964) (Brooklands Museum).
141. This project, embodied in a contract between MoS and Vickers-Armstrongs dated 8 April 1959, was the British part of the agreed work programme to emerge from the Langley discussions. Six months later, RAE Bedford had 'done little or nothing to carry out their part of the programme' (Cascade aircraft: Notes of a meeting with Lord Weeks, 5 October 1959, SM Arch BNW ED1/1).
142. Eric Brown remarks that there was no real contender other than the Phantom, as its performance was so far ahead of any rivals for carrier operations.
143. Warton, between Preston and Blackpool, had been the English Electric works pre-BAC; it was also close to Squire's Gate where many Wellingtons were built.
144. *The BAC P.45 Multi-Role Aircraft* (BAC, June 1964) (Brooklands Museum).
145. Gardner, Charles, *British Aircraft Corporation: a History* (Batsford, 1981), 211.
146. Boorer, Norman W. (private communication).
147. Heath, B.O., 'Problems of Variable-Geometry Aircraft', *Flight International* (12 October 1967), 617–20.
148. Jeffrey Quill did much of the production testing on the Wellesley, before becoming more closely associated with the Spitfire; in the 1960s, he was working in marketing for BAC.
149. Boorer, Norman W. (private communication); Dassault flew the prototype Mirage G in 1967, flight testing continuing until the aircraft was lost in a crash in 1971. Two further prototypes, designated G4 (two-seater) and G8 (single-seater) were flown in 1971 and 1972 respectively, but the type did not go into production.
150. 'Killed by Complexity? The Demise of AVS', *Flight International* (22 February 1968), 262–3.
151. Heath, B.O., 'The MRCA Project', *Aeronautical Journal of the Royal Aeronautical Society*, vol. 74 (June 1970), 444–56.
152. *The Birth of Tornado* (Royal Air Force Historical Society, 2002), 44.
153. Ibid, 86.
154. Three from the USA and six from the USSR in addition to Tornado; see Laming, Tim, *Swing Wings: Tornados, Tomcats and Backfires* (Osprey Aerospace, 1993).
155. Boorer, Norman W. (private communication).
156. Heath, B.O. (private communication).
157. 617 Squadron aircrews (private communication).

Chapter 10

1. Wallis, Barnes N., notes for a meeting with Lord Weeks, 5 October 1959 (SM Arch BNW ED1/1).
2. SM Arch BNW ED1/1; Britain's share of Concorde eventually cost around £1,000 million, and TSR.2 had cost £195 million by the time of its cancellation in 1965.
3. Despite its sleek looks, Concorde would ultimately emerge with an AUW of 400,000lb, half of which was fuel on take-off. This AUW was comparable with the Boeing 707, the largest airliner in service at the time.
4. DCA(RD), report on Cascade, 12 July 1960 (TNA AVIA 73/3).
5. Wallis, Barnes N., *The Development of Aircraft Capable of Economical Performance at all Speeds: The Philosophy of Cascade* (25 April 1960) (SM Arch BNW ED1/2).
6. Patent GB894365, *Improvements in Aeroplanes*, applied for 21 September 1959; this was not the last Wallis patent to be awarded, but the later patents (such as the 'bouncing bomb' patents) had been applied for earlier.
7. Large drawing in TNA AIR 20/10571, same in SM Arch BNW I3/11 and a drawing of a similar variant in Boorer, Norman W., 'Barnes Wallis – Designer (1887–1979)', *Aeronautical Journal* (November 1981), 427.
8. Morgan at RAE to DCAS/VCAS, November 1959 (TNA AIR 20/10571).
9. SM Arch BNW ED1/1.
10. TNA AIR 20/10571.
11. These are commonly referred to as 'Dakota strips' (from the name of the ubiquitous Douglas wartime transport aircraft) and are 500yds long with minimally prepared earth or grass surfaces.
12. SM Arch BNW ED1/1; the drawing in TNA AIR 20/10571 probably shows this aircraft.
13. Jamison papers, 9 June 1960.
14. DCA(RD), report on Cascade, 12 July 1960 (TNA AVIA 73/3).
15. Wallis, Barnes N., *The Command of the Air* (February 1961) (SM Arch BNW ED6/2).
16. George Edwards is quoted as saying that the problems with manufacturing the stainless steel Bristol 188 research aircraft showed how right it was to build Concorde from light alloy; the aircraft companies also had far more experience in fabricating with light alloy.
17. 'Search for new airliner skin', *The Times* (23 February 1960).
18. Wallis, Barnes N., *An interim report on work in connection with vacuum insulation* (Vickers-Armstrongs, November 1957) (SM Arch BNW EC3/12).
19. Patent GB839647, *Improvements relating to Aeroplanes*, applied for 13 February 1957; the corresponding US patent application 708036, was denied due to existence of prior art.
20. Wallis, Barnes N., *The Swallow Project: A Variable Geometry Aircraft* (Vickers-Armstrongs, April 1958), Figure 20.
21. Boorer, Norman W., 'Barnes Wallis – Designer (1887–1979)', *Aeronautical Journal* (November 1981), 414–29.
22. As reported by agents who examined the wreckage of prototype V-2s.
23. Wallis to Major Oliver Stewart, 30 April 1965 (RAFM B493).
24. Wallis, Barnes N., *The Command of the Air* (February 1961) (SM Arch BNW ED6/2).
25. Limited jet lift is for high-speed flight only, and should not be confused with direct jet lift, such as on the Harrier, which is used for V/STOL operation.
26. Wallis diary for 1960 (RAFM X001-2371/121).
27. SM Arch BNW I4/1.
28. SM Arch BNW I4/3.
29. Wallis, Barnes N., *A note on variable camber aircraft*, 31 August 1960 (SM Arch BNW ED 3/3).
30. Wallis, Barnes N., *Note on the Development of Variable Geometry Aircraft* (Vickers-Armstrongs, 14 October 1960) (SM Arch BNW ED6/1).
31. SM Arch BNW EC7/12.
32. SM Arch BNW ED6/3.
33. Witt, D.T. (DDOR1), 26 September 1961 (TNA AIR 2/14232).
34. Esplin, I.G. (DOR(A)), to DCAS, 10 August 1961 (TNA AIR 2/14232).
35. SM Arch BNW ED4/1.
36. British Aircraft Corporation Ltd, Patent Application No. 40479/1965, *Ducted Wing*, applied for 22 September 1965 (SM Arch BNW EC7/12), superseding the earlier Patent Application No. 38495/1964; both patents were unpublished.
37. Wallis to Sawyers, 5 August 1968 (SM Arch BNW EC7/12).
38. Gibson, Chris and Buttler, Tony, *British Secret Projects: Hypersonics, Ramjets and Missiles* (Midland Publishing, 2007), chapters 10–12.
39. Bristol Aero Engines became Bristol-Siddeley in 1959 following a merger, and was sold to Rolls-Royce in 1966, then being known as Rolls-Royce (Bristol); Stanley Hooker, who worked for the company, was also involved in discussions with Wallis.
40. Wallis, Barnes N., *A note on aircraft design and manufacture* (1970) (SM Arch BNW ED3/10).
41. Jamison to Wallis, 27 July 1961 (Jamison papers DM1717-D96).
42. Jamison papers D1717-D98.
43. Wallis, Barnes N., *A note on the design of power units for high speed aircraft* (undated, but 1970 or later) (SM Arch BNW ED3/10).
44. Jamison to Wallis, 6 January 1972 (Jamison papers DM1717-D100).
45. Hall to Jamison, 2 March 1971 (Jamison papers D1717-D99).
46. Panel discussions at meeting of the Barnes Wallis Memorial Trust, Howden, June 2007.
47. Wallis, Barnes N., 'The Strength of England', *Advancement of Science* (November 1965), 393–408 (Presidential Address to Engineering Section of the British Association for the Advancement of Science, Cambridge, 2 September 1965).
48. Wallis, Barnes N., *Programme of work at Research & Development Department* (25 October 1966) (SM Arch BNW ED3/10).
49. That is, not any bigger/heavier than a Boeing 737 or similar.
50. These are the standard cargo containers often seen on ships, trains and lorries; dimensions are typically 8ft × 8ft with length 20ft or multiples thereof, empty weight is 2,200kg (though a lighter type for aircraft use might have been developed).
51. Wallis, Barnes N., *Universal Aircraft* (undated but *c.*1966) (SM Arch BNW ED3/10).
52. Wallis, Barnes N., *A note on a proposal to create a Universal type of aircraft* (undated but *c.*1966) (SM Arch BNW ED3/10).
53. For long-haul flights, payload would have been 10–15 per cent of AUW; for short-haul flights, payload would have been 30–40 per cent of AUW.
54. Wallis, Barnes N., *The Rectangular Fuselage* (undated but *c.*1966) (SM Arch BNW ED3/10).
55. RAFM B3249 has an illustration.
56. Boorer lecture.
57. Wallis, Barnes N., *All-purpose Aircraft* (undated but *c.*1966) (SM Arch BNW ED3/10).
58. Wallis, Barnes N., *A note on a proposed new type of aircraft* (undated but *c.*1966; intended to update his January 1957 paper of the same title) (SM Arch BNW ED3/10).
59. SM Arch BNW I5.
60. RAFM B3249.
61. SM Arch BNW ED3/10.
62. Stopes-Roe, Mary (private communication).
63. Wallis, Barnes N., *A note on aircraft design and manufacture* (1970) (SM Arch BNW ED3/10).
64. Wallis to Jamison, 22 December 1973 (Jamison papers DM1717-D100).
65. Morpurgo, 1981 edn, 378.
66. Wallis, Barnes N., 'Is a third London airport necessary?', letter to *The Times* (28 January 1971), 13.
67. Wallis, Barnes N., 'Local fears over third London airport', letter to *The Times* (8 March 1971), 13.

Chapter 11

1. Morgan, Eric B., 'Barnes Wallis' Glider', *Air-Britain Aeromilitaria*, vol. 27, no. 106 (Summer 2001).
2. *Experiments with Rocket-Propelled S.C. Apparatus* (24 November 1941) (TNA ADM 1/11767).
3. 'The Italian Naval Attack on Grand Harbour', *After the Battle*, No. 10 (1975), 33–7.
4. TNA DEFE 2/951.
5, Ladd, James D., *SBS The Invisible Raiders* (Fontana, 1984), 145–52; 'boom patrol boats' was a deliberate pun on 'boom'.
6. TNA AIR 14/204.
7. Marks, John, 'Drop Boats and Tallboys', *Air Force News,* magazine of the RNZAF (October 2006), 41; also private communication.
8. Wallis diary for 1945 (RAFM X001-2371/087).
9. SM Arch BNW E1/3.
10. Boorer, Norman W., *The Stratosphere Chamber* (Brooklands Museum, 2008); Boorer and his team drew the plans for the chamber, and he remained amazed that Wallis ever managed to persuade Kilner to build it.
11. Heller, Dagmar, 'Weather to Order', *Engineering* (July 1972), 675–7.
12. 'Synthetic Stratospherics', *Flight* (10 June 1948), 641–2.
13. Stratosphere Chamber advertising leaflet (BAC, 1968) (Brooklands Museum).
14. Boorer, Norman W., op. cit.; a longer report on the chamber by the same author and dating from *c.*1980 is in SM Arch BNW E1/3.
15. 'Ice Cause of Ships' Loss', *The Times* (12 August 1955), 5.
16. Heller, Dagmar, op. cit.; Morpurgo, 352, states that the £1,200 cost of these experiments was met by Vickers itself as the BSRA showed little interest in the experiments, and that Wallis's report was 'decently buried' by the BRSA, but other sources suggest that this is incorrect.
17. Boorer lecture.
18. 'Measures Taken for Trawler Safety: Improvements in Design', *The Times* (16 February 1968), 11.
19. 'Boat to Beat Trawler Ice Danger', *The Times* (29 January 1969), 2.
20. SM Arch BNW I7/1.
21. Robertson, Peter, *Beyond Southern Skies* (Cambridge University Press, 1992); the observatory was built eventually, and in 1981 was relocated to the Canary Islands, where it remains.
22. Wallis, Barnes N., *Giant Radio Telescopes* (September 1955) (CAC WLIS2).
23. Ibid.
24. Patent GB731665, *Improved Means for Controlling the Deflection of Loaded*

Structures; this was submitted in 1951 and granted in 1955, so it predates his work on telescopes. Robertson, op. cit., calls them 'incompressible columns', but it is not clear where this term came from.
25. Patent GB798953, *Improvements in Radio Telescopes*, applied for October 1955 and granted July 1958; reference is made to the possibility of using the active deflection control described in GB731665 within the structure.
26. Morpurgo, 338.
27. The story of the Parkes contribution to Apollo 11 is told in the film *The Dish* (Icon Home Entertainment, 2001) and comment on which parts of the film are fact and which are fiction is made on the CSIRO website at http://outreach.atnf.csiro.au/visiting/parkes/looselybased.html
28. Patent GB820166, *Improvements in Telescope Mountings*.
29. Robertson, Peter, op. cit.
30. SM Arch BNW EA1/5 and Patent GB1148492, *Improvements relating to Bombs*, applied for 10 October 1957; not published until 10 April 1969.
31. SM Arch BNW EC7/9.
32. Boorer lecture.
33. SM Arch BNW EC7/9.
34. Rhodes, C.W., *Aerodynamic Feasibility Studies for an Unpowered Momentum Bomb* (RAE Technical Note ARM 678, November 1960) (TNA AVIA 6/17818).
35. SM Arch BNW I2/1 shows a three-view drawing of the aircraft.
36. TNA AIR 20/11344; Edwards was reported as 'very keen'.
37. 'Spacecraft Study by Britain', *The Times* (6 September 1962), 10.
38. 'Aerospace Plane – No Design Study Yet', *Flight International* (15 November 1962), 802.
39.Wallis, Barnes N., *The Vickers Proposal for a New Type of High Pressure Submarine* (12 July 1965) (Barrow Records Office BDB 16L/560); this file also contains contemporary correspondence relating to the report, and plans of two variants of the submarine.
40. Jamison papers, DM1717–D97; 25,000 SHP compared to the 15,000 SHP of the machinery in the *Dreadnought*-class of nuclear submarines.
41. The liquid oxygen tankage would occupy over three times as much volume as the fuel.
42. The removal of the excess carbon dioxide from the exhaust stream was seen as problematic (British Oxygen Company to BNW, 29 December 1970).
43. Wallis to Jamison, 20 May 1965 (Jamison papers, D1717–D97).
44. CAC BLRD J154.
45. SM Arch BNW film K13 and SM Arch BNW film K15.
46. BNW to British Oxygen Company, 6 August 1970 (Jamison papers, D1717–D97).
47. Barrow Records Office BDB 16L/560; this review appears to have been unrelated to the design of the *Vanguard*-class submarines, design of which was already completed at this time.
48. 'Restoring sea supremacy for England', *The Times* (3 September 1965), 13.
49. SM Arch BNW G5/1.
50. SM Arch BNW G5.
51. Professor Stuart Moy (private communication); now at the University of Southampton, Professor Moy was previously at the CEGB, including working on the cooling tower repair projects.
52. SM Arch BNW G2/1.
53. SM Arch BNW G2/2; refers to Jardine, D.R., 'Keeping Cricket Alive', letter to *The Times* (5 July 1947), 5.
54. Correspondence 1949–64 between BNW, ball manufacturers and others (SM Arch BNW G2/3).
55. SM Arch BNW G1/3.
56. Stopes-Roe, Mary (private communication).
57. SM Arch BNW G1/4.
58. SM Arch BNW G7/3.
59. Patent GB1342343, *Improvements in or relating to the Spanning of Bodies of Water.*
60. SM Arch BNW G7/1 and SM Arch BNW I7/4.
61. No bridge or tunnel has yet been built across the Strait of Messina, though there are current plans to span the strait with the world's longest suspension bridge.
62. Morpurgo, 338.
63. Ibid.
64. Patent GB731665, op. cit.
65. Boorer, Norman W., 'Barnes Wallis – Designer (1887-1979)', *Aeronautical Journal* (November 1981), 414–29 and private communication.
66. Boorer, Norman W. (private communication).
67. Wallis, Barnes W. (private communication).
68. Some examples are in the collection of the Barnes Wallis Memorial Trust.
69. Miller, David, *Sir Barnes Wallis, Kt, CBE, FRS and the Christ's Hospital RAF Foundationer's Trust 1951–2003* (Christ's Hospital Club, 2003), 37.
70. 'Virtue spurns the clogging earth on soaring wings'.
71. SM Arch BNW A1/20.

Chapter 12
1. With hindsight, this may have been conservative – the swing-wing American Rockwell B-1 Lancer can fly at an AUW over 400,000lb, and although more than a dozen have been lost in non-combat crashes, none of these have been due to problems with the variable-geometry wings.
2. B. Oliver Heath (private communication).
3. Patent GB741718, *Improvements in the Control of Flying Bodies*, applied for 7 July 1948.
4. B. Oliver Heath (private communication).
5. The Grumman F-14 Tomcat had engines within the fuselage which were quite widely spaced compared to similar designs, and this contributed to control problems following loss of one engine.
6. Morpurgo, 354.
7. Wallis, Barnes W. (private communication).
8. Turnill, Reginald (private communication), quoting Wallis from a 1971 interview (Turnill interviewed Wallis several times between 1959 and 1971).
9. Boorer, Norman W., 'Barnes Wallis – Designer (1887–1979)', *Aeronautical Journal* (November 1981), 414–29.
10. SM Arch BNW ED6/1.
11. Staff of BAE SYSTEMS Submarine Solutions, Barrow (private communication).
12. B. Oliver Heath; although it was not his actual job title, he fulfilled the traditional role of the Chief Designer.
13. Barfield, Norman and others (private communication).
14. Turnill, Reginald (private communication).
15. Wallis, Barnes W. (private communication).
16. Brasher, Christopher, 'Master of the Skies', *The Listener* (22 November 1979).
17. Concorde's supersonic L/D was between 7 and 8.
18. Boorer, Norman W. (private communication); in fact, Wallis does admit in a 1960s TV documentary film that 'As a piece of machining, it's a very fine example of engineering, but as an aeroplane, I think it has no future before it at all.' (SM Arch BNW K17).
19. Boorer, Norman W. (private communication).
20. Robinson, Tim, 'The Meccano Set Computers: a history of differential analyzers made from children's toys', *IEEE Control Systems Magazine* (June 2005), 74–83.
21. Robinson, Tim (private communication); Robinson is an expert in the early history of computing.
22. Cairns, W.J., Crank, J., and Lloyd, E.C., *Some Improvements in the Construction of a Small Scale Differential Analyser and a Review of Recent Applications* (Armament Research Department, Theoretical Research Memo No. 27/44, Fort Halstead, September 1944) (TNA DEFE 15/751); includes a section 'Detonation Wave in High Explosive'.
23. Discussion at meeting of the Barnes Wallis Memorial Trust, Howden, June 2007.
24. Owen, Kenneth, *Concorde: Story of a Supersonic Pioneer* (Science Museum, 2001), chapter 14.
25. In a 1950 letter to Cochrane discussing various methods of missile homing, including sound homing, Wallis notes that 'it is fortunate that all aircraft capable of making sustained horizontal flight must make a large amount of noise'; very much true at the time, decreased noise emission is now an important consideration in the design of new aircraft.
26. Bourdin, P., Gatto, A., and Friswell, M.I, 'The Application of Variable Cant Angle Winglets for Morphing Aircraft Control', *Proceedings of the 24th Applied Aerodynamics Conference* (5–8 June 2006, San Francisco, California); see also http://www.aer.bris.ac.uk/research/dynamicsandsystems/morphingprojects.html
27. Spall, Nick, 'Whatever happened to the SST?', *Aerospace International* (June 2008), 30–3.
28. Turnill, Reginald (private communication), quoting Wallis from a 1971 interview.
29. Boorer, Norman W. (private communication).

Further Reading

Due to the range of projects which Wallis was involved with, there is a wide selection of further reading to cover these areas. The following are recommended:

Books

Andrews, C.F., and Morgan, E.B., *Vickers Aircraft Since 1908* (Putnam, 1988)

Brickhill, Paul, *The Dam Busters* (Evans Brothers, 1951)

Buttler, Tony, *British Secret Projects: Jet Bombers Since 1949* (Midland Publishing, 2003)

Cooper, Alan, *The Men Who Breached the Dams* (William Kimber, 1982)

——, *Beyond the Dams to the Tirpitz* (William Kimber, 1983)

Curtis, Des, *Most Secret Squadron: The Story of 618 Squadron* (Skitten Books, 1995)

Euler, Helmuth, *The Dams Raid: Through the Lens* (After the Battle, 2001)

Falconer, Jonathan, *The Dam Busters* (Sutton, 2003)

Flower, Stephen, *A Hell of a Bomb* (Tempus, 2001)

Gardner, Charles, *British Aircraft Corporation: A History* (Batsford, 1981)

Gardner, Robert, *From Bouncing Bombs to Concorde: The Authorised Biography of Aviation Pioneer Sir George Edwards OM* (Sutton, 2006)

Gibson, Chris, and Buttler, Tony, *British Secret Projects: Hypersonics, Ramjets and Missiles* (Midland Publishing, 2007)

Gibson, Guy P., *Enemy Coast Ahead* (Michael Joseph, 1946)

Harvey, Maurice, *The Allied Bomber War 1939–45* (Book Club Associates, 1992)

Hastings, Max, *Bomber Command* (Michael Joseph, 1979)

Hautefeuille, Richard, *Construciones Spéciales* (Richard Hautefeuille, 1995)

Holmes, Robin, *One of Our Aircraft: The Story of 'R for Robert' the Loch Ness Wellington* (Quiller Press, 1991)

Lumsden, Alec, *Wellington Special* (Ian Allen, 1974)

MacBean, John A., and Hogben, Arthur S., *Bombs Gone: The Development and Use of British Air-dropped Weapons from 1912 to the Present Day* (Patrick Stephens Limited, 1990)

Morpurgo, Jack E., *Barnes Wallis* (St Martin's, 1972); also available in paperback (Penguin, 1973) and in a revised edition following Wallis's death (Ian Allan, 1981)

Morris, Richard, *Guy Gibson* (Viking, 1994)

Mowthorpe, Ces, *Battlebags: British Airships of the First World War* (Sutton Publishing, 1995)

Ovcacik, Michal, and Susa, Karel, *Vickers-Armstrongs Wellington* (Mark I, 2003)

Owen, Kenneth, *Concorde: Story of a Supersonic Pioneer* (Science Museum, 2001)

Pawle, Gerald, *The Secret War* (Harrap, 1956)

Payne, Richard, *Stuck on the Drawing Board: Unbuilt British Commercial Aircraft Since 1945* (History Press, 2004)

Pugh, Peter, *Barnes Wallis: Dambuster* (Icon, 2005)

Saward, Dudley, *'Bomber' Harris* (Cassell, 1984)

Scott, J.D., *Vickers: A History* (Weidenfeld & Nicolson, 1962)

Shute, Nevil, *Slide Rule* (William Heinemann, 1954)

Stopes-Roe, Mary, *Mathematics with Love* (Macmillan, 2005)

Sweetman, John, *The Dambusters Raid* (Cassell Military Classics, 1999); also available in several other editions

——, *Tirpitz: Hunting the Beast* (Sutton, 2000)

Ward, Chris, Lee, Andy, and Wachtel, Andreas, *The Dambusters: The Definitive Story of 617 Squadron at War 1939–1945* (Red Kite, 2003)

Williamson, Gordon, *U-boat Bases and Bunkers 1941–45* (Osprey Publishing, 2003)

Wood, Derek, *Project Cancelled: British Aircraft That Never Flew* (Bobbs-Merrill, 1975)

Websites

Airship Heritage Trust website (http://www.aht.ndirect.co.uk)

The Man-Made Earthquake (http://members.cox.net/nukeinfo1/)

Index

Note: Wallis aircraft designs are listed individually by name; other Vickers aircraft are listed alphabetically under 'Vickers Aircraft'; other aircraft are listed alphabetically under 'Aircraft'.